REVIEWING INTEGRATED MATHEMATICS

COURSE III

With Sample Examinations

Marilyn Occhiogrosso

Former Assistant Principal, Mathematics
Erasmus Hall High School, New York City

REVISED EDITION

When ordering this book, please specify *either* **R 599 P** *or* REVIEWING INTEGRATED MATHEMATICS: COURSE III

AMSCO SCHOOL PUBLICATIONS, INC.
315 Hudson Street New York, N.Y. 10013

Electronic Prepress Production
A. W. Kingston Publishing, Inc. • Tempe, AZ 85282

ISBN 0-87720-290-7

PRINTED IN THE UNITED STATES OF AMERICA

8 9 10 02

CONTENTS

Chapter 4 Relations and Functions

Chapter 5 Circles

Chapter 6 Trigonometry, Part I

CHAPTER 1

The Real Number System, Part I

1.1 THE REAL NUMBERS

Subsets

Real Numbers
Rational Numbers
Integers
Whole Numbers
Naturals
Zero
Irrational Numbers

RATIONAL NUMBERS are numbers that can be expressed as a *ratio* of two integers (excluding the case where the denominator is 0.)

In general, the following are rational numbers:

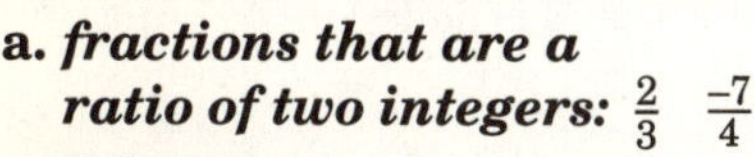

a. ***fractions that are a ratio of two integers:*** $\frac{2}{3}$ $\frac{-7}{4}$

b. ***integers:*** $6 = \frac{6}{1}$ $-5 = \frac{10}{-2}$

c. ***terminating decimals:*** $0.125 = \frac{1}{8}$

d. ***repeating decimals:*** $0.333... = \frac{1}{3}$

e. ***nth roots of perfect nth powers:*** $\sqrt{25} = 5$ $\sqrt[3]{8} = 2$

IRRATIONAL NUMBERS are *not* rational and *cannot* be expressed as the ratio of two integers.

In general, the following are irrational numbers:

a. ***nth roots of nonperfect nth powers:*** $\sqrt{3}$ $\sqrt[3]{2}$

b. ***the number*** π

c. ***decimals that do not end or repeat:*** 0.010010001...

Even roots of negative numbers are not real numbers.

Operations and Properties

Six basic operations that can be performed on real numbers are INVERSES of each other:

addition, subtraction • multiplication, division • raising to a power, extracting a root

Under these operations, the real numbers evidence:

Closure Properties For all real a and b, the following are also real:

$a + b$ $a - b$ $a \cdot b$ $a \div b\ (b \neq 0)$

a^b $\sqrt[b]{a}$ ($a \nless 0$ when b is even)

Commutative Properties For all real a, b:

$a + b = b + a$ $a \cdot b = b \cdot a$

Associative Properties For all real a, b, c:

$(a + b) + c = a + (b + c)$

$(a \cdot b) \cdot c = a \cdot (b \cdot c)$

Distributive Property For all real a, b, c:

$a \cdot (b + c) = a \cdot b + a \cdot c$

Identities For every real a:

0 is the ADDITIVE IDENTITY

$a + 0 = a$ *and* $0 + a = a$

1 is the MULTIPLICATIVE IDENTITY

$a \cdot 1 = a$ *and* $1 \cdot a = a$

Inverses For every real a, there is:

an ADDITIVE INVERSE $-a$ such that

$a + (-a) = 0$

a MULTIPLICATIVE INVERSE $\frac{1}{a}$ such that

$a \cdot \frac{1}{a} = 1$ where $a \neq 0$

Fields

A FIELD consists of a set, together with two operations, usually an addition and a multiplication, such that the system:

1. is *closed* with respect to both operations
2. is *associative* with respect to both operations
3. is *commutative* with respect to both operations
4. has an *identity* element for each operation
5. has an *inverse* for each element under both operations, excluding the 0 under the multiplication
6. is *distributive* with respect to the multiplication over the addition

Examples

Determine if the given set forms a field under the operations of addition and multiplication.

Set under +, ×	Field
1. {real numbers}	yes
2. {integers}	no (except for ±1, the nonzero integers do not have inverses under ×)
3. {positive even powers of 4} $\{4^2, 4^4, 4^6, 4^8, \ldots\}$	no (there is no identity under + or ×, and there are no inverses under + or ×)

EXERCISES

In 1–4, choose the number that is rational.

1. (1) $\sqrt{6}$ (2) $\sqrt{16}$ (3) $\sqrt{18}$ (4) $\sqrt{24}$

2. (1) $\sqrt[3]{3}$ (2) $\sqrt[3]{9}$ (3) $\sqrt[4]{8}$ (4) $\sqrt[4]{16}$

3. (1) $\sqrt{8}$ (2) $\sqrt[3]{9}$ (3) $6\sqrt{2}$ (4) $5\sqrt{1}$

4. (1) $\sqrt{32}$ (2) $\sqrt[3]{32}$ (3) $\sqrt[4]{32}$ (4) $\sqrt[5]{32}$

In 5–9, choose the number that is irrational.

5. (1) $\sqrt{2}$ (2) $\sqrt{4}$ (3) $\frac{1}{2}$ (4) 0

6. (1) $\sqrt{\frac{9}{25}}$ (2) $\sqrt{0.81}$ (3) $\sqrt{9}$ (4) $\sqrt{3}$

7. (1) $-\frac{4}{5}$ (2) π (3) $\sqrt{9}$ (4) 0

8. (1) $\sqrt{3}$ (2) $\sqrt[3]{8}$ (3) $\sqrt{16}$ (4) $\sqrt[4]{16}$

9. (1) 0.375 (2) 0.375375375 ... (3) 0.375337533375 ... (4) 37.5

In 10–11, choose the number that is not real.

10. (1) $-\sqrt{25}$ (2) $\sqrt{-25}$ (3) -5 (4) $\sqrt[3]{-5}$

11. (1) $\sqrt{-2}$ (2) $-\sqrt{2}$ (3) $\sqrt[3]{-2}$ (4) $-\sqrt[3]{2}$

12. Which value of x will make $\sqrt{29 - x}$ a positive integer? (1) 1 (2) 29 (3) 0 (4) 4

13. Which value of x will make $\sqrt{100 - x}$ an irrational number? (1) 0 (2) 100 (3) 25 (4) 75

14. For which value of x is the expression $\sqrt{65 - x}$ not a real number? (1) 1 (2) 2 (3) 65 (4) 66

15. What is the smallest integral value of x for which $\sqrt{3x - 7}$ represents a real number?

16. Write the numeral preceding the set, chosen from the following list, that best completes each of the sentences **a–e**.

Names of Sets

(1) the set of positive integers
(2) the set of rational numbers
(3) the set of irrational numbers

a. The set that contains all the natural numbers and does not contain the member $\frac{1}{2}$ is ____ .

b. The set that contains the member $\sqrt{2}$ is ____ .

c. The set that has a smallest member is ____ .

d. The set that contains the member $\frac{1}{2}$ is ____ .

e. The set that contains the member π is ____ .

17. The additive inverse of -3 is
(1) $-\frac{1}{3}$ (2) $\frac{1}{3}$ (3) 3 (4) 0

18. The multiplicative inverse of $-\frac{1}{3}$ is
(1) $\frac{1}{3}$ (2) -3 (3) 3 (4) $0.33\frac{1}{3}$

19. If the additive inverse of 7 is added to the multiplicative inverse of $\frac{1}{2}$, what is the sum?

20. If the quotient of two real numbers is -1, what is the sum of these numbers?

In 21–22, select from the choices:
(1) 0 (2) 1 (3) $\sqrt{2}$ (4) there is no such number

21. Which real number does not have an additive inverse?

22. Which real number does not have a multiplicative inverse?

23. If x and y are real numbers and $xy > 0$, then which statement is true?
(1) $x > 0$ and $y > 0$ *or* $x < 0$ and $y < 0$
(2) $x > 0$ and $y > 0$ *or* $x < 0$ and $y > 0$
(3) $x > 0$ and $y < 0$ *or* $x < 0$ and $y < 0$
(4) $x > 0$ and $y < 0$ *or* $x < 0$ and $y > 0$

24. Which number has an additive inverse and a multiplicative inverse that are equal?
(1) 0 (2) 1 (3) -1 (4) there is no such real number

25. Which set is not closed under addition?
(1) {odd integers} (2) {even integers} (3) {multiples of 3} (4) {whole numbers}

26. The set {1, 3, 9, 27, 81, ...} is closed under
(1) addition (2) subtraction (3) multiplication (4) division

27. If a and b are natural numbers, which expression must represent a natural number?
(1) $a - b$ (2) $a + b$ (3) $\frac{a}{b}$ (4) $b \div a$

28. Under which operation is the set of positive rational numbers not closed?
(1) addition (2) subtraction (3) multiplication (4) division

29. Which set is closed under subtraction?

(1) {counting numbers} (3) {odd integers}
(2) {whole numbers} (4) {even integers}

30. The set of odd integers is closed under

(1) addition (3) multiplication
(2) subtraction (4) division

31. Which set is not closed under multiplication?

(1) {whole numbers} (3) {negative integers}
(2) {counting numbers} (4) {even integers}

32. The set {1, 3, 5, 7, ...} is closed under

(1) addition (3) multiplication
(2) subtraction (4) division

33. Given $A \odot B$, a binary operation defined such that $A \odot B \neq B \odot A$. Which property does this illustration contradict?

(1) commutative (3) distributive
(2) associative (4) closure

34. Which computation uses the associative property for multiplication?

(1) $5(6) = 6(5) = 30$
(2) $4(10 + 2) = 40 + 8 = 48$
(3) $7(4) + 7(6) = 7(10) = 70$
(4) $\frac{1}{2}(6 \cdot 7) = 3(7) = 21$

35. If the blank in each statement below is replaced by one of the words *addition*, *subtraction*, *multiplication*, or *division*, the statement will be true. Write the name of the operation required to make each of the statements **a–e** true.

a. The set of natural numbers has the associative property under addition and ____.

b. In the set of integers, 0 is the identity element under ____.

c. The set of odd integers is closed under ____.

d. For the rational numbers, the commutative property is not valid under division and ____.

e. In the set of real numbers, multiplication is distributive over subtraction and ____.

36. Write the number of the property of the real number system, chosen from the following list, that justifies each of the statements **a–j**:

Properties

(1) additive inverse property
(2) additive identity property
(3) multiplicative inverse property
(4) multiplicative identity property
(5) commutative property of addition
(6) commutative property of multiplication
(7) associative property of addition
(8) associative property of multiplication
(9) distributive property of multiplication over addition

a. $7 + (3 + 2) = (7 + 3) + 2$

b. $(-5)(1) = -5$

c. $3(x + 2) = 3x + 6$

d. $4 + (-4) = 0$

e. $7(8) = 8(7)$

f. $2\left(\frac{1}{2}\right) = 1$

g. $2(1 + 3) = 2(1) + 2(3)$

h. $2 + 1 = 1 + 2$

i. $(1 \cdot 2) \cdot 3 = 1 \cdot (2 \cdot 3)$

j. $2 + 0 = 2$

37. Each set of numbers below is followed by four properties. Each set has only three of the four properties. Write the number preceding the property that the set in **a–e** does not have.

a. {1, 2, 3, 4, ...}

(1) distributive property of multiplication over addition
(2) commutative property of multiplication
(3) multiplicative identity
(4) multiplicative inverse

b. {0, 1, 2, 3, ...}

(1) associative property of addition
(2) additive inverse
(3) multiplicative identity
(4) additive identity

c. {..., –3, –2, –1, 0, 1, 2, 3, ...}

(1) closure property under division
(2) additive inverse
(3) associative property of multiplication
(4) additive identity

d. {1, –1}

(1) multiplicative inverse
(2) multiplicative identity
(3) closure property under multiplication
(4) closure property under addition

e. $\{-2, -1, -\frac{1}{2}, \frac{1}{2}, 1, 2\}$

(1) multiplicative inverse
(2) multiplicative identity
(3) additive identity
(4) commutative property of addition

In 38–42, determine if the given set forms a field under the operations of addition and multiplication. If the system is not a field, write the field properties that are not satisfied.

38. {positive integers}
39. {positive even integers}
40. {rational numbers}
41. {whole numbers}
42. {rational numbers that are not integers}

In 43–46, list the members of the given set and determine if it forms a field under the operations of addition and multiplication. If the system is not a field, write the field properties that are not satisfied.

43. {integral multiples of 3}
44. {positive integral multiples of 5}
45. {positive integral powers of 3}
46. {integral powers of 2}

1.2 FACTORING

The process of factoring is an application of the distributive property.

Common Monomial Factor

Factor out the greatest common factor.

Examples

1. $3x + 6x^2 = 3x(1 + 2x)$
2. $6x^3y - 8x^2y^2 = 2x^2y(3x - 4y)$

Factoring a Trinomial

To factor a trinomial that is a product of two binomials:

1. **The first term of each binomial is a result of factoring the first term of the trinomial.**
2. **The second term of each binomial, including signs, is a result of factoring the last term of the trinomial.**
3. **The only acceptable terms of the binomials are those that produce the exact middle term of the trinomial when the binomials are multiplied.**

Examples

1. $2x^2 - 5x - 3 = (2x + 1)(x - 3)$
2. $12a^2 - 19a + 4 = (4a - 1)(3a - 4)$
3. $x^4 + 2x^2 + 1 = (x^2 + 1)(x^2 + 1) = (x^2 + 1)^2$

The Difference of Two Perfect Squares

$$a^2 - b^2 = (a + b)(a - b)$$

Examples

1. $9x^2 - 49 = (3x + 7)(3x - 7)$
2. $100 - \frac{1}{36}x^2 = (10 + \frac{1}{6}x)(10 - \frac{1}{6}x)$
3. $25z^2 - 0.09 = (5z + 0.3)(5z - 0.3)$

Example 4 demonstrates a "hidden" perfect square, requiring recognition of a perfect-square trinomial.

4. $x^2 - 6x + 9 - 4y^2 = (x^2 - 6x + 9) - 4y^2$
$= (x - 3)^2 - 4y^2$
$= [(x - 3) + 2y][(x - 3) - 2y]$
$= (x - 3 + 2y)(x - 3 - 2y)$

Combining Types of Factoring

First look for a greatest common factor. After the greatest common factor has been factored out, the remaining factor may still be factorable, either as a difference of two perfect squares or as a trinomial.

Examples

1. $2x^2 - 50 = 2(x^2 - 25) = 2(x + 5)(x - 5)$
2. $6x^3 + 27x^2 - 15x = 3x(2x^2 + 9x - 5)$
$= 3x(2x - 1)(x + 5)$
3. $3x^4 - 243 = 3(x^4 - 81)$
$= 3(x^2 + 9)(x^2 - 9)$
$= 3(x^2 + 9)(x + 3)(x - 3)$

Example 4 demonstrates the use of separate common factors.

4. $ma + mb - na - nb = m(a + b) - n(a + b)$
$= (a + b)(m - n)$

EXERCISES

In 1–8, factor out the greatest common factor.

1. $8y^2 + 16xy$
2. $\pi r^2 + \pi R^2$
3. $35a^3b^4 - 10a^2b^5$
4. $3\sqrt{2} + 7\sqrt{2} - 4\sqrt{2}$
5. $34def - 51d^2ef^3$
6. $\frac{1}{4}x^3 - \frac{1}{8}x^2 + \frac{3}{4}x^5$
7. $3(x - 1) + x(x - 1)$
8. $(a - 2)^2 + 3(a - 2)$

In 9–14, factor the trinomial.

9. $2x^2 + 7x + 3$
10. $5a^2 + 14a - 3$
11. $9m^2 + 6m + 1$
12. $16z^2 - 8z + 1$
13. $3 - r - 10r^2$
14. $x^2 - 8xy + 16y^2$

In 15–20, factor the difference of two perfect squares.

15. $4x^2 - 25$
16. $25 - 0.16a^2$
17. $81y^4 - \frac{4}{25}$
18. $121m^6 - p^{16}$
19. $x^2 + 10x + 25 - 9z^4$
20. $b^2 - 8b + 16 - 16a^2$

In 21–36, factor as completely as possible.

21. $ax^2 - 49a$
22. $2a^2 - 11a - 21$
23. $9x^3 - 36x$
24. $y^4 - 9y^2$
25. $x^2 + y^2$
26. $a^2m^2 - 81m^2$
27. $4x^2 - 6x - 4$
28. $t^4 - 10t^2 + 9$
29. $30z^3 + 5z^2 - 5z$
30. $2a - 4ab - 30ab^2$
31. $81x^2 - 0.0009$
32. $ax + xy + ay + y^2$
33. $x^2 + 6x + 9 - y^4$
34. $m^2 + mn - mp - np$
35. $3q^2 - 6q + 3 - 12r^2$
36. $144t^2 - 9x^2 - 6x - 1$

In 37–40, write as a product of two binomial factors.

37. $x + ax + ay + y$
38. $x^2 + ax + bx + ab$
39. $a^2 + a - 3(a + 1)$
40. $a^3 - 2a^2 + a - 2$

1.3 EXPONENTS

Laws of Exponents

An EXPONENT tells how many times a base is used as a factor.

Law of Exponents Relating to	Examples
Multiplication With Like Bases $x^a \cdot x^b = x^{a+b}$ (add exponents)	a. $x^2 \cdot x^3 = x^{2+3} = x^5$ b. $2^2 \cdot 2^3 = 2^{2+3} = 2^5 = 32$ c. $3x^2y^3 \cdot 5xy^4$ $= 3 \cdot 5 \cdot x^{2+1}y^{3+4}$ $= 15x^3y^7$
Division With Like Bases $x^a \div x^b = x^{a-b}$ where $x \neq 0$ (subtract exponents)	a. $x^5 \div x^2 = x^{5-2} = x^3$ b. $3^5 \div 3^3 = 3^{5-3} = 3^2 = 9$ c. $(14x^5y^3) \div (7xy^2)$ $= (14 \div 7)x^{5-1}y^{3-2}$ $= 2x^4y$
Powers $(x^a)^b = x^{a \cdot b}$ (multiply exponents) $(xy)^a = x^ay^a$ (distribute exponents)	a. $(x^3)^2 = x^{3 \cdot 2} = x^6$ b. $(2^4)^3 = 2^{4 \cdot 3} = 2^{12}$ c. $(3x^2y^3)^4 = 3^4x^{2 \cdot 4}y^{3 \cdot 4}$ $= 81x^8y^{12}$
Zero Exponent $x^0 = 1$ where $x \neq 0$	a. $3x^0 = 3(1) = 3$ b. $(3x)^0 = 1$
Negative Exponent $x^{-n} = \frac{1}{x^n}$ where $x \neq 0$	a. $5^{-1} = \frac{1}{5^1} = \frac{1}{5}$ b. $5^{-2} = \frac{1}{5^2} = \frac{1}{25}$ c. $\frac{32x^3y^2z^4}{16x^4yz^6} = 2x^{-1}yz^{-2}$ $= \frac{2y}{xz^2}$

Note: This section is limited to integral exponents. For fractional exponents, see page 12.

Example

If $2^a = y$, then 2^{a+1} equals

(1) $y + 1$ (2) ay (3) $2y$ (4) y^2

Solution: Establish a connection between the given expression and the expression in question.

2^a must be multiplied by 2^1 to get 2^{a+1}

Balance the equation.
Since the left side is multiplied by 2, the right side must be multiplied by 2.

$$\begin{array}{rcl} 2^a & = & y \\ \times 2 & = & \times 2 \\ \hline 2^{a+1} & = & 2y \end{array}$$

Answer: **(3)**

Evaluating / Simplifying Expressions

For calculations, the ORDER OF OPERATIONS is:

1. **Do all work within parentheses first.**
2. **Do all other work with exponents next.**
3. **Complete multiplications and divisions next, working from left to right.**
4. **Do additions and subtractions last, working from left to right.**

In general, an expression in SIMPLEST FORM contains *no parentheses* and *no like terms.*

The distributive property removes parentheses.

Examples

1. For $x = 2$ and $y = 4$, evaluate: $3x^0 + (xy)^2 - y^{-1}$

Solution:

$$\begin{aligned} 3x^0 + (xy)^2 - y^{-1} &= 3 \cdot 2^0 + (2 \cdot 4)^2 - 4^{-1} \\ &= 3 \cdot 1 + (8)^2 - \tfrac{1}{4} \\ &= 3 + 64 - \tfrac{1}{4} \\ &= 67 - \tfrac{1}{4} = 66\tfrac{3}{4} \end{aligned}$$

2. Simplify: $(3x - 1)^2 - 2(3x^2 + 1)$

Solution:

$$\begin{aligned} &(3x - 1)^2 - 2(3x^2 + 1) \\ &= 9x^2 - 6x + 1 - 6x^2 - 2 \\ &= 3x^2 - 6x - 1 \end{aligned}$$

EXERCISES

In 1–14, perform the indicated operations.

1. $3x^4 \cdot 5x^7$
2. $(5y^{n+1})^2$
3. $4a^{n-1} \cdot 3a^{-n+2}$
4. $2^3 \cdot 2^{-1}(-2)^3$
5. $z^n(z^{n+1})$
6. $(-5y^n)(3y^{2n})$
7. $(4x^2y)^2(3xy^3)$
8. $2(a + b) \cdot 4\frac{1}{2}(a + b)$
9. $(12x^8) \div (3x^2)$
10. $(28a^{11}b^4) \div (7a^2b)$
11. $(42a^5b^6c^4) \div (-7a^2bc^4)$
12. $(3^5 \cdot 2^7) \div (2 \cdot 3^3)$
13. $\frac{10x^{n+3} - 6x^{n+2}}{-2x}$
14. $\frac{32x^3y^2z^4}{4x^4yz^6}$

In 15–21, choose the value of the expression.

	(1)	(2)	(3)	(4)
15. $5x^0$	0	1	5	$\frac{1}{5}$
16. $4(2x)^0$	0	4	8	$\frac{1}{8}$
17. 3^{-2}	-9	-6	$-\frac{1}{9}$	$\frac{1}{9}$
18. $2 \cdot 5^{-2}$	$\frac{2}{25}$	$\frac{1}{50}$	50	-20
19. $3^0 \cdot 3^{-1}$	$\frac{1}{9}$	-9	$\frac{1}{3}$	-3
20. $(\frac{1}{2})^{-3}$	$\frac{1}{8}$	$\frac{1}{6}$	6	8
21. $\frac{2}{4^{-2}}$	$\frac{1}{4}$	4	32	64

In 22–27, rewrite the expression using only positive exponents, and evaluate as possible. Assume the variables are not equal to 0.

22. $3xy^{-2}z^{-4}$

23. $\dfrac{5a^4b^{-5}}{c^{-3}}$

24. $\dfrac{4^{-1}x^{-3}}{2^{-2}xy^{-6}}$

25. $777^0 + 0^{777}$

26. $\dfrac{a^0x^3}{2^{-1}a^{-1}x^{-3}}$

27. $3^{-1}(x^2y^{-5})^{-1}$

28. The expression $\left(\dfrac{x^2y^3}{ab^0}\right)^{-1}$ is equivalent to

(1) $x^{-2}y^{-2}$ (2) ax^2y^3 (3) $\dfrac{a}{x^2y^3}$ (4) $\dfrac{x^2y^3}{a}$

In 29–34, evaluate if $x = 2$ and $y = -3$.

29. $3x^3 + (xy)^2 + xy^2$

30. $(x^0 + y^0)^{-1} + \left(\dfrac{x}{y}\right)^{-1}$

31. $(3 + x)^0y + (x^{-1}y^{-1})^0$

32. $y^{-2} - \left(\dfrac{2y}{x}\right)^{-2}$

33. $(x + y)^x + y^{-x}$

34. $\left(\dfrac{1}{y}\right)^x + \left(\dfrac{y}{x}\right)^{-x}$

35. When $a = 4$, $r = 3$, and $n = 4$, find the value of S:

$$S = \frac{a(r^n - 1)}{r - 1}$$

In 36–40, tell which statement is true.

36. (1) $(2)^2(3)^3 = 6^5$ (2) $(5 - 2)^2 = 5^2 - 2^2$ (3) $2^0 = 123^0$ (4) $(-5)^3 > -5$

37. (1) $2^{-1} + 3^{-1} = 5^{-1}$ (2) $\left(\frac{1}{2}\right)^{-1} + \left(\frac{1}{3}\right)^{-1} = \left(\frac{1}{5}\right)^{-1}$ (3) $5^0 - 3^0 = 2^0$ (4) $\dfrac{1}{2^0} = \dfrac{2}{1^0}$

38. (1) $(-3)^2 = -3^2$ (2) $(2 + 3)^2 = 2 + 3^2$ (3) $(2^2)^3 = (2^3)^2$ (4) $[(-2)^2]^3 = [-(2^2)]^3$

39. If $x = 5^a$, then the value of $5x$ is

(1) $x + 1$ (2) 6^a (3) $a + 5$ (4) 5^{a+1}

40. If $10^x = m$, then 10^{3x} equals

(1) $3m$ (2) $3 + m$ (3) 3^m (4) m^3

In 41–46, remove parentheses and combine.

41. $7a + \frac{1}{4}(2a - 8)^2$

42. $b(b - 2) - 5(b^2 - 1)$

43. $(2x + 1)^2 - 2(2x^2 - 1)$

44. $3x^2 - [2x + 3(x - 7) - 6x^2]$

45. $y^2 + 36 - (y^2 - 4) - [12 - (4 - y)^2]$

46. $[a^2 + b^2 - (a - b)^2]^2$

Scientific Notation

A number in SCIENTIFIC NOTATION is expressed as a product of two factors:

(first factor is between 1 and 10) • (second factor is an integral power of 10)

Scientific notation is used to express:

1. **very large numbers, in which case the power of 10 is a *positive* integer.**

   $430{,}000{,}000 = 4.3 \times 10^8$

2. **very small numbers, in which case the power of 10 is a *negative* integer.**

   $0.0000057 = 5.7 \times 10^{-6}$

***To convert from* scientific notation, look at the power of 10 to tell how many places and which way to move the decimal point.**

Examples

Evaluate: **1.** 4.12×10^6 **2.** 3.4×10^{-5}

Solutions:

1. 10^6 tells you to move the decimal point of the first factor 6 places to the right.

$4.12 \times 10^6 = 4.1\,2\,0\,0\,0\,0 = 4{,}120{,}000$

1 2 3 4 5 6

2. 10^{-5} tells you to move the decimal point of the first factor 5 places to the left.

$3.4 \times 10^{-5} = 0\,0\,0\,0\,3.4 = 0.000034$

5 4 3 2 1

***To convert to* scientific notation:**

1. **Determine the first factor, the number between 1 and 10.**
2. **Determine the power of 10 by counting from where the decimal point will be to where the decimal point is.**

Examples

Express in scientific notation: **1.** 32,000,000 **2.** 0.0000000712

Solutions:

1. 3 2,0 0 0,0 0 0. = 3.2×10^7

1 2 3 4 5 6 7

will be ... is

2. 0.0 0 0 0 0 0 0 7 1 2 = 7.12×10^{-8}

8 7 6 5 4 3 2 1

is ... will be

To calculate **in scientific notation, follow the laws of exponents and use the properties of real numbers.**

Example

$$\frac{(4.6 \times 10^3) \times (3 \times 10^{-2})}{(2 \times 10^4)}$$

$$= \frac{(4.6)(3) \times 10^{3+(-2)}}{2 \times 10^4} = \frac{13.8 \times 10^1}{2 \times 10^4}$$

$$= \frac{13.8}{2} \times 10^{1-4}$$

$$= 6.9 \times 10^{-3}$$

or 0.0069

EXERCISES

In 1–6, write as a decimal.

1. 8×10^5 **3.** 7.1×10^{-4} **5.** 3.14×10^8

2. 9.4×10^6 **4.** 6.3×10^{-7} **6.** 5.23×10^{-5}

In 7–12, convert to scientific notation.

7. 41,000 **9.** 0.00064 **11.** 1,370,000,000

8. 358,000 **10.** 0.00000091 **12.** 0.00000836

13. The expression 2.3×10^{-5} is equivalent to
(1) 0.0000023 **(3)** 230,000
(2) 0.000023 **(4)** 2,300,000

14. 0.0000703 is equivalent to
(1) 70.3×10^{-5} **(3)** 7.03×10^5
(2) 7.03×10^{-5} **(4)** 70.3×10^5

15. 6,340,000 is equivalent to
(1) 63.4×10^5 **(3)** 6.34×10^6
(2) 634×10^4 **(4)** $6,340 \times 10^3$

16. In scientific notation, $0.0000000364 = 3.64 \times 10^n$. The value of n is
(1) 8 **(2)** 10 **(3)** –10 **(4)** –8

In 17–22, write the value of n.

17. $3,100,000 = 3.1 \times 10^n$

18. $0.00026 = 2.6 \times 10^n$

19. $0.00238 = 2.38 \times 10^n$

20. $774,000,000 = 7.74 \times 10^n$

21. $\frac{287}{1,000,000} = 2.87 \times 10^n$

22. $2.5(10)^4 \times 5.6(10)^2 = 1.4 \times 10^n$

23. The rational number 0.0000036 is equivalent to
(1) $(0.006)^2$ **(3)** 3.6×10^{-6}
(2) 3.6×10^6 **(4)** $\frac{36}{10,000}$

24. The velocity of light is approximately 186,000 miles per second. In 10 seconds, the distance light travels would be most nearly
(1) 1.86×10^4 miles **(3)** 1.86×10^{-6} miles
(2) 1.86×10^6 miles **(4)** 1.86×10^7 miles

In 25–32, choose the value of the expression.

25. $(1.2 \times 10^8) \times (1.2 \times 10^{-4})$ is
(1) 1.2×10^4 **(3)** 1.44×100^4
(2) 1.44×10^4 **(4)** 1.44×10^{-32}

26. $\frac{6 \times 10^8}{3 \times 10^2}$ is
(1) 2×10^6 **(3)** 2×10^{-6}
(2) 2×10^4 **(4)** 2×10^{-4}

27. $\frac{4 \times 10^{-10}}{2 \times 10^{-5}}$ is
(1) 0.0002 **(3)** 2,000
(2) 0.00002 **(4)** 20,000

28. $(0.007)^2$ is
(1) 4.9×10^6 **(3)** 4.9×10^{-5}
(2) 4.9×10^{-2} **(4)** 4.9×10^{-6}

29. (0.002)(0.0003) is
(1) 6×10^7 **(3)** 6×10^{-7}
(2) 6×10^9 **(4)** 6×10^{-9}

30. $(2.5 \times 10^5)^2$ is
(1) 6.25×10^7 **(3)** 2.5×10^7
(2) 6.25×10^{10} **(4)** 2.5×10^{10}

31. $\frac{(8 \times 10^6) \times (3 \times 10^{-3})}{(4 \times 10^4)}$ is
(1) 60 **(3)** 0.6
(2) 6 **(4)** 0.06

32. $\frac{(5 \times 10^3) \times (15 \times 10^4) + (6 \times 10^5)}{(3 \times 10^2)}$ is
(1) 3,100,000 **(3)** 25,020,000
(2) 2,502,000 **(4)** 31,002,000

1.4 RADICALS

Simplifying Radicals

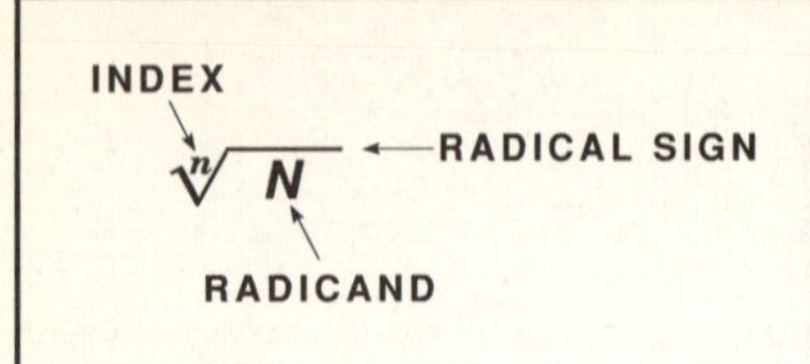

For a square root, factor the radicand so that one factor is the largest perfect square possible. The square root of the perfect-square factor multiplies the remaining radical.

Indexes other than 2 are treated in a similar fashion.

If the perfect-*n* factor chosen is not the largest one possible, the procedure has to be performed more than once.

Examples

Write each of the following irrational numbers in *simplest radical form.*

1. $2\sqrt{108}$
$= 2\sqrt{36} \cdot \sqrt{3}$
$= 2 \cdot 6 \cdot \sqrt{3}$
$= 12\sqrt{3}$

2. $5\sqrt[3]{16}$
$= 5\sqrt[3]{8} \cdot \sqrt[3]{2}$
$= 5 \cdot 2 \cdot \sqrt[3]{2}$
$= 10\sqrt[3]{2}$

The coefficient and exponent of a radicand are affected differently by an index:

1. **For an index *n*, the coefficient is factored using a perfect-*n* factor.**
2. **The exponent is factored using the highest exponent that is divisible by *n*.**

Examples

1. $\sqrt{x^8} = \sqrt{(x^4)^2} = x^4$

2. $\sqrt{y^7} = \sqrt{y^6} \cdot \sqrt{y}$
$= \sqrt{(y^3)^2} \cdot \sqrt{y}$
$= y^3\sqrt{y}$

3. $\sqrt{72a^6b^9}$
$= \sqrt{36} \cdot \sqrt{2} \cdot \sqrt{a^6} \cdot \sqrt{b^8} \cdot \sqrt{b}$
$= 6 \cdot \sqrt{2} \cdot a^3 \cdot b^4 \cdot \sqrt{b}$
$= 6a^3b^4\sqrt{2b}$

The process of simplification depends upon the product and quotient properties of radicals, shown here for square roots. When *a* and *b* are positive:

$$\sqrt{ab} = \sqrt{a} \cdot \sqrt{b} \quad \text{and} \quad \sqrt{\frac{a}{b}} = \frac{\sqrt{a}}{\sqrt{b}}$$

These properties are also true for indexes other than 2.

Since the real numbers are not closed under the operation of extracting a root, there is a restriction on the nature of the radicand, namely, the radicand must be positive when the index is even.

EXERCISES

In 1–11, choose the equivalent value.

1. $\sqrt{300}$ (1) $50\sqrt{6}$ (2) $12\sqrt{5}$ (3) $3\sqrt{10}$ (4) $10\sqrt{3}$
2. $\sqrt{48}$ (1) $16\sqrt{3}$ (2) $4\sqrt{12}$ (3) $4\sqrt{3}$ (4) $2\sqrt{3}$
3. $\sqrt{90}$ (1) $9\sqrt{10}$ (2) $6\sqrt{15}$ (3) $3\sqrt{10}$ (4) $10\sqrt{3}$
4. $3\sqrt{18}$ (1) $9\sqrt{2}$ (2) $3\sqrt{2}$ (3) $3\sqrt{6}$ (4) $9\sqrt{3}$
5. $5\sqrt{3}$ (1) $\sqrt{15}$ (2) $\sqrt{53}$ (3) $\sqrt{75}$ (4) 225
6. $\frac{1}{2}\sqrt{28}$ (1) $\sqrt{14}$ (2) $2\sqrt{7}$ (3) $\sqrt{7}$ (4) 7
7. $\sqrt{\frac{2}{7}}$ (1) $\frac{\sqrt{2}}{\sqrt{7}}$ (3) $\frac{2}{\sqrt{7}}$
(2) $\frac{\sqrt{2}}{7}$ (4) $\frac{\sqrt{2}}{7}$ and $\frac{2}{\sqrt{7}}$
8. $\sqrt{16x^{16}}$ (1) $4x^4$ (2) $8x^8$ (3) $4x^8$ (4) $8x^4$
9. $\sqrt[3]{27x^{27}}$ (1) $9x^9$ (2) $3x^3$ (3) $9x^3$ (4) $3x^9$
10. $\sqrt{6x^6y^8}$ (1) $3x^3y^4$ (2) $x^3y^4\sqrt{6}$ (3) $x^{\sqrt{6}}y^{\sqrt{8}}\sqrt{6}$
11. $\sqrt[3]{8x^8y^9}$ (1) $2x^2y^3$ (2) $2x^5y^3$ (3) $2x^2y^3\sqrt[3]{x^2}$
12. Which is not equal to $\sqrt{200}$?
(1) $10\sqrt{2}$ (2) $8\sqrt{5}$ (3) $5\sqrt{8}$ (4) $2\sqrt{50}$
13. Which is equal to $\sqrt{1{,}000x^{1{,}000}}$?
(1) $500x^{500}$ (3) $10x^{10\sqrt{10}}\sqrt{10}$
(2) $10x^{500}\sqrt{10}$ (4) $100x^{100}$
14. Which is not equal to $\sqrt{\frac{5}{4}}$?
(1) $\sqrt{1\frac{1}{4}}$ (2) $\frac{\sqrt{5}}{\sqrt{4}}$ (3) $\frac{\sqrt{5}}{2}$ (4) $\frac{5}{2}$

In 15–37, express the radical in simplest form. Radicands and exponents should be positive.

15. $2\sqrt{45}$

16. $5\sqrt[3]{32}$

17. $0.3\sqrt[4]{64}$

18. $-\sqrt{50x^6}$

19. $\sqrt{\frac{4}{9}x^{10}}$

20. $\sqrt[3]{-54a^3}$

21. $4\sqrt{\frac{9}{16}x^6y^8}$

22. $\sqrt{0.0625q^{10}}$

23. $\sqrt[3]{\frac{81}{64}x^3y^4}$

24. $\sqrt[3]{0.729x^{12}}$

25. $\sqrt{x^{2a}y^{4b}}$

26. $\sqrt[a]{x^{2a}}$

27. $\frac{3}{4}\sqrt{32x^2y^3}$

28. $-\frac{1}{2}\sqrt[3]{-16a^6}$

29. $\sqrt[3]{48x^7}$

30. $\sqrt{x^0y^{-4}z^5}$

31. $\frac{1}{25}\sqrt[3]{4{,}000a^{-3}}$

32. $7\sqrt[4]{1{,}250m^4n^8}$

33. $\sqrt[4]{\frac{81}{16}x^8y^{10}}$

34. $\sqrt[3]{1{,}728y^{-3}}$

35. $0.2\sqrt[4]{0.0001x^{-4}}$

36. $\sqrt{r^2 - 4r + 4}$

37. $\sqrt{\frac{24x^{-4}z^{-8}}{y^{-6}}}$

Combining Radicals by Addition or Subtraction

Numbers in radical form are *alike* if the radical parts are the same in index and in radicand.

like radicals

$\sqrt{3}$ and $2\sqrt{3}$ $\qquad 5\sqrt[3]{2}$ and $3\sqrt[3]{2}$

unlike radicals

different radicands: $\sqrt{3}$ and $\sqrt{5}$ $\quad \sqrt{x}$ and $\sqrt{3x}$

different indexes: $\sqrt{3}$ and $\sqrt[3]{3}$

Like radicals are combined by adding or subtracting the coefficients, thus applying the distributive property.

$$3\sqrt{2x} + 5\sqrt{2x} = (3 + 5)\sqrt{2x} = 8\sqrt{2x}$$

Sometimes numbers in radical form do not look alike, but after simplifying, they are alike.

Example

$$x\sqrt{3} + \sqrt{75x^2} = x\sqrt{3} + \sqrt{25}\cdot\sqrt{3}\cdot\sqrt{x^2}$$
$$= x\sqrt{3} + 5x\sqrt{3}$$
$$= (x + 5x)\sqrt{3} = 6x\sqrt{3}$$

EXERCISES

In 1–8, choose the equivalent value.

1. The sum of $6\sqrt{6}$ and $\sqrt{54}$ is
(1) $3\sqrt{6}$ **(2)** $6\sqrt{60}$ **(3)** $9\sqrt{6}$ **(4)** $15\sqrt{6}$

2. $\sqrt{48} - \sqrt{12}$ is
(1) 6 **(2)** 2 **(3)** $3\sqrt{2}$ **(4)** $2\sqrt{3}$

3. $\sqrt{125} - \sqrt{20}$ is
(1) $5\sqrt{3}$ **(2)** $3\sqrt{5}$ **(3)** $21\sqrt{5}$ **(4)** $\sqrt{105}$

4. $\sqrt{27} + \sqrt{12}$ is
(1) $\sqrt{39}$ **(2)** $13\sqrt{3}$ **(3)** $5\sqrt{6}$ **(4)** $5\sqrt{3}$

5. $a\sqrt{8} + \sqrt{50a^2}$ is
(1) $29a$ **(2)** $7a\sqrt{2}$ **(3)** $29a\sqrt{2}$ **(4)** $27a$

6. $\sqrt[3]{16} + 5\sqrt[3]{54}$ is
(1) $5\sqrt[3]{70}$ **(2)** $6\sqrt[3]{70}$ **(3)** $17\sqrt[3]{2}$ **(4)** $13\sqrt[3]{2}$

7. $3\sqrt[4]{162} + \sqrt[4]{1{,}250}$ is
(1) $3\sqrt[4]{1{,}412}$ **(2)** $4\sqrt[4]{1{,}412}$ **(3)** 28 **(4)** $14\sqrt[4]{2}$

8. $\frac{1}{2}\sqrt{112} - \sqrt{28} + 2\sqrt{63}$ is
(1) $6\sqrt{7}$ **(2)** $7\sqrt{7}$ **(3)** $8\sqrt{7}$ **(4)** $10\sqrt{7}$

In 9–15, combine into a single term in simplest radical form.

9. $\sqrt{18} + 15\sqrt{2}$

10. $\sqrt{27a^2} + a\sqrt{3}$

11. $x\sqrt{72} - \sqrt{50x^2}$

12. $7\sqrt[3]{16} + \sqrt[3]{432}$

13. $\sqrt[3]{0.001} - x^0$

14. $\sqrt{5\frac{4}{9}a^2b^3} + \sqrt{a^2b^3}$

15. $3\sqrt{\frac{1}{m^{-2}}} + \left(\sqrt{m^{-2}}\right)^{-1}$

In 16–21, simplify and combine.

16. $5\sqrt{27} - \sqrt{108} - 3\sqrt{75}$

17. $7\sqrt{18} - \frac{3}{4}\sqrt{32} + \frac{1}{2}\sqrt{8}$

18. $\frac{1}{5}\sqrt{150} - 4\sqrt{48} + 2\sqrt{54}$

19. $\sqrt{72} + \sqrt[3]{-8} + \sqrt{1{,}250}$

20. $\frac{1}{7}\sqrt{343} + \sqrt{121} - 5\sqrt{175}$

21. $\frac{1}{3}\sqrt[3]{-0.081} + \sqrt[3]{192} - 0.1\sqrt[3]{0.375}$

Multiplying and Dividing Radicals

Any two numbers in radical form can be multiplied or divided when the *indexes are the same.*

1. Multiply or divide the coefficients.

2. Multiply or divide the radicands.

3. Simplify.

Examples

1. $6\sqrt{5}\cdot 2\sqrt{15}$
$= 6\cdot 2\sqrt{5\cdot 15}$
$= 12\sqrt{75}$
$= 12\sqrt{25}\cdot\sqrt{3}$
$= 12\cdot 5\cdot\sqrt{3}$
$= 60\sqrt{3}$

2. $16\sqrt{125} \div 8\sqrt{5}$

$= \frac{16}{8}\sqrt{\frac{125}{5}}$

$= 2\sqrt{25}$

$= 2 \cdot 5 = 10$

3. $(3 + \sqrt{2})(4 - \sqrt{2}) = 3 \cdot 4 + 4\sqrt{2} - 3\sqrt{2} - \sqrt{2} \cdot \sqrt{2}$

$= 12 + (4 - 3)\sqrt{2} - \sqrt{4}$

$= 12 + \sqrt{2} - 2$

$= 10 + \sqrt{2}$

EXERCISES

In 1–10, choose the equivalent value.

1. $(4\sqrt{5})(\sqrt{10})$
(1) $5\sqrt{50}$ (2) $8\sqrt{5}$ (3) $20\sqrt{2}$ (4) $\sqrt{200}$

2. $(3\sqrt{18})(4\sqrt{2})$
(1) 12 (2) 72 (3) $36\sqrt{2}$ (4) $\sqrt{72}$

3. $\left(\frac{1}{2}\sqrt{\frac{1}{2}}\right)(8\sqrt{56})$
(1) $16\sqrt{7}$ (2) $8\sqrt{7}$ (3) $4\sqrt{7}$ (4) $2\sqrt{7}$

4. $(\sqrt[4]{2})(\sqrt[4]{24})$
(1) $\sqrt[4]{6}$ (2) $2\sqrt[4]{3}$ (3) $3\sqrt{6}$ (4) $4\sqrt{3}$

5. $(3\sqrt{6xy})(\sqrt{6xy^2})$
(1) $108xy$ (3) $108xy\sqrt{y}$
(2) $18xy$ (4) $18xy\sqrt{y}$

6. $\sqrt{3} \cdot \sqrt[3]{3} \cdot \sqrt{8}$
(1) $\sqrt[6]{72}$ (3) $\sqrt[5]{72}$
(2) $\sqrt[12]{72}$ (4) $2\sqrt{6} \cdot \sqrt[3]{3}$

7. $\dfrac{48\sqrt{54x^5y}}{4\sqrt{3xy}}$
(1) $72x^2$ (2) $36x^2\sqrt{2}$ (3) $72x^2y$ (4) $36x^2y$

8. $(\sqrt{128} - \sqrt{72}) \div \sqrt{8}$
(1) 1 (2) $8\sqrt{2} - 3$ (3) $\sqrt{7}$ (4) $4 - 6\sqrt{2}$

9. If $x = 3 + \sqrt{2}$, then x^2 is
(1) 11 (2) $11 + 6\sqrt{2}$ (3) $9 + \sqrt{2}$ (4) 5

10. $(9 - \sqrt{5})(3 + \sqrt{5})$
(1) 22 (3) $22 + 6\sqrt{5}$
(2) $27 - \sqrt{5}$ (4) $27 - 6\sqrt{5}$

In 11–35, perform the operations and simplify.

11. $(5\sqrt{8})(3\sqrt{2})$

12. $(3\sqrt{60})(3\sqrt{30})$

13. $(4\sqrt{3})^2$

14. $(3\sqrt{5})(-2\sqrt{15})$

15. $\left(x\sqrt{\frac{9}{16}}\right)(xy\sqrt{32})$

16. $(3\sqrt[3]{2})(\sqrt[3]{16})$

17. $(4x\sqrt{10x})(5\sqrt{20x})$

18. $(6\sqrt[5]{-64})(\sqrt[5]{4})$

19. $(\sqrt{2})(\sqrt[3]{2})(\sqrt{6})$

20. $\sqrt{3}(3\sqrt{2} + \sqrt{3})$

21. $4\sqrt{3}(\sqrt{3} - 3\sqrt{6})$

22. $(2 + \sqrt{5})^2$

23. $(6 - \sqrt{2})(4 + \sqrt{2})$

24. $(\sqrt{3} + 5)(\sqrt{3} - 4)$

25. $(\sqrt{3} - 1)(\sqrt{2} + 3)$

26. $\sqrt{60} \div \sqrt{3}$

27. $(10\sqrt{80}) \div (2\sqrt{5})$

28. $(3\sqrt{54}) \div (6\sqrt{3})$

29. $(16\sqrt{512xy}) \div (2\sqrt{32x})$

30. $\dfrac{\sqrt{360x^3y^5}}{\sqrt{8xy}}$

31. $(\sqrt{2} \cdot \sqrt[3]{3}) \div \sqrt{6}$

32. $\dfrac{\sqrt{150} + \sqrt{75}}{\sqrt{3}}$

33. $\dfrac{4\sqrt{20} + 6\sqrt{30}}{2\sqrt{10}}$

34. $\dfrac{15\sqrt{48} - 30\sqrt{24}}{3\sqrt{6}}$

35. $\dfrac{\sqrt[3]{16} + \sqrt[3]{128}}{\sqrt[3]{2}}$

Rationalizing Denominators

A fraction that contains a radical in its denominator can be rewritten as an equivalent fraction with a *rational denominator*.

When the denominator is a monomial:

1. Multiply both the numerator and the denominator of the fraction by the smallest factor that will make the denominator a perfect *n*th power.

***Note:* The multiplication property of 1 allows a fraction to be changed in form without changing its value.**

2. Simplify.

Examples

Rewrite each expression as an equivalent fraction with a rational denominator:

1. $\dfrac{1}{\sqrt{2}}$ **2.** $\dfrac{4}{\sqrt{12}}$ **3.** $\dfrac{2}{\sqrt[3]{4}}$ **4.** $9\sqrt{\frac{5}{3}}$

Solutions:

1. The next higher perfect square that the denominator $\sqrt{2}$ could become is $\sqrt{4}$. Multiply numerator and denominator by $\sqrt{2}$, and simplify.

$$\frac{1}{\sqrt{2}} = \frac{1}{\sqrt{2}} \cdot \frac{\sqrt{2}}{\sqrt{2}} = \frac{\sqrt{2}}{\sqrt{4}} = \frac{\sqrt{2}}{2}$$

2. The next higher perfect square that the denominator $\sqrt{12}$ could become is $\sqrt{36}$. Multiply numerator and denominator by $\sqrt{3}$, and simplify.

$$\frac{4}{\sqrt{12}} = \frac{4}{\sqrt{12}} \cdot \frac{\sqrt{3}}{\sqrt{3}} = \frac{4\sqrt{3}}{\sqrt{36}} = \frac{4\sqrt{3}}{6} = \frac{2\sqrt{3}}{3}$$

3. The next higher perfect cube that the denominator $\sqrt[3]{4}$ could become is $\sqrt[3]{8}$. Multiply numerator and denominator by $\sqrt[3]{2}$, and simplify.

$$\frac{2}{\sqrt[3]{4}} = \frac{2}{\sqrt[3]{4}} \cdot \frac{\sqrt[3]{2}}{\sqrt[3]{2}} = \frac{2\sqrt[3]{2}}{\sqrt[3]{8}} = \frac{2\sqrt[3]{2}}{2} = \sqrt[3]{2}$$

4. Rewrite the fraction.

$$9\sqrt{\tfrac{5}{3}} = \frac{9\sqrt{5}}{\sqrt{3}} = \frac{9\sqrt{5}}{\sqrt{3}} \cdot \frac{\sqrt{3}}{\sqrt{3}}$$

$$= \frac{9\sqrt{15}}{3} = 3\sqrt{15}$$

When the denominator is a binomial of the form $a + \sqrt{b}$, multiply numerator and denominator by its CONJUGATE $a - \sqrt{b}$.

Examples

In 1–3, write the conjugate of the given binomial.

Binomial	Conjugate
1. $2 + \sqrt{5}$	$2 - \sqrt{5}$
2. $-1 + \sqrt{3}$	$-1 - \sqrt{3}$
3. $5 - \sqrt{2}$	$5 + \sqrt{2}$

In 4–5, rationalize the denominator, and simplify.

4. $$\frac{3}{4+\sqrt{3}} = \frac{3}{4+\sqrt{3}} \cdot \frac{4-\sqrt{3}}{4-\sqrt{3}} = \frac{12-3\sqrt{3}}{16+4\sqrt{3}-4\sqrt{3}-3}$$
$$= \frac{12-3\sqrt{3}}{13}$$

5. $$\frac{\sqrt{3}-1}{-\sqrt{3}-1} = \frac{\sqrt{3}-1}{-\sqrt{3}-1} \cdot \frac{-\sqrt{3}+1}{-\sqrt{3}+1} = \frac{-3+\sqrt{3}+\sqrt{3}-1}{3+\sqrt{3}-\sqrt{3}-1}$$
$$= \frac{-4+2\sqrt{3}}{2}$$
$$= -2 + \sqrt{3}$$

EXERCISES

In 1–6, rationalize the denominator, and simplify.

1. $\frac{1}{\sqrt{5}}$
2. $\sqrt{\frac{2}{3}}$
3. $\frac{3}{\sqrt{18}}$
4. $\frac{4}{\sqrt[3]{16}}$
5. $\frac{8}{\sqrt[4]{64}}$
6. $\frac{3\sqrt{5}-\sqrt{3}}{\sqrt{3}}$

In 7–10, express as a monomial in simplest form.

7. $\sqrt{24} - 6\sqrt{\frac{2}{3}}$
8. $3\sqrt{8} + 4\sqrt{\frac{1}{2}}$
9. $3\sqrt{60} - 6\sqrt{\frac{5}{3}}$
10. $\frac{9}{\sqrt{27}} + \sqrt{12}$

In 11–14, choose the equivalent value.

11. $\frac{\sqrt{50}}{3\sqrt{8}}$ (1) $\frac{2}{3}$ (2) $\frac{5}{3}$ (3) $\frac{5}{6}$ (4) $\frac{7}{6}$

12. $\sqrt{\frac{4}{3}} - \sqrt{\frac{3}{4}}$ (1) 1 (2) 0 (3) $\frac{\sqrt{3}}{6}$ (4) $2\sqrt{3}$

13. $\frac{b}{\sqrt{b}}$ for $b > 0$ (1) 1 (2) $\frac{1}{\sqrt{1}}$ (3) $\frac{1}{\sqrt{b}}$ (4) $\sqrt{b}$

14. $\frac{\sqrt{3}-\sqrt{2}}{\sqrt{2}}$
(1) $\sqrt{3}$ (2) $\frac{\sqrt{6}-2}{2}$ (3) $\frac{\sqrt{3}-2}{2}$ (4) $\sqrt{3}-1$

15. What is the multiplicative inverse of $\frac{\sqrt{b}}{a}$ where $a \neq 0$ and $b > 0$?
(1) $\frac{a\sqrt{b}}{b}$ (2) $\frac{\sqrt{a}}{b}$ (3) $\sqrt{ab}$ (4) $a\sqrt{b}$

16. The reciprocal of $3 - \sqrt{5}$ is
(1) $\frac{3-\sqrt{5}}{4}$ (2) $\frac{3+\sqrt{5}}{4}$ (3) $\frac{3+\sqrt{5}}{14}$ (4) $\frac{3-\sqrt{5}}{14}$

17. Which value of x satisfies the equation $(\sqrt{3}-1)x = 1$?
(1) $\sqrt{3}+2$ (2) $\frac{\sqrt{3}+1}{2}$ (3) $\sqrt{3}$ (4) $\frac{\sqrt{3}}{2}$

18. The solution of $(1-\sqrt{2})y = 3$ is
(1) $1-\sqrt{2}$ (3) $3+3\sqrt{2}$
(2) $1+\sqrt{2}$ (4) $-3-3\sqrt{2}$

19. The area of a square is represented by $\frac{1}{K}$. What is the perimeter of this square in terms of K?
(1) $\frac{4}{K}$ (2) $\sqrt{K}$ (3) $\frac{4\sqrt{K}}{K}$ (4) $\frac{K}{4}$

20. If $\sqrt{3} = 1.732$, what is the value of $\sqrt{\frac{1}{12}}$ to the nearest tenth?
(1) 0.8 (2) 0.2 (3) 0.3 (4) 0.4

In 21-30, choose the equivalent value.

21. $\frac{2}{\sqrt{3}-1}$
(1) $\sqrt{3}+1$ (3) $\sqrt{3}+2$
(2) $\frac{\sqrt{3}+3}{2}$ (4) $2\sqrt{3}+1$

22. $\frac{2}{3-\sqrt{3}}$
(1) $3+\sqrt{3}$ (3) $\frac{3+\sqrt{3}}{3}$
(2) $\frac{3+\sqrt{3}}{2}$ (4) $\frac{1}{3}$

23. $\frac{3}{\sqrt{6}-1}$
(1) $\frac{3\sqrt{6}-3}{5}$ (3) $3\sqrt{6}-3$
(2) $\frac{3\sqrt{6}+3}{5}$ (4) $3\sqrt{6}+3$

24. $\dfrac{5}{2-\sqrt{3}}$

(1) $10+5\sqrt{3}$ (3) $-10-5\sqrt{3}$
(2) $-2-\sqrt{3}$ (4) $2+\sqrt{3}$

25. $\dfrac{3}{\sqrt{3}-\sqrt{2}}$

(1) $3\sqrt{6}$ (3) $\dfrac{\sqrt{3}-\sqrt{2}}{2}$
(2) $3(\sqrt{3}+\sqrt{2})$ (4) $\dfrac{3(\sqrt{3}+\sqrt{2})}{2}$

26. $\dfrac{\sqrt{3}+1}{\sqrt{3}-1}$

(1) -1 (2) 2 (3) $2+\sqrt{3}$ (4) $5+\sqrt{3}$

27. $\dfrac{3+\sqrt{2}}{3-\sqrt{2}}$

(1) $\dfrac{17\sqrt{2}}{7}$ (3) $\dfrac{7-6\sqrt{2}}{7}$
(2) $\dfrac{11+6\sqrt{2}}{7}$ (4) $\dfrac{11}{7}$

28. $\dfrac{3+\sqrt{5}}{3-\sqrt{5}}$

(1) $\dfrac{7}{2}$ (2) $\dfrac{7+3\sqrt{5}}{7}$ (3) $\dfrac{10\sqrt{5}}{7}$ (4) $\dfrac{7+3\sqrt{5}}{2}$

29. $\dfrac{1-\sqrt{3}}{6-\sqrt{3}}$

(1) $\dfrac{3-5\sqrt{3}}{33}$ (2) $\dfrac{3+5\sqrt{3}}{-33}$ (3) $\dfrac{9-5\sqrt{3}}{33}$ (4) $\dfrac{9+5\sqrt{3}}{-33}$

30. $\dfrac{\sqrt{5}+\sqrt{2}}{\sqrt{5}-\sqrt{2}}$

(1) -1 (3) $\dfrac{7+2\sqrt{10}}{3}$
(2) $\dfrac{29+2\sqrt{10}}{21}$ (4) $\dfrac{7}{3}$

In 31-40, rationalize the denominator, and simplify.

31. $\dfrac{1}{3-\sqrt{3}}$

32. $\dfrac{4}{4+\sqrt{2}}$

33. $\dfrac{3}{\sqrt{5}+1}$

34. $\dfrac{3}{2\sqrt{2}-1}$

35. $\dfrac{7\sqrt{2}}{5-\sqrt{2}}$

36. $\dfrac{\sqrt{2}+1}{\sqrt{2}-1}$

37. $\dfrac{4+\sqrt{3}}{4-\sqrt{3}}$

38. $\dfrac{6-\sqrt{2}}{1+\sqrt{2}}$

39. $\dfrac{3+\sqrt{5}}{2-\sqrt{5}}$

40. $\dfrac{\sqrt{2}+\sqrt{3}}{\sqrt{2}-\sqrt{3}}$

Fractional Exponents

$x^{\frac{m}{n}} = \sqrt[n]{x^m}$ **where $n \neq 0$ and $x > 0$ when n is even**

To evaluate an expression containing a fractional exponent:

1. **Use the law of exponents to rewrite the expression in radical form.**
2. **Evaluate the root.**
3. **Evaluate the power.**

Examples

1. $16^{\frac{1}{2}} = \sqrt{16} = 4$
2. $27^{\frac{2}{3}} = \sqrt[3]{27^2}$

   $= 3^2$ Take the cube root.

   $= 9$ Evaluate the square.

Alternate Method: Using the laws of exponents

$27^{\frac{2}{3}} = (3^3)^{\frac{2}{3}} = 3^{3\left(\frac{2}{3}\right)} = 3^2 = 9$

EXERCISES

1. Find the value of $16^{\frac{3}{4}}$.
2. Find the value of $(-8)^{\frac{2}{3}}$.
3. Evaluate $x^{\frac{3}{4}} - x^0$ if $x = 16$.
4. If $a = 4$, find the value of $(4a^0)^{\frac{3}{2}}$.
5. The value of $\left(\frac{8}{27}\right)^{-\frac{2}{3}}$ is

   (1) $\frac{4}{9}$ (2) $-\frac{4}{9}$ (3) $-\frac{2}{3}$ (4) $\frac{9}{4}$
6. Evaluate $a^{-\frac{2}{3}}$ where $a = 27$.
7. Evaluate $(a^{-1})^{\frac{2}{3}}$ where $a = 8$.
8. Find the value of $4a^{-\frac{1}{2}}$ if $a = 9$.
9. Find the value of $2p^0 - p^{\frac{2}{3}}$ if $p = 8$.
10. Express in simplest form the value of $2x^0 + x^{\frac{2}{3}}$ if $x = 27$.
11. Find the value of $A^0 + A^{-\frac{1}{2}}$ when $A = 16$.
12. The expression $8^{\frac{2}{3}} + 8^0 + 8^{-1}$ is equivalent to

    (1) $\frac{97}{8}$ (2) $\frac{33}{8}$ (3) -3 (4) $\frac{41}{8}$
13. When $x = 8$, the value of $[(x^{-2})(27x^0)]^{\frac{1}{3}}$ is

    (1) $\frac{3}{4}$ (2) $\frac{1}{8}$ (3) 12 (4) 4
14. Evaluate the following if $x = 8$:

    $x^{-1}(3x^{\frac{1}{3}} + x^0)$

1.5 FRACTIONS

The Domain of the Variable

Over the set of real numbers, an algebraic fraction is defined only for those values of the variable that:

1. do not yield a denominator of 0

2. do not yield a negative radicand for an even index

Examples

In 1-4, tell the value(s) of the variable for which the fraction is not defined.

	Fraction	Not Defined for
1.	$\frac{4}{x-3}$	$x = 3$
2.	$\frac{2}{y^2-9}$	$y = \pm 3$
3.	$\frac{1}{\sqrt{3-x}}$	$x \geq 3$
4.	$\frac{x-7}{\sqrt{x-5}}$	$x \leq 5$

EXERCISES

In 1-26, write the value(s) of the variable, if any, for which the expression is *not* defined.

1. $\frac{7}{a}$

2. $\frac{5}{2-x}$

3. $\frac{12}{y+8}$

4. $\frac{x}{9}$

5. $\frac{12r}{r}$

6. $\frac{10m}{10m}$

7. $\frac{x-2}{x^2+4}$

8. $\frac{w-4}{4-w}$

9. $\frac{z-3}{7}$

10. $\frac{x+2}{3x-6}$

11. $\frac{10}{x^2-25}$

12. $\frac{b-4}{b^2-16}$

13. $\frac{r-2}{9-r^2}$

14. $\frac{15}{x^2+3x-10}$

15. $\frac{(x+1)(x-2)}{(x-1)(x+2)}$

16. $\frac{x^2-49}{2x^2-3x}$

17. $\frac{x}{x+2} - \frac{x}{x-4}$

18. $\frac{x-2}{7} + \frac{3-x}{14}$

19. $\frac{3}{\sqrt{x}}$

20. $\frac{\sqrt{x}}{\sqrt{y}}$

21. $\frac{2}{\sqrt{x-4}}$

22. $\frac{2}{\sqrt{2-y}}$

23. $\frac{3}{\sqrt{x^2-1}}$

24. $\frac{2-x}{\sqrt{3-x}}$

25. $\frac{\frac{1}{x}}{\frac{1}{x-2}}$

26. $\frac{\frac{1}{x}+\frac{1}{x-2}}{\frac{1}{3-x}}$

Simplifying Fractions

A fraction is in *simplest form*, or *lowest terms*, if its numerator and denominator have no common factors other than 1 or –1.

To simplify a fraction:

1. completely factor the numerator and the denominator

2. cancel common factors

A factor of the form $a - b$ will cancel a factor of the form $b - a$ with a resulting factor of –1.

$$\frac{\overset{1}{\cancel{a-b}}}{\underset{-1}{\cancel{b-a}}} = -1$$

Examples

1. $\frac{x^2+2x-3}{x^2-1} = \frac{(x+3)(x-1)}{(x+1)(x-1)}$ Factor completely.

$= \frac{(x+3)\cancel{(x-1)}}{(x+1)\cancel{(x-1)}}$ Cancel common factors.

$= \frac{x+3}{x+1}$ The x's here are not common factors.

Note: The domain of the variable depends on the *original* fraction. Thus, in Example 1, the fraction is not defined for $x = \pm 1$.

2. $\frac{10-5x}{15x-30} = \frac{5(2-x)}{15(x-2)}$ Factor completely.

$= \frac{\overset{1}{\cancel{5}}\,\overset{-1}{\cancel{(2-x)}}}{\underset{3}{\cancel{15}}\,\underset{1}{\cancel{(x-2)}}}$ Cancel common factors.

Note: $2 - x = (-1)(x - 2)$

$= \frac{-1}{3}$ or $-\frac{1}{3}$

3. $\frac{5x^2-15x}{27x-3x^3} = \frac{5x(x-3)}{3x(9-x^2)} = \frac{5x(x-3)}{3x(3+x)(3-x)}$ Factor completely.

$= \frac{5\overset{1}{\cancel{x}}\overset{-1}{\cancel{(x-3)}}}{3\underset{1}{\cancel{x}}(3+x)\underset{1}{\cancel{(3-x)}}}$ Cancel common factors.

$= \frac{-5}{3(3+x)}$

EXERCISES

In 1–9, choose the equivalent form.

1. $\frac{-12x^6y^2}{3x^2y}$

(1) $9x^3y^2$ (2) $4x^4y$ (3) $-4x^3y$ (4) $-4x^4y$

2. $\frac{x^2+2x-3}{x^2+3x}$

(1) $\frac{x-1}{x}$ (2) $\frac{2x-3}{3x}$ (3) $-\frac{1}{3}$ (4) $\frac{3}{x}$

3. $\frac{4a-4b}{8b-8a}$

(1) $\frac{1}{2}$ (2) $-\frac{1}{2}$ (3) $-\frac{1}{4}$ (4) $\frac{1}{4}$

4. $\frac{3x-6}{12-3x^2}$

(1) $-\frac{1}{2+x}$ (2) $\frac{-1}{-2-x}$ (3) $-\frac{1}{x-2}$ (4) $\frac{-1}{x-2}$

5. $\frac{y^4}{y^5-y^4}$

(1) $\frac{1}{y-1}$ (2) $y-1$ (3) $-\frac{1}{y}$ (4) $\frac{1}{y}$

6. $\frac{(x+h)^2-x^2}{h}$

(1) h (2) 0 (3) $2x^2+2x+h$ (4) $2x+h$

7. $\frac{3x^3-27xy^2}{12x^2+36xy}$

(1) $\frac{x+3y}{4}$ (2) $\frac{x^2-3xy}{4x}$ (3) $\frac{x-3y}{4}$ (4) $\frac{x^2+3xy}{4}$

8. $\frac{x^2-x-6}{9-x^2}$

(1) $\frac{-x-2}{x+3}$ (2) $\frac{-x+2}{x+3}$ (3) $\frac{-x-2}{-x-3}$ (4) $\frac{-(x-2)}{3+x}$

9. $\frac{ay+xy}{a^2+3ax+2x^2}$

(1) $\frac{-y}{2x}$ (2) $\frac{y}{2x}$ (3) $\frac{y}{a-2x}$ (4) $\frac{y}{a+2x}$

In 10–27, simplify.

10. $\frac{8x^4y^4}{2xy^4}$

11. $3^{-1}(9a-15)$

12. $\frac{x^2+3x}{2(x+3)}$

13. $\frac{2x-2y}{3y-3x}$

14. $\frac{n^2-n-6}{4n-12}$

15. $\frac{2x-10}{25-x^2}$

16. $\frac{x+3}{x^2-2x-15}$

17. $\frac{x^2-4x}{x^2-2x-8}$

18. $\frac{5y-15y^2}{9y^2-1}$

19. $\frac{x^2+3x-10}{x^2+5x}$

20. $\frac{(1-m)^3}{(m-1)^4}$

21. $(r^2-1)^{-1}(3-3r)$

22. $\frac{m^2-6m}{m^2-7m+6}$

23. $\frac{x^2-4x-5}{x^2-2x-15}$

24. $\frac{z^2-z-6}{3z^2-15z+18}$

25. $\frac{2a^2-7a+3}{(a-3)^2}$

26. $\frac{2w^2-50}{w^2+8w+15}$

27. $\frac{48+8m-m^2}{m^2+m-12}$

28. If $a = c$, then $\frac{a+b}{c+d}$ is equal to

(1) $\frac{b}{d}$ (2) $1+\frac{b}{d}$ (3) $\frac{c+b}{c+d}$ (4) $\frac{1+b}{1+d}$

29. If a, b and c represent positive unequal numbers, then $\frac{a+b}{c+b}$ is

(1) always equal to $\frac{a}{c}$
(2) only sometimes equal to $\frac{a}{c}$
(3) never equal to $\frac{a}{c}$
(4) undefined

30. If a and b are additive inverses, which expression is undefined?

(1) $\frac{a+b}{a-b}$ (2) $\frac{b-a}{a+b}$ (3) $\frac{b-a}{a-b}$ (4) $\frac{a-b}{a-b}$

Multiplying Fractions

Fractions can be multiplied by multiplying the numerators and multiplying the denominators.

The multiplication is made easier by first factoring and cancelling common factors, which also avoids having to reduce later.

Example

$$\frac{x^2-x-6}{x-3}\cdot\frac{2}{x+2}=\frac{\overset{1}{\cancel{(x+2)}}\overset{1}{\cancel{(x-3)}}}{\underset{1}{\cancel{(x-3)}}}\cdot\frac{2}{\underset{1}{\cancel{(x+2)}}}$$

$$=\frac{2}{1}=2$$

EXERCISES

In 1–18, express the product in lowest terms.

1. $\left(\frac{ay^2}{b^4}\right)^3\left(\frac{b}{y^3}\right)^5$

2. $\left(\frac{m^2x^3}{y^3}\right)^2\left(\frac{n}{mx}\right)^2$

3. $\frac{(x+y)^2}{4}\cdot\frac{2}{x+y}$

4. $\frac{15}{a^2-9}\cdot\frac{a+3}{30}$

5. $\frac{7r-14}{40}\cdot\frac{10}{2r-4}$

6. $\left(\frac{y^2-16}{2y+6}\right)\left(\frac{y+3}{y-4}\right)$

7. $\frac{x^2-1}{x}\cdot\frac{4x^2}{x+1}$

8. $\frac{x^2-y^2}{2xy}\cdot\frac{x^2}{x-y}$

9. $\frac{4x - 8ax^2}{3} \cdot \frac{3 + 6ax}{8a^2x^2 - 2}$

10. $(y + 1)\left(\frac{y}{1 - y^2}\right)$

11. $\frac{a^2 - b^2}{2a} \cdot \frac{10a^2}{b - a}$

12. $\frac{x^2 - x}{3} \cdot \frac{6}{1 - x^2}$

13. $\left(\frac{3x + 6}{x^2 - 7x + 10}\right)\left(\frac{x - 5}{2 + x}\right)$

14. $\frac{(x - 3)^2}{x^2 - x - 6} \cdot \frac{x + 2}{x - 3}$

15. $\frac{x^2 - 25}{3x - 9} \cdot \frac{x - 3}{x^2 + 10x + 25}$

16. $\left(\frac{a^2 - 25}{5a^2}\right)\left(\frac{a^2 - 5a}{a^2 - 10a + 25}\right)$

17. $\frac{x^2 + 7x + 12}{x^2 - 4} \cdot \frac{4 - 2x}{x + 3}$

18. $\frac{6a^2 - 7ab + 2b^2}{5x} \cdot \frac{10x}{2b - 4a}$

19. The product of $\frac{x^2 - 1}{x}$ and $\frac{4x^2}{x + 1}$ is

(1) $\frac{x - 1}{4x^3}$ (3) $4x(x + 1)$

(2) $\frac{(x^2 - 1)(x + 1)}{4x^3}$ (4) $4x(x - 1)$

20. The product $\frac{x - 2}{x - 1} \cdot \frac{x^2 - 1}{x^2 + x - 6}$ is

(1) 1 (3) $\frac{x + 1}{x + 3}$

(2) $\frac{x^3 - 2}{x^3 - x^2 + x + 6}$ (4) $\frac{x - 1}{x - 6}$

In 21–24, express the product in lowest terms.

21. $\frac{x^2 + 8x + 12}{x^2 - 8x + 16} \cdot \frac{x^2 + x - 20}{x^2 + 11x + 30}$

22. $\frac{3 - x}{x^2 - 4x} \cdot \frac{x^2 - 16}{x^2 + x - 12}$

23. $\frac{x + 2}{3x + 3} \cdot \frac{x^2 + 5x + 4}{2x + 4}$

24. $\frac{x^2 - 6x + 9}{9 - x^2} \cdot \frac{4x^2 + 4x + 1}{2x^2 + 7x + 3}$

Dividing Fractions

Turn a division problem into a multiplication problem by inverting the second fraction. That is, division by a fraction is equivalent to multiplication by the multiplicative inverse, or reciprocal, of that fraction.

Example

$$\frac{x^2 - 9}{x^2 + 5x - 6} \div \frac{x^2 + x - 12}{3x - 3} = \frac{x^2 - 9}{x^2 + 5x - 6} \cdot \frac{3x - 3}{x^2 + x - 12}$$

$$= \frac{(x + 3)\cancel{(x - 3)}}{(x + 6)\cancel{(x - 1)}} \cdot \frac{3\cancel{(x - 1)}}{(x + 4)\cancel{(x - 3)}}$$

$$= \frac{3(x + 3)}{(x + 6)(x + 4)} \text{ or } \frac{3x + 9}{x^2 + 10x + 24}$$

EXERCISES

In 1–12, for all values of the variable for which the expressions are defined, perform the indicated division and express the result in lowest terms.

1. $\frac{a - 1}{3} \div \frac{2a - 2}{5}$

2. $\frac{x^2 - 25}{18} \div \frac{x - 5}{36}$

3. $\frac{3r - 3t}{rt^2} \div \frac{r^2 - t^2}{r^2t}$

4. $\frac{a}{b^2 - 49} \div \frac{4a^3}{2b + 14}$

5. $\frac{6x + 12}{2x + 6} \div \frac{x^2 - 4}{7x + 21}$

6. $\frac{b^2 - 4}{2b - 6} \div \frac{2 - b}{b - 3}$

7. $\frac{r^2 - 25}{5r^2} \div \frac{(5 - r)^2}{r^2 - 5r}$

8. $\frac{x^2 - 4}{x^2 - 5x + 6} \div \frac{x - 2}{9 - 3x}$

9. $\frac{w^2 + 4w + 4}{3w + 6} \div (2 + w)$

10. $\frac{x^2 - 16}{4x} \div \frac{x^2 - 2x - 8}{8x + 16}$

11. $\frac{(2 - x)^2}{x^2 - 16} \div \frac{x^2 + 2x - 8}{x^2 + 6x + 8}$

12. $\frac{x^2 + 2x}{x - 1} \div \frac{x^2 - x - 6}{x^2 + 2x - 3}$

13. $\frac{x - 7}{3x^2 - 8x + 4} \div \frac{3x - 21}{6x^2 - 24}$ is

(1) $\frac{2x + 2}{3x - 2}$ (2) $\frac{2x + 2}{3(x - 2)}$ (3) $\frac{2(x + 2)}{3x - 2}$ (4) $\frac{2(x + 2)}{3(x - 2)}$

14. Which is not a multiplicative inverse for the rational number $\frac{m}{v}$?

(1) $\frac{1}{\frac{m}{v}}$ (2) $\frac{v}{m}$ (3) $-\frac{m}{v}$ (4) $\frac{-v}{-m}$

15. If $x^8 - y^8$ is divided by $x^4 - y^4$, then the quotient is

(1) $x^2 + y^2$ (3) $x^4 + x^2y^2 + y^4$

(2) $x^4 + y^4$ (4) $x^4 - x^2y^2 + y^4$

In 16–19, for all values of the variable for which the expressions are defined, perform the indicated operations and express the result in lowest terms.

16. $\left(\frac{x^2 + 4x + 3}{x^2 + x} \cdot \frac{12 - 3x}{2x}\right) \div \frac{x^2 - x - 12}{4x^3}$

17. $\frac{x^2 - 16}{x^2 - 25} \div \left(\frac{x^2 - 16}{x^2 - x - 20} \cdot \frac{x + 4}{x - 4}\right)$

18. $\left(\frac{x^2 - 9}{x^2 - 3x - 10} \div \frac{3 - x}{5 - x}\right) \cdot \frac{4 + 4x + x^2}{9 + 6x + x^2}$

19. $\frac{x^2 - 9}{27 + 3x^2} \cdot \left(\frac{x^2 + x - 6}{x - 4} \div \frac{6 - x - x^2}{3x - 12}\right)$

Combining Fractions by Addition or Subtraction

CASE 1: **If the *denominators are alike*, keep the denominator and add or subtract the numerators. Reduce the single fraction as needed.**

Examples

1. $\frac{3x}{7} + \frac{4x}{7} = \frac{3x + 4x}{7} = \frac{\cancel{7}x}{\cancel{7}} = x$

2. $\frac{19}{7 + x} + \frac{2}{7 + x} = \frac{19 + 2}{7 + x} = \frac{21}{7 + x}$

3. $\frac{4}{x - 2} + \frac{7}{2 - x} = \frac{4}{x - 2} - \frac{7}{x - 2} = \frac{4 - 7}{x - 2} = \frac{-3}{x - 2}$

CASE 2: If the *denominators are different*, rewrite fractions so that the denominators are alike. Use the lowest common denominator, or L.C.D. To determine the L.C.D., use prime factors.

Examples

1. Express as a single fraction in lowest terms:

$\frac{x+1}{3} - \frac{x-1}{5}$

Solution: The L.C.D. of 3 and 5 is 15.

$$\begin{aligned}\frac{x+1}{3} - \frac{x-1}{5} &= \frac{x+1}{3}\cdot\frac{5}{5} - \frac{x-1}{5}\cdot\frac{3}{3}\\ &= \frac{5(x+1)}{15} - \frac{3(x-1)}{15}\\ &= \frac{5(x+1)-3(x-1)}{15} \quad \text{Note sign.}\\ &= \frac{5x+5-3x+3}{15} = \frac{2x+8}{15}\end{aligned}$$

2. Express as a single fraction in simplest form:

$\frac{5}{1-x} - \frac{1}{x}$

Solution: The L.C.D. of $(1-x)$ and x is $x(1-x)$.

$$\begin{aligned}\frac{5}{1-x} - \frac{1}{x} &= \frac{5}{1-x}\cdot\frac{x}{x} - \frac{1}{x}\cdot\frac{1-x}{1-x}\\ &= \frac{5x}{x(1-x)} - \frac{1-x}{x(1-x)}\\ &= \frac{5x-(1-x)}{x(1-x)}\\ &= \frac{5x-1+x}{x(1-x)}\\ &= \frac{6x-1}{x(1-x)} \text{ or } \frac{6x-1}{x-x^2}\end{aligned}$$

3. Combine and simplify: $\frac{x}{x^2-4} - \frac{1}{x+2}$

Solution: Since $x^2-4 = (x+2)(x-2)$, the L.C.D. of x^2-4 and $x+2$ is $(x+2)(x-2)$.

$$\begin{aligned}\frac{x}{x^2-4} - \frac{1}{x+2} &= \frac{x}{(x+2)(x-2)} - \frac{1}{x+2}\\ &= \frac{x}{(x+2)(x-2)} - \frac{1}{x+2}\cdot\frac{x-2}{x-2}\\ &= \frac{x-(x-2)}{(x+2)(x-2)}\\ &= \frac{x-x+2}{(x+2)(x-2)}\\ &= \frac{2}{(x+2)(x-2)} \text{ or } \frac{2}{x^2-4}\end{aligned}$$

Sometimes several operations are involved.

Example

Perform the indicated operations and express the result in simplest form.

$$\begin{aligned}&\left(1+\frac{1}{x}\right)\left(\frac{1}{x+1}-1\right)\\ &= \left(\frac{1}{1}\cdot\frac{x}{x}+\frac{1}{x}\right)\left(\frac{1}{x+1}-\frac{1}{1}\cdot\frac{x+1}{x+1}\right)\\ &= \left(\frac{x}{x}+\frac{1}{x}\right)\left(\frac{1}{x+1}-\frac{x+1}{x+1}\right)\\ &= \left(\frac{x+1}{x}\right)\left(\frac{1-(x+1)}{x+1}\right)\\ &= \left(\frac{x+1}{x}\right)\left(\frac{1-x-1}{x+1}\right)\\ &= \left(\frac{\cancel{x+1}^{\,1}}{\cancel{x}_{\,1}}\right)\left(\frac{\cancel{-x}^{\,-1}}{\cancel{x+1}_{\,1}}\right) = -1\end{aligned}$$

EXERCISES

1. The expression $\frac{x}{3}+\frac{x}{5}$ is equivalent to

(1) $\frac{8}{15}$ (2) $\frac{8x}{15}$ (3) $\frac{2x}{15}$ (4) $\frac{2x}{8}$

2. The expression $\frac{x}{8}-\frac{x}{2}$ is equivalent to

(1) $\frac{x}{6}$ (2) 0 (3) $\frac{-3x}{8}$ (4) $\frac{-3x}{-8}$

3. Which is equivalent to $\frac{8}{x}-\frac{3}{x}$?

(1) 5 (2) $5x$ (3) $\frac{5}{x}$ (4) $-\frac{5}{x}$

4. What is the sum of $\frac{x-1}{2}$ and $\frac{x-1}{4}$?

(1) $\frac{3x-3}{4}$ (2) $\frac{x-1}{6}$ (3) $\frac{3x-2}{4}$ (4) $\frac{3x-3}{8}$

5. When combined into a single fraction, the expression $\frac{b}{c}-\frac{-c}{g}$ is equivalent to

(1) $\frac{b+c}{cg}$ (2) $\frac{b}{g}$ (3) $\frac{b+c}{c+g}$ (4) $\frac{bg+c^2}{cg}$

6. What is the numerical value of $3^{-1}+4^{-1}$?

(1) $\frac{1}{7}$ (2) 7^{-2} (3) $\frac{1}{12}$ (4) $\frac{7}{12}$

7. The expression $\frac{\sqrt{2}}{3}+\frac{2}{\sqrt{2}}$ is equivalent to

(1) $\frac{3\sqrt{2}}{5}$ (2) $\frac{4\sqrt{2}}{3}$ (3) $3\sqrt{2}$ (4) $\frac{2}{3}$

8. Expressed in simplest form, $\frac{x-7}{6}-\frac{3x-2}{12}$ is equivalent to

(1) $\frac{2x+5}{6}$ (2) $\frac{2x+9}{6}$ (3) $\frac{-x-12}{12}$ (4) $\frac{-x-16}{12}$

9. What is the sum of $\frac{2}{x-2}$ and $\frac{x}{2-x}$?

(1) 1 (2) −1 (3) 0 (4) $\frac{2+x}{2-x}$

10. $\frac{b^2}{b-3}+\frac{9}{3-b}$ is equivalent to

(1) −1 (2) $\frac{1}{3-b}$ (3) $b-3$ (4) $b+3$

11. The expression $x^{-1} + y^{-1}$ is equal to

(1) $(x + y)^{-2}$ (2) $\frac{1}{x + y}$ (3) $\frac{2}{x + y}$ (4) $\frac{x + y}{xy}$

12. What is the sum of $\frac{1}{x + 1}$ and $\frac{1}{x}$?

(1) $2x + 1$ (2) $\frac{2x + 1}{x(x + 1)}$ (3) $\frac{x(x + 1)}{2x + 1}$ (4) $\frac{2}{2x + 1}$

13. When combined into a single fraction, $\frac{3}{x + 2} - \frac{2}{x - 2}$ is equal to

(1) $\frac{1}{x}$ (2) $\frac{5}{x + 2}$ (3) $\frac{x - 10}{x^2 - 4}$ (4) $\frac{x - 4}{x^2 - 4}$

14. When combined into a single term and simplified, the expression $\frac{3}{3x - 1} - \frac{1}{x}$ becomes

(1) $\frac{6x - 1}{x(3x - 1)}$ (2) $\frac{-1}{x(3x - 1)}$ (3) 1 (4) $\frac{1}{x(3x - 1)}$

15. The expression $\frac{x}{x - 1} + \frac{x}{x + 1}$ is equivalent to

(1) 1 (2) $\frac{2x}{x^2 - 1}$ (3) -2 (4) $\frac{2x^2}{x^2 - 1}$

16. The expression $\frac{a}{a - b} - \frac{b}{a + b}$ is equivalent to

(1) 1 (2) $\frac{a + b}{a - b}$ (3) $\frac{1}{a + b}$ (4) $\frac{a^2 + b^2}{a^2 - b^2}$

17. The expression $\frac{x - y}{x + y} - \frac{x + y}{x - y}$ is equivalent to

(1) $\frac{2x^2}{x^2 - y^2}$ (2) $\frac{2y^2}{x^2 - y^2}$ (3) $\frac{-2y^2}{x^2 - y^2}$ (4) $\frac{-4xy}{x^2 - y^2}$

18. The sum of $\frac{2}{x + 1}$ and $\frac{3}{x^2 - 1}$ expressed as a single fraction is

(1) $\frac{2}{x - 1}$ (3) $\frac{2x + 1}{(x + 1)(x - 1)}$

(2) $\frac{5}{(x + 1)(x - 1)}$ (4) $\frac{2}{x + 1}$

19. The expression $\frac{a^2 + 1}{a^2 - 1} - \frac{a}{a + 1}$ is equivalent to

(1) $\frac{-1}{a + 1}$ (2) $\frac{1}{a + 1}$ (3) $\frac{1}{a - 1}$ (4) $\frac{1}{1 - a}$

20. The expression $\frac{x}{x^2 - 9} + \frac{1}{3 - x}$ is equivalent to

(1) $\frac{2x + 3}{x^2 - 9}$ (2) $\frac{3}{x^2 - 9}$ (3) $\frac{-3}{x^2 - 9}$ (4) $\frac{-1}{x^2 - 3}$

21. If $x = \frac{1}{a}$, express $2x + 3$ as a single fraction in terms of a.

22. If $x = \frac{1}{1 + a}$, express $2x - 1$ as a single fraction in terms of a.

In 23–49, for all values of the variable for which the expressions are defined, combine and simplify.

23. $\frac{2x}{3} + \frac{3x}{5}$ **28.** $\frac{3}{x^2} + \frac{6}{x^4}$ **33.** $2 - \frac{x - a}{a - x}$

24. $\frac{3}{x} + \frac{5}{2x}$ **29.** $\frac{x}{3} - \frac{2x - 1}{6}$ **34.** $\frac{x}{x - 2} - 1$

25. $\frac{3}{2x} + \frac{2}{3x}$ **30.** $5 + \frac{1}{a}$ **35.** $\frac{3}{x - 2} - \frac{2}{x}$

26. $\frac{3b}{2a} - \frac{2a}{3b}$ **31.** $6 - \frac{3}{r - 3}$ **36.** $\frac{3}{x - 1} - \frac{1}{x}$

27. $\frac{8}{x} + \frac{2}{x^2}$ **32.** $1 - \frac{x - 1}{x + 1}$ **37.** $\frac{3}{1 - x} - \frac{2}{x}$

38. $\frac{2}{x - 2} + \frac{1}{2 - x}$ **44.** $\frac{4x}{2x + 6} + \frac{x}{x + 3}$

39. $\frac{3}{2x} - \frac{x}{6x - 9}$ **45.** $\frac{3a + 1}{a^2 - 1} - \frac{1}{a + 1}$

40. $\frac{1}{a + b} - \frac{1}{a - b}$ **46.** $\frac{y - 20}{y^2 - 16} + \frac{2}{y - 4}$

41. $\frac{5}{1 - x} - \frac{1}{x}$ **47.** $\frac{1}{a^2 - 1} - \frac{1}{a - 1}$

42. $\frac{3}{x + 1} - \frac{1}{x + 2}$ **48.** $\frac{3}{x^2 - 4} - \frac{2}{2 - x}$

43. $\frac{a}{a - 2} + \frac{2}{2 - a}$ **49.** $\frac{1}{9 - m^2} - \frac{m - 1}{m - 3}$

50. For all values of n for which the expressions are defined, $\left(1 + \frac{1}{n}\right) \div \left(\frac{n + 1}{n^2}\right)$ is equivalent to

(1) $\frac{(n + 1)^2}{n^3}$ (2) $\frac{2n}{n + 1}$ (3) $\frac{n^2}{n + 1}$ (4) n

In 51–54, for all values of the variable for which the expressions are defined, perform the indicated operations and express the result in simplest form.

51. $\left(\frac{1}{t} + \frac{1}{s}\right)\left(\frac{t}{s + t}\right)$ **53.** $\left(1 - \frac{1}{y}\right)\left(\frac{1}{y - 1} + 1\right)$

52. $\left(x - \frac{1}{x}\right)\left(\frac{1}{x + 1} - 1\right)$ **54.** $\left(x^{-1} + y^{-1}\right)\left(\frac{x}{x + y}\right)$

Complex Fractions

A fraction that contains other fractions is called a COMPLEX FRACTION.

There are two methods for simplifying a complex fraction:

1. **Multiply numerator and denominator by the L.C.D. of all the denominators, or**
2. **Treat the complex fraction as a division.**

Example

Simplify: $\dfrac{1+\frac{1}{x}}{1-\frac{1}{x^2}}$

Solution 1: Multiply each term of the numerator and denominator by x^2, which is the L.C.D. of 1, x, and x^2.

$$\frac{1+\frac{1}{x}}{1-\frac{1}{x^2}} = \frac{\frac{1}{1}\cdot x^2+\frac{1}{x}\cdot x^2}{\frac{1}{1}\cdot x^2-\frac{1}{x^2}\cdot x^2}$$

$$= \frac{x^2+x}{x^2-1}$$

$$= \frac{x\cancel{(x+1)}}{\cancel{(x+1)}(x-1)} \quad \text{Factor and cancel to reduce.}$$

$$= \frac{x}{x-1}$$

Solution 2: Treat the complex fraction as a division.

$$\frac{1+\frac{1}{x}}{1-\frac{1}{x^2}} = \left(1+\frac{1}{x}\right) \div \left(1-\frac{1}{x^2}\right)$$

$$= \left(\frac{1}{1}\cdot\frac{x}{x}+\frac{1}{x}\right) \div \left(\frac{1}{1}\cdot\frac{x^2}{x^2}-\frac{1}{x^2}\right)$$

$$= \frac{x+1}{x} \div \frac{x^2-1}{x^2}$$

$$= \frac{x+1}{x} \cdot \frac{x^2}{x^2-1}$$

$$= \frac{\overset{1}{\cancel{x+1}}}{\underset{1}{\cancel{x}}} \cdot \frac{\overset{x}{\cancel{x^2}}}{\underset{1}{\cancel{(x+1)}}(x-1)}$$

$$= \frac{x}{x-1}$$

Note that a complex fraction can also appear with negative exponents. For example, here is another form for the complex fraction of this example.

$$\frac{1+x^{-1}}{1-x^{-2}} = \frac{1+\frac{1}{x}}{1-\frac{1}{x^2}}$$

EXERCISES

1. The value of $\dfrac{1}{\frac{1}{2}+\frac{1}{2}}$ is

   (1) 1 (2) 2 (3) 3 (4) 4

2. Given: $s=\dfrac{a}{1-r}$ Express in simplest form the value of s when $a = 3$ and $r = \frac{2}{3}$.

3. Given the equation $y=\dfrac{3}{2+x}$. If $x = -\frac{1}{2}$, find the numerical value of y in simplest form.

4. What is the value of the expression $\dfrac{2-\frac{1}{x}}{8}$ when $x = \frac{3}{2}$?

   (1) $\frac{1}{6}$ (2) $\frac{2}{3}$ (3) $\frac{3}{8}$ (4) $\frac{1}{4}$

5. The expression $\dfrac{6}{\frac{1}{2}+\frac{1}{3}}$ is equivalent to

   (1) 30 (2) $\frac{36}{5}$ (3) 5 (4) $\frac{6}{5}$

6. Find in simplest form the value of $\dfrac{r+s}{1-rs}$ when $r = \frac{1}{3}$ and $s = \frac{1}{7}$.

7. Given: $h=\dfrac{2s}{a+b}$ What is the value of h when $s = 5\frac{1}{2}$, $a = \frac{1}{3}$, and $b = \frac{1}{2}$?

   (1) $\frac{33}{5}$ (2) $\frac{66}{5}$ (3) 33 (4) 55

In 8–26, choose the equivalent form of the given complex fraction.

8. $\dfrac{x-y}{\frac{1}{y}-\frac{1}{x}}$ (1) −1 (2) 0 (3) $\dfrac{1}{xy}$ (4) xy

9. $\dfrac{2+\frac{1}{n}}{\frac{1}{n^2}}$

   (1) $\dfrac{2n+1}{n}$ (3) $2n + 1$

   (2) $\dfrac{n}{2n+1}$ (4) $n(2n+1)$

10. $\dfrac{\frac{a}{2}-1}{a^2-1}$

    (1) $\dfrac{a-2}{2a^2-2}$ (3) $\dfrac{a-1}{2a^2-1}$

    (2) $\dfrac{a-2}{a^2-1}$ (4) $\dfrac{1}{2a+2}$

11. $\dfrac{1}{\frac{1}{x-1}+1}$

    (1) $\dfrac{x}{x-1}$ (2) $\dfrac{x-1}{x}$ (3) $\dfrac{1-x}{x}$ (4) $\dfrac{x}{1-x}$

12. $\dfrac{\frac{x}{x+3}}{1-\frac{x}{x+3}}$

    (1) $\dfrac{3x}{x+3}$ (2) $\dfrac{3x}{x^2+9}$ (3) $\dfrac{3}{x}$ (4) $\dfrac{x}{3}$

13. $\dfrac{x^{-1}}{x^{-1}+y^{-1}}$

(1) y (2) $\dfrac{y}{x+y}$ (3) $\dfrac{x+y}{x}$ (4) $\dfrac{x}{x+y}$

14. $\dfrac{x-\frac{1}{3}}{3-\frac{1}{x}}$

(1) 1 (2) $\dfrac{x-1}{2}$ (3) $\dfrac{x}{3}$ (4) $\dfrac{x^2-1}{3x-1}$

15. $\dfrac{1+\frac{1}{z}}{1-\frac{1}{z^2}}$

(1) z (2) $-z$ (3) $\dfrac{z}{z+1}$ (4) $\dfrac{z}{z-1}$

16. $\dfrac{1-\frac{x}{2}}{\frac{x}{2}-1}$

(1) 1 (2) -1 (3) $x-2$ (4) $2-x$

17. $\dfrac{1+\frac{1}{x}}{\frac{1}{x}-x}$

(1) 1 (2) -1 (3) $\dfrac{1}{x-1}$ (4) $\dfrac{1}{1-x}$

18. $\dfrac{\frac{2}{x}+\frac{5}{y}}{\frac{2}{x}-\frac{5}{y}}$

(1) $\dfrac{2y+5x}{2y-5x}$ (2) $\dfrac{4}{xy}$ (3) $-\dfrac{7}{3xy}$ (4) $\dfrac{2y+5x}{x^2+y^2}$

19. $\dfrac{m-\frac{1}{m}}{1-\frac{1}{m}}$

(1) $m-1$ (2) $m+1$ (3) $\dfrac{1}{m-1}$ (4) $\dfrac{1}{1-m}$

20. $\dfrac{s-\frac{s}{c}}{\frac{1}{c}-1}$

(1) s (2) $-s$ (3) $\dfrac{1}{s}$ (4) $-\dfrac{1}{s}$

21. $\dfrac{\frac{1}{a}-1}{1-\frac{1}{a}}$

(1) 1 (2) $\dfrac{1}{a-1}$ (3) $\dfrac{1}{1-a}$ (4) -1

22. $\dfrac{1+\frac{1}{x}}{1+\frac{1}{y}}$

(1) 1 (2) $\dfrac{y}{x}$ (3) $\dfrac{xy+1}{xy}$ (4) $\dfrac{xy+y}{xy+x}$

23. $\dfrac{1+\frac{1}{a}}{a-\frac{1}{a}}$

(1) 1 (2) $a-1$ (3) $\dfrac{1}{a-1}$ (4) $\dfrac{1}{a^2-1}$

24. $\dfrac{1+\frac{a}{b}}{\frac{a}{b}-1}$

(1) 1 (2) -1 (3) $\dfrac{b+a}{a-b}$ (4) $\dfrac{a^2-b^2}{b^2}$

25. $\dfrac{\frac{m}{n}-\frac{n}{m}}{\frac{1}{n}+\frac{1}{m}}$

(1) $m-n$ (2) $m+n$ (3) nm (4) $\dfrac{m-n}{nm}$

26. $\dfrac{b+\frac{b}{a}}{a-\frac{1}{a}}$

(1) b (2) $\dfrac{b}{a-1}$ (3) $\dfrac{2ab}{a^2-1}$ (4) $\dfrac{a-1}{b}$

27. The reciprocal of $\left(\frac{1}{n}+2\right)$ is

(1) $2n+1$ (2) $n+2$ (3) $\dfrac{n}{1+2n}$ (4) $\dfrac{2n+1}{n}$

28. The reciprocal of $\left(2+\frac{1}{x}\right)$ is

(1) $2+x$ (2) $\dfrac{1+2x}{x}$ (3) $\dfrac{x}{2x+1}$ (4) $\dfrac{x+2}{2x}$

29. The reciprocal of $\left(1-\frac{1}{x}\right)$ is

(1) $\dfrac{1}{x}-1$ (2) $1-x$ (3) $\dfrac{x-1}{x}$ (4) $\dfrac{x}{x-1}$

30. The multiplicative inverse of the sum $\frac{1}{r}+\frac{1}{s}$ is

(1) $\dfrac{rs}{r+s}$ (2) $\dfrac{r+s}{rs}$ (3) $\dfrac{1}{r}-\dfrac{1}{s}$ (4) $-\left(\dfrac{1}{r}+\dfrac{1}{s}\right)$

In 31–69, for the values of the variables for which the expressions are defined, write the complex fraction in simplest form.

31. $\dfrac{\frac{1}{2}}{\frac{1}{x}-1}$

32. $\dfrac{\frac{1}{x}}{1+\frac{1}{x}}$

33. $\dfrac{\frac{1}{ab}}{\frac{1}{a}-\frac{1}{b}}$

34. $\dfrac{\frac{a+b}{a}}{\frac{1}{a}+\frac{1}{b}}$

35. $\dfrac{\frac{b-a}{a}}{\frac{1}{a}-\frac{1}{b}}$

36. $\dfrac{\frac{a-b}{a}}{\frac{a}{b}-1}$

37. $\dfrac{2-\frac{2}{x}}{x-1}$

38. $\dfrac{\frac{1}{2}+x^{-1}}{x^{-1}}$

39. $\dfrac{1-\frac{2}{x}}{\frac{1}{x}}$

40. $\dfrac{\frac{1}{\sqrt{3}}-\frac{4}{\sqrt{3}}}{\sqrt{3}}$

41. $\dfrac{x-\frac{1}{x}}{1-\frac{1}{x}}$

42. $\dfrac{\frac{1}{a}+\frac{1}{b}}{\frac{2}{ab}}$

43. $\dfrac{x^{-1}+y^{-1}}{x^{-1}}$

44. $\dfrac{\frac{x}{4}-\frac{1}{x}}{1-\frac{2}{x}}$

45. $\dfrac{1+\frac{2}{x}}{x-\frac{4}{x}}$

46. $\dfrac{x-\frac{4}{x}}{1+\frac{2}{x}}$

47. $\dfrac{\frac{1}{4x^2}-1}{2-\frac{1}{x}}$

48. $\dfrac{\frac{a^2}{4}-1}{\frac{a}{4}-\frac{1}{2}}$

49. $\dfrac{1+a^{-1}}{a-a^{-1}}$

50. $\dfrac{a-\frac{1}{b}}{\frac{1}{a}-b}$

51. $\dfrac{\frac{1}{a}-b}{\frac{1}{b}-a}$

52. $\dfrac{\frac{1}{b}-a}{b-\frac{1}{a}}$

53. $\dfrac{\frac{1}{x}-\frac{1}{y}}{\frac{1}{x}+\frac{1}{y}}$

54. $\dfrac{\frac{a}{b}-\frac{b}{a}}{\frac{a}{b}-1}$

55. $\dfrac{\frac{x}{y}+z}{\frac{x}{z}+y}$

56. $\dfrac{x^{-1}+y^{-1}}{x^{-1}-y^{-1}}$

57. $\dfrac{\frac{b}{a}-\frac{a}{b}}{\frac{1}{a}-\frac{1}{b}}$

58. $\dfrac{n-\frac{1}{n}}{\frac{1-n^2}{n}}$

59. $\dfrac{\frac{a}{4}-\frac{1}{2}}{\frac{a^2}{4}-1}$

60. $\dfrac{2+\frac{1}{x}}{4-\frac{1}{x^2}}$

61. $\dfrac{x^{-2}-1}{1+x^{-1}}$

62. $\dfrac{3-\frac{3}{x}}{x-1}$

63. $\dfrac{\frac{1}{x+h}-\frac{1}{x}}{h}$

64. $\dfrac{\frac{x}{x+1}}{1-\frac{x}{x+1}}$

65. $\dfrac{\frac{a}{a+b}}{1-\frac{b}{a+b}}$

66. $\dfrac{1+\frac{b}{a-b}}{1-\frac{a}{a-b}}$

67. $\dfrac{1-\frac{1}{x}}{x-2+\frac{1}{x}}$

68. $\dfrac{m-\frac{1}{m}}{m-2+\frac{1}{m}}$

69. $\dfrac{x+\frac{2}{x}-3}{x-1-\frac{2}{x}}$

1.6 SUMMARY EXERCISES

1. Which is an irrational number?
(1) $\sqrt{\frac{16}{36}}$ (2) $\sqrt{90}$ (3) $\sqrt[3]{125}$ (4) $-\sqrt{4}$

2. If $x = -2$, which is not an expression for zero?
(1) $\frac{0}{x}$ (2) $x - 2$ (3) $x^2 - 4$ (4) $x + (-x)$

3. If n is an odd integer, which of the following represents an even integer?
(1) $3n$ (2) n^3 (3) $n^2 + 1$ (4) $n + 2$

4. If the product of two consecutive integers is 0, one of the integers may be
(1) 1 (2) 2 (3) 3 (4) 4

5. The set of odd counting numbers is closed under which operation?
(1) addition (3) multiplication
(2) subtraction (4) division

6. The set of integers fails to meet the requirements for a field with respect to addition and multiplication because it lacks
(1) multiplicative inverse (3) additive identity
(2) multiplicative identity (4) closure

7. Which is true for the set of whole numbers?
(1) The multiplicative identity element is 0.
(2) The additive identity element is 1.
(3) The multiplicative identity element is 1.
(4) The multiplicative identity element is –1.

8. The set of real numbers has the commutative property under the operations of
(1) addition, subtraction, and multiplication
(2) addition and subtraction, but not multiplication
(3) subtraction and multiplication, but not addition
(4) addition and multiplication, but not subtraction

9. The replacement of $2a + 2b$ by $2(a + b)$ is justified by the
(1) commutative property of multiplication
(2) associative property of multiplication
(3) associative property of addition
(4) distributive property

10. Which illustrates the associative property of addition?
(1) $(87 + 2)8 = 87 \cdot 8 + 2 \cdot 8$
(2) $(87 + 2) + 8 = 8 + (87 + 2)$
(3) $87(2 + 8) = 87 \cdot 2 + 87 \cdot 8$
(4) $(87 + 2) + 8 = 87 + (2 + 8)$

11. Factor completely: $3x^2 - 12$

12. Factor completely: $x^3 - x^2 - 6x$

13. Find the two binomial factors: $ax + bx + ay + by$

14. $3^3 + 3^0 + 3^{-3}$ equals
(1) 0 (2) 1 (3) $10\frac{1}{9}$ (4) $28\frac{1}{27}$

15. Which statement is true?
(1) $3^{-1} + 4^{-1} = 7^{-1}$ (3) $7^0 - 3^0 = 4^0$
(2) $\left(\frac{1}{3}\right)^{-1} + \left(\frac{1}{4}\right)^{-1} = \left(\frac{1}{7}\right)^{-1}$ (4) $\frac{3^0}{4^0} = \frac{3}{7^0}$

16. If $3^m = a$, then 3^{m+3} equals
(1) $a + 3$ (2) $3a$ (3) a^3 (4) $27a$

17. The expression $(2x + 1)^2 - 2(2x^2 - 1)$ is equivalent to
(1) $4x + 3$ (2) $2x + 3$ (3) 3 (4) –1

18. Write the number 4.86×10^{-3} in ordinary decimal notation.

19. If the number 34,500,000 is written in the form 3.45×10^n, find the value of n.

20. The wavelength of sodium light is 0.000000589 meter. If this number is written in the form 5.89×10^n, what is the value of n?

21. The additive inverse of $2 - \sqrt{3}$ is
(1) 1 (2) 0 (3) $2 + \sqrt{3}$ (4) $-2 + \sqrt{3}$

22. $(\sqrt{5})(\sqrt{12})$ is equivalent to
(1) $\sqrt{7}$ (2) $2\sqrt{15}$ (3) $\sqrt{17}$ (4) $4\sqrt{15}$

23. The sum of $2\sqrt{18}$ and $\sqrt{50}$ is
(1) $10\sqrt{2}$ (2) $11\sqrt{2}$ (3) $2\sqrt{68}$ (4) $3\sqrt{68}$

24. If $x = 3 + \sqrt{2}$, find the value of $x^2 - 11$.

25. If $(\sqrt{128} - \sqrt{72})$, is divided by $\sqrt{8}$, the result is
(1) 1 (3) $\sqrt{7}$
(2) $8\sqrt{2} - 3$ (4) $4 - 6\sqrt{2}$

26. The expression $\frac{2}{3-\sqrt{3}}$ is equivalent to
(1) $1 + 2\sqrt{3}$ (3) $\frac{3-\sqrt{3}}{3}$
(2) $1 - 2\sqrt{3}$ (4) $\frac{3+\sqrt{3}}{3}$

27. Express $\frac{3}{2+\sqrt{3}}$ as an equivalent fraction with a rational denominator.

28. The expression $\frac{3+\sqrt{2}}{3-\sqrt{2}}$ is equivalent to
(1) $\frac{7}{11+6\sqrt{2}}$ (3) $\frac{11}{7}$
(2) $\frac{11-6\sqrt{2}}{7}$ (4) $\frac{11+6\sqrt{2}}{7}$

29. Evaluate $m^{-\frac{3}{2}}$ when $m = 4$.

30. Evaluate $x^{\frac{2}{3}} + x^{-1}$ when $x = 8$.

31. Evaluate $a^0 + a^{-\frac{1}{2}}$ when $a = 9$.

32. For which ordered pair, (x, y), is the fraction $\frac{3}{y-x}$ undefined?
(1) $(-1, 1)$ (2) $(-3, -2)$ (3) $(2, 3)$ (4) $(4, 4)$

33. If $h \neq 0$, when the fraction $\frac{(x+h)^2 - x^2}{h}$ is simplified, the result is
(1) h (2) 0 (3) $2x^2 + 2x + h$ (4) $2x + h$

34. For all values of y, where $y \neq 1$, the expression $\frac{6}{y-1} \cdot \frac{5-5y}{10}$ is equivalent to
(1) $-\frac{1}{3}$ (2) $3(y - 1)$ (3) -3 (4) $\frac{3}{5}(1 - y)$

35. Express the product in simplest form:
$$\left(\frac{a}{a^2-25}\right)\left(\frac{a^2+2a-15}{a-3}\right)$$

36. Perform the indicated operation and express in simplest form:
$$\frac{x^2-3x}{2x^2+x-6} \div \frac{x^2-5x+6}{x^2-4}$$

37. Perform the indicated operation and express in simplest terms:
$$\frac{x^2-9}{x^2-5x} \cdot \frac{5x-x^2}{x^2-x-12} \div \frac{x-4}{x^2-8x+16}$$

38. Expressed in simplest form, $\frac{x-7}{6} - \frac{3x-2}{12}$ is equivalent to
(1) $\frac{2x+5}{6}$ (3) $\frac{-x-12}{12}$
(2) $\frac{2x+9}{6}$ (4) $\frac{-x-16}{12}$

39. When combined, $\frac{2}{x+3} + \frac{1}{x}$ is equivalent to
(1) $\frac{3x+3}{x^2+3x}$ (3) $\frac{3x+3}{2x+3}$
(2) $\frac{3x+1}{x^2+3x}$ (4) $\frac{3}{2x+3}$

40. Express as a single fraction in lowest terms:
$$\frac{3}{x-2} + \frac{4}{x^2-4}$$

41. For all values of b for which the expressions are defined, $\frac{b^2}{b-3} + \frac{9}{3-b}$ is equivalent to
(1) -1 (3) $b - 3$
(2) $\frac{1}{3-b}$ (4) $b + 3$

42. The complex fraction $\frac{1+\frac{1}{x}}{x-\frac{1}{x}}$, where $x \neq -1, 0, 1$, is equivalent to
(1) 1 (3) $\frac{1}{x-1}$
(2) -1 (4) $\frac{1}{1-x}$

43. Simplify:
$$\frac{\frac{2}{x}-2}{\frac{1-x}{x}}$$

44. Express as a fraction in simplest form:
$$\frac{\frac{1}{n}-\frac{1}{3n^2}}{1-\frac{1}{9n^2}}$$

CHAPTER 2

The Real Number System, Part II, and The Complex Numbers

2.1 PROPERTIES OF EQUALITY

For all real numbers a, b, and c:

Reflexive Property $a = a$

Symmetric Property **If $a = b$, then $b = a$.**

Transitive Property **If $a = b$ and $b = c$, then $a = c$.**

Substitution Property **If $a = b$, then a may be replaced by b or b may be replaced by a.**

Addition Property
If $a = b$, then $a + c = b + c$.
If $a = b$ and $c = d$, then $a + c = b + d$.

Multiplication Property
If $a = b$, then $a \cdot c = b \cdot c$.
If $a = b$ and $c = d$, then $a \cdot c = b \cdot d$.

The properties of equality, along with the properties of the real numbers, justify the techniques used in solving an equation or simplifying an expression.

Example

Identify the property that justifies each step of the solution of $5x = 2x + 12$.

Solution:

$5x = 2x + 12$	
$5x + (-2x) = 2x + (-2x) + 12$	addition
$3x = 2x + (-2x) + 12$	substitution
$3x = 0 + 12$	additive inverse
$3x = 12$	additive identity
$\frac{1}{3} \cdot 3x = \frac{1}{3} \cdot 12$	multiplication
$1 \cdot x = \frac{1}{3} \cdot 12$	multiplicative inverse
$x = \frac{1}{3} \cdot 12$	multiplicative identity
$x = 4$	substitution

These properties are also applied when you are changing the subject of a formula (solving for one quantity in terms of the others) or solving a LITERAL EQUATION (an equation that uses letters for certain constants).

Example

Solve for x in terms of a, b, c, and d:

$$ax + b = d - cx$$

Solution: Apply inverse operations to isolate the variable x.

$ax + b = d - cx$	
$ax + cx + b = d$	x-terms on left.
$ax + cx = d - b$	Constant terms on right.
$x(a + c) = d - b$	Factor out x.
$x = \frac{d-b}{a+c}$	Divide by the coefficient of x.

EXERCISES

1. The first three steps in solving the equation $2x = 10$ are

   Step 1 $2x = 10$
   Step 2 $\frac{1}{2} \cdot 2x = \frac{1}{2} \cdot 10$
   Step 3 $1 \cdot x = \frac{1}{2} \cdot 10$

   Name the property that justifies deriving Step 3 from Step 2.

   (1) multiplicative inverse (3) multiplication
   (2) multiplicative identity (4) reflexive

2. The first three steps in simplifying the expression $3x + (x + 4)$ are

   Step 1 $3x + (x + 4)$
   Step 2 $(3x + x) + 4$
   Step 3 $4x + 4$

   Name the property that justifies deriving Step 2 from Step 1.

   (1) closure (3) associative
   (2) distributive (4) commutative

3. Four consecutive steps in the solution of the equation $4x + 3 = 7x$ could be

Step 1 $4x + 3 = 7x$
Step 2 $4x + (-4x) + 3 = 7x + (-4x)$
Step 3 $0 + 3 = 7x + (-4x)$
Step 4 $3 = 7x + (-4x)$

Name the property that justifies deriving Step 4 from Step 3.

(1) additive inverse (3) addition
(2) additive identity (4) symmetric

4. The last three steps in solving the equation $16 = 3x + 4$ could be

Step 7 $\frac{1}{3} \cdot 12 = x$
Step 8 $4 = x$
Step 9 $x = 4$

Name the property that justifies deriving Step 9 from Step 8.

(1) identity (3) reflexive
(2) inverse (4) symmetric

In 5–14, solve for the indicated quantity in terms of the other quantities.

5. Solve for h: $V = \frac{s^2h}{3}$

6. Solve for b: $A = \frac{1}{2}h(b + c)$

7. Solve for t : $A = P(1 + rt)$

8. Solve for n: $P = T(n - 2)$

9. Solve for c : $S = \pi a(b + c)$

10. Solve for h: $T = 2\pi rh + 2\pi r^2$

11. Solve for m: $r(m + 3) = w$

12. Solve for x: $ax = b - cx$

13. Solve for x: $ax + b = bx + c$

14. Solve for w: $gt = wv - wt$

2.2 ABSOLUTE-VALUE EQUATIONS

An algebraic definition of ABSOLUTE VALUE is:

$$|x| = \begin{cases} x & \text{if } x \geq 0 \\ -x & \text{if } x < 0 \end{cases}$$

Example: If $x = 3$, then $|3| = 3$, since $3 > 0$.
If $x = -3$, then $|-3| = -(-3)$, or 3, since $-3 < 0$.

In an equation, when a variable is involved in an absolute value, two cases must be considered:

CASE 1: Consider the variable expression in the absolute value as ≥ 0, and replace the absolute value by the variable expression.

CASE 2: Consider the variable expression in the absolute value as < 0, and replace the absolute value by the negative of the variable expression.

It is essential to check in the original equation both values obtained, since the actual solution may contain two values, one value, or no values.

Examples

1. Solve: $|2x - 3| = 5$

Solution: Since there are two cases, the given equation leads to two equations.

If $2x - 3 \geq 0$, replace $|2x - 3|$ by $2x - 3$.

$$2x - 3 = 5$$
$$2x = 8$$
$$x = 4$$

If $2x - 3 < 0$, replace $|2x - 3|$ by $-(2x - 3)$.

$$-(2x - 3) = 5$$
$$-2x + 3 = 5$$
$$-2x = 2$$
$$x = -1$$

Check both values in the original equation.

$$|2x - 3| = 5$$
$$|2(4) - 3| \stackrel{?}{=} 5$$
$$|8 - 3| \stackrel{?}{=} 5$$
$$|5| \stackrel{?}{=} 5$$
$$5 = 5 \checkmark$$

$$|2x - 3| = 5$$
$$|2(-1) - 3| \stackrel{?}{=} 5$$
$$|-2 - 3| \stackrel{?}{=} 5$$
$$|-5| \stackrel{?}{=} 5$$
$$5 = 5 \checkmark$$

Answer: The solution set is $\{-1, 4\}$.

2. Solve: $2x - |x + 2| = 11$

Solution:

If $x + 2 \geq 0$, replace $|x + 2|$ by $x + 2$.

$$2x - |x + 2| = 11$$
$$2x - (x + 2) = 11$$
$$2x - x - 2 = 11$$
$$x - 2 = 11$$
$$x = 13$$

If $x + 2 < 0$, replace replace $|x + 2|$ by $-(x + 2)$.

$$2x - |x + 2| = 11$$
$$2x - [-(x + 2)] = 11$$
$$2x - (-x - 2) = 11$$
$$2x + x + 2 = 11$$
$$3x = 9$$
$$x = 3$$

Check both values in the original equation.

$$2x - |x + 2| = 11$$
$$2(13) - |13 + 2| \stackrel{?}{=} 11$$
$$26 - |15| \stackrel{?}{=} 11$$
$$26 - 15 \stackrel{?}{=} 11$$
$$11 = 11 \checkmark$$

$$2x - |x + 2| = 11$$
$$2(3) - |3 + 2| \stackrel{?}{=} 11$$
$$6 - |5| \stackrel{?}{=} 11$$
$$6 - 5 \stackrel{?}{=} 11$$
$$1 \neq 11$$

Answer: The solution set is $\{13\}$.

EXERCISES

1. The solution set of $|x - 1| = 2$ is
   (1) $\{1, 3\}$ (2) $\{-3, 3\}$ (3) $\{-1, 3\}$ (4) $\{\ \}$

2. What is the solution set of the equation $|2 - 3x| = 5$?
   (1) $\{-1\}$ (2) $\left\{-1, \frac{7}{3}\right\}$ (3) $\{5, -5\}$ (4) $\{\ \}$

3. What is the solution set of the equation $|3 - 2x| = 5$?
   (1) $\{-1, 4\}$ (2) $\{1, -4\}$ (3) $\{-1\}$ (4) $\{4\}$

4. What is the solution set of the equation $|5 - 2x| = 7$?
   (1) $\{6, -1\}$ (2) $\{6\}$ (3) $\{-1\}$ (4) $\{\ \}$

5. What is the solution set of the equation $|3x + 2| = 5$?
   (1) $\{1\}$ (2) $\left\{\frac{7}{3}\right\}$ (3) $\left\{1, -\frac{7}{3}\right\}$ (4) $\left\{-1, \frac{7}{3}\right\}$

6. The solution set of $|2x + 1| = -3$ is
   (1) $\{\pm 2\}$ (2) $\{2\}$ (3) $\{-2\}$ (4) $\{\ \}$

7. The solution set of $|8x + 20| = 7x + 10$ is
   (1) $\{-10, -2\}$ (2) $\{-10\}$ (3) $\{-2\}$ (4) $\{\ \}$

In 8–9, find the negative member of the solution set.

8. $|2x - 4| = 6$
9. $1 + |3y - 2| = 11$

In 10–25, find the solution set.

10. $|2x + 1| = 9$
11. $|2x - 1| = 3$
12. $|3y + 1| = 7$
13. $|4z + 1| = 3$
14. $|2 - 3x| = 14$
15. $|1 - 2t| = 11$
16. $13 = |7 + 4w|$
17. $\left|\frac{4t - 1}{3}\right| = 15$
18. $|1 - \frac{1}{2}x| = 6$
19. $-|x + 1| = 7$
20. $-|1 - x| = -2$
21. $|5q - 2| + 3 = 11$
22. $7 + |6x - 1| = 18$
23. $2x - |x + 3| = 9$
24. $2y - |y + 1| = 10$
25. $|3z + 2| = 4z + 5$

2.3 QUADRATIC EQUATIONS

Standard Form

A QUADRATIC EQUATION is of degree 2, and, in general, has two elements in the solution set. STANDARD FORM of a quadratic equation is:

$$ax^2 + bx + c = 0 \text{ where } a \neq 0$$

Solution by Factoring

Solution by factoring applies this principle:

If the product of two factors is 0, then at least one of the factors must be 0.

To solve a quadratic equation by factoring:

1. **Write the equation in standard form.**
2. **Factor the quadratic member of the equation.**
3. **Set each factor = 0, thus obtaining two first-degree equations.**
4. **Solve each of the two first-degree equations, thus obtaining two values.**
5. **Check both values in the *original* equation.**

Examples

1. Solve: $x^2 - 8x = -15$

Solution:

$x^2 - 8x = -15$	
$x^2 - 8x + 15 = 0$	Standard form.
$(x - 5)(x - 3) = 0$	Factor the trinomial.
$x - 5 = 0 \quad \vert \quad x - 3 = 0$	Set each factor = 0, and solve for x.
$x = 5 \quad \vert \quad x = 3$	

Check both values in the *original* equation.

Answer: $x = 5$ or $x = 3$; the solution set is $\{3, 5\}$.

2. Solve: $x^2 + 4x = 0$

Solution:

$x^2 + 4x = 0$	Standard form, $c = 0$.
$x(x + 4) = 0$	There is a common factor.
$x = 0 \quad \vert \quad x + 4 = 0$	Set each factor = 0, and solve.
$x = -4$	One value is $x = 0$.

Check both values in the *original* equation.

Answer: $x = 0$ or $x = -4$; the solution set is $\{0, -4\}$.

3. Solve: $x^2 - 16 = 0$

Solution:

$x^2 - 16 = 0$	Standard form, $b = 0$.
$(x + 4)(x - 4) = 0$	Factor the difference of two perfect squares.
$x + 4 = 0 \quad \mid \quad x - 4 = 0$	Set each factor = 0, and solve.
$x = -4 \quad \mid \quad x = 4$	

Check both values in the *original* equation.

Answer: $x = 4$ or $x = -4$; the solution set is $\{\pm 4\}$.

Alternate Solution:

$x^2 - 16 = 0$	
$x^2 = 16$	Add 16.
$x = \pm\sqrt{16}$	Take the square root of both sides of the equation.
$x = \pm 4$	

The alternate solution produces answers for this form of the quadratic equation ($b = 0$) even if the constant term is not a perfect square. See Example 4 below.

The alternate solution is helpful at other times as well. See Examples 5 and 6 below.

Examples

4. $x^2 - 17 = 0$

Solution:

$x^2 - 17 = 0$
$x^2 = 17$
$x^2 = \pm\sqrt{17}$

5. $3x^2 = 75$

Solution:

$3x^2 = 75$
$x^2 = 25$
$x = \pm\sqrt{25}$
$x = \pm 5$

6. $x^2 + 2 = 38$

Solution:

$x^2 + 2 = 38$
$x^2 = 36$
$x = \pm\sqrt{36}$
$x = \pm 6$

EXERCISES

1. The solution set for $x^2 - 7x + 12 = 0$ is
(1) $\{3, -4\}$ **(3)** $\{3, 4\}$
(2) $\{-3, 4\}$ **(4)** $\{-3, -4\}$

2. Which is the solution set of $x^2 - 3x - 10 = 0$?
(1) $\{-5, 2\}$ **(3)** $\{2, 5\}$
(2) $\{5, -2\}$ **(4)** $\{-2, -5\}$

3. The solution set of $x^2 - x - 6 = 0$ is
(1) $\{1, -6\}$ **(3)** $\{3, -2\}$
(2) $\{-3, 2\}$ **(4)** $\{5, 1\}$

4. What is the positive root of the equation $(x - 4)(x + 3) = 0$?

5. Write the solution set of $x^2 - 2x - 35 = 0$.

6. The solution set of the equation $x^2 - 3x = 0$ is
(1) $\{3\}$ **(2)** $\{-3\}$ **(3)** $\{3, -3\}$ **(4)** $\{0, 3\}$

7. The solution set $x^2 = 6x$ is
(1) $\{6\}$ **(2)** $\{0, 6\}$ **(3)** $\{0, -6\}$ **(4)** $\{-6\}$

8. The solution set of $2x^2 - 8x = 0$ is
(1) $\{0, 4\}$ **(2)** $\{0, -4\}$ **(3)** $\{2, 4\}$ **(4)** $\{2, -4\}$

9. The solution set of $x^2 - 25 = 0$ is
(1) $\{5\}$ **(2)** $\{-5\}$ **(3)** $\{\pm 5\}$ **(4)** $\{0, 5\}$

10. The solution set of $(2x - 8)(5x - 4) = 0$ is
(1) $\{-8, 4\}$ **(2)** $\{4, -\frac{1}{5}\}$ **(3)** $\{-4, \frac{4}{5}\}$ **(4)** $\{4, \frac{4}{5}\}$

In 11–32, solve and check. Express irrational answers in simplest radical form.

11. $x^2 + 7x + 12 = 0$	**22.** $4x^2 = 15$
12. $y^2 + 3y - 10 = 0$	**23.** $y^2 = 2 - y^2$
13. $z^2 - 8z + 15 = 0$	**24.** $3q^2 = 10 - 2q^2$
14. $a^2 - 5a = 24$	**25.** $2x^2 + 9x + 9 = 0$
15. $x^2 = 9x - 20$	**26.** $2r^2 = 5r - 2$
16. $x^2 - 3x = 18$	**27.** $3y^2 - 8y = -4$
17. $3z^2 = 12z$	**28.** $3z - 5 = -2z^2$
18. $a^2 - 100 = 0$	**29.** $1 - 3x^2 = 2x$
19. $x^2 - 0.36 = 0$	**30.** $7q^2 = 30 - 11q$
20. $y^2 + 4 = 44$	**31.** $10m^2 = 13m + 3$
21. $2t^2 - 5 = 11$	**32.** $24u + 6 = 30u^2$

Solution by the Quadratic Formula

To solve a quadratic equation by using the QUADRATIC FORMULA:

1. **Match the given equation against the standard form $ax^2 + bx + c = 0$ to identify the values for a, b, and c.**
2. **Substitute the values for a, b, c into the quadratic formula:**

$$x = \frac{-b \pm \sqrt{b^2 - 4ac}}{2a}$$

3. **Evaluate the results to obtain two values for x.**
4. **Check in the original equation.**

Example

Solve and check: $x^2 = 6x - 1$

Solution:

Rewrite the equation in standard form and identify the values of *a, b, and c.*

$$x^2 = 6x - 1$$
$$x^2 - 6x + 1 = 0$$
$$ax^2 + bx + c = 0$$
$$a = 1, b = -6, c = 1$$

Substitute into the formula.

$$x = \frac{-b \pm \sqrt{b^2 - 4ac}}{2a}$$
$$x = \frac{-(-6) \pm \sqrt{(-6)^2 - 4(1)(1)}}{2(1)} = \frac{6 \pm \sqrt{36 - 4}}{2}$$
$$x = \frac{6 \pm \sqrt{32}}{2} = \frac{6 \pm 4\sqrt{2}}{2} = 3 \pm 2\sqrt{2}$$

Check: It is sufficient to check one of the two irrational roots since they occur in pairs.

$$x^2 = 6x - 1$$
$$(3 + 2\sqrt{2})(3 + 2\sqrt{2}) \stackrel{?}{=} 6(3 + 2\sqrt{2}) - 1$$
$$9 + 12\sqrt{2} + 8 \stackrel{?}{=} 18 + 12\sqrt{2} - 1$$
$$17 + 12\sqrt{2} = 17 + 12\sqrt{2} \checkmark$$

Answer: The solution set is $\{3 \pm 2\sqrt{2}\}$.

EXERCISES

In 1–26, solve by using the quadratic formula. Express irrational roots in simplest radical form.

1. $x^2 - 3x + 2 = 0$
2. $y^2 + 2y - 3 = 0$
3. $z^2 + 5z + 6 = 0$
4. $x^2 + 6x + 5 = 0$
5. $x^2 + x - 2 = 0$
6. $r^2 - r = 6$
7. $s^2 + 2s = 15$
8. $t^2 - 3t = 4$
9. $2x^2 + 3x - 2 = 0$
10. $2x^2 + 7x + 6 = 0$
11. $u^2 - 8u + 15 = 0$
12. $t^2 + 2t = 8$
13. $2r^2 - r - 6 = 0$
14. $2t^2 + 5t = 3$
15. $3x^2 - 16 = 2x$
16. $y^2 - 10y + 11 = 0$
17. $h^2 - 2h = 35$
18. $b^2 + 10 = 8b$
19. $3t^2 = 5t - 1$
20. $x(x + 4) = 6$
21. $k^2 - 3k = 0$
22. $q^2 - 8 = 0$
23. $3r^2 = 11$
24. $x(x - 3) + 3x = 5$
25. $(2m - 1)^2 = 7$
26. $(x + 3)(x - 2) = 1$

In 27–32, find the roots correct to the nearest tenth.

27. $2x^2 + 3x - 3 = 0$
28. $3x^2 = 7x - 1$
29. $2x^2 - 5x = 1$
30. $2x^2 - 7 = 3x$
31. $2x^2 - 7x = 3$
32. $3x^2 - 5x = 4$

2.4 SYSTEMS OF EQUATIONS

Linear Systems

METHOD 1: ELIMINATION OF ONE VARIABLE BY SUBSTITUTION

This method is especially useful if one variable is already expressed in terms of the other in one of the two equations.

1. ***Replace one variable in terms of the other,* thus reducing the problem to one equation in one variable.**
2. ***Solve for the remaining variable.***
3. ***Substitute* the now known value in any equation involving both variables, and solve for the second variable.**
4. ***Check* both values in *each original* equation.**

Example

Solve the system of equations and check:

$$y = 3x - 1$$
$$7x + 2y = 37$$

Solution: substitution method

Replace y by $3x - 1$ in the second equation, and solve for x.

$$7x + 2y = 37$$
$$7x + 2(3x - 1) = 37$$
$$7x + 6x - 2 = 37$$
$$13x - 2 = 37$$
$$13x = 39$$
$$\boxed{x = 3}$$

Substitute $x = 3$ into either of the original equations, and solve for y.

$$y = 3x - 1$$
$$y = 3(3) - 1$$
$$y = 9 - 1$$
$$\boxed{y = 8}$$

Check both values in *each* of the *original* equations.

Answer: $x = 3, y = 8$ or $(3, 8)$

METHOD 2: ELIMINATION OF ONE VARIABLE BY ADDITION OR SUBTRACTION

This method requires that the coefficients of one variable be equal in absolute value. This may be the case from the beginning, or one or two multipliers may be needed.

1. ***Decide on the variable that is to have equal or opposite coefficients.*** **Use multipliers if needed.**
2. ***Combine the two equations*** **by addition or subtraction, thus reducing the problem to one equation in one variable.**
3. ***Solve for the one variable.***
4. ***Substitute*** **the now known value in any equation involving both variables, and solve for the second variable.**
5. ***Check*** **both values in** ***each original*** **equation.**

Example

Solve the system of equations and check:

$$5x - 2y = 20$$
$$2x + 3y = 27$$

Solution: To obtain coefficients for x that are opposites, multiply the first equation by 2 and the second equation by -5.

To eliminate x, add the two equations.

Multiply.
$$\begin{array}{r|rcl} 2 & 5x - 2y &=& 20 \\ -5 & 2x + 3y &=& 27 \end{array}$$

Add, and solve for y.
$$\begin{array}{rcl} 10x - 4y &=& 40 \\ -10x - 15y &=& -135 \\ \hline -19y &=& -95 \\ \boxed{y = 5} \end{array}$$

Return to any equation containing x and y. Substitute $y = 5$, and solve for x.
$$\begin{array}{rcl} 5x - 2y &=& 20 \\ 5x - 2(5) &=& 20 \\ 5x - 10 &=& 20 \\ 5x &=& 30 \\ \boxed{x = 6} \end{array}$$

Check both values in *each* of the *original* equations.

Answer: $x = 6$, $y = 5$ or $(6, 5)$

Alternate Solution: To eliminate y, multiply the first equation by 3 and the second equation by 2. Then, add.

Graphing

For a system of two lines, it is possible that the graphs:

intersect (one solution)

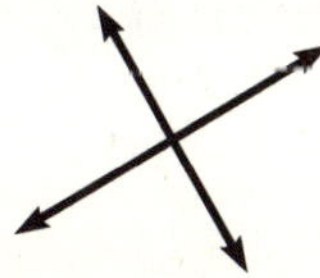

are parallel (no solution)

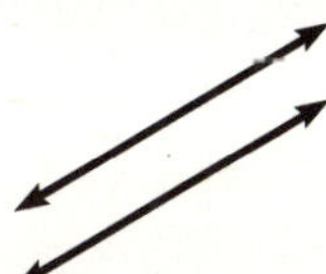

coincide (infinite solutions)

A quick way to sketch a line is by its intercepts.

Horizontal Line $y = b$

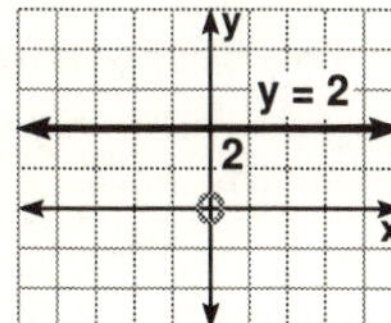

Vertical Line $x = a$

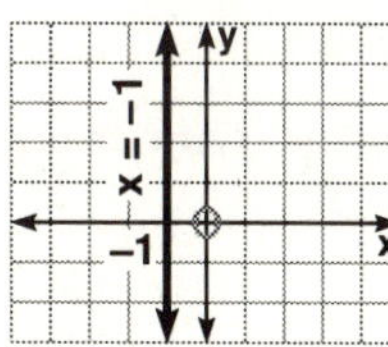

Oblique Line $ax + by = c$

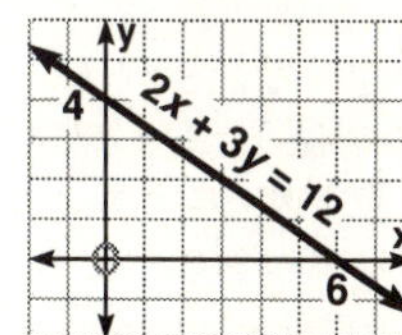

To find the y-intercept, let $x = 0$.

To find the x-intercept, let $y = 0$.

EXERCISES

In 1–24, solve the system of equations algebraically.

1. $5x - y = 20$, $y = 3x$

2. $2a - b = 5$, $b = 7 - a$

3. $2u - v = 3$, $v = 3 - u$

4. $x + y = 7$, $2x - y = 2$

5. $2c + 3d = 7$, $c - 3d = 8$

6. $3p + q = 7$, $2p - q = 8$

7. $3x + 2y = 19$, $x - 2y = 9$

8. $a - b = 9$, $a + 4b = 24$

9. $m + 4n = 1$
$2m - 2n = -8$

10. $r + 6s = 28$
$r - 2s = -4$

11. $x + y = 4$
$2x + y = 10$

12. $3x - y = 7$
$2x + y = 8$

13. $4x + y = 3$
$x + y = 12$

14. $c - 3d = 7$
$2c - 3d = 11$

15. $3u - 2v = 42$
$2u - v = 26$

16. $3p - 5q = -9$
$2p - q = 1$

17. $2x + y = -1$
$y = x + 5$

18. $4x + 3y = 27$
$y = 2x - 1$

19. $2r + s = 6$
$r = 3s + 10$

20. $2h + 3k = 6$
$3h + 5k = 9$

21. $3x - 2y = 16$
$4x + 3y + 7 = 0$

22. $2a + 3b = -4$
$5a + 2b = 1$

23. $3x + 2y = 1$
$2x + 3y = 9$

24. $3h - 4k = 12$
$4h - 3k = 2$

In 25-32, solve the system of equations graphically.

25. $x + y = 6$
$y = 3$

26. $y = x + 2$
$x = 1$

27. $2x = y + 5$
$x + y = -2$

28. $2y = x + 6$
$3x - y = 2$

29. $y = x + 7$
$2x + y = 1$

30. $2x + y = 8$
$y = 3x - 2$

31. $2y - x = 4$
$2y - 8 = x$

32. $3x - y = 6$
$6x - 12 = 2y$

Linear-Quadratic Systems

To obtain an algebraic solution for a linear-quadratic system:

1. ***Rewrite the linear equation*** **so that one variable is expressed in terms of the other, for example, y in terms of x.**
2. ***Substitute the expression for y*** **obtained from the linear equation into the quadratic equation, thus obtaining a quadratic equation in one variable, x.**
3. ***Solve the quadratic equation*** **in one variable, thus obtaining two values for x.**
4. ***Substitute each value of x*** **into the linear equation to obtain the corresponding y-values.**
5. ***Check both sets*** **of ordered pairs in each of the original equations.**

Example

Find the solution set of the system:

$$y - 2x = -6$$
$$2y = x^2 - 4x$$

Solution:

Rewrite the linear equation. $y - 2x = -6$
$y = 2x - 6$

Substitute for y. $2y = x^2 - 4x$
$2(2x - 6) = x^2 - 4x$

Solve the quadratic. $4x - 12 = x^2 - 4x$
$0 = x^2 - 8x + 12$
$0 = (x - 6)(x - 2)$

$x - 6 = 0$	$x - 2 = 0$
$x = 6$	$x = 2$

Substitute each value of x into the linear equation.

$y = 2x - 6$	$y = 2x - 6$
$y = 2(6) - 6$	$y = 2(2) - 6$
$y = 12 - 6$	$y = 4 - 6$
$y = 6$	$y = -2$

Check: Substitute each set of ordered pairs into each of the original equations.

Answer: $\{(6, 6), (2, -2)\}$

For a linear-quadratic system, it is possible that the graphs intersect in:

2 points **1 point** **no points**

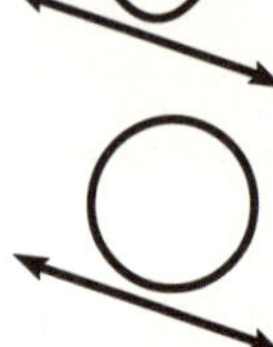

To Sketch a Parabola

$$y = ax^2 + bx + c$$

When $a > 0$, the parabola opens upward.

When $a < 0$, the parabola opens downward.

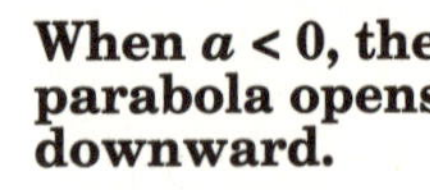

Vertical Axis of Symmetry

$$x = \frac{-b}{2a}$$

$$x = ay^2 + by + c$$

When $a > 0$, the parabola opens to the right.

When $a < 0$, the parabola opens to the left.

Horizontal Axis of Symmetry

$$y = \frac{-b}{2a}$$

To Sketch a Circle

The graph of $x^2 + y^2 = r^2$ is a circle with center at the origin and radius of length r.

Example

If the graphs of $y = -x^2$ and $y = 1$ are sketched on the same set of axes, how many points of intersection are there?

Solution:

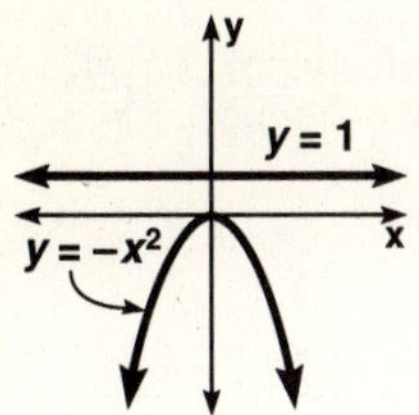

$y = -x^2$ is a parabola with turning point at the origin, and opening down.

$y = 1$ is a horizontal line.

Answer: There are no points of intersection.

EXERCISES

1. Which is a solution for the system of equations $y = x - 2$ and $y = x^2 - 4x - 8$?
   (1) $(1, -1)$ **(2)** $(-1, -3)$ **(3)** $(-1, -1)$ **(4)** $(3, 1)$
2. Which is a solution for the system of equations $x^2 + y^2 = 10$ and $y = x - 2$?
   (1) $(1, 3)$ **(2)** $(1, -3)$ **(3)** $(-1, -3)$ **(4)** $(-1, 3)$
3. Which is a solution for the system of equations $y = x^2 + 2x + 3$ and $y = x + 3$?
   (1) $(-2, 1)$ **(2)** $(2, -1)$ **(3)** $(-1, 2)$ **(4)** $(-1, -2)$

In 4–25, solve the system of equations and check.

4. $y = x^2 - x - 6$; $y = 2x - 2$

5. $y = 2x^2 + 3x - 1$; $y = 2x$

6. $y = x^2 + 4x + 3$; $y = 2x + 6$

7. $y = -x^2 + 4x - 3$; $y = x - 1$

8. $y = x^2 + 2x$; $x + y = -2$

9. $y^2 - 8x = 0$; $2x - y = 0$

10. $y + x^2 = 2$; $y + x = 0$

11. $y = x^2 + 3x + 1$; $y - x = 4$

12. $y = x^2 - x - 6$; $y = x - 7$

13. $y = x^2 - 3x - 10$; $3x - y = 19$

14. $y = 3x^2 - 3x + 2$; $y - x = 2$

15. $x^2 + y^2 = 26$; $x - y = 6$

16. $x^2 + y^2 = 50$; $x + y = 0$

17. $x^2 + y^2 = 34$; $x - y = 8$

18. $x^2 + y^2 = 18$; $x + y = 6$

19. $x^2 + y^2 = 25$; $3x - y = 5$

20. $y = \frac{1}{2}x^2 - 2x$; $y - 2x + 6 = 0$

21. $y = 4 - x^2$; $y - x = 2$

22. $y = x^2 - 4x + 4$; $y = \frac{1}{3}x$

23. $y = x^2 - 2x + 1$; $y = \frac{1}{2}x$

24. $y = x^2 - 6x + 8$; $2y + x = 4$

25. $y = -x^2 + x + 5$; $2y - x = 4$

In 26–33, tell how many points of intersection there are if the two graphs are sketched on the same set of axes.

26. $y = x^2$; $y = -2$

27. $y = -x^2$; $x = 1$

28. $x = y^2$; $y = 3$

29. $x = -y^2$; $x = -1$

30. $x^2 + y^2 = 25$; $y = 5$

31. $x^2 + y^2 = 16$; $y = x$

32. $x^2 + y^2 = 9$; $x + y = 3$

33. $x^2 + y^2 = 36$; $y = x^2$

2.5 FRACTIONAL EQUATIONS

An equation that contains the variable in a denominator is called a FRACTIONAL EQUATION.

To solve a fractional equation:

1. Determine the L. C. D. of *all* the denominators.

2. Multiply both sides of the equation (*each* term) by the L.C.D.

3. Cancel common factors and multiply. Solve the resulting equation, which has no fractions.

4. Check in the *original* equation by substituting and separately doing the arithmetic on each side of the equality. *Do not repeat the solution.*

Note that the solution set cannot contain a value that makes any denominator of the original equation = 0.

Examples

1. Find the solution set: $\frac{4}{x} + \frac{2}{7} = \frac{8}{x}$

Solution:

$$\frac{4}{x} + \frac{2}{7} = \frac{8}{x}$$

$$7x \cdot \frac{4}{x} + 7x \cdot \frac{2}{7} = \frac{8}{x} \cdot 7x \qquad \text{Multiply by the L.C.D., } 7x.$$

$$\overset{1}{7\cancel{x}} \cdot \frac{4}{\underset{1}{\cancel{x}}} + \overset{1}{\cancel{7}x} \cdot \frac{2}{\underset{1}{\cancel{7}}} = \frac{8}{\underset{1}{\cancel{x}}} \cdot \overset{1}{7\cancel{x}} \qquad \text{Cancel.}$$

$$28 + 2x = 56 \qquad \text{Multiply.}$$

$$2x = 28 \qquad \text{Subtract 28.}$$

$$x = 14 \qquad \text{Divide by 2.}$$

Check: $\frac{4}{14} + \frac{2}{7} \stackrel{?}{=} \frac{8}{14}$

$\frac{4}{14} + \frac{4}{14} \stackrel{?}{=} \frac{8}{14}$

$\frac{8}{14} = \frac{8}{14}$ ✓

Answer: The solution set is $\{14\}$.

2. Find the solution set: $\frac{6x+18}{x+3} = 5$

Solution: $\frac{6x+18}{x+3} = 5$

$(x+3)\left(\frac{6x+18}{x+3}\right) = 5(x+3)$	Multiply by the L.C.D., $x + 3$.
$\overset{1}{\cancel{(x+3)}}\left(\frac{6x+18}{\underset{1}{\cancel{x+3}}}\right) = 5(x+3)$	Cancel.
$6x + 18 = 5x + 15$	Multiply.
$x + 18 = 15$	Subtract $5x$.
$x = -3$	Subtract 18.

Alternate Solution: Use cross-multiplication as in a proportion.

Check: $x = -3$ leads to a denominator of 0 and, thus, cannot be a solution.

Answer: The solution set is empty.

A fractional equation can lead to a quadratic.

Example

Solve: $\frac{2x}{x+5} + \frac{1}{x-5} = \frac{10}{x^2-25}$

Solution: Multiply by the L.C.D., $(x + 5)(x - 5)$, and cancel common factors.

$$\frac{2x}{x+5} + \frac{1}{x-5} = \frac{10}{(x+5)(x-5)}$$

$$\overset{1}{\cancel{(x+5)}}(x-5)\cdot\frac{2x}{\underset{1}{\cancel{x+5}}} + (x+5)\overset{1}{\cancel{(x-5)}}\cdot\frac{1}{\underset{1}{\cancel{x-5}}} = \frac{10}{\underset{1}{\cancel{(x+5)}}\underset{1}{\cancel{(x-5)}}}\cdot\overset{1}{\cancel{(x+5)}}\overset{1}{\cancel{(x-5)}}$$

$2x(x-5) + (x+5) = 10$	Multiply.
$2x^2 - 10x + x + 5 = 10$	Distribute.
$2x^2 - 9x - 5 = 0$	Standard form of quadratic.
$(2x+1)(x-5) = 0$	Factor.
$2x + 1 = 0$ | $x - 5 = 0$	Set each factor = 0.
$2x = -1$ | $x = 5$	
$x = -\frac{1}{2}$ (does check) | $x = 5$: reject (makes a denominator = 0)	

Answer: $x = -\frac{1}{2}$

A fractional equation can be involved in a system of equations.

Examples

1. Solve the system: $\frac{x-1}{y} = \frac{1}{2}$
$2y - 3x = 6$

Solution: Work first with the fractional equation to clear of fractions.

$\frac{x-1}{y} = \frac{1}{2}$	
$y = 2x - 2$	Cross multiply.
$2y - 3x = 6$ $2(2x-2) - 3x = 6$ $4x - 4 - 3x = 6$ $x = 10$	In the second equation, replace y by $2x - 2$, and solve for x.
$y = 2x - 2$ $y = 2(10) - 2$ $y = 18$	Use any equation with x and y to evaluate y.

Check in the original equations.

$\frac{10-1}{18} \stackrel{?}{=} \frac{1}{2}$	$2(18) - 3(10) \stackrel{?}{=} 6$
$\frac{9}{18} \stackrel{?}{=} \frac{1}{2}$	$36 - 30 \stackrel{?}{=} 6$
$\frac{1}{2} = \frac{1}{2}$ ✓	$6 = 6$ ✓

Answer: $x = 10$, $y = 18$, or $(10, 18)$

2. Solve the system: $y = -x^2$, $\dfrac{y+1}{x+1} = \dfrac{1}{2}$

Solution: Since y is expressed in terms of x in the first equation, substitute for y in the second equation.

$$\frac{y+1}{x+1} = \frac{1}{2}$$

$$\frac{-x^2+1}{x+1} = \frac{1}{2} \quad \text{Substitute } -x^2 \text{ for } y.$$

$$2(-x^2+1) = x+1 \quad \text{Cross multiply.}$$

$$-2x^2+2 = x+1$$

$$2x^2+x-1 = 0 \quad \text{Standard form.}$$

$$(2x-1)(x+1) = 0 \quad \text{Factor.}$$

$2x-1=0$ | $x+1=0$ Set each factor = 0.

$2x = 1$ | $x = -1$ ← reject (makes a denominator = 0)

$x = \frac{1}{2}$

$y = -x^2$ Use the first equation to evaluate y.

$$y = -\left(\frac{1}{2}\right)^2 = -\frac{1}{4}$$

Answer: $x = \frac{1}{2}$, $y = -\frac{1}{4}$, or $\left(\frac{1}{2}, -\frac{1}{4}\right)$

EXERCISES

In 1–12, solve the equation.

1. $\frac{2}{x} + 1 = \frac{1}{4}$
2. $\frac{1}{R} = \frac{1}{2} + \frac{1}{3}$
3. $\frac{1}{15} + \frac{1}{10} = \frac{1}{x}$
4. $\frac{1}{x} + 1 = \frac{3}{2x}$
5. $\frac{1}{2x} = \frac{1}{x} - 2$
6. $\frac{3}{y} = 2 + \frac{5}{y}$
7. $\frac{3}{2x-1} = \frac{1}{3x-5}$
8. $\frac{1}{2x-3} = \frac{5}{4x+1}$
9. $\frac{2q}{q+1} = \frac{2q-1}{q-1}$
10. $\frac{3}{2a-1} + 2 = \frac{9}{2a-1}$
11. $\frac{2}{z-3} + 1 = \frac{z-1}{z-3}$
12. $\frac{m}{m-2} - \frac{m+4}{3(m-2)} = \frac{1}{3}$

13. The solution of $\frac{1}{x} + \frac{1}{2x} = 1$ is
(1) $\frac{1}{2}$ (2) $\frac{1}{3}$ (3) $\frac{2}{3}$ (4) $\frac{3}{2}$

14. If the sum of a number n and ten times its reciprocal is 7, then a value of n may be
(1) $\frac{1}{2}$ (2) 2 (3) 3 (4) 4

15. If the reciprocal of $(x + 2)$ is equal to $\frac{2}{x}$, then x is equal to
(1) −2 (2) 2 (3) −4 (4) 4

16. The statement $\dfrac{1}{1+\frac{1}{x}} = 1$ is true for
(1) all real values of x
(2) some but not all real values of x
(3) no real values of x

In 17–26, solve for the indicated quantity in terms of the other quantities.

17. Solve for x: $a = b + \frac{1}{x}$
18. Solve for m: $\frac{a}{m} - b = c$
19. Solve for b: $\frac{1}{R} = \frac{1}{a} + \frac{1}{b}$
20. Solve for y: $\frac{1}{y} - \frac{1}{x} = \frac{1}{x}$
21. Solve for x: $\frac{1}{y} - \frac{1}{x} = \frac{1}{x}$
22. Solve for r: $S = \frac{a}{1-r}$
23. Solve for S: $R = \frac{ST}{S+T}$
24. Solve for R: $C = \frac{E}{R+S}$
25. Solve for n: $c = \frac{en}{s+nr}$
26. Solve for x: $\frac{x}{a} - \frac{a}{x-a} = \frac{x}{2a}$

27. If $\frac{1}{s} = \frac{1}{x} - \frac{1}{y}$, then x equals
(1) $s + y$ (2) $\frac{sy}{s+y}$ (3) $\frac{sy}{y-s}$ (4) $\frac{y+s}{sy}$

In 28–49, find the solution set. Express irrational answers in simplest radical form.

28. $\frac{2}{x} = \frac{x}{8}$
29. $\frac{5}{b} + 3b = \frac{17}{b}$
30. $d - 2 = \frac{3}{d}$
31. $\frac{3}{y-1} = \frac{y}{2}$
32. $\frac{a}{3} - \frac{5}{3} = \frac{2}{a}$
33. $\frac{6m}{m} + 2m = 0$
34. $x + 7 = \frac{47}{x-7}$
35. $\frac{1}{15-r} = \frac{15+r}{9}$
36. $\frac{54}{z} = 3z + 9$
37. $\frac{x-3}{x} = \frac{2x}{x-2}$
38. $m - \frac{3}{m} = 2$
39. $\frac{6}{m} + \frac{m-9}{2m} = m$
40. $\frac{3x+3}{x+1} = \frac{2x}{x}$
41. $\frac{2r-2}{r-1} = \frac{r}{5}$
42. $\frac{2}{y-2} = \frac{3y}{2}$
43. $6 + 2r = \frac{1}{r}$
44. $\frac{1}{q+1} + \frac{1}{q-1} = 1$
45. $\frac{1}{t+3} + \frac{1}{t+1} = 1$
46. $\frac{5}{x+1} + \frac{x-1}{4} = 2$
47. $\frac{x}{x-1} + \frac{2}{x^2-1} = \frac{8}{x+1}$
48. $\frac{x}{x-2} - \frac{8}{x+3} = \frac{10}{x^2+x-6}$
49. $\frac{x}{x-2} - \frac{2}{x+4} = \frac{12}{x^2+2x-8}$

In 50–68, solve the system of equations.

50. $\frac{y}{2} = x + 1$
$4x - y = 6$

51. $3a - 2b = 6$
$\frac{b-1}{a} = \frac{1}{2}$

52. $\frac{t-u}{2} = 1$
$\frac{t+u}{2} = 4$

53. $3s + t = 9$
$\frac{3s}{2} + \frac{4t}{5} = \frac{27}{5}$

54. $\frac{x}{2} + \frac{3y}{4} = 8$
$x + \frac{y}{4} = 6$

55. $\frac{3x}{2} + \frac{y}{5} = 6$
$\frac{x+2}{4} - \frac{y-3}{6} = 2$

56. $\frac{x}{5} - \frac{y}{10} = 1$
$\frac{x}{3} - \frac{y}{5} = 1$

57. $\frac{x}{2} + \frac{4y}{3} = 4$
$x + \frac{3y}{2} = 1$

58. $\frac{m}{n+1} = \frac{2}{3}$
$m + n = 9$

59. $m + 2n = 12$
$\frac{m}{n} = 1 + \frac{6}{n}$

60. $r - 8t = -2$
$\frac{3r}{2t} + 1 = \frac{10}{t}$

61. $2u + v = 23$
$\frac{u-6}{3v} = \frac{1}{5}$

62. $3x - 4y = 1$
$\frac{y+2}{x} + \frac{8}{5} = \frac{20y+4}{5x}$

63. $y = x^2 + 1$
$\frac{y-10}{x-3} = 2$

64. $y = x^2 + 4x$
$\frac{y-3}{x-1} = 1$

65. $y = x^2 - 4$
$\frac{y+5}{x+1} = 1$

66. $y = \frac{1}{2}x^2$
$\frac{y-2}{2-x} = \frac{6}{5}$

67. $x = y^2$
$\frac{y-2}{x-4} = \frac{1}{3}$

68. $x = -y^2$
$\frac{x+2}{y+4} = \frac{1}{2}$

2.6 RADICAL EQUATIONS

An equation that contains the variable inside a radical is called a RADICAL EQUATION.

To solve a square-root radical equation:

1. **Isolate the term with the radical on one side of the equation.**
2. **Square both sides of the equation, and solve the resulting equation.**
3. **Check in the *original* equation by substituting and separately calculating on each side of the equality. *Do not repeat the solution.***

Note that one or both of the solutions of the squared equation may not satisfy the original equation.

Examples

1. Find the solution set: $\sqrt{2x+1} - 1 = 4$

Solution:

$\sqrt{2x+1} - 1 = 4$	
$\sqrt{2x+1} = 5$	Add 1 to isolate the radical term.
$(\sqrt{2x+1})^2 = (5)^2$	Square both sides.
$2x + 1 = 25$	Solve for x.
$2x = 24$	
$x = 12$	

Check in the original equation, by substituting and working separately on each side.

$\sqrt{2x+1} - 1 = 4$
$\sqrt{2(12)+1} - 1 \stackrel{?}{=} 4$
$\sqrt{25} - 1 \stackrel{?}{=} 4$
$5 - 1 \stackrel{?}{=} 4$
$4 = 4$ ✔

Answer: The solution set is {12}.

2. Find the solution set: $x - \sqrt{9-2x} = 3$

Solution:

$x - \sqrt{9-2x} = 3$	Subtract 3 and add $\sqrt{9-2x}$ to isolate the radical term.
$x - 3 = \sqrt{9-2x}$	
$(x-3)^2 = (\sqrt{9-2x})^2$	Square both sides.
$x^2 - 6x + 9 = 9 - 2x$	Expand the square.
$x^2 - 4x = 0$	Quadratic standard form.
$x(x-4) = 0$	Factor.
$x = 0$ | $x - 4 = 0$, $x = 4$	Set each factor = 0, and solve for x.

Check both values in the original equation.

$0 - \sqrt{9-2(0)} \stackrel{?}{=} 3$
$-\sqrt{9} \stackrel{?}{=} 3$
$-3 \neq 3$

$4 - \sqrt{9-2(4)} \stackrel{?}{=} 3$
$4 - \sqrt{1} \stackrel{?}{=} 3$
$3 = 3$ ✔

Answer: The solution set is {4}.

EXERCISES

1. The solution set of $\sqrt{x+1} + 5 = 0$ is
(1) ∅ (2) {24} (3) {–26} (4) {0}

2. The equation $\sqrt{x} + 3 = 1$ has
(1) one positive root only
(2) one negative root only
(3) one positive and one negative root
(4) no roots

3. The solution set of $5 + \sqrt{2x-4} = 1$ is
(1) {10} (2) {±10} (3) {0} (4) ∅

4. The solution set of $\sqrt{3x-8} = \sqrt{x}$ is
(1) {4} (2) {±4} (3) {2} (4) {±2}

5. If $3\sqrt{2} = \sqrt{a}$, the value of a is
(1) 6 (2) 2 (3) 12 (4) 18

6. What value of x satisfies the equation $x^{\frac{3}{2}} = 64$?

In 7–14, find the solution set.

7. $\sqrt{3x-5} = 5$
8. $\sqrt{6x-2} = 4$
9. $\sqrt{3x-2} - 4 = 0$
10. $8 = 2 + \sqrt{2x-4}$
11. $2\sqrt{x-1} = 1$
12. $\sqrt{x+2} - 3 = 0$
13. $\sqrt{2x+3} - 5 = 0$
14. $\sqrt{x^2+7} = x + 1$

15. When 4 is subtracted from 2 times a certain number, the square root of the result is 6. Find the number.

In 16–17, solve the equation for the indicated quantity.

16. Solve for e: $S = \sqrt{\frac{20e}{k}}$

17. Solve for C: $f = \frac{1}{2\pi\sqrt{LC}}$

18. The equation $\sqrt{x} = x$ has two distinct roots. These roots are
(1) 1 and 0 (3) 1 and –1
(2) –1 and 0 (4) 4 and 2

19. The equation $\sqrt{2-x} = x$ has
(1) 1 as its only root (3) both –2 and 1 as roots
(2) –2 as its only root (4) neither –2 nor 1 as roots

20. The solution set of $\sqrt{3x+4} = x$ is
(1) {–1} (2) {–4, 1} (3) {4, –1} (4) {4}

21. The equation $x = \sqrt{2x+3}$ has
(1) 3 and –1 as solutions
(2) 3 as its only solution
(3) –1 as its only solution
(4) no solution

22. The equation $\sqrt{y-3} = 5 - y$ has
(1) both 7 and 4 as roots
(2) 7 as its only root
(3) 4 as its only root
(4) neither 7 nor 4 as roots

23. The solution set of $\sqrt{y-2} = 2 - y$ is
(1) {2, 3} (2) {2} (3) {3} (4) ∅

24. The roots of $\sqrt{x-1} + x = 7$ are
(1) 10 only
(2) –10 only
(3) both 5 and 10
(4) 5 only

25. The equation $x - 3 = \sqrt{x-3}$ has
(1) both 4 and 3 as roots
(2) 4 as its only root
(3) 3 as its only root
(4) neither 4 nor 3 as roots

26. Which equation has both 3 and 6 as roots?
(1) $\sqrt{x-2} = \frac{3}{x}$ (3) $\sqrt{x-2} = \frac{x}{3}$
(2) $\sqrt{x-2} = 4 - x$ (4) $\sqrt{x-2} = x - 4$

In 27–36, find the solution set.

27. $\sqrt{x^2+3x} = x + 3$
28. $\sqrt{2x+3} = x$
29. $\sqrt{x^2+27} = 2x$
30. $2\sqrt{2x+3} + x = 1$
31. $2\sqrt{x-1} = x - 1$
32. $y = \sqrt{8y-7}$
33. $y = \sqrt{y^2+5}$
34. $2y = \sqrt{4y^2-1}$
35. $1 - y = \sqrt{7+y^2}$
36. $2 - y - 2\sqrt{y+1} = 0$

2.7 SOLUTIONS OF INEQUALITIES

Linear Inequalities

Applying basic properties, the solution of a linear inequality is similar to that of an equality.

A major difference is that *when multiplying or dividing by a negative number, you must reverse the order of the inequality.*

Example

Find the solution set and graph: $-3x + 2 < 11$

Solution:

$-3x + 2 < 11$
$-3x < 9$ Subtract 2.
$x > -3$ Divide by –3. Reverse the order of the inequality.

Answer: The solution set is $\{x \mid x > -3\}$.

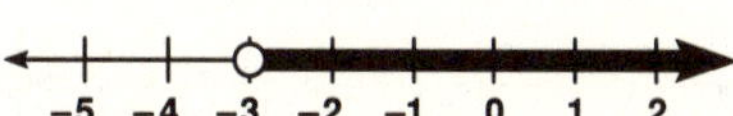

Note that the open hole at –3 indicates that –3 is not included in the solution set.

A COMPOUND INEQUALITY is a combination of two simpler inequalities.

Two simple inequalities may be combined into a single sentence that is a *conjunction*.

Example: The combination of inequalities $-1 < x$ ***and*** $x < 2$ can be written $-1 < x < 2$, which is the conjunction $(-1 < x) \wedge (x < 2)$.

$\{x \mid -1 < x < 2\}$

−2 −1 0 1 2 3

Two simple inequalities may be combined into a *disjunction*.

Example: The combination of inequalities $x \leq -1$ ***or*** $x > 2$ is the disjunction $(x \leq -1) \vee (x > 2)$.

$\{x \mid (x \leq -1) \vee (x > 2)\}$

−2 −1 0 1 2 3

As the simple inequalities increase in complexity, finding the solution set to a compound inequality requires initial solution of the simple inequalities.

Example

Find and graph the solution set of the inequality:

$$8 < -3x + 2 \leq 14$$

Solution: The given compound inequality is equivalent to the conjunction of two simpler inequalities.

$$8 < -3x + 2 \leq 14 \Leftrightarrow (8 < -3x + 2) \wedge (-3x + 2 \leq 14)$$

Find the solution set for each simple inequality. Remember to reverse the order of the inequality when dividing by a negative number.

$8 < -3x + 2$	$-3x + 2 \leq 14$
$6 < -3x$	$-3x \leq 12$
$-2 > x$	$x \geq -4$

Answer: The solution set is $\{x \mid -2 > x \geq -4\}$, or $\{x \mid -4 \leq x < -2\}$.

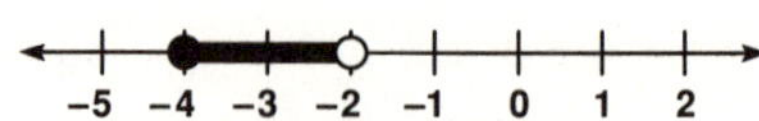

EXERCISES

1. If $a > b$ and $b > c$, which statement is *not* true?

(1) $b < a$ **(2)** $c < b$ **(3)** $a > c$ **(4)** $a < c$

2. If $a > b$ and $c < 0$, which statement is true?

(1) $a + c < b + c$ **(3)** $ac < bc$
(2) $a - c < b - c$ **(4)** $ac > bc$

3. If $a < b$ and $c > 0$, which statement is true?

(1) $a + c > b + c$ **(3)** $ac > bc$
(2) $a - c > b - c$ **(4)** $ac < bc$

4. If $a > b$ and $c > d$, which statement is always true?

(1) $a + c < b + d$ **(3)** $a + c > b + d$
(2) $a - c < b - d$ **(4)** $a + d > b + c$

5. Which statement is true?

(1) For positive a and b: if $a < b$, then $a^2 < b^2$
(2) For positive a and b: if $a < b$, then $a^2 > b^2$
(3) For negative a and b: if $a < b$, then $a^2 < b^2$
(4) For negative a and b: if $a > b$, then $a^2 > b^2$

6. Which graph represents the solution set of the inequality $-4x < 8$?

(1)
(2)

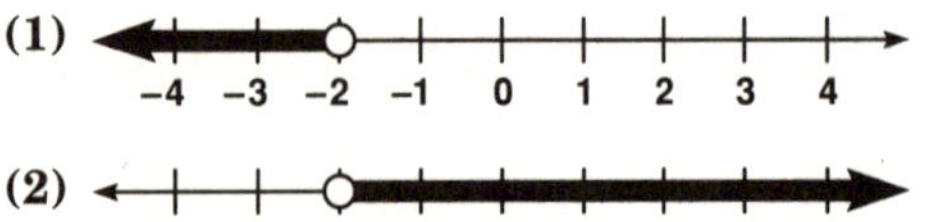

(3)

(4)

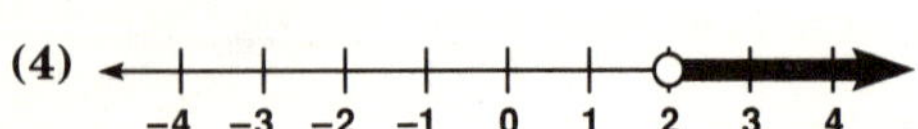

7. Which graph represents the solution set of $3x + 4 > 13$?

(1)

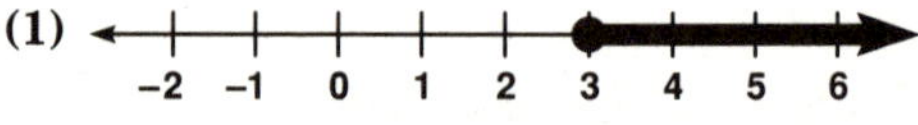

(2)

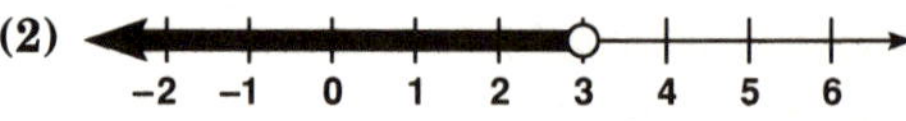

(3)

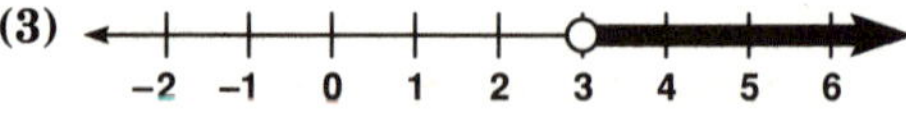

(4)

8. Which graph represents the solution set of $2x - 1 \leq 9$?

(1)

(2)

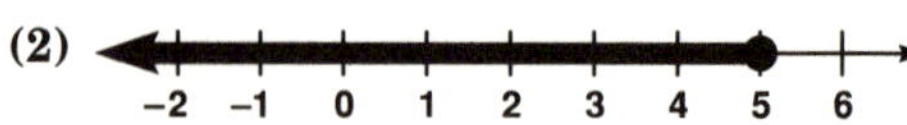

(3)

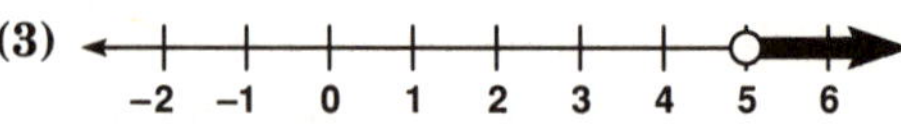

(4)

−2 −1 0 1 2 3 4 5 6

9. Which inequality is represented by the graph?

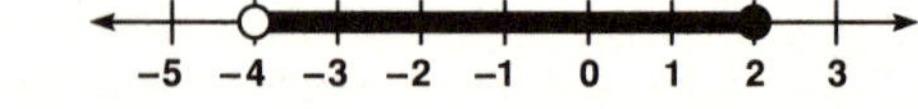

(1) $2 \leq x < -4$ **(3)** $-4 < x \leq 2$
(2) $-4 \leq x \leq 2$ **(4)** $-4 \leq x < 2$

10. Which inequality is represented by the graph?

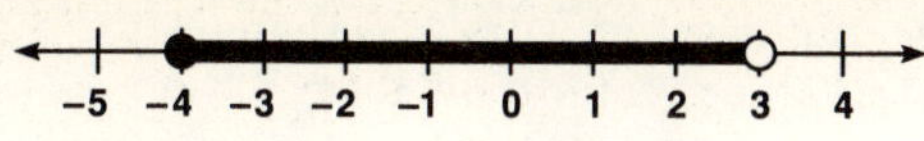

(1) $3 \le x < -4$ (3) $-4 < x \le 3$
(2) $-4 \le x \le 3$ (4) $-4 \le x < 3$

11. Which graph shows the solution to $(x < -1) \vee (x \ge 3)$?

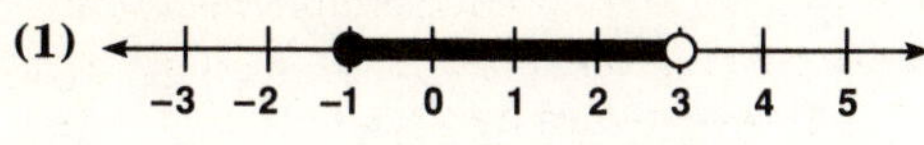

(1)
(2)
(3)
(4)

12. Which is the graph of $(-x > 4) \vee (2x - 1 > 7)$?

(1)
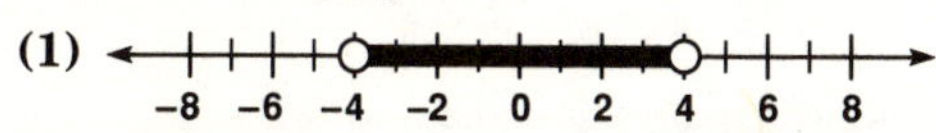

(2)
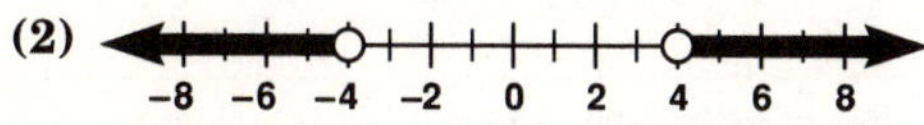

(3)
(4)

13. Which sentence is equivalent to $x \ge 5$?

(1) $(x > 5) \wedge (x = 5)$ (3) $(x > 5) \wedge (x < 5)$
(2) $(x > 5) \vee (x = 5)$ (4) $(x > 5) \vee (x < 5)$

14. Which sentence is equivalent to $-4 \le x < 5$?

(1) $(-4 \le x) \vee (x < 5)$ (3) $(x \le -4) \vee (x < 5)$
(2) $(-4 \le x) \wedge (x < 5)$ (4) $(x \le -4) \wedge (x < 5)$

In 15–21, find the solution set.

15. $4x - 1 < x + 8$

16. $3(2k - 1) \le 2(k + 3)$

17. $3(y + 6) > 6 + 5y$

18. $2z - 1 < \frac{8 - z}{2}$

19. $\frac{4x - 3}{2} \ge \frac{2 - x}{3}$

20. $\frac{2y + 7}{2} < \frac{4y + 5}{3}$

21. $\frac{2m - 5}{3} - \frac{m - 7}{4} \ge 0$

In 22–31, find and graph the solution set.

22. $1 < 3x - 2 < 10$

23. $-13 \le 4x - 1 \le 3$

24. $0 < 2 - 2x < 6$

25. $1 < 3 - 2x < 12$

26. $7 \le \frac{2 + 3x}{2} \le 10$

27. $13 > 6x + 1 > -11$

28. $0 > 8x + 5 > -3$

29. $14 \ge 2 - 2x \ge 8$

30. $25 > 4 - 3x > 16$

31. $3 > \frac{1 - 2x}{3} > -1$

Absolute-Value Inequalities

To solve an absolute-value inequality:

1. Consider two cases.

CASE 1: **Consider the variable expression in the absolute value as ≥ 0, and replace the absolute value by the variable expression.**

CASE 2: **Consider the variable expression in the absolute value as < 0, and replace the absolute value by the negative of the variable expression.**

2. Reverse the order of the inequality when multiplying or dividing by a negative number.

3. The results of solving the two simple inequalities are a compound inequality:

a conjunction if the original inequality is of the form $|x| < a$

a disjunction if the original inequality is of the form $|x| > a$

4. Choose value(s) in the domain of the compound inequality to check in the original inequality.

Examples

1. Find the solution set and graph: $|2x - 1| < 7$

Solution: Since there are two cases, the given inequality leads to two inequalities.

If $2x - 1 \ge 0$, replace $|2x - 1|$ by $2x - 1$.	If $2x - 1 < 0$, replace $|2x - 1|$ by $-(2x - 1)$.
$2x - 1 < 7$	$-(2x - 1) < 7$
$2x < 8$	$-2x + 1 < 7$
$x < 4$	$-2x < 6$
	$x > -3$ or $-3 < x$

The results combine as a conjunction: $-3 < x$ AND $x < 4$, written $-3 < x < 4$

Check: Substitute a value between −3 and 4, say 0, into the original inequality.

$|2x - 1| < 7$

$|2(0) - 1| \stackrel{?}{<} 7$

$|-1| \stackrel{?}{<} 7$

$1 < 7$ ✓

Answer: $\{x \mid -3 < x < 4\}$

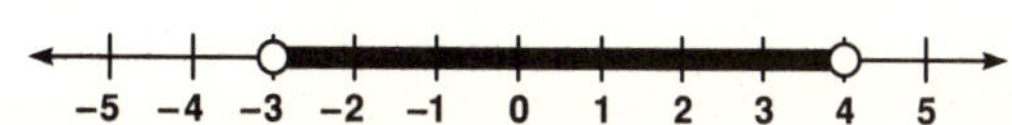

2. Find the solution set and graph: $|2x - 1| \geq 7$

Solution: Since there are two cases, the given inequality leads to two inequalities.

If $2x - 1 \geq 0$, replace $|2x - 1|$ by $2x - 1$.	If $2x - 1 < 0$, replace $|2x - 1|$ by $-(2x - 1)$.
$2x - 1 \geq 7$	$-(2x - 1) \geq 7$
$2x \geq 8$	$-2x + 1 \geq 7$
$x \geq 4$	$-2x \geq 6$
	$x \leq -3$

The results combine as a disjunction: $x \leq -3$ OR $x \geq 4$, written $(x \leq -3) \vee (x \geq 4)$

Check: Substitute a value less than −3, say −4, and a value greater than 4, say 5.

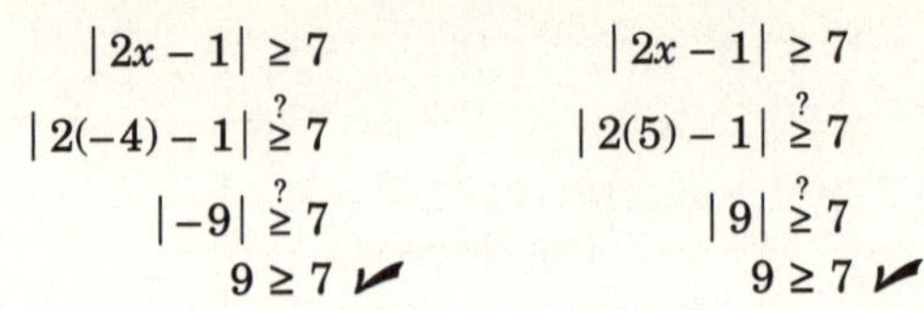

$|2x - 1| \geq 7$	$|2x - 1| \geq 7$
$|2(-4) - 1| \overset{?}{\geq} 7$	$|2(5) - 1| \overset{?}{\geq} 7$
$|-9| \overset{?}{\geq} 7$	$|9| \overset{?}{\geq} 7$
$9 \geq 7$ ✓	$9 \geq 7$ ✓

Answer: $\{x \mid (x \leq -3) \vee (x \geq 4)\}$

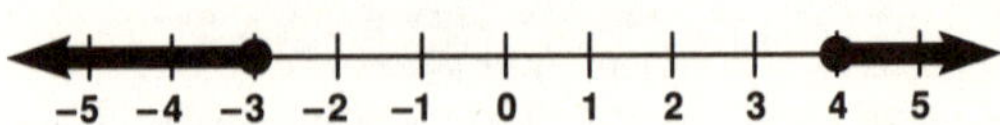

EXERCISES

1. The solution of $|3x - 2| < 4$ is

(1) $-\frac{2}{3} < x < 2$ (3) $x > -\frac{2}{3}$
(2) $x < 2$ (4) $x < -\frac{2}{3}$ or $x > 2$

2. The solution to $|3x - 4| > 5$ is

(1) $x > 3$ or $x < -\frac{1}{3}$ (3) $x < 3$ and $x > -\frac{1}{3}$
(2) $x \geq 3$ or $x \leq -\frac{1}{3}$ (4) $x \leq 3$ and $x \geq -\frac{1}{3}$

3. The solution set of $|2x - 5| \leq 11$ is

(1) $\{x \mid -5 \leq x \leq 22\}$ (3) $\{x \mid -3 \leq x \leq 8\}$
(2) $\{x \mid x \leq 8\}$ (4) $\{x \mid x \leq -3 \vee x \geq 8\}$

4. Which represents the solution set for x in the inequality $|2x + 1| < 9$?

(1) $\{x \mid x < -5 \text{ or } x > 4\}$ (3) $\{x \mid -5 < x < 4\}$
(2) $\{x \mid x < -4 \text{ or } x > 5\}$ (4) $\{x \mid -4 < x < 5\}$

5. The solution set of $|x - 2| < 3$ is

(1) $\{x \mid x > 5\}$ (3) $\{x \mid -1 < x < 5\}$
(2) $\{x \mid x < -1\}$ (4) $\{x \mid x < -1 \text{ or } x > 5\}$

6. The solution set of $|3 - x| < 5$ is

(1) $\{x \mid (x < -2) \vee (x > 8)\}$
(2) $\{x \mid -2 < x < 8\}$
(3) $\{x \mid -8 < x < 2\}$
(4) $\{x \mid (x < -8) \vee (x > 2)\}$

7. Which is the graph of the solution set of $|x + 3| > 2$?

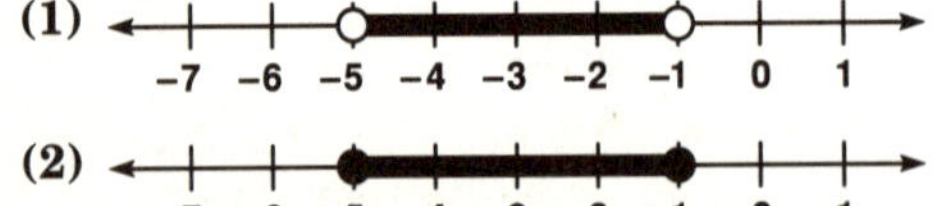

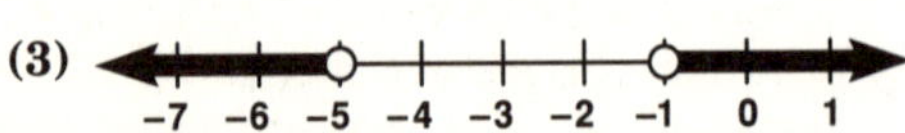

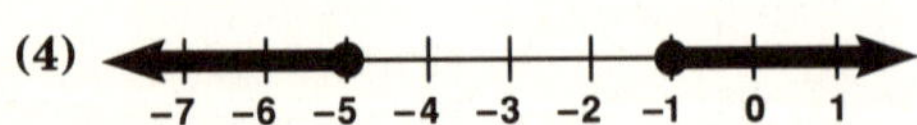

8. Which graph represents the solution set of $|x + 1| < 2$?

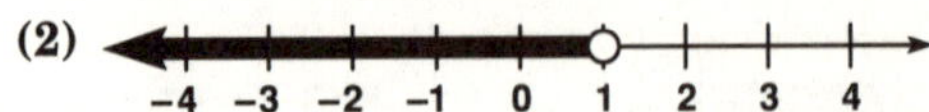

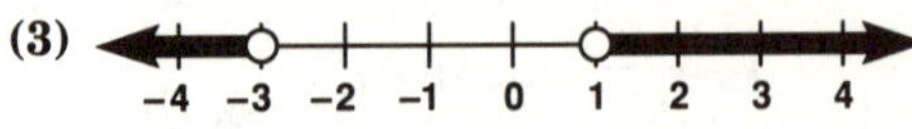

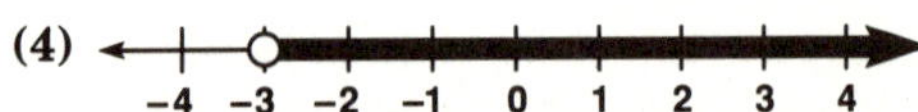

9. Which is the graph of the solution set of $|x - 3| < 5$?

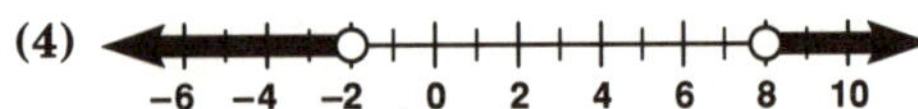

10. Which is the graph of the solution set of $|2x - 3| < 7$?

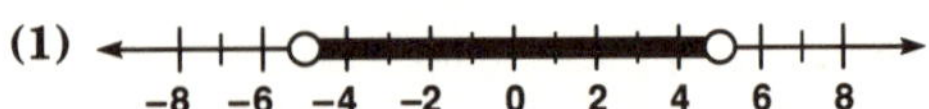

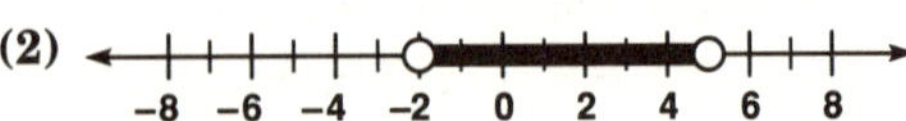

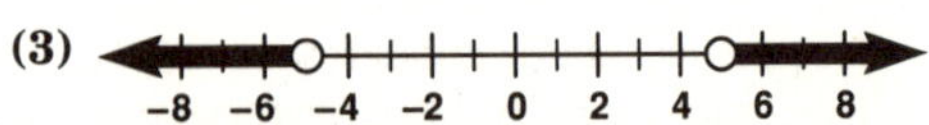

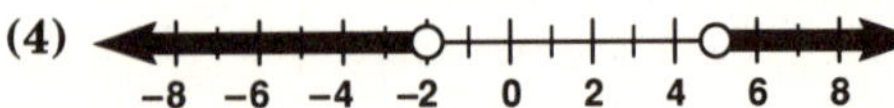

11. Which graph represents the solution set of $|5x - 15| < 10$?

(1) 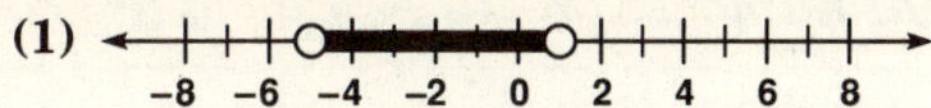

(2) 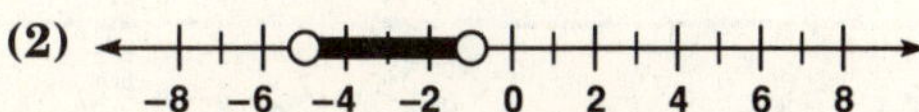

(3) −8 −6 −4 −2 0 2 4 6 8

(4) −8 −6 −4 −2 0 2 4 6 8

12. Which is the graph of the solution set of $|1 - 2x| < 7$?

(1) −8 −6 −4 −2 0 2 4 6 8

(2) −8 −6 −4 −2 0 2 4 6 8

(3) −8 −6 −4 −2 0 2 4 6 8

(4) −8 −6 −4 −2 0 2 4 6 8

In 13–23, find and graph the solution set.

13. $|x - 2| > 5$

14. $|5 - x| > 7$

15. $|x + 3| \le 4$

16. $|2x - 3| < 5$

17. $|4x - 1| \ge 7$

18. $5 + |2x + 1| > -4$

19. $|2x + 3| > x$

20. $|2 + 3x| < x$

21. $|5x - 12| \ge x$

22. $x > |2x + 1|$

23. $|5x + 3| \le 2x$

Quadratic Inequalities

METHOD 1: USING THE POSSIBILITIES FOR THE SIGNS OF THE FACTORS

To solve a quadratic inequality by factoring:

1. Break the quadratic inequality into simple inequalities by considering the possibilities for the signs of the factors.

a. If the inequality involves > 0, the two factors must have the same sign.

b. If the inequality involves < 0, the two factors must have opposite signs.

2. Write the results of solving the two simple inequalities as a compound inequality.

3. Choose values to check in the original inequality.

Examples

1. Find the solution set: $x^2 - 5x - 6 > 0$

Solution:

$x^2 - 5x - 6 > 0$ Standard form.

$(x - 6)(x + 1) > 0$ Factor.

Since the inequality involves > 0, the factors must have the same signs.

CASE 1: BOTH FACTORS > 0

$x - 6 > 0$ AND $x + 1 > 0$

$x > 6 \downarrow$ $x > -1$

Conjunction: $x > 6$

CASE 2: BOTH FACTORS < 0

$x - 6 < 0$ AND $x + 1 < 0$

$x < 6 \downarrow$ $x < -1$

Conjunction: $x < -1$

Check: Choose a value from each case, say $x = 7$ and $x = -2$, to substitute into the original inequality.

Answer: $\{x | (x > 6) \vee (x < -1)\}$

2. Find the solution set: $x^2 - 5x - 6 < 0$

Solution:

$x^2 - 5x - 6 < 0$ Standard form.

$(x - 6)(x + 1) < 0$ Factor.

Since the inequality involves < 0, the factors must have opposite signs.

CASE 1: FIRST FACTOR > 0 AND SECOND FACTOR < 0

$x - 6 > 0$ AND $x + 1 < 0$

$x > 6 \downarrow$ $x < -1$

Conjunction: impossible

CASE 2: FIRST FACTOR < 0 AND SECOND FACTOR > 0

$x - 6 < 0$ AND $x + 1 > 0$

$x < 6 \downarrow$ $x > -1$

Conjunction: $-1 < x < 6$

Check: Choose a value between −1 and 6, say 0, to substitute into the original inequality.

Answer: $\{x | -1 < x < 6\}$

The solution to a quadratic inequality can also be determined by working with the roots of the related quadratic equation. That is, the solution to a quadratic inequality is either: ***the set of real numbers between the roots or the set of real numbers on either side of the roots***

	Quadratic Equation	Related Quadratic Inequalities	
Solution	$ax^2 + bx + c = 0$ r_1 or r_2	$ax^2 + bx + c < 0$ $\{x \mid r_1 < x < r_2\}$	$ax^2 + bx + c > 0$ $\{x \mid (x < r_1) \vee (x > r_2)\}$

METHOD 2: USING THE ROOTS OF THE RELATED EQUATION

To solve a quadratic inequality:

1. **Find, by factoring, the solutions, $\{r_1, r_2\}$, to the related quadratic equation $ax^2 + bx + c = 0$.**
2. **Determine from the order of the inequality, or by checking values, whether the solution set is:**
   the set of real numbers between r_1 and r_2, or
   the set of real numbers on either side of r_1 and r_2

Example

3. Find the solution set: $x^2 + x - 6 > 0$

Solution: First, by factoring, find the roots of the related equation.

$$x^2 + x - 6 = 0$$
$$(x + 3)(x - 2) = 0$$
$$x + 3 = 0 \quad \Big| \quad (x - 2) = 0$$
$$x = -3 \quad \Big| \quad x = 2$$

Choose a check point: say 0, between the roots. Substitute into the given inequality.

$x^2 + x - 6 > 0$

$0^2 + 0 - 6 \overset{?}{>} 0$ false

Thus, the solution is *not* between the roots.

Answer: $\{x \mid (x < -3) \vee (x > 2)\}$

The solution can also be found on a number line by marking the intervals determined by r_1 and r_2. Use + to mark where a factor is positive and – where a factor is negative.

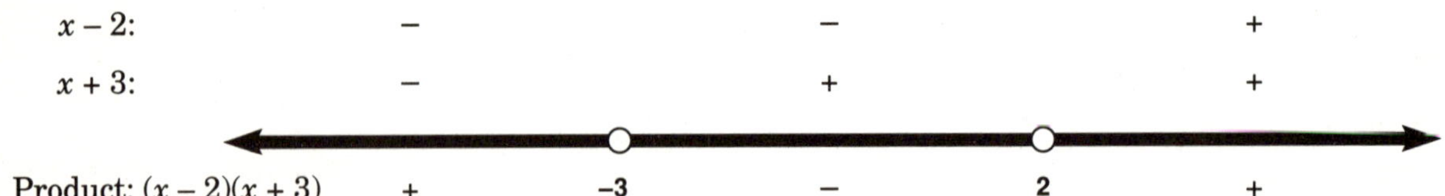

Where the product is positive the values are the solution to >: $\{x \mid (x < -3) \vee (x > 2)\}$
Where the product is negative the values are the solution to <: $\{x \mid -3 < x < 2\}$

EXERCISES

1. The solution set of $x^2 + 4x + 3 < 0$ is

(1) $\{x \mid -3 < x < -1\}$
(2) $\{x \mid (x < -3) \vee (x > -1)\}$
(3) $\{x \mid 1 < x < 3\}$
(4) $\{x \mid (x < 1) \vee (x > 3)\}$

2. The solution set of $x^2 - 6x + 8 \geq 0$ is

(1) $\{x \mid 2 \leq x \leq 4\}$
(2) $\{x \mid (x \leq 2) \vee (x \geq 4)\}$
(3) $\{x \mid -4 \leq x \leq -2\}$
(4) $\{x \mid (x \leq -4) \vee (x \geq -2)\}$

3. What is the solution set for $x^2 - 4x - 5 < 0$?

(1) $\{x \mid -1 < x < 5\}$
(2) $\{x \mid -5 < x < 1\}$
(3) $\{x \mid x > 5 \text{ or } x < -1\}$
(4) $\{x \mid x < -1\}$

4. What is the solution set of the inequality $x^2 - 6x - 7 > 0$?

(1) $\{x \mid -1 < x < 7\}$
(2) $\{x \mid x = -1 \text{ or } x = 7\}$
(3) $\{x \mid x < -7 \text{ or } x > 1\}$
(4) $\{x \mid x > 7 \text{ or } x < -1\}$

5. The solution set of $2x^2 + 5x - 3 \leq 0$ is

(1) $\{x \mid -3 \leq x \leq \frac{1}{2}\}$
(2) $\{x \mid -\frac{1}{2} \leq x \leq 3\}$
(3) $\{x \mid (x \leq -3) \vee (x \geq \frac{1}{2})\}$
(4) $\{x \mid (x \leq -\frac{1}{2}) \vee (x \geq 3)\}$

6. What is the solution set for $(x + 3)(x - 2) > 0$?

(1) –4 –3 –2 –1 0 1 2 3 4

(2) 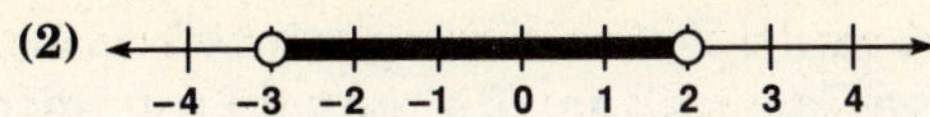

(3) 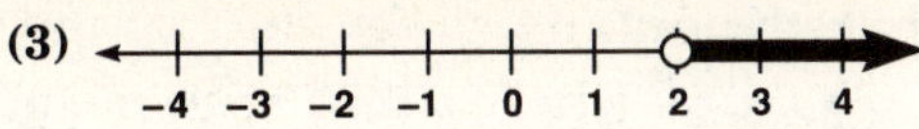

(4)

7. Which is the graph of the solution set of $x^2 - x - 6 < 0$?

(1) 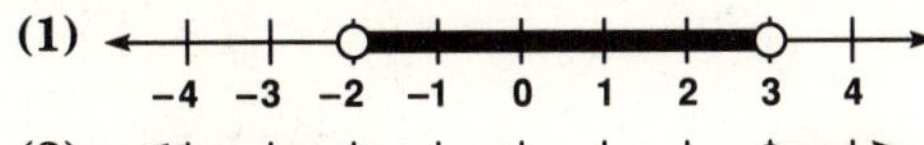

(2)

(3)

(4)

8. Which is the graph of the solution set of the inequality $x^2 + 3x - 4 < 0$?

(1) 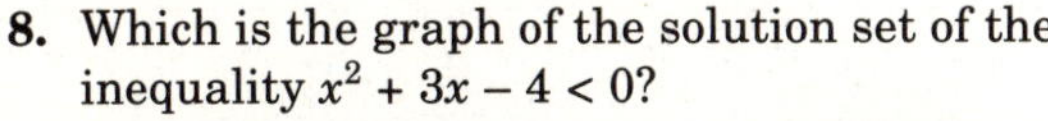

(2)

(3)

(4)

9. Which graph is the solution set of $x^2 + 3x < 10$?

(1)

(2)

(3)

(4)

10. Which is the graph of the solution set for $x^2 > 4x$?

(1)

(2)

(3)

(4)

In 11–20, find the solution set.

11. $x^2 + 9x + 8 > 0$
12. $x^2 + 8x - 9 < 0$
13. $x^2 - 7x + 12 \le 0$
14. $x^2 - 6x - 7 > 0$
15. $x^2 - 3x > 0$
16. $x^2 + 4x < 0$
17. $x^2 - 16 > 0$
18. $25 - x^2 \le 0$
19. $x^2 > 3 - 2x$
20. $2x^2 < 3x + 2$

2.8 THE COMPLEX NUMBERS

The Imaginary Unit

The IMAGINARY UNIT i is defined as $i = \sqrt{-1}$.
Square roots involving negative radicands are rewritten in terms of i.

Examples

1. $\sqrt{-128} = \sqrt{64} \cdot \sqrt{2} \cdot \sqrt{-1}$
$= 8i\sqrt{2}$

Factor to separate the imaginary unit, the perfect square, and the irrational factor.

2. $\sqrt{-81} + 3\sqrt{-25}$
$= \sqrt{81} \cdot \sqrt{-1} + 3\sqrt{25} \cdot \sqrt{-1}$
$= 9i + 15i$
$= 24i$

To combine square roots with negative radicands, first rewrite each in terms of i, simplifying as possible.

Powers of i are cyclical, repeating exactly four values: $i, -1, -i, 1$
All powers of i can be expressed as one of these four values.

$i = \sqrt{-1}$
$i^2 = -1$
$i^3 = i^2 \cdot i = -1 \cdot i = -i$
$i^4 = i^2 \cdot i^2 = -1 \cdot -1 = 1$
$i^5 = i^4 \cdot i = 1 \cdot i = i$
etc.

To simplify higher powers of i:

1. **Identify the greatest power of i^4, or 1, that is contained in the given power of i. The remaining factor is i, i^2, or i^3.**
2. **Apply two laws of exponents:**
   $x^{ab} = (x^a)^b$ **to rewrite the power of i^4**
   $x^{a+b} = x^a \cdot x^b$ **to rewrite the term as a product**
3. **Replace the basic powers of i by their values.**

Example

i^{47}

$= i^{44+3}$ Identify the greatest power of i^4.

$= (i^4)^{11} \cdot i^3$ $x^{ab} = (x^a)^b$ and $x^{a+b} = x^a \cdot x^b$

$= (1)^{11} \cdot (-i)$ Replace the basic powers of i by their values: $i^4 = 1$, $i^3 = -i$

$= -i$

When multiplying square roots involving negative radicands, do not immediately multiply radicands.

$\sqrt{a} \cdot \sqrt{b} \neq \sqrt{ab}$ **where a and b are negative**

Rewrite the numbers in terms of i. When the radicands are positive, they may be multiplied.

Example

$\sqrt{-8} \cdot \sqrt{-2}$

$= \sqrt{4} \cdot \sqrt{2} \cdot \sqrt{-1} \cdot \sqrt{2} \cdot \sqrt{-1}$ Factor to separate the imaginary unit and the squares.

$= 2i\sqrt{2} \cdot i\sqrt{2}$

$= 2i^2 \cdot \sqrt{4}$ Multiply coefficients and radicands.

$= 2(-1) \cdot 2$ Replace i^2 by -1.

$= -4$

EXERCISES

In 1–6, write in simplest form in terms of i.

1. $\sqrt{-121}$ **3.** $\sqrt{-80}$ **5.** $\sqrt{-108}$

2. $\sqrt{-225}$ **4.** $\sqrt{-625}$ **6.** $\sqrt{-324}$

7. The sum of $\sqrt{-2}$ and $\sqrt{-18}$ is
(1) $6i$ **(2)** $2i\sqrt{5}$ **(3)** $5i\sqrt{2}$ **(4)** $4i\sqrt{2}$

8. The sum of $\sqrt{-27}$ and $\sqrt{-12}$ is
(1) $-5\sqrt{3}$ **(2)** $i\sqrt{39}$ **(3)** $5i\sqrt{3}$ **(4)** $3i\sqrt{5}$

9. The sum of $\sqrt{-8}$ and $2\sqrt{-50}$ is
(1) $12\sqrt{2}$ **(2)** $-12\sqrt{2}$ **(3)** $12i\sqrt{2}$ **(4)** $-12i\sqrt{2}$

10. The sum of $\sqrt{-18}$ and $\sqrt{-72}$ is
(1) $6i$ **(2)** $36i$ **(3)** $3\sqrt{10}$ **(4)** $9i\sqrt{2}$

11. When $\sqrt{-3}$ is subtracted from $\sqrt{-12}$, the difference is
(1) $i\sqrt{3}$ **(2)** $-i\sqrt{3}$ **(3)** $3i\sqrt{3}$ **(4)** $-3i\sqrt{3}$

In 12–21, combine as a monomial in terms of i.

12. $\sqrt{-25} + 2\sqrt{-36}$ **17.** $2\sqrt{-50} + \sqrt{-32}$

13. $\sqrt{-49} + 2\sqrt{-16}$ **18.** $\sqrt{-75} + 2\sqrt{-48}$

14. $\sqrt{-25} + 3\sqrt{-16}$ **19.** $3\sqrt{-63} + 4\sqrt{-28}$

15. $\sqrt{-64} + 2\sqrt{-16}$ **20.** $5\sqrt{-4} + \sqrt{-1} - 2\sqrt{-9}$

16. $\sqrt{-9} + 2\sqrt{-64}$ **21.** $3\sqrt{-8} - \sqrt{-2} + 5\sqrt{-72}$

22. Expressed in simplest form, $\frac{\sqrt{-36}}{-\sqrt{4}}$ is equivalent to
(1) $3i$ **(2)** $-3i$ **(3)** 3 **(4)** -3

23. The value of i^{16} is
(1) 1 **(2)** -1 **(3)** i **(4)** $-i$

24. The product $i^3 \cdot i^7$ is
(1) 1 **(2)** -1 **(3)** i **(4)** $-i$

25. The value of $i^8 - i^{20}$ is
(1) 0 **(2)** 1 **(3)** -1 **(4)** i

26. $i^3 + i(2 - i)$ is equivalent to
(1) $1 + i$ **(2)** $1 - i$ **(3)** $-1 + 3i$ **(4)** $1 + 3i$

In 27–34, express in simplest form.

27. i^{12} **29.** i^{39} **31.** $i^5 + i^{12}$ **33.** $i^{16} - i^{22}$

28. i^{10} **30.** i^{100} **32.** $2i^6 - 3i^2$ **34.** $-i^{50} + i^{51}$

35. The value of $\sqrt{-4} \cdot \sqrt{-25}$ is
(1) 10 **(2)** -10 **(3)** ± 10 **(4)** $10i$

36. The value of $\sqrt{-4} + \sqrt{-25}$ is
(1) $\sqrt{-29}$ **(2)** $29i$ **(3)** $-7i$ **(4)** $7i$

In 37–40, express in simplest form.

37. $\sqrt{-9} \cdot \sqrt{-16}$ **39.** $\sqrt{-48} \cdot \sqrt{-75}$

38. $\sqrt{-32} \cdot \sqrt{-50}$ **40.** $\sqrt{-72} \cdot \sqrt{-27}$

Standard form of a COMPLEX NUMBER is:
$a + bi$ **where** a **and** b **are real numbers**

The set of complex numbers consists of the set of real numbers and the set of imaginary numbers.

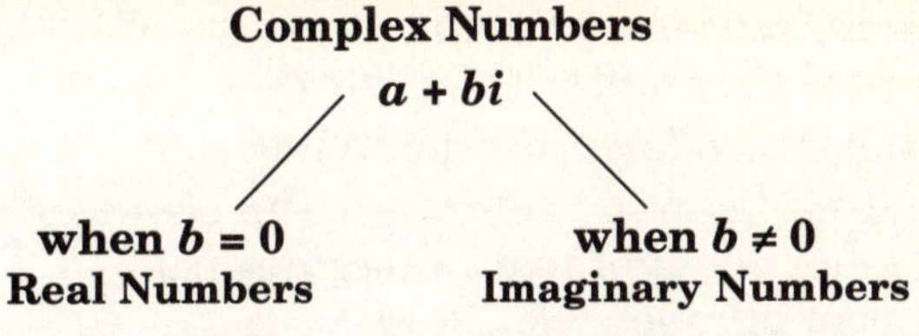

In the complex plane, the horizontal axis is the real axis and the vertical axis is the imaginary axis.

A complex number can be represented by a point or by a VECTOR (a directed length).

The absolute value of $a + bi$ **is** $\sqrt{a^2 + b^2}$. **Graphically, the absolute value of a complex number represents the distance of the point from the origin, or the length of the vector that represents the number.**

Calculating $|-3 + 2i|$, or the distance of P (shown on the graph) from the origin, or the length of the vector:

$$|-3 + 2i| = \sqrt{(-3)^2 + 2^2} = \sqrt{13}$$

Point P or vector OP, written $\overrightarrow{OP}$, represents the complex number $-3 + 2i$.

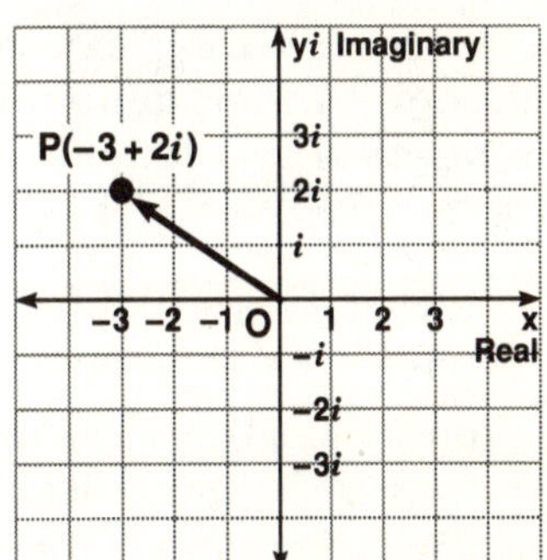

Two complex numbers that differ only by the sign of b **are called CONJUGATES.**	$a + bi$ **and** $a - bi$ **are conjugates**	The conjugate of $-3 + 2i$ is $-3 - 2i$
Two complex numbers are equal when their real parts are equal and their imaginary parts are equal.	$a + bi = c + di$ **if and only if** $a = c$ **and** $b = d$	If $3 + (x - 2)i = 3 + 7i$, $x - 2 = 7$, $x = 9$
To add two complex numbers, add their corresponding real and imaginary parts.	$(a + bi) + (c + di)$ $= (a + c) + (b + d)i$	$(3 + 2i) + (-4 + i)$ $= [3 + (-4)] + (2 + 1)i$ $= -1 + 3i$
To subtract a complex number, add its additive inverse. Note that the additive inverse of $a + bi$ is $-a - bi$, which is not the same as the conjugate $a - bi$.	$(a + bi) - (c + di)$ $= (a + bi) + (-c - di)$ $= (a - c) + (b - d)i$	$(3 + 2i) - (-4 + i)$ $= (3 + 2i) + (4 - i)$ $= (3 + 4) + (2 - 1)i$ $= 7 + i$

Graphic Addition

$(3 + 2i) + (-4 + i) = -1 + 3i$

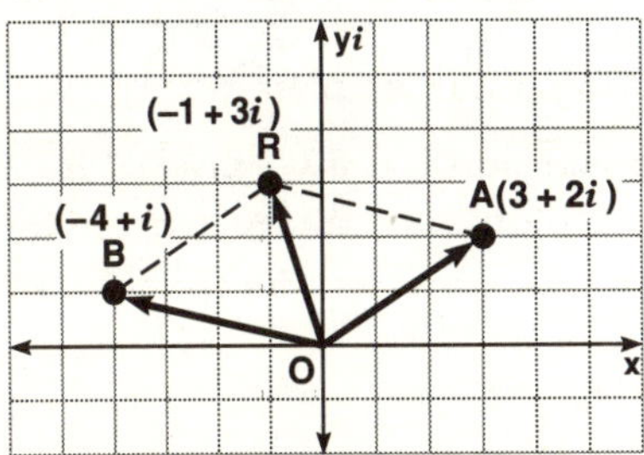

The sum of $\overrightarrow{OA}$ and $\overrightarrow{OB}$ is the resultant $\overrightarrow{OR}$, the diagonal in parallelogram $OARB$.

Graphic Subtraction

$(3 + 2i) - (-4 + i) = 7 + i$

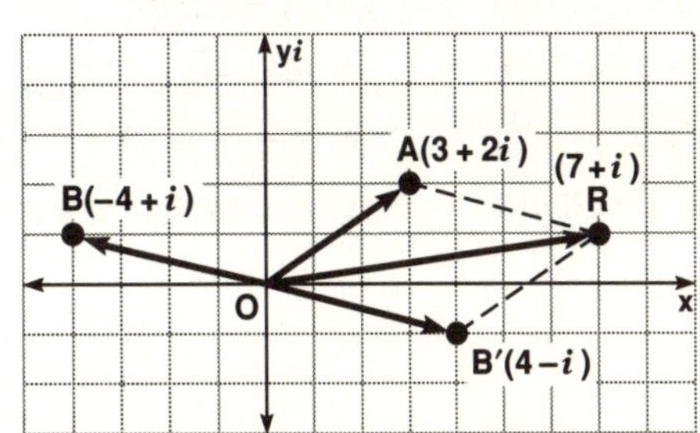

To subtract $\overrightarrow{OB}$, add the additive inverse $\overrightarrow{OB'}$.

To multiply two complex numbers, use binomial multiplication. Replace i^2 by –1.	$(5 + 4i) \cdot (-4 + 3i) = (5)(-4) + (-16i + 15i) + (4i)(3i)$ [inner product $-16i$, outer product $+15i$] $= -20 \quad -i \quad + 12i^2$ $= -20 \quad -i \quad + 12(-1)$ $= -32 - i$
The product of two conjugates is a real number.	$(a + bi) \cdot (a - bi) = a^2 + (abi - abi) - b^2i^2$ [inner product abi, outer product $-abi$] $= a^2 + \quad - b^2(-1)$ $= a^2 + b^2$
To divide two complex numbers, multiply numerator and denominator by the conjugate of the denominator. Express the result in *a* + *bi* form.	$\frac{3 + 2i}{1 - i} \cdot \frac{1 + i}{1 + i}$ $= \frac{3 + 5i + 2i^2}{1 - i^2} = \frac{1 + 5i}{2}$ or $\frac{1}{2} + \frac{5}{2}i$

EXERCISES

1. The conjugate of $-4 + i$ is
   (1) $4 - i$ (2) $-4 - i$ (3) $i - 4$ (4) $i + 4$

2. The additive inverse of $2 - 3i$ is
   (1) $-2 + 3i$ (2) $\frac{1}{2 - 3i}$ (3) $-2 - 3i$ (4) $2 + 3i$

3. What is the conjugate of $7 - i$?

4. What is the additive inverse of $-2 + 3i$?

5. Which set together with the operations of addition and multiplication does *not* form a field?
   (1) complex numbers (3) pure imaginaries
   (2) reals (4) rationals

6. In which quadrant does the graph of the complex number $-4 - 2i$ lie?

7. What is the distance of $P(-3 + i)$ from the origin?

8. Find the absolute value of $7 - 2i$.

9. Evaluate: $|-2 + i|$

10. If $7 + 2xi = y + 16i$, find the value of x.

11. Express the sum of $(3 + \sqrt{-16})$ and $(7 - \sqrt{-81})$ in the form $a + bi$.

12. Express the sum of $4 + \sqrt{-16}$ and $5 - \sqrt{-25}$ in $a + bi$ form.

13. If $(3 + 2i) + (2 + bi) = 5 - 4i$, the value of b is
    (1) –2 (2) 2 (3) –6 (4) 6

14. Solve for x: $(5 - 2i) - (x + 4i) = 7 - 6i$

15. In which quadrant does the graph of the sum of $(2 + 3i)$ and $(-1 - 6i)$ lie?

In 16–19, show the indicated sum or difference graphically.

16. $(4 + 2i) + (1 - 3i) = 5 - i$

17. $(-2 + i) + (-4 - 4i) = -6 - 3i$

18. $(1 - i) - (2 + i) = -1 - 2i$

19. $(-3 + 2i) - (-1 - 2i) = -2 + 4i$

In 20–23, find the indicated sum or difference graphically.

20. $(7 + i) + (2 - 2i)$

21. $(-3 - 2i) + (-1 + 4i)$

22. $(5 - 2i) - (3 - 2i)$

23. $(6 + 3i) - (6 - i)$

24. The product of $(2 - 2i)$ and $(2 + 2i)$ is
    (1) 0 (2) 8 (3) $4 - 4i$ (4) 4

25. Express the product of $4 - 3i$ and its conjugate in simplest terms.

26. The expression $(2 + i)^2$ is equivalent to
    (1) $3 + 4i$ (2) $5 + 4i$ (3) 3 (4) 5

27. The square of $(2 - 2i)$ is
    (1) 0 (2) $-8i$ (3) $4 - 4i$ (4) 4

In 28–35, express the product in $a + bi$ form.

28. $5i(3i - 2)$

29. $(3 - 2i)(1 + i)$

30. $(4 - 5i)(2 + i)$

31. $(1 + i)(1 - i)$

32. $(2 + i)(1 - i)$

33. $(2 + \sqrt{-9})(3 - \sqrt{-16})$

34. $(1 - \sqrt{-4})(1 + \sqrt{-4})$

35. $(3 - 2i)^2$

36. The expression $\frac{5}{4 - 3i}$ is equivalent to
    (1) $\frac{20 + 15i}{7}$ (2) $\frac{4 + 3i}{5}$ (3) $\frac{20 - 15i}{7}$ (4) $\frac{7i}{5}$

37. What is the multiplicative inverse of $2 + i$?
    (1) $2 - i$ (2) $-2 - i$ (3) $\frac{2 - i}{3}$ (4) $\frac{2 - i}{5}$

38. What is the multiplicative inverse of $2 - i$?
    (1) $2 - i$ (2) $2 + i$ (3) $\frac{2 + i}{3}$ (4) $\frac{2 + i}{5}$

39. What is the multiplicative inverse of $3 - i$?
    (1) $\frac{3 - i}{8}$ (2) $\frac{3 + i}{8}$ (3) $\frac{3 - i}{10}$ (4) $\frac{3 + i}{10}$

More About Quadratic Equations

Complex Roots

When the roots of a quadratic equation with real coefficients are imaginary, they occur as a conjugate pair.

Example

Solve the equation $x + \frac{3}{x} = 2$ and express its roots in $a + bi$ form.

Solution:

$$x + \frac{3}{x} = 2$$

$$x \cdot x + \frac{3}{x} \cdot x = 2 \cdot x$$ To clear of fractions, multiply each term by the L.C.D., x.

$$x^2 + 3 = 2x$$

$$x^2 - 2x + 3 = 0$$ Standard form.

$$x = \frac{-b \pm \sqrt{b^2 - 4ac}}{2a}$$ Quadratic formula. $a = 1, b = -2, c = 3$

$$x = \frac{-(-2) \pm \sqrt{(-2)^2 - 4(1)(3)}}{2(1)}$$

$$x = \frac{2 \pm \sqrt{-8}}{2}$$

$$x = \frac{2 \pm \sqrt{4} \cdot \sqrt{-1} \cdot \sqrt{2}}{2} = \frac{2 \pm 2i\sqrt{2}}{2} = 1 \pm i\sqrt{2}$$

EXERCISES

In 1–18, solve the equation and express its roots in $a + bi$ form.

1. $x^2 + 8x + 20 = 0$
2. $x^2 + 2x + 10 = 0$
3. $x^2 - 2x + 5 = 0$
4. $2x^2 - 6x + 5 = 0$
5. $x^2 - 4x = -13$
6. $x^2 - 6x = -25$
7. $x^2 - 4x = -10$
8. $x^2 = 4x - 20$
9. $x^2 = 4x - 5$
10. $3x^2 + 3 = 5x$
11. $2x^2 = -3(2x + 3)$
12. $\frac{x^2}{2} = x - 1$
13. $x + \frac{5}{x} = 3$
14. $2(x + 3) = -\frac{5}{x}$
15. $2x + \frac{4}{x} = 5$
16. $1 + \frac{2}{x^2} = \frac{4}{2x}$
17. $\frac{x+8}{5} + \frac{x+5}{x} = 1$
18. $\frac{3}{x-2} - \frac{1}{x-1} = -2$

The General Roots

The quadratic formula states that for the general equation $ax^2 + bx + c = 0$ where a, b, and c are real and $a \neq 0$, the roots are:

$$r_1 = \frac{-b + \sqrt{b^2 - 4ac}}{2a} \text{ and } r_2 = \frac{-b - \sqrt{b^2 - 4ac}}{2a}$$

The Discriminant and the Nature of the Roots

For information about the roots of a quadratic equation, examine the DISCRIMINANT $b^2 - 4ac$.

If the value of the discriminant, $b^2 - 4ac$, is:	*The roots of the quadratic equation are:*
positive and a perfect square	**real, rational, and unequal**
positive and not a perfect square	**real, irrational, and unequal**
0	**real, rational, and equal**
negative	**imaginary**

Examples

1. If the value of the discriminant is 37, the roots of the quadratic equation are

   (1) real, rational, and unequal
   (2) real, rational, and equal
   (3) real, irrational, and unequal
   (4) imaginary

   Solution: Since 37 is positive and not a perfect square, the roots of the equation are real, irrational, and unequal.

   Answer: (3)

2. Find the value of c for which the roots of the equation $x^2 + 8x + c = 0$ will be equal.

   Solution: For the roots to be equal, the discriminant must be 0.

$$b^2 - 4ac = 8^2 - 4(1)c = 0$$
$$64 - 4c = 0$$
$$-4c = -64$$
$$c = 16$$

EXERCISES

1. If a quadratic equation with real coefficients has a discriminant of -2, then its two roots must be

   (1) equal
   (2) imaginary
   (3) real and irrational
   (4) real and rational

2. If the discriminant of an equation is 10, then the roots are

   (1) real, rational, and unequal
   (2) real, irrational, and unequal
   (3) real, rational, and equal
   (4) imaginary

In 3–10, describe the nature of the roots as one of the following: **(1)** real, rational, and unequal **(2)** real, irrational, and unequal **(3)** real, rational, and equal **(4)** imaginary

3. $x^2 + x + 1 = 0$

4. $x^2 + 2x + 1 = 0$

5. $2x^2 + 3x + 2 = 0$

6. $x^2 - 2x - 2 = 0$

7. $-x^2 + x + 6 = 0$

8. $x^2 - 9 = 0$

9. $x^2 + 10 = 0$

10. $2x^2 = 5$

11. The roots of the equation $ax^2 + 4x + 2 = 0$ are real and equal when a is equal to
(1) 1 **(2)** 2 **(3)** 3 **(4)** 4

12. The roots of $x^2 + bx + 3 = 0$ are real when b is equal to
(1) 0 **(2)** 2 **(3)** 3 **(4)** 4

13. The roots of $x^2 + bx + 2 = 0$ will be imaginary when b equals: **(1)** 1 **(2)** 7 **(3)** 3 **(4)** 9

14. What is the positive value of m in the equation $4x^2 + mx + 9 = 0$ that makes the roots equal?
(1) 12 **(2)** 9 **(3)** 3 **(4)** 4

15. If the equation $9x^2 - 12x + k = 0$ has equal roots, find the value of k.

16. For what value of k are the roots of $2x^2 - 8x + k = 0$ equal?

17. Find the largest integral value of k in the equation $kx^2 - 5x + 3 = 0$ that will make its roots real.

18. Find the largest integral value of c for which the roots of $2x^2 - 8x + c = 0$ are real.

19. Find the smallest integral value of c for which the roots of $x^2 - 6x + c = 0$ are imaginary.

Relationships Between Roots and Coefficients

Operating with the general roots leads to the following relationships between those roots r_1, r_2 and the coefficients a, b, c.

Sum of the Roots $\quad$ ***Product of the Roots***

$$r_1 + r_2 = \frac{-b}{a} \qquad r_1 \cdot r_2 = \frac{c}{a}$$

Examples

1. What is the value of the sum of the roots of the equation $x^2 - 2x + 10 = 0$?

Solution: sum of the roots $= \frac{-b}{a} = \frac{-(-2)}{1} = 2$

2. If $2 + i$ and $2 - i$ are the roots of $x^2 + bx + c = 0$, what is the value of c?

Solution: The coefficient c is related to the product of the roots. Since the roots are known, find the actual product and then use the product-coefficient relation.

$$r_1 \cdot r_2 = (2 + i)(2 - i) = 4 + 2i - 2i - i^2 = 5$$

$$r_1 \cdot r_2 = \frac{c}{a} = 5$$

$$\frac{c}{1} = 5$$

$$c = 5$$

The relationships between roots and coefficients can be used to check solutions. Both conditions, sum and product, must be satisfied.

Example

Verify that $1 \pm 2i$ are the roots of the equation $x^2 - 2x + 5 = 0$.

Solution: Match the results obtained from the actual values, $r_1 = 1 + 2i$ and $r_2 = 1 - 2i$, against the results of the coefficient formulas.

$$r_1 + r_2 = (1 + 2i) + (1 - 2i) = 2$$

$$r_1 + r_2 = \frac{-b}{a} = \frac{-(-2)}{1} = 2 \quad ✓$$

$$r_1 \cdot r_2 = (1 + 2i)(1 - 2i) = 1 + 2i - 2i - 4i^2 = 5$$

$$r_1 \cdot r_2 = \frac{c}{a} = \frac{5}{1} = 5 \quad ✓$$

The sum and product relationships can be used to write a quadratic equation whose roots are known.

Example

Write a quadratic equation with roots $2 \pm 3i$.

Solution: Use the sum and product of the roots to determine values for a, b, c.

$$r_1 + r_2 = (2 + 3i) + (2 - 3i) = 4 = \frac{-b}{a}$$

$$r_1 \cdot r_2 = (2 + 3i)(2 - 3i) = 4 + 6i - 6i - 9i^2 = 13 = \frac{c}{a}$$

What has been determined so far is the value of two ratios for which there are infinitely many possible values of a, b, and c.

$$\frac{-b}{a} = 4 \text{ and } \frac{c}{a} = 13$$

One possible solution is to let $a = 1$. Then $b = -4$ and $c = 13$.

Answer: $x^2 - 4x + 13 = 0$ has the roots $2 \pm 3i$.

A combination of discriminant and coefficient relationships can be used to select the correct set of roots for a given quadratic equation. (An alternate method is to use the quadratic formula to solve.)

Example

The roots of $2x^2 + 5x - 1 = 0$ are

(1) $\frac{5 \pm \sqrt{17}}{4}$ (2) $\frac{-5 \pm \sqrt{17}}{4}$ (3) $\frac{5 \pm \sqrt{33}}{4}$ (4) $\frac{-5 \pm \sqrt{33}}{4}$

Solution: Begin by evaluating the discriminant.

$b^2 - 4ac = 5^2 - 4(2)(-1) = 33$

Thus, eliminate choices (1) and (2).

Note from the equation that the sum of the roots is negative. Thus, eliminate choice (3).

Answer: **(4)**

EXERCISES

1. What is the product of the roots of the equation $-2x^2 + 3x + 8 = 0$?

(1) $\frac{3}{2}$ (2) -4 (3) $\frac{3}{4}$ (4) 4

2. What is the sum of the roots of the equation $-x^2 = 3x + 4$?

(1) -3 (2) 3 (3) 4 (4) -4

3. Given the equation $x^2 + 3x - 9 = 0$. What is the product of the roots?

(1) 9 (2) -9 (3) 3 (4) -3

4. For which equation does the sum of the roots equal the product of the roots?

(1) $x^2 - 2x + 3 = 0$ (3) $4x^2 - 4x + 1 = 0$
(2) $x^2 - 13x + 13 = 0$ (4) $5x^2 - 5x = 0$

5. If the sum of the roots of $x^2 + kx - 3 = 0$ is equal to the product of the roots, the value of k is

(1) -6 (2) -3 (3) 3 (4) 6

6. What is the value of c if $x^2 - 4x + c = 0$ and the roots of the equation are $(2 + i)$ and $(2 - i)$?

7. If $1 + i$ and $1 - i$ are the roots of the quadratic equation $x^2 + bx + c = 0$, what is the value of c?

8. If the solution set of $x^2 + px + q = 0$ is $\{1 + i, 1 - i\}$, find the value of p.

9. A quadratic equation having the roots $(2 - 3i)$ and $(2 + 3i)$ is

(1) $x^2 + 4x + 13 = 0$ (3) $x^2 + 4x - 9 = 0$
(2) $x^2 - 4x + 13 = 0$ (4) $x^2 - 4x + 9 = 0$

10. Which quadratic equation has roots of $(1 + 3i)$ and $(1 - 3i)$?

(1) $x^2 + 2x - 10 = 0$ (3) $x^2 + 2x - 8 = 0$
(2) $x^2 - 2x + 10 = 0$ (4) $x^2 - 2x - 8 = 0$

In 11–16, write a quadratic equation with the given roots.

11. $\pm i$ **13.** $\pm 2i$ **15.** $2 \pm 5i$
12. $\pm\sqrt{3}$ **14.** $3 \pm i$ **16.** $\frac{1}{2} \pm \frac{3}{2}i$

17. The roots of the equation $x^2 - 4x + 9 = 0$ are

(1) $2 \pm i\sqrt{5}$ (3) $2 \pm i\sqrt{13}$
(2) $2 \pm \sqrt{5}$ (4) $2 \pm \sqrt{13}$

18. What are the roots of the equation $x^2 - x + 1 = 0$?

(1) $\frac{1 \pm \sqrt{3}}{2}$ (3) $\frac{1 \pm i\sqrt{3}}{2}$
(2) $\frac{1 \pm \sqrt{5}}{2}$ (4) $\frac{1 \pm i\sqrt{5}}{2}$

19. The roots of the equation $x^2 - 3x + 7 = 0$ are

(1) $\frac{3 \pm \sqrt{19}}{2}$ (3) $3 \pm \frac{\sqrt{19}}{2}$
(2) $\frac{3 \pm i\sqrt{19}}{2}$ (4) $3 \pm \frac{i\sqrt{19}}{2}$

20. The roots of $3x^2 - 4x + 2 = 0$ are

(1) $\frac{1 \pm \sqrt{2}}{3}$ (3) $\frac{2 \pm \sqrt{10}}{3}$
(2) $\frac{2 \pm i\sqrt{2}}{3}$ (4) $4 \pm \frac{i\sqrt{2}}{3}$

Using a Parabola to Solve $ax^2 + bx + c = 0$

The x-intercepts of the parabola $y = ax^2 + bx + c$ are the roots of the equation $ax^2 + bx + c = 0$.

If the parabola:	*Possible Graph*	*Then the roots of $ax^2 + bx + c = 0$ are:*
intersects the x-axis in two distinct points		**real and unequal** ($b^2 - 4ac > 0$)
touches the x-axis in exactly one point (is tangent to the x-axis)		**real and equal** ($b^2 - 4ac = 0$)
does not intersect the x-axis		**imaginary** ($b^2 - 4ac < 0$)

Example

The graph of $y = x^2 - 9x + 18$

(1) is tangent to the x-axis
(2) intersects the x-axis in two points
(3) does not intersect the x-axis
(4) lies entirely above the x-axis

Solution: Evaluate the discriminant to determine the nature of the roots of $x^2 - 9x + 18 = 0$.

$$b^2 - 4ac = (-9)^2 - 4(1)(18) = 9$$

Since the roots are real and unequal, the parabola $y = x^2 - 9x + 18$ intersects the x-axis in two points.

Answer: **(2)**

EXERCISES

1. If the roots of the equation $ax^2 + bx + c = 0$ are imaginary, the graph of $y = ax^2 + bx + c$ will
   (1) intersect the x-axis at two points
   (2) not intersect the y-axis
   (3) not intersect the x-axis
   (4) be tangent to the x-axis

2. The graph of $y = ax^2 + bx + c$ is tangent to the x-axis. The roots of the equation $ax^2 + bx + c = 0$ are
   (1) real, rational, and unequal
   (2) real, rational, and equal
   (3) imaginary
   (4) real, irrational, and unequal

3. The graph of the equation $y = x^2 + 2x - 8$ intersects the x-axis at
   (1) 2 and −4 (3) −2 and −4
   (2) −2 and 4 (4) 2 and 4

4. Which is true of the graph of $y = x^2 + 4x + 6$?
   (1) It intersects the x-axis in two real points.
   (2) It is tangent to the x-axis.
   (3) It lies entirely below the x-axis.
   (4) It lies entirely above the x-axis.

5. Which parabola touches the x-axis at one point?
   (1) $y = x^2 + 8x + 16$ (3) $y = x^2 - 5x + 6$
   (2) $y = x^2 - 16$ (4) $y = x^2 + 4$

6. Which parabola does not have an x-intercept?
   (1) $y = x^2 + 3x + 1$ (3) $y = x^2 + x + 3$
   (2) $y = x^2 + 3x - 1$ (4) $y = x^2 + x - 3$

7. Which parabola intersects the x-axis in two distinct points?
   (1) $y = (x + 5)^2$ (3) $y = x^2 - 25$
   (2) $y = (x - 5)^2$ (4) $y = x^2 + 25$

8. If the graph of $y = 2x^2 + 4x + c$ does not intersect the x-axis, then c may be equal to
   (1) 1 (2) 2 (3) −2 (4) 5

9. If the graph of $y = 4x^2 + bx + 1$ intersects the x-axis in two distinct points, then b may be equal to
   (1) 3 (2) 4 (3) −4 (4) 5

10. If the graph of $y = x^2 - 6x + c$ is tangent to the x-axis, then c equals
    (1) 3 (2) −3 (3) 9 (4) −9

2.9 SUMMARY EXERCISES

1. Solve for y in terms of a, b, and c:
   $ay - 2c = b$

2. What is the solution set of the equation $|2x - 1| = 9$?
   (1) { } (2) {5, −4} (3) {−5, 4} (4) {5}

3. What is the solution set for the equation $2x - |x + 3| = 9$?
   (1) {12} (2) {2} (3) {2, 12} (4) { }

4. Solve for all the values of x: $|6 - x| = 4$

5. What is the negative root of the equation $|2x + 3| = 11$?

6. Three consecutive integers that satisfy the condition that the square of the second exceeds the product of the first and third by 1 are
   (1) −3, −2, −1 only
   (2) 1, 2, 3 only
   (3) any three consecutive integers
   (4) never possible

7. Solve: $6x^2 - x = 2$

8. Express in simplest radical form the roots of the equation $x^2 - 4x + 1 = 0$.

9. Solve for the positive value of x: $\frac{2x}{3\sqrt{2}} = \frac{3\sqrt{2}}{x}$

10. Solve the set of equations:
    $2x + y = 8$
    $3x + 2y = 9$

11. Solve the system of equations:
    $y = x^2 - 2x + 1$
    $2x - y = 3$

12. When the graphs of $y = x^2$ and $y = 3$ are sketched on the same set of axes, how many points of intersection are there?

13. Solve for x: $\frac{3}{2x - 1} = \frac{1}{3x - 5}$

14. Solve for y: $\frac{5}{3y} - \frac{6}{4y} = \frac{1}{6}$

15. Solve for x: $\frac{x}{x - 2} - \frac{8}{x + 3} = \frac{10}{x^2 + x - 6}$

16. If $4\sqrt{5} = \sqrt{n}$, the value of n is
    (1) 10 (2) 20 (3) 80 (4) 100

17. What is the solution set for $\sqrt{3x + 1} + 1 = x$?
    (1) {0, 5} (2) {0} (3) {5} (4) { }

18. Solve for x: $3\sqrt{2x + 5} - 15 = 0$

19. If a and b are real numbers and $ab > 0$, which is never true?
    (1) $a > b$ (3) $a > 0$ and $b > 0$
    (2) $a > 0$ and $b < 0$ (4) $a < 0$ and $b < 0$

20. Solve for x: $5 < 2 - 3x < 14$

21. Which is the solution set for $|x - 1| < 5$?
    (1) $\{x|\ -6 < x < 4\}$ (3) $\{x|\ x < -4 \text{ or } x > 6\}$
    (2) $\{x|\ -4 < x < 6\}$ (4) $\{x|\ x < -6 \text{ or } x > 4\}$

22. Which graph represents the solution set of $|5x - 15| < 10$?

(1) 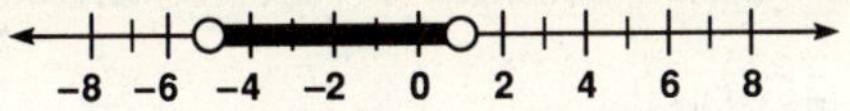 −8 −6 −4 −2 0 2 4 6 8

(2) 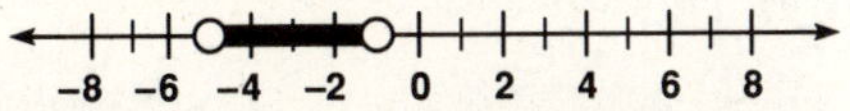 −8 −6 −4 −2 0 2 4 6 8

(3) 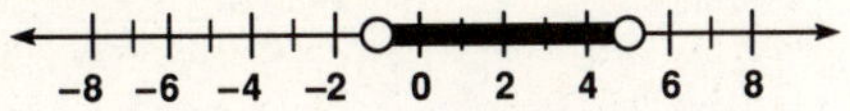 −8 −6 −4 −2 0 2 4 6 8

(4) −8 −6 −4 −2 0 2 4 6 8

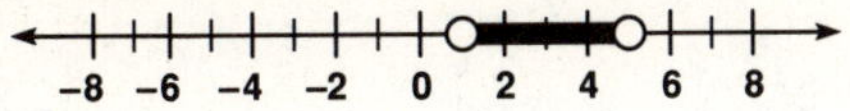

23. What is the solution set for $x^2 - 4x - 5 < 0$?

(1) $\{x \mid -1 < x < 5\}$
(2) $\{x \mid -5 < x < 1\}$
(3) $\{x \mid x > 5 \text{ or } x < -1\}$
(4) $\{x \mid x < -1\}$

24. Which is the solution set of the inequality $x^2 - x - 6 > 0$?

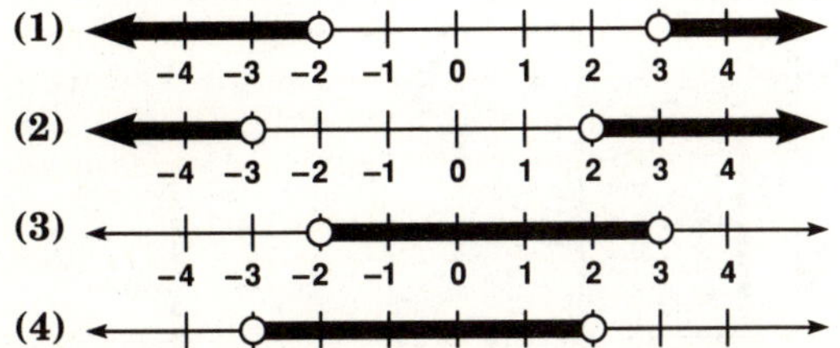

25. A number whose square is less than zero is called

(1) a whole number
(2) an imaginary number
(3) a negative real number
(4) a negative rational number

26. Which set does not form a field with the operations of addition and multiplication?

(1) complex numbers (3) integers
(2) rational numbers (4) real numbers

27. The quotient $\frac{i^6}{i^3}$ is equivalent to

(1) 1 (2) −1 (3) i (4) $-i$

28. The value of $2i^8$ is equivalent to

(1) $2i$ (2) 2 (3) −2 (4) $-2i$

29. If $x^2 + y^2 = 9$ and $x = 5$, then a value of y is

(1) i (2) 2 (3) $4i$ (4) 4

30. Consider:

$$\sqrt[3]{x^2} = (\sqrt[3]{x})^2$$

Tell whether the statement is true for

(1) all real values of x
(2) some, but not all, real values of x
(3) no real values of x

31. Express as a monomial in terms of i:

$$3\sqrt{-32} - \sqrt{-8}$$

32. Simplify and express in terms of i:

$$3\sqrt{-49} - 2\sqrt{-25} - \sqrt{-9}$$

33. Expressed in simplest form, $2\sqrt{-50} - 3\sqrt{-8}$ is equivalent to

(1) $16i\sqrt{2}$ (2) $3i\sqrt{2}$ (3) $4i\sqrt{2}$ (4) $-\sqrt{-42}$

34. Expressed in simplest form, $\frac{\sqrt{-36}}{-\sqrt{4}}$ is equivalent to

(1) $3i$ (2) $-3i$ (3) 3 (4) −3

35. What is the additive inverse of $3 + 2i$?

(1) $3 - 2i$ (2) $-3 - 2i$ (3) $-3 + 2i$ (4) 0

36. Express the sum of $(2 - \sqrt{-4})$ and $(-3 + \sqrt{-16})$ in $a + bi$ form.

37. Show graphically that $(2 + 3i) + (4 - 5i) = 6 - 2i$.

38. Show graphically that $(1 - i) - (2 - 3i) = -1 + 2i$.

39. Express the product $(3 - i)(4 + i)$ in the form $a + bi$.

40. The expression $(2 + 3i)^2$ is equal to

(1) −5 (2) 13 (3) $-5 + 12i$ (4) $13 + 12i$

41. The multiplicative inverse of $4 + i$ is

(1) $\frac{4-i}{17}$ (2) $\frac{4+i}{17}$ (3) $\frac{4-i}{15}$ (4) $\frac{4+i}{14}$

42. If one root of the equation $x^2 - 10x + 26 = 0$ is $5 + i$, what is the other root?

43. Express the roots of the equation $3x^2 = -2(2x + 3)$ in $a + bi$ form.

44. Solve the equation $2x + \frac{3}{x} = -2$ and express the roots in $a + bi$ form.

45. The roots of the equation $3n^2 + 2n - 3 = 0$ are best described as

(1) real, rational, and unequal
(2) real, irrational, and unequal
(3) real, rational, and equal
(4) imaginary

46. Which equation has imaginary roots?

(1) $x^2 - 2x + 1 = 0$ (3) $x^2 - 2x + 5 = 0$
(2) $x^2 - 2x - 1 = 0$ (4) $x^2 - 2x - 5 = 0$

47. For which value of k will the roots of $2x^2 + kx + 1 = 0$ be real?

(1) 1 (2) 2 (3) 3 (4) 0

48. For which value of k will the roots of the equation $2x^2 - 4x + k = 0$ be real and equal?

(1) 1 (2) 2 (3) −1 (4) 0

49. What are the sum (s) and the product (p) of the roots of the equation $x^2 + 2x - 35 = 0$?

(1) $s = 2, p = -35$ (3) $s = -2, p = -35$
(2) $s = -35, p = 2$ (4) $s = 35, p = -2$

50. In the equation $ax^2 + bx + c = 0$, a, b, and c are real numbers. If $\frac{1}{3} - \frac{2}{3}i$ is a root of this equation, the sum of the roots is

(1) 1 (2) $-\frac{2}{3}$ (3) $\frac{2}{3}$ (4) 0

51. Which parabola intersects the x-axis in two points?

(1) $y = x^2 - 25$ (3) $y = x^2 + x + 1$
(2) $y = x^2 + 4$ (4) $y = x^2 + x + 6$

CHAPTER 3

Transformations

3.1 TYPES OF TRANSFORMATIONS

Descriptions

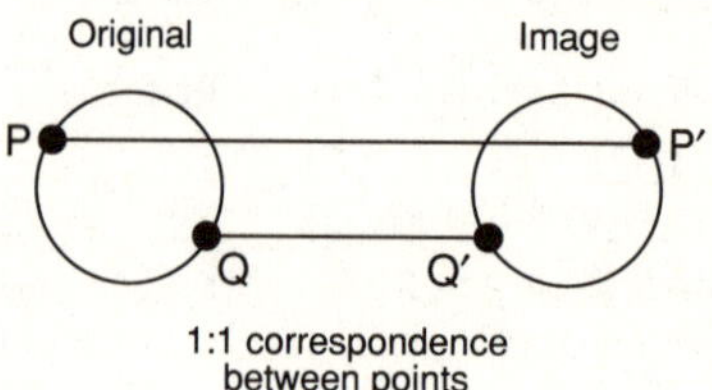

A TRANSFORMATION moves each point of a plane figure according to some rule, mapping the original figure onto an *image* in a 1:1 correspondence of points.

Reflection	*Rotation*	*Translation*	*Dilation*
a mirror image	a turning	a slide	an enlargement or reduction
The letter **F** is reflected in line ℓ.	The letter **F** is rotated 90° clockwise about point *O*.	The letter **F** is translated 3 units right and 1 unit up.	The letter **F** is dilated from center *O*.

Reflection in a Line

By Definition	Illustration
If P' is the image of P under a REFLECTION IN A LINE ℓ, then ℓ is the perpendicular bisector of $\overline{PP'}$. Notation: r_ℓ	

Special Line Reflection	Example	Special Line Reflection	Example
Under a reflection in the *y*-axis: $P(x,y) \to P'(-x,y)$	P′ (−2, 3); P (2, 3)	Under a reflection in the line $y = x$: $P(x,y) \to P'(y,x)$	(1, 2) P′; P(2, 1); y = x
Under a reflection in the *x*-axis: $P(x,y) \to P'(x,-y)$	P(2, 3); (2, −3) P′	Under a reflection in the line $y = -x$: $P(x,y) \to P'(-y,-x)$	P(−1, 3); P′ (−3, 1); y = −x

Example

$\triangle ABC$ has vertices $A(0, 1)$, $B(2, 6)$, and $C(2, 4)$. Graph the image under a reflection in the :

a. x-axis **c.** line $y = x$ **e.** line $y = 2$
b. y-axis **d.** line $y = -x$ **f.** line $x = 2$

Solution: On a graph, use a ruler as a guide to ensure that the line of reflection is the perpendicular bisector of the distance between a vertex of the original triangle and its image.

a.

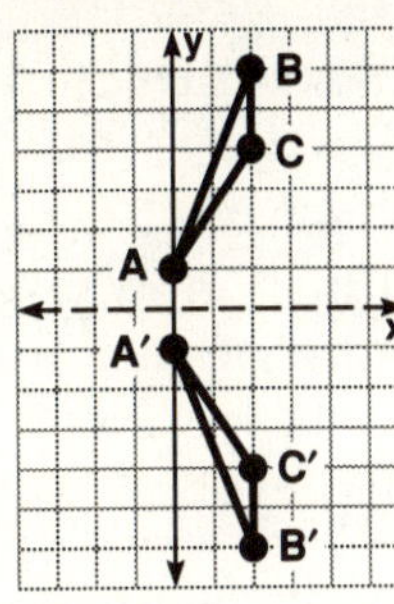

b.

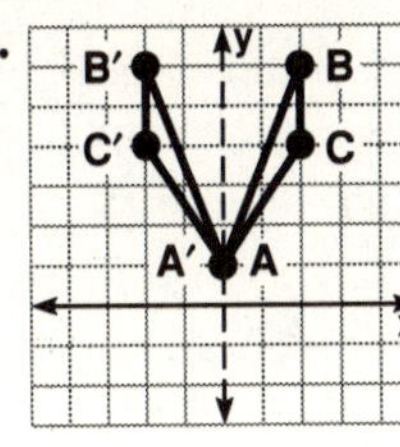

c.

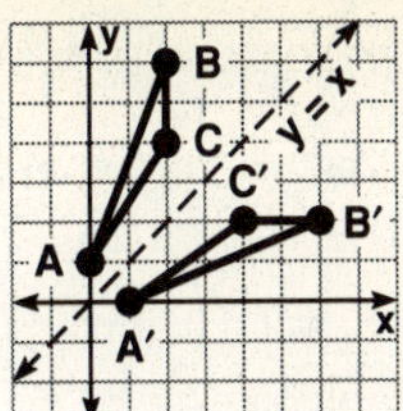

e.

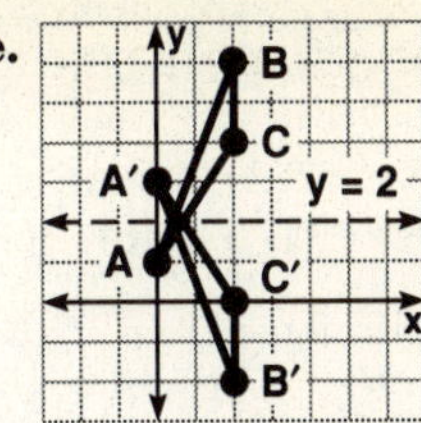

d.

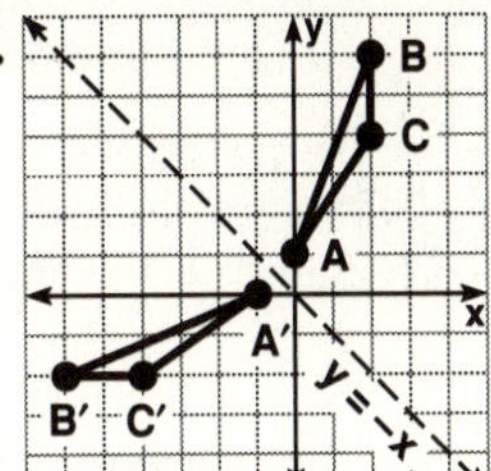

f.

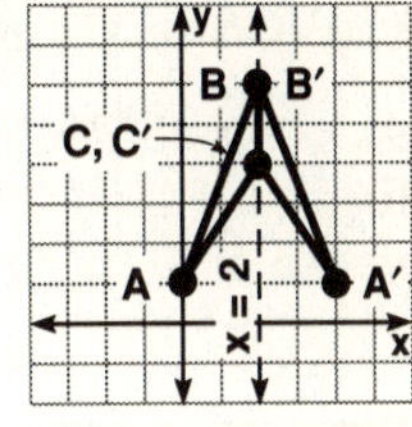

Reflection in a Point

By Definition	Illustration
If A' is the image of A under a REFLECTION IN A POINT P, then P is the midpoint of $\overline{AA'}$.	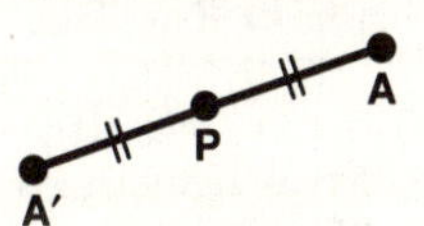
Special Point Reflection	**Example**
Under a reflection in the origin: **$P(x, y) \rightarrow P'(-x, -y)$**	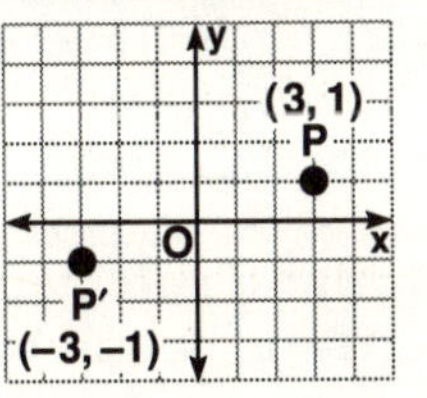

Example

The image of $A(1, 1)$ under a reflection in a point P is $A'(-5, 3)$.

Find B', the image of $B(3, 2)$ under a reflection in P.

Solution: To locate P, find the midpoint of $\overline{AA'}$.

$$P\left(\frac{1 + (-5)}{2}, \frac{1 + 3}{2}\right)$$

$P(-2, 2)$ is now to be the midpoint of $\overline{BB'}$.

$B(3, 2)$, $P(-2, 2)$, $B'(x, y)$

$$\frac{3 + x}{2} = -2 \qquad \frac{2 + y}{2} = 2$$

$$3 + x = -4 \qquad 2 + y = 4$$

$$x = -7 \qquad y = 2$$

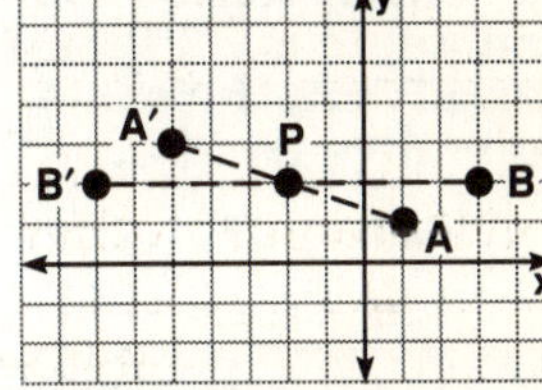

Answer:
$B'(-7, 2)$

EXERCISES

In 1–14, find the image of the point under the given reflection.

1. (3, 4) in the y-axis
2. (–2, –1) in the x-axis
3. (1, 5) in the line $y = x$
4. (–1, 2) in the line $y = -x$
5. (3, –2) in the origin
6. (0, –1) in the line $y = 1$
7. (–1, 0) in the line $x = -1$
8. (1, –1) under $r_{x\text{-axis}}$
9. (3, –2) under $r_{y\text{-axis}}$
10. (–5, –1) under $r_{y = -x}$
11. (–2, 4) under $r_{y = x}$
12. (–2, –1) under $r_{(0, 0)}$
13. (3, –4) under $r_{(3, 0)}$
14. (2, –3) under $r_{(-1, 0)}$
15. Reflecting (5, 1) in the y-axis yields an image of
 (1) (5, –1) **(2)** (–5, –1) **(3)** (5, 1) **(4)** (–5, 1)
16. What is the image of (–3, 6) when reflected in the x-axis?
 (1) (–3, 6) **(2)** (3, –6) **(3)** (3, 6) **(4)** (–3, –6)
17. The point (–3, –2) is reflected in the origin. The coordinates of its image are
 (1) (–2, –3) **(2)** (3, 2) **(3)** (2, 3) **(4)** (–3, 2)
18. If $P(3, -4)$ is reflected in the point (3, 0), what are the coordinates of P', the image of P?
 (1) (3, 4) **(2)** (–3, 4) **(3)** (–4, 3) **(4)** (4, –3)
19. The coordinates of any point (x, y) after a reflection in the x-axis can always be represented by
 (1) (x, y) **(2)** $(-x, y)$ **(3)** $(x, -y)$ **(4)** $(-x, -y)$

20. When point $A(-2, 5)$ is reflected in the line $x = 1$, the image is

(1) (5, 2) **(2)** (−2, −3) **(3)** (4, 5) **(4)** (0, 5)

21. Write an equation of the line of reflection that maps $A(1, 5)$ onto $A'(5, 1)$.

22. The image of $L(2, 0)$ under a reflection in a point P is $L'(0, -4)$. Find K', the image of $K(4, -5)$ under a reflection in P.

23. The image of $Q(-3, -2)$ under a reflection in a point P is $Q'(1, -4)$. R', the image of $R(4, 0)$ under a reflection in P, is

(1) (−4, −4) **(3)** (−6, −6)
(2) (−5, −5) **(4)** (−7, −7)

24. $\overline{OP}$ forms an angle of 15° with the x-axis. The reflection of $\overline{OP}$ in the y-axis is $\overline{OP'}$. What is the measure of $\angle POP'$?

(1) 30° **(2)** 75° **(3)** 135° **(4)** 150°

25. Given a parabola whose axis of symmetry is the y-axis. The point (1, 5) lies on the parabola. Which point also lies on the parabola?

(1) (1, −5) **(2)** (−1, 5) **(3)** (−1, −5) **(4)** (0, 5)

26. In the diagram of circle O, diameter $\overline{AB}$ is perpendicular to chord $\overline{CD}$ at point E. What is the image of $\overline{AC}$ in $\overline{AB}$?

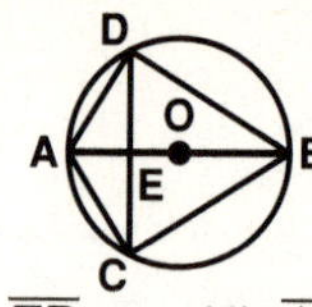

(1) $\overline{AD}$ **(2)** $\overline{BD}$ **(3)** $\overline{ED}$ **(4)** $\overline{AE}$

27. If the graph of the equation $y = 2x$ is reflected in the line $y = x$, the equation of the image is

(1) $y = 2x$ **(2)** $y = \frac{x}{2}$ **(3)** $y = 2$ **(4)** $y = -\frac{x}{2}$

28. Given $\triangle ABC$ with $A(0, 4)$, $B(-3, 6)$, $C(-3, 8)$. Write the coordinates and graph its image when it is reflected in the:

a. x-axis **e.** origin
b. y-axis **f.** line $y = 4$
c. line $y = x$ **g.** line $x = 2$
d. line $y = -x$ **h.** point (0, 4)

Rotation

By Definition	Illustration	Special Rotation	Example
If P' is the image of P under a ROTATION about a center point C through an angle of $\theta°$, then P and P' are the same distance from C. **Notation: $R_{C,\theta°}$ or $\text{Rot}_{C,\theta°}$**	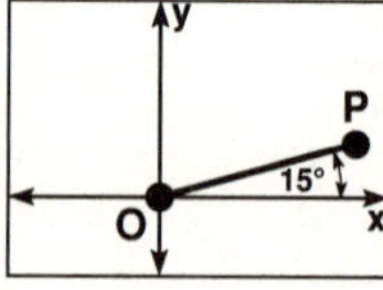	**Under a rotation about the origin of 180°, $R_{O,180°}$: $P(x,y) \rightarrow P'(-x,-y)$** **This rotation, also called a *half turn*, is equivalent to a reflection in the origin.**	(−3, 1) P′; O; P (3, −1)
Special Rotation	**Example**	**Under a rotation about the origin of 270° in a counterclockwise direction, $R_{O,270°}$: $P(x,y) \rightarrow P'(y,-x)$** **This rotation is the same as a clockwise rotation of −90°, written: $R_{O,-90°}$**	O; P (3, −1); P′ (−1, −3)
Under a rotation about the origin of 90° in a counterclockwise direction, $R_{O,90°}$ or $R_{90°}$: $P(x,y) \rightarrow P'(-y,x)$	P′(1, 3); O; P(3, −1)		

Example

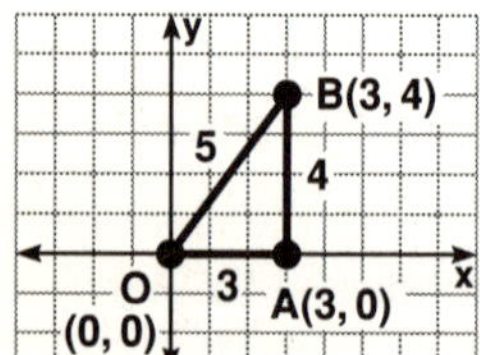

Rotate $\triangle OAB$:

a. $R_{O,90°}$ **d.** $R_{A,90°}$
b. $R_{O,180°}$ **e.** $R_{A,-90°}$
c. $R_{O,270°}$ **f.** $R_{A,180°}$

Solution: The center of the rotation remains fixed.

a.

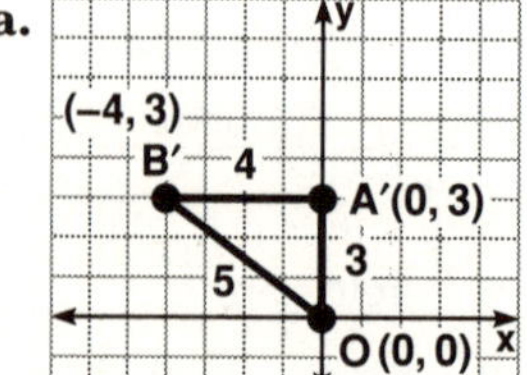

b.

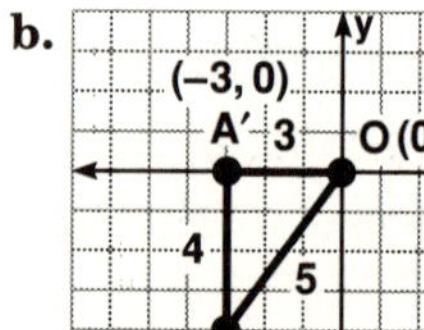

c.

O (0, 0)
3
5
A′
4
B′
(0, –3)
(4, –3)

d. 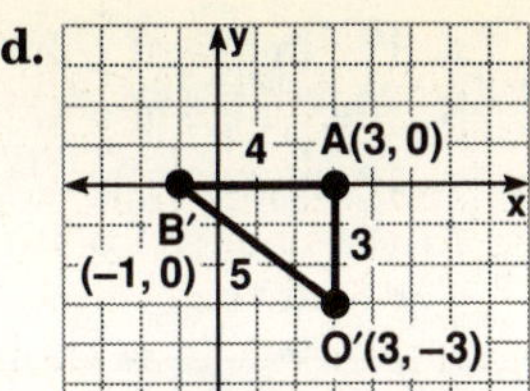

e. 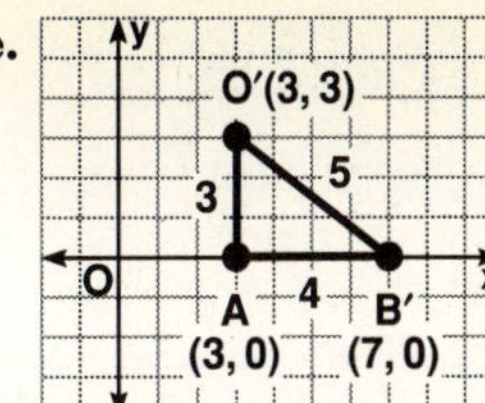

f. 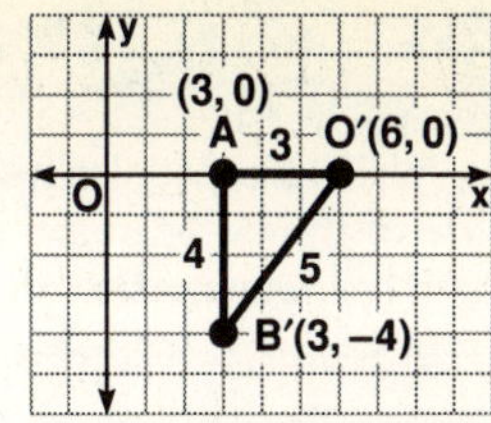

EXERCISES

1. What are the coordinates of M', the image of $M(2, 4)$ after a counterclockwise rotation of 90° about the origin?
   (1) (–2, 4) **(2)** (–2, –4) **(3)** (–4, 2) **(4)** (–4, –2)

2. What are the coordinates of B', the image of $B(-2, 3)$ after a clockwise rotation of 90° about the origin?
   (1) (–3, 2) **(2)** (3, 2) **(3)** (2, –3) **(4)** (2, 3)

In 3–6, write the coordinates of the image of the point under a rotation about the origin of:

a. 90° clockwise, or $R_{O,-90°}$
b. 90° counterclockwise, or $R_{O,90°}$

3. (1, 5) **4.** (3, –1) **5.** (–1, –3) **6.** (–6, –1)

7. What are the coordinates of P', the image of $P(-2, 4)$ after a rotation of 180° about the origin?
   (1) (–2, –4) **(2)** (2, –4) **(3)** (2, 4) **(4)** (–2, 4)

8. If the letter **P** is rotated 180°, which is the resulting figure?
   (1) **d** **(2)** **ɑ** **(3)** **ᑫ** **(4)** **b**

9. If the point (3, 0) is rotated 270° counterclockwise about the origin ($R_{270°}$), its image is on the line
   (1) $x = 0$ **(2)** $y = 0$ **(3)** $y = x$ **(4)** $y = -x$

10. Which of the following rotations about the origin is not equivalent to the other three?
    (1) 90° counterclockwise **(3)** –270°
    (2) 270° clockwise **(4)** –90°

11. If △OAB with vertices $O(0, 0)$, $A(-3, 0)$, and $B(-3, 4)$ is rotated 180° about point A, which of the following is the image?

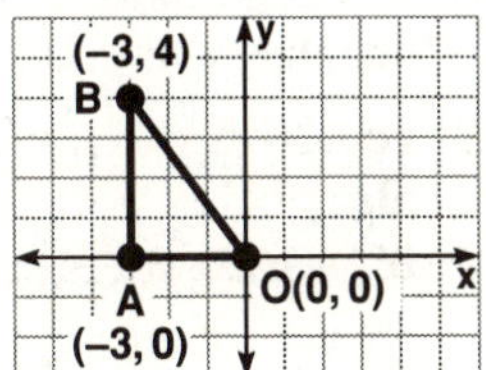

(1) 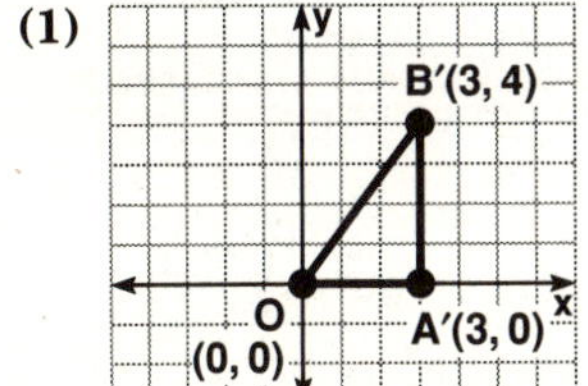

(2) 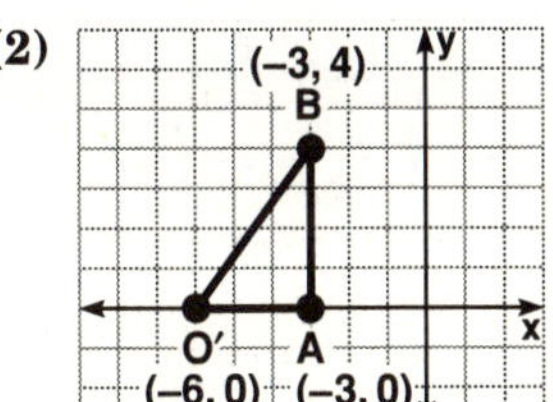

(3) 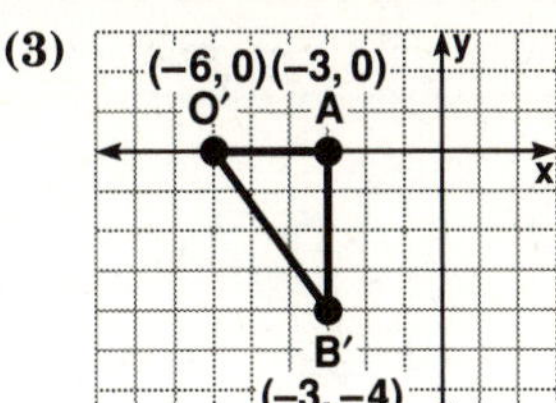

(4) 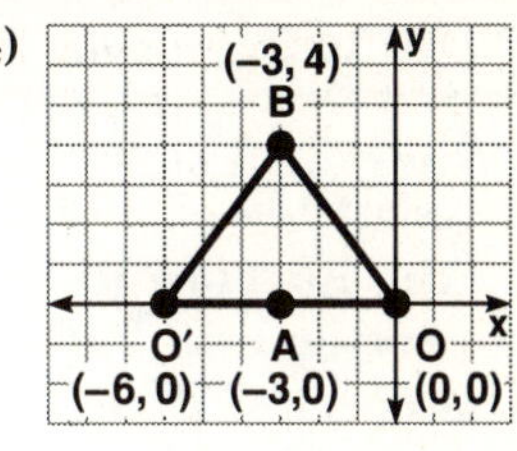

12. Graph △OAB with vertices $O(0, 0)$, $A(-3, 0)$, and $B(-3, -4)$. Graph the rotation of △OAB about point A as indicated:
    a. 180° clockwise **c.** 270° counterclockwise
    b. 90° clockwise **d.** 360° counterclockwise

13. Graph rectangle $OABC$ with vertices $O(0, 0)$, $A(6, 0)$, $B(6, 2)$ and $C(0, 2)$. Graph the rotation of rectangle $OABC$ about point C as indicated:
    a. 90° clockwise **b.** 90° counterclockwise

14. *Given:* △ABC with $A(2, 3)$, $B(0, 6)$, and $C(2, 6)$
    Graph and state the coordinates of:
    a. △$A'B'C'$, the image of △ABC after a reflection in the y-axis
    b. △$A''B''C''$, the image of △$A'B'C'$ after a reflection in the line $y = x$
    c. △$A'''B'''C'''$, the image of △$A''B''C''$ after a rotation of 90° clockwise about the origin

15. *Given:* △ABC with $A(6, 1)$, $B(6, 5)$, and $C(2, 1)$
    a. Reflect the figure over the line $y = x$. What are the coordinates of △$A'B'C'$, the image of △ABC?
    b. Using the origin as the center of rotation, rotate the figure obtained in part **a** 90° counterclockwise. What are the coordinates of △$A''B''C''$, the image of △$A'B'C'$?
    c. Reflect the figure obtained in part **b** through the origin. What are the coordinates of △$A'''B'''C'''$, the image of △$A''B''C''$?

16. *Given:* △ABC with $A(9, 1)$, $B(2, 5)$, and $C(2, 1)$
    a. Reflect △ABC over the y-axis. What are the coordinates of the vertices of the image △$A'B'C'$?
    b. Reflect △$A'B'C'$ over the line $y = x$. What are the coordinates of the vertices of the image △$A''B''C''$?
    c. What is the name of the single transformation that maps △ABC onto △$A''B''C''$?

17. *Given:* Hexagon *ABCDEF* with $A(2, 2)$, $B(4, 0)$, $C(2, -2)$, $D(-2, -2)$, $E(-4, 0)$, and $F(-2, 2)$.

Write the letters **a–e**, and next to each letter, write the coordinates of the stated image after the transformation described.

a. the image of point *A*; reflection in $y = -x$
b. the image of point *F*; reflection in the *y*-axis
c. the image of point *B*; reflection in the origin
d. the image of point *C* rotated 90° clockwise about the origin

Translation

By Definition	Example
Under $T_{(a,b)}$, a TRANSLATION of *a* units in the horizontal direction and *b* units in the vertical direction: **$P(x,y) \rightarrow P'(x + a, y + b)$**	y, x, $T_{(3,4)}$, P'(5,7), 4, 3, P (2, 3)

Example

The coordinates of the vertices of $\triangle PQR$ are $P(2, 3)$, $Q(4, 0)$, and $R(-3, -2)$.

Graph the image of $\triangle PQR$ under $T_{(4, -5)}$.

Solution: This translation shifts each point 4 units to the right and 5 units down.

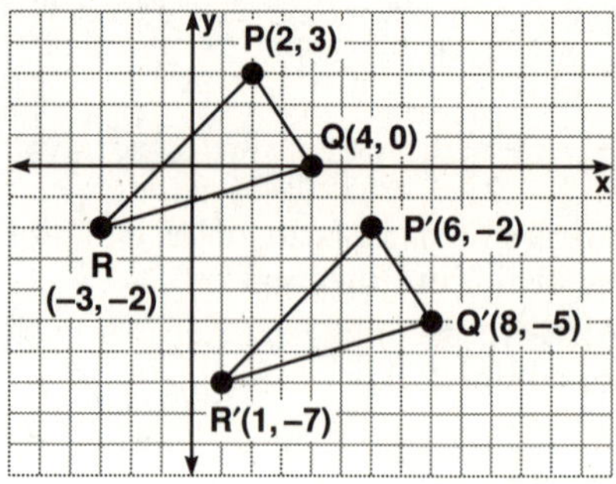

EXERCISES

1. What is the image of the point $(5, -2)$ under the translation $T_{(2, 1)}$?

2. What is the image of the point $(3, -4)$ under the translation $T_{(-2, 0)}$?

3. A translation maps $(-2, -3)$ onto $(4, 2)$. What is the image of the origin under this translation?

4. A translation maps $(2, 1)$ onto $(-3, 2)$. Find the image of $(4, -1)$ under the same translation.

5. A translation maps $A(0, 2)$ onto $A'(2, 0)$. Find the coordinates of B', the image of $B(1, 1)$ under the translation.

6. A translation maps $P(4, -3)$ onto $P'(0, 0)$. Find the coordinates of Q', the image of $Q(-2, 1)$, under the same translation.

7. A translation maps $P(3, -2)$ onto $P'(5, 0)$. Find the coordinates of the image of $Q(4, -6)$ under the same translation.

8. A translation maps the point $(0, 0)$ to a point $(-2, 4)$. What is the image of the point $(3, -2)$ under the same translation?

9. Under a given translation, the origin maps onto the point $(3, 5)$. What is the image of the point $(7, -1)$ under this same translation?

10. Translation *T* is defined by $(x, y) \rightarrow (x + 2, y - 1)$. Find the image of $(-1, 5)$ under translation *T*.

11. A transformation maps the point $P(x, y)$, onto $P'(x + 3, y - 2)$. Find the coordinates of *Q*, whose image under the same transformation is $Q'(6, 2)$.

12. If translation *T* maps point $A(-3, 1)$ onto point $A'(5, 5)$, which is the translation *T*?
(1) $T_{2,4}$ **(2)** $T_{2,6}$ **(3)** $T_{8,6}$ **(4)** $T_{8,4}$

13. The transformation $T_{(-2, 3)}$ maps the point $(7, 2)$ onto the point whose coordinates are
(1) $(9, 5)$ **(2)** $(5, 5)$ **(3)** $(5, -1)$ **(4)** $(-14, 6)$

14. Given $A(0, 2)$ and $B(4, 0)$, which translation maps *A* onto the midpoint of $\overline{AB}$?
(1) $T_{(2,-1)}$ **(2)** $T_{(-1,2)}$ **(3)** $T_{(-2,-1)}$ **(4)** $T_{(-1,-2)}$

15. $\triangle DEF$ has vertices $D(3, -1)$, $E(3, 4)$, and $F(6, 2)$. Find the coordinates of the vertices of $\triangle D'E'F'$, the image of $\triangle DEF$ under the translation $T_{(-3, 4)}$.

16. $\triangle ABC$ has vertices $A(6, 1)$, $B(8, 5)$, and $C(5, 4)$. Find the coordinates of the vertices of $\triangle A'B'C'$, the image of $\triangle ABC$ after a translation that maps $P(0, 0)$ onto $P'(3, -1)$.

17. *Given:* $\overline{AB}$ with endpoints $A(4, 1)$ and $B(5, 4)$

a. Graph and state the coordinates of:
(1) $\overline{A'B'}$, the image of $\overline{AB}$ after a reflection over the line $y = x$
(2) $\overline{A''B''}$, the image of $\overline{A'B'}$ after the transformation $(x, y) \rightarrow (x - 5, y - 5)$
(3) $\overline{A'''B'''}$, the image of $\overline{A''B''}$ after a reflection through the origin

b. Write a translation that will map $\overline{A'B'}$ onto $\overline{B'''A'''}$.

18. *Given:* $\triangle ABC$ with $A(1, 2)$, $B(0, 5)$, and $C(5, 4)$
Graph and state the coordinates of:

a. $\triangle A'B'C'$, the image of $\triangle ABC$ after the translation $T_{-6, 3}$

b. $\triangle A''B''C''$, the image of $\triangle A'B'C'$ after a reflection in the x-axis

c. $\triangle A'''B'''C'''$, the image of $\triangle A''B''C''$ after a reflection in the origin

19. *Given:* $\triangle ABC$; $A(-1, -2)$, $B(0, -4)$, and $C(3, -1)$
Graph and state the coordinates of:

a. $\triangle A'B'C'$, the image of $\triangle ABC$ after the translation $T_{(4, -3)}$

b. $\triangle A''B''C''$, the image of $\triangle ABC$ after a reflection in the origin

c. $\triangle A'''B'''C'''$, the image of $\triangle ABC$ after a reflection in the line $y = -x$

20. *Given:* Vertices $A(-3, -7)$, $B(-3, -3)$, and $C(0, -3)$
Graph and state the coordinates of:

a. $\triangle A'B'C'$, the image of $\triangle ABC$ after a point reflection in the origin

b. $\triangle A''B''C''$, the image of $\triangle A'B'C'$ reflected in the line $y = 2$

c. $\triangle A'''B'''C'''$, the image of $\triangle A''B''C''$ after translation $T_{(-8, 2)}$

21. *Given:* $\triangle ABC$ with $A(2, 1)$, $B(6, 4)$, and $C(8, 1)$
Graph and state the coordinates of:

a. $\triangle A'B'C'$, the reflection of $\triangle ABC$ through the x-axis

b. $\triangle A''B''C''$, the image of $\triangle A'B'C'$ after the translation $T_{-6, -2}$

c. $\triangle A'''B'''C'''$, the result of rotating $\triangle A''B''C''$ 90° clockwise about the origin

22. *Given:* $\triangle ABC$ with $A(-2, 2)$, $B(-7, 4)$, and $C(-5, 6)$
What are the coordinates of:

a. the vertices of $\triangle A'B'C'$, the image of $\triangle ABC$ reflected over the x-axis?

b. the vertices of $\triangle A''B''C''$, the image of $\triangle A'B'C'$, reflected over the line $y = -x$?

c. the vertices of $\triangle A'''B'''C'''$, the image of $\triangle A''B''C''$, under the translation $T_{(3, -4)}$?

23. *Given:* $\triangle ABC$ with $A(-1, 3)$, $B(3, 7)$, and $C(0, 6)$
Graph and state the coordinates of:

a. $\triangle A'B'C'$, the image of $\triangle ABC$ after a reflection in the line $y = x$

b. $\triangle A''B''C''$, the image of $\triangle A'B'C'$ following $r_{y\text{-axis}}(\triangle A'B'C')$

c. $\triangle A'''B'''C'''$, the image of $\triangle A''B''C''$ after a translation that maps $P(0, 0)$ onto $P(0, -5)$

24. *Given:* $\triangle ABC$ with $A(-3, -7)$, $B(-3, -3)$, and $C(0, -3)$
Graph and state the coordinates of:

a. $\triangle A'B'C'$, the image of $\triangle ABC$ after a point reflection in the origin

b. $\triangle A''B''C''$, the image of $\triangle A'B'C'$ reflected in the line $y = 2$

c. $\triangle A'''B'''C'''$, the image of $\triangle A''B''C''$ after the translation $T_{(-8, 2)}$

Dilation

By Definition	Illustration
Under a DILATION D_c with respect to the origin O, $\overline{OA}$ stretches or shrinks to $\overline{OA'}$ by a constant *scale factor* c. $A(x, y) \rightarrow A'(cx, cy)$	y, A′, A, O, x **If $\lvert c \rvert > 1$, $OA' > OA$.** **If $\lvert c \rvert < 1$, $OA' < OA$.** **If $c = 1$, $OA' = OA$.**

Examples

1. Find the image of $P(-3, -1)$ under the dilation D_2.

Solution: The scale factor of 2 stretches $\overline{OP}$ to $\overline{OP'}$. Multiply each coordinate by 2.

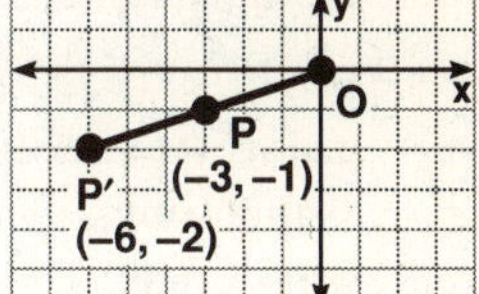

$P(-3, -1) \rightarrow P'(-6, -2)$

2. Under a dilation with respect to the origin, the image of $A(1, 3)$ is $A'(4, 12)$. Find the coordinates of B', the image of $B(2, 1)$, under the same dilation.

Solution: The coordinates of A' and A have the same scale factor, 4.

$$\frac{\text{abscissa of } A'}{\text{abscissa of } A} = \frac{4}{1} \qquad \frac{\text{ordinate of } A'}{\text{ordinate of } A} = \frac{12}{3} = \frac{4}{1}$$

Use the scale factor 4 to find the image of B.

$$B(2, 1) \rightarrow B'(8, 4)$$

EXERCISES

1. The image of $A(3, 1)$ under the dilation D_3 is
(1) $(1, \frac{1}{3})$ **(2)** $(\frac{1}{3}, 1)$ **(3)** $(3, 9)$ **(4)** $(9, 3)$

2. Find the image of $(3, -2)$ under the dilation D_2.

3. Find the coordinates of the image of $A(-1, 2)$ under the dilation D_4.

4. What are the coordinates of the point (2, –4) under the dilation D_{-2}?
(1) (8, –4) **(2)** (4, –8) **(3)** (–8, 4) **(4)** (–4, 8)

5. If $P(4, -3)$ is transformed under the dilation D_{-3}, what is the image P'?

6. What are the coordinates of the point $P(-2, 3)$ under the dilation D_2?

7. Under a dilation with center P and scale factor k, A' is the image of A. Find k if $PA = 7$ and $PA' = 28$.

8. If the distance from the origin to point A is $\sqrt{10}$ and $A' = D_3(A)$, the distance from the origin to point A' is
(1) $3\sqrt{10}$ **(2)** $2\sqrt{10}$ **(3)** $3 + \sqrt{10}$ **(4)** $\frac{\sqrt{10}}{3}$

9. $\triangle ABC$ has vertices $A(1, 3)$, $B(0, 4)$, and $C(-2, 2)$. Write the coordinates of its image $\triangle A'B'C'$ under the dilation D_2.

10. $\triangle JKL$ has vertices $J(0, -6)$, $K(6, 3)$, and $L(-3, 6)$. Write the coordinates of its image $\triangle J'K'L'$ under the dilation $D_{\frac{1}{3}}$.

11. $EFGH$ has vertices $E(-2, 2)$, $F(2, 2)$, $G(2, 4)$, and $H(-2, 4)$. Write the coordinates of its image:
a. $E'F'G'H'$ under D_3 **c.** $E'''F'''G'''H'''$ under D_1
b. $E''F''G''H''$ under $D_{\frac{1}{2}}$

12. *Given:* $\triangle ABC$ with $A(0, 0)$, $B(8, 6)$, and $C(8, 0)$
Graph and state the coordinates of:
a. $\triangle A'B'C'$, the image of $\triangle ABC$ after the transformation $D: (x, y) \rightarrow (\frac{3}{2}x, \frac{3}{2}y)$
b. $\triangle A''B''C''$, the image of $\triangle ABC$ after a reflection in the line $x = 2$
c. $\triangle A'''B'''C'''$, the image of $\triangle ABC$ under the transformation $G: (x, y) \rightarrow (x + 3, y - 7)$

13. *Given:* $\triangle ABC$ with $A(2, 0)$, $B(6, -2)$, and $C(4, -4)$
Graph and state the coordinates of:
a. $\triangle A'B'C'$, the image of $\triangle ABC$ after the transformation: $(x, y) \rightarrow (\frac{1}{2}x, \frac{1}{2}y)$
b. $\triangle A''B''C''$, the image of $\triangle ABC$ after a 90° counterclockwise rotation about the origin
c. $\triangle A'''B'''C'''$, the image of $\triangle ABC$ after a reflection in the origin

14. *Given:* $\triangle ABC$ with $A(0, 9)$, $B(-3, 0)$, and $C(-6, 9)$
Graph and state the coordinates of:
a. A', B', C', the images of A, B, C after a reflection in the origin
b. A'', B'', C'', the images of A', B', C' after the dilation $D_{\frac{1}{3}}$
c. A''', B''', C''', the images of A'', B'', C'' after the translation $T_{(5, 4)}$

Summary of Coordinate Rules

Under the transformation	(x, y) becomes:	Under the transformation	(x, y) becomes:
$r_{y\text{-axis}}$	$(-x, y)$	$r_{(0,0)}$	$(-x, -y)$
$r_{x\text{-axis}}$	$(x, -y)$	$R_{O, 90°}$	$(-y, x)$
$r_{y=x}$	(y, x)	$R_{O, 180°}$	$(-x, -y)$
$r_{y=-x}$	$(-y, -x)$	$R_{O, 270°}$	$(y, -x)$
$r_{x=a}$	$(2a - x, y)$	$T_{a,b}$	$(x + a, y + b)$
$r_{y=b}$	$(x, 2b - y)$	D_k	(kx, ky)

Implementing a Rule for a Transformation

Given any rule for a transformation, you can write the coordinates for the image of a known point.

Example

The transformation Z maps each point P of the plane according to the rule:

$$P(x, y) \rightarrow P'(-x, y + 2)$$

Write the coordinates of A', the image of $A(-3, -1)$ under the transformation Z.

Solution: Under the rule for Z,

$x \rightarrow -x$ Thus, for A: $-3 \rightarrow -(-3)$, or 3
$y \rightarrow y + 2$ Thus, for A: $-1 \rightarrow -1 + 2$, or 1

Answer: $A'(3, 1)$

Sometimes, you will be able to identify a given rule as one of the basic transformations: reflection, rotation, translation, or dilation.

Example

The mapping that moves every point in the plane under the rule $(x, y) \rightarrow (x - 1, y + 3)$ is called a
(1) translation **(3)** dilation
(2) rotation **(4)** point reflection

Answer: **(1)**

EXERCISES

1. If T is the transformation $(x, y) \to (-x, 2y)$, find the image of $P(-3, 4)$ after the transformation T.

2. If W is the transformation $(x, y) \to (-2x, y + 2)$, find the image of (2, 0) after transformation W.

3. A transformation maps (x, y) onto $(y + 1, x - 1)$. Find the coordinates of B', the image of $B(2, 1)$ under the same transformation.

4. A transformation maps $P(x, y)$ onto $P'(x - 2, y + 3)$. Under the same transformation, find the coordinates of Q', the image of $Q(-4, 1)$.

5. If T is the transformation $(x, y) \to (-x, y - 2)$, find the image of $(-1, 3)$ after the transformation T.

6. A transformation maps (1, 3) onto (−1, −3). This transformation is equivalent to

   (1) rotation $R_{90°}$ (3) dilation D_{-1}
   (2) rotation $R_{-90°}$ (4) translation $T_{-1,-3}$

7. The mapping that moves every point in the plane under the rule $(x, y) \to (x + 2, y - 3)$ is called a

   (1) line reflection (3) translation
   (2) rotation (4) dilation

8. For each transformation listed in **a–e**, select the description, chosen from the list below, that best describes the transformation.

   Transformations

   a. T: $(x, y) \to (x + 3, y)$
   b. R: $(x, y) \to (x, -y)$
   c. S: $(x, y) \to (2 - x, y)$
   d. U: $(x, y) \to (-x, -y)$
   e. V: $(x, y) \to (y, x)$

   Descriptions

   (1) reflects in origin (5) reflects in $x = 1$
   (2) reflects in x-axis (6) translates 3 right
   (3) reflects in y-axis (7) translates 3 left
   (4) reflects in $y = x$

9. *Given:* $\triangle ABC$ with $A(1, 2)$, $B(4, 0)$, and $C(3, -2)$
   F is the transformation $(x, y) \to (-y, -x)$
   U is the transformation $(x, y) \to (x - 2, y + 4)$
   N is the transformation $(x, y) \to (2x, 2y)$

   a. Graph and state the coordinates of:
   (1) $\triangle A'B'C'$, the image of $\triangle ABC$ after the transformation F
   (2) $\triangle A''B''C''$, the image of $\triangle A'B'C'$ after the transformation U
   (3) $\triangle A'''B'''C'''$, the image of $\triangle A''B''C''$ after the transformation N

   b. Which transformation, F, U, or N, is a dilation?

10. *Given:* $A(8, 5)$ and $B(6, 1)$ and the transformations T, R, and S as described below:
    T: $(x, y) \to (x + 1, y - 5)$
    R: $(x, y) \to (y, x)$
    S: $(x, y) \to (-x, y)$

    a. Graph and state the coordinates of:
    (1) $\overline{A'B'}$, the image of $\overline{AB}$ after the transformation T.
    (2) $\overline{A''B''}$, the image of $\overline{AB}$ after the transformation R.
    (3) $\overline{A'''B'''}$, the image of $\overline{AB}$ after the transformation S.

    b. Compare the slopes of the pairs of segments listed below and indicate whether these slopes are *equal*, *reciprocals*, *additive inverses*, or *negative reciprocals*.
    (1) $\overline{AB}$ and $\overline{A'B'}$
    (2) $\overline{AB}$ and $\overline{A''B''}$
    (3) $\overline{AB}$ and $\overline{A'''B'''}$

3.2 COMPOSITION

Composition of Transformations

Definition	Illustration
The COMPOSITION of transformations is the result of a second transformation performed on the image of a first.	**If $r_m(A) = A'$ and $r_n(A') = A''$, then $r_n \circ r_m(A) = A''$.**
In Symbols	
If r_m is a reflection in line m and r_n is a reflection in line n, then $r_n \circ r_m$ is the reflection in line m followed by the reflection in line n. **Note: The order of performing the transformations is from right to left.**	A′ m A n A″

Example

What is the image of (5, 1) under a reflection in the x-axis followed by a half turn about the origin?

Solution:

$(5, 1) \xrightarrow{r_{x\text{-axis}}} (5, -1) \xrightarrow{R_{O, 180^\circ}} (-5, 1)$

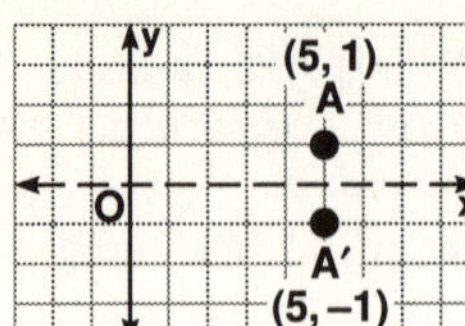

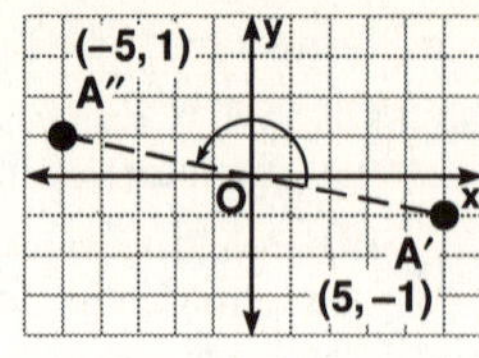

Note: The composition $R_{O, 180^\circ} \circ r_{x\text{-axis}}(5, 1)$ is equivalent to a reflection of (5, 1) in the y-axis.

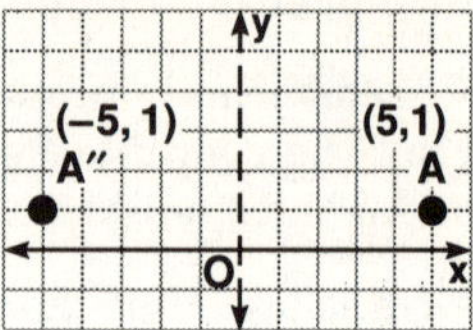

In symbols: $R_{O, 180^\circ} \circ r_{x\text{-axis}}(5, 1) = R_{O, 180^\circ}(5, -1) = (-5, 1)$

EXERCISES

1. What is the image of $P(-4, 6)$ under the composite $r_{x=2} \circ r_{y\text{-axis}}$?
   (1) (–8, 6) (2) (4, –2) (3) (6, 0) (4) (0, 6)

2. Given the transformations:
   $R(x, y) \to (-x, y)$
   $S(x, y) \to (y, x)$
   What is $(R \circ S)(5, -1)$?
   (1) (1, 5) (2) (1, –5) (3) (–1, 5) (4) (–1, –5)

3. Find the coordinates of $r_{y\text{-axis}} \circ r_{y=x}(A)$ if the coordinates of A are (6, 1).

4. What are the coordinates of P', the image of the point $P(2, 3)$, under the transformation $r_{x=4} \circ r_{x\text{-axis}}$?

5. If $A = (-2, 3)$, what is $r_{y\text{-axis}} \circ D_3(A)$?
   (1) (–6, –9) (2) (9, –6) (3) (5, 6) (4) (6, 9)

6. Point A has coordinates (4, 3). What are the coordinates of A', the image of A under $r_{x=2} \circ r_{x=6}(A)$?
   (1) (12, 3) (2) (–4, 3) (3) (4, 11) (4) (4, –5)

7. Referring to the diagram, find the coordinates of $r_\ell \circ r_m(P)$.

   Line ℓ is $x = 2$.
   Line m is $y = x$.

8. Which is the image of A under the transformation $r_{x\text{-axis}} \circ R_{90^\circ}$?
   (1) A (2) ∀ (3) ᐳ (4) ᐸ

9. Find the image of (–3, 2) under: $R_{O, 180^\circ} \circ r_{y\text{-axis}}$

10. Find the image of (4, –6) under: $R_{O, 90^\circ} \circ D_{\frac{1}{2}}$

11. *Given:* $\triangle ABC$ with coordinates $A(6, 1)$, $B(8, 5)$, and $C(5, 4)$.
    Graph and state the coordinates of:
    a. A', B', and C', the images of A, B, and C after a reflection over the line $y = x$.
    b. $\triangle A''B''C''$, the image of original $\triangle ABC$ after $r_{y\text{-axis}} \circ r_{x\text{-axis}}(\triangle ABC)$.
    c. $\triangle A'''B'''C'''$, the image of original $\triangle ABC$ after a translation that maps $P(0, 0)$ onto $P'(3, -1)$.

Composition of Two Line Reflections

When the lines of reflection are *parallel,* the composition of two line reflections is equivalent to a *translation.*

Example

Find the coordinates of the image of $\triangle ABC$, with $A(4, 1)$, $B(1, 2)$, $C(3, 5)$, under: $r_{y\text{-axis}} \circ r_{x=1}$

Solution:

$(4, 1) \xrightarrow{r_{x=1}} (-2, 1) \xrightarrow{r_{y\text{-axis}}} (2, 1)$
$(1, 2) \longrightarrow (1, 2) \longrightarrow (-1, 2)$
$(3, 5) \longrightarrow (-1, 5) \longrightarrow (1, 5)$

The lines of reflection are parallel (line $x = 1 \parallel y$-axis). The given composition is equivalent to a translation:

$r_{y\text{-axis}} \circ r_{x=1} = T_{-2, 0}$

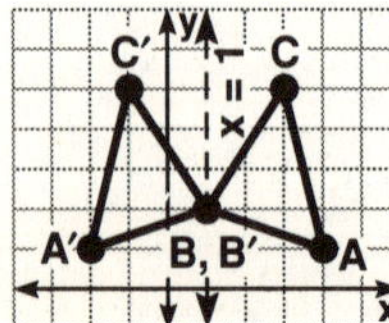

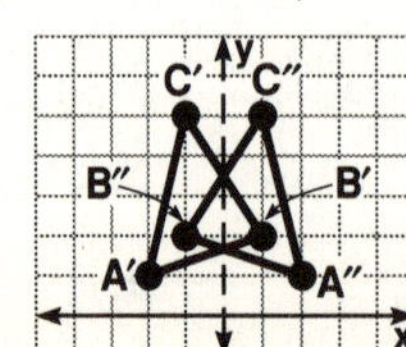

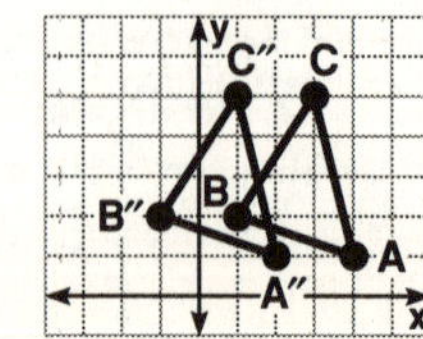

The distance of the translation is twice the distance between the lines of reflection.

When the lines of reflection *intersect*, the composition of two line reflections is equivalent to a *rotation*.

Example

Find the coordinates of the image of $\triangle ABC$, with $A(4, 1)$, $B(1, 2)$, and $C(3, 5)$, under: $r_{y\text{-axis}} \circ r_{y=x}$

Solution:

$$(4, 1) \xrightarrow{r_{y=x}} (1, 4) \xrightarrow{r_{y\text{-axis}}} (-1, 4)$$
$$(1, 2) \longrightarrow (2, 1) \longrightarrow (-2, 1)$$
$$(3, 5) \longrightarrow (5, 3) \longrightarrow (-5, 3)$$

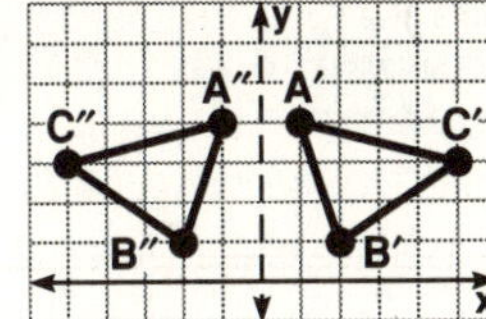

The lines of reflection intersect (line $y = x$ intersects y-axis). The given composition of two line reflections is equivalent to a rotation:

$$r_{y\text{-axis}} \circ r_{y=x} = R_{O,\,90^\circ}$$

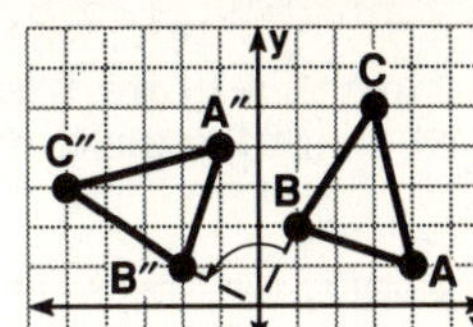

The angle of rotation is twice the measure of the angle between the lines of reflection.

Composition of Two Rotations

The composition of two rotations about the same center is also a rotation.

Example

Find the coordinates of the image of $\triangle ABC$, with $A(4, 1)$, $B(1, 2)$, and $C(3, 5)$ under: $R_{O,\,90^\circ} \circ R_{O,\,180^\circ}$

Solution:

$$(4, 1) \xrightarrow{R_{O,\,180^\circ}} (-4, -1) \xrightarrow{R_{O,\,90^\circ}} (1, -4)$$
$$(1, 2) \longrightarrow (-1, -2) \longrightarrow (2, -1)$$
$$(3, 5) \longrightarrow (-3, -5) \longrightarrow (5, -3)$$

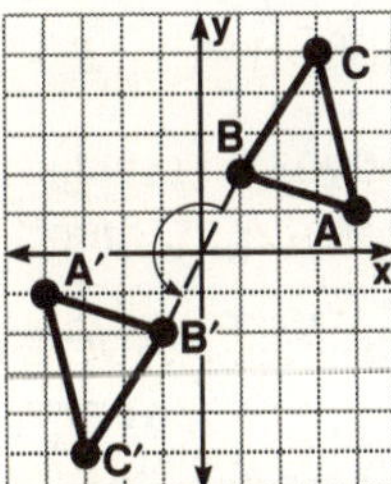

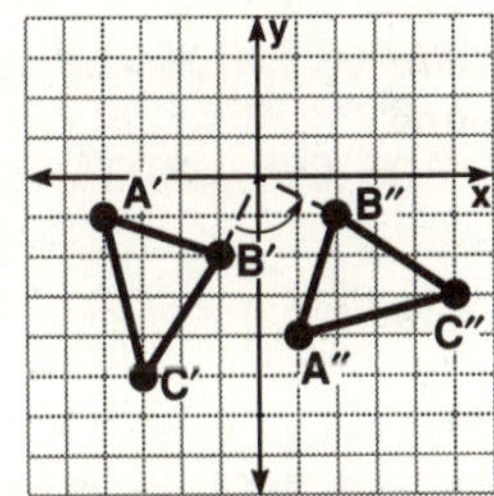

The given composition of two rotations is equivalent to a single rotation with the same center as the two rotations, and angle measure that is the sum of the two angle measures:

$$R_{O,\,90^\circ} \circ R_{O,\,180^\circ} = R_{O,\,270^\circ}$$

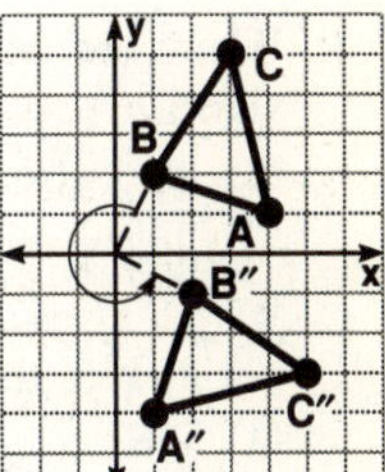

Composition of Two Translations

The composition of two translations is also a translation.

Example

Find the coordinates of the image of $\triangle ABC$, with $A(4, 1)$, $B(1, 2)$, and $C(3, 5)$ under: $T_{1,3} \circ T_{2,-5}$

Solution:

$$(4, 1) \xrightarrow{T_{2,-5}} (6, -4) \xrightarrow{T_{1,3}} (7, -1)$$
$$(1, 2) \longrightarrow (3, -3) \longrightarrow (4, 0)$$
$$(3, 5) \longrightarrow (5, 0) \longrightarrow (6, 3)$$

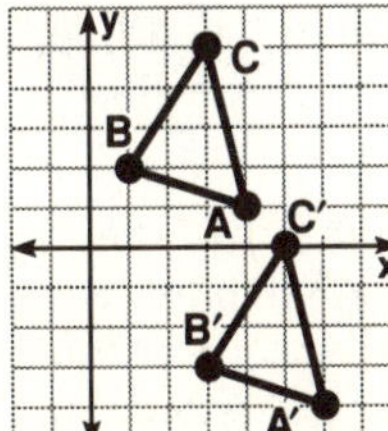

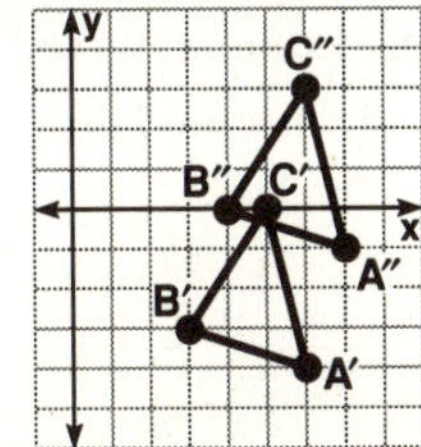

The given composition of two translations is equivalent to a single translation that sums the horizontal and the vertical translations:

$$T_{1,3} \circ T_{2,-5} = T_{3,-2}$$

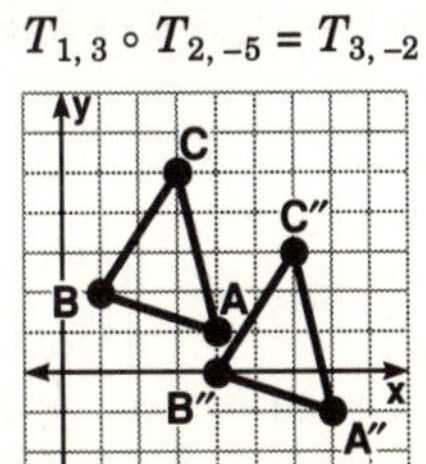

Glide Reflection

The composition of a line reflection and a translation is called a GLIDE REFLECTION. The direction of the translation is parallel to the line of reflection.

***A* is first reflected in the line *m* (to *A*′) and then translated in a direction parallel to line *m* (to *A*″).**

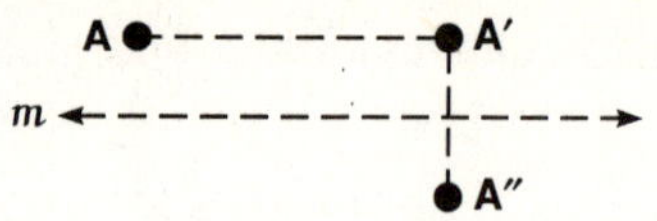

***A* is first translated in a direction parallel to line *m* (to *A*′) and then reflected in the line *m* (to *A*″).**

A glide reflection is a commutative operation, although, in general, composition of transformations is not commutative.

EXERCISES

1. If line s intersects line t, then $r_s \circ r_t$ ($\triangle ABC$) is equivalent to a
   (1) rotation (3) dilation
   (2) translation (4) glide reflection

2. If line s is parallel to line t, which is equivalent to the composition of line reflections $r_s \circ r_t$ ($\triangle ABC$)?
   (1) a rotation (3) a translation
   (2) a line reflection (4) a glide reflection

3. Which transformation is equivalent to the composition $r_{y=2} \circ r_{y=0}$ ($\overline{AB}$)?
   (1) a rotation (3) a translation
   (2) a dilation (4) a line reflection

4. Which transformation is equivalent to the composite line reflections $r_{y\text{-axis}} \circ r_{y=x}$ ($\overline{AB}$)?
   (1) a rotation (3) a translation
   (2) a dilation (4) a glide reflection

5. *Given:* $\triangle ABC$ with $A(-2, 3)$, $B(-6, 7)$, and $C(-3, 8)$.
   a. Graph and state the coordinates of:
   (1) $\triangle A'B'C'$, the image of $\triangle ABC$, after a reflection over the y-axis.
   (2) $\triangle A''B''C''$, the image of $\triangle A'B'C'$ after a reflection over the line $y = x$.
   b. The composite
   $r_{y=x} \circ r_{y\text{-axis}}$ ($\triangle ABC$) = $\triangle A''B''C''$ is a
   (1) rotation (3) dilation
   (2) translation (4) glide reflection
   c. Graph and state the coordinates of $\triangle A'''B'''C'''$, the image of $\triangle ABC$, the original triangle, after the transformation $(x, y) \rightarrow (2x, -y)$.

6. *Given:* $\triangle ABC$ with $A(4, 0)$, $B(8, 1)$, and $C(8, 4)$.
   a. Graph and state the coordinates of $\triangle A'B'C'$, the image of $\triangle ABC$ after the composite transformation $r_{x=0} \circ r_{y=x}$ ($\triangle ABC$).
   b. Which single type of transformation maps $\triangle ABC$ onto $\triangle A'B'C'$?
   (1) rotation (3) glide reflection
   (2) dilation (4) translation
   c. Graph and state the coordinates of $\triangle A''B''C''$, the image of $\triangle ABC$ after the composite transformation $r_{y=-4} \circ r_{y=0}$ ($\triangle ABC$).
   d. Which single type of transformation maps $\triangle ABC$ onto $\triangle A''B''C''$?
   (1) rotation (3) glide reflection
   (2) dilation (4) translation

7. *Given:* $\triangle ABC$ with $A(2, 3)$, $B(9, 1)$, and $C(5, 5)$.
   a. Graph and state the coordinates of:
   (1) $\triangle A'B'C'$, the image of $\triangle ABC$ after a reflection through the origin.
   (2) $\triangle A''B''C''$, the image of $\triangle A'B'C'$ after $r_{y\text{-axis}} \circ r_{x\text{-axis}}$ ($\triangle A'B'C'$).
   b. A series of transformations that reflect point P through the origin, then over the x-axis, and then over the y-axis, is equivalent to a rotation about the origin of
   (1) 90° (2) 180° (3) 270° (4) 360°

8. What is the result of $R_{A, 90°} \circ R_{A, -180°}$ ()?
   (1)  (2)  (3)  (4) 

In 9 and 10, refer to the diagram of $ABCDEF$, a regular hexagon inscribed in circle O.

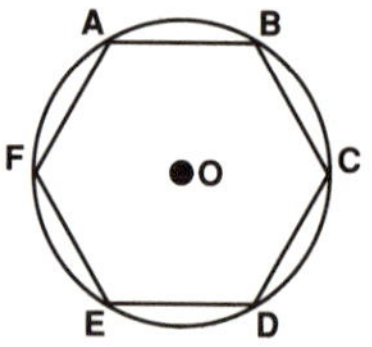

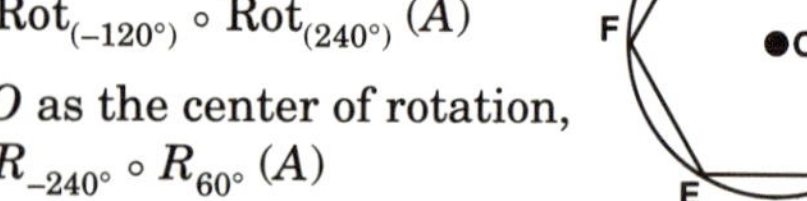

9. With O as the center of rotation, find: $\text{Rot}_{(-120°)} \circ \text{Rot}_{(240°)}$ (A)

10. With O as the center of rotation, find: $R_{-240°} \circ R_{60°}$ (A)

11. Which is equivalent to the composition $T_{-2,3} \circ T_{2,-2}$?
    (1) $r_{-2,3} \circ r_{2,-2}$ (3) $T_{0,1}$
    (2) $r_{2,-2} \circ r_{-2,3}$ (4) $r_{0,1}$

12. The vertices of $\triangle ABC$ are $A(-1, 2)$, $B(0, 4)$, and $C(3, 1)$. Find the coordinates of $\triangle A'B'C'$, the image of $\triangle ABC$ under the composition:
    $$T_{0,3} \circ T_{-2,4}$$

13. In general, which composition of transformations is commutative?
    (1) $r \circ R$ (3) $R \circ D$
    (2) $r \circ T$ (4) $D \circ r$

14. *Given:* $\triangle ABC$ with $A(-7, 4)$, $B(-2, 6)$, and $C(-4, 9)$. Graph and state the coordinates of:

a. $\triangle A'B'C'$, the image of $\triangle ABC$ after the translation $T_{3,0}$.

b. $\triangle A''B''C''$, the image of $\triangle A'B'C'$ after the reflection $r_{y=2}$.

c. Which single transformation maps $\triangle ABC$ onto $\triangle A''B''C''$?

(1) a line reflection (3) a glide reflection
(2) a point reflection (4) a rotation

15. *Given:* $\overline{AB}$ with $A(2, 5)$ and $B(5, 9)$. Graph and state the coordinates of:

a. $\overline{A'B'}$, the image of $\overline{AB}$ after the reflection $r_{y=x}$.

b. $\overline{A''B''}$, the image of $\overline{A'B'}$ after the translation $T_{3,3}$.

c. Which single transformation is equivalent to the composite $r_{y=x} \circ T_{3,3}$?

(1) a dilation (3) a line reflection
(2) a rotation (4) a glide reflection

3.3 ISOMETRY

A transformation that preserves distance is called an ISOMETRY.

For all transformations except dilation, the image is *congruent* to the original figure. Thus, reflection, rotation, translation, and glide reflection are isometries.

Reflection	*Rotation*	*Translation*	*Glide Reflection*	*Dilation*
A, A′, B, B′, ℓ	A, B, C, A′, B′	A, B, A′, B′	A, B, A′, B′, A″, B″	A′, A, B, B′, C
isometry	isometry	isometry	isometry	not an isometry

When distance is preserved, angle measure, parallelism, collinearity, and betweenness are also preserved. Dilation does not preserve distance or, therefore, area. But, dilation does preserve angle measure, parallelism, collinearity, and betweenness.

The vertices of a polygon are read in an order. This order, or ORIENTATION, can be

clockwise order

B
A C
$\triangle ABC$

counterclockwise order

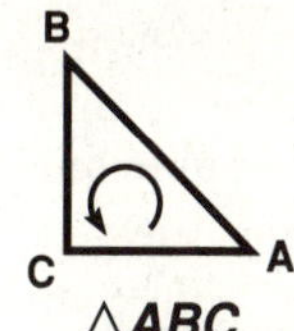

A DIRECT ISOMETRY preserves orientation.	**An OPPOSITE ISOMETRY changes orientation.**
Translation (A, B, C, A′, B′, C′) — *Rotation* (A, B, C, P, A′, B′, C′)	*Reflection* (A, B, C, A′, B′, C′, ℓ) — *Glide Reflection* (A, B, C, ℓ, A′, B′, C′, A″, B″, C″)

1. A line reflection preserves
   (1) distance and orientation
   (2) angle measurement and orientation
   (3) distance, but not angle measurement
   (4) distance and angle measurement

2. A property not preserved under a line reflection is
   (1) angle measure (3) distance
   (2) collinearity (4) orientation

3. Which property is not preserved under a reflection in the x-axis?
   (1) distance (3) parallelism
   (2) orientation (4) betweenness

4. Which properties are preserved under a rotation?
   (1) distance, only
   (2) angle measure, only
   (3) distance and angle measure, only
   (4) distance, angle measure, and orientation

5. Which property is not preserved under a dilation?
   (1) collinearity (3) similarity
   (2) orientation (4) distance

6. Which property is not preserved under a rotation?
   (1) distance (3) betweenness
   (2) orientation (4) all are preserved

7. Which property is not preserved by a glide reflection?
   (1) betweenness (3) orientation
   (2) angle measure (4) collinearity

8. Which transformation does not preserve distance?
   (1) dilation (3) line reflection
   (2) rotation (4) point reflection

9. Which transformation can produce an image triangle with an area not equal to the area of the original triangle?
   (1) translation (3) dilation
   (2) line reflection (4) rotation

10. Which transformation does not preserve orientation?
    (1) a reflection in $y = x$
    (2) the translation $T_{(x+3,\, y-4)}$
    (3) the dilation D_3
    (4) the rotation $R_{90°}$

11. Which transformation is not an isometry?
    (1) $(x, y) \to (x + 6, y - 2)$
    (2) $(x, y) \to (y, -x)$
    (3) $(x, y) \to (\frac{1}{2}x, \frac{1}{2}y)$
    (4) $(x, y) \to (-y, -x)$

12. Which transformation is not an isometry?
    (1) $T_{(5,\,3)}$ (2) D_2 (3) $r_{x\text{-axis}}$ (4) $\text{Rot}_{(O,\,90°)}$

13. Which of the following is always a direct isometry?
    (1) line reflection (3) dilation
    (2) glide reflection (4) rotation

14. Which composition of transformations results in a direct isometry?
    (1) $R_{O,\,90°} \circ r_{y=0}$
    (2) $r_{x\text{-axis}} \circ r_{y=2}$
    (3) $r_{y=x} \circ T_{1,\,3}$
    (4) $r_{y\text{-axis}} \circ R_{O,\,180°}$

15. *Given:* $\triangle ABC$ with $A(1, 1)$, $B(3, 1)$, and $C(1, 4)$.
    a. Graph and state the coordinates of:
       (1) $\triangle A'B'C'$, the image of $\triangle ABC$ after the dilation D_3
       (2) $\triangle A''B''C''$, the image of $\triangle A'B'C'$ after the reflection W: $(x, y) \to (x, -y)$
       (3) $\triangle A'''B'''C'''$, the image of $\triangle A''B''C''$ after the glide reflection G: $(x, y) \to (y, x - 2)$
    b. Which of the transformations, D_3, W, or G, is not an isometry?

16. $\triangle ABC$ has vertices $A(2, -2)$, $B(5, -2)$, and $C(3, -4)$.
    a. On the same set of axes, graph and label $\triangle ABC$ and its image under each of the following transformations. State the coordinates of the vertices for each image of $\triangle ABC$.
       (1) T: $(x, y) \to (-x, y)$
       (2) U: $(x, y) \to (x - 4, y + 4)$
       (3) W: $(x, y) \to (2x, 2y)$
    b. Which transformation, T, U, or W, is not an isometry?
    c. Which transformation, T, U, or W, does not preserve orientation?

Application to Graphing

A graph has SYMMETRY if its reflection about a line or a point is identical to the original.

The graph is symmetric about:	*If the equation is unchanged when you*	Example
the y-axis	**replace x by $-x$**	(x, y) $y = x^2$ $(-x, y)$ $y = (-x)^2$ $y = x^2$
the x-axis	**replace y by $-y$**	(x, y) $x = y^2$ $(x, -y)$ $x = (-y)^2$ $x = y^2$
the origin	**replace x by $-x$ and y by $-y$**	(x, y) $xy = 4$ $(-x, -y)$ $(-x)(-y) = 4$ $xy = 4$
the line $y = x$	**interchange x and y**	(x, y) $xy = 6$ (y, x) $(y)(x) = 6$ $xy = 6$

EXERCISES

1. Which graph has symmetry with respect to the x-axis?

(1)
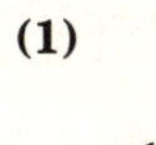
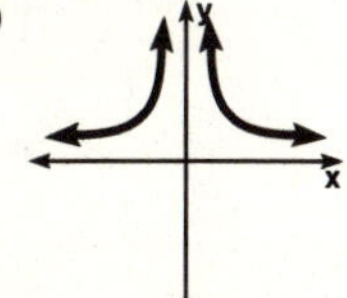

(3)

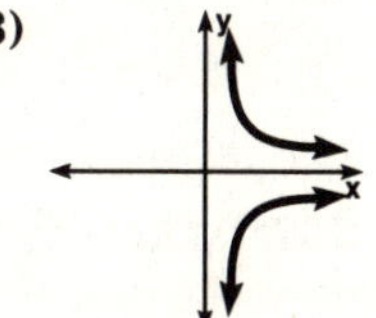

(2)
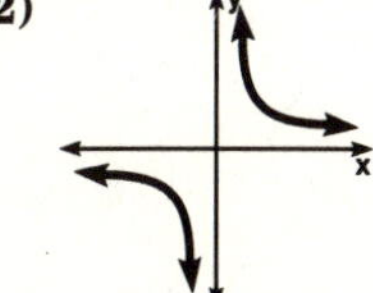

(4)
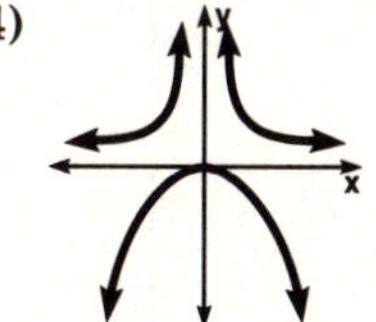

2. Which graph has symmetry with respect to the origin?

(1)

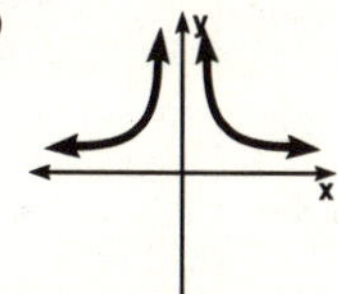

(3)

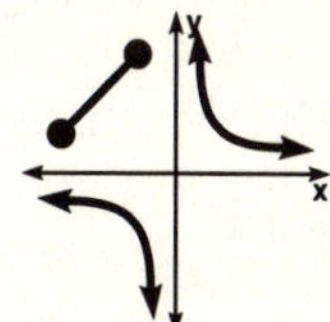

(2)

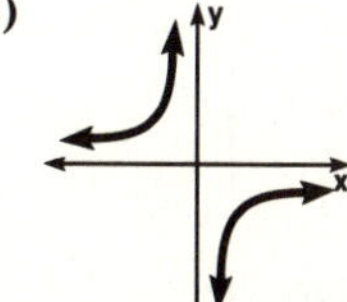

(4)

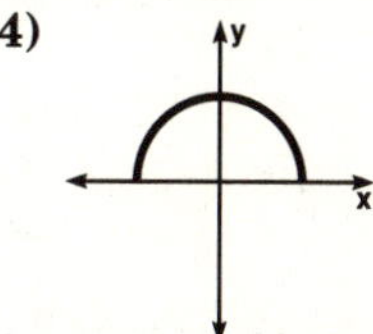

3. Which graph has symmetry with respect to the y-axis?

(1)

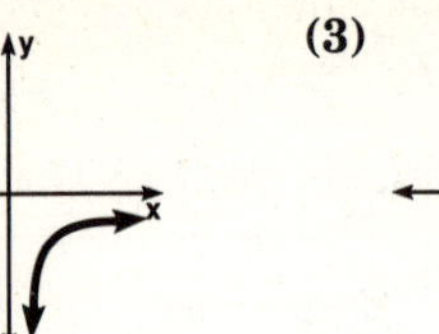

(3)

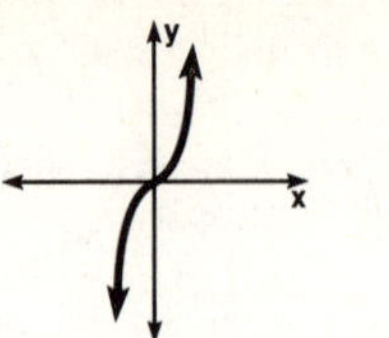

(2)

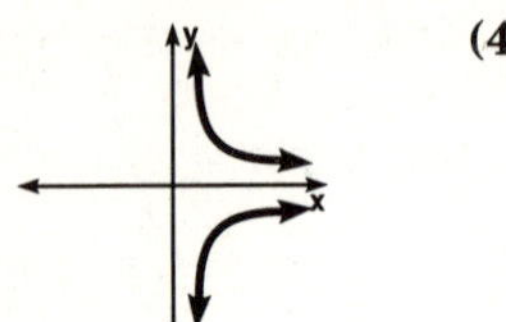

(4)

4. Which graph has symmetry with respect to the line $y = x$?

(1)

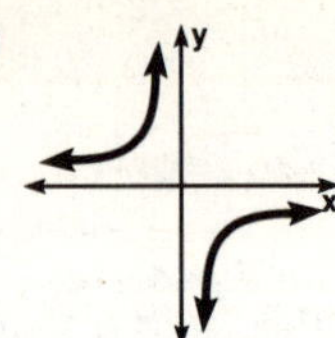

(3)

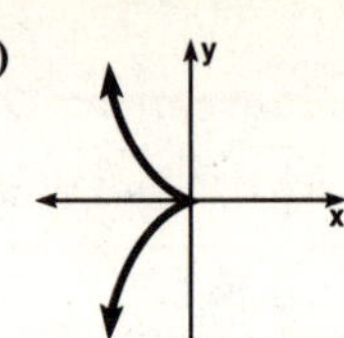

(2)

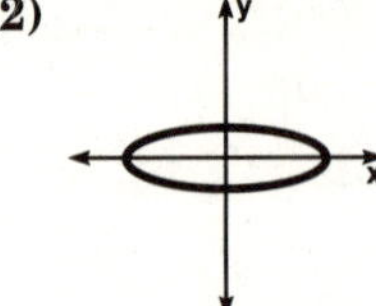

(4)

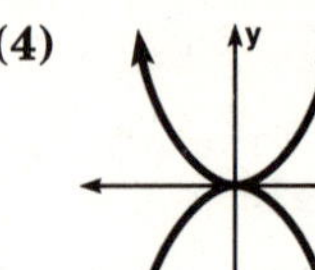

In 5-20, apply the tests for symmetry to tell if the graph of the given function has symmetry with respect to:

(1) the y-axis **(2)** the x-axis **(3)** the origin **(4)** the line $y = x$

List all of the symmetries that the graph has. If there is no symmetry, write "none."

5. $y = |x|$
6. $y = -|x|$
7. $x = |y|$
8. $x = -|y|$
9. $y = x + 2$
10. $y = 2x$
11. $y = 2x^2$
12. $y = x^3$
13. $x = y^3$
14. $y = x^4$
15. $x = y^4$
16. $y = \sqrt{x}$
17. $x = \sqrt{y}$
18. $x^2 + y^2 = 25$
19. $y = \sqrt{25 - x^2}$
20. $xy = 12$

Symmetry in Figures

Line Symmetry	*Rotational Symmetry*	*Point Symmetry*
A figure has LINE SYMMETRY if a line can be drawn through the figure so that the part of the figure on one side of the line is the mirror image of the part on the other side.	**A figure has ROTATIONAL SYMMETRY if the figure coincides with itself when rotated in either direction $n°$, where $n \neq 360$, about a fixed point.**	**A figure has POINT SYMMETRY if there is a central point so that the part of the figure on one side of the central point is the reflection of the part on the other side.** **180° rotational symmetry is also point symmetry.**
Examples of Lines of Symmetry	*Examples of Rotational Symmetry*	*Examples of Point Symmetry*
vertical; horizontal	72°, 72°, 72°, 72°, 72° — 72° rotation about its center	S N
diagonal; vertical, horizontal, and diagonal	120°, 120°, 120° — 120° rotation about its center	

EXERCISES

1. Which letter has horizontal line symmetry?
(1) A (2) F (3) N (4) B

2. Which letter has vertical line symmetry?
(1) A (2) B (3) C (4) D

3. Which letter has both horizontal and vertical line symmetry?
(1) A (2) X (3) T (4) M

4. Which letter has no line symmetry?
(1) C (2) E (3) F (4) K

5. Which letter has horizontal but not vertical line symmetry?
(1) X (2) O (3) V (4) E

6. Which letter has vertical but not horizontal line symmetry?
(1) H (2) W (3) N (4) D

7. Which kind of symmetry does the word TOOT have?
(1) only vertical line symmetry
(2) only horizontal line symmetry
(3) both vertical and horizontal line symmetry
(4) neither horizontal nor vertical line symmetry

8. Which word has horizontal line symmetry?
(1) MOM (2) EVE (3) BOB (4) DAD

9. Which does not have vertical line symmetry?
(1) HAH (2) MUM (3) BOB (4) WOW

10. Which word has horizontal line symmetry?
(1) ODD (3) COMPOSITE
(2) EVEN (4) PRIME

11. Which symbol has two lines of symmetry?
(1) ♣ (2) ♦ (3) ♥ (4) ♠

12. Which figure has both vertical and horizontal line symmetry?
(1) (2) (3) (4)

13. Which quadrilateral has no line symmetry?
(1) parallelogram (3) rhombus
(2) square (4) rectangle

14. What kind of line symmetry does this rhombus have?
(1) only vertical
(2) only horizontal
(3) both vertical and horizontal
(4) diagonal

15. What is the total number of lines of symmetry in any rectangle?
(1) 1 (2) 2 (3) 3 (4) 4

16. Which figure has line symmetry with respect to the line $x = 0$?
(1) (3)
(2) (4)

17. Which symbol has 90° rotational symmetry?
(1) □ (2) H (3) S (4) 8

18. Which figure has 60° rotational symmetry?
(1) square (3) regular octagon
(2) equilateral triangle (4) regular hexagon

19. Which letter has rotational symmetry?
(1) E (2) T (3) C (4) H

20. Which figure has 180° rotational symmetry?
(1) (2) (3) (4)

21. Which figure does not have rotational symmetry?
(1) trapezoid (3) equilateral triangle
(2) square (4) regular pentagon

22. Which graph has point symmetry?

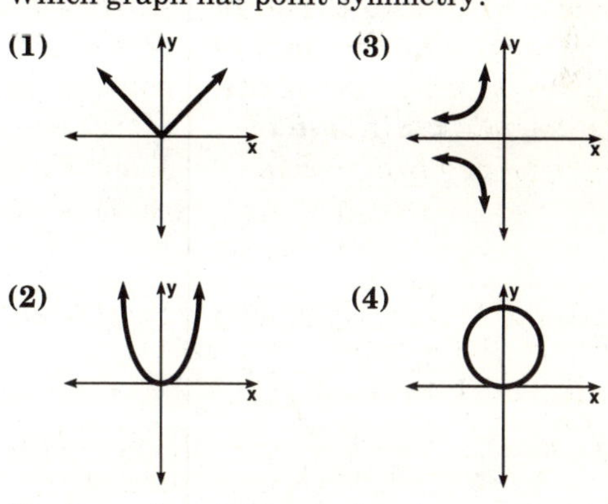

23. If a figure has 180° rotational symmetry, it must have
(1) point symmetry
(2) horizontal line symmetry, only
(3) vertical line symmetry, only
(4) horizontal and vertical line symmetry

24. Which figure has no point symmetry?
(1) square (3) rhombus
(2) regular hexagon (4) isosceles triangle

In 25–31, complete the statement by choosing one of the following answers:

(1) only point symmetry
(2) only line symmetry
(3) both point and line symmetry
(4) neither point nor line symmetry

25. A rectangle has _____.

26. An isosceles trapezoid has _____.

27. The letter H has _____.

28. An equilateral triangle has _____.

29. The letter T has _____.

30. The letter J has _____.

31. A rhombus has _____.

32. Which letter has only point symmetry?
(1) A **(2)** Z **(3)** O **(4)** B

33. Which letter has only line symmetry?
(1) O **(2)** N **(3)** C **(4)** R

34. Which letter has both point and line symmetry?
(1) O **(2)** L **(3)** T **(4)** W

35. In the figure, ℓ and m are symmetry lines for square $ABCD$. What is $r_\ell \circ r_m(\overline{AB})$?

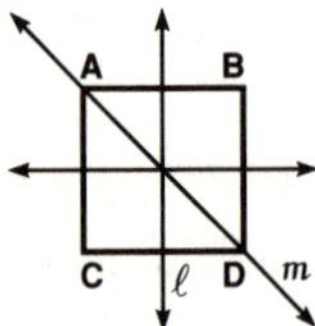

(1) $\overline{AB}$ **(3)** $\overline{CD}$
(2) $\overline{BC}$ **(4)** $\overline{DA}$

36. In the diagram, ℓ and m are symmetry lines for regular octagon $ABCDEFGH$. What is $r_\ell \circ r_m(F)$?

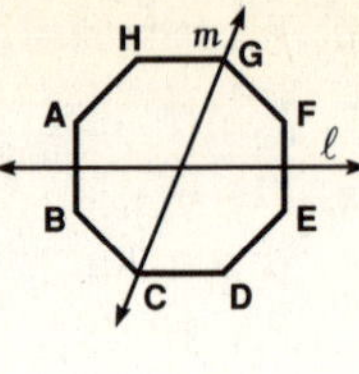

(1) A **(3)** C
(2) B **(4)** D

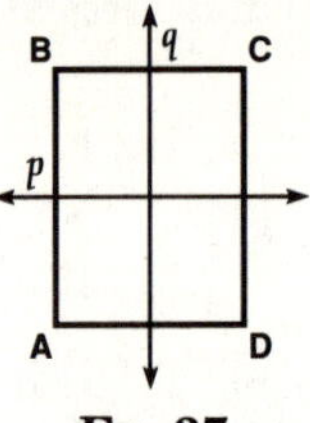

Ex. 37

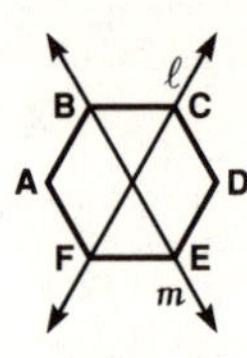

Ex. 38

37. In the diagram, p and q are symmetry lines for rectangle $ABCD$. Find $r_p \circ r_q \circ r_p(A)$.

38. In the figure, ℓ and m are symmetry lines for regular hexagon $ABCDEF$. Find $r_\ell \circ r_m \circ r_\ell(D)$.

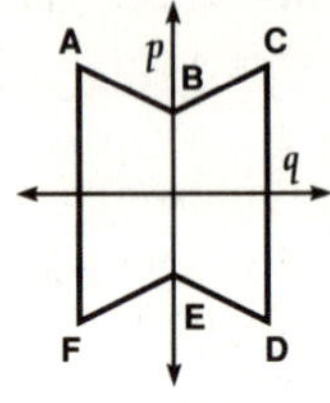

Ex. 39

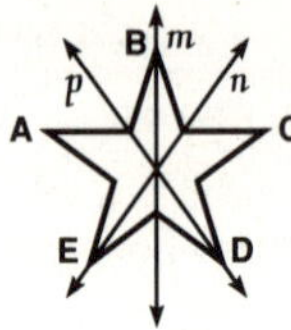

Ex. 40

39. In the figure, p and q are symmetry lines for the figure $ABCDEF$. Find $r_q \circ r_p \circ r_q(A)$.

40. In the figure, p, m, and n are symmetry lines. Find $r_p \circ r_m \circ r_n(A)$.

3.5 SUMMARY EXERCISES

1. If $M(-2, 8)$ is reflected in the y-axis, what are the coordinates of M', the image of M?

2. The coordinates of the image of $P(2, -3)$ under a reflection in the x-axis are
(1) (2, –3) **(2)** (–2, –3) **(3)** (2, 3) **(4)** (–2, 3)

3. What are the coordinates of the image of point $A(-2, -5)$ after a reflection over the line $y = -1$?

4. When point $A(-2, 5)$ is reflected in the line $x = 1$, the image is
(1) (5, 2) **(2)** (–2, –3) **(3)** (4, 5) **(4)** (0, 5)

5. If $B(-2, 5)$ is reflected over the line $y = x$, what are the coordinates of the image of B?

6. If $P(-3, 2)$ is reflected in the line $y = -x$, what are the coordinates of P', the image of P?

7. What are the coordinates of the image of point $M(3, -1)$ after a reflection in the origin?
(1) (–3, 1) **(2)** (–1, 3) **(3)** (1, –3) **(4)** (–3, –1)

8. If the letter L is rotated 90° clockwise, which is the resulting figure?
(1) ¬ **(2)** ⌐ **(3)** ⌋ **(4)** ⌉

9. What is the image of (5, 1) under a counterclockwise rotation of 90°?

10. Find the image of (3, –1) under: $R_{O, -90°}$

11. Find the image of the point (–3, 5) under the rotation $R_{180°}$.

12. **a.** Graph and label $\triangle ABC$ that has coordinates $A(3, 1)$, $B(4, 3)$, and $C(6, 1)$.
b. Reflect $\triangle ABC$ over the line $y = x$. What are the coordinates of $\triangle A'B'C'$, the image of $\triangle ABC$?
c. Using the origin as the center of rotation, rotate $\triangle A'B'C'$ 90° counterclockwise. What are the coordinates of $A''B''C''$, the image of $\triangle A'B'C'$?
d. Reflect $\triangle A''B''C''$ through the origin. What are the coordinates of $\triangle A'''B'''C'''$, the image of $\triangle A''B''C''$?

13. What is the image of the point (5, –2) under the translation $T_{2,1}$?

14. A translation maps the origin to point (4, 3). What is the image of the point (–1, 2) under the same translation?

15. *Given*: $\triangle ABC$ with $A(2, 1)$, $B(6, 4)$, and $C(8, 1)$. Graph and state the coordinates of:
   a. (1) $\triangle A'B'C'$, the reflection of $\triangle ABC$ through the x-axis.
   (2) $\triangle A''B''C''$, the image of $\triangle A'B'C'$ after the translation $T_{-6,-2}$.
   b. Using the origin as the center of rotation, graph and state the coordinates of $\triangle A'''B'''C'''$, the result of rotating $\triangle A''B''C''$ 90° clockwise.

16. Find the coordinates of the image of A (4, 2) under the dilation D_2.

17. Find the coordinates of the image of $P(-6, -4)$ under D_{-2}.

18. P' is the image of P under a dilation, and Q' is the image of Q. Find the value of the constant of dilation if $PQ = 12$ mm and $P'Q' = 42$ mm.

19. Given points $A(3, 0)$ and $B(-4, 6)$, write the coordinates of the images of points A and B under
   a. a reflection in the line $y = x$
   b. a rotation of 90° counterclockwise about the origin
   c. a reflection in the line $x = 2$
   d. a reflection through the origin
   e. a dilation $D_{\frac{1}{2}}$

20. The mapping that moves every point in the plane under the rule $(x, y) \to (x - 2, y + 1)$ is
   (1) a reflection (3) a translation
   (2) a dilation (4) a rotation

21. The transformation $(x, y) \to (3x, 3y)$ represents a
   (1) reflection (3) dilation
   (2) rotation (4) translation

22. $\triangle ABC$ has coordinates $A(2, 1)$, $B(2, 4)$, and $C(4, 2)$. Given the following transformations:
$$T = (x, y) \to (-x, -y)$$
$$U = (x, y) \to (x + 4, y - 6)$$
$$F = (x, y) \to (3x, 2y)$$
   a. Graph and state the coordinates of
   (1) $\triangle A'B'C'$, the image of $\triangle ABC$ after the transformation T.
   (2) $\triangle A''B''C''$, the image of $\triangle ABC$ after the transformation U.
   (3) $\triangle A'''B'''C'''$, the image of $\triangle ABC$ after the transformation F.
   b. Which transformation, T, U, or F, is a translation?

23. Find the coordinates of $r_{y\text{-axis}} \circ r_{x\text{-axis}} (A)$ where A is (–4, 2).

24. Find the coordinates of A', the image of the point A (2, –3) under the transformation $r_{y=2} \circ r_{y\text{-axis}}$.

25. If Q is (–4, 2), what is $r_{x\text{-axis}} \circ D_2(Q)$?

26. Find the coordinates of B', the image of B (6, –1) under the composition: $r_{x\text{-axis}} \circ R_{O,180°}$

27. When the lines of reflection are parallel, the composition of two line reflections is equivalent to
   (1) a translation (3) a line reflection
   (2) a rotation (4) a glide reflection

28. Which of the following statements is false?
   (1) The composition of two rotations about the same center is also a rotation.
   (2) The composition of two translations is also a translation.
   (3) A glide reflection is the composition of a line reflection and a translation.
   (4) When the lines of reflection intersect, the composition of two line reflections is equivalent to a translation.

29. Which transformation is equivalent to the composite line reflections $r_{x\text{-axis}} \circ r_{y\text{-axis}} (A)$?
   (1) a 90° rotation (3) a line reflection
   (2) a 180° rotation (4) a glide reflection

30. Write a single transformation that is equivalent to the composite transformation: $T_{2,1} \circ T_{-3,2}$

31. Figure B is the image of figure A under which single transformation?
   (1) line reflection
   (2) translation
   (3) rotation
   (4) glide reflection

A B

32. Which transformation is not an example of an isometry?
   (1) line reflection (3) translation
   (2) rotation (4) dilation

33. A dilation is a transformation that does not preserve
   (1) distance (3) orientation
   (2) similarity (4) betweenness

34. Which property is not preserved under a line reflection?
   (1) collinearity (3) perpendicularity
   (2) distance (4) orientation

35. $\triangle ABC$ has coordinates $A(1, 1)$, $B(5, 1)$, and $C(4, 3)$. Given the transformations T, U, and W:

$$T = (x, y) \rightarrow (x, -y)$$
$$U = (x, y) \rightarrow (x - 6, y + 6)$$
$$W = (x, y) \rightarrow (-2x, -2y)$$

Graph and state the coordinates of:

a. **(1)** $\triangle A'B'C'$, the image of $\triangle ABC$ after transformation T.
(2) $\triangle A''B''C''$, the image of $\triangle ABC$ after transformation U.
(3) $\triangle A'''B'''C'''$, the image of $\triangle ABC$ after transformation W.

b. Which transformation, T, U, or W, is not an isometry?

c. Which transformation, T, U, or W, does not preserve orientation?

36. Which graph has symmetry with respect to the line $y = x$?

(1) 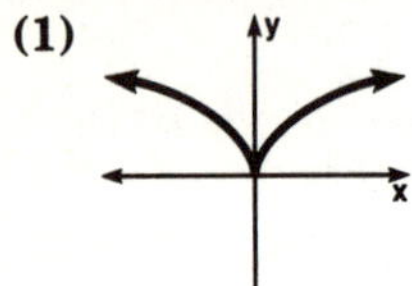

(3) 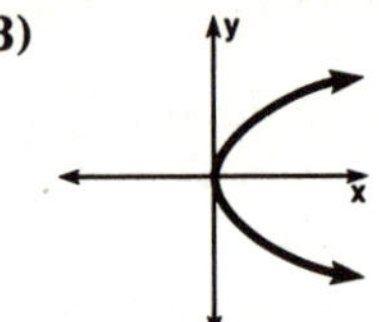

(2) 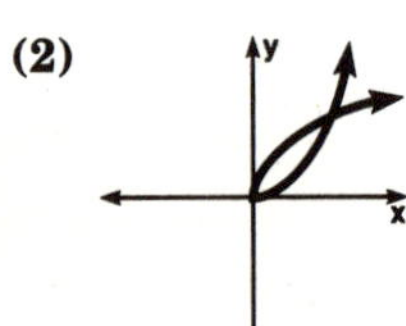

(4) 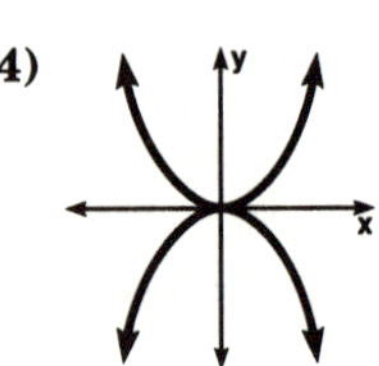

37. Which geometric abbreviation has vertical line symmetry?
(1) SSS (2) SAS (3) AAA (4) ASA

38. Which word has horizontal line symmetry?
(1) ROB (2) BOB (3) ORB (4) BAR

39. Which figure has both vertical and horizontal line symmetry?

(1) (3)

(2) (4)

40. Which graph has point symmetry?

(1) 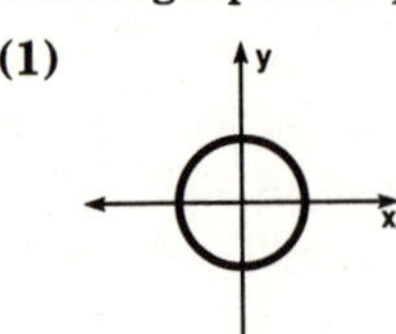

(3) 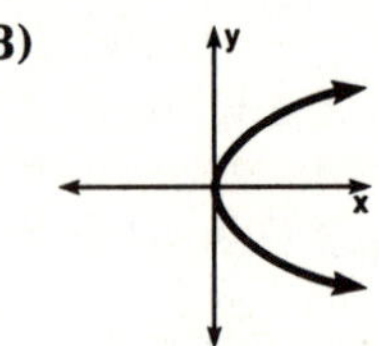

(2) 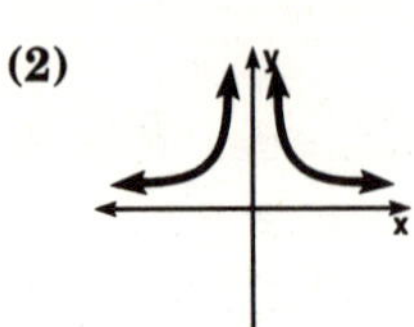

(4) 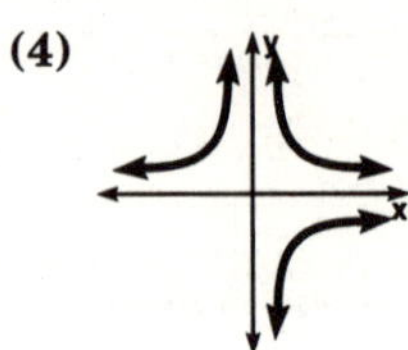

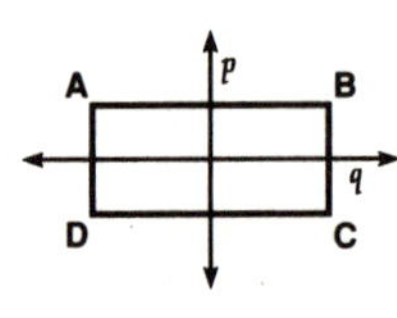

Ex. 41

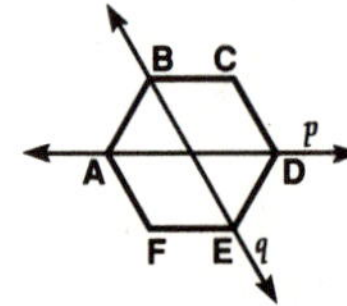

Ex. 42

41. In the figure, p and q are symmetry lines for rectangle $ABCD$. Find $r_p \circ r_p \circ r_q(A)$.

42. In the figure, p and q are symmetry lines for regular hexagon $ABCDEF$. Find $r_q \circ r_p \circ r_q(D)$.

CHAPTER 4

Relations and Functions

4.1 BASIC CONCEPTS

Domain and Range

A RELATION is a set of ordered pairs.

The DOMAIN of a relation is the set of all first components of the ordered pairs.

The RANGE of a relation is the set of all second components of the ordered pairs.

If the domain is not specified, assume the largest subset of the real numbers for which the range consists only of real numbers.

Remember: no negative radicand under square root; no denominator of 0 in fraction.

How to Specify a Relation

(1) *By listing the ordered pairs*

Examples:

1. $\{(1, 2), (3, 4), (5, 6), (7, 8), \ldots\}$
   Domain = $\{1, 3, 5, 7, \ldots\}$
   Range = $\{2, 4, 6, 8, \ldots\}$
2. | Student | Score |
   |---|---|
   | Mary | 87 |
   | Joe | 94 |
   | Peter | 82 |

   Domain = {Mary, Joe, Peter}
   Range = {87, 94, 82}

(2) *By specifying a rule*

Examples:

1. $R = \{(x, y) | y = \sqrt{x - 1}\}$
   Domain = {reals ≥ 1}
   Range = {nonnegative reals}
2. $y = 4x - 5$
   Domain = {reals}
   Range = {reals}

(3) *By specifying a mapping*

Examples:

1. $x \longrightarrow x^2$ Each element x corresponds to an element x^2. For the relation, the set of ordered pairs is $\{(x, x^2)\}$.

2. 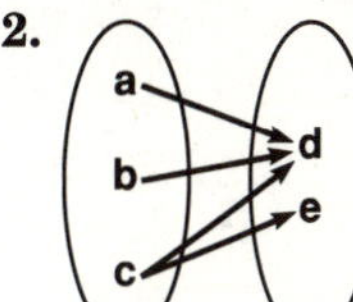

The mapping indicates that for the relation, the set of ordered pairs is:
$\{(a, d), (b, d), (c, d), (c, e)\}$

The Difference Between a Relation and a Function

A FUNCTION is a relation in which each element of the domain corresponds to *exactly one* element of the range. That is, no two ordered pairs have the same first element.

Examples:

1. $y = x^3$ is a function
   For each x, there is exactly one y:
   say $x = 2$, then $y = 8$
2. $|y| = x$ is not a function
   For each x (except $x = 0$), there is more than one y:
   say $x = 2$, then $y = 2$ or -2

Determining Graphically If a Relation Is a Function

VERTICAL-LINE TEST: **When any vertical line intersects a graph that does represent a function, the vertical line intersects the graph in *exactly one* point. If there is more than one point, the graph represents a relation that is not a function.**

Examples:

1. $y = x^2 - 4x + 3$

Vertical lines will intersect this parabola in exactly one point. Thus, the relation is a function.

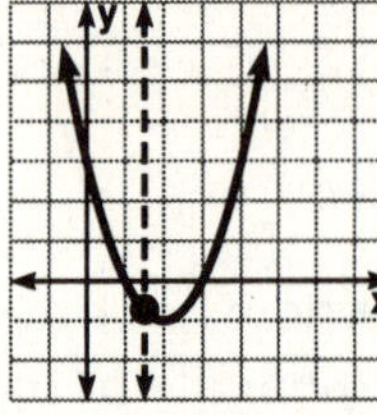

2. $y = \pm\sqrt{9 - x^2}$

Except at the x-intercepts, vertical lines will intersect this circle in more than one point. Thus, the relation is not a function.

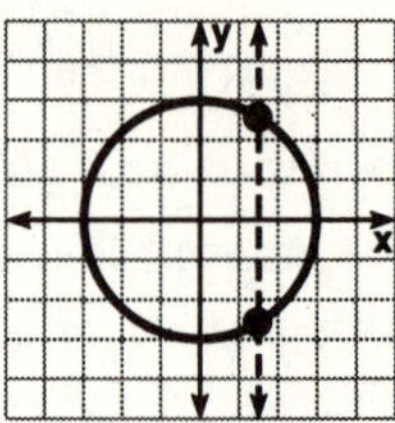

EXERCISES

1. For which value of x is $y = \dfrac{2x^2 + 3x + 1}{x - 1}$ undefined?

2. For which value of x is $y = \dfrac{x^2 - 2x + 1}{3x - 1}$ undefined?

3. For what values of x will the function $y = \sqrt{x - 4}$ be real?

(1) $\{x | x < 0\}$ **(3)** $\{x | x \leq 4\}$
(2) $\{x | x > 0\}$ **(4)** $\{x | x \geq 4\}$

4. The domain of the relation $y = \dfrac{4}{\sqrt{x - 1}}$ is the set

(1) $\{x | x > 1\}$ **(3)** $\{x | x < 1\}$
(2) $\{x | x \geq 1\}$ **(4)** $\{x | x > 2\}$

5. What is the domain of the function $y = \sqrt{x - 2}$?

(1) $\{x | x \geq 0\}$ **(3)** $\{x | x \leq 2\}$
(2) $\{x | x \geq 2\}$ **(4)** $\{x | x \geq -2\}$

6. The domain of the function $y = \dfrac{x}{\sqrt{x - 1}}$ is

(1) $\{x | x \neq 1\}$ **(3)** $\{x | x < 1\}$
(2) $\{x | x \geq 1\}$ **(4)** $\{x | x > 1\}$

7. Which is the range of the relation $y = 2x^2 + 3x$ if the domain is the set $\{-2, -1, 0\}$?

(1) $\{2, 1, 0\}$ **(3)** $\{-1, -5, 0\}$
(2) $\{2, -1, 0\}$ **(4)** $\{10, 1, 0\}$

8. What is the range of the function $y = \sqrt{x - 1}$ where $x \geq 1$?

(1) $y \geq 1$ **(3)** $y \leq 0$
(2) $y \geq 0$ **(4)** all real numbers

9. A function is defined by the equation $y = 8x - 3$. If the domain is $2 \leq x \leq 4$, find the minimum value in the range of the function.

10. The domain for $y = 3x + 2$ is $-3 \leq x \leq 2$. The greatest value in the range is

(1) -7 **(3)** 8
(2) 2 **(4)** 11

11. The domain for $y = x^2 - 1$ is $-3 \leq x \leq 3$. The smallest value in the range is

(1) -1 **(3)** -3
(2) -2 **(4)** 0

12. List the ordered pairs in the relation specified by the mapping.

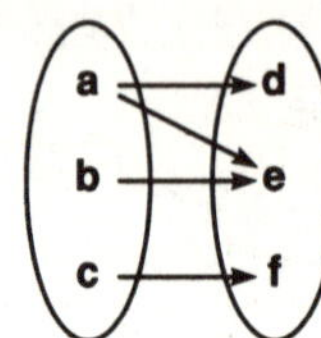

13. The relation defined by the set of ordered pairs $\{(0, 2), (-2, 2), (1, 4), (4, 1), (0, -1)\}$ is not a function. Which of the ordered pairs listed below, if omitted from this relation, will make the resulting set a function?

(1) $(-2, 2)$ **(2)** $(1, 4)$ **(3)** $(4, 1)$ **(4)** $(0, -1)$

14. Given the relation $R = \{(-2, 3), (a, 4), (1, 9), (0, 7)\}$. Which replacement for a makes this relation a function?

(1) 1 **(2)** -2 **(3)** 0 **(4)** 4

15. Which of the following mappings defines a relation that is not a function?

(1)

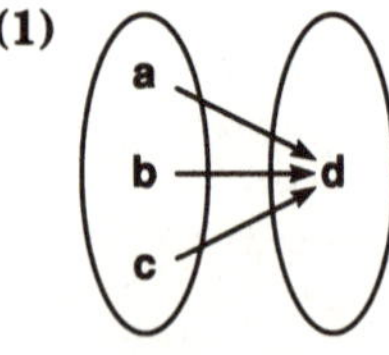

(3)

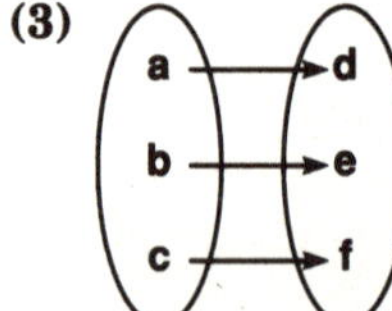

(2)

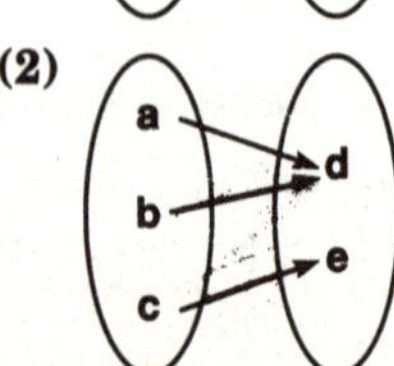

(4)

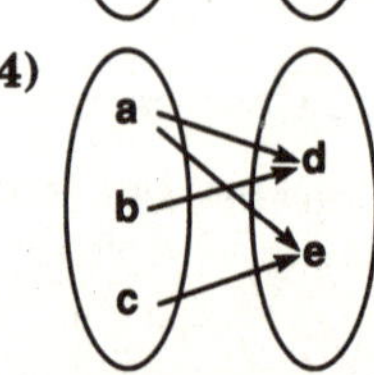

16. Which of the following is not a function?

(1) $3x + 2y = 7$ **(3)** $y = 2x^2 + 3$
(2) $y = 4$ **(4)** $x = 4$

17. Which equation defines a relation that is not a function?

(1) $y = 2x + 3$ (3) $x^2 + y^2 = 25$
(2) $y = x^2$ (4) $y = 3$

18. Which graph represents a function?

(1)
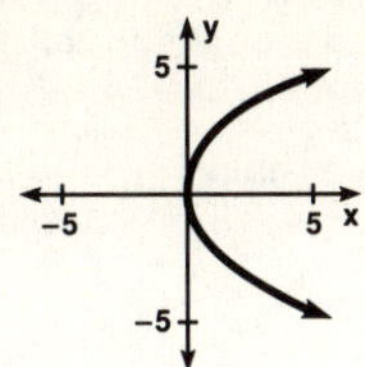

(3)
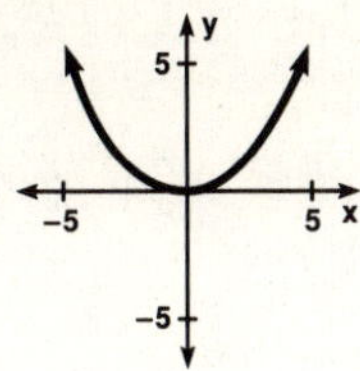

(2)
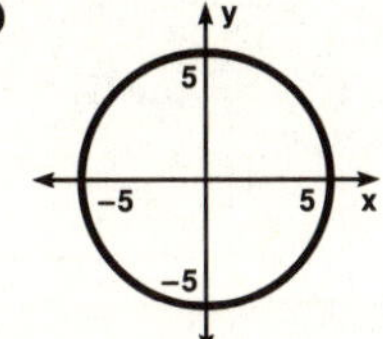

(4)
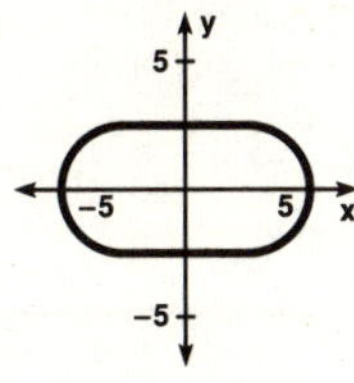

19. Which graph represents a function?

(1)
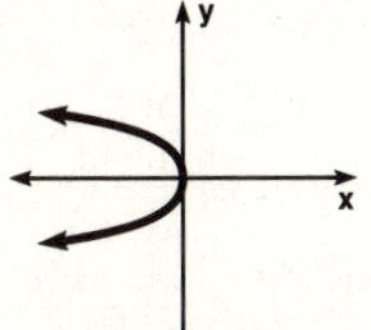

(2)
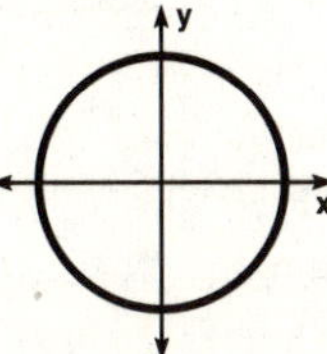

(3)
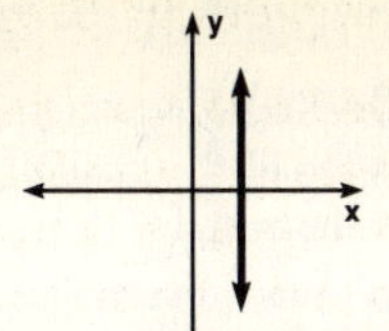

(4)
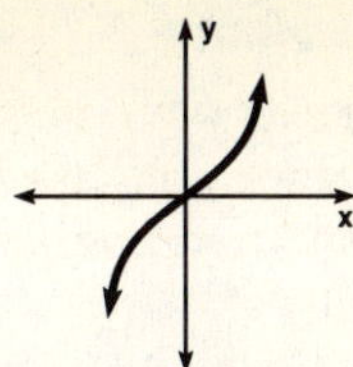

20. Which graph does not represent a function?

(1)
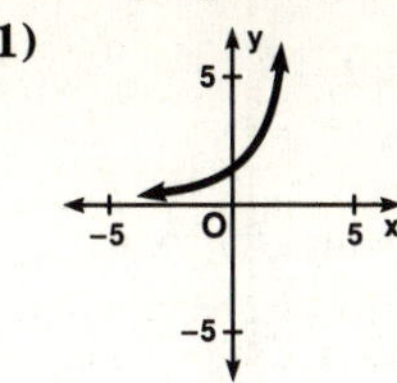

(3)
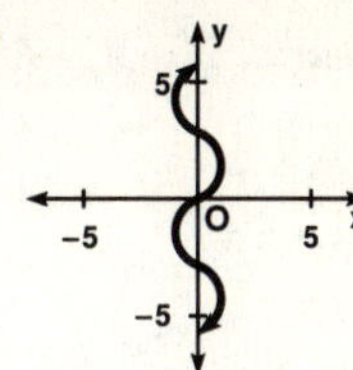

(2)
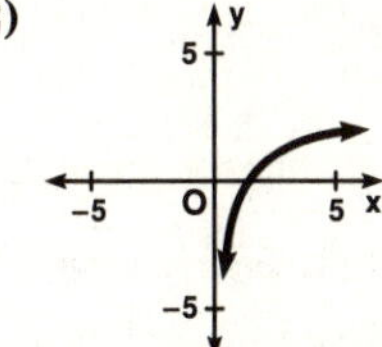

(4)
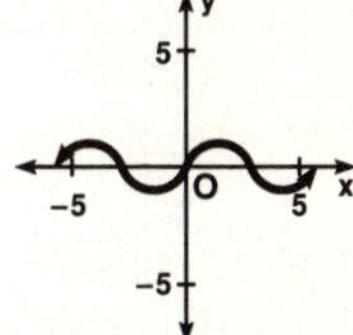

4.2 FUNCTION NOTATION

Expressing a Rule

The rule for a function f is written with the symbol $f(x)$, read "f of x," where x is the variable of the domain. Two different function rules for the same variable are distinguished by using different function letters, say f and g.

Examples:

Rule	Function Notation
$y = x + 2$	$f(x) = x + 2$
$y = x - 4$	$g(x) = x - 4$
$A = s^2$	$A(s) = s^2$

Evaluating a Rule

Determine the element of the range that corresponds to a given element of the domain by evaluating the function rule at the indicated value.

Examples:

If $f(x) = x^0 + x^{-1}$ where $x \neq 0$

then $f(3) = 3^0 + 3^{-1} = 1 + \frac{1}{3} = \frac{4}{3}$

and $f(6) = 6^0 + 6^{-1} = 1 + \frac{1}{6} = \frac{7}{6}$

and $f(a) = a^0 + a^{-1} = 1 + \frac{1}{a} = \frac{a+1}{a}$

Composition of Functions

For two functions f and g, the COMPOSITE $[f \circ g]$ means that the function f "follows" the function g. That is, the second function f is applied to the result of the first function g.

Example

If $f(x) = x^2$ and $g(x) = x + 1$, find:

a. $[f \circ g](3)$ **b.** $[f \circ g](x)$ **c.** $[g \circ f](3)$ **d.** $[g \circ f](x)$

Solution: The first function is the one at the right of the notation. In $f \circ g$, the first function is g. In $g \circ f$, the first function is f.

a. $[f \circ g](3)$

$g(x) = x + 1$	The first function.
$g(3) = 3 + 1 = 4$	Evaluate at the given value of the variable.
$f(x) = x^2$ $f(4) = 4^2 = 16$	In the second function, substitute for the variable the value found for the first function.

Answer: $[f \circ g](3) = 16$

b. $[f \circ g](x)$

$g(x) = x + 1$	The first function.
$f(x) = x^2$ $f(x + 1) = (x + 1)^2$	In the second function, substitute for the variable the rule for the first function.

Answer: $[f \circ g](x) = (x + 1)^2$

c. $[g \circ f](3)$

$f(x) = x^2$	The first function.
$f(3) = 3^2 = 9$	Evaluate at the given value of the variable.
$g(x) = x + 1$ $g(9) = 9 + 1 = 10$	In the second function, substitute for the variable the value found for the first function.

Answer: $[g \circ f](3) = 10$ Note that $[f \circ g](3) \neq [g \circ f](3)$.

d. $[g \circ f](x)$

$f(x) = x^2$	The first function.
$g(x) = x + 1$ $g(x^2) = x^2 + 1$	In the second function, substitute for the variable the rule for the first function.

Answer: $[g \circ f](x) = x^2 + 1$

Since $[f \circ g](x) \neq [g \circ f](x)$, composition is not a commutative operation.

An alternate notation for $[f \circ g](x)$ is $f(g(x))$, read "f of g of x." The method of evaluation is the same.

EXERCISES

1. If the function g is defined by $g(x) = 2x - 4$, find the value of $g(-6)$.

2. If $f(x) = x^3 - 2x$, find $f(-2)$.

3. If $f(x) = (x + 1)^2$, what is the value of $f(-2)$?

4. If $f(x) = |x^3 - 3|$, then $f(-1)$ is equivalent to
(1) 0 (2) 2 (3) −2 (4) 4

5. If a function p is defined by $p(x) = \frac{2x^2 - x^0}{7}$, find the value of $p(-2)$.

6. If $f(x) = 4x^{-2} - 2x^0$, find the value of $f(2)$.

7. If $f(x) = (3x)^{-2}$, find $f(2)$.

8. If $f(x) = x^{\frac{3}{4}}$, find $f(16)$.

9. If $f(x) = x^{-\frac{3}{2}}$, find $f(4)$.

10. If $f(x) = 8^x$, find the value of $f\left(\frac{2}{3}\right)$.

11. If $f(x) = x^0 + x^{\frac{2}{3}}$, compute $f(8)$.

12. If $f(x) = \sqrt{x^2 - 9}$, then $f(4)$ is
(1) imaginary (3) real and irrational
(2) real and rational (4) undefined

13. If $h(x) = x^2$ and $i = \sqrt{-1}$, then $h(2i)$ equals
(1) $4i$ (2) −4 (3) $-4i$ (4) 4

14. If $f(x) = x^2 + 2$, what is the value of $f(3i)$?
(1) 11 (2) 8 (3) −7 (4) −4

15. If $f(x) = x^2$, then $f(2 - 3i)$ equals
(1) −5 (3) $13 - 12i$
(2) $-5 - 12i$ (4) 13

16. If $f(x) = kx^2$ and $f(2) = 12$, then k equals
(1) 1 (2) 2 (3) 3 (4) 4

17. If $f(x) = \frac{x-2}{x+1}$, then $f(n + 1)$ is equal to
(1) $-\frac{1}{2}$ (2) $\frac{n+1}{n-2}$ (3) $\frac{n-1}{n+2}$ (4) $\frac{n-2}{n+1}$

18. If $f(x) = x^2 + 3x$ and $g(x) = x + 3$, for what positive value of x does $f(x) = g(x)$?

19. If $f(x) = 6x$ and $g(x) = x - 3$, what is $[f \circ g](-3)$?
(1) −21 (2) −36 (3) 0 (4) 36

20. If $f(x) = 3x$ and $g(x) = 7x - 1$, what is $[f \circ g](4)$?

21. If $f(x) = 4 + x$ and $g(x) = 3x$, find $f(g(5))$.

22. If $f(x) = x^2 + 1$ and $g(x) = x + 1$, what is $[f \circ g](x)$?
(1) $(x + 1)^2 + 1$ (3) $(x^2 + 1)^2 + 1$
(2) $(x^2 + 1) + 1$ (4) $(x^2 + 1 + 1)^2$

23. If $f(x) = 4 + x$ and $g(x) = 2x$, find $[g \circ f](3)$.

24. If $f(x) = (x + 1)^2$ and $g(x) = x + 1$, find $g(f(-2))$.

25. If $f(x) = \frac{1}{x}$ and $g(x) = 2x$, what is $[g \circ f](x)$?
(1) $\frac{1}{2x}$ (2) $\frac{2}{x}$ (3) $\frac{x}{2}$ (4) $2x$

26. For which pair of functions does $[f \circ g](x) = [g \circ f](x)$?
(1) $f(x) = 2 + x$ $g(x) = 2x$
(2) $f(x) = 2x$ $g(x) = \frac{1}{2}x$
(3) $f(x) = x^2$ $g(x) = x + 1$
(4) $f(x) = \frac{1}{x}$ $g(x) = x + 1$

The General Equation $ax^2 + by^2 = c$

Depending on the values of the coefficients, the general equation $ax^2 + by^2 = c$, where $a, b, c \neq 0$, describes the graph of a *circle*, *ellipse*, or *hyperbola*.

Values of Coefficients	Name of Graph	Example
$a = b$ and have the same sign as c	*circle*	$2x^2 + 2y^2 = 18$ or $x^2 + y^2 = 9$ circle with center at origin and radius = 3
$a \neq b$ and have the same sign as c	*ellipse*	$9x^2 + 25y^2 = 225$ ellipse with center at origin and x-intercepts = ± 5 y-intercepts = ± 3
a, b have different signs	*hyperbola*	$x^2 - y^2 = 9$ hyperbola with center at origin and x-intercepts = ± 3 no y-intercepts

Recall: **The equation of a parabola contains only one square term: either $y = ax^2 + bx + c$ or $x = ay^2 + by + c$**
The equation of a straight line contains no square terms: $ax + by = c$

EXERCISES

In 1-14, identify the graph of the given relation as

(1) a circle
(3) a hyperbola
(2) an ellipse
(4) a parabola

1. $4y^2 = 25 - 4x^2$

2. $2x^2 + 3y^2 = 24$

3. $x^2 = y^2 + 9$

4. $x^2 = 6 - y$

5. $4x^2 - 100 = 25y^2$

6. $3y^2 = 6 - x^2$

7. $3x^2 + 2y^2 = 6$

8. $4x^2 + 16y^2 = 25$

9. $x^2 + y = 9$

10. $2x^2 = 5 - 2y^2$

11. $y^2 = 6 - 3x^2$

12. $2x^2 - 9 = 2y^2$

13. $4x^2 - 4y^2 = 9$

14. $x^2 - \frac{y^2}{16} = 1$

15. Which of the following is the equation of a hyperbola?
(1) $x^2 = 10 - y^2$
(2) $x = y^2 - 9$
(3) $y^2 = x^2 - 1$
(4) $4x^2 + y^2 = 9$

16. The graph of which equation is an ellipse?
(1) $3x^2 - 4y^2 = 7$
(2) $\frac{y+6}{x-1} = 3$
(3) $y = 2x^2 + 3x - 5$
(4) $x^2 + 5y^2 = 2$

17. Which is an equation of a circle?
(1) $2x^2 - 2y^2 = 18$
(2) $2x^2 + 3y^2 = 36$
(3) $3x^2 + 3y^2 = 21$
(4) $x^2 = y^2 + 16$

18. Which equation has a hyperbola as its graph?
(1) $x^2 = 10 + y$
(2) $x^2 = 10 - y^2$
(3) $3x^2 = 10 - 2y^2$
(4) $3x^2 = 10 + 2y^2$

19. Which equation has an ellipse as its graph?
(1) $2x^2 = 8 - 3y$
(2) $2x^2 = 8 + 3y^2$
(3) $2x^2 = 8 - 3y^2$
(4) $2x = 8 - 3y$

20. Which is an equation of a circle?
(1) $2x^2 + y^2 = 7$
(2) $x = \frac{y}{8}$
(3) $x^2 - y^2 = 10$
(4) $5(x^2 + y^2) = 12$

21. Which is an equation of a parabola?

(1) $x^2 = 3 + y^2$ (3) $x = 3 + y$
(2) $x = 3 + y^2$ (4) $y^2 = 3x^2 + 3$

22. The graph of the relation $ay = bx^2 + c$ in which neither a nor b is 0 is

(1) a parabola (3) an ellipse
(2) a straight line (4) a hyperbola

23. If a, b, and c are positive unequal numbers, the graph of $ax^2 + by^2 = c$ is

(1) a circle (3) an ellipse
(2) a parabola (4) a hyperbola

24. The graph of $ax^2 + by^2 = c$, in which a, b, and c are real numbers, is an ellipse if

(1) $a = b, a > 0, b < 0, c > 0$
(2) $a = b, a > 0, b > 0, c < 0$
(3) $a \neq b, a > 0, b > 0, c > 0$
(4) $a \neq b, a > 0, b < 0, c > 0$

25. If $a \neq 0$, $b \neq 0$, and $c \neq 0$, the graph of $ax^2 + by^2 = c$ can not be

(1) an ellipse (3) a parabola
(2) a circle (4) a hyperbola

26. The graph of the equation $\frac{x^2}{4} + \frac{y^2}{16} = 1$ passes through the point whose coordinates are

(1) (0, 0) (2) (0, 2) (3) (0, 4) (4) (4, 0)

27. Which relation is a function?

(1) $\{(x, y) | x^2 + y = 4\}$ (3) $\{(x, y) | x^2 - y^2 = 4\}$
(2) $\{(x, y) | x^2 + y^2 = 4\}$ (4) $\{(x, y) | x^2 + 4y^2 = 4\}$

28. If the replacement set is the set of real numbers, what is the domain of the relation represented by $\{(x, y) | x^2 + 4y^2 = 16\}$?

(1) $\{y | -2 \leq y \leq 2\}$ (3) $\{x | -4 \leq x \leq 4\}$
(2) $\{y | -2 < y < 2\}$ (4) $\{x | -4 < x < 4\}$

29. Which is the graph of a quadratic relation for which the domain consists of all the real numbers?

(1)
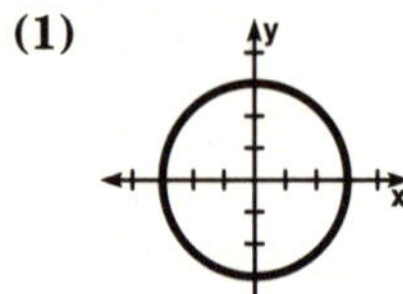

(3)
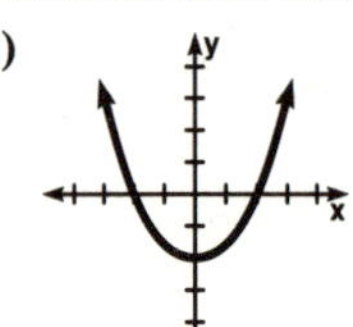

(2)
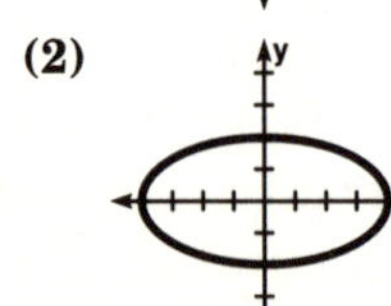

(4)
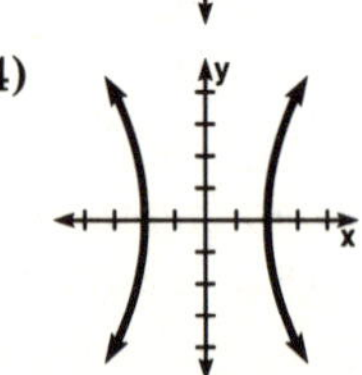

30. If the graphs of the equations $x^2 + y^2 = 9$ and $y = 3$ are drawn on the same set of axes, what is the total number of points common to both graphs?

(1) 1 (2) 2 (3) 3 (4) 0

31. When drawn on the same set of axes, the points of intersection of the graphs of $x^2 + y^2 = 16$ and $x = 2$ are located in quadrants

(1) I and III (3) II and III
(2) I and IV (4) II and IV

32. The graphs of the equations $x^2 + y^2 = 25$ and $y = x^2$ are drawn on the same set of axes. The total number of points common to these graphs is

(1) 1 (2) 2 (3) 3 (4) 4

33. The graph of $x^2 + y^2 = 25$ and the graph of $x - 4 = 0$ are drawn on the same set of axes. A point of intersection of the graphs is

(1) (5, 0) (2) (−4, −3) (3) (4, −3) (4) (−3, 4)

34. What is the graph of the solution set of $x^2 + y^2 > 9$?

(1)
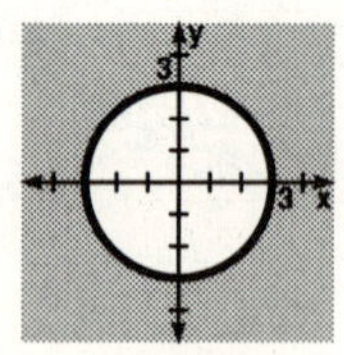

(3)
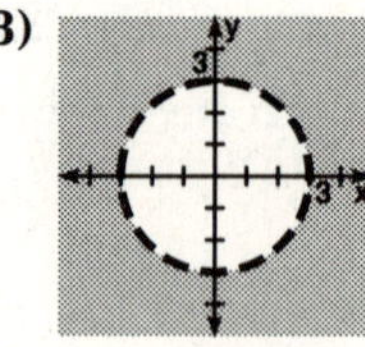

(2)
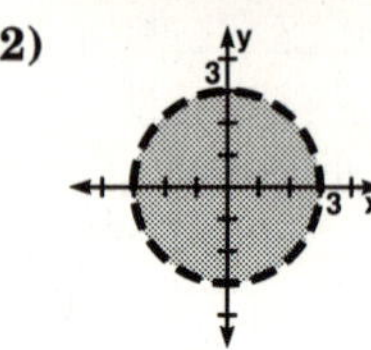

(4)
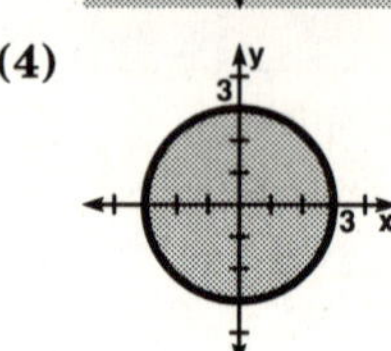

35. Each equation in column A has one of the geometric figures in column B as its graph. List the numbers 1-5 on your answer paper and after each number write the letter that indicates the corresponding graph.

Column A	Column B
(1) $x^2 + y^2 - 4 = 0$	**a.** The point (0, 0)
(2) $4x^2 + y^2 - 1 = 0$	**b.** Two straight lines parallel to the y-axis
(3) $x^2 - y - 4 = 0$	**c.** Two straight lines intersecting at the origin
(4) $x^2 + 4y^2 = 0$	**d.** A parabola that crosses the y-axis at (0, −4)
(5) $x^2 - 4y^2 = 0$	**e.** A circle whose center is the origin and whose radius is 2
	f. An ellipse that crosses the y-axis at (0, 1) and (0, −1)
	g. A hyperbola that crosses the y-axis at (0, 2) and (0, −2)

Direct Variation

Two quantities VARY DIRECTLY if their *ratio* is constant.

$$\frac{y}{x} = k \text{ or } y = kx$$

y varies directly as x,
with k the CONSTANT OF VARIATION

When $y = kx$:
as x increases, y increases by the same factor
as x decreases, y decreases by the same factor

Example: $y = 5x$

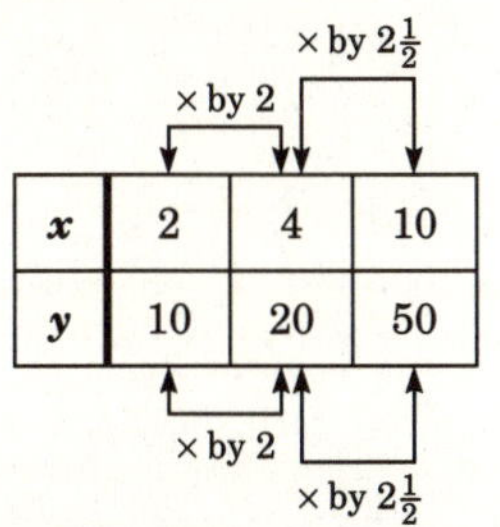

x	2	4	10
y	10	20	50

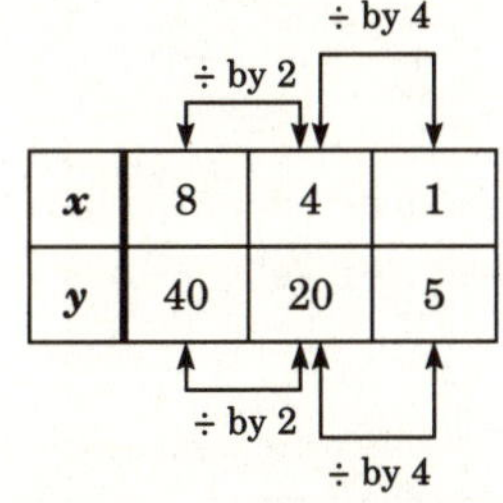

x	8	4	1
y	40	20	5

The graph of the direct variation $y = kx$ is a straight line.

The line passes through the origin and has slope k.

If $k > 0$, the line is in Quadrants I and III.

If $k < 0$, the line is in Quadrants II and IV.

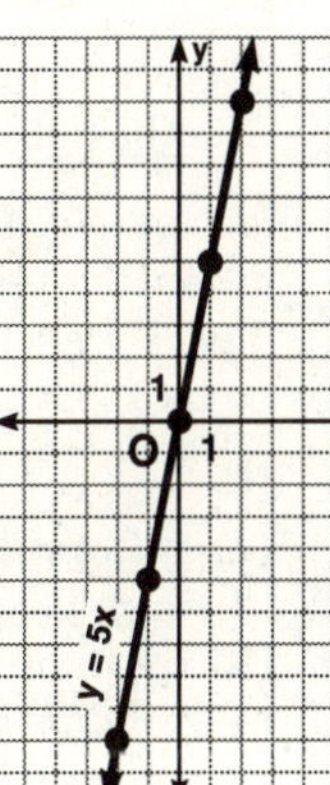

Examples

1. s varies directly as r.
If $s = 18$ when $r = 3$, find s when $r = -2$.

Solution: In direct variation, there is a constant *ratio*.

$$\frac{s_1}{r_1} = \frac{s_2}{r_2}$$
$$\frac{18}{3} = \frac{s}{-2}$$
$$3s = -36$$
$$s = -12$$

Answer: $s = -12$ when $r = -2$

Alternate Solution: First find the constant of variation from the known pair of values.

$$\frac{s}{r} = \frac{18}{3} = 6 = k$$

Write the rule of the variation. $s = 6r$
Substitute to find the unknown element of the second pair. $s = 6(-2)$
$s = -12$

2. y varies directly as the square of x.
If $y = 18$ when $x = 3$, find x when $y = 98$.

Solution:

$$\frac{y_1}{(x_1)^2} = \frac{y_2}{(x_2)^2}$$
$$\frac{18}{3^2} = \frac{98}{x^2}$$
$$18x^2 = 9 \cdot 98$$
$$x^2 = \frac{\overset{1}{\cancel{9}} \cdot \overset{49}{\cancel{98}}}{\underset{\underset{1}{\cancel{2}}}{\cancel{18}}}$$
$$x^2 = 49$$
$$x = \pm 7 \quad \textit{Ans.}$$

Note: The constant of variation is $\frac{18}{3^2}$, or 2. The rule is $y = 2x^2$, whose graph is a parabola.

Inverse Variation

Two quantities VARY INVERSELY if their *product* is constant.

$$xy = k \quad \text{or} \quad y = \frac{k}{x}$$

y varies inversely as x,
with k the constant of variation

When $xy = k$:
as x increases, y decreases by the same factor
as x decreases, y increases by the same factor

Example: $xy = 12$

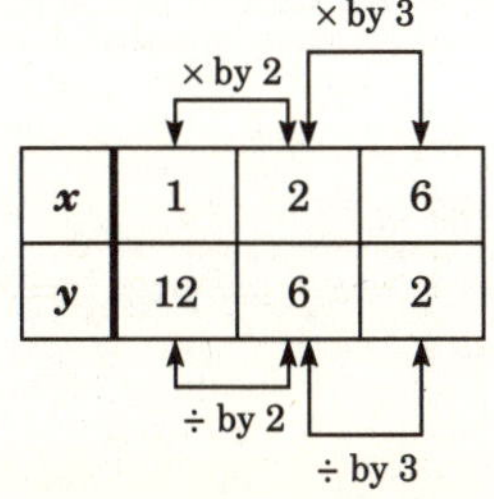

x	1	2	6
y	12	6	2

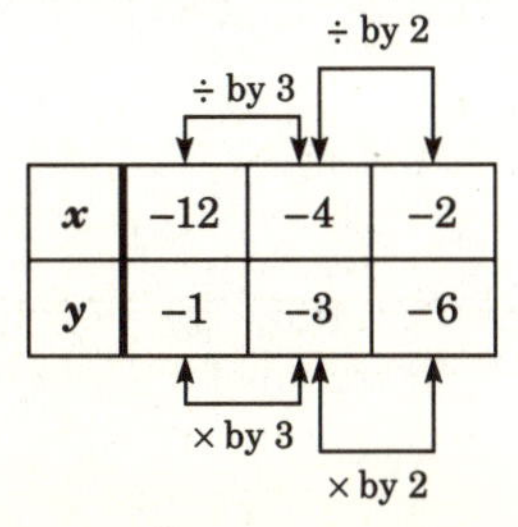

x	−12	−4	−2
y	−1	−3	−6

The graph of the inverse variation $xy = k$ is a hyperbola.

If $k > 0$, the branches of the hyperbola are in Quadrants I and III.

If $k < 0$, the branches of the hyperbola are in Quadrants II and IV.

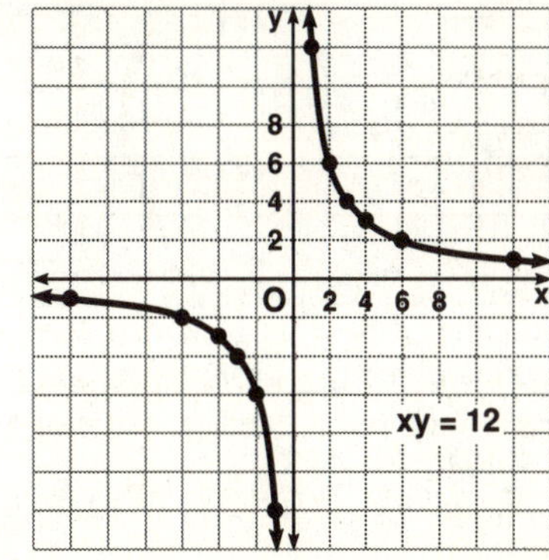

Examples

1. s varies inversely as r.
If $s = 18$ when $r = 3$, find s when $r = -2$.

Solution: Since this is inverse variation, there is a constant *product*.

$$s_1 \cdot r_1 = s_2 \cdot r_2$$
$$18 \cdot 3 = s \cdot (-2)$$
$$54 = -2s$$
$$-27 = s$$

Answer: $s = -27$ when $r = -2$

Alternate Solution: First find the constant of variation from the known pair of values.

$$s \cdot r = 18 \cdot 3 = 54 = k$$

Write the rule of the variation. $sr = 54$
Substitute to find the unknown element of the second pair. $s(-2) = 54$
$s = -27$

2. y varies inversely as the square of x.
If $y = 18$ when $x = 3$, find x when $y = 98$.

Solution: Since this is inverse variation, there is a constant *product*.

$$y_1 \cdot (x_1)^2 = y_2 \cdot (x_2)^2$$
$$18 \cdot 3^2 = 98 \cdot x^2$$
$$\frac{\overset{9}{\cancel{18}} \cdot 9}{\underset{49}{\cancel{98}}} = x^2$$
$$\frac{81}{49} = x^2$$
$$\pm\frac{9}{7} = x$$

Answer: $x = \pm\frac{9}{7}$ when $y = 98$

EXERCISES

1. If a varies directly as b and $a = 1.2$ when $b = 1.5$, find a when $b = 20$.

2. If x varies directly as y and if $x = 6$ when $y = \frac{1}{3}$, find the value of x when $y = 3$.

3. If y varies directly as x, and $y = \pi$ when $x = 180$, find the value of y when $x = 360$.

4. Given that x varies directly as y. If y is multiplied by 3, then x would be multiplied by
(1) $\frac{1}{9}$ (2) $\frac{1}{3}$ (3) 3 (4) 9

5. If d varies directly as the square of t and if $d = 144$ when $t = 3$, find d when $t = 2$.

6. If t varies directly as $\sqrt{x}$ and if $t = 2$ when $x = 25$, what is the value of t when $x = 100$?

7. Given that y varies directly as the square of x. The graph of this relation is a
(1) straight line (3) parabola
(2) circle (4) hyperbola

8. Which of the following tables does not represent direct variation?

(1)

x	1	2	3
y	5	10	15

(3)

r	1	$\frac{1}{2}$	$\frac{1}{3}$
s	2	1	1

(2)

q	−4	3	7
r	8	−6	−14

(4)

a	$\frac{1}{2}$	$\frac{1}{3}$	$\frac{1}{4}$
b	1	$\frac{2}{3}$	$\frac{1}{2}$

9. The graph of all points with coordinates (x, y) such that y varies directly as x is
(1) a hyperbola, only
(2) a parabola
(3) sometimes a straight line and sometimes a hyperbola
(4) a straight line through the origin

10. If $\frac{1}{2}$ inch represents 10 feet in a scale drawing, then how many inches will represent 25 feet?

11. A mass of 48 kilograms causes a beam to bend 8 centimeters. If the amount of bending varies directly as the mass, what mass will cause the beam to bend 11 centimeters?

12. If r varies inversely as s, then their
(1) difference is constant
(2) sum is constant
(3) quotient is constant
(4) product is constant

13. If y varies inversely as x and $y = 6$ when $x = 7$, what is the value of y when $x = 3$?

14. If x varies inversely as y and if $x = 12$ when $y = 8$, find x when $y = 10$.

15. If x varies inversely as y and $x = 2.5$ when $y = 60$, find y when $x = 3$.

16. The relationship between x and y is expressed by $y = \frac{k}{x}$. If x is doubled, then y is
(1) halved (3) unchanged
(2) doubled (4) multiplied by 4

17. L varies inversely as the square of d. If d is multiplied by 3, then L is
(1) multiplied by 3 (3) multiplied by 9
(2) divided by 3 (4) divided by 9

18. If $xy^2 = k$ and $x = 3$ when $y = 4$, what is the value of x when $y = 2$?
(1) 96 (2) 48 (3) 12 (4) $\sqrt{12}$

19. If x varies inversely as y^2 and if $x = 2$ when $y = 6$, the value of x when $y = 12$ is
(1) 1 (2) 2 (3) $\frac{1}{2}$ (4) 8

20. The rate at which Al travels from City *A* to City *B* varies inversely as the time it takes to make the trip. If Al can make the trip in $3\frac{1}{2}$ hours at 60 kilometers per hour, how many kilometers per hour must he travel to make the trip in 3 hours?

21. According to Boyle's law, the volume of a gas, at a constant temperature, varies inversely with pressure applied to it. If the volume of a gas is 120 cubic inches when the pressure is 30 pounds per square inch, find the volume in cubic inches when the pressure is 40 pounds per square inch.

22. Which statement is represented by the formula $yx^2 = k$?

(1) x varies inversely as the square of y.
(2) y varies directly as the square of x.
(3) y varies inversely as the square of x.
(4) x varies directly as the square of y.

23. If x and y are related as shown in the table, which is true?

x	5	10	20
y	25	100	400

(1) y varies directly as x.
(2) y varies inversely as x.
(3) y varies directly as the square of x.
(4) The relationship between x and y is not correctly stated in any of the above.

24. If x varies inversely as y, which graph could show this relationship between x and y?

(1)
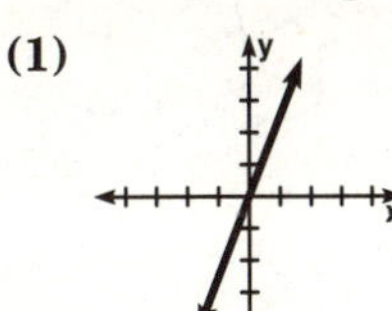

(3)
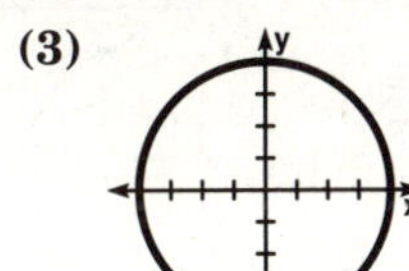

(2)
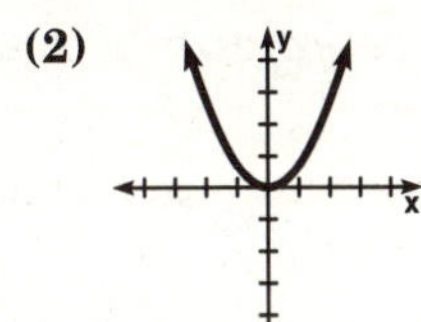

(4)
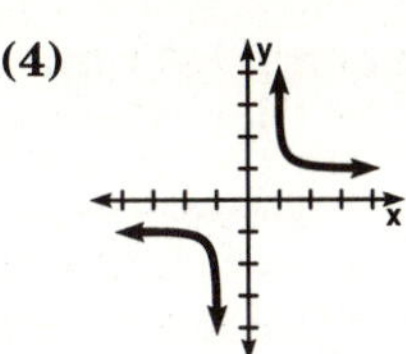

25. The coordinates of which point lie on the graph of $xy = 4$?

(1) $(-1, -3)$ **(2)** $(-2, -2)$ **(3)** $(0, 4)$ **(4)** $(4, 0)$

26. The graph of the equation $xy = 8$ does not pass through the point whose coordinates are

(1) $(-2, -4)$ **(2)** $(0, 8)$ **(3)** $\left(\frac{1}{2}, 16\right)$ **(4)** $(4, 2)$

27. The graph of the equation $xy = -8$ lies in Quadrants

(1) I and II **(3)** I and IV
(2) I and III **(4)** II and IV

28. The graph of the equation $2xy = 7$ will lie in Quadrant(s)

(1) I only **(3)** I and III
(2) I and II **(4)** II and IV

29. If the graphs of $xy = 8$ and $y = x - 2$ are drawn on the same set of axes, what is the total number of points at which they will intersect?

30. Which graph of a quadratic relation is also the graph of a function?

(1)
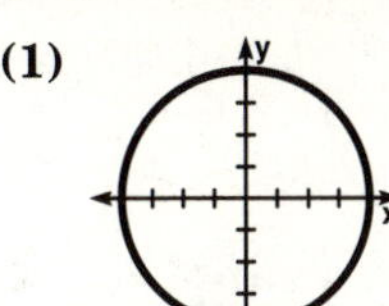

(3)
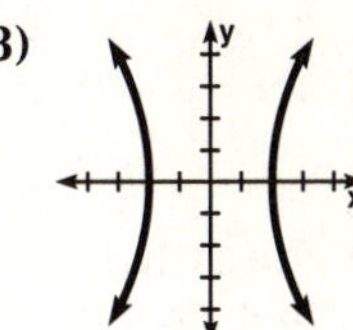

(2)
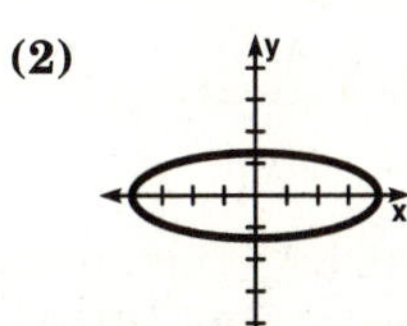

(4)
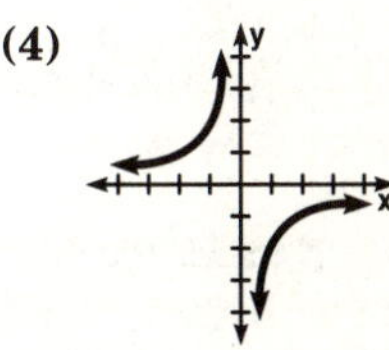

31. a. Sketch the graph of $xy = 8$ from $x = -8$ to $x = 8$.
b. On the same set of axes, reflect the graph drawn in part **a** in the x-axis and label it **b**.
c. Write an equation of the function graphed in part **b**.

32. a. Draw and label the graph of $xy = -12$ in the interval $-12 \le x \le 12$.
b. On the same set of axes, draw and label (with its equation) the image of $xy = -12$ after a reflection in the y-axis.

33. a. Draw and label the graph of the equation $xy = 6$ in the interval $-6 \le x \le 6$.
b. On the same set of axes, draw and label the graph of the image of $xy = 6$ after a rotation of 90°.
c. Write the equation of the graph drawn in part **b**.
d. On the same set of axes, draw and label the graph of the image of $xy = 6$ after a dilation of 2.
e. Write the equation of the graph drawn in part **d**.

34. Identify the image of the graph of $xy = 6$ after the composite transformation:

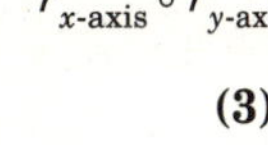
$$r_{x\text{-axis}} \circ r_{y\text{-axis}}$$

(1)
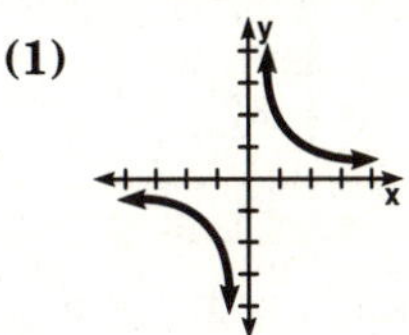

(3)
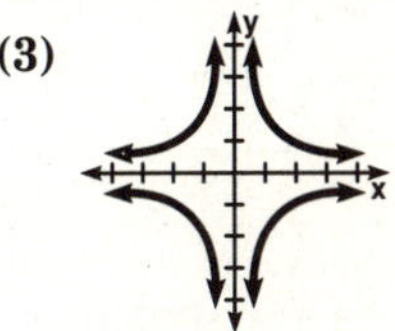

(2)
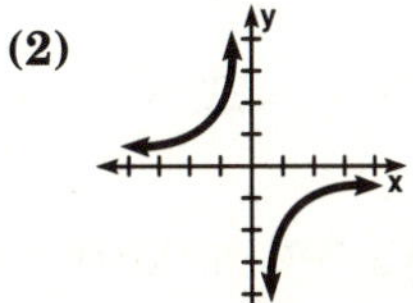

(4)
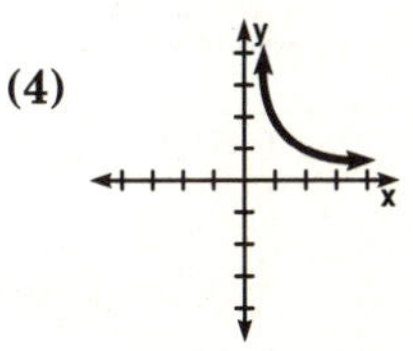

One-to-One Functions

If each second element of a function corresponds to *exactly one* first element, the function is ONE-TO-ONE.

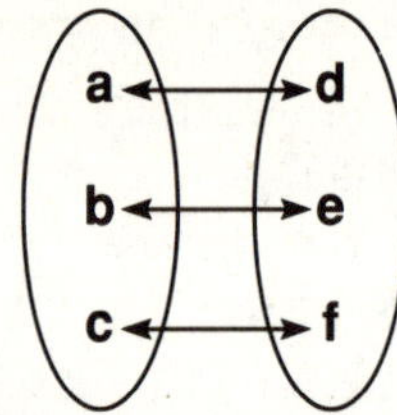

This mapping represents a function since each first element corresponds to exactly one second element: $a \to d, b \to e, c \to f$

The function is one-to-one since each second element corresponds to exactly one first element: $d \to a, e \to b, f \to c$

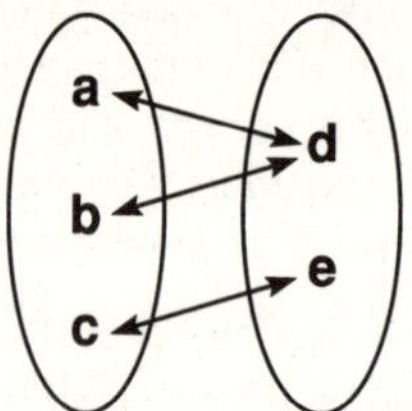

This mapping represents a function since each first element corresponds to exactly one second element: $a \to d, b \to d, c \to e$

The function is not one-to-one since each second element does not correspond to exactly one first element: $d \to a$ and b

HORIZONTAL-LINE TEST: **When any horizontal line intersects a graph that does represent a one-to-one function, the horizontal line intersects the graph in *exactly one* point. If there is more than one point, the graph does not represent a one-to-one function.**

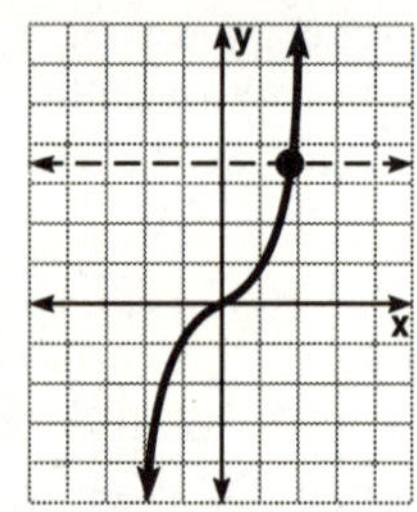

The function $y = x^3$ is one-to-one.

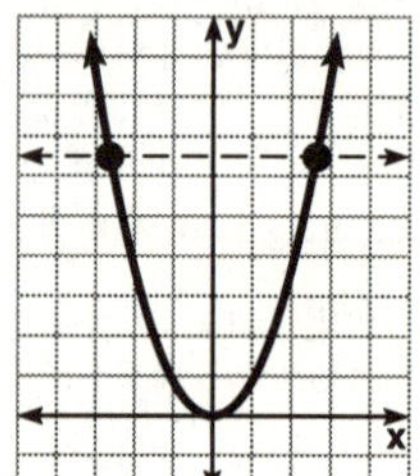

The function $y = x^2$ is not one-to-one.

Determining an Inverse Function

The set of ordered pairs obtained by interchanging the first and second elements of each pair belonging to a one-to-one function f is called the INVERSE FUNCTION f^{-1}.

For the one-to-one function $y = 2x - 1$, the inverse formed by interchanging x and y is $x = 2y - 1$.

Solve the inverse for y:

$$x = 2y - 1$$
$$x + 1 = 2y$$
$$\frac{x+1}{2} = y$$

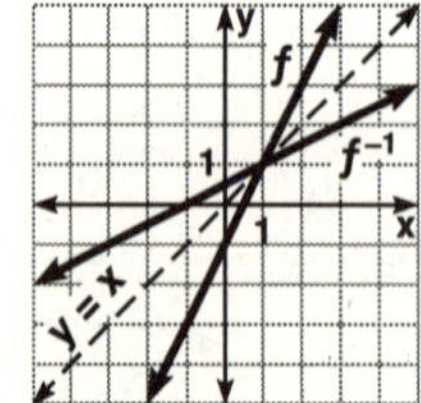

Since the original function $y = 2x - 1$ is one-to-one, its inverse $y = \frac{x+1}{2}$ is a function.

$$f(x) = 2x - 1 \text{ and } f^{-1}(x) = \frac{x+1}{2}$$

For the function $y = x^2$, the inverse formed by interchanging x and y is $x = y^2$.

Solve the inverse for y:

$$x = y^2$$
$$\pm\sqrt{x} = y$$

Since the original function $y = x^2$ is not one-to-one, its inverse $y = \pm\sqrt{x}$ is not a function.

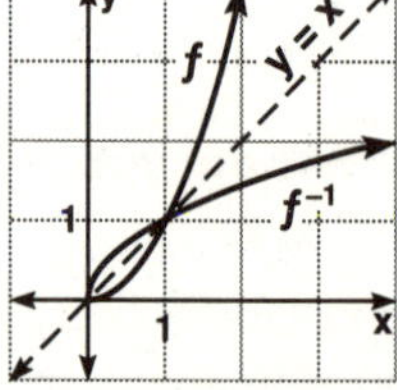

To obtain an inverse that is a function, restrict the domain of the original function.

If the domain of $f(x) = x^2$ is limited to $x \geq 0$, then the inverse is a function.

$$f^{-1} = +\sqrt{x}$$

The graphs of f and f^{-1} are symmetric with respect to the line $y = x$.

Composition of a Function and Its Inverse

In arithmetic: **The sum of a number a and its additive inverse $-a$ yields the identity for addition, 0.**

The product of a nonzero number a and its multiplicative inverse $\frac{1}{a}$ yields the identity for multiplication, 1.

For functions: **The composite of a function f and its inverse f^{-1}, in either order $f \circ f^{-1}$ or $f^{-1} \circ f$, yields the identity function, x.**

Example

For the function $f(x) = \frac{x+1}{2}$:

a. Determine the inverse function: f^{-1}

b. Find: $[f \circ f^{-1}](3)$ c. Find: $[f^{-1} \circ f](3)$ d. Find: $[f \circ f^{-1}](x)$ e. Find: $[f^{-1} \circ f](x)$

Solution:

a.

$y = \frac{x+1}{2}$ The given function.

$x = \frac{y+1}{2}$ Interchange x and y.

$2x = y + 1$ Solve for y.

$2x - 1 = y$

Answer: $f^{-1}(x) = 2x - 1$

b.

$f^{-1}(x) = 2x - 1$

$f^{-1}(3) = 2(3) - 1$

$= 5$

Evaluate the first function of the composite at the given value.

$f(x) = \frac{x+1}{2}$

$f(5) = \frac{5+1}{2}$

$= 3$

In the second function of the composite, substitute for the variable the value found for the first function.

Answer: $[f \circ f^{-1}](3) = 3$

c.

$f(x) = \frac{x+1}{2}$

$f(3) = \frac{3+1}{2}$

$= 2$

Evaluate the first function of the composite at the given value.

$f^{-1}(x) = 2x - 1$

$f^{-1}(2) = 2(2) - 1$

$= 3$

In the second function of the composite, substitute for the variable the value found for the first function.

Answer: $[f^{-1} \circ f](3) = 3$

Note: The value of both composites at $x = 3$ is 3.

d.

$f^{-1}(x) = 2x - 1$ The first function of the composite.

$f(x) = \frac{x+1}{2}$ In the second function of the composite, substitute for the variable the rule for the first function.

$f(2x - 1) = \frac{(2x-1)+1}{2}$

$= \frac{2x}{2}$

$= x$

Answer: $[f \circ f^{-1}](x) = x$

e.

$f(x) = \frac{x+1}{2}$ The first function of the composite.

$f^{-1}(x) = 2x - 1$ In the second function of the composite, substitute for the variable the rule for the first function.

$f^{-1}\left(\frac{x+1}{2}\right) = 2\left(\frac{x+1}{2}\right) - 1$

$= x + 1 - 1$

$= x$

Answer: $[f^{-1} \circ f](x) = x$

Note: The value of both composites is x.

EXERCISES

1. Which mapping represents a one-to-one function?

(1)

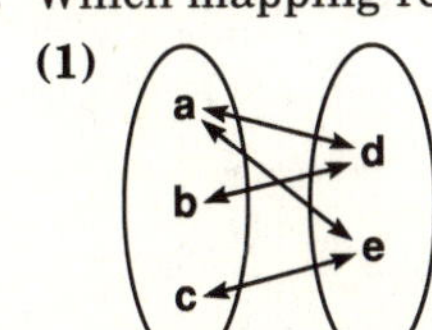

(2)

(3)

(4)

2. Which relation is a one-to-one function?
(1) $\{(a, b), (a, c), (a, d)\}$
(2) $\{(a, b), (a, c), (b, d)\}$
(3) $\{(a, c), (b, c), (a, b)\}$
(4) $\{(a, b), (b, c), (c, d)\}$

3. Which statement is false?
(1) To determine if a relation is a function, apply the vertical-line test to the graph.
(2) To determine if a relation is a function, apply the horizontal-line test to the graph.
(3) To determine if a relation is a one-to-one function, apply both the vertical-line and horizontal-line tests to the graph.
(4) To determine if a function is one-to-one, apply the horizontal-line test to the graph.

4. Which is a one-to-one function?

(1)
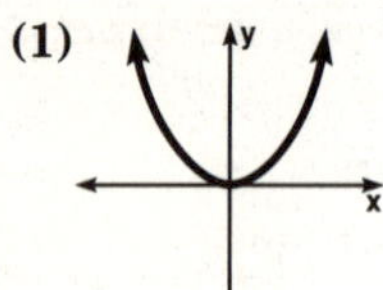

(3)
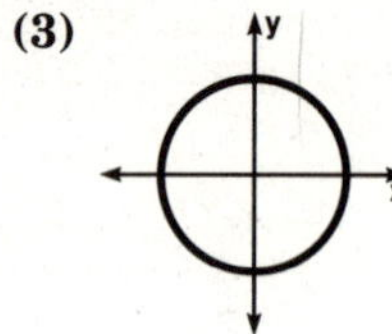

(2)
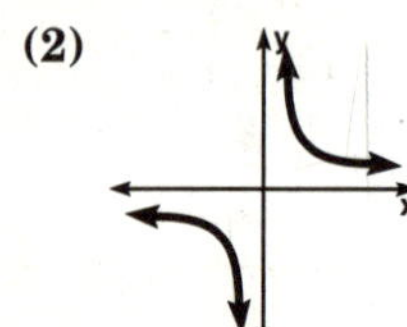

(4)
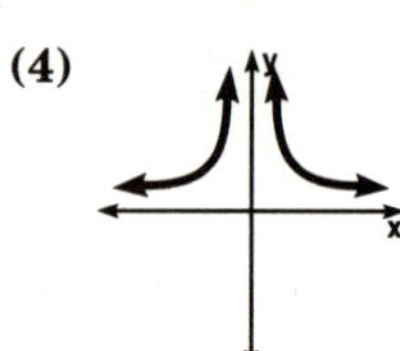

5. Which function is not one to one?

(1)
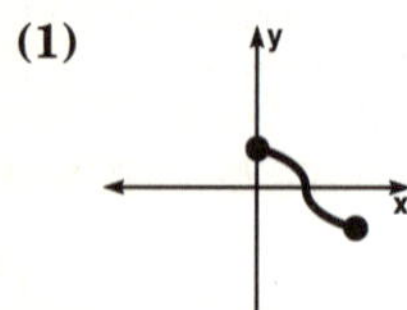

(3)
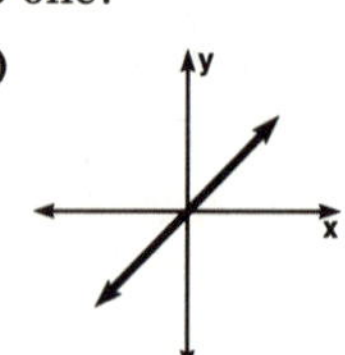

(2)
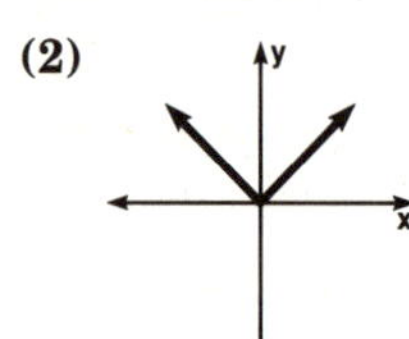

(4)
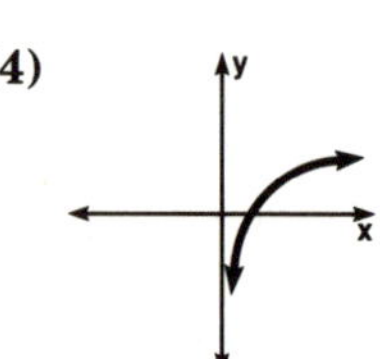

6. Given the relation $\{(1, 2), (2, 3), (3, 4)\}$. What is the inverse of the relation?
(1) $\{(1, \frac{1}{2}), (2, \frac{1}{3}), (3, \frac{1}{4})\}$
(2) $\{(-1, -2), (-2, -3), (-3, -4)\}$
(3) $\{(3, 4), (2, 3), (1, 2)\}$
(4) $\{(2, 1), (3, 2), (4, 3)\}$

7. Which is the inverse function of $\{(-2, 3), (7, 2), (8, -11)\}$?
(1) $\{(-\frac{1}{2}, \frac{1}{3}), (\frac{1}{7}, \frac{1}{2}), (\frac{1}{8}, -\frac{1}{11})\}$
(2) $\{(2, 3), (-7, 2), (-8, -11)\}$
(3) $\{(3, -2), (2, 7), (-11, 8)\}$
(4) $\{(-3, 2), (-2, 7), (11, 8)\}$

8. Given the set $A = \{(1, 2), (3, 4), (5, 1), (2, 5)\}$ and its inverse, A^{-1}. Which describes the two sets?
(1) Both A and A^{-1} are functions.
(2) Neither A nor A^{-1} is a function.
(3) A is a function and A^{-1} is not a function.
(4) A is not a function and A^{-1} is a function.

9. Write the inverse of the given function:

$$\{(5, 3), (-2, 4), (7, -2)\}$$

10. The inverse of the function $y = 2x$ is
(1) $x = -2y$ (3) $y = x - 2$
(2) $x = 2y$ (4) $y = -2x$

11. The inverse of the function $y = x^2$ is
(1) $\frac{1}{y}$ (2) $\frac{1}{x}$ (3) $y^2 = x$ (4) $x^2 = y$

12. The inverse of $y = 2x - 1$ is
(1) $y = -2x + 1$ (3) $y = \frac{1}{2}x + 1$
(2) $y = -\frac{1}{2}x - 1$ (4) $y = \frac{1}{2}x + \frac{1}{2}$

13. What is the inverse of the function $y - 2 = 3x$?
(1) $y = \frac{2 - x}{3}$ (3) $y = 3x - 2$
(2) $y = \frac{2x}{3}$ (4) $y = \frac{x - 2}{3}$

14. What is the inverse of the function $x + 2y + 3 = 0$?
(1) $y = -\frac{1}{2}x - \frac{3}{2}$ (3) $2y + x + 3 = 0$
(2) $y = -2x - 3$ (4) $2x - y + 3 = 0$

15. Which is an equation of the line formed when the line $y = 3x + 1$ is reflected in the line $y = x$?
(1) $y = 3x - 1$ (3) $y = \frac{x}{3} - 1$
(2) $y = \frac{x - 1}{3}$ (4) $x = y$

16. What is the inverse of $f(x) = -\frac{2}{3}x$?
(1) $f^{-1}(x) = \frac{2}{3}x - 3$ (3) $f^{-1}(x) = -\frac{3}{2}x$
(2) $f^{-1}(x) = \frac{3}{2}x$ (4) $f^{-1}(x) = -\frac{2}{3}x$

17. Which is the graph of the inverse of the function $y = 3x + 6$?

(1)
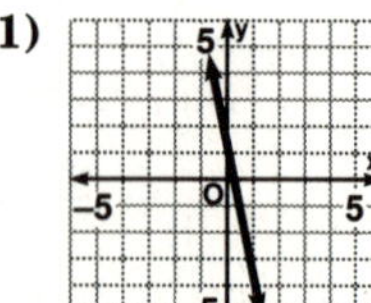

(3)
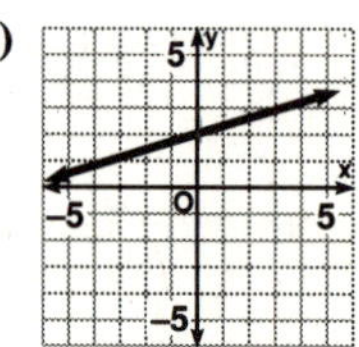

(2)
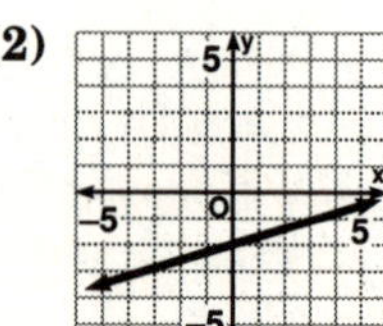

(4)
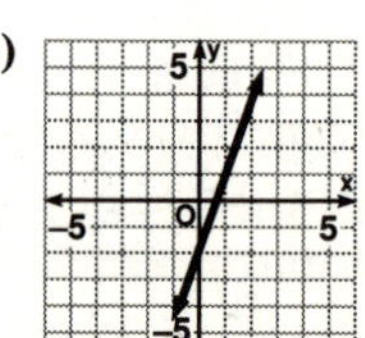

18. Which function represented in the graphs shown has an inverse function?

(1) 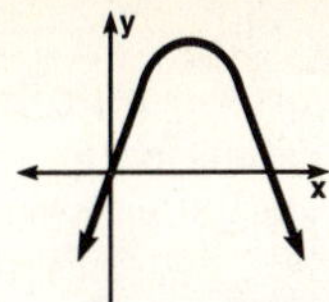
(2) 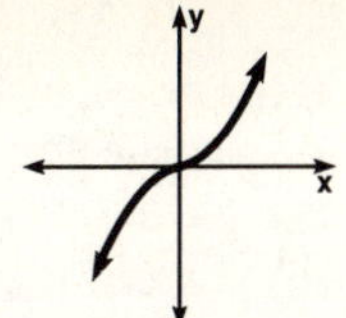
(3) 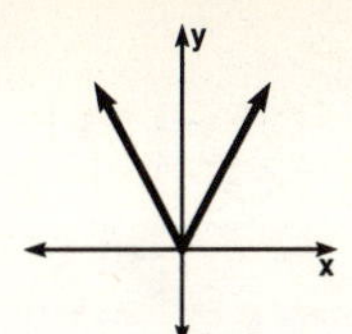
(4) 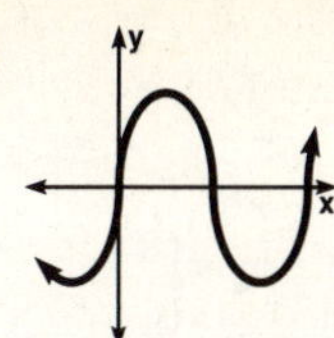

4.5 THE EXPONENTIAL AND LOGARITHMIC FUNCTIONS

Characteristics of the Graphs

A function that contains the variable in the exponent is called an EXPONENTIAL FUNCTION.

$y = a^x$ or $f(x) = a^x$, where $a > 0$ and $a \neq 1$

$y = 2^x$

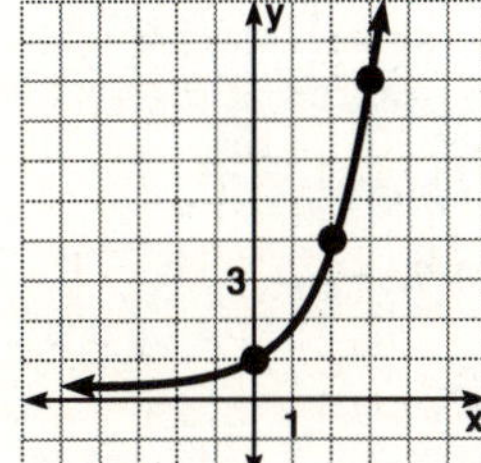

$y = 2^{-x}$ or $y = \left(\frac{1}{2}\right)^x$

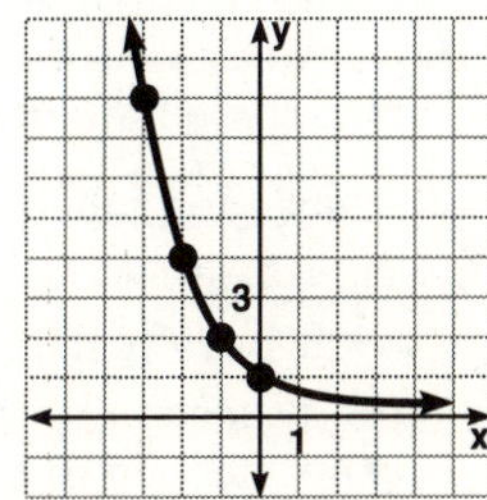

Note from the graphs above, the general characteristics of the exponential function $y = a^x$:

1. **The domain is the set of real numbers.**
2. **The range is the set of positive real numbers.**
3. **The graph includes the point (0, 1).**
4. **The function is one-to-one.**
5. **If $a > 1$, the graph rises. (an *increasing* function) If $0 < a < 1$, the graph falls. (a *decreasing* function)**
6. **The graphs of $y = a^x$ *and* $y = a^{-x}$ are reflections of each other in the y-axis.**

Form the inverse of the exponential function by interchanging x and y.

$y = a^x$	The exponential function.
$x = a^y$	Interchange x and y.

To express the inverse function in the form $y = f(x)$ (called "writing y *explicitly*"), the notation uses a LOGARITHM, abbreviated "log". (Read $\log_a x$ as "log x to the base a.")

$x = a^y$ is equivalent to $y = \log_a x$

A logarithm is equivalent to an exponent.

The inverse of the exponential function is the LOGARITHMIC FUNCTION.

If $f(x) = a^x$, then $f^{-1}(x) = \log_a x$.

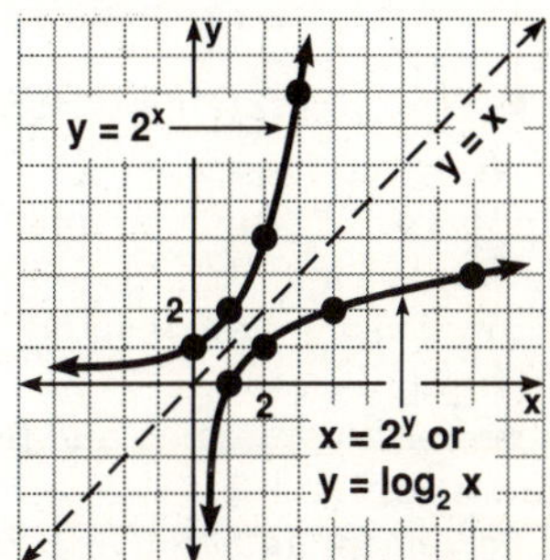

Note from the graph above, the general characteristics of the logarithmic function $y = \log_a x$:

1. **Since the exponential function $y = a^x$ is one-to-one, it has an inverse function, $y = \log_a x$.**
2. **The domain of $y = \log_a x$ is the set of positive real numbers.**
3. **The range is the set of real numbers.**
4. **The graph includes the point (1, 0).**
5. **The graphs of $y = a^x$ and $x = a^y$ (or $y = \log_a x$) are reflections of each other in the line $y = x$.**

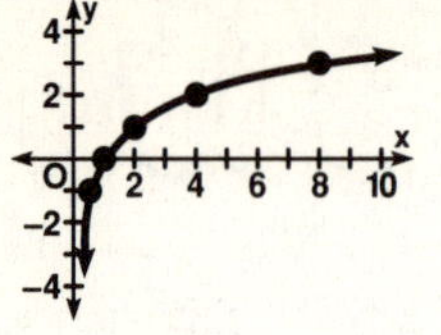

Ex. 1

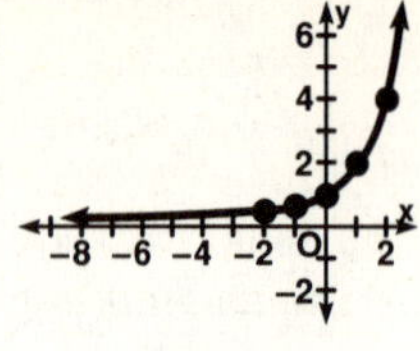

Ex. 2

1. Which is the equation of the graph shown?
(1) $y = 2^x$ (2) $y = 10^x$ (3) $y = \log_2 x$ (4) $y = \log_{10} x$

2. Which is the equation of the graph shown?
(1) $y = \log_2 x$ (3) $y = 2^x$
(2) $y = -\log_2 x$ (4) $y = 2^{-x}$

3. The graph of $y = a^x$, where $a > 0$, contains the point
(1) (1, 0) (2) (−1, 0) (3) (0, 0) (4) (0, 1)

4. The graph of $y = \left(\frac{1}{2}\right)^x$ lies entirely in Quadrants
(1) I and II (3) II and III
(2) I and III (4) I and IV

5. Which statement accurately describes the graph of $y = 10^x$?
(1) It is an increasing function and lies entirely in Quadrants I and II.
(2) It is an increasing function and lies entirely in Quadrants I and IV.
(3) It is a decreasing function and lies entirely in Quadrants I and II.
(4) It is a decreasing function and lies entirely in Quadrants I and IV.

6. The graph of the equation $y = 2^x$ intersects
(1) the x-axis, only
(2) the y-axis, only
(3) the x-axis and the y-axis
(4) neither the x-axis nor the y-axis

7. Given the function $y = 2^x$, express the value of y if $x = -4$.

8. Which is an equation of the inverse of the function $y = 2^x$?
(1) $y = \log_2 x$ (3) $x = y^2$
(2) $y = x^2$ (4) $x = \log_2 y$

9. What is the x-intercept of the graph of the equation $y = \log_2 x$?
(1) 1 (2) 2 (3) 0 (4) 4

10. Which statement is true for the graph of $y = \log_{10} x$?
(1) It is an increasing function and lies entirely in Quadrants I and II.
(2) It is an increasing function and lies entirely in Quadrants I and IV.
(3) It is a decreasing function and lies entirely in Quadrants I and II.
(4) It is a decreasing function and lies entirely in Quadrants I and IV.

11. If the graph of the equation $y = 3^x$ is reflected in the x-axis, the equation of the reflection is
(1) $y = 3^{-x}$ (3) $y = \log_x 3$
(2) $y = -(3^x)$ (4) $y = x^3$

12. If the graphs of $y = 1$ and $y = \log x$ are sketched on the same axes, then the number of points in their intersection is
(1) 1 (2) 2 (3) 3 (4) 0

13. Given the function $f = \{(x, y) | y = \log_2 x\}$.
a. Sketch the graph of f.
b. Write an equation for f^{-1}, the inverse of f.

14. a. Graph and label the function $y = 2^x$ for the restricted domain $-2 \le x \le 3$.
b. On the same set of axes, sketch the reflection of $y = 2^x$ in the x-axis and label the image **b**.
c. On the same set of axes, sketch the reflection in the origin of $y = 2^x$ and label it **c**.
d. On the same set of axes, sketch the translation of $y = 2^x$ under $T_{(6,\ 2)}$ and label it **d**.

15. a. Sketch and label the graph of $y = 2^x$.
b. The graph of $y = 2^x$ is subject to each of these transformations:
(1) reflection in the y-axis
(2) reflection in the line $y = x$
(3) translation : $(x, y) \to (x, y + 1)$
On your answer paper, write the numerals (1), (2), and (3). Next to the appropriate numeral, write the letter of the equation, chosen from the list below, that best describes the image of $y = 2^x$ under each of the given transformations.

Equations
(a) $y = \log_2 x$ (c) $y = 2^{-x}$
(b) $y = -2^x$ (d) $y = 2^x + 1$

16. a. Sketch and label the graph of the equation $y = 2^x$ in the interval $-3 \le x \le 3$.
b. On the same set of axes, sketch and label the graph of the equation $xy = 8$ in the interval $-8 \le x \le 8$.
c. Using the graphs drawn in parts **a** and **b**, solve for x: $2^x = \frac{8}{x}$

17. a. Sketch and label the graph of the equation $y = 3^x$.
b. The graph of the equation $y = 3^x$ is reflected in the y-axis. On the same set of axes used in part **a**, sketch this reflection.
c. Which is an equation of the reflection sketched in part **b**?
(1) $y = -(3^x)$ (3) $y = \log_3 x$
(2) $y = 3^{-x}$ (4) $x = 3^y$

18. **a.** Copy and complete the table for the values of y in the equation $y = 4^x$.

x	$-\frac{3}{2}$	-1	$-\frac{1}{2}$	0	$\frac{1}{2}$	1	$\frac{3}{2}$
y						4	8

b. Using the completed table, draw and label the graph of $y = 4^x$ for $-\frac{3}{2} \le x \le \frac{3}{2}$.

c. On the same set of axes, draw the graph of the reflection of $y = 4^x$ in the x-axis and label it **c**.

d. On the same set of axes, draw the graph of the reflection of $y = 4^x$ through the origin and label it **d**.

19. **a.** Sketch the graph of $F = \{(x, y) | y = 3^x\}$.

b. On the same set of axes, sketch the graph of F^{-1} by reflecting the graph drawn in part **a** over the line $y = x$.

c. Write an equation for F^{-1}.

Exponential Equations

To solve an exponential equation:

1. **Express both sides of the equation as powers of the same base.**
2. **Apply the principal that:**

   if $x^a = x^b$, then $a = b$

   That is, set the exponents of the common base equal to each other.
3. **Solve the resulting linear or quadratic equation.**

Examples

1. Find x if $2^{x+1} = 16$.

Solution:

$2^{x+1} = 16$
$2^{x+1} = 2^4$ — Express both sides as powers of the same base.

$x + 1 = 4$
$x = 3$ — Equate the exponents, and solve the linear equation.

Check:

$2^{3+1} \stackrel{?}{=} 16$

$2^4 \stackrel{?}{=} 16 \leftrightarrow 16 = 16$ ✓

Answer: $x = 3$

2. Solve for x: $4^{x^2+4x} = 4^{-3}$

Solution: $4^{x^2+4x} = 4^{-3}$ — Given powers of the same base.

$x^2 + 4x = -3$ — Equate the exponents.

$x^2 + 4x + 3 = 0$ — Solve the resulting quadratic equation.

$(x + 1)(x + 3) = 0$

$x + 1 = 0 \quad | \quad x + 3 = 0$

$x = -1 \quad | \quad x = -3$

Check:

$4^{x^2+4x} = 4^{-3}$
$4^{(-1)^2+4(-1)} \stackrel{?}{=} 4^{-3}$
$4^{1-4} \stackrel{?}{=} 4^{-3}$
$4^{-3} = 4^{-3}$ ✓

$4^{x^2+4x} = 4^{-3}$
$4^{(-3)^2+4(-3)} \stackrel{?}{=} 4^{-3}$
$4^{9-12} \stackrel{?}{=} 4^{-3}$
$4^{-3} = 4^{-3}$ ✓

Answer: $x = -1$ or $x = -3$

3. Solve for x: $4^{3x} = 8^{x+1}$

Solution:

$4^{3x} = 8^{x+1}$
$(2^2)^{3x} = (2^3)^{x+1}$ — Express both sides as powers of the same base.
$2^{6x} = 2^{3x+3}$ — $(x^a)^b = x^{ab}$
$6x = 3x + 3$ — Equate the exponents, and solve the linear equation.
$3x = 3$
$x = 1$ *Ans.*

EXERCISES

1. The solution set of $3^{2x-1} = 3^{x^2}$ is
   (1) {1} (3) {1, –1}
   (2) {–1} (4) { }

2. The solution set of $2^{x^2+2x} = 2^{-1}$ is
   (1) {1} (3) {1, –1}
   (2) {–1} (4) { }

In 3–14, solve for x.

3. $3^{3x-1} = 3^{2x+2}$
4. $3^{x^2+4x} = 3^{-4}$
5. $3^{x+2} = 9^x$
6. $8^{x-2} = 2^{2x}$
7. $2^{x+3} = 64$
8. $4^x = 2^{3x+1}$
9. $5^{5x+1} = 25^{x+2}$
10. $10^{3x} = 100^{x+2}$
11. $27^x = 3^{2x-1}$
12. $9^{2x} = 3^{3x+1}$
13. $81^x = 9^{x+1}$
14. $8^{\frac{1}{3}} = 2^{x+1}$

15. Which value satifies the equation $9^x = 27$?
   (1) -2 (2) 2 (3) $-\frac{3}{2}$ (4) $\frac{3}{2}$

In 16–25, solve for x.

16. $27^x = 9^{2x-1}$
17. $9^{x+5} = 81^{2x+1}$
18. $4^{2x+1} = 8^{2x}$
19. $\left(\frac{1}{2}\right)^x = 4$
20. $100^{x+1} = 1{,}000^{x-1}$
21. $4^x = 32$
22. $8^{2x} = 16$
23. $25^{x-2} = 125^{x-2}$
24. $\left(\frac{1}{3}\right)^{x+1} = 27$
25. $100^x = 0.001$

Logarithmic Equations

Solving a Logarithmic Equation

To solve a logarithmic equation:
Apply the definition that

$$\log_b n = e \longleftrightarrow b^e = n$$

to rewrite the equation in exponential form, where base $b > 0$ and $b \neq 1$.

Examples

1. Solve for x: $\log_5 x = 2$

Solution:

$\log_5 x = 2$	Convert to exponential form: $\log_b n = e \longleftrightarrow b^e = n$
$5^2 = x$	
$25 = x$	

Check: Note that
$\log_5 25 = 2$ is equivalent to $5^2 = 25$

Answer: $x = 25$

2. Solve for x: $\log_x 81 = 4$

Solution:

$\log_x 81 = 4$	Convert to exponential form:
$x^4 = 81$	$\log_b n = e \longleftrightarrow b^e = n$
$x = 3$	Take the 4th root of each side. Consider positive value only.

Using a Logarithmic Equation to Find the Log of a Number

Finding the log of a number is equivalent to solving a logarithmic equation.

Examples

1. Find: $\log_2 64$

Solution:

$\log_2 64 = x$	
$2^x = 64$	Convert to exponential form: $\log_b n = e \longleftrightarrow b^e = n$
$2^x = 2^6$	Powers of the same base.
$x = 6$	Equate the exponents.

Answer: $\log_2 64 = 6$

Mental Solution: Since a logarithm is equivalent to an exponent, think: 2 to what power is 64?

2. If $f(x) = \log_5 x$, find $f(125)$.

Solution:

$f(x) = \log_5 x$	The requirement is to find the value of the rule at $x = 125$.
$f(125) = \log_5 125$	
$\log_5 125 = y$	Express as a log equation.
$5^y = 125$	Convert to exponential form: $\log_b n = e \longleftrightarrow b^e = n$
$5^y = 5^3$	Powers of the same base.
$y = 3$	Equate the exponents.

Answer: $f(125) = 3$

EXERCISES

1. Which is the equivalent exponential form of $\log_b N = x$?
(1) $b^N = x$ **(2)** $N^b = x$ **(3)** $x^b = N$ **(4)** $b^x = N$

2. Solve for x in terms of a and b: $\log_b x = a$

In 3–18, solve for x.

3. $\log_2 x = 3$
4. $\log_2 x = 5$
5. $\log_3 x = 4$
6. $\log_4 x = 3$
7. $\log_8 x = \frac{2}{3}$
8. $\log_9 x = \frac{1}{2}$
9. $\log_9 x = \frac{3}{2}$
10. $\log_3 (x - 2) = 2$
11. $\log_x 36 = 2$
12. $\log_x 125 = 3$
13. $\log_{(x+1)} 27 = 3$
14. $\log_x 5 = \frac{1}{2}$
15. $\log_x 2 = \frac{1}{3}$
16. $\log_x 3 = \frac{1}{3}$
17. $\log_x \frac{1}{4} = -1$
18. $\log_x 16 = -2$

19. If $\log_2 x = -3$, then x is equal to
(1) 9 **(2)** −6 **(3)** $\frac{1}{8}$ **(4)** −8

20. If $\log_x 9 = \frac{1}{2}$, what is the value of x?
(1) $4\frac{1}{2}$ **(2)** 27 **(3)** 3 **(4)** 81

In 21–36, evaluate.

21. $\log_2 8$
22. $\log_2 64$
23. $\log_4 64$
24. $\log_3 81$
25. $\log_9 81$
26. $\log_5 625$
27. $\log_{25} 625$
28. $\log_{10} 1{,}000$
29. $\log_{10} 0.01$
30. $\log_{10} 0.001$
31. $\log_2 \left(\frac{1}{2}\right)$
32. $\log_3 \left(\frac{1}{3}\right)$
33. $\log_a \left(\frac{1}{a}\right)$
34. $\log_8 2$
35. $\log_{16} 4$
36. $\log_{27} 3$

37. If a function is defined by $f(x) = \log_{10} x$, find the value of $f(10)$.

38. If $f(x) = \log_{10} (x^2)$, find $f(10)$.

39. If $f(x) = \log_2 x$, find $f(8)$.

40. If $f(x) = \log_3 x$, find $f(27)$.

41. For what value of k will the graph of $y = \log_{10} x$ contain the point $(1, k)$?

4.6 CALCULATING WITH LOGARITHMS

Laws of Logarithms

Since logarithms represent exponents, laws of logarithms are derived from the laws of exponents. These laws of logarithms apply to any base b, where $b > 0$ and $b \neq 1$.

When base 10 is used, by convention the base value is understood rather than written.

***Example:* $\log N$ is equivalent to $\log_{10} N$**

To simplify notation, the laws in the following table are indicated in base 10.

Law of Logarithms to Calculate	In Symbols	How Operations are Treated When Using Logarithms
a product	$\log (A \cdot B) = \log A + \log B$	**log of product = sum of logs** (With logs, multiplication converts to addition.)
a quotient	$\log (A \div B) = \log A - \log B$	**log of quotient = difference of logs** (With logs, division converts to subtraction.)
a power	$\log (A^n) = n \cdot \log A$	**log of power = multiplier of log** (With logs, a power converts to multiplication.)
a root	$\log (\sqrt[n]{A}) = \frac{1}{n} \cdot \log A$	**log of root = multiplier of logs** (With logs, a root (*fractional power*) converts to multiplication.)

Examples

1. Write an equivalent expression for: $\log \frac{x^2}{y}$

Solution: Describe the operations verbally to fix on a starting point.

$\log \frac{x^2}{y}$	The expression is the log of a quotient.
$= \log x^2 - \log y$	In logs, division converts to subtraction.
$= 2 \log x - \log y$	In logs, a power converts to a multiplier.

Answer: $\log \frac{x^2}{y} = 2 \log x - \log y$

2. The expression $2 + \log x$ is equivalent to

(1) $2 \log x$ **(3)** $\log x^2$
(2) $\log 2x$ **(4)** $\log 100x$

Solution: Examine the choices.

For choice **(1)** to be equivalent to the given expression, the sum of two quantities would be equal to their product, which is not true. Since choice **(1)** is equivalent to choice **(3)**, eliminate both.

Choice **(2)** is equivalent to $\log 2 + \log x$. For this to be equal to the given expression, 2 would have to be equal to log 2, which is not true. Eliminate choice **(2)**.

Choice **(4)** is equivalent to $\log 100 + \log x$. For this to be equal to the given expression, 2 would have to be equal to log 100, which is true: $\log_{10} 100 = 2$

Answer: **(4)**

3. If $\log m = x$ and $\log n = y$, write in terms of x and y an equivalent expression for: $\log \sqrt{mn}$

Solution:

$\log \sqrt{mn}$	The log expression shows the square root of a product.
$= \log (mn)^{\frac{1}{2}}$	The square root converts to a fractional exponent.
$= \frac{1}{2} \log mn$	In logs, a power converts to a multiplier.
$= \frac{1}{2} (\log m + \log n)$	In logs, multiplication converts to addition.
$= \frac{1}{2} (x + y)$ *Ans.*	Substitute: $\log m = x$, $\log n = y$

4. If $\log 2 = m$ and $\log 6 = n$, then log 48 equals

(1) $m^3 + n$ **(3)** $3m + n$
(2) $(mn)^3$ **(4)** $3(m + n)$

Solution:

$\log 48$	
$= \log (2^3 \cdot 6)$	Express 48 in terms of 2 and 6.
$= \log 2^3 + \log 6$	In logs, multiplication converts to addition.
$= 3 \log 2 + \log 6$	In logs, a power converts to a multiplier.
$= 3m + n$	Substitute: $\log 2 = m$, $\log 6 = n$

Answer: **(3)**

EXERCISES

1. The expression $\log 3x$ is equivalent to
(1) $(\log 3)(\log x)$ **(3)** $\log 3 + \log x$
(2) $3 \log x$ **(4)** $\log (3 + x)$

2. If $A = \pi r^2$, which equation is true?
(1) $\log A = \log \pi + 2 \log r$
(2) $\log A = 2\pi(\log r)$
(3) $\log A = \pi + 2 \log r$
(4) $\log A = \log \pi + \log 2 + \log r$

3. The expression $\log\sqrt{xy}$ is equivalent to
(1) $2 \log x \log y$ **(3)** $\frac{1}{2} \log x \log y$
(2) $2 (\log x + \log y)$ **(4)** $\frac{1}{2}(\log x + \log y)$

4. Which is equivalent to $\log \sqrt{\frac{a}{b}}$?
(1) $(\log a - \log b)$ **(3)** $\dfrac{\log a}{\log b}$
(2) $\frac{1}{2} (\log a - \log b)$ **(4)** $\sqrt{\dfrac{\log a}{\log b}}$

5. The expression $\log \dfrac{\sqrt[3]{a}}{b}$ is equivalent to
(1) $\frac{1}{3} \log a - \log b$ **(3)** $3 \log a - \log b$
(2) $\frac{1}{3} \log (a - b)$ **(4)** $3 \log (a - b)$

6. The expression $\log \sqrt[3]{\frac{a}{b}}$ is equivalent to
(1) $\frac{1}{3} (\log a - \log b)$ **(3)** $\frac{1}{3}\left(\dfrac{\log a}{\log b}\right)$
(2) $\frac{1}{3} \log a + \log b$ **(4)** $3 (\log a - \log b)$

7. The expression $(a + b) \log x$ is equivalent to
(1) $\log ax + \log bx$ **(3)** $a \log x + b \log x$
(2) $\log (a + x) + \log (b + x)$ **(4)** $\log abx$

8. The expression $\log b^{m+1}$ is equivalent to
(1) $10 \log b^m$ **(3)** $m \log b + b$
(2) $m \log b + \log b$ **(4)** $m \log b$

9. $\log \dfrac{\sqrt{xy}}{z}$ is equal to
(1) $\frac{1}{2} \log x + \frac{1}{2} \log y - \log z$
(2) $\frac{1}{2} \log x + \log y - \log z$
(3) $\frac{1}{2} (\log x + \log y - \log z)$
(4) $\dfrac{\frac{1}{2} \log xy}{\log z}$

10. The expression $2 \log a - \log b$ is equivalent to
(1) $\dfrac{2 \log a}{\log b}$ **(3)** $\log (a^2 - b)$
(2) $\log \left(\frac{a}{b}\right)^2$ **(4)** $\log \dfrac{a^2}{b}$

11. The expression $\log a - \frac{1}{2} \log b$ is equivalent to
(1) $\dfrac{\log a}{\frac{1}{2} \log b}$ **(2)** $\dfrac{\log a}{\log \sqrt{b}}$ **(3)** $\log \dfrac{a}{\sqrt{b}}$ **(4)** $\log \dfrac{a}{b^2}$

12. The expression $3 \log x - \frac{1}{2} \log y$ is equal to
(1) $\log \dfrac{x^3}{y^2}$ **(3)** $\log \sqrt{\dfrac{3x}{y}}$
(2) $\log \dfrac{x^3}{\sqrt{y}}$ **(4)** $\dfrac{\log 3x}{\frac{1}{2} \log y}$

13. The expression $2 \log_5 m + \log_5 n$ is equivalent to
(1) $\log_5 m^2n$ **(3)** $\log_5 \sqrt{mn}$
(2) $\log_5 \dfrac{m^2}{n}$ **(4)** $\log_5 \dfrac{2m}{n}$

14. If $x = \dfrac{\sqrt{r}}{s}$, which expression is equivalent to $\log x$?
(1) $\dfrac{2 \log r}{\log s}$ **(3)** $\frac{1}{2} \log r - \log s$
(2) $2 \log r - \log s$ **(4)** $\dfrac{\log r - \log s}{2}$

15. If $N = \dfrac{7^3}{\sqrt[4]{6}}$, which is equivalent to $\log N$?
(1) $3(\log 7 - \frac{1}{4} \log 6)$ **(3)** $\dfrac{3 \log 7}{\frac{1}{4} \log 6}$
(2) $\frac{1}{3} \log 7 - 4 \log 6$ **(4)** $3 \log 7 - \frac{1}{4} \log 6$

16. If $x = u^2v$, which expression is equivalent to $\log x$?
(1) $2 \log u + \log v$ **(3)** $\dfrac{2 \log u}{\log v}$
(2) $\log 2u + \log v$ **(4)** $2 \log u \log v$

17. If $x = \dfrac{a\sqrt{b}}{c}$, then $\log x$ is equal to
(1) $\log a + \frac{1}{2} \log b - \log c$
(2) $\log a + 2 \log b - \log c$
(3) $\log a - \frac{1}{2} \log b + \log c$
(4) $\log a - 2 \log b - \log c$

18. If $x = (8^2)(\sqrt{5})$, which expression is equivalent to $\log x$?
(1) $2 \log 8 + 2 \log 5$ **(3)** $2 \log 8 + \frac{1}{2} \log 5$
(2) $2(\log 8 + \frac{1}{2} \log 5)$ **(4)** $(2 \log 8)(\frac{1}{3} \log 5)$

19. $\log \sqrt{\dfrac{100}{n}}$ equals
(1) $1 - \dfrac{\log n}{2}$ **(3)** $2 - \log n$
(2) $10 - \dfrac{\log n}{2}$ **(4)** $\dfrac{2}{\log n}$

20. If $\log 100ab^2$ is expressed as a function of $\log a$ and $\log b$, the result will be
(1) $2 \log a + 2 \log b$ **(3)** $2 + \log a + 2 \log b$
(2) $100 \log a + 2 \log b$ **(4)** $2 + 2 \log a + 2 \log b$

21. $\log \dfrac{x^3}{100}$ equals
(1) $3 \log x - 2$ **(3)** $3x - 100$
(2) $\dfrac{3 \log x}{2}$ **(4)** $\dfrac{3x}{100}$

22. If $\log a = m$ and $\log b = n$, an equivalent expression for $\log a^2b$ is

(1) $2(m+n)$ (2) m^2+n^2 (3) $2m+n$ (4) $m+2n$

23. If $\log 3 = x$ and $\log 5 = y$, express $\log \sqrt{\frac{3}{5}}$ in terms of x and y.

24. If $\log m = 1.2970$, then $\log 100m$ equals

(1) 129.7 (3) 3.2970
(2) 12.97 (4) 8.2970 − 10

25. If $\log 4.72 = m$, then $\log 472$ equals

(1) $m+2$ (2) $2m$ (3) $100m$ (4) $100+m$

26. If $\log a = 0.4262$, find $\log \sqrt{a}$.

27. If $\log N = \log A + 3 \log B$, solve for N in terms of A and B.

28. If $\log 2 = A$ and $\log 3 = B$, then $\log 6$ is equal to

(1) $A+B$ (2) $A-B$ (3) AB (4) $\frac{A}{B}$

29. If $\log 3 = a$ and $\log 5 = b$, then $\log 45$ is equal to

(1) a^2+b (2) $2a+b$ (3) $2ab$ (4) a^2b

30. If $\log 2 = p$, $\log 3 = q$, and $\log 5 = r$, write an expression for $\log 150$ in terms of p, q, and r.

Common Logarithms, Base 10

Characteristic, Mantissa

All positive real numbers can be expressed as powers of 10. Numbers such as 100, 1000, 0.01, and 0.001 are integral powers of 10. Nonintegral powers of 10 are fitted between integral powers.

Powers of 10	*Real Numbers*
⋮	⋮
10^2	100
$10^{2.1847}$	153
10^3	1000
⋮	⋮

Each positive real number has a logarithm in base 10.

$10^{2.1847} = 153$ means $\log 153 = 2.1847$

CHARACTERISTIC — the integral part of the logarithm (2)

MANTISSA — the decimal part of the logarithm (.1847)

To determine the characteristic, think of the number in scientific notation.

$$\begin{pmatrix}\text{first factor is}\\ \text{between 1 and 10}\end{pmatrix} \times \begin{pmatrix}\text{second factor is an}\\ \text{integral power of 10}\end{pmatrix}$$

The characteristic is the integral exponent of 10.

Example:

In scientific notation: $153 = 1.53 \times 10^2$

For log 153, the characteristic is 2.

Some numbers share the same characteristic but differ in mantissa.

Example:

All the numbers from 100 to 999 have the characteristic 2, but all have different mantissas.

You can determine the characteristic of a logarithm by inspection, but you need a calculator (or table) to determine the mantissa. A calculator will give you the complete logarithm of a number—that is, the characteristic and the mantissa.

Example: To read log 153 to four decimal places,

ENTER: 153 [LOG] or, on some calculators [LOG] 153

DISPLAY: [2.1846914]

Answer: $\log 153 \approx 2.1847$

Some numbers share the same mantissa but differ in characteristic.

Example: If $\log 1.53 = 0.1847$

then	since
$\log 1{,}530 = 3.1847$	$1{,}530 = 1.53 \times 10^3$
$\log 153{,}000 = 5.1847$	$153{,}000 = 1.53 \times 10^5$
$\log 0.0153 = -2 + 0.1847 = -1.8153$	$0.0153 = 1.53 \times 10^{-2}$
$\log 0.153 = -1 + 0.1847 = -0.8153$	$0.153 = 1.53 \times 10^{-1}$

Note that when a characteristic is negative, a calculator will display the simplified sum.

Example: $\log 0.0153 = -2 + 0.1847$
$= -1.8153$ ← simplified sum

ENTER: 0.0153 [LOG]

DISPLAY: [-1.8153085]

ROUNDED: −1.8153

Antilogarithm

If log $N = x$, then N is the number whose logarithm is x.

When N is known, you can find x, which is the logarithm of N.

That is, you are finding the exponent x to which the base 10 must be raised to produce the number N.

When x is known, you can find N, which is the ANTILOGARITHM of x.

That is, you are finding the number N that is the result of raising the base 10 to the exponent x.

To use a calculator to find antilog, press [10ˣ], which is usually accessed by [2nd].

Examples

1. If log N = 0.7745, find N rounded to the nearest hundredth.

ENTER: 0.7745 [2nd] [10ˣ]

DISPLAY: 5.9497675

Answer: $N \approx 5.95$

Verify the value of the antilog by finding: log 5.95

ENTER: 5.95 [LOG]

DISPLAY: 0.7745169

ROUNDED: 0.7745

Verifies that: If log N = 0.7745, then $N \approx 5.95$.

2. If log N = –1.3130, find N rounded to five decimal places.

ENTER: 1.3130 [+/–] [2nd] [10ˣ]

DISPLAY: 0.0486407

Answer: $N \approx 0.04864$

Verify the value of the antilog by finding: log 0.04864

ENTER: 0.04864 [LOG]

DISPLAY: –1.3130064

ROUNDED: –1.3130

Verifies that: If log N = –1.3130, then $N \approx 0.04864$.

EXERCISES

1. The mantissa of log 3.07 is
(1) 3.07 **(2)** 0 **(3)** 0.4871 **(4)** 10

2. The characteristic of log 0.173 is
(1) 0.2380 **(2)** 0.173 **(3)** 0 **(4)** –1 or 9–10

3. Which logarithm has the same characteristic as log 14?
(1) log 1.4 **(2)** log 0.14 **(3)** log 140 **(4)** log 99

4. Which logarithm does not have the same characteristic as log 3047?
(1) log 30.47 **(2)** log 3048 **(3)** log 7000 **(4)** log 9999

5. Which two logarithms have the same characteristic?
(1) log 34.5 and log 543
(2) log 3.45 and log 54.3
(3) log 3.45 and log 34.5
(4) log 0.345 and log 0.543

6. Which logarithm does not have the same mantissa as log 2.13?
(1) log 0.0213 **(2)** log 2130 **(3)** log 2.03 **(4)** log 21,300

7. If $10^{3.5922} = 3910$, then the value of $10^{0.5922}$ is
(1) 0.391 **(2)** 3.91 **(3)** 39.1 **(4)** 3,910,000

8. If $10^{0.9370} = 8.65$, then $10^{2.9370}$ is equal to
(1) 865 (2) 86.5 (3) 17.3 (4) 0.0865

9. If $10^{0.4771} = 3$, then what is the value of $10^{2.4771}$?

10. If $10^{0.5623} = 3.65$, what is the numerical value of $10^{2.5623}$?

11. If $10^{0.8338} = 6.82$, find the value of $10^{2.8338}$.

12. If $10^{3.5551} = 3590$, find the value of $10^{0.5551}$.

13. If $10^{2.5729} = 374$, find the value of $10^{0.5729}$.

14. If $4 = 10^{0.6021}$, then the value of $10^{-2 + 0.6021}$ is
(1) 40 (2) 400 (3) 0.04 (4) 0.4

In 15-28, find the indicated logarithm to the nearest ten-thousandth.

15. log 7.62
16. log 24
17. log 0.346
18. log 2000
19. log 0.0005
20. log 10.1
21. log 2001
22. log 37.62
23. log 429.7
24. log 0.1264
25. log 58.43
26. log 1985
27. log 742.6
28. log 9.012

29. If $\log N = 0.7388$,
then N is approximately equal to
(1) 7388 (3) 5480
(2) 7.388 (4) 5.48

30. If $\log N = -0.3261$,
then N is approximately equal to
(1) 471 (3) 0.472
(2) 0.8286 (4) 4.72

31. If $\log N = 3.8609$, find the value of N to the nearest integer.

32. If $\log N = 0.9175$, find the value of N to the nearest hundredth.

33. If $\log N = -1.4868$, find the value of N to the nearest ten-thousandth.

34. If $\log N = 0.5459$, find N to the nearest thousandth.

In 35-38, for the indicated value of $\log N$, find the value of N to the nearest thousandth.

35. $\log N = 1.7390$
36. $\log N = 0.5959$
37. $\log N = 9.8373 - 10$
38. $\log N = 8.8080 - 10$

Using Logarithms to Solve an Exponential Equation

When the terms of an exponential equation cannot be expressed as *integral* powers of a common base, use base 10 and logarithms to solve.

Example

Solve for x to the nearest tenth: $5^x = 17$

Solution: Since 17 cannot be expressed as an integral power of 5, use 10 as a common base.

$5^x = 17$	
$\log 5^x = \log 17$	When two numbers are equal, their common logs are equal.
$x \log 5 = \log 17$	In logs: power $\rightarrow$ multiplier
$x = \dfrac{\log 17}{\log 5}$	Divide by the coefficient of x.
Answer: $x \approx 1.8$	Use a calculator and round.

Note: The original equation might first need to be rewritten as exponential form, if it is given in logarithmic form.

$$\log_5 17 = x \longleftrightarrow 5^x = 17$$

EXERCISES

In 1–16, using logarithms, solve for x to the nearest tenth.

1. $2^x = 5$

2. $3^x = 21$

3. $4^x = 70$

4. $5^x = 30$

5. $(2.1)^x = 32$

6. $(1.95)^x = 54$

7. $2^{3x} = 7$

8. $3^{2x} = 4$

9. $x = \log_2 9$

10. $x = \log_5 29.5$

11. $\log_3 5 = x$

12. $\log_3 4 = x$

13. $x^3 = 7$

14. $x^3 = 52$

15. $\log_x 5 = 3$

16. $x = 2^y$ when $y = 2$

4.7 SUMMARY EXERCISES

1. Which relation is not a function?

(1) $\{(x, y) \mid y = x\}$ (3) $\{(1, 3), (2, 5), (1, 7)\}$
(2) $\{(1, 2), (2, 3), (3, 4)\}$ (4) $\{(1, 4), (2, 4), (3, 4)\}$

2. Which relation is also a function?

(1) $x^2 + y^2 = 36$ (3) $9x^2 + 4y^2 = 36$
(2) $x^2 - y^2 = 36$ (4) $y = 4x^2$

3. What is the domain of the function $f(x) = \sqrt{x - 1}$?

(1) $\{x \mid x \geq 1\}$ (3) $\{x \mid x \leq 1\}$
(2) $\{x \mid x \geq 2\}$ (4) $\{x \mid x \leq -2\}$

4. The diagram shows the graph of the function $\{(x, y) \mid y = x^2 - 3\}$, where the domain is the set of real numbers. What is the range of this function?

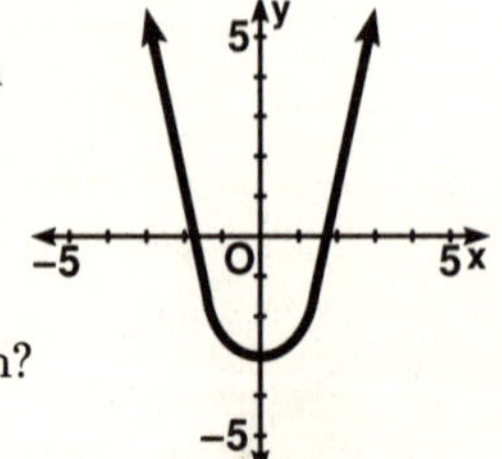

5. The domain for $f(x) = 2x - 1$ is $-3 \leq x \leq 3$. The greatest value in the range of f is

(1) –12 (2) –7 (3) 5 (4) 12

6. In which function is the range equal to the domain?

(1) $y = 2^x$ (3) $y = \log x$
(2) $y = x^2$ (4) $y = x$

7. Which graph is not a representation of a function?

(1)

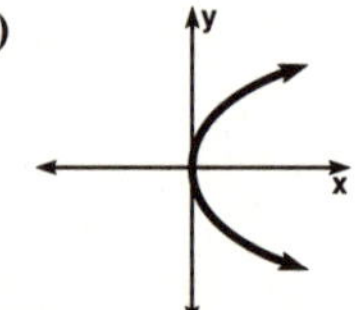

(3)
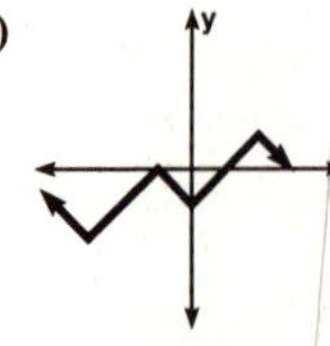

(2)
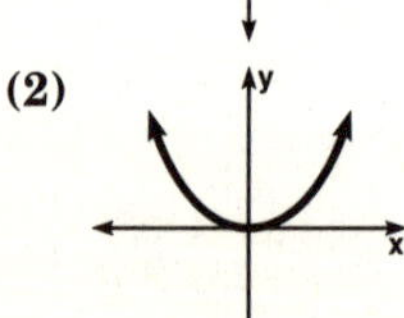

(4)
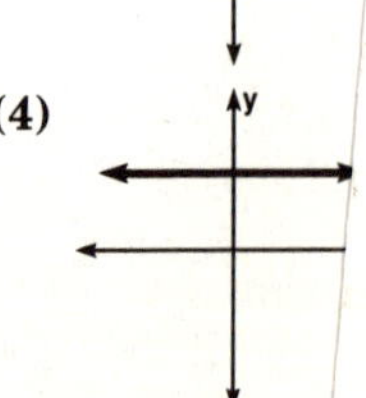

8. In the diagram at the right, the function $f(x) = x^2$ is represented graphically. Which graph below represents the inverse relation of $f(x)$?

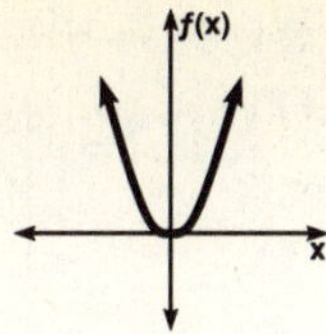

(1)
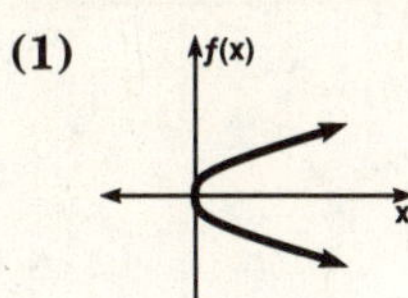

(3)
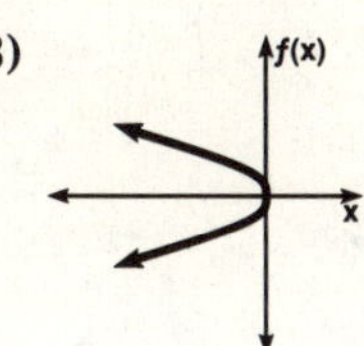

(2)
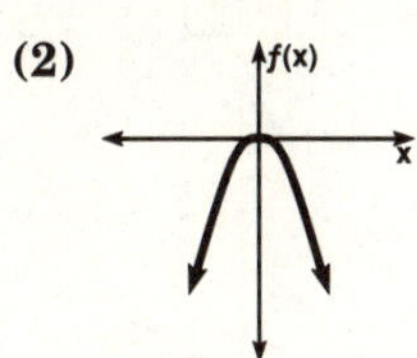

(4)
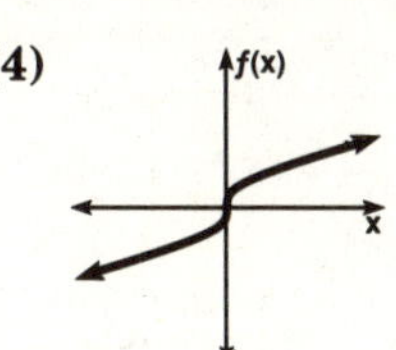

9. The diagram at the right represents the graph of $f(x)$. Which graph below represents $f^{-1}(x)$?

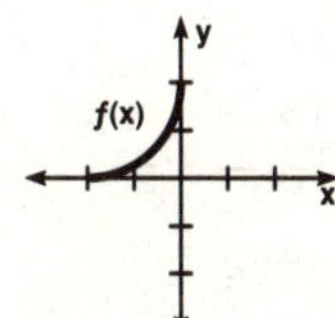

(1)
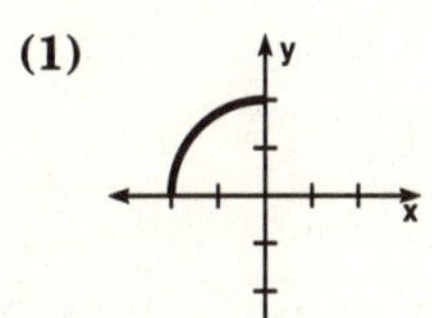

(3)
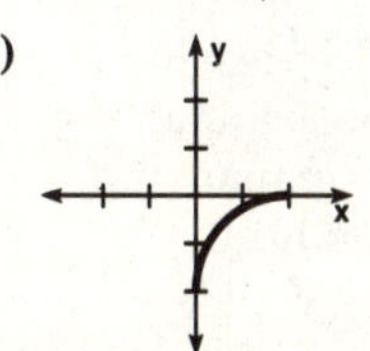

(2)
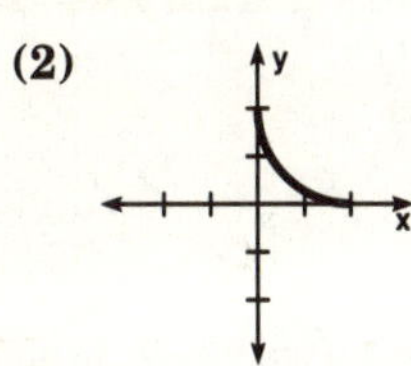

(4)
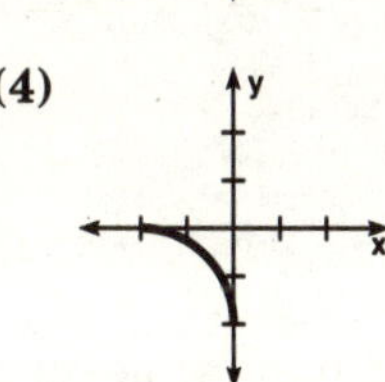

10. If $f(x) = x^{-2} + x^0$, find the value of $f(2)$.

11. If $f(x) = x^{\frac{2}{3}}$, find $f(-27)$.

12. If $f(x) = 2x^{-\frac{1}{2}}$, find $f(16)$.

13. If $f(x) = 3 + x$ and $g(x) = 6x$, what is $[f \circ g]\,(-2)$?
(1) 6 (2) 12 (3) −9 (4) −12

14. If $f(x) = x^2 - 3$, then $f(a - b)$ is equivalent to
(1) $a^2 - b^2 - 3$
(2) $a^2 - 2ab - b^2 - 3$
(3) $a^2 - 2ab + b^2 - 3$
(4) $a^2 + b^2 - 3$

15. If $f(x) = \dfrac{x-4}{x+4}$, then $f(4a)$ equals
(1) $\dfrac{a-1}{a+1}$
(2) $\dfrac{a+1}{a-1}$
(3) $\dfrac{4a-1}{4a+1}$
(4) $\dfrac{4a+1}{4a-1}$

16. If $h(x) = 2x - 1$ and $g(x) = 3x + 1$, what is $[h \circ g](2)$?

17. Given: $f(x) = 11x + 3$ and $g(x) = \sqrt{x}$
Find:
a. $f(2)$ **b.** $g(f(2))$ **c.** $g(100)$ **d.** $f^{-1}(x)$ **e.** $g^{-1}(3)$

18. For which pair of functions does $f(g(x)) = g(f(x))$?
(1) $f(x) = x + 3$ $g(x) = 3x$
(2) $f(x) = 3x$ $g(x) = \frac{1}{3}x$
(3) $f(x) = 3x$ $g(x) = \frac{1}{3x}$
(4) $f(x) = x + 3$ $g(x) = 3 - x$

19. Which equation has a circle as its graph?
(1) $x^2 = 10 - y^2$
(2) $x^2 = 10 + y^2$
(3) $2x^2 = 10 - y^2$
(4) $2x^2 = 10 + y^2$

20. Which of the following is the equation of a parabola?
(1) $9x^2 = 4y^2 + 36$
(2) $xy = -8$
(3) $x^2 = 25 - 4y^2$
(4) $x^2 = y - 16x + 4$

21. Which equation represents an ellipse?
(1) $x^2 + y^2 = 400$
(2) $25x^2 + 16y^2 = 400$
(3) $x^2 - y^2 = 400$
(4) $xy = 400$

22. Which graph illustrates a quadratic relation whose domain is all real numbers?

(1)
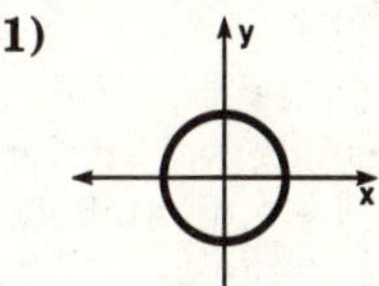

(3)
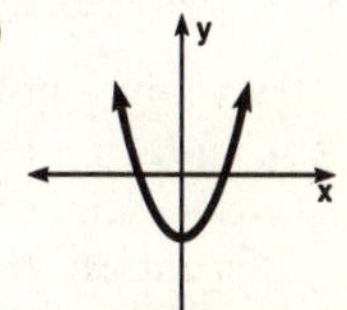

(2)
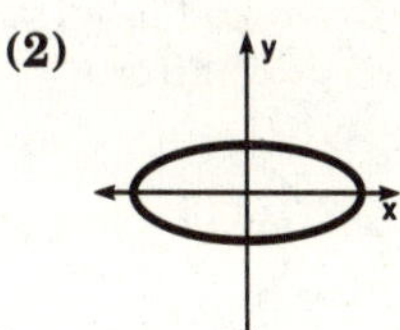

(4)
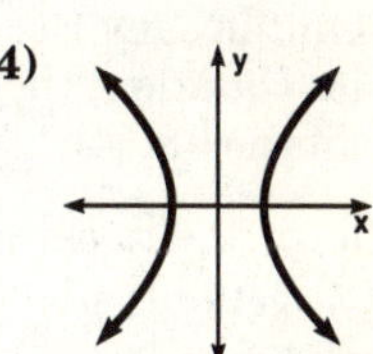

23. The graphs of $x^2 + y^2 = 9$ and $y = -3$ are drawn on the same set of axes. How many points do these graphs have in common?
(1) 1 (2) 2 (3) 0 (4) 4

24. What is the total number of points in which the graphs of $x^2 - y^2 = 4$ and $x = 2$ intersect?
(1) 1 (2) 2 (3) 0 (4) 4

25. If y varies directly as the square of x, and $y = 32$ when $x = 4$, find the value of y when $x = 5$.

26. If b varies inversely as h and if $b = 8$ when $h = 9$, find b when $h = 6$.

27. If x and y vary inversely and x is doubled, then y is
(1) doubled
(2) unchanged
(3) halved
(4) four times as large

28. The cabbage harvest (h) from the Stuyvesant Farm varies inversely as the local population of the cabbage worm (w). Which graph best illustrates this relationship?

(1)
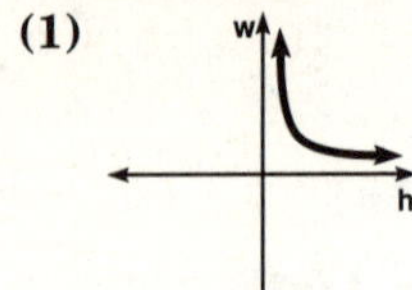

(3)
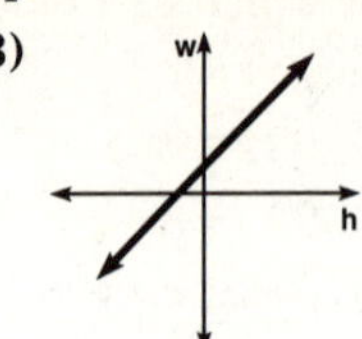

(2)
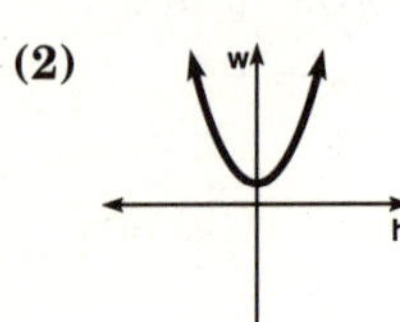

(4)
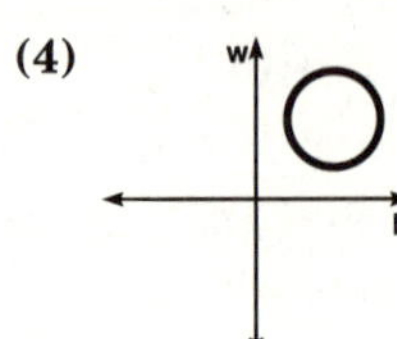

29. The graph of the equation $xy = 4$ is

(1) a hyperbola **(3)** an ellipse
(2) a parabola **(4)** a circle

30. If the graphs of the equations $xy = 12$ and $x - y = 3$ were drawn on the same set of axes, the total number of points common to these graphs would be

(1) 1 **(2)** 2 **(3)** 0 **(4)** 4

31. a. Draw and label, with its equation, the graph of the equation $xy = 8$ in the interval $-8 \le x \le 8$.

b. On the same set of axes, draw and label, with its equation, the graph of the image of $xy = 8$ after a reflection in the x-axis.

c. On the same set of axes, draw and label, with its equation, the image of $xy = 8$ after a dilation of -2.

32. What is the inverse of the function $\{(-1, 2), (0, 5), (3, -2)\}$?

(1) $\{(1, -2), (0, -5), (-3, 2)\}$
(2) $\{(-1, -2), (0, -5), (3, 2)\}$
(3) $\{(2, -1), (5, 0), (-2, 3)\}$
(4) $\{(-2, 1), (-5, 0), (2, -3)\}$

33. The inverse of the function $2x + 3y = 6$ is

(1) $y = -\frac{2}{3}x + 2$
(2) $y = -\frac{3}{2}x + 3$
(3) $y = \frac{3}{2}x + 2$
(4) $y = \frac{2}{3}x + 3$

34. Which equation defines a function whose inverse is not a function?

(1) $y = |x|$ **(3)** $y = 3x + 2$
(2) $y = -x$ **(4)** $y = 2^x$

35. For the function $f(x) = \frac{x-2}{3}$:

a. write $f^{-1}(x)$
b. find $[f^{-1} \circ f](8)$

36. Which function is one-to-one?

(1)
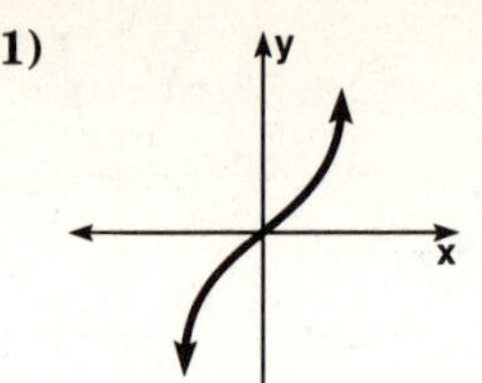

(3)
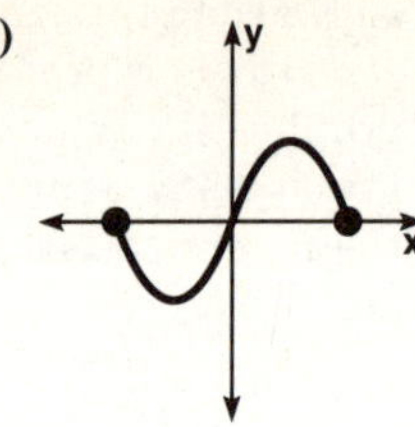

(2)
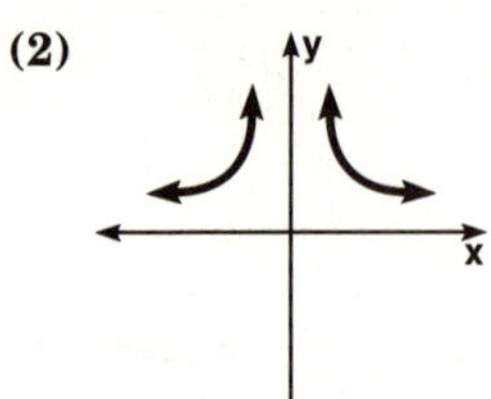

(4)
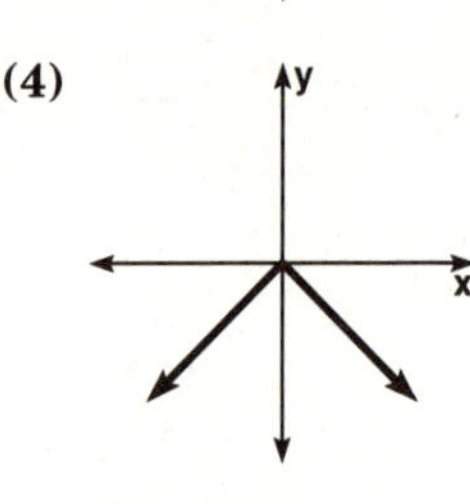

37. The accompanying diagram is the graph of which equation?

(2, 1)
(1, 0)
$(\frac{1}{2}, -1)$
$(\frac{1}{4}, -2)$

(1) $y = |x|$
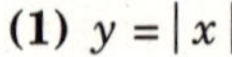
(2) $y = \sqrt{x}$
(3) $y = 2^x$
(4) $y = \log_2 x$

38. Which equation is represented by the graph in the accompanying diagram?

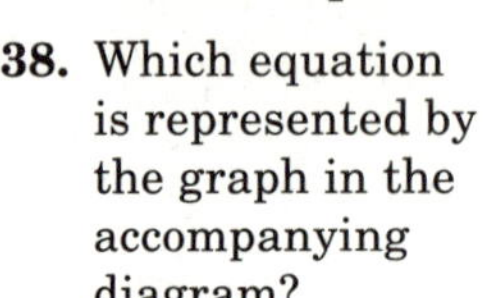

(1) $y = \log x$
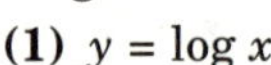
(2) $y = \log_2 x$
(3) $y = 2^x$
(4) $y = 10^x$

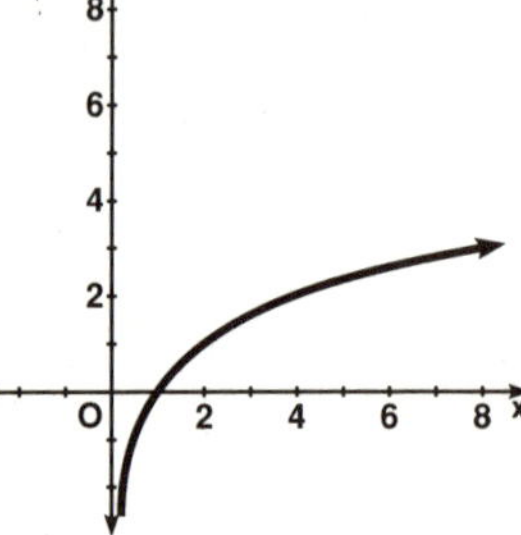

39. a. Sketch the graph of the equation $y = 2^x$ and label the graph a.

b. On the same set of axes, graph the reflection of $y = 2^x$ in the y-axis and label the graph b.

c. Using logarithms, find x, to the *nearest hundredth*: $2^x = 5$

40. Given: $f(x) = 2^x$

a. On graph paper, sketch the graph of $f(x)$ in the interval $-1 \le x \le 3$. Label the graph a.

b. On the same set of axes, sketch the image of the graph drawn in part **a** after $(T_{2,-1} \circ r_{x\text{-axis}})$. Label the graph b.

c. On the same set of axes, sketch the image of the graph drawn in part **b** after D_{-1}. Label the graph c.

41. a. On the same set of axes, sketch and label the graphs of $y = \log_2 x$ and $y = 2^x$.

b. The graphs of $y = \log_2 x$ and $y = 2^x$ are symmetrical to each other with respect to a line. What is an equation of the line of symmetry?

c. Write an equation of the inverse of the function $y = \log_2 x$.

42. The graph of which equation has symmetry to the origin?

(1) $y = x^2$ (3) $xy = 10$
(2) $x = y^2$ (4) $x + y = 7$

43. Solve for x: $9^{2x-3} = 81$

44. Solve each of the following equations for the real value of x:

a. $3^x = \frac{1}{27}$ **c.** $\log_8 x = -\frac{2}{3}$
b. $\log_x 8 = 3$ **d.** $x^{\frac{3}{2}} = 125$

45. Using logarithms, solve for x to the nearest tenth: $2^x = 7$

46. Which equation is equivalent to $y = 10^x$?

(1) $y = -10^{-x}$ (3) $y = \left(\frac{1}{10}\right)^{-x}$
(2) $y = 10^{-x}$ (4) $y = \left(\frac{1}{10}\right)^x$

47. Find $\log \sqrt[3]{0.691}$ to four decimal places.

48. The equation $y = a^x$ expressed in logarithmic form is

(1) $y = \log_a x$ (3) $x = \log_a y$
(2) $a = \log_x y$ (4) $x = \log_y a$

49. If $\log a = x$ and $\log b = y$ then $\log \sqrt{ab}$ is equivalent to

(1) $\frac{1}{2}x + y$ (3) $\frac{1}{2}xy$
(2) $\frac{1}{2}(x + y)$ (4) $\frac{1}{4}xy$

50. The expression $\log \frac{a^3}{b}$ is equivalent to

(1) $3 \log a - \log b$ (3) $3\left(\frac{\log a}{\log b}\right)$
(2) $3(\log a - \log b)$ (4) $\frac{1}{3}(\log a - \log b)$

51. If $\log_9 x = \frac{3}{2}$, what is the value of x?

(1) $\frac{3}{2}$ (2) 8 (3) $\frac{27}{2}$ (4) 27

52. Log $\sqrt{\frac{a}{b}}$ is equivalent to

(1) $\frac{1}{2} \log a - \log b$ (3) $\frac{1}{2}(\log a + \log b)$
(2) $\frac{1}{2}(\log a - \log b)$ (4) $\frac{1}{2} \log a + \log b$

53. The expression $2 - \log a$ is equivalent to

(1) $\log \frac{100}{a}$ (3) $\log \frac{2}{a}$
(2) $\frac{2}{\log a}$ (4) $\sqrt{\log a}$

54. Find: log 62.43

55. If $\log N = 9.9011 - 10$, find N.

56. If $\log 28 = \log 4 + \log x$, what is the value of x?

(1) 7 (2) 14 (3) 24 (4) 32

57. The expression $\log \sqrt[4]{\frac{a^2}{b}}$ is equivalent to

(1) $\frac{1}{4}\left(\frac{\log a^2}{\log b}\right)$ (3) $\frac{1}{2}(4 \log a - \log b)$
(2) $4(\log a^2 - \log b)$ (4) $\frac{1}{4}(2 \log a - \log b)$

58. If $\log 7 = x$ and $\log 3 = y$, express in terms of x and y:

a. $\log \sqrt{\frac{3}{7}}$ **b.** log 63

59. If $\log 2 = x$ and $\log 3 = y$, express in terms of x and y:

a. $\log \frac{\sqrt{2}}{9}$ **b.** $\log \sqrt[3]{6}$

CHAPTER 5

Circles

5.1 ANGLE MEASURE

Basic Definitions

A CIRCLE is a set of points in a plane that are equidistant from a fixed point, which is the CENTER of the circle. The perimeter of a circle is called its CIRCUMFERENCE, with degree measure 360.

A RADIUS is a line segment from the center to any point on the circumference.

A CENTRAL ANGLE has its vertex at the center of the circle and its sides are radii.

A CHORD is a line segment that connects two points on the circumference.

A DIAMETER is a chord that passes through the center.

An INSCRIBED ANGLE has its vertex on the circumference, and its sides are chords.

A TANGENT is a line that intersects the circle in exactly one point.

A SECANT is a line that intersects the circle in two points.

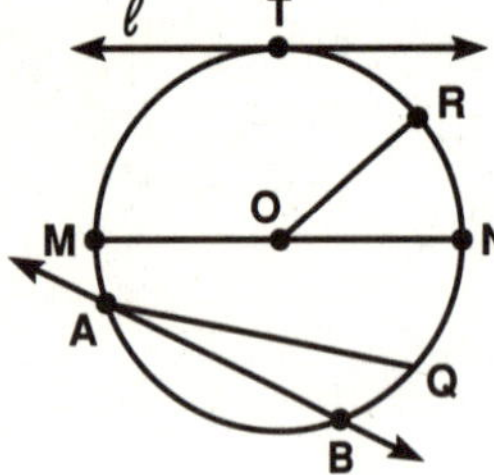

In circle O:
$\overline{RO}$ and $\overline{NO}$ are radii.
$\angle RON$ is a central angle.
$\overline{AQ}$ is a chord.
$\overline{MN}$ is a diameter.
$\angle QAB$ is an inscribed angle.
ℓ is a tangent.
$\overleftrightarrow{AB}$ is a secant.

An ARC is any portion of the circumference.

A SEMICIRCLE measures exactly half of the circumference, = 180°.

A MINOR ARC is an arc with measure less than a semicircle, < 180°.

A MAJOR ARC is an arc with measure greater than a semicircle, > 180°.

The degree measure of an arc equals the measure of the central angle that intercepts the arc.

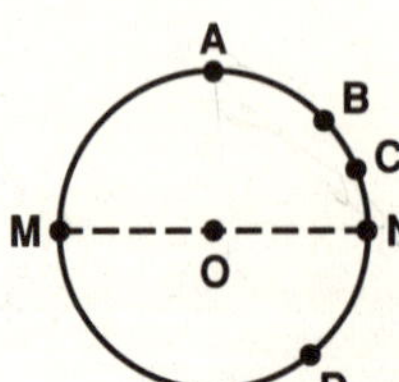

m semicircle $\widehat{MAN} = 180°$
m minor $\widehat{ABC} < 180°$
m major $\widehat{MBD} > 180°$

Applying Theorems

The measure of a central angle is the same as the measure of its intercepted arc.

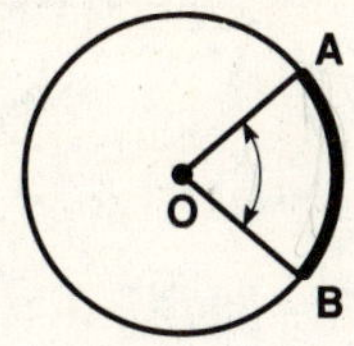

$m\angle AOB = m\widehat{AB}$

The measure of an inscribed angle is one-half the measure of its intercepted arc.

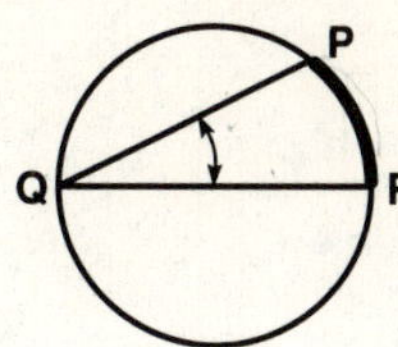

$m\angle PQR = \frac{1}{2} m\widehat{PR}$

An angle inscribed in a semicircle is a right angle.

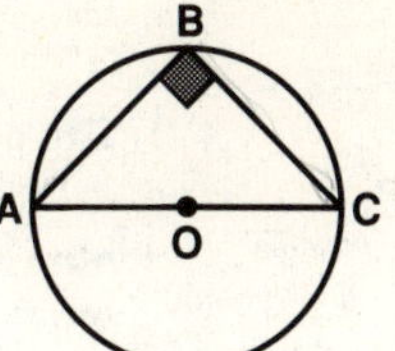

$m\angle ABC = 90°$

The measure of an angle formed by two chords intersecting in a circle is one-half the sum of the measures of the arcs intercepted by the angle and by its vertical angle.

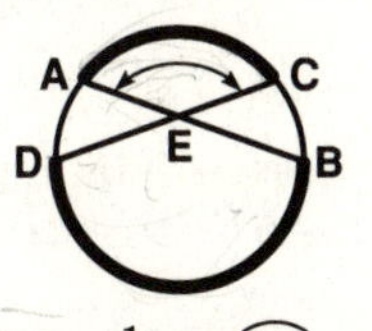

$m\angle AEC = \frac{1}{2}(m\widehat{AC} + m\widehat{BD})$

The measure of an angle formed by a tangent and a chord intersecting at the point of tangency is one-half the measure of the intercepted arc.

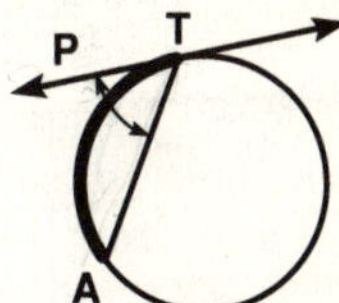

$m\angle PTA = \frac{1}{2} m\widehat{AT}$

The measure of an angle formed by a tangent and a secant, or two tangents, or two secants intersecting outside a circle is one-half the difference of the measures of the intercepted arcs.

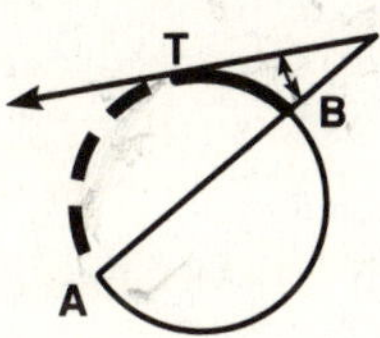

$m\angle P = \frac{1}{2}(m\widehat{AT} - m\widehat{TB})$

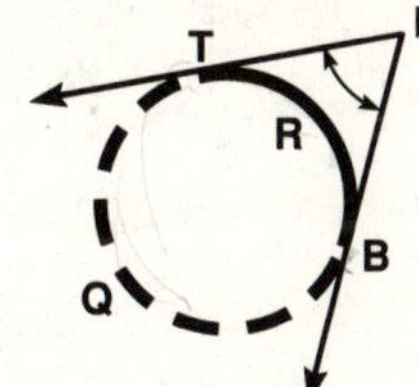

$m\angle P = \frac{1}{2}(m\widehat{TQB} - m\widehat{TRB})$

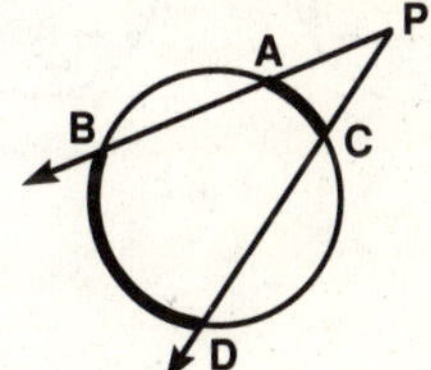

$m\angle P = \frac{1}{2}(m\widehat{BD} - m\widehat{AC})$

Examples

1. If $\overrightarrow{PA}$ and $\overrightarrow{PB}$ are tangents to a circle and the ratio of major arc $\widehat{AB}$ to minor arc $\widehat{AB}$ is 2 : 1, what is $m\angle P$?

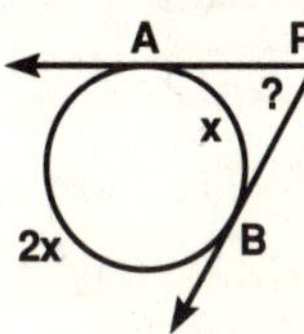

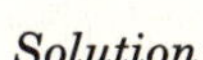

Solution:

Let x = the common ratio factor.

$$\begin{aligned} m \text{ major } \widehat{AB} + m \text{ minor } \widehat{AB} &= 360 \\ 2x + x &= 360 \\ 3x &= 360 \\ x &= 120 \\ 2x &= 240 \end{aligned}$$

$m\angle P = \frac{1}{2}(m \text{ major } \widehat{AB} - m \text{ minor } \widehat{AB})$

$m\angle P = \frac{1}{2}(240 - 120) = 60°$ *Ans.*

2. *Given:* $\overline{AB} \parallel \overline{CD}$

$m\widehat{AC} = 50°$

Find: $m\widehat{BD}$

Plan: Prove $m\widehat{BD} = m\widehat{AC}$.

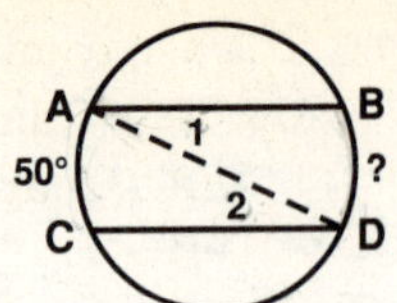

Statements	*Reasons*
1. Draw $\overline{AD}$.	1. Two points determine a line.
2. $\overline{AB} \parallel \overline{CD}$	2. Given
3. $m\angle 1 = m\angle 2$	3. Alternate interior ∠s of ∥ lines are equal in measure.
4. $m\angle 1 = \frac{1}{2}m\widehat{BD}$ $m\angle 2 = \frac{1}{2}m\widehat{AC}$	4. In a circle, the measure of an inscribed ∠ is one-half the measure of its intercepted arc.
5. $\frac{1}{2}m\widehat{BD} = \frac{1}{2}m\widehat{AC}$	5. Things = to = things are =.
6. $m\widehat{BD} = m\widehat{AC}$	6. Multiplication property

Answer: $m\widehat{BD} = 50°$

Note: The results of this example may be taken as a theorem, extended for different cases.

In a circle, parallel lines intercept congruent arcs between them.

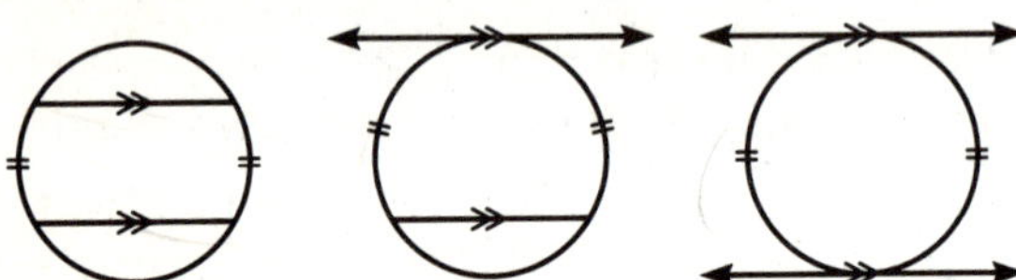

3. *Given:* Circle *O* with diameter $\overline{AOD}$, tangent $\overline{CD}$, secant $\overline{CFB} \parallel \overline{DA}$, $\overline{AF}$ and $\overline{BD}$ intersecting at *E*, and $m\angle BAF = 20°$

Find: **a.** $m\widehat{AB}$
b. $m\angle BEF$
c. $m\angle CDB$
d. $m\angle BCD$
e. $m\angle CFE$

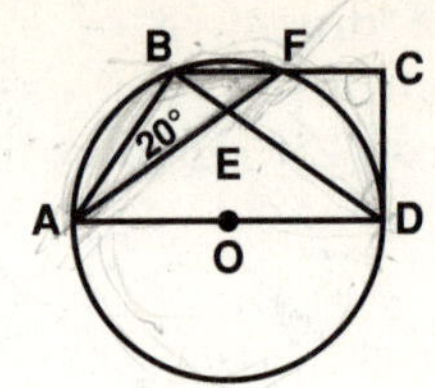

Solution:

a. m inscribed $\angle BAF = 20° = \frac{1}{2}m\widehat{BF}$ Thus, $m\widehat{BF} = 40°$.
$\overline{CFB} \parallel \overline{DA}$ making $m\widehat{AB} = m\widehat{FD}$.
Since $\overline{AD}$ is a diameter, $\widehat{ABFD}$ is a semicircle:

$$m\widehat{AB} + m\widehat{BF} + m\widehat{FD} = 180$$
$$m\widehat{AB} + 40 + m\widehat{AB} = 180$$
$$2(m\widehat{AB}) = 140$$
$$m\widehat{AB} = 70° \quad \textit{Ans.}$$

b. $\angle BEF$ is formed by two intersecting chords.
$$m\angle BEF = \tfrac{1}{2}(m\widehat{BF} + m\widehat{AD}) = \tfrac{1}{2}(40 + 180) = 110° \quad \textit{Ans.}$$

c. $\angle CDB$ is formed by a tangent and a chord.
$$m\angle CDB = \tfrac{1}{2}(m\widehat{BFD}) = \tfrac{1}{2}(40 + 70) = 55° \quad \textit{Ans.}$$

d. $\angle BCD$ is formed by a secant and a tangent.
$$m\angle BCD = \tfrac{1}{2}(m\widehat{BAD} - m\widehat{FD}) = \tfrac{1}{2}[(70 + 180) - 70] = 90° \quad \textit{Ans.}$$

e. $\angle CFE$ is the supplement of inscribed $\angle BFA$.
$$m\angle CFE = 180 - m\angle BFA$$
$$= 180 - \tfrac{1}{2}m\angle \widehat{BA}$$
$$= 180 - \tfrac{1}{2}(70) = 145° \quad \textit{Ans.}$$

EXERCISES

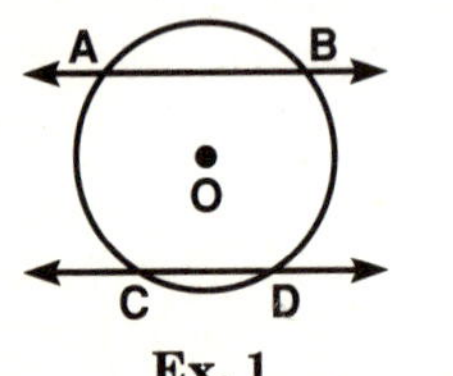

Ex. 1

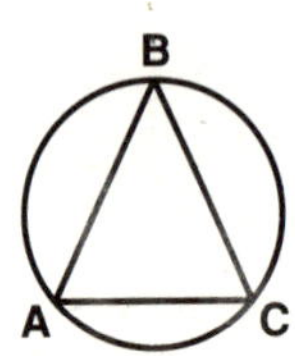

Ex. 2

1. Secants $\overleftrightarrow{AB}$ and $\overleftrightarrow{CD}$ intersect circle *O* at *A*, *B*, *C*, and *D*. If $\overleftrightarrow{AB} \parallel \overleftrightarrow{CD}$, $m\widehat{AB} = 100°$, and $m\widehat{AC} = 100°$, what is $m\widehat{CD}$?

2. $\triangle ABC$ is inscribed in the circle. If $\angle A \cong \angle C$ and $m\widehat{AC} = 100°$, find $m\angle C$.

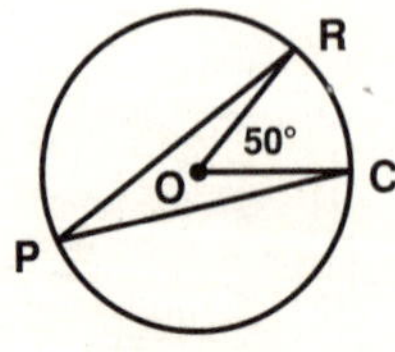

Ex. 3

3. If $m\angle ROC = 50°$, find $m\angle RPC$.

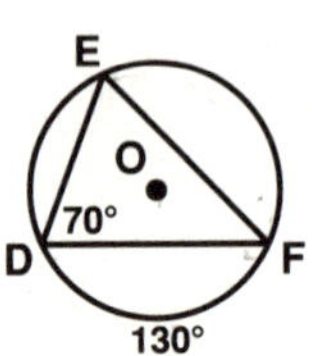

Ex. 4

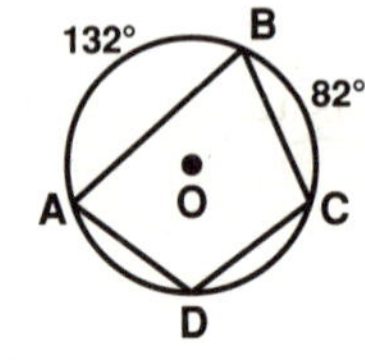

Ex. 5

4. $\triangle DEF$ is inscribed in circle *O*. If $m\angle D = 70°$ and $m\widehat{DF} = 130°$, find $m\angle F$.

5. Quadrilateral *ABCD* is inscribed in circle *O*. If $m\widehat{AB} = 132°$ and $m\widehat{BC} = 82°$, find $m\angle ADC$.

6. Chord $\overline{CD}$ is parallel to diameter $\overline{AB}$. If $m\widehat{AC} = 25°$, what is $m\angle COD$?
(1) 25° **(3)** 130°
(2) 65° **(4)** 155°

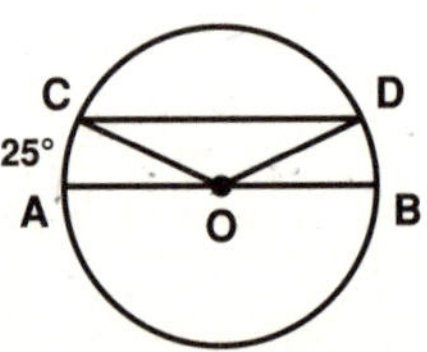

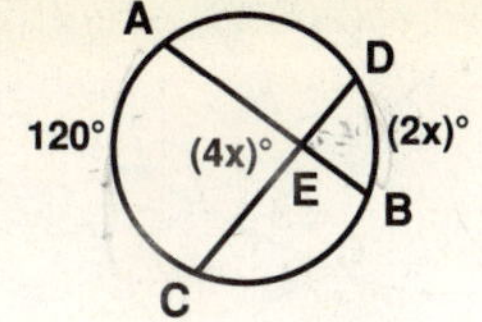

Ex. 7 Ex. 8

7. Chords $\overline{AB}$ and $\overline{CD}$ intersect at E. If $m\angle AEC = (4x)°$, $m\widehat{AC} = 120°$, and $m\widehat{DB} = (2x)°$, what is the value of x?
(1) 12 (2) 20 (3) 30 (4) 60

8. Chords $\overline{CD}$ and $\overline{AB}$ intersect at E. If $m\angle BED$ is 50°, what is the sum of $m\widehat{BC}$ and $m\widehat{DA}$?
(1) 50° (2) 100° (3) 130° (4) 260°

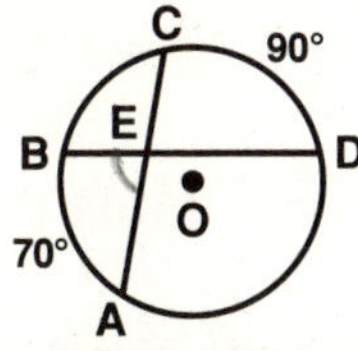

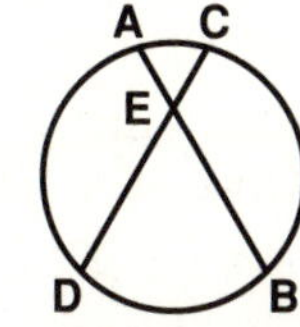

Ex. 9 Ex. 10

9. $\overline{AC}$ and $\overline{BD}$ are chords of circle O and intersect at E. If $m\widehat{AB} = 70°$ and $m\widehat{CD} = 90°$, find $m\angle BEA$.

10. Chords $\overline{AB}$ and $\overline{CD}$ intersect at E. If $m\widehat{AC} = 30°$ and $m\angle DEB = 70°$, find $m\widehat{DB}$.

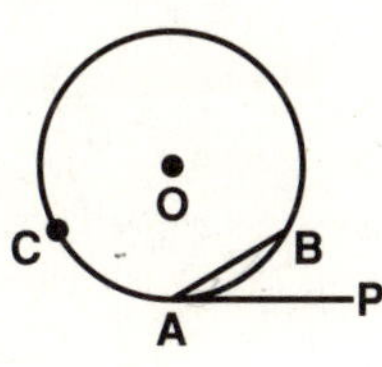

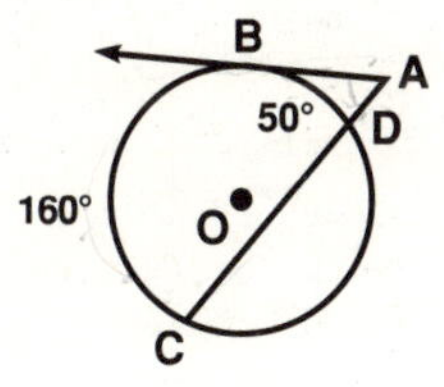

Ex. 11 Ex. 12

11. $\overline{PA}$ is tangent to circle O, and $\overline{AB}$ is a chord. If $m\widehat{ACB} = 300°$, find the measure of $\angle BAP$.

12. $\overrightarrow{AB}$ is tangent to circle O at B and $\overline{ADC}$ is a secant. If $m\widehat{BD} = 50°$ and $m\widehat{BC} = 160°$, find $m\angle A$.

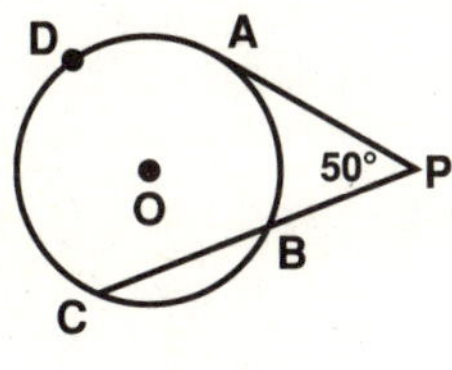

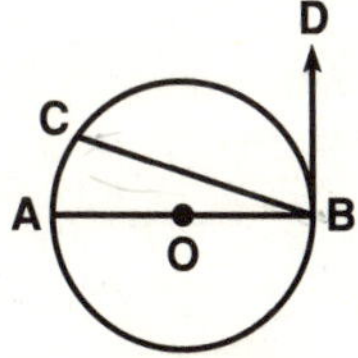

Ex. 13 Ex. 14

13. Tangent $\overline{PA}$ and secant $\overline{PBC}$ are drawn to circle O. If $m\widehat{ADC}$ is twice $m\widehat{AB}$ and $m\angle P$ is 50°, what is $m\widehat{AB}$?
(1) 25° (2) 50° (3) 100° (4) 200°

14. $\overrightarrow{BD}$ is a tangent to circle O at B, $\overline{BC}$ is a chord, and $\overline{BOA}$ is a diameter. If $m\widehat{AC} : m\widehat{CB} = 1:4$, find $m\angle DBC$. (Diagram: page bottom, at left.)

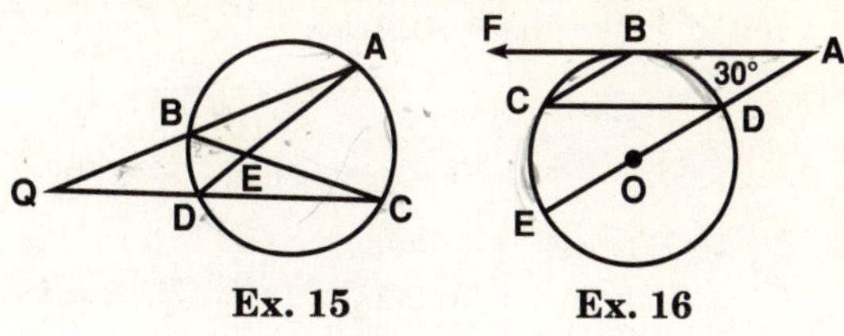

Ex. 15 Ex. 16

15. Secants $\overline{QBA}$ and $\overline{QDC}$ are drawn to a circle from external point Q. Chords $\overline{AD}$ and $\overline{CB}$ intersect at point E. If $m\angle ABC = 40°$ and $m\angle DCB = 20°$, what is $m\angle AEC$?
(1) 120° (2) 60° (3) 20° (4) 15°

16. Tangent $\overleftrightarrow{ABF}$ is parallel to chord $\overline{CD}$ and secant $\overline{ADOE}$ is parallel to chord $\overline{BC}$. If $m\angle A = 30°$, find $m\widehat{BD}$.

17. For circle O,
tangent $\overline{PA} \perp$ radius $\overline{OA}$,
tangent $\overline{PB} \perp$ radius $\overline{OB}$,
and $m\angle AOP = 35°$.
What is $m\angle APB$?

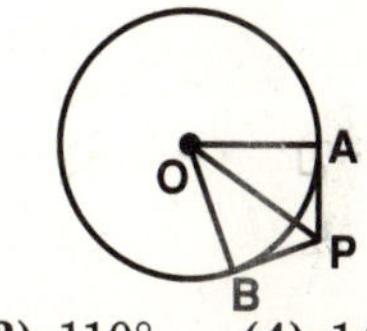

(1) 70° (2) 55° (3) 110° (4) 145°

18. From the same external point, two tangents are drawn to a circle. The tangents intercept arcs whose measures are 300° and 60°. The measure of the angle formed by the tangents is
(1) 60° (2) 120° (3) 240° (4) 300°

19. Two tangents to a circle from an external point intercept a major arc of 200°. Find the number of degrees in the angle formed by the two tangents.

20. Tangents $\overline{PA}$ and $\overline{PB}$ are drawn from point P to the same circle. The measure of the major arc intercepted by the tangents is three times that of the minor arc. Find $m\angle APB$.

21. Two tangents drawn to a circle from an external point are perpendicular. Find the measure of the smaller of the intercepted arcs.

22. $\overline{AOB}$ is a diameter of circle O, $\overline{CB}$ is tangent to the circle at B, $\overline{EAC}$ and $\overline{EFB}$ are secants, $m\widehat{AD} = 70°$, and $m\angle ABF = 40°$.

Find:
a. $m\angle CAB$
b. $m\widehat{AF}$
c. $m\angle E$
d. $m\angle C$
e. $m\angle ABC$

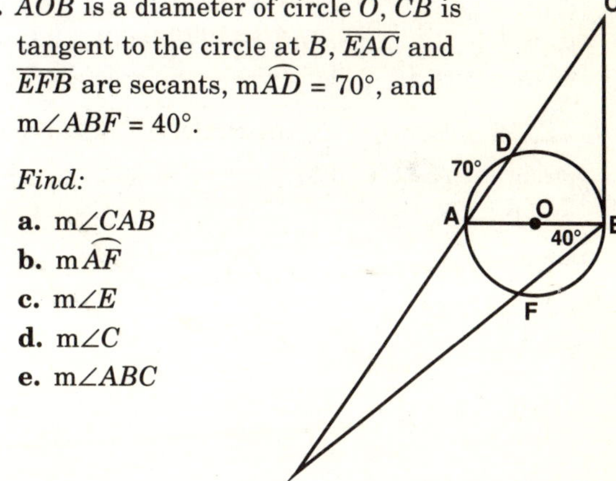

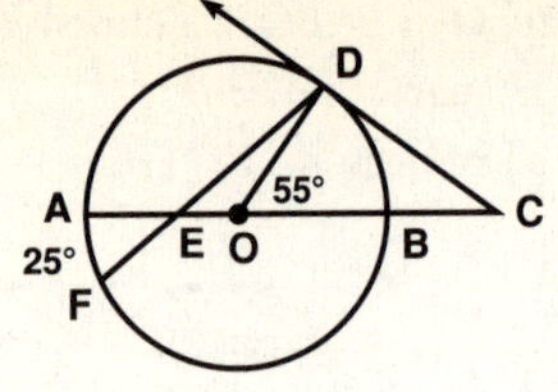

Ex. 23

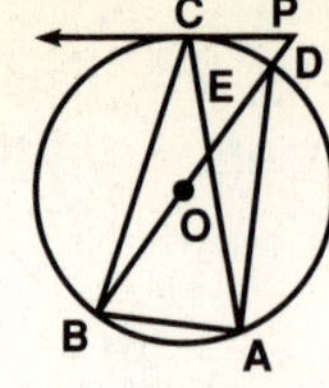

Ex. 24

23. In circle O, $\overline{AB}$ is a diameter, $\overline{OD}$ is a radius, $\overrightarrow{CD}$ is tangent to circle O at D, $m\angle DOB = 55°$, and $m\widehat{AF} = 25°$.

Find:

a. $m\widehat{DB}$

b. $m\angle DCA$

c. $m\angle AEF$

d. $m\angle CDF$

e. $m\angle EDO$

24. $\triangle ABC$ is inscribed in circle O. Diameter $\overline{BD}$ is extended through D to point P and intercepts chord $\overline{AC}$ at E, $\overrightarrow{PC}$ is tangent to the circle at C, chord $\overline{AD}$ is drawn, $m\widehat{AD} = 122°$, and $m\angle BAC = 73°$.

Find:

a. $m\widehat{BC}$

b. $m\angle ABC$

c. $m\angle P$

d. $m\angle BEA$

e. $m\angle PDA$

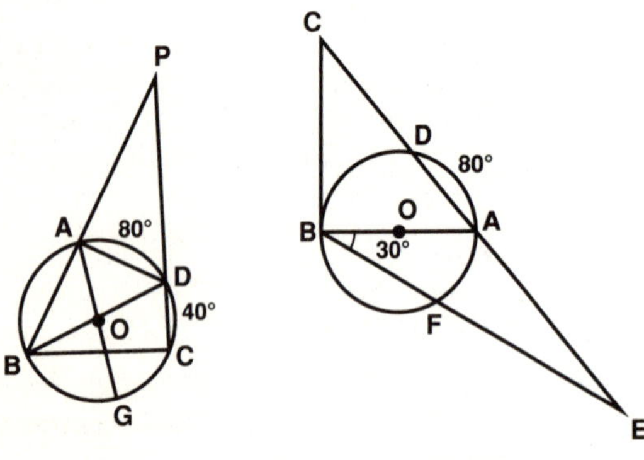

Ex. 25 **Ex. 26**

25. Quadrilateral $ABCD$ is inscribed in circle O, $\overline{BD}$ and $\overline{AG}$ are diameters, $\overline{PAB}$ and $\overline{PDC}$ are secants, $m\widehat{AD} = 80°$, and $m\widehat{DC} = 40°$.

Find:

a. $m\widehat{AB}$

b. $m\angle BCD$

c. $m\angle BOG$

d. $m\angle P$

e. $m\angle BAG$

26. $\overline{AOB}$ is a diameter of circle O, $\overline{CB}$ is tangent to the circle at B, $\overline{EAC}$ and $\overline{EFB}$ are secants, $m\widehat{AD} = 80°$, and $m\angle ABF = 30°$.

Find:

a. $m\angle CAB$

b. $m\widehat{AF}$

c. $m\angle E$

d. $m\angle C$

e. $m\angle ABC$

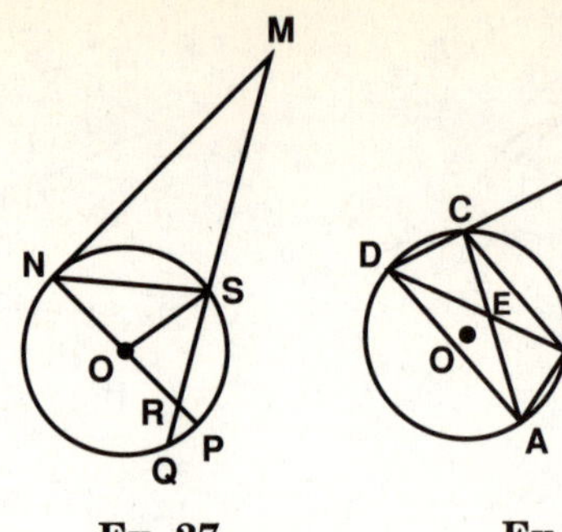

Ex. 27 **Ex. 28**

27. In circle O, $\overline{MN}$ is a tangent, $\overline{NP}$ is a diameter, $\overline{MQ}$ is a secant, $\overline{OS}$ is a radius, $m\widehat{QN} = 160°$, and $m\angle PNS = 40°$.

Find:

a. $m\widehat{QP}$

b. $m\widehat{PS}$

c. $m\angle QRP$

d. $m\angle NOS$

e. $m\angle M$

28. $\overline{PCD}$ and $\overline{PBA}$ are secants from external point P to circle O. Chords $\overline{DA}$, $\overline{DEB}$, $\overline{CEA}$, and $\overline{CB}$ are drawn, $m\widehat{AB} = m\widehat{DC}$, $m\widehat{BC}$ is twice $m\widehat{AB}$, and $m\widehat{AD}$ is 60° more than $m\widehat{BC}$.

Find:

a. $m\widehat{AB}$

b. $m\angle P$

c. $m\angle DAC$

d. $m\angle DEA$

e. $m\angle PCB$

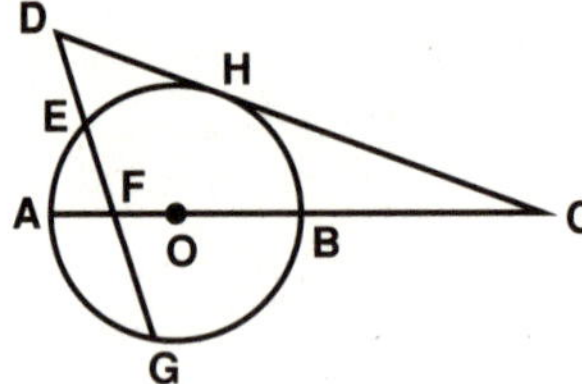

Ex. 29

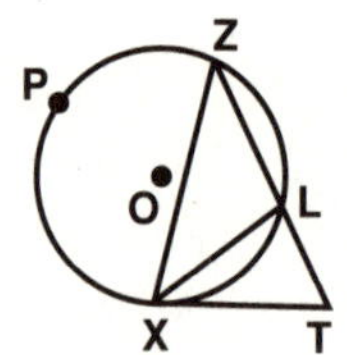

Ex. 30

29. $\overline{DC}$ is tangent to circle O at H, $\overline{AFOBC}$, secant $\overline{DEG}$ intersects secant $\overline{CBA}$ at F, $m\widehat{AEH} = 110°$, $m\widehat{AG} = 80°$, and the ratio between $m\widehat{AE}$ and $m\widehat{EH}$ is $2 : 3$.

Find:

a. $m\widehat{GB}$ **b.** $m\widehat{EA}$ **c.** $m\angle EFA$ **d.** $m\angle DCA$

30. *Given:* Circle O, tangent $\overline{TX}$, secant $\overline{TLZ}$, chords $\overline{ZX}$ and $\overline{XL}$, $m\widehat{XL} : m\widehat{LZ} : m\widehat{XPZ} = 2 : 2 : 5$.

Find:

a. $m\widehat{XL}$

b. $m\angle Z$

c. $m\angle T$

d. $m\angle ZXT$

e. $m\angle XLT$

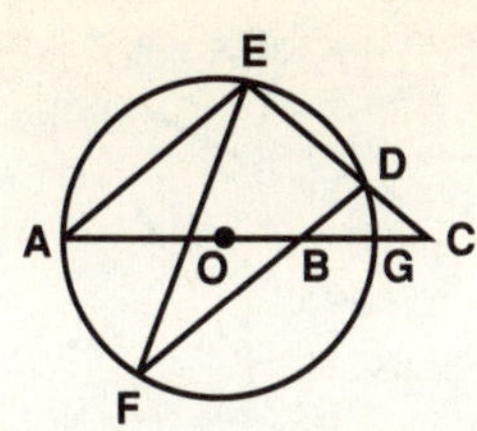

Ex. 31

Ex. 32

31. In circle O, $\overline{AE}$ and $\overline{FD}$ are chords, $\overline{AOBG}$ is a diameter and is extended to C, $\overline{CDE}$ is a secant, $\overline{AE} \parallel \overline{FD}$, and $m\widehat{AE} : m\widehat{ED} : m\widehat{DG} = 5 : 3 : 1$.
Find:

a. $m\widehat{DG}$ **b.** $m\angle AEF$ **c.** $m\angle DBG$ **d.** $m\angle DCA$ **e.** $m\angle CDF$

32. Quadrilateral $ABCD$ is inscribed in circle O. Diagonals $\overline{AC}$ and $\overline{BD}$ meet at F, and $\overline{AD}$ is a diameter. Chords $\overline{AB}$ and $\overline{DC}$ are extended to meet at E. B is the midpoint of $\widehat{AC}$, and $m\widehat{AB} : m\widehat{CD} = 4 : 1$.
Find:

a. $m\widehat{CD}$ **b.** $m\angle BDA$ **c.** $m\angle BFC$ **d.** $m\angle E$ **e.** $m\angle EBD$

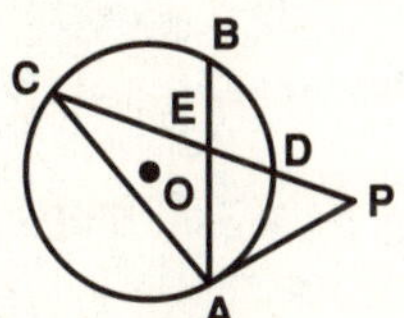

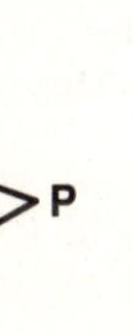

Ex. 33

Ex. 34

33. $\overline{PA}$ is tangent to circle O at A and secant $\overline{PC}$ intersects circle O at C and D. Chord $\overline{CA}$ is drawn, chords $\overline{BA}$ and $\overline{CD}$ intersect at E, $m\widehat{BC} = 50°$, $m\angle BEC = 60°$, $m\widehat{BD} = x°$, and $m\widehat{CA} = (2x + 30)°$.
Find:

a. $m\widehat{DA}$ **b.** $m\widehat{BD}$ **c.** $m\angle CPA$ **d.** $m\angle BAC$

34. $\overrightarrow{ABS}$ is tangent to circle O, $\overline{APMT}$ is a secant, and $\overline{BP}$, $\overline{BV}$, and $\overline{BT}$ are chords.

a. If $m\widehat{BP}$, $m\widehat{PV}$, $m\widehat{VT}$, and $m\widehat{TB}$ are represented by x, $3y$, y, and $5x$ respectively, express each of the following in terms of x and y:

(1) $m\angle AMB$ **(2)** $m\angle TBS$ **(3)** $m\angle PBT$ **(4)** $m\angle TAB$

b. If $x = 42°$, find the number of degrees represented by y.

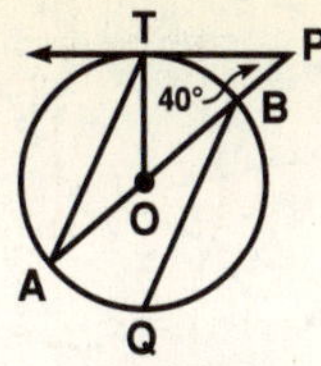

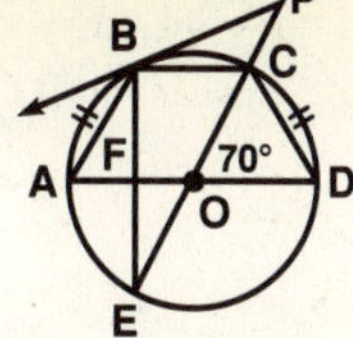

Ex. 35

Ex. 36

35. In circle O, $\overline{PBOA}$ is a secant, tangent $\overrightarrow{PT} \perp$ radius $\overline{OT}$, $m\angle P = 40°$, and $\overline{QB} \parallel \overline{AT}$.
Find:

a. $m\angle BOT$ **b.** $m\angle A$ **c.** $m\widehat{AT}$ **d.** $m\angle ATO$ **e.** $m\angle PBQ$

36. $ABCD$ is inscribed in circle O, $m\angle COD = 70°$, $\overline{AOD}$ is a diameter, $\overrightarrow{PB}$ is tangent to circle O at B, $\overline{PCOE}$ is a secant, and $m\widehat{BA} = m\widehat{CD}$.
Find:

a. $m\widehat{BC}$ **b.** $m\angle PBC$ **c.** $m\angle A$ **d.** $m\angle BPE$ **e.** $m\angle AFE$

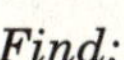

37. Regular pentagon $ABCDE$ is inscribed in circle O. $\overline{FEGB}$ is a secant, $\overrightarrow{FD}$ is tangent to the circle at D, and $\overline{AGC}$ is a chord.
Find:

a. $m\widehat{AB}$ **b.** $m\angle ABE$ **c.** $m\angle CGE$ **d.** $m\angle BFD$ **e.** $m\angle DEF$

38. 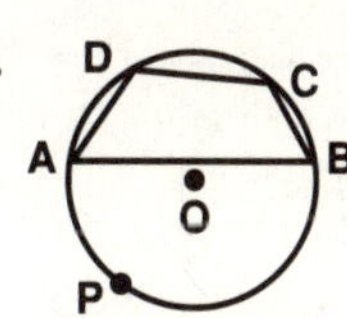

$ABCD$ is a quadrilateral inscribed in circle O. The measures of $\widehat{AD}$, $\widehat{DC}$, $\widehat{CB}$ are represented by $(2y - 30)°$, $(x + 10)°$, $(y - 20)°$, respectively. The measures of angles A and B are 70° and 80°, respectively.

a. In terms of x and y, write a set of equations that can be used to solve for x and y.
b. Solve the set of equations in part **a**.
c. Find the number of degrees in $\widehat{APB}$.

39. Secants $\overline{PAB}$ and $\overline{PCD}$ are drawn to a circle from external point P so that $m\angle P = 20°$ and $m\angle ADC = 10°$. $m\widehat{AC}$ is represented by $(3x + y)°$ and $m\widehat{BD}$ by $(8x + 4y)°$.

a. Write a pair of equations that can be used to solve for x and y.
b. Solve these equations to find values for x and y.
c. Find $m\angle BAD$.

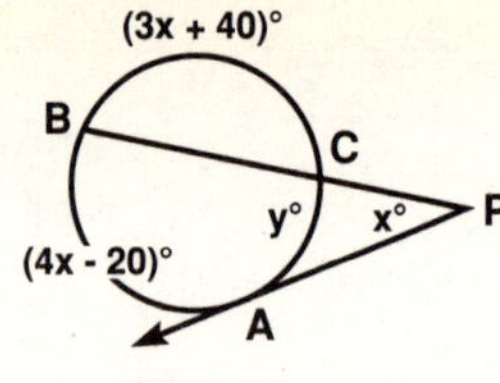

Ex. 40

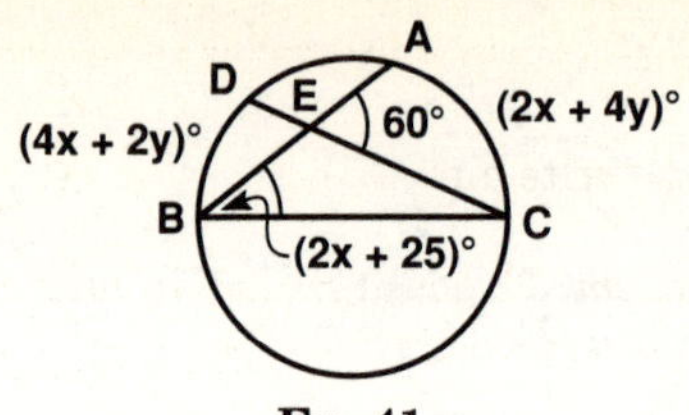

Ex. 41

40. $\overrightarrow{PA}$ is a tangent and $\overline{PCB}$ is a secant to the circle. $m\angle P$ is represented by $x°$ and the measures of $\widehat{AB}$, $\widehat{BC}$ and $\widehat{CA}$ are represented by $(4x - 20)°$, $(3x + 40)°$ and $y°$, respectively.

a. In terms of x and y, write a set of equations that can be used to solve for x and y.

b. Solve the set of equations written in answer to part **a**.

c. Find the number of degrees in $\widehat{BAC}$.

41. Chords $\overline{AB}$ and $\overline{CD}$ intersect at point E and chord $\overline{BC}$ is drawn. The number of degrees in the measures of $\widehat{AC}$ and $\widehat{BD}$ are represented by $(2x + 4y)°$ and $(4x + 2y)°$, respectively. The degree measure of $\angle ABC$ is represented by $(2x + 25)°$ and $m\angle AEC$ is $60°$.

a. In terms of x and y, write a set of equations that can be used to solve for x and y.

b. Solve the set of equations written in answer to **a** to obtain the values of x and y.

c. Find the number of degrees in $\widehat{AC}$ and $\widehat{BD}$.

Proving Theorems

Examples

1. *Theorem:* The measure of an inscribed angle of a circle is one-half the measure of its intercepted arc.

CASE 1: The center of the circle lies on one side of the angle. (One side of the angle is a diameter.)

Given: $\angle PQR$ inscribed in circle O, where $\overline{QR}$ is a diameter.

Prove: $m\angle PQR = \frac{1}{2}m\widehat{PR}$

Plan: Draw $\overline{OP}$. For $\triangle OQP$, use m exterior $\angle POR$ = 2(m interior $\angle PQR$).

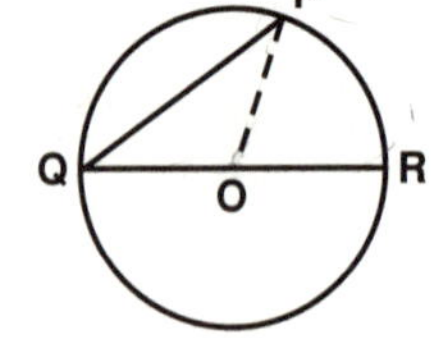

Statements	*Reasons*
1. Draw radius $\overline{OP}$.	1. Two points determine line.
2. $\overline{OQ} \cong \overline{OP}$	2. Radii of a circle are $\cong$.
3. $\triangle OQP$ isosceles.	3. Definition: isosceles $\triangle$.
4. $m\angle P = m\angle Q$	4. Base $\angle$s of isosceles $\triangle$.
5. $m\angle POR = m\angle P + m\angle Q$	5. m exterior $\angle$ of $\triangle$ is sum of measures of two remote interior $\angle$s.
6. $m\angle POR = m\angle Q + m\angle Q = 2(m\angle Q)$	6. Substitution.
7. $m\angle POR = m\widehat{PR}$	7. In $\odot$, m central $\angle$ = m arc.
8. $2m\angle Q = m\widehat{PR}$	8. Transitive property.
9. $m\angle Q = \frac{1}{2}m\widehat{PR}$	9. Division property.

Note: Other cases appear as Exercises.

2. *Theorem:* The measure of an angle formed by a tangent and a secant, or two secants, or two tangents intersecting outside a circle is one-half the difference of the measures of the intercepted arcs.

CASE 1: An angle formed by a tangent and a secant intersecting outside a circle.

Given: Tangent $\overleftrightarrow{PTR}$ and secant $\overline{PBA}$ to a circle.

Prove: $m\angle P = \frac{1}{2}(m\widehat{TA} - m\widehat{TB})$

Plan: Draw $\overline{TA}$. For $\triangle TAP$, use exterior $\angle$ relation.

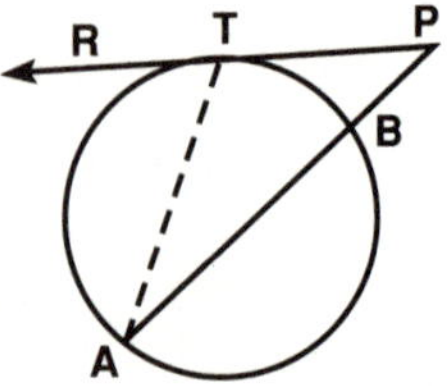

Statements	*Reasons*
1. Tangent $\overleftrightarrow{PTR}$, secant $\overline{PBA}$.	1. Given.
2. Draw $\overline{TA}$.	2. Two points determine line.
3. $m\angle A + m\angle P = m\angle RTA$	3. m exterior $\angle$ of $\triangle$ is sum of measures of two remote interior $\angle$s.
4. $m\angle P = m\angle RTA - m\angle A$	4. Subtraction property
5. $m\angle RTA = \frac{1}{2}m\widehat{TA}$	5. m tan-chord $\angle = \frac{1}{2}$ m arc
6. $m\angle A = \frac{1}{2}m\widehat{TB}$	6. m inscribed $\angle = \frac{1}{2}$ m arc
7. $m\angle P = \frac{1}{2}m\widehat{TA} - \frac{1}{2}m\widehat{TB}$	7. Substitution
8. $m\angle P = \frac{1}{2}(m\widehat{TA} - m\widehat{TB})$	8. Factoring

Note: Other cases appear as Exercises.

EXERCISES

In 1–4, write a proof.

1. *Theorem:* The measure of an inscribed angle of a circle is one-half the measure of its intercepted arc.

a. CASE 2: The center of the circle is inside the angle.

Given: $\angle PQR$ inscribed in circle O, with O in the interior of the angle.
Prove: $m\angle PQR = \frac{1}{2}m\widehat{PR}$
Plan: Draw diameter $\overline{QT}$. Assume CASE 1. Add angle measures.

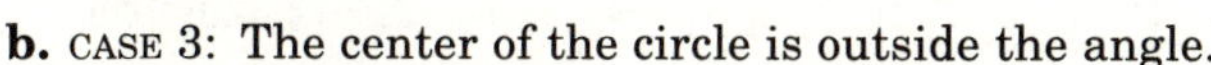

b. CASE 3: The center of the circle is outside the angle.

Given: $\angle PQR$ inscribed in circle O, with O in the exterior of the angle.
Prove: $m\angle PQR = \frac{1}{2}m\widehat{PR}$
Plan: Draw diameter $\overline{QT}$.
Assume CASE 1. Subtract angle measures.

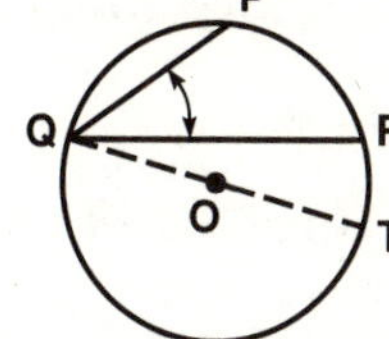

2. *Theorem:* The measure of an angle formed by two chords intersecting in a circle is one-half the sum of the measures of the arcs intercepted by the angle and its vertical angle.

Given: Chords $\overline{AB}$ and $\overline{CD}$ intersect at E inside a circle.
Prove: $m\angle AEC = \frac{1}{2}(m\widehat{AC} + m\widehat{DB})$
Plan: Draw $\overline{AD}$. For $\triangle AED$, use exterior $\angle$ relation.

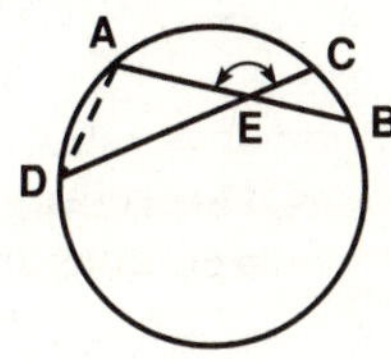

3. *Theorem:* The measure of an angle formed by a tangent and a chord intersecting at the point of tangency is one-half the measure of the intercepted arc.

Given: $\overleftrightarrow{TP}$ tangent to circle O at T, chord $\overline{AT}$.
Prove: $m\angle PTA = \frac{1}{2}m\widehat{AT}$
Plan: Draw diameter $\overline{TOM}$ and chord $\overline{AM}$.
$\triangle TAM$ is a right $\triangle$ ($\angle$ inscribed in semicircle).
$\angle MTP$ is a right $\angle$ (diameter $\perp$ tangent). Use complements of same angle.

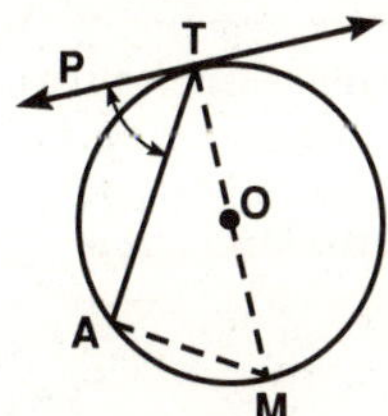

4. *Theorem:* The measure of an angle formed by a tangent and a secant, or two secants, or two tangents intersecting outside a circle is one-half the difference of the measures of the intercepted arcs.

a. CASE 2: An angle formed by two secants intersecting outside the circle.

Given: Secants $\overrightarrow{PAB}$ and $\overrightarrow{PCD}$ to a circle.
Prove: $m\angle P = \frac{1}{2}(m\widehat{BD} - m\widehat{AC})$
Plan: Draw $\overline{BC}$. For $\triangle PBC$, use exterior $\angle$ relation. Use inscribed $\angle$.

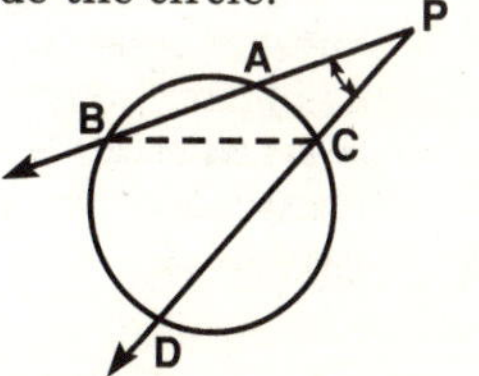

b. CASE 3: An angle formed by two tangents intersecting outside the circle.

Given: Tangents $\overrightarrow{PT}$ and $\overrightarrow{PB}$ to a circle.
Prove: $m\angle P = \frac{1}{2}(m\widehat{TQB} - m\widehat{TRB})$
Plan: Draw $\overline{TB}$. For $\triangle PTB$, use exterior $\angle$ relation. Use tan-chord $\angle$.

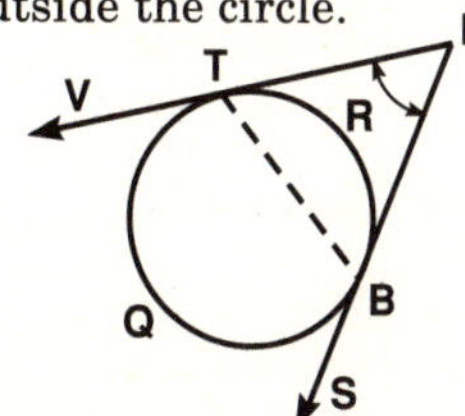

5.2 PROOFS INVOLVING CONGRUENCE

Methods of Proving Triangles Congruent

To prove that two triangles are congruent, it is sufficient to show that three strategic pairs of corresponding parts are congruent.

Two triangles are congruent if:

Two pairs of corresponding sides and the *included* pair of corresponding angles are congruent.

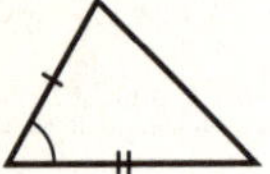
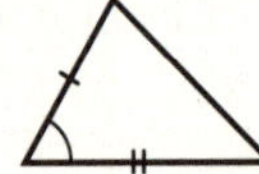

1. If s.a.s. ≅ s.a.s., the triangles are congruent.

Two pairs of corresponding angles and *any* pair of corresponding sides are congruent.

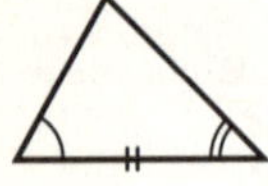
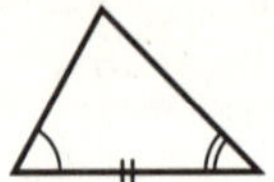

2. If a.s.a. ≅ a.s.a., the triangles are congruent.

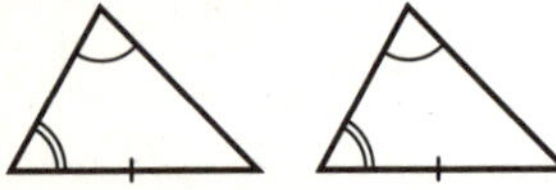

3. If a.a.s. ≅ a.a.s., the triangles are congruent.

Three pairs of corresponding sides are congruent.

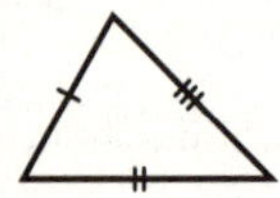
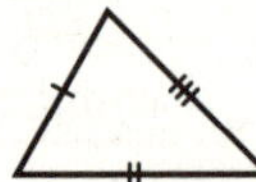

4. If s.s.s. ≅ s.s.s., the triangles are congruent.

Two right triangles are congruent if their hypotenuses and a pair of legs are respectively congruent.

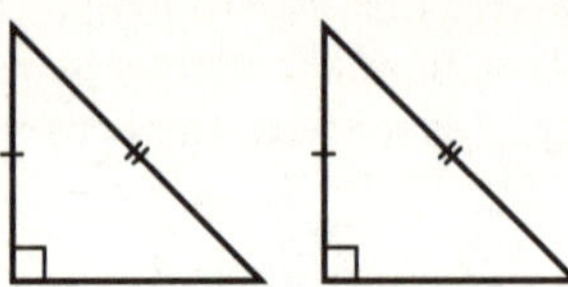

5. If hy-leg ≅ hy-leg, the right triangles are congruent.

Theorems About Circles

CONGRUENT CIRCLES are circles that have congruent radii.

***Theorem 1:* In a circle, or in congruent circles, if two central angles are congruent, then the arcs that they intercept are congruent, and conversely.**

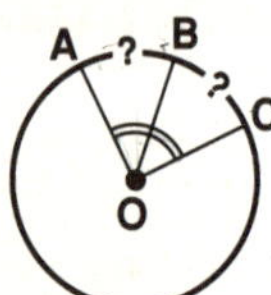

If $\angle AOB \cong \angle BOC$, then $\overset{\frown}{AB} \cong \overset{\frown}{BC}$.

If $\overset{\frown}{AB} \cong \overset{\frown}{BC}$, then $\angle AOB \cong \angle BOC$.

***Theorem 2:* In a circle, or in congruent circles, if two chords are congruent, then the arcs that they intercept are congruent, and conversely.**

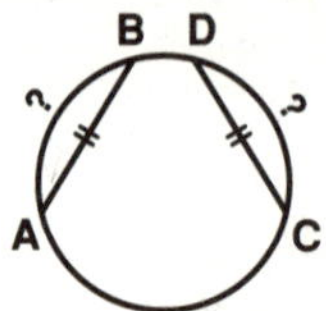

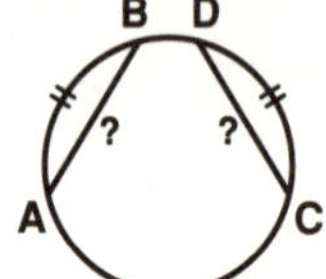

If $\overline{AB} \cong \overline{CD}$, then $\overset{\frown}{AB} \cong \overset{\frown}{CD}$.

If $\overset{\frown}{AB} \cong \overset{\frown}{CD}$, then $\overline{AB} \cong \overline{CD}$.

***Theorem 3:* A diameter (or radius) perpendicular to a chord bisects the chord, and conversely.**

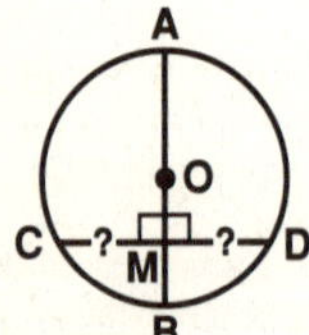

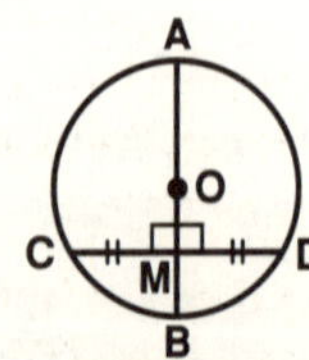

If diameter $\overline{AOB} \perp \overline{CD}$, then $\overline{CM} \cong \overline{MD}$.

If $\overline{CM} \cong \overline{MD}$, and $\overline{AB} \perp \overline{CD}$, then $\overline{AB}$ passes through the center O.

***Theorem 4:* If two chords are congruent, then they are equidistant from the center of a circle, and conversely. (Distance is measured along a perpendicular.)**

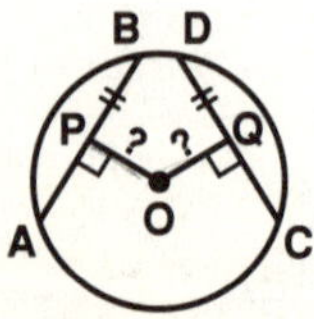

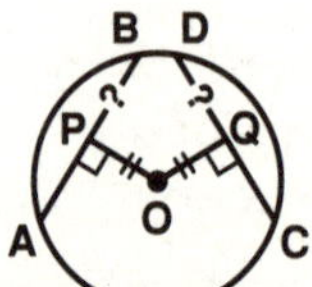

If $\overline{AB} \cong \overline{CD}$, then $\overline{OP} \cong \overline{OQ}$.

If $\overline{OP} \cong \overline{OQ}$, then $\overline{AB} \cong \overline{CD}$.

Theorem 5: **A diameter (or radius) drawn to a point of tangency is perpendicular to the tangent, and conversely.**

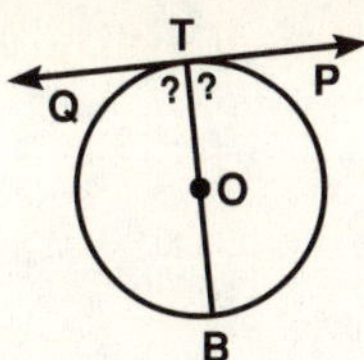

If $\overline{BOT}$ is a diameter and $\overleftrightarrow{PTQ}$ is a tangent, then $\overline{BOT} \perp \overleftrightarrow{PTQ}$.

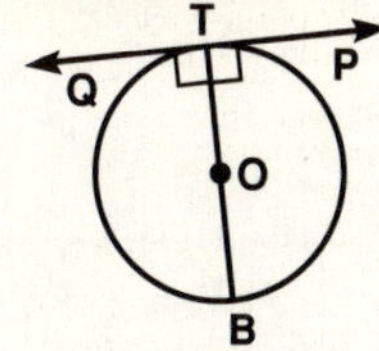

If tangent $\overleftrightarrow{PTQ} \perp \overline{BT}$, then $\overline{BT}$ passes through the center O.

Theorem 6: **In a circle, parallel lines intercept congruent arcs between them, and conversely.**

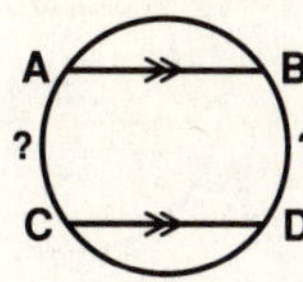

If $\overline{AB} \parallel \overline{CD}$, then $\widehat{AC} \cong \widehat{BD}$.

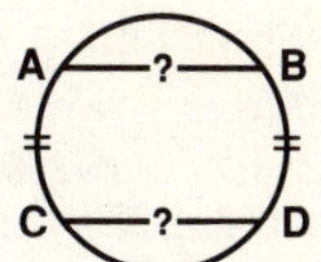

If $\widehat{AC} \cong \widehat{BD}$, then nonintersecting chords $\overline{AB}$ and $\overline{CD}$ are parallel.

Proving Theorems

Examples

1. *Theorem:* In a circle, if two central angles are congruent, then the arcs that they intercept are congruent.

Given: Circle O with $\angle AOB \cong \angle BOC$.

Prove: $\widehat{AB} \cong \widehat{BC}$

Plan: Use the definition of arc measure.

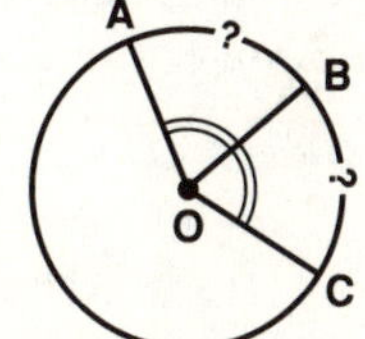

Statements	*Reasons*
1. $\angle AOB \cong \angle BOC$	1. Given
2. $m\angle AOB = m\angle BOC$	2. Definition: congruence
3. $m\angle AOB = m\widehat{AB}$ $m\angle BOC = m\widehat{BC}$	3. Definition: degree measure of an arc
4. $m\widehat{AB} = m\widehat{BC}$	4. Things = to = things are =.
5. $\widehat{AB} \cong \widehat{BC}$	5. Definition: congruence

2. *Theorem:* In a circle, if two chords are congruent, then the arcs that they intercept are congruent.

Given: $\overline{AB} \cong \overline{CD}$ in circle O.

Prove: $\widehat{AB} \cong \widehat{CD}$

Plan: Draw radii $\overline{OA}$, $\overline{OB}$, $\overline{OC}$, $\overline{OD}$. Show $\triangle AOB \cong \triangle COD$ by s.s.s. $\cong$ s.s.s. to get congruent central angles.

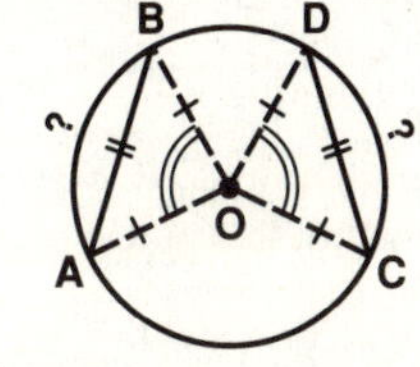

Statements	*Reasons*
1. Draw radii $\overline{OA}$, $\overline{OB}$, $\overline{OC}$, $\overline{OD}$.	1. Two points determine a line.
(s) 2. $\overline{OA} \cong \overline{OC}$ (s) $\overline{OB} \cong \overline{OD}$	2. Radii of a circle are congruent.
(s) 3. $\overline{AB} \cong \overline{CD}$	3. Given
4. $\triangle AOB \cong \triangle COD$	4. s.s.s. $\cong$ s.s.s.
5. $\angle AOB \cong \angle COD$	5. Corresponding $\angle$s of $\cong$ $\triangle$s are $\cong$.
6. $\widehat{AB} \cong \widehat{CD}$	6. In $\odot$, congruent central $\angle$s intercept congruent arcs.

3. *Theorem:* If two chords are congruent, then they are equidistant from the center of a circle.

Given: $\overline{AB} \cong \overline{CD}$ in circle O. $\overline{OP} \perp \overline{AB}$, $\overline{OQ} \perp \overline{CD}$.

Prove: $\overline{OP} \cong \overline{OQ}$

Plan: Draw radii $\overline{OA}$, $\overline{OC}$. Show $\triangle POA \cong \triangle QOC$ by hy-leg $\cong$ hy-leg.

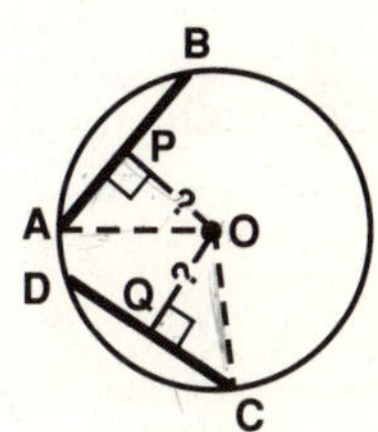

Statements	*Reasons*
1. Draw radii $\overline{OA}$, $\overline{OC}$.	1. 2 points determine line.
2. $\overline{OP} \perp \overline{AB}$, $\overline{OQ} \perp \overline{CD}$.	2. Given
3. $\angle OPA$ is right $\angle$, $\angle OQC$ is right $\angle$.	3. $\perp$s form right $\angle$s.
4. $\overline{OP}$ bisects $\overline{AB}$, $\overline{OQ}$ bisects $\overline{CD}$.	4. Diameter $\perp$ chord bisects chord.
5. $\overline{AP} \cong \frac{1}{2}\overline{AB}$ $\overline{CQ} \cong \frac{1}{2}\overline{CD}$	5. Definition: bisect
(leg) 6. $\overline{AP} \cong \overline{CQ}$	6. Halves of =s are =.
(hy) 7. $\overline{OA} \cong \overline{OC}$	7. Radii of a $\odot$ are $\cong$.
8. $\triangle POA \cong \triangle QOC$	8. hy-leg $\cong$ hy-leg
9. $\overline{OP} \cong \overline{OQ}$	9. Corr. sides of $\cong$ $\triangle$s.

EXERCISES

In 1–7, write a proof.

1. *Theorem:* In a circle, if two arcs are congruent, then the central angles that intercept them are congruent.

Given: Circle O with radii $\overline{OA}$, $\overline{OB}$, $\overline{OC}$. $\widehat{AB} \cong \widehat{BC}$.

Prove: $\angle AOB \cong \angle BOC$

Plan: Use the definition of arc measure.

2. *Theorem:* In a circle, if two arcs are congruent, then the chords that they intercept are congruent.

Given: $\overset{\frown}{AB} \cong \overset{\frown}{CD}$ in circle O.

Prove: $\overline{AB} \cong \overline{CD}$

Plan: Draw radii $\overline{OA}$, $\overline{OB}$, $\overline{OC}$, $\overline{OD}$. Show $\triangle AOB \cong \triangle COD$ by s.a.s. $\cong$ s.a.s.

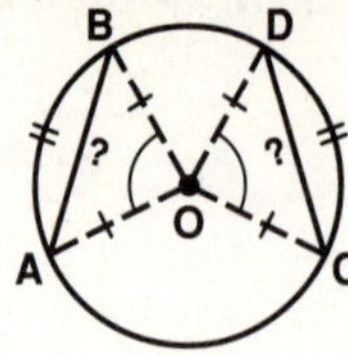

3. *Theorem:* In a circle, if two central angles are congruent, then the chords that they subtend are congruent.

Given: $\angle AOB \cong \angle COD$. Chords $\overline{AB}$ and $\overline{CD}$.

Prove: $\overline{AB} \cong \overline{CD}$

Plan: Show $\triangle AOB \cong \triangle COD$ by s.a.s. $\cong$ s.a.s.

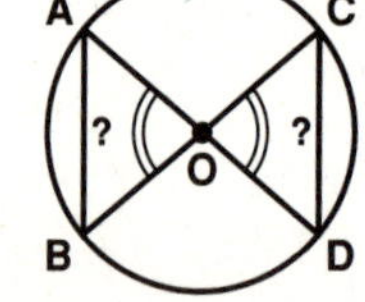

4. *Theorem:* A diameter perpendicular to a chord of a circle bisects the chord and its arcs.

Given: In circle O, diameter $\overline{AB} \perp \overline{CD}$.

Prove:

a. $\overline{CM} \cong \overline{DM}$

b. $\overset{\frown}{CB} \cong \overset{\frown}{DB}$

c. $\overset{\frown}{CA} \cong \overset{\frown}{DA}$

Plan: Draw radii $\overline{OC}$, $\overline{OD}$. Show $\triangle OCM \cong \triangle ODM$ by hy-leg $\cong$ hy-leg. Then use:

a. Corresponding sides of congruent $\triangle$s.

b. Congruent central $\angle$s intercept congruent arcs.

c. Subtract congruent minor arcs, $\overset{\frown}{CB}$ and $\overset{\frown}{DB}$, from semicircles $\overset{\frown}{ACB}$ and $\overset{\frown}{ADB}$.

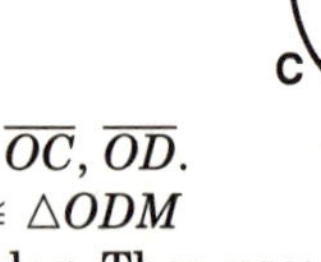

5. *Theorem:* If two chords are equidistant from the center of a circle, then they are congruent.

Given: Circle O with $\overline{AB}$ and $\overline{CD}$. $\overline{OP} \perp \overline{AB}$, $\overline{OQ} \perp \overline{CD}$, $\overline{OP} \cong \overline{OQ}$.

Prove: $\overline{AB} \cong \overline{CD}$

Plan: Draw radii $\overline{OA}$, $\overline{OC}$. Show $\triangle POA \cong \triangle QOC$ by hy-leg $\cong$ hy-leg.

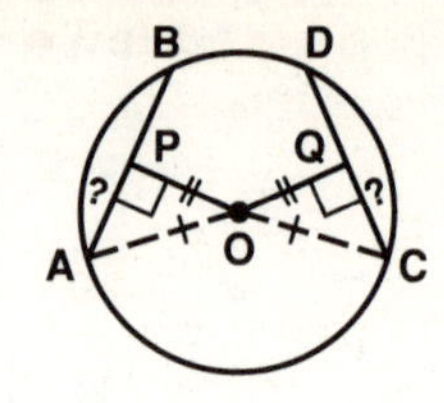

6. *Theorem:* In a circle, parallel lines intercept congruent arcs between them.

Given: $\overline{AB} \parallel \overline{CD}$ in circle O.

Prove: $\overset{\frown}{AC} \cong \overset{\frown}{BD}$

Plan: Draw transversal $\overline{AD}$. Congruent alternate interior angles of parallel lines are congruent inscribed angles of the circle, making the arcs congruent.

7. In a circle, if two congruent arcs are intercepted by nonintersecting chords, the chords are parallel.

Given: $\overset{\frown}{AC}$ and $\overset{\frown}{BD}$ are intercepted by $\overline{AB}$ and $\overline{CD}$. $\overset{\frown}{AC} \cong \overset{\frown}{BD}$.

Prove: $\overline{AB} \parallel \overline{CD}$

Plan: Draw transversal $\overline{AD}$. Congruent inscribed angles of the circle are congruent alternate interior angles of the chords, making the chords parallel.

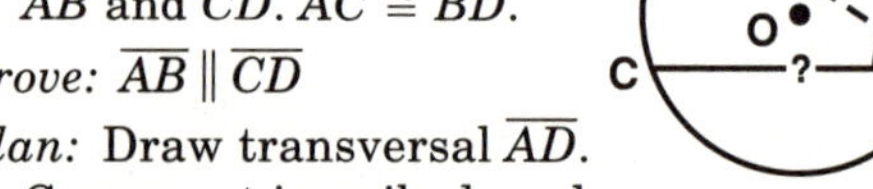

Applying Theorems

Using Congruent Triangles

Look for congruent angles.

Angles in a circle are congruent if they are measured in the same way by the same arc or by congruent arcs.

An angle of a circle is a right angle if:

(1) inscribed in a semicircle

(2) formed by a diameter and a tangent

(3) formed by a diameter bisecting a chord

Look for congruent sides.

Segments in a circle are congruent if:

(1) radii or diameters

(2) chords of congruent arcs

(3) the result of a diameter perpendicular to a chord

Example

Given: Circle O with diameter $\overline{AOB}$, $\overset{\frown}{BC} \cong \overset{\frown}{BD}$.

Prove: $\overline{AC} \cong \overline{AD}$

Plan: Show $\triangle ACB \cong \triangle ADB$, by a.a.s. $\cong$ a.a.s.

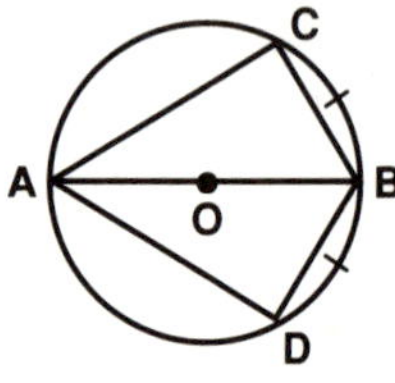

	Statements	*Reasons*
	1. $\overline{AOB}$ is a diameter.	1. Given
	2. $\overset{\frown}{ACB}$ is a semicircle. $\overset{\frown}{ADB}$ is a semicircle.	2. Diameter cuts ⊙ into 2 semicircles.
	3. $\angle ACB$ and $\angle ADB$ are right angles.	3. An $\angle$ inscribed in a semicircle is a rt. $\angle$.
(a)	4. $\angle ACB \cong \angle ADB$	4. All right $\angle$s are $\cong$.
	5. $\overset{\frown}{BC} \cong \overset{\frown}{BD}$	5. Given
(a)	6. $\angle CAB \cong \angle DAB$	6. Inscribed $\angle$s intercepting $\cong$ arcs are $\cong$.
(s)	7. $\overline{AB} \cong \overline{AB}$	7. Reflexive property
	8. $\triangle ACB \cong \triangle ADB$	8. a.a.s. $\cong$ a.a.s.
	9. $\overline{AC} \cong \overline{AD}$	9. Corr. sides of $\cong$ $\triangle$s

Using Addition or Subtraction

Congruent segments or angles of a circle can be added or subtracted, with congruent results.

Example

Given: Circle O, chords $\overline{AB}$, $\overline{CD}$, $\overline{AD}$, $\overline{CB}$, $\overline{AC}$. $\widehat{AD} \cong \widehat{CB}$

Prove: $\overline{EB} \cong \overline{ED}$

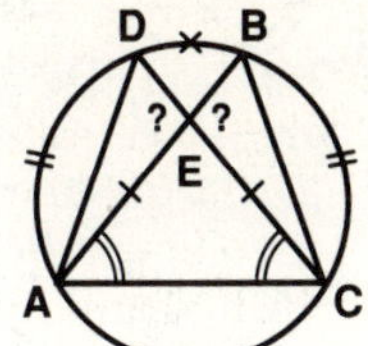

Statements	*Reasons*
1. $\widehat{AD} \cong \widehat{BC}$	1. Given
2. $\angle DCA \cong \angle BAC$	2. Inscribed $\angle$s subtended by $\cong$ arcs are $\cong$.
3. $\triangle AEC$ is isosceles.	3. If base $\angle$s are equal in measure, $\triangle$ is isosceles.
4. $\overline{AE} \cong \overline{CE}$	4. Definition: isosceles $\triangle$
5. $\widehat{DB} \cong \widehat{DB}$	5. Reflexive property
6. $\widehat{AD} + \widehat{DB} \cong \widehat{CB} + \widehat{BD}$ $\widehat{ADB} \cong \widehat{CBD}$	6. Addition property
7. $\overline{AB} \cong \overline{CD}$	7. In a $\odot$, congruent arcs intercept congruent chords.
8. $\overline{AB} - \overline{AE} \cong \overline{CD} - \overline{CE}$ $\overline{EB} \cong \overline{ED}$	8. Subtraction property

EXERCISES

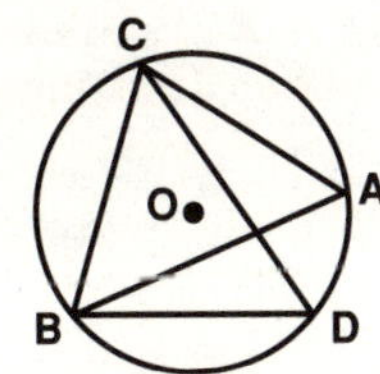

Ex. 1

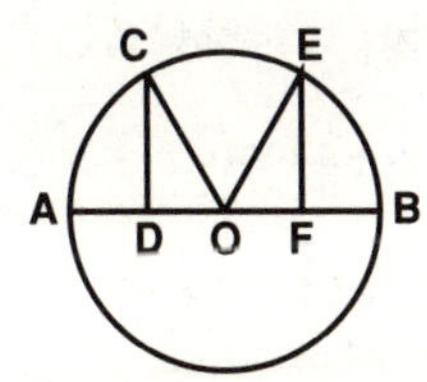

Ex. 2

1. *Given:* Circle O, chords $\overline{AC}$, $\overline{BD}$, $\overline{BC}$, $\overline{CD}$, $\overline{AB}$. $\overline{AC} \cong \overline{BD}$.

Prove: $\triangle CAB \cong \triangle BDC$

2. *Given:* Circle O, diameter $\overline{ADOFB}$, $\widehat{ACEB}$, $\overline{AD} \cong \overline{BF}$, $\overline{CD} \perp \overline{AB}$, $\overline{EF} \perp \overline{AB}$.

Prove: $\widehat{AC} \cong \widehat{BE}$

3. *Given:* Circle O, inscribed $\triangle SAB$. $\overline{SA} \cong \overline{SB}$, diameter $\overline{ST}$ intersecting $\overline{AB}$ at R.

Prove: $\overline{ST} \perp \overline{AB}$

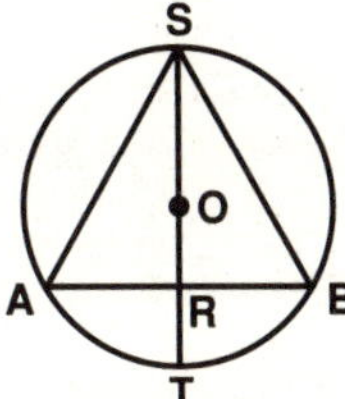

4. *Given:* In circle O, E and F are midpoints of radii $\overline{OD}$ and $\overline{OC}$, and $\widehat{AD} \cong \widehat{BC}$.

Prove:

a. $\triangle AOE \cong \triangle BOF$ **b.** $\angle DAE \cong \angle CBF$

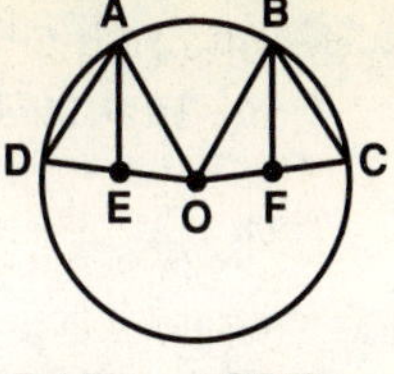

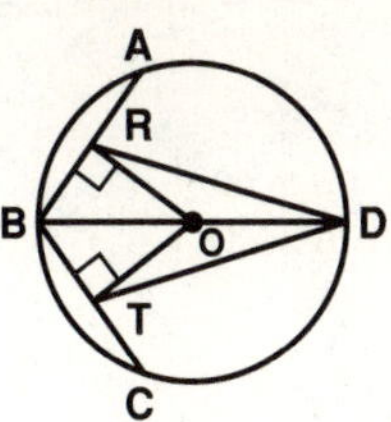

Ex. 5

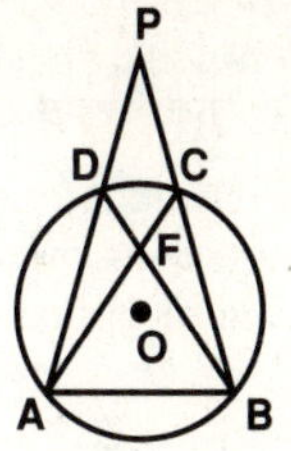

Ex. 6

5. *Given:* Circle O, diameter $\overline{BD}$, $\overline{BA} \cong \overline{BC}$, $\overline{OR} \perp \overline{AB}$, $\overline{OT} \perp \overline{BC}$.

Prove:

a. $\angle ABD \cong \angle CBD$ **b.** $\triangle RDB \cong \triangle TDB$

6. *Given:* Secants $\overline{PDA}$ and $\overline{PCB}$ are drawn to circle O, $\overline{PDA} \cong \overline{PCB}$, chords $\overline{AC}$ and $\overline{BD}$ intersect at F.

Prove: $\overline{FC} \cong \overline{FD}$

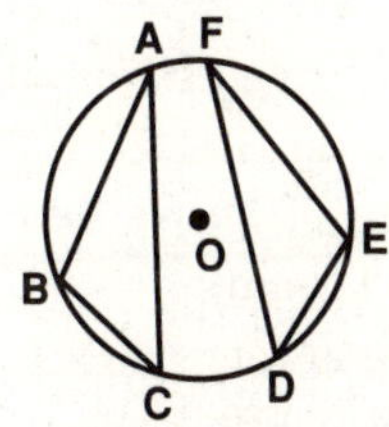

Ex. 7

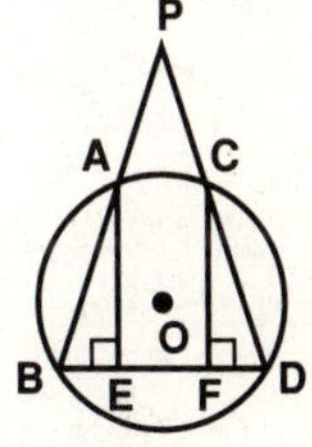

Ex. 8

7. *Given:* Circle O with points A, B, C, D, E, F on the circle so that $\overline{AB} \cong \overline{FE}$ and $\overline{BC} \cong \overline{ED}$

Prove: $\overline{AC} \cong \overline{FD}$

8. *Given:* Secants $\overline{PAB}$ and $\overline{PCD}$ drawn to circle O, $\overline{PAB} \cong \overline{PCD}$, and $\overline{AE}$ and $\overline{CF}$ are perpendicular to $\overline{BD}$ at points E and F, respectively.

Prove: $\overline{AE} \cong \overline{CF}$

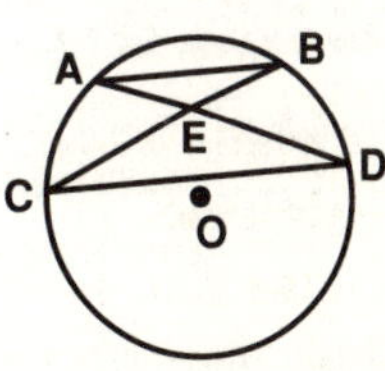

Ex. 9

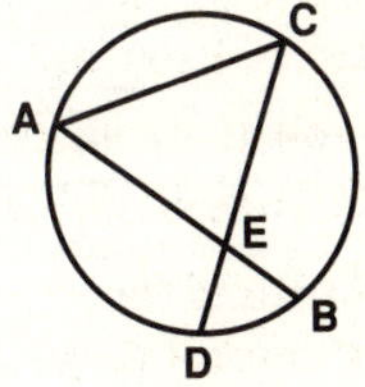

Ex. 10

9. *Given:* Circle O with chord $\overline{AB}$ parallel to chord $\overline{CD}$, chords $\overline{AD}$ and $\overline{BC}$ intersect at E.

Prove: $\overline{AD} \cong \overline{BC}$

10. *Given:* Chords $\overline{AB}$ and $\overline{CD}$ intersecting at E so that $\overline{DE} \cong \overline{BE}$. Chord $\overline{AC}$ is drawn.

Prove: $\triangle ACE$ is isosceles.

11. Secants $\overline{PAB}$ and $\overline{PCD}$ are drawn to a circle from an external point P and chords $\overline{AB}$ and $\overline{CD}$ thus formed are congruent. Chord $\overline{BD}$ is drawn.
Prove: **a.** $\angle B \cong \angle D$ **b.** $\overline{AP} \cong \overline{CP}$

12. *Theorem:* Tangent segments to a circle from an external point are congruent.

Given: Circle O, tangents $\overrightarrow{PA}$ and $\overrightarrow{PB}$.
Prove: $\overline{PA} \cong \overline{PB}$
Plan: Draw $\overline{AB}$. Show congruent tangent-chord angles, $\angle PAB$ and $\angle PBA$, to get $\triangle PAB$ isosceles.

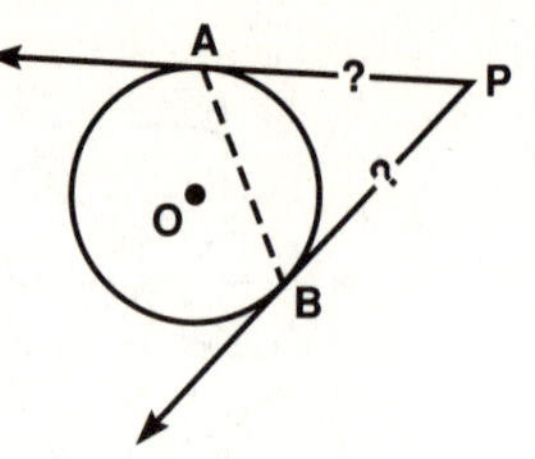

13. *Theorem:* If two tangents are drawn to a circle from an external point, the line determined by that point and the center of the circle bisects the angle formed by the tangents.

Given: Circle O, tangents $\overrightarrow{PA}$ and $\overrightarrow{PB}$.
Prove: $\overline{OP}$ bisects $\angle P$.
Plan: Draw radii $\overline{OA}$, $\overline{OB}$. Show $\triangle AOP \cong \triangle BOP$ by hy-leg $\cong$ hy-leg.

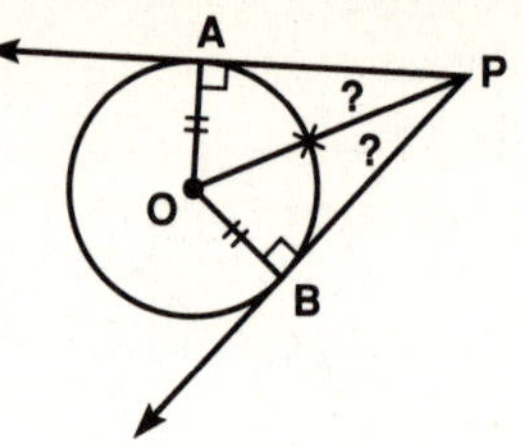

5.3 PROOFS INVOLVING SIMILAR TRIANGLES

Proving a Proportion

Goal: **To prove that the required statement is a proportion by showing it involves corresponding sides of similar triangles.**

Method: **To determine which triangles you must prove similar, read the proportion and then look at the diagram.**

To read the proportion, use either of the following two procedures.

Procedure	Example
1. Read the numerators and the denominators of the proportion. **If the four letters of the numerators have a common letter, read the common letter only once. If the four letters of the denominators have a common letter, read the common letter only once. Look at the diagram to see if the triangles read from the numerators and denominators exist. If they do exist, try to prove them similar.**	$\frac{AB}{} = \frac{BC}{} \rightarrow \triangle ABC$ $\frac{}{RS} = \frac{}{SQ} \rightarrow \triangle RSQ$
2. Read each ratio of the proportion. **If the four letters of each ratio have a common letter, read the common letter only once. Look at the diagram to see if the triangles read from the ratios exist. If they do exist, try to prove them similar.**	$\triangle ABC \left\{ \frac{AB}{BC} = \frac{RS}{ST} \right\} \triangle RST$

It is possible that:	Example
a. only the numerators and denominators will yield a pair of triangles	$\frac{AB}{RS} = \frac{BC}{TR}$ $\begin{matrix}\rightarrow \triangle ABC \\ \rightarrow \triangle RST\end{matrix}$
b. only the ratios will yield a pair of triangles	$\triangle ABC \left\{ \frac{AB}{BC} = \frac{RS}{ST} \right\} \triangle RST$
c. both procedures will yield the same pair of triangles	$\triangle ABC \left\{ \frac{AB}{AC} = \frac{BF}{AB} \right\} \triangle ABF$ $\begin{matrix}\rightarrow \triangle ABF \\ \rightarrow \triangle ABC\end{matrix}$
d. each procedure will yield a different pair of triangles	$\triangle ABR \left\{ \frac{AB}{BR} = \frac{BC}{RC} \right\} \triangle BRC$ $\begin{matrix}\rightarrow \triangle ABC \\ \rightarrow \triangle BRC\end{matrix}$

The final determination of which pair of triangles to use comes from looking at the diagram to see if the pair of triangles exists and if that pair of triangles can be proved similar.

The method you will use to prove triangles similar is to show two pairs of corresponding angles congruent (a.a. ≅ a.a.).

Examples

1. *Theorem:* If a tangent and a secant are drawn to a circle from an external point, then the measure of the tangent segment is the mean proportional between the measures of the secant segment and its external segment.

Given: Tangent $\overline{PA}$ and secant $\overline{PBC}$ to a circle.

Prove: $\frac{PC}{PA} = \frac{PA}{PB}$

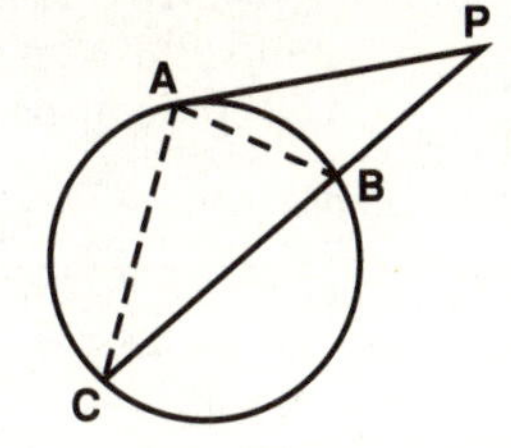

Plan: Read the numerators and denominators of the proportion to obtain $\triangle PCA$ and $\triangle PAB$.

Lines must be drawn to create these $\triangle$s, which can then be proved similar by a.a. ≅ a.a.

Statements	*Reasons*
1. Tangent $\overline{PA}$, secant $\overline{PBC}$	1. Given
2. Draw $\overline{BA}$, $\overline{CA}$.	2. Two points determine line.
3. $m\angle PAB = \frac{1}{2} m\widehat{AB}$	3. m tan-chord $\angle = \frac{1}{2}$ m arc
4. $m\angle ACB = \frac{1}{2} m\widehat{AB}$	4. m inscribed $\angle = \frac{1}{2}$ m arc
5. $m\angle PAB = m\angle ACB$	5. Transitive property
(a) 6. $\angle PAB \cong \angle ACB$	6. Definition: congruence
(a) 7. $\angle P \cong \angle P$	7. Reflexive property
8. $\triangle PCA \sim \triangle PAB$	8. a.a. ≅ a.a.
9. $\frac{PC}{PA} = \frac{PA}{PB}$	9. Corr. sides of similar $\triangle$s are in proportion.

2. *Given:* $\overline{CEB}$ is tangent to circle O at B, secants $\overline{DFB}$ and $\overline{EFA}$ intersect circle O at F, and diameter $\overline{AB} \parallel \overline{DC}$.

Prove: $\frac{BD}{AE} = \frac{CD}{BE}$

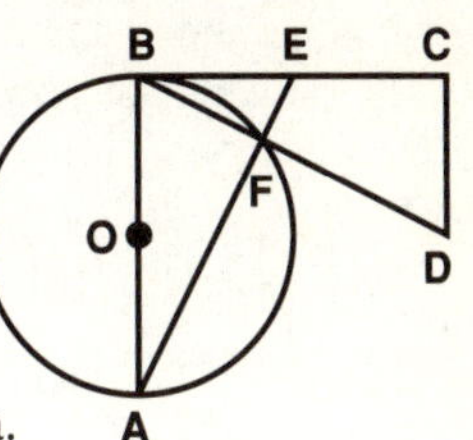

Plan: Read the numerators and denominators of the proportion to obtain $\triangle BDC$ and $\triangle ABE$.

These $\triangle$s exist in the diagram and can then be proved similar by a.a. ≅ a.a.

Statements	*Reasons*
1. Tangent $\overline{CEB}$, secant $\overline{DFB}$, (chord $\overline{BF}$), diameter $\overline{AB}$	1. Given
2. $m\angle CBD = \frac{1}{2} m\widehat{BF}$	2. m tan-chord $\angle = \frac{1}{2}$ m arc
3. $m\angle BAE = \frac{1}{2} m\widehat{BF}$	3. m inscribed $\angle = \frac{1}{2}$ m arc
4. $m\angle CBD = m\angle BAE$	4. Transitive property
(a) 5. $\angle CBD \cong \angle BAE$	5. Definition: congruence
6. $\overline{AB} \perp \overline{CEB}$ at B.	6. Diameter ⊥ tangent at point of tangency.
7. $\angle ABC$ right $\angle$	7. ⊥s form right angles.
8. $\overline{AB} \parallel \overline{DC}$	8. Given
9. $\overline{CEB} \perp \overline{DC}$	9. Line ⊥ 1 of 2 parallel lines ⊥ the other.
10. $\angle BCD$ right $\angle$	10. ⊥s form right angles
(a) 11. $\angle ABC \cong \angle BCD$	11. All right $\angle$s are ≅.
12. $\triangle BDC \sim \triangle AEB$	12. a.a. ≅ a.a.
13. $\frac{BD}{AE} = \frac{CD}{BE}$	13. Corr. sides of similar $\triangle$s are in proportion.

EXERCISES

1. *Given:* $\overleftrightarrow{DB}$ is tangent to circle O at B, $\overline{AB}$ is a diameter of circle O, and chord $\overline{AC}$ extended intersects $\overleftrightarrow{DB}$ at D.

Prove:

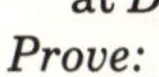

a. $\triangle ACB \sim \triangle BCD$

b. $\frac{AB}{BD} = \frac{AC}{BC}$

2.

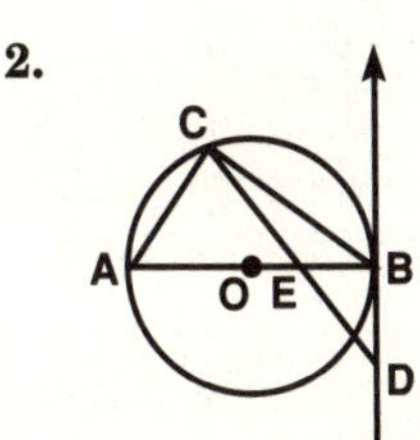

Given: $\triangle ABC$ is inscribed in circle O, $\overline{AB}$ is a diameter, $\overrightarrow{BD}$ is tangent to circle O at point B, $\overline{CD}$ is drawn and intersects $\overline{AB}$ at point E such that $\overline{AC} \cong \overline{CE}$.

Prove: $\frac{AB}{ED} = \frac{AC}{EB}$

3. *Given:* Diameter $\overline{AB}$ of circle O, $\overleftrightarrow{RB}$ is tangent to O at B, chords $\overline{AE}$ and $\overline{AC}$ are drawn. $\overline{AE}$ is extended to meet $\overleftrightarrow{RB}$ at D, and $\widehat{BE} \cong \widehat{BC}$.

Prove: $\frac{AD}{AB} = \frac{AB}{AC}$

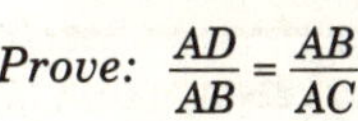

4.

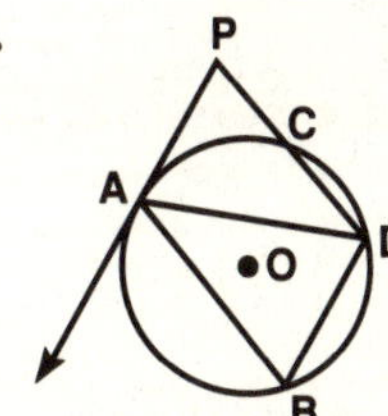

Given: $\overrightarrow{PA}$ is tangent to circle O at A and intersects secant $\overline{PCD}$ at P. Chord $\overline{AB}$ is parallel to $\overline{PCD}$.

Prove: $\frac{PD}{AD} = \frac{AD}{AB}$

5. *Given:* Secants $\overline{AD}$ and $\overline{EC}$ intersect circle O at F, $\overline{BD}$ is tangent to the circle at D, and $\overline{AB} \perp \overline{BD}$.

Prove: $\frac{AB}{BD} = \frac{CD}{DE}$

6. *Given:* $\overrightarrow{PA}$ is a tangent to circle O at point A. Secant $\overline{PDC}$ passes through the center O and is perpendicular to chord $\overline{AB}$ at E. Radii $\overline{OA}$ and $\overline{OB}$ are drawn.

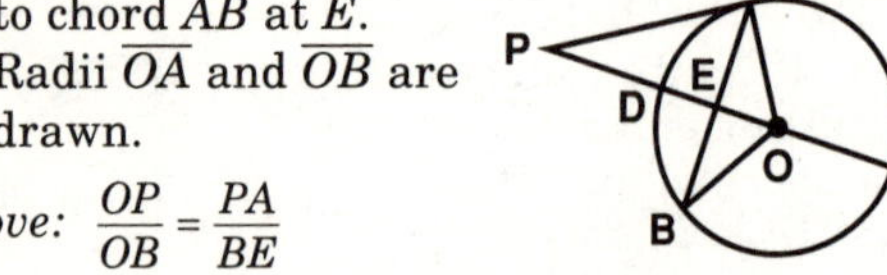

Prove: $\frac{OP}{OB} = \frac{PA}{BE}$

7. *Given:* $\overline{AB}$ is a diameter of circle O and $\overline{AC}$ and $\overline{BD}$ are tangents to the circle at points A and B, respectively. $\overline{AD}$ and $\overline{BC}$ intersect on the circle at E.

Prove: $AC : AB = AB : BD$

8. *Given:* $\overleftrightarrow{AT}$ is tangent to the circle. Chord $\overline{CE} \parallel \overleftrightarrow{AT}$, and B is any point on $\widehat{AE}$. $\overline{AC}$, $\overline{BC}$, and $\overline{AB}$ are drawn. $\overline{AB}$ and $\overline{CE}$ are extended to meet at D.

Prove: AC is the mean proportional between AB and AD.

9. *Given:* $\triangle ABC$ is inscribed in a circle and point P lies on chord $\overline{BC}$. $\overrightarrow{AP}$ extended meets the circle at point D. Chord $\overline{BD}$ is drawn.

Prove: $AC : BD = AP : BP$

10. In circle O, diameter $\overline{AB} \perp$ diameter $\overline{CD}$, and $\overline{AM}$ is any chord intersecting $\overline{CD}$ at P. $\overline{MB}$ and $\overline{BP}$ are drawn.

Prove:
a. $AP = BP$ **b.** $\frac{OB}{MA} = \frac{OP}{MB}$

Proving a Product

Goal: **To show that the required statement displays the product of the means and the product of the extremes of a proportion.**

Method:

1. Rewrite the product as a proportion.

Procedure	Example
Use one pair of lengths as the means and other pair as the extremes. **To avoid confusion, split the first pair immediately, and write them as the extremes. Then, place the other pair.**	*Given:* $AB \times PR = BC \times RS$ First do $\frac{AB}{} = \frac{}{PR}$ Then $\frac{AB}{RS} = \frac{BC}{PR}$
If one product is a square, write that product as a mean proportional.	*Given:* $PR \times RS = (AB)^2$ *Write:* $\frac{PR}{AB} = \frac{AB}{RS}$

2. Determine the triangles to prove similar **by reading the proportion.**

3. Begin your proof by establishing the two pairs of angles **that show the triangles are similar.**

Examples

1. *Theorem:* If two chords intersect inside a circle, then the product of the measures of the segments of one chord equals the product of the measures of the segments of the other.

Given: Chords $\overline{AB}$ and $\overline{CD}$ intersect at E inside a circle.

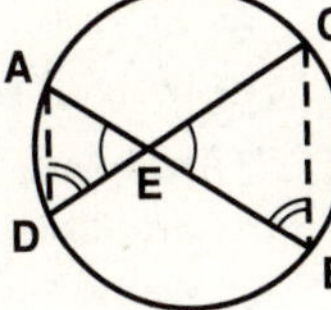

Prove: $AE \times EB = CE \times ED$

Plan: Rewrite the product as a proportion:

$$\frac{AE}{CE} = \frac{ED}{EB}$$

Read the proportion to determine the triangles that must be proved similar.

Show $\triangle AED \sim \triangle CEB$ by a.a. $\cong$ a.a.

Statements	Reasons
1. Chords $\overline{AB}, \overline{CD}$	1. Given
2. Draw $\overline{AD}, \overline{CB}$.	2. Two points determine line.
(a) 3. $\angle AED \cong \angle CEB$	3. Vertical $\angle$s are $\cong$.
4. $m\angle ADC = \frac{1}{2} m\widehat{AC}$ $m\angle CBA = \frac{1}{2} m\widehat{AC}$	4. m inscribed $\angle = \frac{1}{2}$ m arc.
5. $m\angle ADC = m\angle CBA$	5. Transitive property
(a) 6. $\angle ADC \cong \angle CBA$	6. Definition: congruence
7. $\triangle AED \sim \triangle CEB$	7. a.a. $\cong$ a.a.
8. $\frac{AE}{CE} = \frac{ED}{EB}$	8. Corr. sides of similar $\triangle$s are in proportion.
9. $AE \times EB = CE \times ED$	9. In a proportion, product of means = product of extremes.

2. *Given:* $\overline{RN}$ tangent to circle T at N, and diameter $\overline{AN}$.

Prove: $(AN)^2 = AR \times AB$

Plan: Rewrite the product as a proportion:

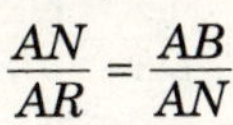

$$\frac{AN}{AR} = \frac{AB}{AN}$$

Show $\triangle ANB \sim \triangle ARN$ by a.a. $\cong$ a.a.

Statements	Reasons
1. Tangent $\overline{RN}$, diameter $\overline{AN}$	1. Given
2. $\overline{AN} \perp \overline{RN}$	2. Diameter $\perp$ tangent.
3. $\angle ANR$ right $\angle$	3. $\perp$s form right $\angle$s.
4. $\widehat{ABN}$ semicircle	4. Diameter $\div$ circle.
5. $\angle ABN$ right $\angle$	5. $\angle$ inscribed in semicircle.
(a) 6. $\angle ANR \cong \angle ABN$	6. All right $\angle$s are $\cong$.
(a) 7. $\angle A \cong \angle A$	7. Reflexive property
8. $\triangle ANB \sim \triangle ARN$	8. a.a. $\cong$ a.a.
9. $\frac{AN}{AR} = \frac{AB}{AN}$	9. Corresponding sides of similar $\triangle$s are in prop.
10. $(AN)^2 = AR \times AB$	10. In a proportion, product of means = product of extremes.

EXERCISES

1. *Given:* Diameter $\overline{AC}$ of circle O is extended to point D, $\overline{DF} \perp \overline{AD}$, $\overline{AEF}$, where E is a point on circle O, and $\overline{EC}$ is drawn.

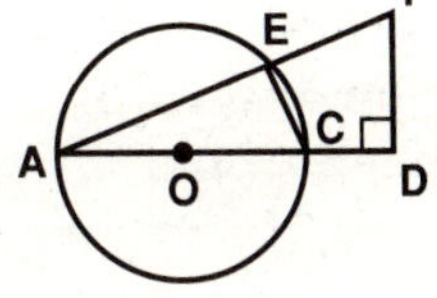

Prove: $AF \times EC = AC \times FD$

2. *Given:* $\triangle ABC$ is inscribed in circle O so that the center of the circle lies in the interior of the triangle. Diameter $\overline{AE}$ and altitude $\overline{AD}$ are drawn.

Prove: $AB \times AC = AD \times AE$

3. *Given:* Quadrilateral $ABCD$ is inscribed in the circle. Diagonals $\overline{AC}$ and $\overline{BD}$ meet at point E and $\overline{AD} \cong \overline{CD}$.

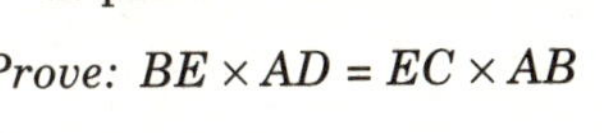

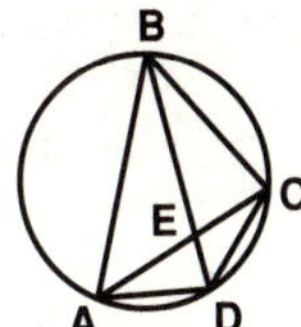

Prove: $BE \times AD = EC \times AB$

4. *Given:* $\overline{AB}$ is a diameter of circle O, $\overrightarrow{DC}$ is tangent to the circle at C, and $\overline{AD} \perp \overrightarrow{DC}$. Chords $\overline{AC}$ and $\overline{BC}$ are drawn.

Prove: $AB \times AD = (AC)^2$

5. *Given:* A circle with secants $\overline{PAB}$ and $\overline{PCD}$, chord $\overline{BC}$ is extended to R, and $\overline{PR} \parallel \overline{AD}$.

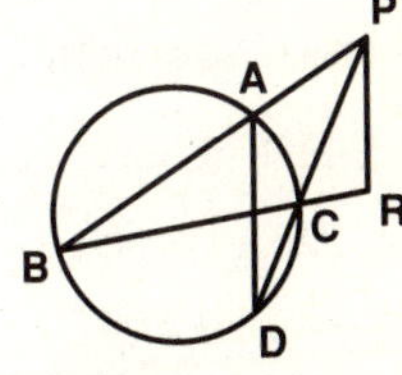

Prove: $(PR)^2 = BR \times CR$

6. *Given:* Isosceles $\triangle ABC$, with $\overline{AB} \cong \overline{AC}$, is inscribed in a circle. Chord $\overline{AE}$ intersects side $\overline{BC}$ at D. Chord $\overline{BE}$ is drawn.

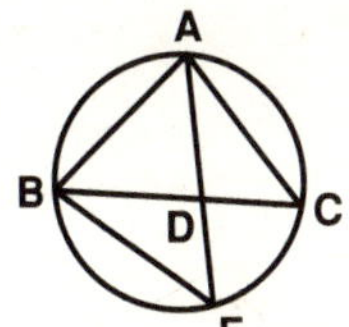

Prove: $(AB)^2 = AD \times AE$

7. *Given:* $\overleftrightarrow{PR}$ is a tangent, $\overline{PA}$ and $\overline{PE}$ are chords, and $\overline{AE}$ is a diameter of circle O. $\overline{AB} \perp \overleftrightarrow{PR}$.

Prove: $AB \times AE = (AP)^2$

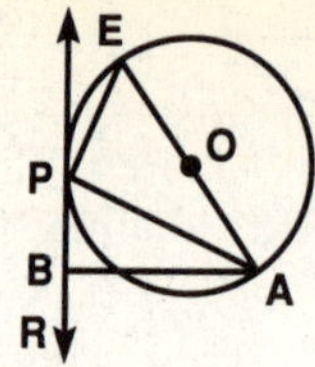

8. *Given:* $\overline{AB}$ is a diameter of circle O, $\overrightarrow{DB}$ is tangent to the circle at B, and $\overline{AB}$ bisects $\angle DAC$.

Prove: $AC \times AD = (AB)^2$

9. *Given:* In circle O, point E lies between A and O on diameter $\overline{AB}$. Chord $\overline{CD} \perp \overline{AB}$ at E. $\overline{CA}$, $\overline{CB}$, and $\overline{DB}$ are drawn.

Prove: $EB \times AB = CB \times DB$

10. *Given:* Isosceles $\triangle ABC$ inscribed in circle O with $\overline{AC} \cong \overline{BC}$. Chords $\overline{CD}$ and $\overline{AB}$ intersect at E. Chord $\overline{AD}$ is drawn.

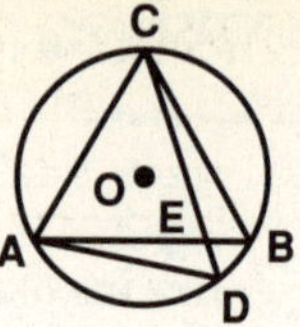

Prove:

a. $\angle CAD \cong \angle CEA$

b. $(AC)^2 = CE \times CD$

11. *Theorem:* If two secants are drawn to a circle from an external point, then the product of the measures of one secant segment and its external segment equals the product of the measures of the other secant segment and its external segment.

Given: Secants $\overrightarrow{PAB}$ and $\overrightarrow{PCD}$ to a circle.

Prove: $PB \times PA = PD \times PC$

Plan: Rewrite the product as a proportion, leading to $\triangle PBC$ and $\triangle PDA$. Draw $\overline{BC}$, $\overline{AD}$.

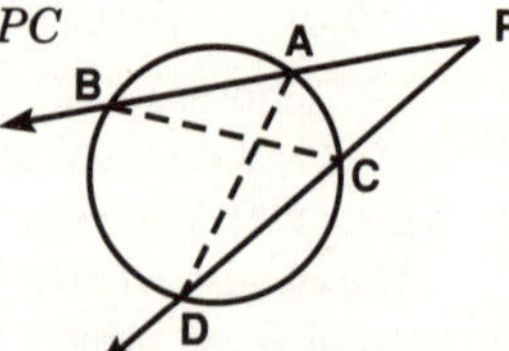

5.4 LENGTHS OF SEGMENTS

Common Tangents

A COMMON TANGENT is a line, $\overleftrightarrow{TT'}$, that is tangent to each of two circles. The distance between the centers of two circles is measured along the LINE OF CENTERS, $\overline{OO'}$.

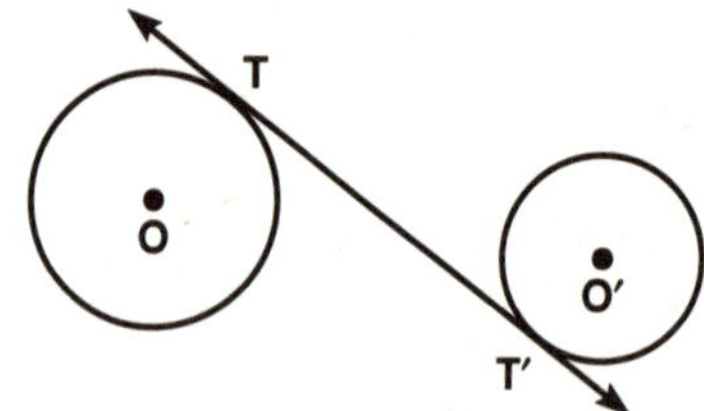

COMMON INTERNAL TANGENT LINE

The circles are on opposite sides of the tangent line.

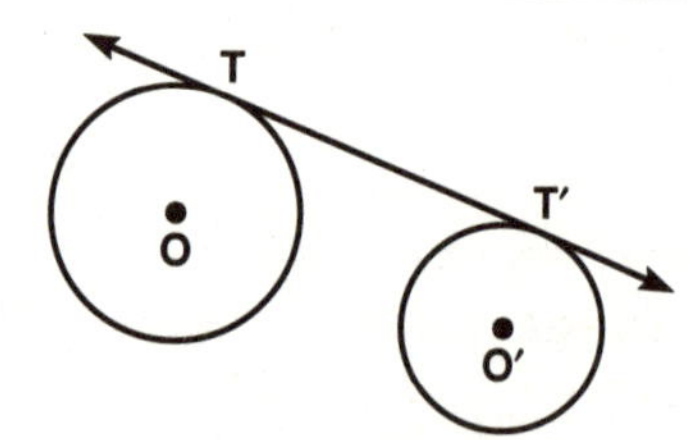

COMMON EXTERNAL TANGENT LINE

The circles are on the same side of the tangent line.

EXTERNALLY TANGENT CIRCLES

have a common internal tangent line.

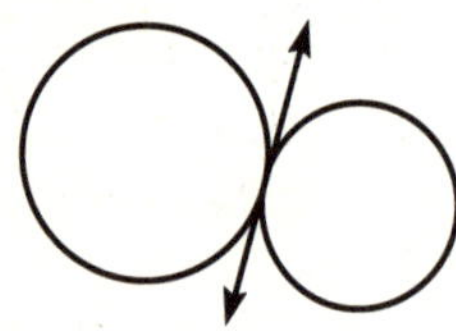

INTERNALLY TANGENT CIRCLES

have a common external tangent line.

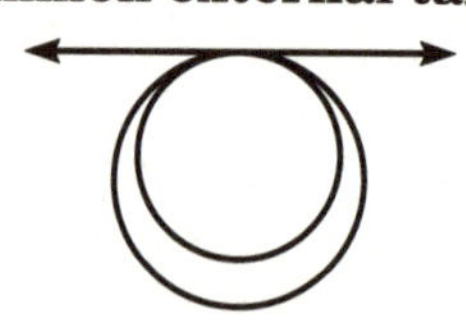

Two circles can have 0, 1, 2, 3 or 4 common tangent lines.

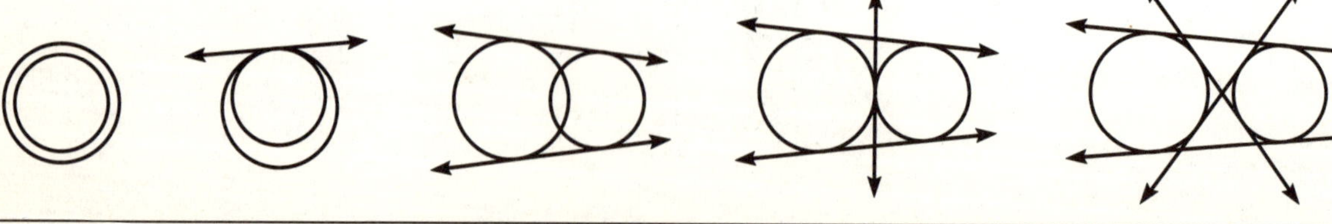

Applying Theorems

Theorem	*Example*

A diameter perpendicular to a chord bisects the chord and its arcs.

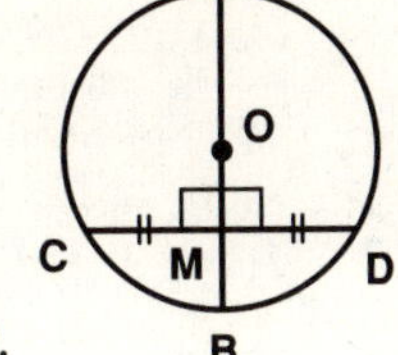

If $\overline{AOB} \perp \overline{CD}$, then $\overline{CM} \cong \overline{MD}$, $\widehat{CB} \cong \widehat{BD}$, $\widehat{AC} \cong \widehat{AD}$.

In a circle, chord $\overline{AB}$ is 9 cm from the center. If the length of $\overline{AB}$ is 24 cm, find the length of the radius.

Solution:

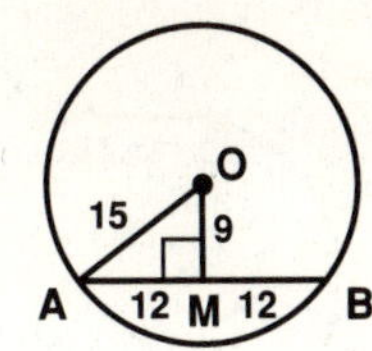

Distance from the center is measured along a perpendicular, $\overline{OM}$, which extends to a diameter. Thus, $\overline{OM}$ bisects chord $\overline{AB}$. Draw radius $\overline{OA}$ as the hypotenuse of a right △. Lengths are a multiple of the 3-4-5 Pythagorean Triple (3×3, 3×4, 3×5).

Answer: radius = 15 cm

If two chords intersect in a circle, then the product of the measures of the segments of one chord equals the product of the measures of the segments of the other.

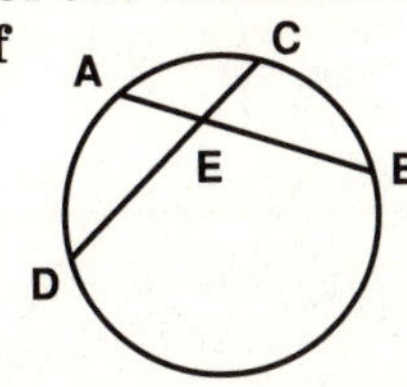

If chords $\overline{AB}$ and $\overline{CD}$ intersect at E in the circle, then $AE \times EB = CE \times ED$.

In a circle, chords $\overline{AB}$ and $\overline{CD}$ intersect at E. If $AE = x + 1$, $EB = x$, $CE = 2$, and $ED = 3$, find x.

Solution:

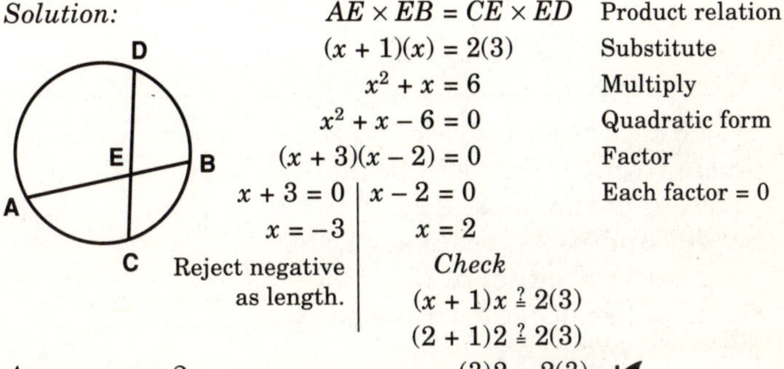

$AE \times EB = CE \times ED$	Product relation
$(x + 1)(x) = 2(3)$	Substitute
$x^2 + x = 6$	Multiply
$x^2 + x - 6 = 0$	Quadratic form
$(x + 3)(x - 2) = 0$	Factor
$x + 3 = 0$ | $x - 2 = 0$	Each factor = 0

$x + 3 = 0$, $x = -3$ — Reject negative as length.

$x - 2 = 0$, $x = 2$

Check

$(x + 1)x \stackrel{?}{=} 2(3)$

$(2 + 1)2 \stackrel{?}{=} 2(3)$

$(3)2 = 2(3)$ ✓

Answer: $x = 2$

Tangent segments to a circle from an external point are congruent.

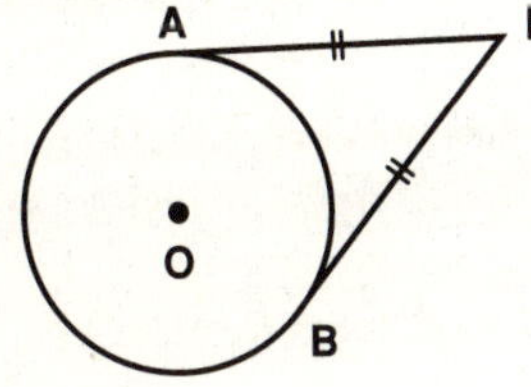

If $\overline{PA}$ and $\overline{PB}$ are tangent to circle O, then $\overline{PA} \cong \overline{PB}$.

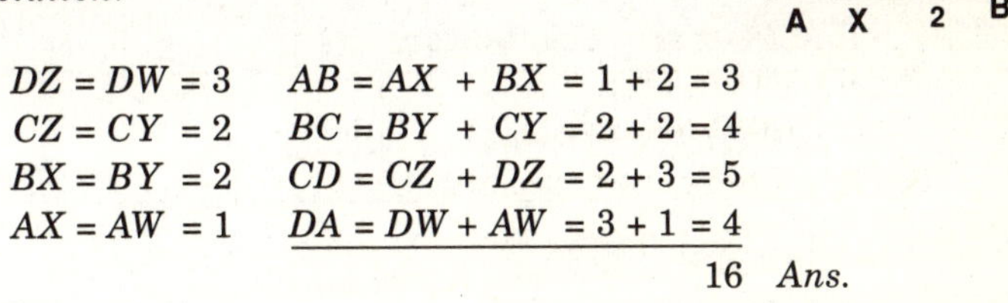

A circle is inscribed in quadrilateral $ABCD$ and W, X, Y, and Z are points of tangency of the sides. If $DZ = 3$, $CY = 2$, $BX = 2$, and $AW = 1$, find the perimeter of the quadrilateral.

Solution:

$DZ = DW = 3$	$AB = AX + BX = 1 + 2 = 3$
$CZ = CY = 2$	$BC = BY + CY = 2 + 2 = 4$
$BX = BY = 2$	$CD = CZ + DZ = 2 + 3 = 5$
$AX = AW = 1$	$DA = DW + AW = 3 + 1 = 4$
	16 *Ans.*

(Theorems continue on next page)

Theorem	*Example*
If a tangent and a secant are drawn to a circle from an external point, the measure of the tangent segment is the mean proportional between the measures of the secant and its external segment. 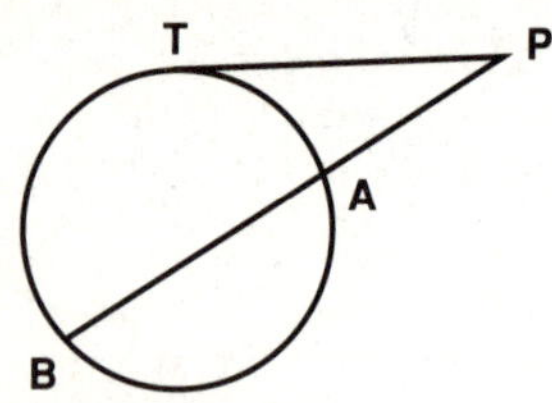 If $\overline{PT}$ is a tangent and $\overline{PAB}$ a secant, then $\frac{PB}{PT} = \frac{PT}{PA}$	Tangent $\overline{AB}$ and secant $\overline{ACD}$ are drawn to circle O from external point A. If $AB = 6$ and $CD = 5$, find AD. *Solution:* Let $AD = x$, then $AC = x - 5$. 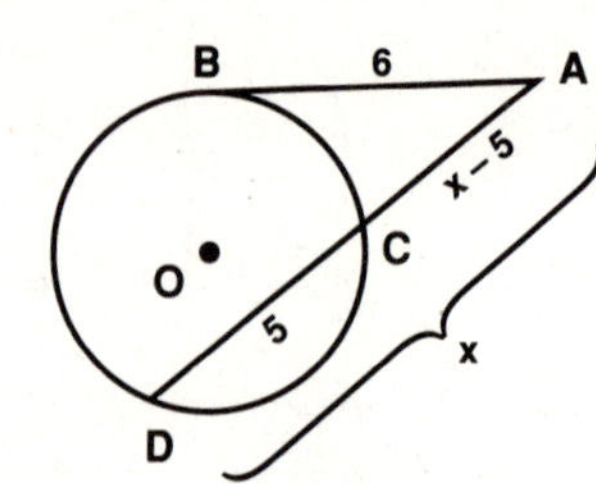 $\frac{\text{whole secant}}{\text{tangent}} = \frac{\text{tangent}}{\text{external segment of secant}}$ $\frac{AD}{AB} = \frac{AB}{AC}$ $\frac{x}{6} = \frac{6}{x-5}$ $x^2 - 5x = 36$ $x^2 - 5x - 36 = 0$ $(x - 9)(x + 4) = 0$ $x - 9 = 0$ | $x + 4 = 0$ $x = 9$ | $x = -4$ Reject *Answer:* $AD = 9$
If two secants are drawn to a circle from an external point, the product of the measures of one secant and its external segment equals the product of the measures of the other secant and its external segment. 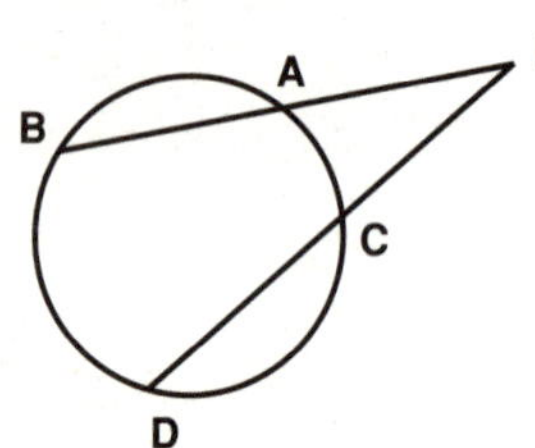 If $\overline{PAB}$ and $\overline{PCD}$ are secants from external point P, then $PB \times PA = PD \times PC$	Secants $\overline{ABC}$ and $\overline{ADE}$ are drawn to a circle from external point A. If $AB = 8$ and $BC = 4$, and DE is 4 more than AD, find AE. *Solution:* Let $AD = x$, then $DE = x + 4$. 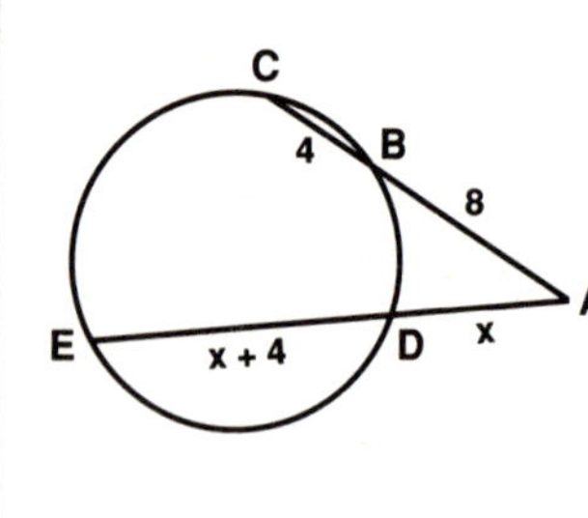 whole secant × external segment = whole secant × external segment $AC \times AB = AE \times AD$ $12 \times 8 = (2x + 4)x$ $96 = 2x^2 + 4x$ $48 = x^2 + 2x$ $x^2 + 2x - 48 = 0$ $(x + 8)(x - 6) = 0$ $x + 8 = 0$ | $x - 6 = 0$ $x = -8$ Reject | $x = 6$ $AE = AD + DE = 6 + 10 = 16$ *Ans.*

EXERCISES

1. If two circles are internally tangent, what is the total number of common tangents that can be drawn to the circles?

(1) 1 **(2)** 2 **(3)** 3 **(4)** 0

2. Each of two circles has a radius of 5 centimeters. Their centers are 8 centimeters apart. The total number of common tangents that can be drawn to these circles is

(1) 1 **(2)** 2 **(3)** 3 **(4)** 4

3. If two circles with radii 2 and 5 are drawn such that the distance between their centers is 6, what is the maximum number of common tangents they may have?

(1) 0 **(2)** 2 **(3)** 3 **(4)** 4

4. If two circles have exactly one common tangent, then the circles must be

(1) concentric (same center)
(2) congruent
(3) internally tangent
(4) externally tangent

In 5–6, find the length of $\overline{OO'}$.

5.

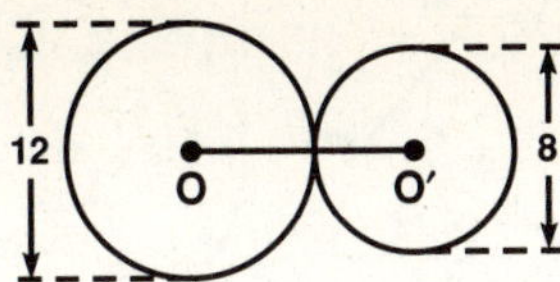

6.

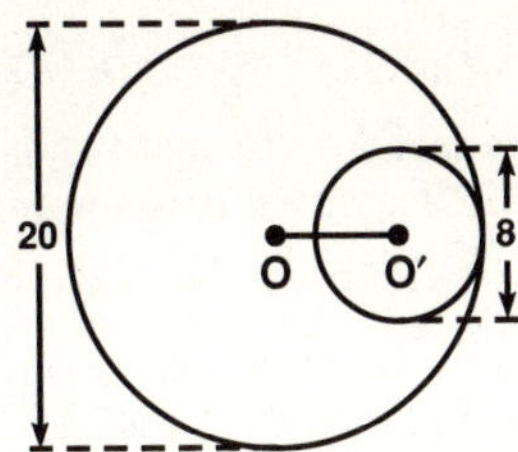

7. *Given:* Circle $O \cong$ circle O', radii $\overline{OA}$ and $\overline{O'B}$, $\overleftrightarrow{AB}$ is a common internal tangent, and $\overline{OO'}$ intersects $\overleftrightarrow{AB}$ at C.

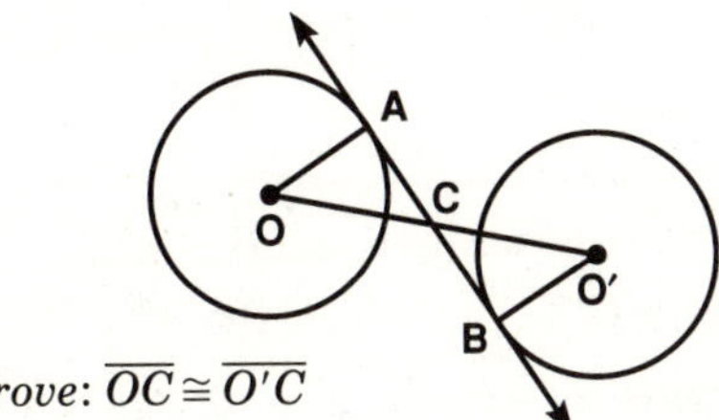

Prove: $\overline{OC} \cong \overline{O'C}$

Ex. 8

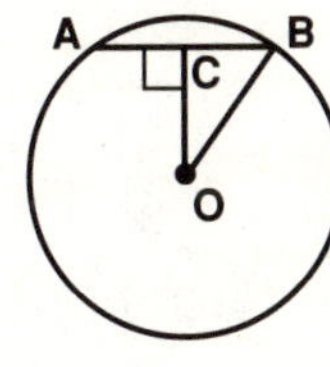

Ex. 9

8. In the diagram of circle O, chord $\overline{CD}$ is perpendicular to diameter $\overline{AB}$ at E. If $AE = 4$ and $EB = 9$, find CE.

9. In the diagram, the length of the radius of circle O is 13 and the length of chord $\overline{ACB}$ is 10. If $\overline{CO}$ is perpendicular to $\overline{AB}$, find CO.

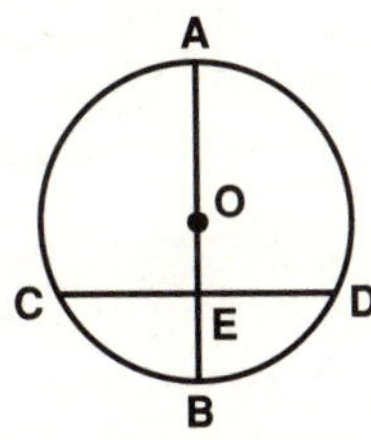

Ex. 10

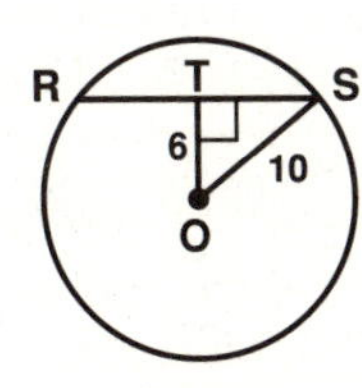

Ex. 11

10. In the diagram of circle O, diameter $\overline{AB}$ is perpendicular to chord $\overline{CD}$ at E. If $CD = 8$ and $OE = 3$, find the length of the radius of the circle.

11. In the diagram of circle O, the length of radius $\overline{OS} = 10$ and the distance from center O to chord $\overline{RTS}$ is 6. Find RS.

12. In a circle of radius 10 cm, how far from the center is a chord that measures 16 cm?

13. *Given:* $\overline{BD}$ is a diameter of circle O. Chord $\overline{AC} \perp \overline{BD}$ at E and chord $\overline{BC}$ is drawn.

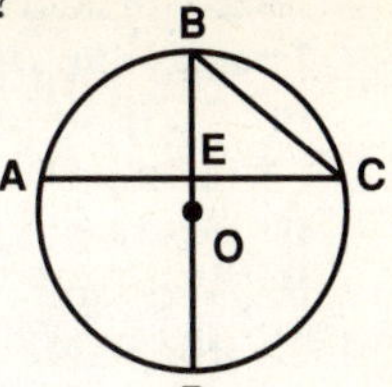

a. *Prove:* $BE \times BD = (BC)^2$

b. If $BE = 8$ and $ED = 10$, find BC.

Ex. 14

Ex. 15

14. In the diagram, chords $\overline{AB}$ and $\overline{CD}$ of the circle intersect at E. If $AE = 6$, $EB = 8$, and $CE = 4$, find the length of $\overline{ED}$.

15. In the diagram, $\overline{AB}$ and $\overline{CD}$ are chords of the circle and intersect at E. If $AE = 10$, $EB = 9$, and $CE = 6$, find CD.

16. In circle O, chords $\overline{AB}$ and $\overline{CD}$ intersect at E. If $AE = 8$, $EB = 6$, and $ED = 12$, find the length of $\overline{CE}$.

17. In a circle, a chord of 10 cm bisects a chord of 8 cm. The length of the shorter segment of the 10-cm chord is

(1) 5 cm (2) 2 cm (3) 8 cm (4) 4 cm

18. In circle O, chords $\overline{AB}$ and $\overline{CD}$ intersect at P. If $AP = a$, $PB = b$, and $CP = c$, what is the length of $\overline{PD}$?

(1) $\frac{ab}{c}$ (3) $\frac{bc}{a}$

(2) $\frac{ac}{b}$ (4) $\frac{a+b}{c}$

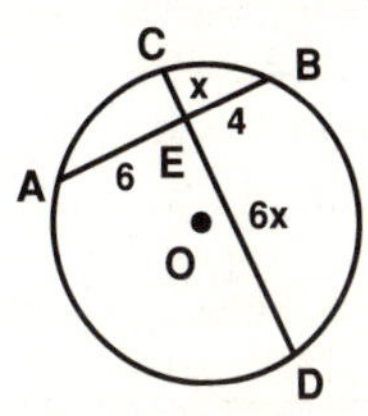

Ex. 19

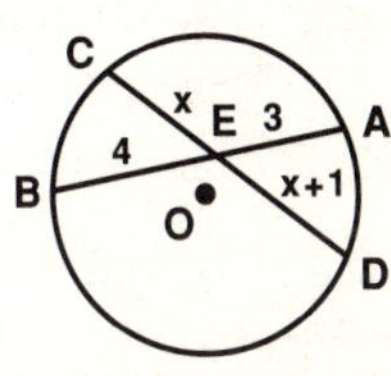

Ex. 20

19. Chords $\overline{AB}$ and $\overline{CD}$ of circle O intersect in E. If $AE = 6$, $EB = 4$, $CE = x$, and $ED = 6x$, find CE.

20. In circle O, chords $\overline{AB}$ and $\overline{CD}$ intersect at E. If $AE = 3$, $EB = 4$, $CE = x$, and $ED = x + 1$, find CE.

21. Chords $\overline{AB}$ and $\overline{CD}$ of circle O intersect at E. If $AE = x$, $EB = x - 6$, and $CE = ED = 4$, find AE.

22. In circle O, diameter $\overline{AB}$ is perpendicular to chord $\overline{CD}$ at E. If $AE = 16$ and $EB = 4$, what is CD?

(1) 32 (2) 16 (3) 10 (4) 8

23. In circle O, diameter $\overline{AB} \perp$ chord $\overline{CD}$ at point E. The length of chord $\overline{CD}$ is 12 inches, and AE is 5 inches longer than BE.

a. If BE is represented by x, represent AE in terms of x.

b. State a reason why E is the midpoint of $\overline{CD}$.

c. Write an equation that can be used to find the value of x.

d. Find the number of inches in the length of $\overline{BE}$ by solving the equation obtained in answer to part **c**.

e. Find the number of inches in the length of diameter $\overline{AB}$.

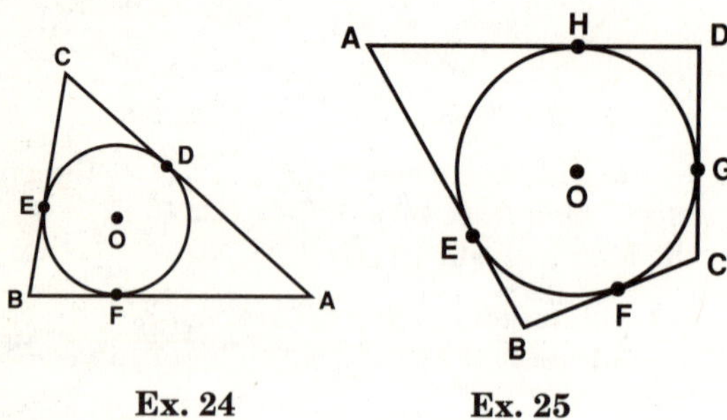

Ex. 24 **Ex. 25**

24. In the diagram, circle O is inscribed in $\triangle ABC$. If $AB = 6$, $AF = 4$, and $EC = 3$, what is the perimeter of $\triangle ABC$?

25. In the diagram, circle O is inscribed in quadrilateral $ABCD$ and E, F, G, and H are the points of tangency of the sides. If $AH = 6$, $DG = 4$, $CF = 2$, and $BF = 3$, what is the perimeter of quadrilateral $ABCD$?

(1) 15 (2) 21 (3) 24 (4) 30

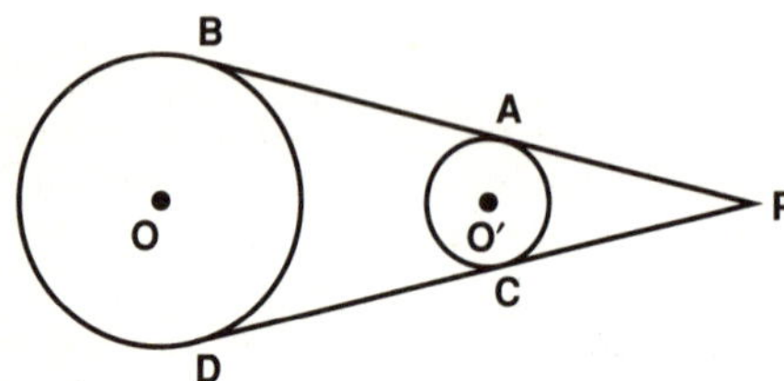

Ex. 26

26. In the diagram, $\overline{PAB}$ and $\overline{PCD}$ are externally tangent to circles O and O'. If $PB = 16$ and $CD = 10$, find PA.

27. Tangents $\overline{PA}$ and $\overline{PB}$ are drawn to circle O from external point P, and chord $\overline{AB}$ is drawn. If $m\angle APB = 60°$ and $AB = 8$, PB is equal to

(1) 8 (2) 10 (3) 6 (4) 4

28. *Given*: Two unequal circles are tangent externally at point A. $\overline{BC}$ is a common external tangent touching the circles at B and C, respectively. The common internal tangent at A intersects $\overline{BC}$ at D.

a. *Prove*: D is the midpoint of $\overline{BC}$.

b. If $m\angle CAD$ is represented by x and $m\angle BAD$ is represented by y, find the value of $x + y$.

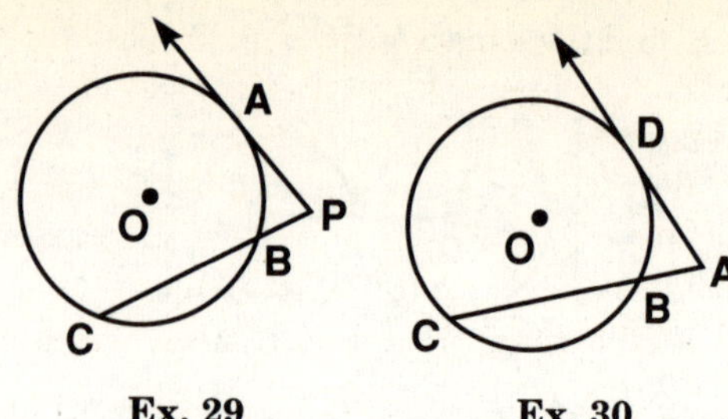

Ex. 29 **Ex. 30**

29. In the diagram, $\overrightarrow{PA}$ is tangent to circle O at A. If $CB = 12$ and $PB = 4$, what is the length of $\overline{PA}$?

(1) $4\sqrt{3}$ (2) 48 (3) $16\sqrt{3}$ (4) 8

30. In the diagram, $\overrightarrow{AD}$ is tangent to circle O at D and $\overline{ABC}$ is a secant. If $AD = 4$ and $AC = 8$, find AB.

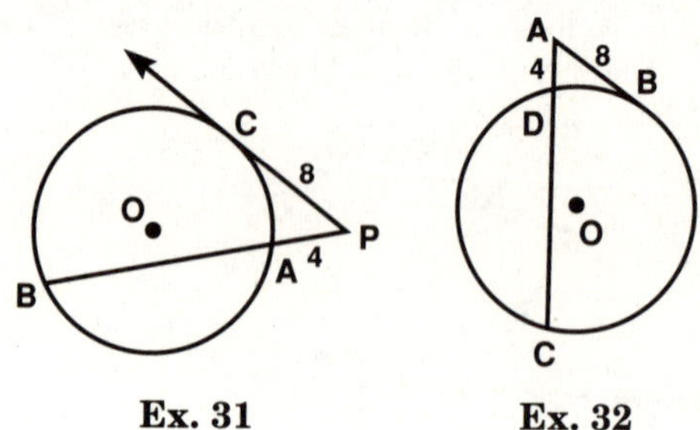

Ex. 31 **Ex. 32**

31. In the diagram, $\overrightarrow{PC}$ is tangent to circle O at C and $\overline{PAB}$ is a secant. If $PC = 8$ and $PA = 4$, find AB.

32. In the diagram, secant $\overline{ADC}$ and tangent $\overline{AB}$ are drawn to circle O from external point A. If $AB = 8$ and $AD = 4$, what is the length of $\overline{AC}$?

(1) 16 (2) 12 (3) 8 (4) 4

33. *Given*: Circle O with tangent $\overline{PA}$ and secant $\overline{PBC}$; chord $\overline{DE}$ bisects chord $\overline{BC}$ at M and $PA = 3$ and $PB = 1$.

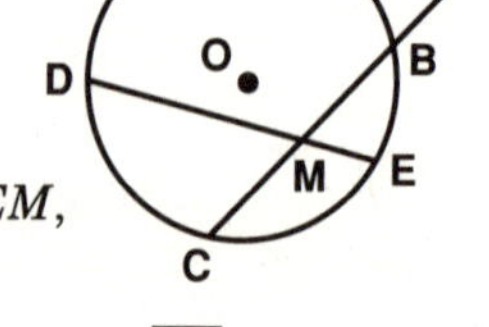

a. Find BC.

b. If $DE = 10$ and $DM > EM$, find EM.

34. From external point A, tangent $\overline{AD}$ and secant $\overline{ABC}$ are drawn to circle O. If $AD = 6$, $AB = x$, and $BC = 5$, find AB.

35. From external point P, tangent $\overline{PA}$ and secant $\overline{PBC}$ are drawn to circle O. If $PA = 4$, $PB = x$, and $BC = 8$, find PBC.

36. In circle O, diameter $\overline{COB}$ is extended to external point P and tangent $\overline{PA}$ is drawn. If the radius of the circle is 4 and PA is 3, find PB.

37. From a point P outside a circle, tangent $\overrightarrow{PA}$ and secant $\overline{PCB}$ are drawn. $PA = 10\sqrt{3}$ and $BC = 20$.

a. Represent the length of $\overline{PC}$ by x and write an equation that may be used to find the value of x.

b. Solve the equation written in answer to part **a** and state the length of $\overline{PC}$.

38. At A on circle O, tangent $\overrightarrow{PA}$ is drawn. $\overline{PCD}$ is a secant that passes through O. $PA = x$, $PC = 2$, and $PD = x + 4$.

a. Write an equation that can be used to solve for x.

b. Find the length of the tangent.

c. Find the length of the radius of the circle.

39. Diameter $\overline{AB}$ of circle O is 12 inches in length. $\overline{AB}$ is extended through B to a point C and tangent $\overrightarrow{CD}$ is drawn, meeting the circle at D. $\overline{CD}$ is 2 inches longer than $\overline{BC}$.

a. Let x represent the number of inches in BC, and express CD and CA in terms of x.

b. Express as an equation in the variable x, the relationship that exists among BC, CA, and CD.

c. Find the length of $\overline{BC}$ by solving the equation in part **b**.

40. 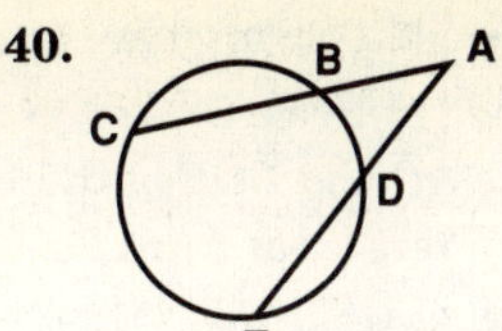

In the diagram of a circle, secants $\overline{ABC}$ and $\overline{ADE}$ are drawn from external point A. If $AD = 3$, $DE = 5$, and $AB = 4$, find AC.

41. In the diagram of a circle, secants $\overline{FGH}$ and $\overline{FJK}$ are drawn from external point F. If $FG = 2$, $GH = 6$, and $JK = 4$, find FJ.

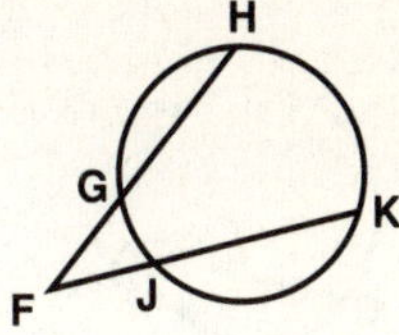

42. Secants $\overline{ABC}$ and $\overline{ADE}$ are drawn to a circle from external point A. If $AB = 1$, $BC = 3$, and DE is 4 more than AD, find AE.

43. *Given:* $\overline{PB} \cong \overline{PD}$

Prove: $\overline{PA} \cong \overline{PC}$

5.5 SUMMARY EXERCISES

1. Congruent circles may be defined as circles with congruent

(1) centers (3) central angles
(2) chords (4) radii

2. Two arcs in the same circle have central angles with measures in the ratio of 2 : 3. The lengths of the arcs are in the ratio of

(1) 1 : 9 (2) 2 : 3 (3) 2 : 9 (4) 4 : 9

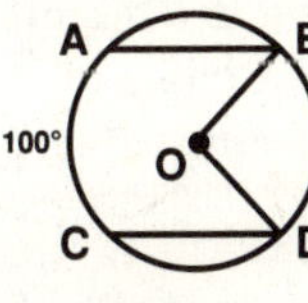

Ex. 3

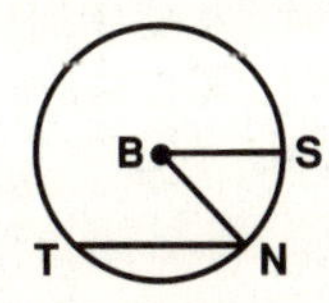

Ex. 4

3. In circle O, chord $\overline{AB}$ is parallel to chord $\overline{CD}$. If $m\widehat{AC} = 100°$, find $m\angle BOD$.

4. In circle B, chord $\overline{TN}$ is parallel to radius $\overline{BS}$. If $m\angle N = 48°$, what is $m\widehat{NS}$?

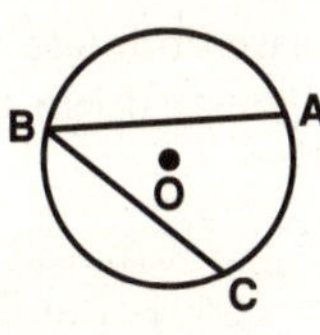

Ex. 5

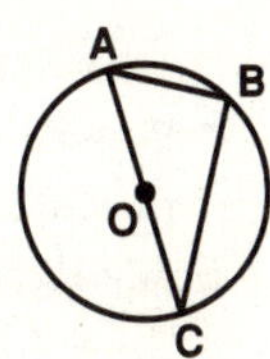

Ex. 6

5. In circle O, $m\widehat{AC}$ is 84°. Find $m\angle ABC$.

(1) 21° (2) 42° (3) 84° (4) 168°

6. In circle O, the ratio of $m\widehat{BC}$ to $m\widehat{AB}$ is 2 : 1. What is $m\angle ACB$?

(1) 30° (2) 45° (3) 60° (4) 90°

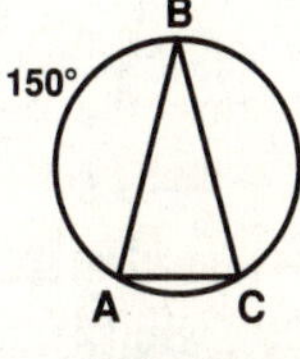

Ex. 7

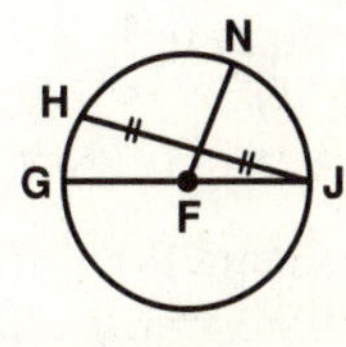

Ex. 8

7. Isosceles triangle ABC is inscribed in the circle. If $\overline{AB} \cong \overline{CB}$ and $m\widehat{AB} = 150°$, find $m\angle B$.

8. In circle F, $\overline{FN}$ bisects $\overline{HJ}$ and $m\widehat{NJ} = 68°$. Find $m\widehat{HG}$.

9. The sides of a triangle divide a circumscribed circle into three arcs. If the measures of the arcs are in the ratio 2 : 3 : 5, the measure of the largest angle of the triangle is

(1) 18° (2) 36° (3) 54° (4) 90°

10. Triangle DEF is inscribed in circle O. If $m\angle D = 85°$ and $m\angle E = 65°$, which side of triangle DEF lies nearest to the center of circle O?

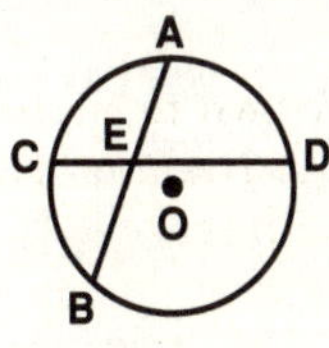

Ex. 11

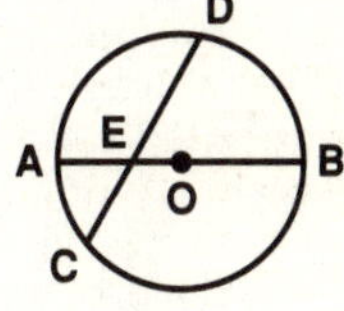

Ex. 12

11. Chords $\overline{AB}$ and $\overline{CD}$ intersect in the circle at E. If $m\widehat{BC} = 60°$ and $m\widehat{AD} = 80°$, find $m\angle AEC$.

12. $\overline{AB}$ is a diameter of circle O and chord $\overline{CD}$ intersects diameter $\overline{AB}$ at E. If $m\widehat{AD} = 100°$ and $m\widehat{AC} = 40°$, find $m\angle DEB$.

13. 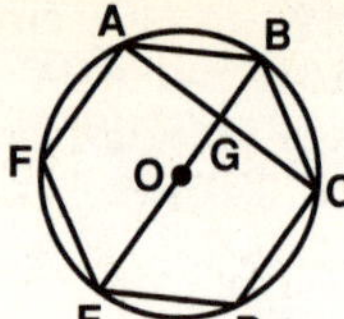

Regular hexagon $ABCDEF$ is inscribed in circle O. Diagonals $\overline{AC}$ and $\overline{BOE}$ of the hexagon intersect at point G. What is m$\angle EGC$?

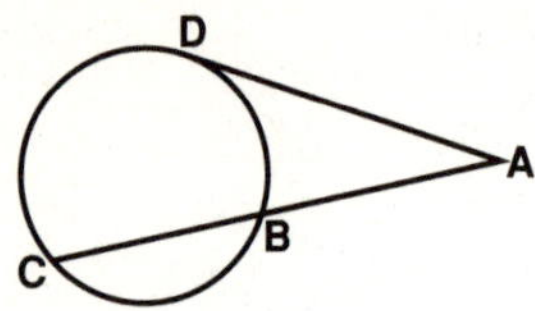

Ex. 14

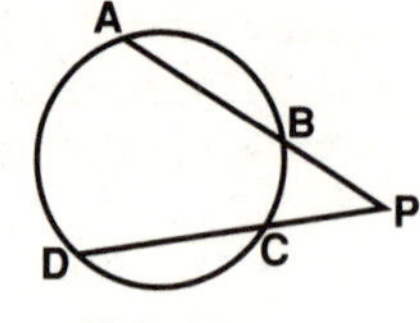

Ex. 15

14. $\overline{AD}$ is tangent to the circle at D and $\overline{ABC}$ is a secant. If m$\overset{\frown}{DC} = 150°$ and m$\overset{\frown}{BD} = 90°$, find m$\angle A$.

15. $\overline{PBA}$ and $\overline{PCD}$ are secants to the circle. If m$\angle P = 40°$ and m$\overset{\frown}{AD} = 120°$, find m$\overset{\frown}{BC}$.

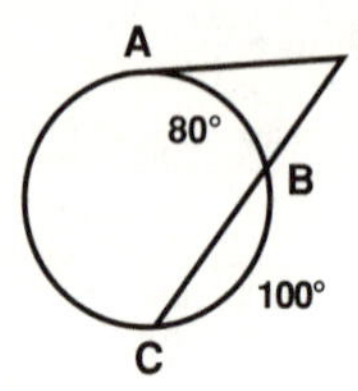

Ex. 16

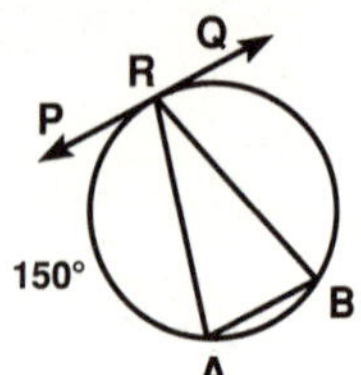

Ex. 17

16. $\overline{PA}$ is tangent to the circle at A and $\overline{PBC}$ is a secant. If m$\overset{\frown}{AB} = 80°$ and m$\overset{\frown}{BC} = 100°$, what is m$\angle APB$?

17. $\overleftrightarrow{PQ}$ is tangent to the circle at R and $\overleftrightarrow{PQ} \parallel \overline{AB}$. If m$\overset{\frown}{RA} = 150°$, find m$\angle ARB$.

18. Two tangents $\overline{PA}$ and $\overline{PB}$ are drawn to circle O from an external point P. If the measure of major $\overset{\frown}{AB}$ is 250°, find the measure of $\angle P$.

19. Given: Circle O with $\overline{QR}$ tangent to the circle at R. If m$\angle OQR = 20°$, find m$\angle ROQ$.

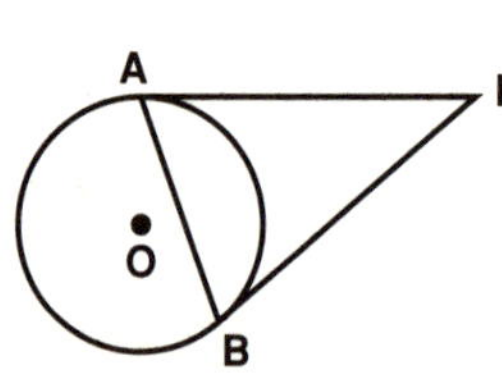

Ex. 20

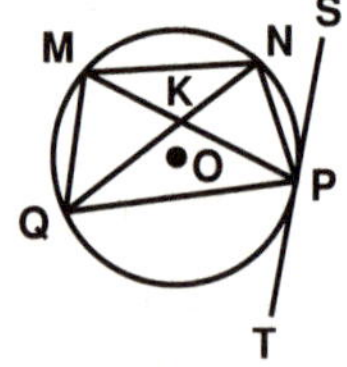

Ex. 21

20. $\overline{PA}$ and $\overline{PB}$ are tangent to circle O. If m$\angle PBA = 70°$, find m$\angle P$.

21. Quadrilateral $MNPQ$ is inscribed in circle O with $\overline{ST}$ tangent to the circle at P. Diagonals $\overline{PM}$ and $\overline{QN}$ intersect at K and m$\overset{\frown}{MN}$: m$\overset{\frown}{NP}$: m$\overset{\frown}{PQ}$: m$\overset{\frown}{QM}$ = 5 : 3 : 8 : 4.

Find:

a. m$\overset{\frown}{MN}$ **c.** m$\angle SPQ$
b. m$\angle MQP$ **d.** m$\angle PKQ$

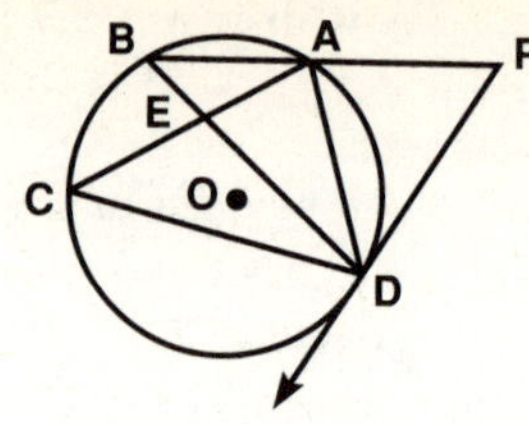

Ex. 22

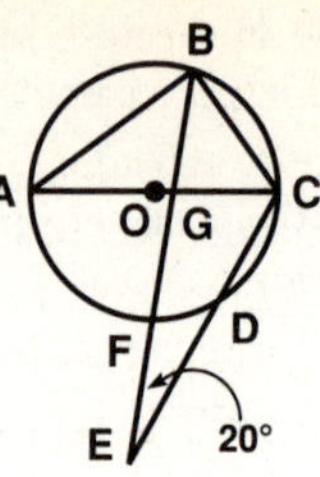

Ex. 23

22. B is the midpoint of $\overset{\frown}{AC}$, $\triangle ADC$ is inscribed in circle O, chords $\overline{AC}$ and $\overline{BD}$ intersect at E, $\overrightarrow{PD}$ is tangent to circle O at D, $\overline{PAB}$ is a secant, and m$\overset{\frown}{BA}$: m$\overset{\frown}{AD}$: m$\overset{\frown}{DC}$ = 2 : 3 : 5.

Find:

a. m$\overset{\frown}{BC}$ **c.** m$\angle AEB$ **e.** m$\angle P$
b. m$\angle ADC$ **d.** m$\angle ADP$

23. $\triangle ABC$ is inscribed in circle O. Secant $\overline{EFB}$ bisects $\angle ABC$ and intersects diameter $\overline{AOC}$ at G, $\overline{EDC}$ is a secant, m$\angle E = 20°$, and m$\overset{\frown}{AB}$: m$\overset{\frown}{BC}$ = 3 : 2.

Find:

a. m$\overset{\frown}{BC}$ **c.** m$\angle ABE$ **e.** m$\angle ACD$
b. m$\overset{\frown}{FD}$ **d.** m$\angle FGC$

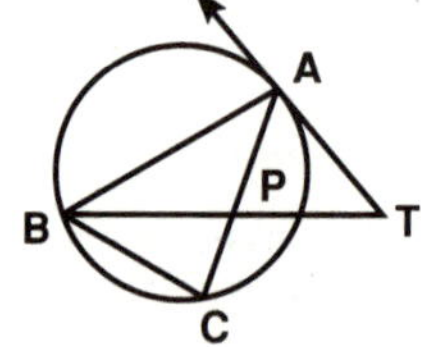

Ex. 24

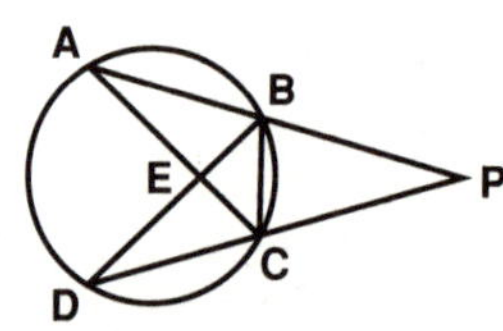

Ex. 25

24. $\triangle ABC$ is inscribed in a circle, $\overline{BT}$ bisects $\angle CBA$, $\overrightarrow{TA}$ is tangent to the circle, and m$\angle BAC$: m$\angle CBA$: m$\angle ACB$ = 2 : 3 : 4.

Find:

a. m$\angle BAC$ **c.** m$\angle CPT$ **e.** m$\angle T$
b. m$\overset{\frown}{BC}$ **d.** m$\angle PAT$

25. $\overline{PBA}$ and $\overline{PCD}$ are secants, chords $\overline{AC}$ and $\overline{BD}$ intersect at E, $\overset{\frown}{BA} \cong \overset{\frown}{CD}$, chord $\overline{BC}$ is drawn, m$\angle ABD = 60°$, and m$\overset{\frown}{BC} = 40°$.

Find: **a.** m$\angle ACD$
b. m$\angle P$
c. m$\angle DBC$
d. m$\angle AED$
e. m$\angle PCB$

26. Chords $\overline{AB}$ and $\overline{CD}$ are extended to meet at E. Chords $\overline{AD}$ and $\overline{BC}$ intersect at F. $m\angle AEC = 51°$ and $m\angle AFC = 92°$. Let $m\widehat{AC}$ be represented by $(23y - 8x)°$ and $m\widehat{BD}$ by $(y + 4x)°$.

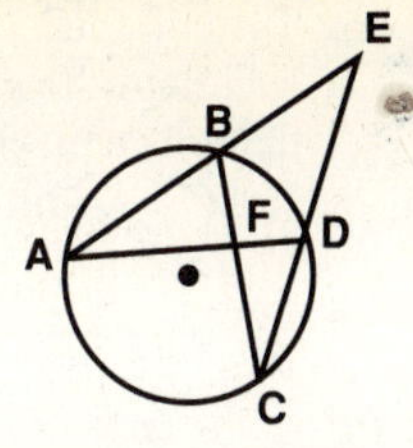

a. In terms of x and y, write a set of equations that can be used to solve for x and y.

b. Solve for x and y the set of equations written in answer to part **a**.

c. Find $m\widehat{AC}$.

d. Find $m\widehat{BD}$.

27. *Given:* Point M is the midpoint of minor arc $\widehat{BC}$ of circle O. A tangent $\overleftrightarrow{DME}$ is drawn to the circle at M.

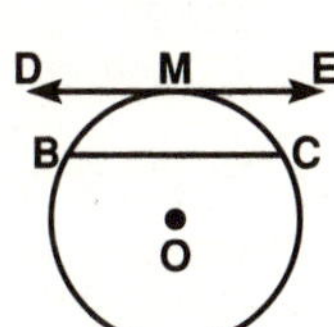

Prove: Tangent $\overleftrightarrow{DME} \parallel$ chord $\overline{BC}$

28.

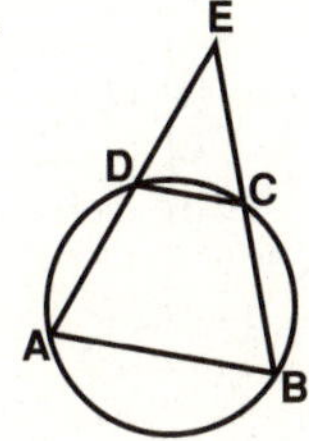

Given: Quadrilateral $ABCD$ is inscribed in a circle, with $\overline{AD} \cong \overline{BC}$. Chords $\overline{AD}$ and $\overline{BC}$ are extended to meet at E.

Prove: $\overline{AE} \cong \overline{BE}$

29. *Given:* Circle O with tangents $\overline{PA}$ and $\overline{PB}$, secant $\overline{PCOD}$, chords $\overline{AD}$ and $\overline{DB}$, and $\widehat{AD} \doteq \widehat{DB}$.

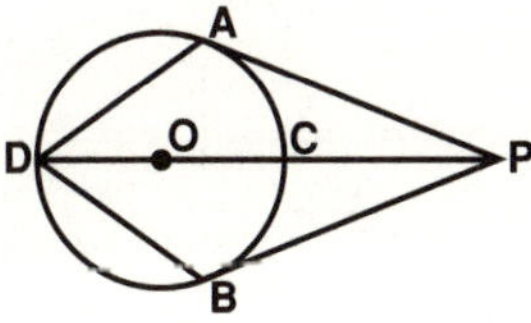

a. *Prove:* $\angle APD \cong \angle BPD$

b. If $m\widehat{AD} = 110°$, find $m\angle BPD$.

30.

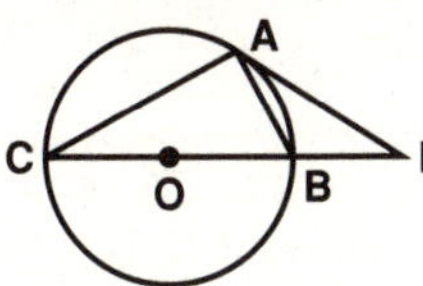

Given: Diameter $\overline{CB}$ of circle O is extended to point P, $\overline{PA}$ is tangent to the circle at A, and chords $\overline{AB}$ and $\overline{AC}$ are drawn.

Prove: $\angle PAB \cong \angle ACB$

31. *Given:* $\overline{PA}$ and $\overline{PB}$ are tangent to the circle at A and B, respectively, R lies in the interior of the circle, $\overline{AR}$ and $\overline{BR}$ are drawn, and $\overline{RP}$ does not bisect $\angle APB$.

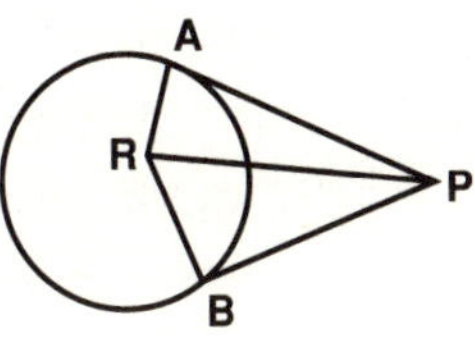

Prove: R is not the center of the circle.

32. *Given:* Triangle MAB is inscribed in a circle. $\overleftrightarrow{XY}$ is tangent to the circle at point M. Chord $\overline{CD}$ is parallel to $\overleftrightarrow{XY}$ and intersects $\overline{MA}$ and $\overline{MB}$ at points E and K, respectively.

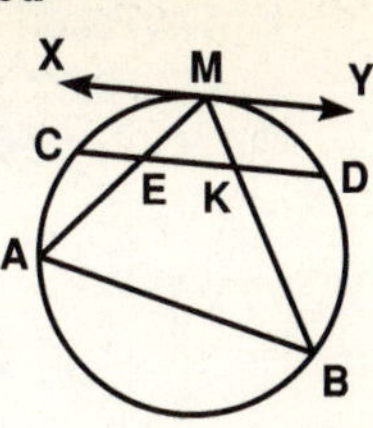

Prove: $\dfrac{ME}{MB} = \dfrac{MK}{MA}$

33.

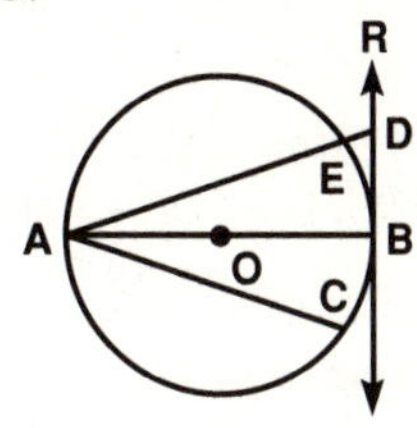

Given: $\overline{AB}$ is a diameter of circle O, $\overleftrightarrow{RB}$ is a tangent at B, chords $\overline{AE}$ and $\overline{AC}$ are drawn on opposite sides of $\overline{AB}$ such that $m\widehat{BE} = m\widehat{BC}$, and chord $\overline{AE}$ is extended to meet $\overleftrightarrow{RB}$ at D.

Prove: $\dfrac{AD}{AB} = \dfrac{AB}{AC}$

34. *Given:* In circle O, diameter $\overline{AB} \perp \overline{DE}$ at E.

Prove: $BA \times BE = BC \times BD$

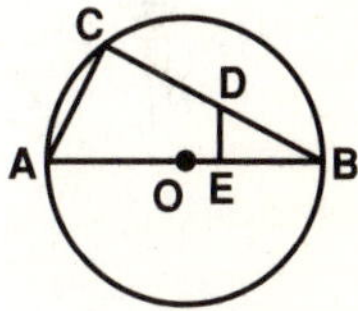

35. *Given:* $\overline{RN}$ tangent to circle T at N, and diameter $\overline{AN}$.

Prove: $(AN)^2 = AR \times AB$

36. *Given:* B is the midpoint of major $\widehat{AC}$. Chords $\overline{BD}$ and $\overline{AC}$ intersect at E. Chords $\overline{AD}$ and $\overline{AB}$ are drawn.

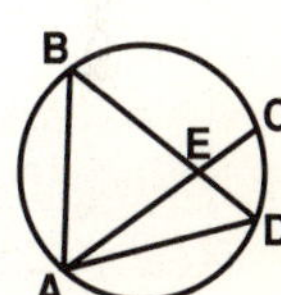

Prove: $BD \times BE = (AB)^2$

37. In circle O, diameter $\overline{AB} \perp \overline{CD}$, and $CD = 14$.

Find: CE

38. In a circle, a chord of 13 centimeters bisects a chord of 12 centimeters. The length of the shorter segment of the 13-centimeter chord is

(1) 5 cm **(2)** 2 cm **(3)** 8 cm **(4)** 4 cm

39. In circle O, chords $\overline{AB}$ and $\overline{CD}$ intersect at E. If $AE = 2$, $CD = 9$, and $CE = 4$, find BE.

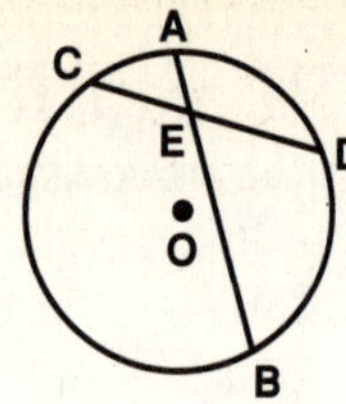

40.

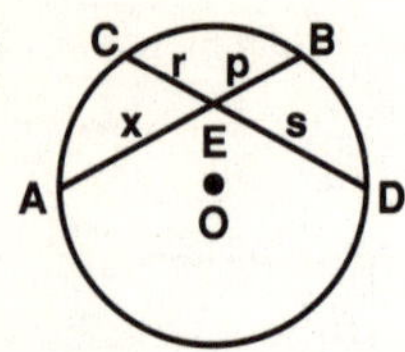

Chords $\overline{AB}$ and $\overline{CD}$ of circle O intersect at E. If $AE = x$, $EB = p$, $CE = r$, and $ED = s$, express x in terms of p, r, and s.

41. In circle O, chords $\overline{AB}$ and $\overline{CD}$ intersect at E. If $AE = 4$, $EB = 12$, and $ED = 16$, then CE equals

(1) 19 **(2)** 16 **(3)** 3 **(4)** 48

42. In circle O, chords $\overline{AB}$ and $\overline{CD}$ intersect at point E. If $AE = EB$, $CE = 4$, and $ED = 9$, find the length of $\overline{AE}$.

43. In circle O, chords $\overline{AB}$ and $\overline{CD}$ intersect at E. If $AE = 3$, $EB = 4$, $CE = x$, and $ED = x + 1$, find CE.

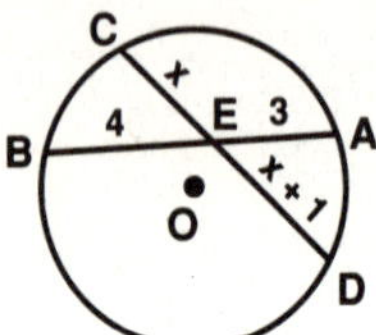

44. If two circles with radii 3 cm and 5 cm are drawn such that the distance between their centers is 10 cm, what is the maximum number of common tangents they may have?

45. Tangent $\overline{AB}$ and secant $\overline{ACD}$ are drawn to circle O. If $AC = 4$ and $CD = 5$, find AB.

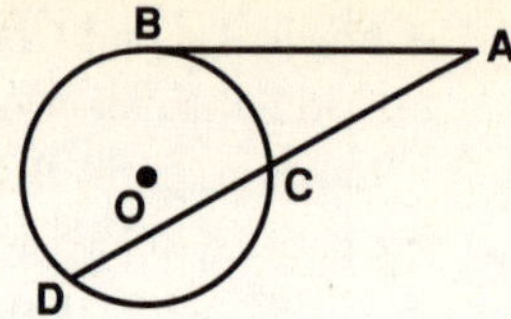

46.

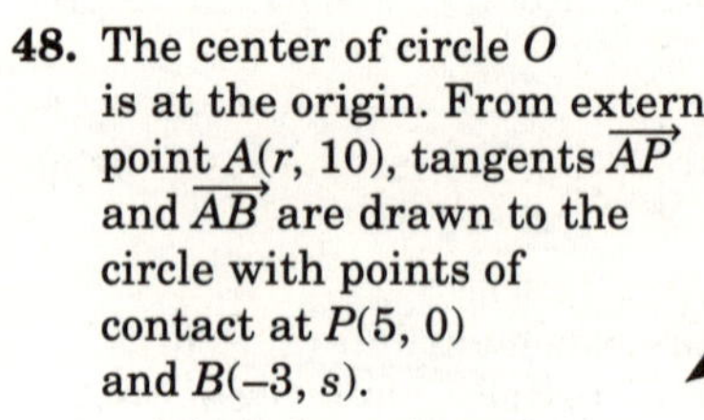

$\overrightarrow{PA}$ is tangent to circle O at A, and $\overline{PBC}$ is a secant. If $PC = 16$ and $BC = 12$, find PA.

47. Secants $\overline{PAB}$ and $\overline{PCD}$ are drawn to a circle from an external point P. If $PA = 3$, $AB = 17$, and $PC = 4$, find PCD.

48. The center of circle O is at the origin. From external point $A(r, 10)$, tangents $\overrightarrow{AP}$ and $\overrightarrow{AB}$ are drawn to the circle with points of contact at $P(5, 0)$ and $B(-3, s)$.

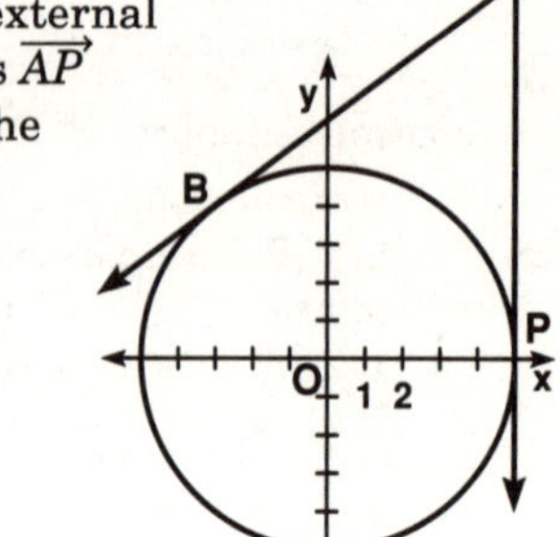

a. Find the value of r.

b. Write an equation of tangent $\overrightarrow{AP}$.

c. Write an equation of circle O.

d. Find the value of s.

e. Find AB.

CUMULATIVE SUMMARY EXERCISES

CHAPTERS 1–5

1. What is the smallest integral value of x for which $\sqrt{2x-3}$ represents a real number?

2. If n represents an even integer, then an odd integer may be represented by the expression

(1) $5n$ **(2)** n^2+1 **(3)** n^3 **(4)** $n+2$

3. $6(\frac{1}{2}x + \frac{1}{3}y) = 3x + 2y$ is an illustration of the

(1) associative law of addition
(2) associative law of multiplication
(3) commutative law
(4) distributive law

4. For the set of integers, which operations are commutative?

(1) addition and multiplication
(2) addition and subtraction
(3) subtraction and division
(4) multiplication and division

5. If a and b are both real numbers, which statement represents the fact that b is the multiplicative inverse of a?

(1) $a \times b = a$ **(3)** $a \times b = 0$
(2) $a \times b = b$ **(4)** $a \times b = 1$

6. Which set of numbers forms a field with respect to the operations of addition and multiplication?

(1) integers **(3)** whole numbers
(2) rational numbers **(4)** natural numbers

In 7–10, factor completely.

7. $9x^3 - x$

8. $3x^3y^2 - 147x$

9. $2x^3 - 11x^2 + 5x$

10. $a^2 - ab - bc + ac$

11. Find the numerical value of $8^{\frac{2}{3}} + 4^0$.

12. If $x = 27$, evaluate $x^{-\frac{1}{3}}$.

13. If the number 0.0031 is written in the form 3.1×10^n, then n is equal to

(1) $\frac{1}{3}$ **(2)** -2 **(3)** 3 **(4)** -3

14. The expression $\frac{1}{3+\sqrt{5}}$ is equivalent to

(1) $\frac{3-\sqrt{5}}{4}$ **(3)** $\frac{3+\sqrt{5}}{13}$

(2) $\frac{\sqrt{5}}{8}$ **(4)** $\frac{3-\sqrt{5}}{8}$

15. Express $\frac{2}{5-2\sqrt{3}}$ as a fraction with a rational denominator.

16. For which ordered pair is the fraction $\frac{3}{x-y}$ undefined?

(1) (1, –1) **(3)** (–2, –3)
(2) (3, 2) **(4)** (1, 1)

17. The fraction $\dfrac{1+\frac{1}{x}}{1-\frac{1}{x^2}}$ is equivalent to

(1) x **(3)** $\frac{x}{x+1}$

(2) $-x$ **(4)** $\frac{x}{x-1}$

18. Express in simplest form: $\dfrac{5-\frac{25}{x}}{x-5}$

19. Perform the indicated operations and simplify:

$$\frac{x^2+4xy+3y^2}{x^2-y^2} \cdot \frac{x^2+xy}{x-y} \div \frac{x^2+3xy}{(x-y)^2}$$

20. Solve for h: $V = \frac{1}{3}\pi r^2 h$

21. Solve for all values of x: $|3x - 1| = 5$

22. The solution set of $|4x - 2| = 3x + 2$ is

(1) {4} **(3)** {4, 0}
(2) {0} **(4)** ∅

23. The solution set of $|8x + 20| = 7x + 10$ is

(1) {–10, –2} **(3)** {–2}
(2) {–10} **(4)** ∅

24. Find the solution set of: $3x^2 = 9x$

25. Find the roots in simplest radical form:
$x^2 - 6x + 1 = 0$

26. Find the roots to the nearest tenth:
$3x^2 + 6x = 5$

27. Solve the following set of equations:
$3y = 2x + 14$
$x - 2y = -8$

28. Find the solution set of the system:
$x - 2y = -6$
$2x = y^2 - 4y$

In 29-32, tell how many points of intersection there are if the two graphs are sketched on the same set of axes.

29. $x + y = 0$
$x - y = 0$

30. $x + y = 6$
$x^2 + y^2 = 36$

31. $x = -y^2$
$x = -2$

32. $y = x^2$
$y = 0$

33. Solve for x: $\frac{2}{x} = \frac{9}{2} + \frac{1}{2x}$

34. Express a in simplest radical form:

$$\frac{2}{a^2 - 7a + 10} = \frac{3}{a-5} - \frac{a}{a-2}$$

35. The solution set of $\frac{3x+15}{x+5} = 7$ is

(1) $\{-5\}$ (2) $\{0\}$ (3) $\{-5, 0\}$ (4) $\varnothing$

36. What is the solution set of the equation $\sqrt{9x^2 - 11} = 5$?

(1) $\{0\}$ (2) $\{2\}$ (3) $\{-2\}$ (4) $\{2, -2\}$

37. If $\sqrt{5 - y} = 2$, find the numerical value of $(5 - y)^2$.

38. Solve for x: $6 - \sqrt{x - 2} = 2$

39. Which graph is the solution set of the inequality $11 < 2 - 3x < 17$?

(1) 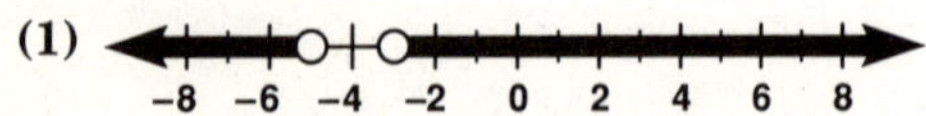

(2) 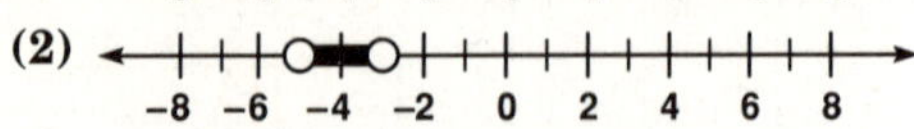

(3) 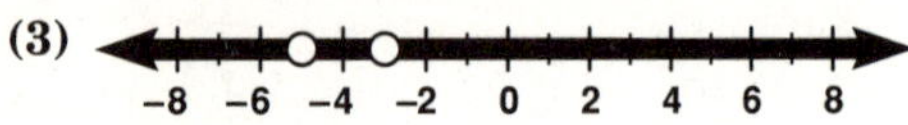

(4) 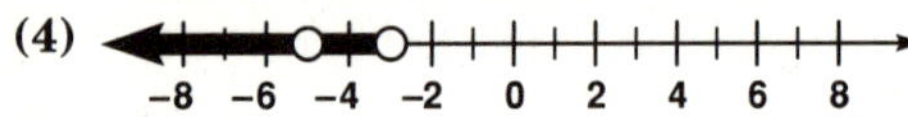

40. Which graph is the solution set of the inequality $|5 - 2x| \le 7$?

(1) 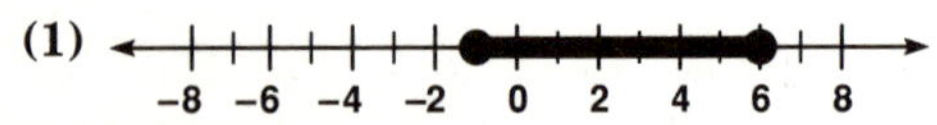

(2) 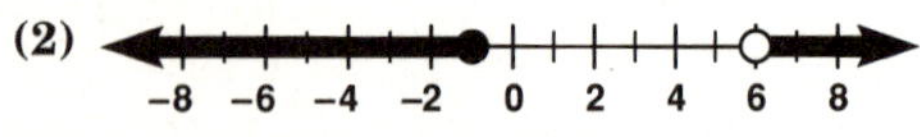

(3)

-8 -6 -4 -2 0 2 4 6 8

(4)

-8 -6 -4 -2 0 2 4 6 8

41. If a, b, c, and d are positive integers, and $\frac{a}{b} > \frac{c}{d}$, then which must always be true?

(1) $a > c$ (3) $ad > bc$

(2) $a < c$ (4) $ad < bc$

42. If a and b are real numbers, then the inequality $|a + b| < |a| + |b|$ is true for all values of a and b when

(1) a and b are both positive

(2) a and b are both negative

(3) a is positive and b is negative

(4) a and b are equal

43. The solution set of $|2x - 5| \le 11$ is

(1) $\{x \mid -5 \le x \le 22\}$

(2) $\{x \mid x \le 8\}$

(3) $\{x \mid -3 \le x \le 8\}$

(4) $\{x \mid (x \le -3) \vee (x \ge 8)\}$

44. What is the solution set of $x^2 - 8x + 12 < 0$?

(1) $\{x \mid (x < 2) \vee (x > 6)\}$

(2) $\{x \mid (x < -6) \vee (x > -2)\}$

(3) $\{x \mid 2 < x < 6\}$

(4) $\{x \mid -6 < x < -2\}$

45. Which graph is the solution set of $x^2 + 3x < 10$?

(1) 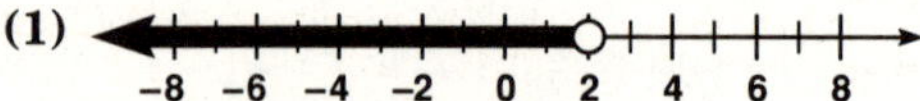

(2)

-8 -6 -4 -2 0 2 4 6 8

(3)

-8 -6 -4 -2 0 2 4 6 8

(4)

-8 -6 -4 -2 0 2 4 6 8

46. What is the solution set for $x^2 - x - 6 > 0$?

(1) $\{x \mid x < -2 \text{ or } x > 3\}$

(2) $\{x \mid x < -3 \text{ or } x > 2\}$

(3) $\{x \mid -3 < x < 2\}$

(4) $\{x \mid -2 < x < 3\}$

47. If $\sqrt{-28}$ is subtracted from $\sqrt{-63}$, the difference is

(1) i (2) $i\sqrt{7}$ (3) $-i\sqrt{7}$ (4) $\sqrt{-35}$

48. Express $5\sqrt{-18} + 6\sqrt{-98}$ as a monomial in terms of i.

49. If a, b, n and m are positive real numbers, which represents an incorrect application of the laws of exponents?

(1) $\sqrt[n]{a^m} = (\sqrt[n]{a})^m$ (3) $\sqrt[n]{a} + \sqrt[n]{b} = \sqrt[n]{a+b}$

(2) $\sqrt[n]{a} \cdot \sqrt[n]{b} = \sqrt[n]{ab}$ (4) $\sqrt[n]{a} \div \sqrt[n]{b} = \sqrt[n]{\frac{a}{b}}$

50. i^{13} is equivalent to

(1) i (2) $-i$ (3) 1 (4) -1

51. Write the conjugate of $4 - 3i$.

52. Write the additive inverse of $-3 + 2i$.

53. The product of $(3 - 2i)$ and $(7 + 6i)$ is

(1) $21 - 12i$ (3) $9 + 4i$

(2) $33 + 4i$ (4) $21 + 16i$

54. Express $(3 - 2i)^2$ in $a + bi$ form.

55. The expression $\frac{1}{4+i}$ is equivalent to

(1) $4 - i$ (2) $\frac{4-i}{15}$ (3) $\frac{4+i}{17}$ (4) $\frac{4-i}{17}$

56. When represented graphically, in which quadrant does the sum of $-4 - i$ and $3 + 4i$ lie?

57. Show graphically: $(3 - i) + (2 + 3i) = 5 + 2i$

58. Show graphically: $(7 + 2i) - (4 - i) = 3 + 3i$

59. Solve for x: $(3 - 2i) - (x - i) = 8 - i$

60. What is the solution set of the equation $x^2 + 9 = 0$?

(1) $\{3i\}$ (2) $\{-3i\}$ (3) $\{\ \}$ (4) $\{3i, -3i\}$

61. Express, in terms of i, the roots of the equation $\frac{2}{3}x^2 + 18 = 0$.

62. Solve the equation $6x - 34 = x^2$ and express the roots in simplest $a + bi$ form.

63. Solve the equation $x = 2 - \frac{8}{x}$ and express the roots in simplest $a + bi$ form.

64. Find the value of k if the roots of the equation $x^2 - 6x + k = 0$ are equal.

65. What is the sum of the roots of the equation $3x^2 = 9x + 1$?

(1) $\frac{1}{3}$ (2) -3 (3) 3 (4) 9

66. If the sum of the roots of the equation $2x^2 - 5x - 3 = 0$ is added to the product of the roots, the result is

(1) 1 (2) $-\frac{1}{4}$ (3) -1 (4) 4

67. The roots of $2x^2 - 3x + c = 0$ are imaginary if c equals

(1) 1 (2) 2 (3) -1 (4) 0

68. The roots of the equation $2x^2 - 7x - 3 = 0$ are

(1) rational (3) imaginary
(2) irrational (4) equal

69. The roots of the equation $2x^2 = 2x + 1$ are

(1) real, unequal, and irrational
(2) real, equal, and rational
(3) real, unequal, and rational
(4) imaginary

70. Which parabola touches the x-axis at one point?

(1) $x^2 - 6x - 16 = y$ (3) $x^2 + 8x + 16 = y$
(2) $x^2 - 16 = y$ (4) $x^2 + 16 = y$

71. Which is true of the parabola $x^2 + 5x + 6 = y$?

(1) It intersects the x-axis in two distinct points.
(2) It is tangent to the x-axis.
(3) It lies entirely below the x-axis.
(4) It lies entirely above the x-axis.

72. The diagram shows the graph of $y = x^2 - 2x - 3$ when $-2 \le x \le 4$. For which values of k will the solutions of $x^2 - 2x - 3 = k$ be imaginary?

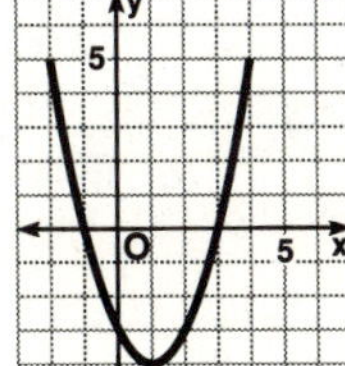

(1) $k > 0$ (3) $k > -4$
(2) $k < 0$ (4) $k < -4$

73. Which solution set gives all values of K that will place the turning point of the graph of $y = x^2 - 6x + K$ below the x-axis?

(1) $\{K > 36\}$ (3) $\{K < 9\}$
(2) $\{K > 9\}$ (4) $\{K < 36\}$

74. If the blank in each of the following statements is replaced by one of the words *always, sometimes* or *never,* the resulting statement will be true. Write the numbers 1–5 on your answer paper and opposite each number write the word that will correctly complete the corresponding statement.

(Consider only the cases where a, b, and c are real numbers and $a \neq 0$.)

(1) The graph of the equation $y = ax^2 + bx + c$ __?__ passes through the origin when $c = 0$.
(2) The graph of the equation $y = ax^2 + bx + c$ is __?__ tangent to the x-axis when $b^2 = 4ac$.
(3) The graph of the equation $y = ax^2 + bx + c$ is __?__ symmetric to the y-axis when $b \neq 0$.
(4) The roots of the equation $ax^2 + bx + c = 0$ are __?__ real if a, b, and c have the same sign.
(5) Both roots of the equation $ax^2 + bx + c = 0$ __?__ have the same sign if a and c have opposite signs.

75. Which could be the graph of the equation $y = bx - ax^2$ when both a and b are positive?

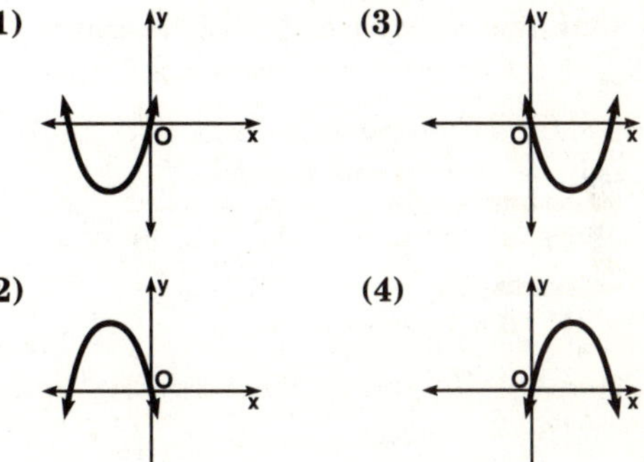

76. If the point $(-5, 1)$ is reflected over the y-axis, what are the coordinates of its image point?

(1) $(1, -5)$ (2) $(-1, 5)$ (3) $(-5, -1)$ (4) $(5, 1)$

77. The point $(-3, -2)$ is reflected in the origin. The coordinates of its image are

(1) $(-2, -3)$ (2) $(3, 2)$ (3) $(2, 3)$ (4) $(-3, 2)$

78. Write the coordinates of P', the image of $P(5, -1)$ after a clockwise rotation of 180° about the origin.

79. What is the image of $A(3, 4)$ under $R_{90°}$?

(1) $(3, -4)$ (2) $(-4, 3)$ (3) $(-3, -4)$ (4) $(-4, -3)$

80. What is the image of $R_{-180°}(-4, -7)$?

81. A translation maps the point $(5, -2)$ to a point $(0, -2)$. What is the image of the point $(0, -2)$ under the same translation?

82. Find the image of the point $(7, -3)$ under the translation $T_{(-4, 6)}$.

83. Given: $\triangle ABC$ with $A(2, 3)$, $B(0, 6)$, and $C(2, 6)$

Graph and state the coordinates of:

a. $\triangle A'B'C'$, the image of $\triangle ABC$ after a reflection in the y-axis.

b. $\triangle A''B''C''$, the image of $\triangle A'B'C'$ after a translation that maps $(0, 0)$ onto $(0, -5)$.

c. $\triangle A'''B'''C'''$, the image of $\triangle A''B''C''$ after a rotation of 90° clockwise about the origin.

84. Under a dilation, P' is the image of P and Q' is the image of Q. Find the value of the constant of dilation if $PQ = 96$ cm and $P'Q' = 76.8$ cm.

85. If $P(4, -3)$ is transformed under the dilation D_{-2}, what is the image P'?

86. *Given*: Points $A(3, 0)$ and $B(-4, 6)$

Write the coordinates of the images of points A and B after each transformation described.

a. a rotation of 90° counterclockwise about the origin

b. a reflection in the line $x = 2$

c. a translation $T_{3,-2}$

d. a dilation $D_{\frac{1}{2}}$

87. The transformation Z maps each point P of the plane according to the rule:

$$P(x, y) \rightarrow P'(y, x - 2)$$

Write the coordinates of A', the image of $A(3, -2)$ under the transformation Z.

88. A transformation maps (1, 5) onto (−1, −5). This transformation is equivalent to

(1) $R_{90°}$ (3) D_{-1}
(2) $R_{-90°}$ (4) $T_{-1,-5}$

89. Find the coordinates of $r_{x\text{-axis}} \circ r_{y=x}(A)$ if the coordinates of A are $(3, -4)$.

90. If $A = (-4, -2)$, what is $r_{y=-x} \circ D_2(A)$?

91. *Given*: $\triangle ABC$ with $A(-1, 4)$, $B(3, 7)$, $C(5, 1)$

a. Graph and state the coordinates of $\triangle A'B'C'$, the image of $\triangle ABC$ under the composition: $R_{0,90°} \circ r_{x\text{-axis}}$

b. State the single transformation equivalent to: $R_{0,90°} \circ r_{x\text{-axis}}$

92. If ℓ and m are parallel lines, then $r_\ell \circ r_m(\overline{AB})$ is equivalent to a

(1) rotation (3) translation
(2) dilation (4) glide reflection

93. Write the coordinates of A', the image of $A(-3, 1)$ under the composition: $R_{90°} \circ R_{180°}$

94. Write the coordinates of P', the image of $P(-4, -2)$ under the composition: $T_{2,1} \circ T_{-1,-3}$

95. Which single transformation is equivalent to the composite $r_{y=-x} \circ T_{1,-2}$?

(1) a rotation (3) a glide reflection
(2) a dilation (4) a point reflection

96. Which is not an isometry?

(1) rotation (3) translation
(2) reflection (4) dilation

97. Which transformation does not preserve orientation?

(1) reflection (3) dilation
(2) rotation (4) translation

98. Which graph has symmetry with respect to the origin?

(1)
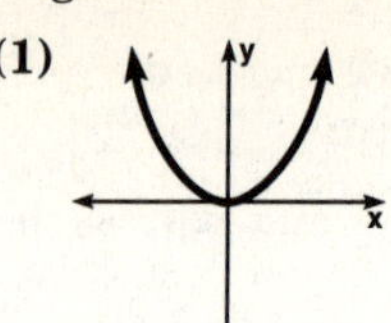

(3)
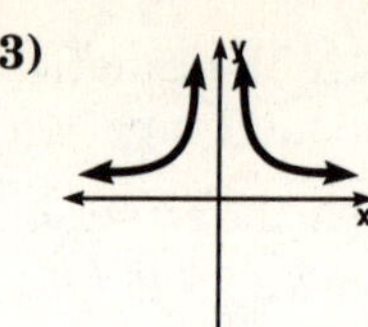

(2)
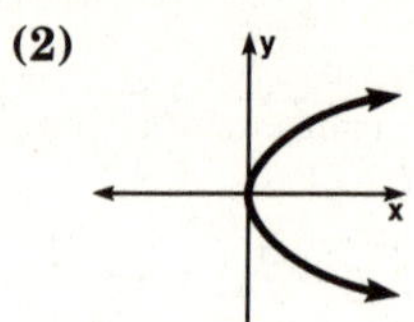

(4)
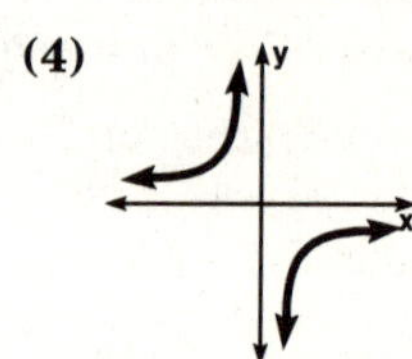

99. A graph may have symmetry with respect to:
I the x-axis II the y-axis III the origin
The graph of $y = x^4$ has symmetry with respect to

(1) I only
(2) II only
(3) I and II only
(4) I, II, and III

100. Which letter has point symmetry?

(1) A (2) C (3) N (4) W

101. Which letter has horizontal line symmetry but not vertical line symmetry?

(1) H (2) K (3) S (4) T

102. ℓ and m are symmetry lines for regular pentagon $ABCDE$. What is $r_m \circ r_\ell(\overline{DC})$?

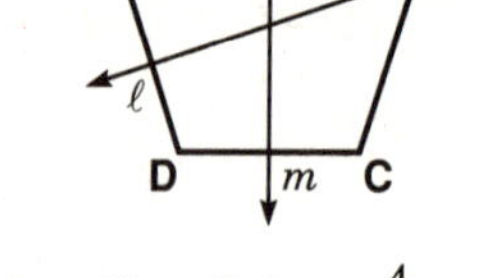

(1) $\overline{BA}$
(2) $\overline{AE}$
(3) $\overline{CB}$
(4) $\overline{DC}$

103. What is the domain of the function $f(x) = \frac{4}{\sqrt{x+1}}$ over the set of real numbers?

(1) $\{x \mid x = 1\}$
(2) $\{x \mid x \geq -1\}$
(3) $\{x \mid x < -1\}$
(4) $\{x \mid x > -1\}$

104. Let $x \rightarrow x^2$ be a mapping of all the real numbers onto their squares. Which numbers will map onto themselves?

(1) 0, only
(2) 1, only
(3) 0 and 1, only
(4) 0, 1, and −1

105. The relation defined by the set of ordered pairs, {(0, 1), (1, 1), (0, 0), (−1, 1), (−2, −2)}, is not a function. Which ordered pair, if omitted from this relation, will make the resulting set a function?

(1) (1, 1) (3) (−1, 1)
(2) (0, 0) (4) (−2, −2)

106. Which is not the graph of a function?

(1) 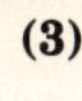

(3) 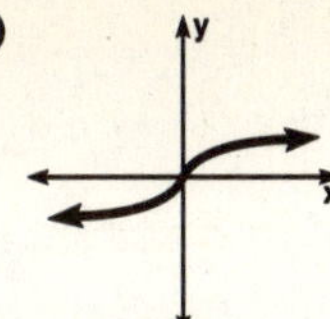

(2)

(4) 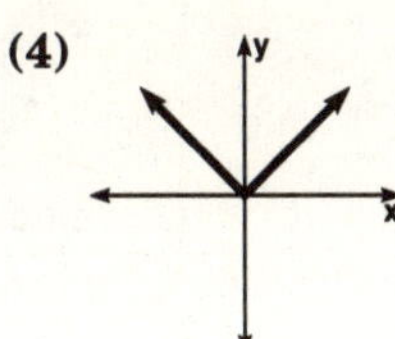

107. If $f(x) = x^{-\frac{1}{2}}$, find $f(9)$.

108. If $f(x) = \frac{x+3}{x-1}$, then $f(a + 1)$ is equal to

(1) $\frac{a+4}{a}$ (2) $\frac{a+3}{a-1}$ (3) 5 (4) 4

109. If $f(x) = x^2$ and $g(x) = x - 1$, what is $[f \circ g](x)$?

(1) $(x - 1)^2$
(3) $x^2(x - 1)$
(2) $x^2 - 1$
(4) $x^2 + x - 1$

110. If $f(x) = x - 1$ and $g(x) = x^2 + 1$, find $f(g(-2))$.

111. Which is the equation of a circle?

(1) $2x^2 + 3y^2 = 12$
(3) $2x^2 - 3y^2 = 12$
(2) $3x^2 + 3y^2 = 12$
(4) $3x^2 - 3y^2 = 12$

112. Which equation does not represent a hyperbola?

(1) $xy = 12$
(3) $x = y^2 + 12$
(2) $x^2 = y^2 + 12$
(4) $2x^2 = y^2 + 12$

113. The solutions of the system of equations $x + y = 0$ and $x^2 + y^2 = 9$ are found in which quadrants?

(1) I and II
(3) II and III
(2) I and III
(4) II and IV

114. Which relation is a function?

(1) $\{(x, y) | x^2 + y^2 = 25\}$
(2) $\{(x, y) | x^2 - y^2 = 25\}$
(3) $\{(x, y) | x + y = 25\}$
(4) $\{(x, y) | x = y^2 + 25\}$

115. Every year a band is paid \$350 to play at the county fair. Let a represent the amount each member receives and let n represent the number of members in the band. The inverse variation relationship between a and n is best represented as

(1) $\frac{350}{a} = \frac{1}{n}$
(3) $a + n = 350$
(2) $\frac{n}{a} = 350$
(4) $an = 350$

116. R varies inversely as the square of T. If T is multiplied by 16, then R is

(1) multiplied by 256
(3) divided by 256
(2) multiplied by 4
(4) divided by 4

117. If x varies inversely as y and $x = 1.5$ when $y = 30$, find y when $x = 6$.

118. Which mapping represents a one-to-one function?

(1)

(3) 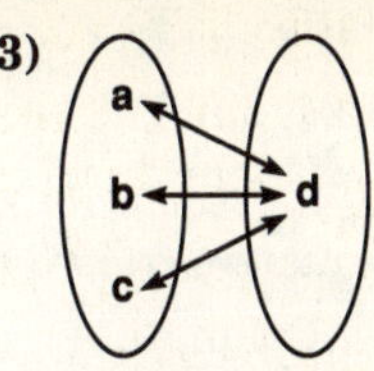

(2)

(4) 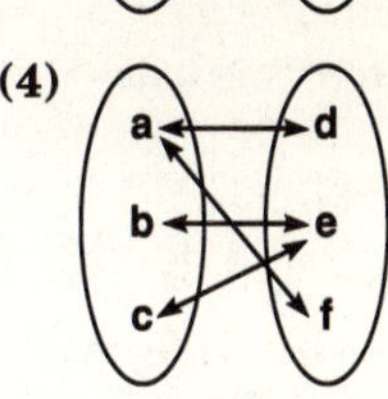

119. Which graph represents a function that is one-to-one?

(1) 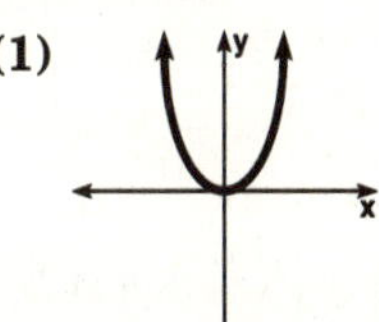

(3) 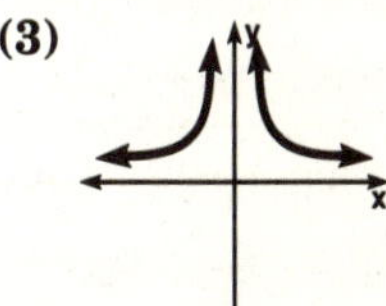

(2) 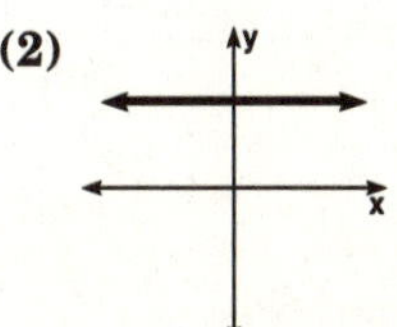

(4) 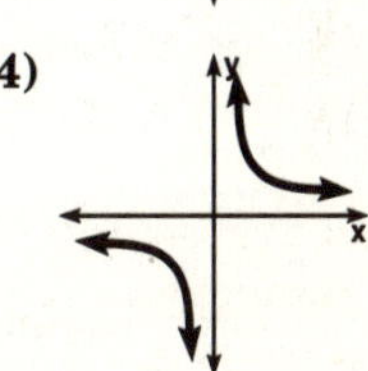

120. The inverse function of $\{(2, 6), (-3, 4), (7, -5)\}$ is

(1) $\{(-2, 6), (3, 4), (-7, -5)\}$
(2) $\{(2, -6), (-3, -4), (7, 5)\}$
(3) $\{(6, 2), (4, -3), (-5, 7)\}$
(4) $\{(-6, -2), (-4, 3), (5, -7)\}$

121. What is the inverse of the function $y = 2x + 1$?

(1) $y = \frac{1}{2}x + 1$
(3) $y = \frac{x-1}{2}$
(2) $y = 2x - 1$
(4) $y = \frac{x+1}{2}$

122. If the graph of the equation $y = 2x$ is reflected in the line $y = x$, the equation of the image is

(1) $y = 2x$
(3) $y = 2$
(2) $y = \frac{x}{2}$
(4) $y = -\frac{x}{2}$

123. *Given*: $f(x) = x^2 - 4$, $x \geq 0$

a. State the range of $f(x)$.
b. Graph $f(x)$ over its domain. Label the graph $f(x)$.
c. On the same set of axes, sketch $f^{-1}(x)$, the inverse of $f(x)$. Label the graph $f^{-1}(x)$.
d. Write an equation for $f^{-1}(x)$.
e. Find $(f \circ f^{-1})(5)$.

124. The graph of the equation $y = 10^x$ lies entirely in which quadrants?

(1) I and II
(3) I and IV
(2) I and III
(4) III and IV

125. The graph of $y = \log_{10} x$ lies entirely in which quadrants?

(1) I and II (3) I and III
(2) I and IV (4) III and IV

126. Match each transformation in Column I with an equation from Column II.

Column I	Column II
a. reflection of $y = 3^x$ in the y-axis	(1) $y = \log_3 x$
b. reflection of $y = 3^x$ in the line $y = x$	(2) $y = 3^x + 2$
	(3) $y = 3^{-x}$
c. translation of $y = 3^x$ such that $(x, y) \to (x, y - 2)$	(4) $y = -3^x$

127. Solve for x: $8^x = 2^{2x+1}$

128. Solve for x: $3^{x^2+2x} = \frac{1}{3}$

129. If $\log_b n = y$, then n equals

(1) $y \cdot b$ (2) $\frac{y}{b}$ (3) y^b (4) b^y

130. If $\log_x 2 = \frac{1}{3}$, what is the value of x?

(1) $2\frac{1}{3}$ (2) $\sqrt[3]{2}$ (3) 8 (4) 4

131. If $f(x) = \log_4 x$, find $f(64)$.

132. If $L = \frac{x^2}{k}$, then $\log L$ is equal to

(1) $2 \log \frac{x}{k}$ (3) $2 \log x - \log k$
(2) $2(\log x - \log k)$ (4) $\frac{2 \log x}{\log k}$

133. The expression $\frac{1}{3} \log a - 3 \log b$ is equal to

(1) $\log (\sqrt[3]{a} - b^3)$ (3) $\log \frac{\sqrt[3]{a}}{b^3}$
(2) $\log \frac{a}{3b^3}$ (4) $\log \frac{\sqrt[3]{a}}{3b}$

134. $\text{Log } \frac{\sqrt{b}}{a^2}$ is equivalent to

(1) $\frac{1}{2} \log b + 2 \log a$ (3) $2 \log b - \frac{1}{2} \log a$
(2) $\frac{1}{2} \log b - 2 \log a$ (4) $\frac{\frac{1}{2} \log b}{2 \log a}$

135. Solve for x: $\log_{10}(x + 3) - \log_{10} x = 2$

136. Find: log 4273

137. If $\log N = 1.7697$, find N.

138. The value of $10^{1.9047}$ is

(1) 0.0803 (2) 0.803 (3) 8.03 (4) 80.3

139. Using logarithms, compute the value of $\sqrt[3]{80}$ to the nearest tenth.

140. Using logarithms, solve for x to the nearest tenth:

$$3^{2x} = 5$$

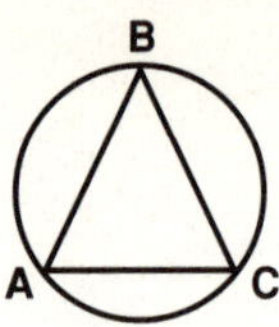

Ex. 141

141. $\triangle ABC$ is inscribed in the circle. If $\overline{AB} \cong \overline{CB}$ and $m\widehat{AC} = 80°$, find $m\angle C$.

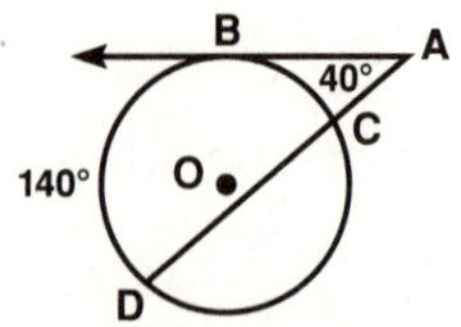

Ex. 142

142. $\overrightarrow{AB}$ is tangent to circle O at B and $\overline{ACD}$ is a secant. If $m\angle A = 40°$ and $m\widehat{BD} = 140°$, find $m\widehat{BC}$.

143. *Given:* Circle O, tangent $\overline{DE}$, secant $\overline{DAC}$, diameter $\overline{AOB}$, $\overline{OE}$, $\overline{BE} \cong \overline{BC}$, $m\angle x : m\angle y = 2:1$

Find:

a. $m\angle y$
b. $m\widehat{EB}$
c. $m\angle EOA$
d. $m\angle D$

144. 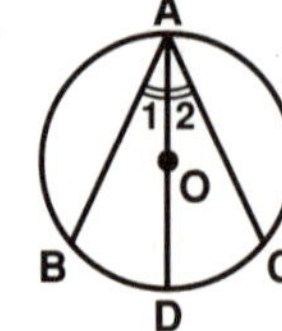

Given: Diameter $\overline{AD}$ forms congruent angles with chords $\overline{BA}$ and $\overline{CA}$.

Prove: $\overline{BA} \cong \overline{CA}$

145. *Given:* Circle O, chord $\overline{BGF}$ is parallel to secant $\overline{CDE}$, B is the midpoint of $\widehat{AD}$, secant $\overline{CBA}$, and chords $\overline{AF}$ and $\overline{AGD}$.

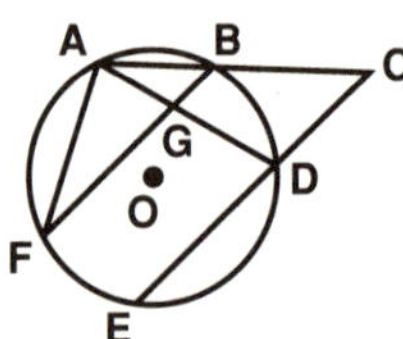

Prove: $\frac{CD}{BA} = \frac{CA}{BF}$

146. *Given:* $\overrightarrow{CE}$ is tangent to circle O at point A. $\overline{BD}$ is a diameter, $\overline{AB}$ is a chord, and $\overline{BC} \perp \overline{CE}$ at C.

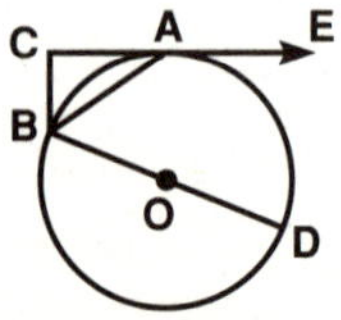

Prove: $(AB)^2 = BC \times BD$

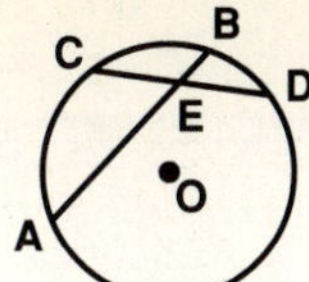

Ex. 147

147. Chords $\overline{AB}$ and $\overline{CD}$ of circle O intersect at E. If $AE = x$, $EB = x - 6$, and $CE = ED = 4$, find AE.

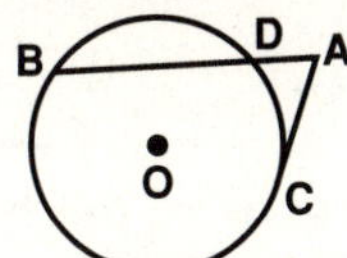

Ex. 148

148. Secant $\overline{ADB}$ and tangent $\overline{AC}$ are drawn to circle O from external point A. If $AD = 3$ and $DB = 9$, what is the length of $\overline{AC}$?

(1) 6 (2) $\sqrt{6}$ (3) 27 (4) $\sqrt{27}$

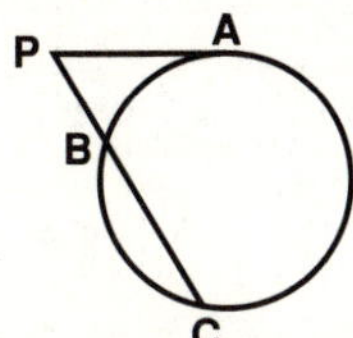

Ex. 149

149. $\overrightarrow{PA}$ is tangent to the circle at A and $\overline{PBC}$ is a secant. If $PA = 2\sqrt{3}$ and $PB = 2$, what is PC?

(1) 6 (2) 2 (3) 8 (4) 4

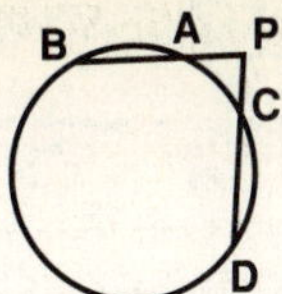

Ex. 150

150. $\overline{PAB}$ and $\overline{PCD}$ are secants to the circle. If $PA = 4$, $AB = 5$, and $PD = 12$, what is PC?

151. On a set of coordinate axes, circle O is drawn with its center at the origin. Segment $\overline{PA}$ is drawn tangent to circle O at A and secant $\overline{PBC}$ is drawn passing through point O. The coordinates of A and P are (0, 4) and (3, 4) respectively.

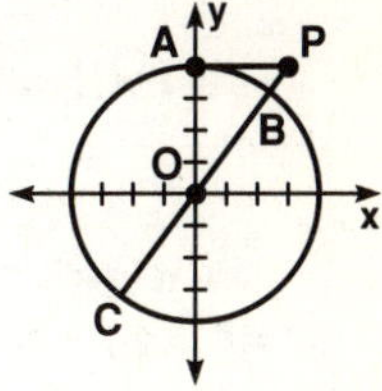

a. Find PO.

b. Find PC.

c. Find PB.

d. Write an equation of $\overleftrightarrow{AP}$.

e. Write an equation of circle O.

CHAPTER 6

Trigonometry, Part I

6.1 RIGHT-TRIANGLE TRIGONOMETRY

Definitions of Trigonometric Functions

In a right triangle, consider three ratios involving the lengths of pairs of sides of the triangle. Each of these TRIGONOMETRIC FUNCTIONS is *constant* with respect to an acute angle of fixed measure.

$$\text{SINE } A = \frac{\textbf{length of side } \textbf{\textit{opposite}} \ \angle A}{\textbf{length of } \textbf{\textit{hypotenuse}}}$$

$$\text{COSINE } A = \frac{\textbf{length of side } \textbf{\textit{adjacent}} \textbf{ to } \angle A}{\textbf{length of } \textbf{\textit{hypotenuse}}}$$

$$\text{TANGENT } A = \frac{\textbf{length of side } \textbf{\textit{opposite}} \ \angle A}{\textbf{length of side } \textbf{\textit{adjacent}} \textbf{ to } \angle A}$$

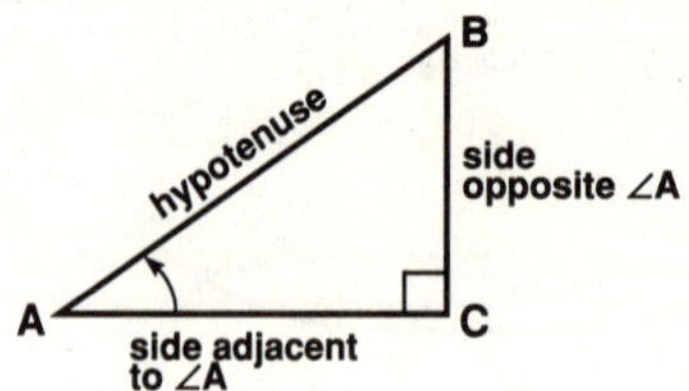

S O H C A H T O A

$$\text{Sin} \angle = \frac{\text{Opposite}}{\text{Hypotenuse}} \qquad \text{Cos} \angle = \frac{\text{Adjacent}}{\text{Hypotenuse}} \qquad \text{Tan} \angle = \frac{\text{Opposite}}{\text{Adjacent}}$$

For right $\triangle ABC$, with right $\angle C$:

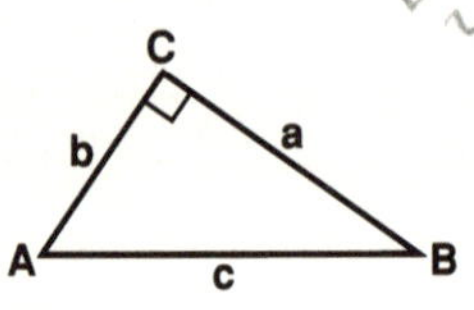

$\sin A = \frac{a}{c}$ $\quad \sin B = \frac{b}{c}$

$\cos A = \frac{b}{c}$ $\quad \cos B = \frac{a}{c}$

$\tan A = \frac{a}{b}$ $\quad \tan B = \frac{b}{a}$

The sine of an acute angle has the same value as the cosine of its complement. $\sin A = \cos B \quad \cos A = \sin B$

The tangent of an acute angle is the reciprocal of the tangent of its complement. $\tan A \cdot \tan B = 1$

The reciprocal ratio of tangent is cotangent.

$$\tan A = \frac{\text{opposite}}{\text{adjacent}} \qquad \cot A = \frac{\text{adjacent}}{\text{opposite}}$$

The tangent of an acute angle has the same value as the cotangent of its complement. $\tan A = \cot B \quad \cot A = \tan B$

Examples

1. sin 24° is equivalent to

(1) cos 24° **(3)** cos 66°

(2) sin 66° **(4)** $\frac{1}{\sin 24°}$

Solution: The sine of an angle has the same value as the cosine of its complement.

Answer: **(3)**

2. If $\cot x = \tan(x + 20°)$, find x.

Solution: When the cotangent and tangent functions are equal in value, the angles must be complements.

$$x + (x + 20) = 90$$
$$2x + 20 = 90$$
$$2x = 70$$
$$x = 35° \quad \textit{Ans.}$$

EXERCISES

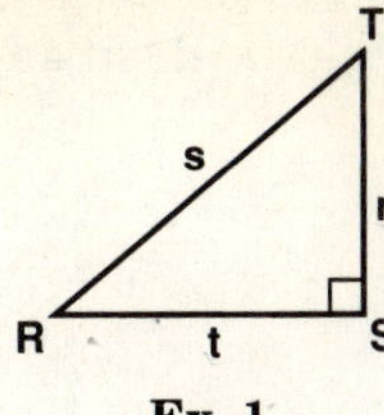

Ex. 1

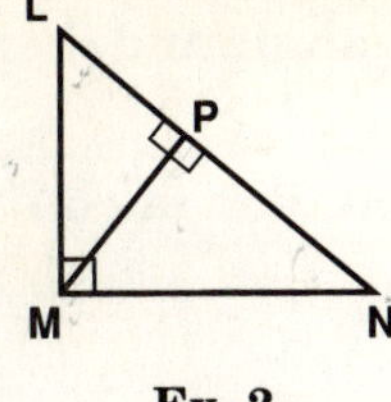

Ex. 2

1. *Given:* Right $\triangle RST$ as shown.
   Required: Write, in terms of r, s, and t, the sine, cosine, and tangent ratios for
   a. $\angle R$ **b.** $\angle T$

2. *Given:* $\overline{LM} \perp \overline{MN}$ and $\overline{MP} \perp \overline{LN}$ as shown.
   Required: Complete the following ratios.
   a. $\sin L = \frac{MN}{?}$
   b. $\sin L = \frac{MP}{?}$
   c. $\cos LMP = \frac{?}{LM}$
   d. $\cos PMN = \frac{?}{MN}$
   e. $\tan L = \frac{MP}{?}$
   f. $\tan N = \frac{LM}{?}$
   g. $\tan N = \frac{MP}{?}$
   h. $\tan PMN = \frac{PN}{?}$
   i. $\cos N = \frac{PN}{?}$
   j. $\cos N = \frac{MN}{?}$
   k. $\sin N = \frac{LM}{?}$
   l. $\tan PML = \frac{?}{MP}$

3. Which is equivalent to sin 73°?
   (1) cos 17° **(2)** cos 73° **(3)** sin 17° **(4)** –sin 73°

4. If $\cos(x + 30°) = \sin x$, a measure of angle x is
   (1) 15° **(2)** 30° **(3)** 45° **(4)** 60°

5. If $\tan x = \cot(2x - 6°)$, then $m\angle x$ is
   (1) 28° **(2)** 32° **(3)** 45° **(4)** 84°

6. If x is a positive acute angle and $\sin x = \cos(x + 20°)$, find the value of x.

In 7–10, find the value of x.

7. $\sin x = \cos 2x$
8. $\cos x = \sin x$
9. $\tan(x + 10°) = \cot x$
10. $\cot(2x + 40°) = \tan(x - 10°)$

Using a Calculator to Work With Trigonometric Functions

Angle Units

Angles measured in degrees can have a whole number of degrees, such as 40° or 41°

Angle measures between 40° and 41° can be written
- **by using decimals: 40.5° is halfway between 40° and 41°, or**
- **by using division of degrees called *minutes* and *seconds*, 60 minutes = 1 degree and 60 seconds = 1 minute:**
  40.5° = 40° 30′ (read 40 degrees 30 minutes)

On a calculator, minutes are entered using two decimal places.
To record 40° 30′, ENTER: 40.30
To read the decimal equivalent of 40° 30′, ENTER: [2nd] [DD] DISPLAY: [40.5]
To read the equivalent in minutes, access [DMS], degree/minute/second format.
ENTER: [2nd] [DMS], or your calculator may require [3rd] [DMS].

Example

Record and display 72 degrees 5 minutes 27 seconds.

Solution: ENTER: 72.0527 [2nd] [DD] DISPLAY: [72.090833] ← decimal degrees

ENTER: [2nd] [DMS] DISPLAY: [72°05′27″]

Reading Trigonometric Functions

To read the value of a trigonometric function:

Enter the number of degrees in the measure of the angle and then press the desired ratio. On some calculators, you do this in reverse.

If you enter an angle in degree/minute/second format, you must first convert it to decimal degrees before using the trigonometric functions.

Examples

1. Find sin 72° rounded to four decimal places.

Solution: ENTER: 72 [SIN]

DISPLAY: [0.9510565]

Answer: sin 72° ≈ 0.9511

2. Find cos 16° 20′ rounded to four decimal places.

Solution: ENTER: 16.20 [2nd] [DD] [COS]

DISPLAY: [0.959641]

Answer: cos 16° 20′ ≈ 0.9596

Reading Angle Measures

To find the measure of an angle for which you know the value of a trigonometric function:

Enter the value of the trigonometric function, and then press the inverse key for that function.

Note that the inverse for each function is over (or at the top of) the key with the function and is accessed by pressing [2nd].

At first, the calculator displays the angle measure in decimal degrees. If you wish to see the angle measure in the degree/minute/second format, press [2nd] [DMS].

Examples

1. If sin A = 0.4695, find m∠A rounded to the nearest degree.

Solution: ENTER: 0.4695 [2nd] [SIN⁻¹]

DISPLAY: [28.001845] ← decimal degrees

Answer: m∠A ≈ 28°

2. If tan A = 3.4424, find m∠A rounded to: **a.** the nearest minute **b.** the nearest ten minutes

Solution: ENTER: 3.4424 [2nd] [TAN⁻¹]

DISPLAY: [73.801683] ← decimal degrees

ENTER: [2nd] [DMS]

DISPLAY: [73°48′06″]

Answer: **a.** m∠A ≈ 73° 48′
b. m∠A ≈ 73° 50′

EXERCISES

In 1–10, use a calculator to record and display the angle measure in degree/minute/second format.

1. 39° 42′ 27″
2. 86° 19′ 31″
3. 12° 26′ 14″
4. 27° 09′ 19″
5. 31° 05′ 21″
6. 46° 9′ 3″
7. 71° 9′ 9″
8. 62° 8′ 4″
9. 31° 2′ 8″
10. 10° 1′ 9″

In 11–32, use a calculator to find the value of the trigonometric function correct to 4 decimal places.

11. sin 23°
12. cos 48°
13. tan 19°
14. sin 61°
15. cos 12°
16. tan 82°
17. sin 45°
18. cos 45°
19. tan 45°
20. sin 18° 40′
21. cos 72° 20′
22. tan 30° 50′
23. cos 0° 30′
24. sin 41° 19′
25. tan 18° 42′
26. cos 63° 16′
27. tan 29° 05′
28. sin 89° 7′
29. cos 63° 4′
30. sin 7° 7′
31. cos 9° 2′
32. tan 4° 8′

In 33–42, use a calculator to find the value of the trigonometric function correct to 4 decimal places.

33. sin 12° 43′ 16″
34. cos 41° 38′ 47″
35. tan 36° 5′ 19″
36. tan 81° 9′ 6″
37. sin 26° 4′ 3″
38. cos 5° 18′ 4″
39. tan 9° 9′ 9″
40. sin 5° 4′ 31″
41. sin 39° 9′ 7″
42. cos 70° 4′ 4″

In 43–52, use a calculator to find $m\angle\theta$
a. correct to the nearest minute
b. correct to the nearest ten minutes

43. $\sin\theta = 0.2012$
44. $\tan\theta = 0.1148$
45. $\cos\theta = 0.5380$
46. $\sin\theta = 0.9186$
47. $\cos\theta = 0.8380$
48. $\tan\theta = \frac{4}{5}$
49. $\sin\theta = \frac{3}{4}$
50. $\tan\theta = \frac{5}{3}$
51. $\cos\theta = \frac{2}{3}$
52. $\cos\theta = \frac{12}{13}$

Solving a Right Triangle

Given two measures in a right triangle (either one side and one angle or two sides), you can find the measures of the remaining sides and angles using trigonometry. To choose the appropriate trigonometric function, first identify the placement of the sides of the triangle with respect to a particular angle.

Examples

1. Find, to the nearest tenth, the length of the side whose measure is represented by x.

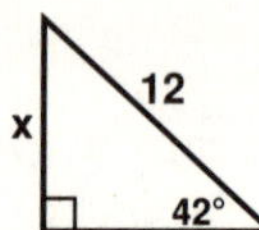

Solution: Identify the placement of the sides with respect to the 42° angle.

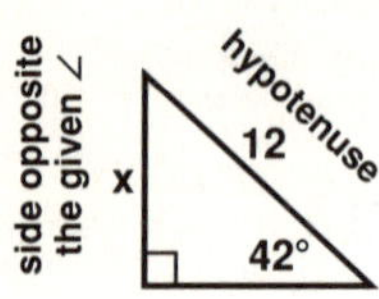

$$\sin \angle = \frac{\text{opposite}}{\text{hypotenuse}}$$

$$\sin 42^\circ = \frac{x}{12}$$

$$x = 12(\sin 42^\circ)$$

$$x \approx 8.0296$$

$$x \approx 8.0$$

2. Find m$\angle x$ to the nearest minute.

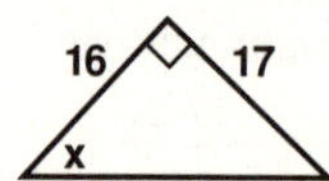

Solution: Identify the placement of the sides with respect to $\angle x$.

$$\tan \angle = \frac{\text{opposite}}{\text{adjacent}}$$

$$\tan x = \frac{17}{16}$$

ENTER: [( ] 17 [÷] 16 [ )] [2nd] [TAN⁻¹]

DISPLAY: 46.735705 ← decimal degrees

ENTER: [2nd] [DMS]

DISPLAY: 46°44'8.5"

$$m\angle x \approx 46^\circ 44'$$

3. *Given:* Isosceles $\triangle ABC$ with altitude $\overline{CD}$ to base $\overline{AB}$. $AC = BC = 11$ units and $AB = 8$ units.

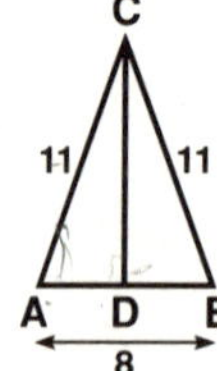

Find:

a. m$\angle A$ to the nearest degree

b. CD to the nearest unit

Solution: In an isosceles triangle, the altitude to the base is also the median.

a. Work in right $\triangle ACD$ to find m$\angle A$.

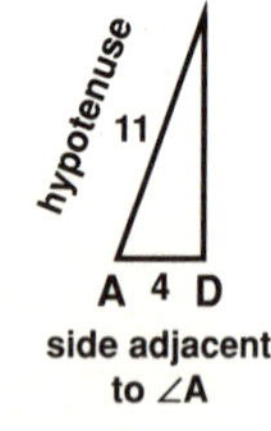

$$\cos \angle = \frac{\text{adjacent}}{\text{hypotenuse}}$$

$$\cos A = \frac{4}{11}$$

ENTER: [( ] 4 [÷] 11 [ )] [2nd] [COS⁻¹]

$$m\angle A \approx 69^\circ$$

b. Now that you know the measure of $\angle A$, you can use either of two trigonometric functions to find CD.

$$\sin 69^\circ = \frac{CD}{11} \quad \text{or} \quad \tan 69^\circ = \frac{CD}{4}$$

$$CD = 11(\sin 69^\circ) \qquad CD = 4(\tan 69^\circ)$$

$$CD \approx 10.2694 \qquad CD \approx 10.4204$$

$$CD \approx 10 \textit{ Ans.} \qquad CD \approx 10 \textit{ Ans.}$$

Alternate Solution: Use the Pythagorean Relation.

$$(AC)^2 = (AD)^2 + (CD)^2$$

4. Tangents $\overline{PA}$ and $\overline{PB}$ are drawn to circle O from external point P. If $OA = 12$ cm and m$\angle APB = 40°$, find the length of the tangent to the nearest tenth of a centimeter.

Solution: $\overline{OP}$ bisects $\angle APB$.

Radius $\overline{OA} \perp$ tangent $\overline{PA}$.

$$\tan 20° = \frac{OA}{PA}$$

$$(\tan 20°)PA = 12$$

$$PA = \frac{12}{\tan 20°}$$

$$PA \approx 33.0 \text{ cm}$$

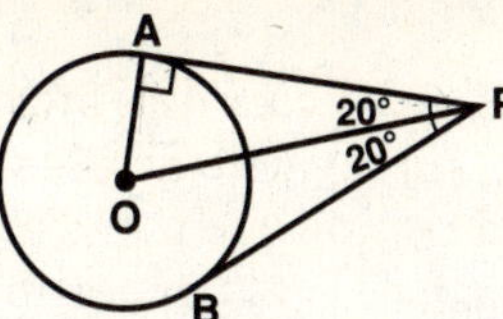

EXERCISES

In 1–4, find the value of x to the nearest tenth.

1.

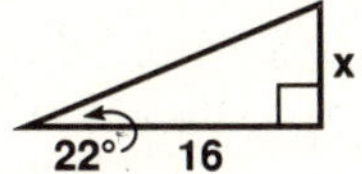

2.

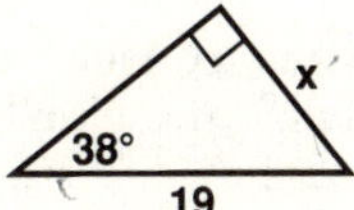

3.

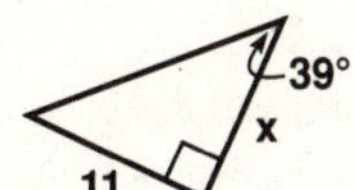

4.

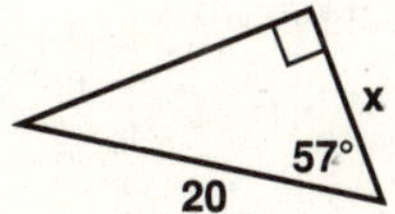

5. In right $\triangle ABC$, m$\angle A = 38°$, m$\angle C = 90°$, and $BC = 10$ cm. Find AC to the nearest cm.

6. Find, to the nearest foot, the length of the hypotenuse of an isosceles right triangle each of whose legs measures 12 feet.

In 7–9, find m$\angle x$ to the nearest 10 minutes.

7.

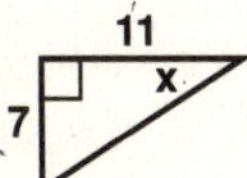

8.

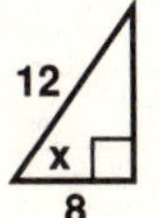

9.

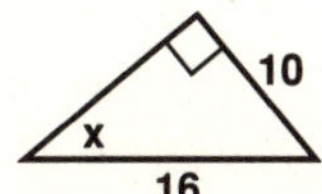

10. In cm, the legs of a right triangle measure 4 and 7. Find, to the nearest degree, the measure of the smaller acute angle.

11. Find, to the nearest 10 minutes, the measure of the smaller acute angle of a right triangle whose sides measure 5 cm, 12 cm, and 13 cm.

12. Find, to the nearest minute, the measure of the larger acute angle of a right triangle whose sides measure 8 in., 15 in., and 17 in.

13. In cm, the lengths of the sides of a rectangle are 30 and 24. Find, to the nearest degree, the measure of the angle formed by a diagonal and one of the longer sides.

14. In $\triangle ABC$, altitude $\overline{BD}$ is drawn to side $\overline{AC}$. m$\angle A = 62°$, m$\angle C = 20°$, and $BC = 50$ in. Find, to the nearest integer:

a. BD

b. AD

15. In $\square ABCD$, altitude $\overline{DH}$ is drawn to base $\overline{AB}$. m$\angle A = 47°$, $AD = 16$ ft., and $AB = 43$ ft. Find:

a. DH to the nearest tenth of a foot

b. the area of the parallelogram to the nearest square foot

16. In rhombus $ABCD$, diagonals $\overline{AC}$ and $\overline{BD}$ are drawn. Each side measures 20 units and m$\angle DAB = 52°$. Find:

a. AC to the nearest integer

b. BD to the nearest integer

c. the area of the rhombus

17. In rhombus $ABCD$ with diagonals $\overline{BD}$ and $\overline{AC}$ intersecting at E, $AB = 13$ cm and $AC = 24$ cm.

Find:

a. BD

b. the area of the rhombus

c. m$\angle EAB$ to the nearest degree

18. In rhombus $ABCD$ with diagonals $\overline{BD}$ and $\overline{AC}$ intersecting at E, $AE = 14$ ft., and $m\angle CAB = 25°$.

Find:

a. EB to the nearest ft.

b. the area of the rhombus

c. AB to the nearest ft.

d. to the nearest ft., the length of the altitude from D to $\overline{AB}$

19. Isosceles trapezoid $ABCD$ has bases $\overline{AB}$ and $\overline{DC}$, with $AB > DC$. Each leg of the trapezoid measures 14 in., and $\overline{AB}$ and $\overline{DC}$ measure 20 in. and 12 in. respectively.

Find:

a. $m\angle A$ to the nearest degree

b. the length of the altitude of the trapezoid to the nearest inch

c. the area of the trapezoid

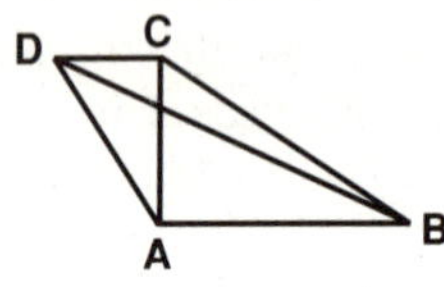

Ex. 20

20. $ABCD$ is a quadrilateral with $\overline{AB}$ parallel to $\overline{DC}$. $AB = 28.0$ in. and $DC = 12.0$ in. Diagonal $\overline{AC}$ is perpendicular to $\overline{AB}$. The angle between diagonal $\overline{DB}$ and $\overline{AB}$ measures 24°.

Find:

a. AC to the nearest tenth of an inch

b. the area of quadrilateral $ABCD$ to the nearest square inch

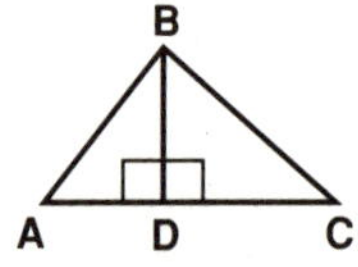

Ex. 21

21. In scalene $\triangle ABC$, $m\angle A = 51°$, $AB = 17$, $AC = 26$, and $\overline{BD}$ is an altitude.

Find:

a. BD to the nearest integer

b. AD to the nearest integer

c. DC to the nearest integer

d. $m\angle C$ to the nearest degree

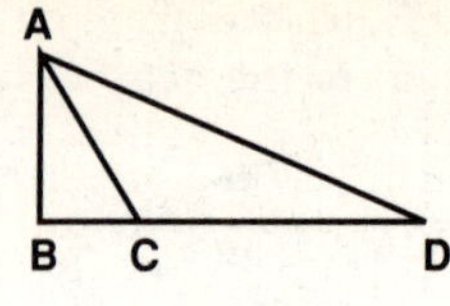

Ex. 22

22. In the diagram, $m\angle B = 90°$, $m\angle ACB = 58°$, $m\angle D = 23°$, and $BC = 60$.
Find, to the nearest integer:

a. AB

b. CD

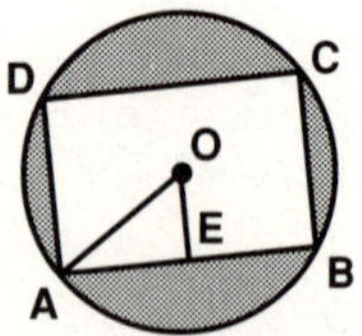

Ex. 23

23. Rectangle $ABCD$ is inscribed in circle O. Side $\overline{AB}$ is 12 inches long and OE, the distance of $\overline{AB}$ from the center of the circle, is 4 inches.

Find:

a. $m\angle AOE$ to the nearest degree

b. the radius of the circle to the nearest inch

c. the area of the circle to the nearest square inch (Use the approximation $\pi = \frac{22}{7}$ and the length of the radius as determined in part **b.**)

d. the area of the shaded portion to the nearest square inch

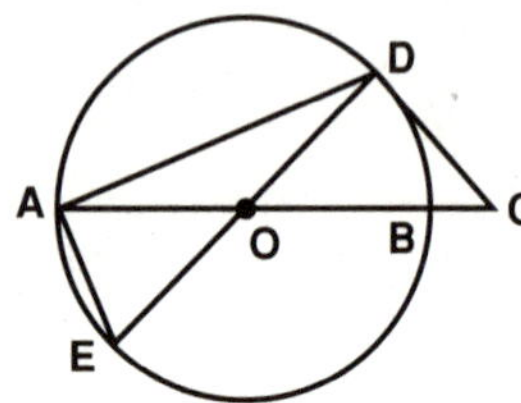

Ex. 24

24. In circle O, diameter $\overline{AB}$ is extended to point C, $\overline{CD}$ is tangent to the circle at D, diameter $\overline{DE}$ has length 20 cm, and $m\overset{\frown}{BD} : m\overset{\frown}{AD} = 1:4$. Chords $\overline{AE}$ and $\overline{AD}$ are drawn.

Find:

a. $m\overset{\frown}{BD}$

b. $m\angle E$

c. $m\angle C$

d. CD to the nearest tenth

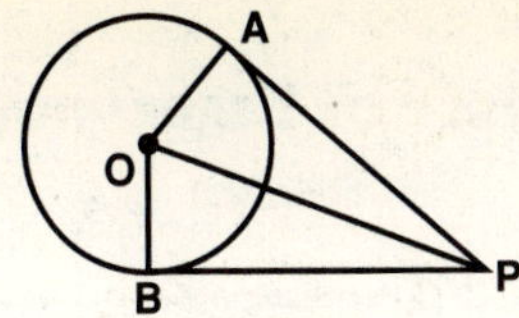

Ex. 25

25. Tangents $\overline{PA}$ and $\overline{PB}$ are drawn from external point P to points A and B of circle O, respectively. $PA = 25$, $m\angle APB = 40°$.

Find:

a. OA to the nearest integer

b. $m\angle AOB$

26. Two tangents are drawn from an external point to a circle whose radius is 12 inches. The arcs intercepted by the tangents are in the ratio 1:4.

a. Find the number of degrees in the smaller intercepted arc.

b. Find the number of degrees in the angle formed by the two tangents.

c. Find to the nearest inch the distance from the external point to the center of the circle.

27. In circle O, whose radius is 10 in., $m\overset{\frown}{AB} = 60°$. The tangents to the circle at A and B meet in point C. $\overline{OC}$ is drawn. Find, to the nearest square inch, the area of the quadrilateral $OACB$.

28. Point A lies outside a circle whose center is at O. OA is 37 inches long. From A, a tangent $\overline{AB}$ is drawn to the circle. If this tangent forms an angle of 27° with $\overline{OA}$, find to the nearest inch the length of:

a. the radius

b. tangent $\overline{AB}$

Solving Problems

ANGLE OF ELEVATION

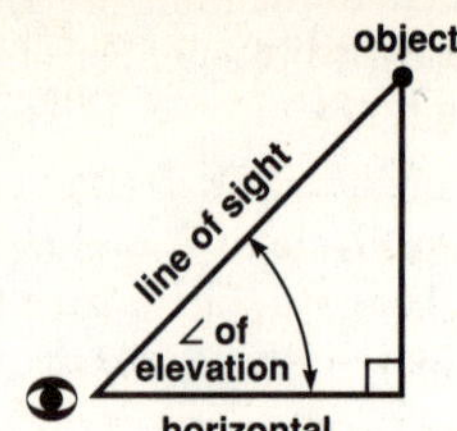

The observer is looking up at the object.

ANGLE OF DEPRESSION

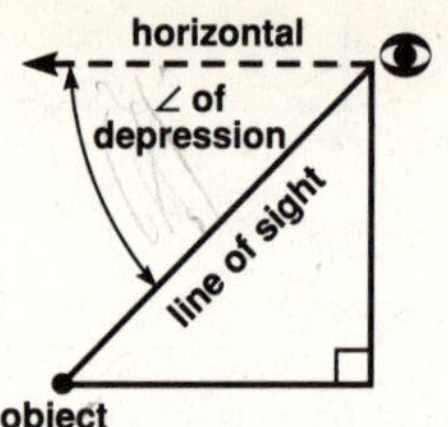

The observer is looking down at the object.

Examples

1. From a point on the ground 36 feet from the foot of a tree, the angle of elevation of the top of the tree contains 40°. Find the height of the tree to the nearest foot.

Solution: Draw a diagram to represent the situation. Let x = the height of the tree.

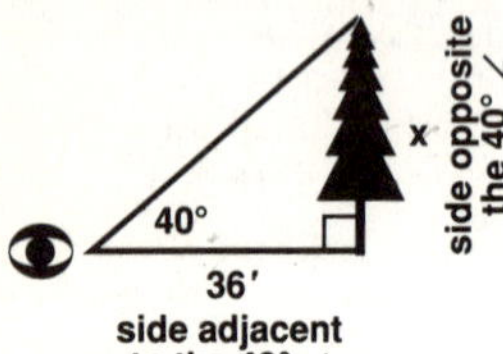

$$\tan \angle = \frac{\text{opposite}}{\text{adjacent}}$$

$$\tan 40° = \frac{x}{36}$$

$$x = 36(\tan 40°)$$

$$x \approx 30.2076$$

Answer: The height of the tree is about 30 feet.

2. From the top of a lighthouse 200 feet high, an observer measures the angle of depression of a boat at sea to be 24°. Find, to the nearest foot, the distance from the boat to the base of the lighthouse.

Solution: Since the angle of depression is outside the triangle, use the complement.

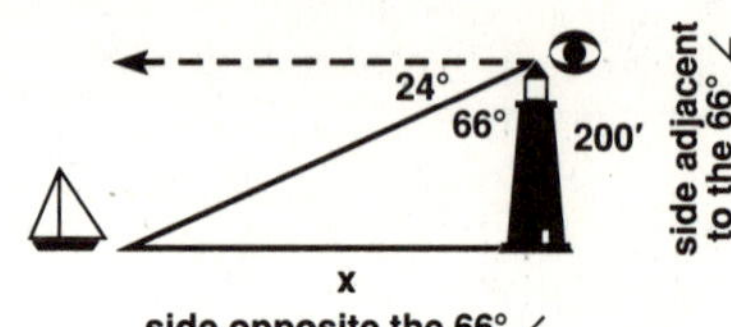

$$\tan \angle = \frac{\text{opposite}}{\text{adjacent}}$$

$$\tan 66° = \frac{x}{200}$$

$$x = 200(\tan 66°)$$

$$x \approx 449.2$$

Answer: The boat is about 449 feet from the foot of the lighthouse.

---

3. A pole ($\overline{TF}$) is on the roof of a shed ($\overline{FB}$). From a point (P) on the ground 27 feet from the foot of the shed, the angle of elevation of the top of the pole (T) contains 38° and the angle of elevation of the foot of the pole (F) contains 32°. Find, to the nearest foot, the height of:

a. the shed **b.** the pole

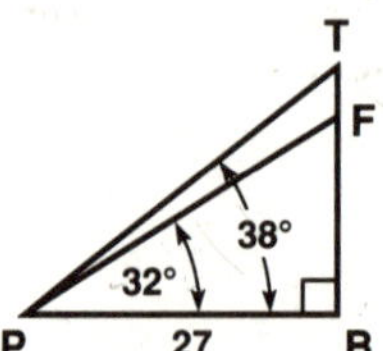

Solution:

a. To find the height of the shed $\overline{FB}$, work in right $\triangle FPB$:

$$\tan 32° = \frac{FB}{27}$$

$$FB = 27(\tan 32°)$$

$$FB \approx 16.8715$$

$$FB \approx 17 \text{ feet} \quad \textit{Ans.}$$

b. Since the pole $\overline{TF}$ is not a side of a right triangle, work indirectly.

First find TB.

In right $\triangle TPB$:

$$\tan 38° = \frac{TB}{27}$$

$$TB = 27(\tan 38°)$$

$$TB \approx 21.0947$$

Now, subtract to find TF.

$$TF = TB - FB$$

$$TF \approx 21.0947 - 16.8715$$

$$TF \approx 4.2232$$

$$TF \approx 4 \text{ feet} \quad \textit{Ans.}$$

EXERCISES

1. If a tree 28 meters tall casts a shadow 32 meters long, what is the measure of the angle of elevation of the sun to the nearest degree?

   (1) 29 (2) 41 (3) 50 (4) 61

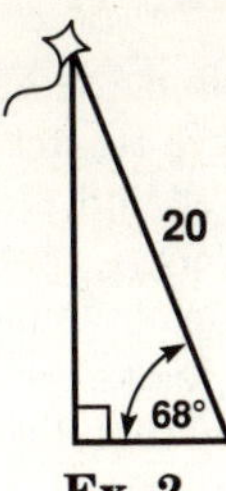

Ex. 2

2. A kite is flying at the end of a 20-meter string. If the string makes an angle of 68° with the ground, how high, to the nearest meter, is the kite?

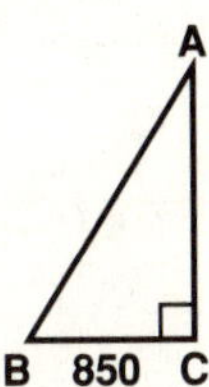

Ex. 3

3. The height of a cloud over an airport at night is determined by projecting a light vertically upward to the cloud. At a point on the ground 850 feet from the light, the angle of elevation of the spot where the light hits the cloud is found to contain 58°. Find, to the nearest foot, the height of the cloud.

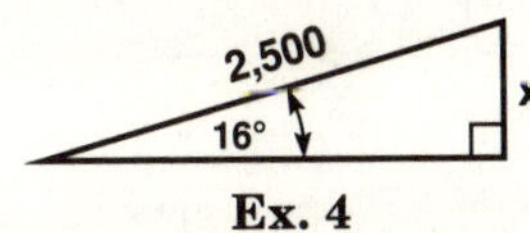

Ex. 4

4. A straight road is inclined upward at an angle of 16° with the horizontal. If a horse walked a distance of 2,500 feet up the road, find, to the nearest foot, his increase in altitude.

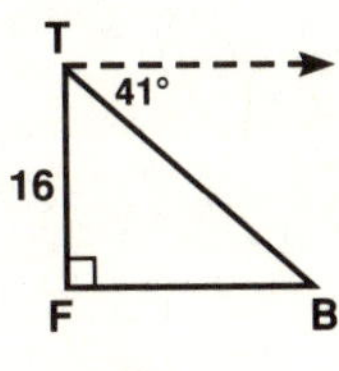

Ex. 5

5. From the top of a tree 16 feet tall, an observer measures the angle of depression of an object on the ground as 41°. Find, to the nearest foot, the distance from the foot of the tree to the object.

6. One angle of a rhombus measures 76°. The shorter diagonal has a length of 18 cm. Find to the nearest centimeter the length of the side of the rhombus.

7. For each 12-foot horizontal distance, a wheelchair ramp rises one foot. Find, to the nearest 10 minutes, the measure of the angle that the ramp makes with the horizontal.

8. A vertical pole 20 meters high casts a shadow 16 meters long on level ground. Find, to the nearest 10 minutes, the measure of the angle of elevation of the sun.

9. A monument stands on level ground. The measure of the angle of elevation of the top of the monument, taken at a point 325 feet from the foot of the monument, is found to be 27° 20′. Find, to the nearest foot, the height of the monument.

10. A 27-foot-long wire stretches from the top of a vertical pole to a stake in the ground 21 feet from the foot of the pole. Find, to the nearest 10 minutes, the measure of the acute angle that the wire makes with the ground.

11. From the top of a 108-foot-high building, an observer measures the angle of depression of a bicycle on the sidewalk as 29° 40′. Find, to the nearest foot, the distance from the bicycle to the base of the building.

12. An 18-foot ladder leans against the side of a house that stands on level ground. The foot of the ladder is 10 feet from the house.

    Find:

    a. to the nearest 10 minutes, the measure of the angle that the foot of the ladder makes with the ground

    b. to the nearest foot, the distance from the point where the top of the ladder touches the house to the ground

13. A telephone pole stands on level ground. A wire is attached to the pole at a point 30 feet above the ground. The wire makes an angle of 61° 20′ with the ground. Find, to the nearest foot:

    a. the distance from the base of the pole to the point on the ground where the wire is fastened

    b. the length of the wire

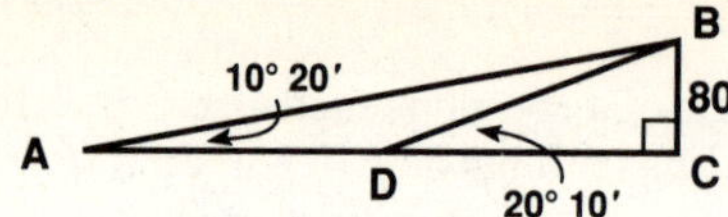

Ex. 14

14. A ship is headed directly toward a coastline formed by a vertical cliff $\overline{BC}$ that is 80 meters high. At point A, from the ship, the measure of the angle of elevation of B, the top of the cliff, is 10° 20′. A few minutes later, at point D, the measure of the angle of elevation has increased to 20° 10′. Find, to the nearest meter:

a. DC

b. AC

c. the distance between the two sightings

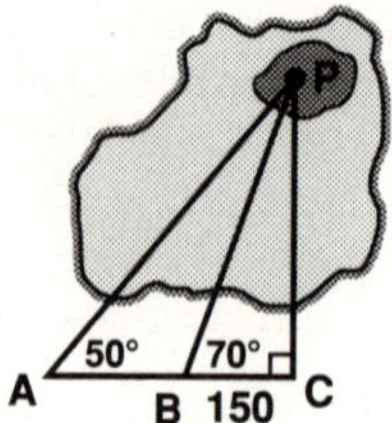

Ex. 15

15. Point P is on an island in a small lake. To find the distance from P to a point on the shore of the lake, a convenient base line, $\overline{ABC}$, was taken along the shore and the following measurements were made: m∠A = 50°, m∠PBC = 70°, m∠C = 90°, and BC = 150 yards. Find, to the nearest yard:

a. PC **b.** AP

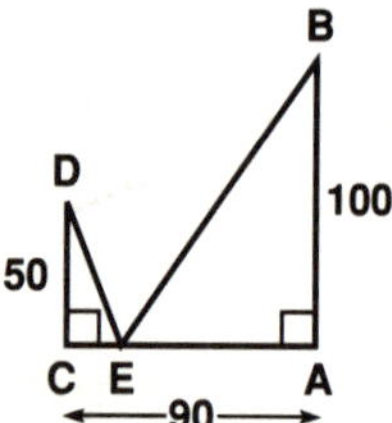

Ex. 16

16. The heights AB and CD of buildings on opposite sides of an avenue 90 feet wide are, respectively, 100 feet and 50 feet. From a point E on the avenue, the measure of the angle of elevation of B is 55° 20′.

Find:

a. to the nearest tenth of a foot, the distance from E to A

b. to the nearest 10 minutes, the measure of the angle of elevation of D from E

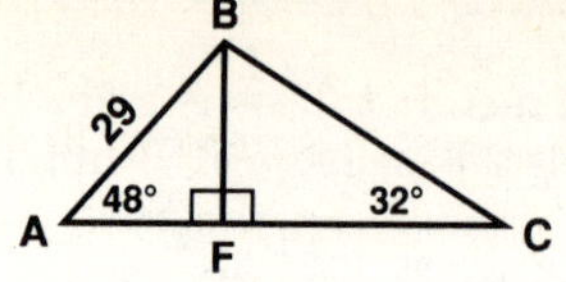

Ex. 17

17. From the top of pole $\overline{BF}$ that is standing on level ground, two wires are stretched to the ground and fastened at points A and C that are on opposite sides of the pole. From A, the measure of the angle of elevation of the top of the pole is 48°. From C, the measure of the angle of elevation of the top of the pole is 32°. If AB = 29 feet, find, to the nearest foot:

a. the height of pole $\overline{BF}$

b. the length of wire $\overline{BC}$

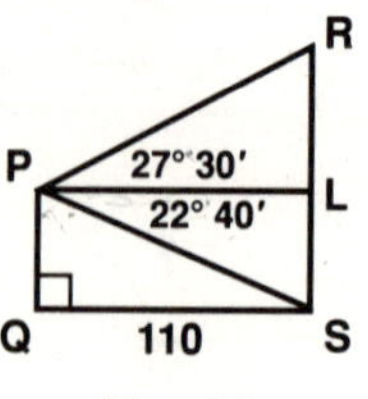

Ex. 18

18. $\overline{PQ}$ and $\overline{RS}$ represent buildings on opposite sides of a highway 110 feet wide. From P, the measure of the angle of elevation of R is 27° 30′ and the measure of the angle of depression of S is 22° 40′. Find, to the nearest foot:

a. the height of $\overline{PQ}$

b. the height of $\overline{RS}$

6.3 EXTENDING TRIGONOMETRY

Redefining the Trigonometric Functions

The trigonometric functions, redefined in a more general sense, apply to an angle of any size, not just to an acute angle.

A UNIT CIRCLE has a radius of one unit, with each point (x, y) on the circle satisfying the equation $x^2 + y^2 = 1$ when the center of the circle is at the origin.

When an angle is in STANDARD POSITION, its INITIAL SIDE is a ray coincident with the nonnegative x–axis. The other ray of the angle is its TERMINAL SIDE.

Counterclockwise motion is positive.

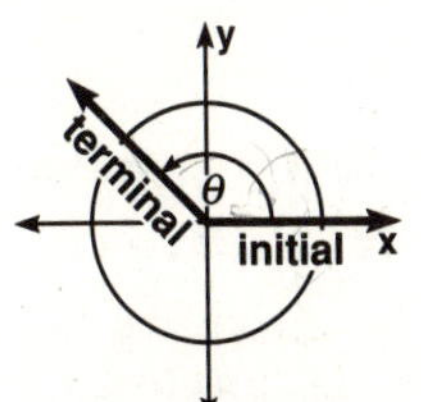

Clockwise motion is negative.

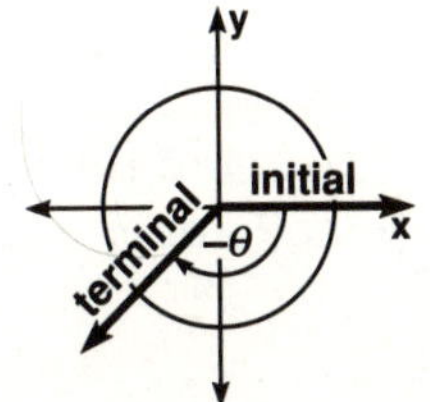

There may be more than one rotation.

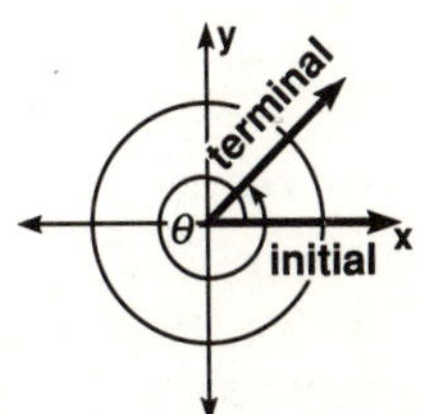

For point $P(x, y)$ on a unit circle, which is where the terminal side of a central angle θ intersects the circle, the directed distances x and y are defined as cosine and sine. The ratio $y : x$ is tangent.

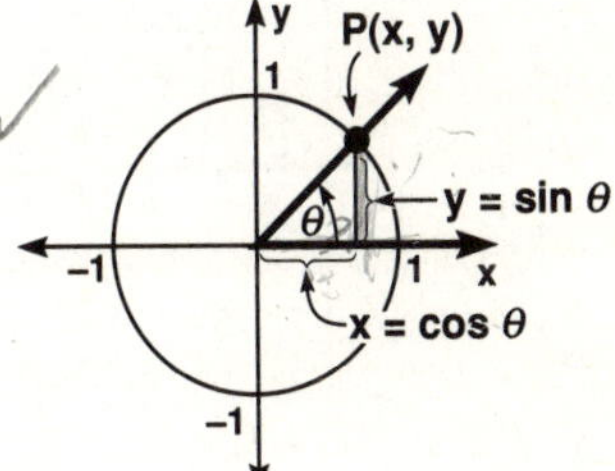

$x = \cos\theta$ $\qquad$ $y = \sin\theta$ $\qquad$ $\frac{y}{x} = \tan\theta$

Three additional functions, called *cosecant*, *secant*, and *cotangent*, are defined using the respective *reciprocals* of the function values of sine, cosine, and tangent.

RECIPROCAL FUNCTIONS:

$\csc\theta = \frac{1}{\sin\theta}$ where $\sin\theta \neq 0$ $\qquad$ $\sec\theta = \frac{1}{\cos\theta}$ where $\cos\theta \neq 0$ $\qquad$ $\cot\theta = \frac{1}{\tan\theta}$ where $\tan\theta \neq 0$

EXERCISES

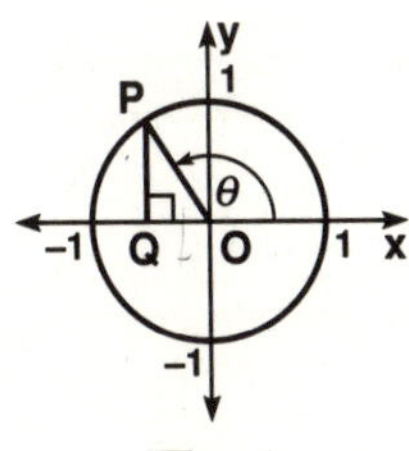

Ex. 1

1. Circle O is a unit circle. Which function is represented by the length of $\overline{PQ}$?

(1) $\sin\theta$ **(2)** $\cos\theta$ **(3)** $\tan\theta$ **(4)** $\cot\theta$

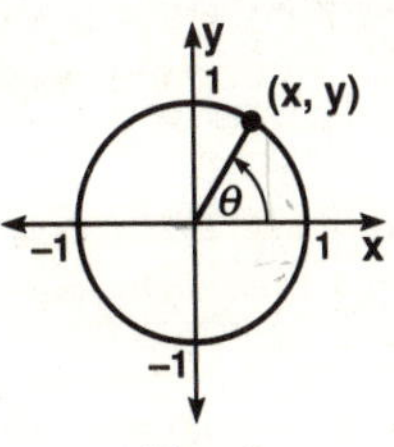

Ex. 2

2. In a unit circle, the ordered pair (x, y) represents the locus of points forming the circle. Which ordered pair is equivalent to (x, y)?

(1) $(\sin\theta, \cos\theta)$

(2) $(\cot\theta, \tan\theta)$

(3) $(\tan\theta, \cot\theta)$

(4) $(\cos\theta, \sin\theta)$

In 3–5, the diagram shows part of a unit circle with radius $OA = 1$. Angle θ is in Quadrant I, $\overline{AD} \perp \overline{OC}$, and $\overline{BC} \perp \overline{OC}$.

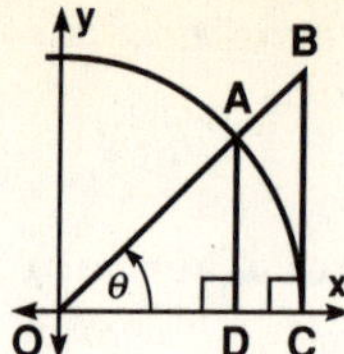

3. Which line segment has a length equivalent to $\sin \theta$?
   (1) $\overline{AD}$ (2) $\overline{BC}$ (3) $\overline{OD}$ (4) $\overline{OC}$

4. Which line segment has a length equivalent to $\cos \theta$?
   (1) $\overline{OB}$ (2) $\overline{OA}$ (3) $\overline{OC}$ (4) $\overline{OD}$

5. Which line segment has a length equivalent to $\tan \theta$?
   (1) $\overline{OA}$ (2) $\overline{OB}$ (3) $\overline{AD}$ (4) $\overline{BC}$

In 6–11, the diagram represents trigonometric functions of θ and of $-\theta$ by line segments. $\angle AOP = \theta$ and $\angle AOP' = -\theta$. The equation of the circle is $x^2 + y^2 = 1$, and the equation of line BC is $x = 1$. $\overline{PDP'}$ is $\perp$ to the x-axis. From the diagram, select a line segment that represents each of the following:

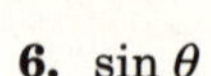

6. $\sin \theta$
7. $\cos \theta$
8. $\tan \theta$
9. $\cos(-\theta)$
10. $\tan(-\theta)$
11. $\sin(-\theta)$

Signs of the Trigonometric Functions

As the terminal side of an angle in standard position moves through the different quadrants, the directed distances $x = \cos \theta$ and $y = \sin \theta$ have different positive or negative orientations.

Quadrant I	**Quadrant II**	**Quadrant III**	**Quadrant IV**
	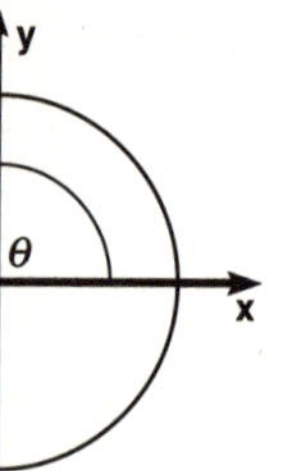	 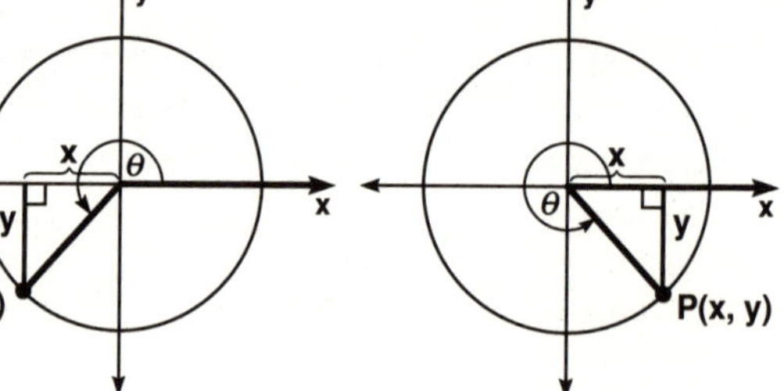	
$y > 0$, or $\sin \theta > 0$	$y > 0$, or $\sin \theta > 0$	$y < 0$, or $\sin \theta < 0$	$y < 0$, or $\sin \theta < 0$
$x > 0$, or $\cos \theta > 0$	$x < 0$, or $\cos \theta < 0$	$x < 0$, or $\cos \theta < 0$	$x > 0$, or $\cos \theta > 0$
$\frac{y}{x} > 0$, or $\tan \theta > 0$	$\frac{y}{x} < 0$, or $\tan \theta < 0$	$\frac{y}{x} > 0$, or $\tan \theta > 0$	$\frac{y}{x} < 0$, or $\tan \theta < 0$

I	II	III	IV
All	***Sin***	***Tan***	***Cos***

Only these functions and their reciprocals are positive in the quadrants shown.

To remember the order *A–S–T–C*, think:

All Students Take Calculus

Summary of Function Signs in the Quadrants

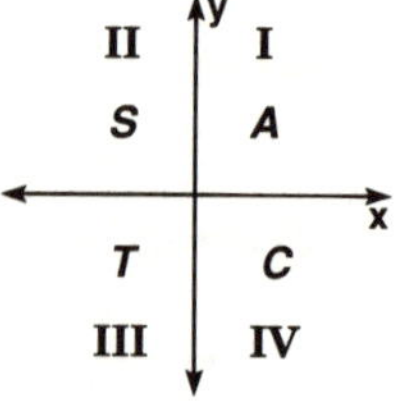

Examples

1. If $\sin \theta > 0$ and $\cos \theta < 0$, in which quadrant does angle θ lie?

   Solution: $\sin \theta > 0$ in Quadrants I and II.
   $\cos \theta < 0$ in Quadrants II and III.

   Quadrant II satisfies both conditions.

2. If $\sec \theta > 0$ and $\cot \theta < 0$, in which quadrant does angle θ lie?

   Solution: $\sec \theta$, like $\cos \theta$, > 0 in Q I, IV.
   $\cot \theta$, like $\tan \theta$, < 0 in Q II, IV.

   Quadrant IV satisfies both conditions.

EXERCISES

In 1–6, determine the quadrants in which $\angle\theta$ may lie if:

1. $\sin\theta > 0$

2. $\cos\theta < 0$

3. $\tan\theta > 0$

4. $\cot\theta < 0$

5. $\csc\theta < 0$

6. $\sec\theta > 0$

In 7–13, determine the quadrant in which $\angle\theta$ may lie if:

7. $\sin\theta < 0$ and $\cos\theta > 0$

8. $\tan\theta > 0$ and $\sin\theta > 0$

9. $\tan\theta < 0$ and $\cos\theta < 0$

10. $\sec\theta > 0$ and $\csc\theta < 0$

11. $\cot\theta > 0$ and $\sin\theta < 0$

12. $\csc\theta < 0$ and $\cot\theta > 0$

13. $\sec\theta > 0$ and $\csc\theta > 0$

In 14–17, determine the quadrant in which $\angle\theta$ may lie if:

14. $\cos\theta = -\frac{4}{5}$ and $\tan\theta > 0$

15. $\sin\theta = -\frac{3}{5}$ and $\cos\theta < 0$

16. $\tan\theta < 0$ and $\sin\theta = \frac{3}{5}$

17. $\tan\theta = -3$ and $\sin\theta > 0$

18. If $\sin x = \cos x$, in which quadrant(s) may angle x lie?
(1) I only **(2)** II only **(3)** I or III **(4)** II or IV

19. If $\cos x > 0$, then which must always be true?
(1) $\sin x > 0$ **(3)** $\sec x > 0$
(2) $\tan x > 0$ **(4)** $\csc x > 0$

20. If $\sin x \tan x > 0$ and $\tan x > 0$, which is true?
(1) $\cos x > 0$ **(3)** $\sec x < 0$
(2) $\cos x < 0$ **(4)** $\cot x < 0$

Finding a Function Value From Coordinates or From a Known Function Value

The value of a specific function can be determined if you know either of the following conditions.

1. the coordinates of a point on the terminal side of the angle

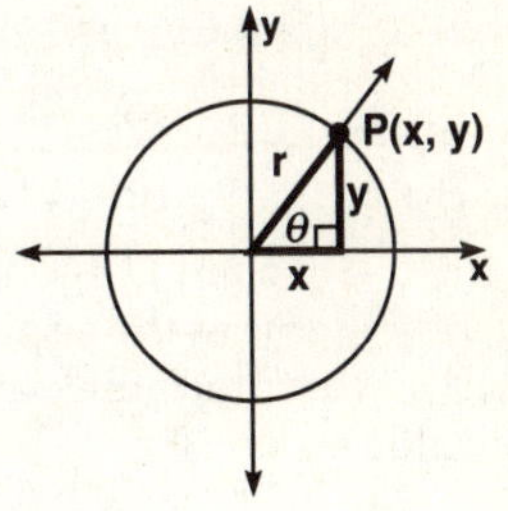

For point *P* on a circle of radius *r*:

$P(x, y) \rightarrow P(r\cos\theta, r\sin\theta)$

$r\cos\theta = x$ $\quad r\sin\theta = y$ $\quad \tan\theta = \frac{y}{x}$

$\cos\theta = \frac{x}{r}$ $\quad \sin\theta = \frac{y}{r}$ $\quad \tan\theta = \frac{\sin\theta}{\cos\theta}$

2. the quadrant in which the angle lies and the value of any other function

Examples

1. Point $P(-\sqrt{3}, 1)$ is on a circle whose center is the origin. If θ is an angle in standard position whose terminal ray passes through point P, find the value of $\sin\theta$.

Solution: To evaluate sine, you will need to know the values of y and r.

From the given coordinates: $x = -\sqrt{3}$, $y = 1$

Determine the value of r from the equation of the circle:

$x^2 + y^2 = r^2$

$(-\sqrt{3})^2 + 1^2 = r^2$

$3 + 1 = r^2$

$4 = r^2$

Reject −2. $2 = r$

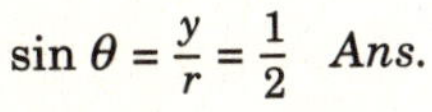
$\sin\theta = \frac{y}{r} = \frac{1}{2}$ *Ans.*

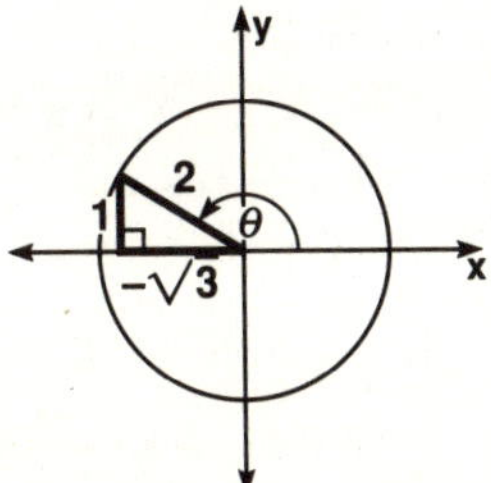

2. If $\tan\theta = \frac{3}{4}$ and θ is in Quadrant III, find $\csc\theta$.

Solution: In Q III, $x < 0$ and $y < 0$.

$\tan\theta = \frac{y}{x} = \frac{3}{4} = \frac{-3}{-4}$ Since x and y are known to be negative.

Use: $y = -3$, $x - 4$

To evaluate cosecant, you will need to know the value of r. Either substitute in the equation of the circle, or use the Pythagorean Relation.

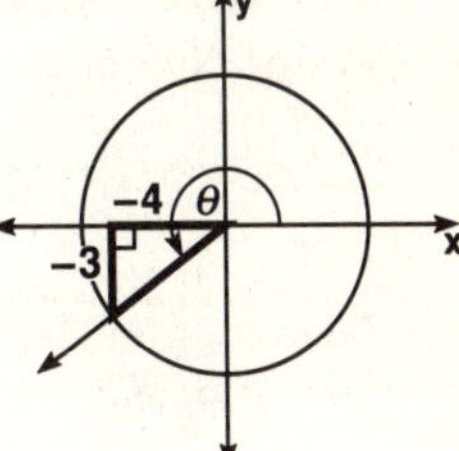

$r = 5$

$\csc\theta = \frac{r}{y} = \frac{5}{-3} = -\frac{5}{3}$ *Ans.*

Note: It is helpful to remember some Pythagorean Triples: 3, 4, 5 $\quad$ 5, 12, 13 $\quad$ 8, 15, 17

3. If $\cos\theta = -\frac{1}{2}$ and $\tan\theta = \sqrt{3}$, find $\csc\theta$.

Solution: Since $\cos\theta < 0$ and $\tan\theta > 0$, angle θ lies in Q III, where $x < 0$ and $y < 0$.

$\cos\theta = \frac{x}{r} = -\frac{1}{2} = \frac{-1}{2}$ Since x is known to be negative.

Thus: $x = -1, r = 2$

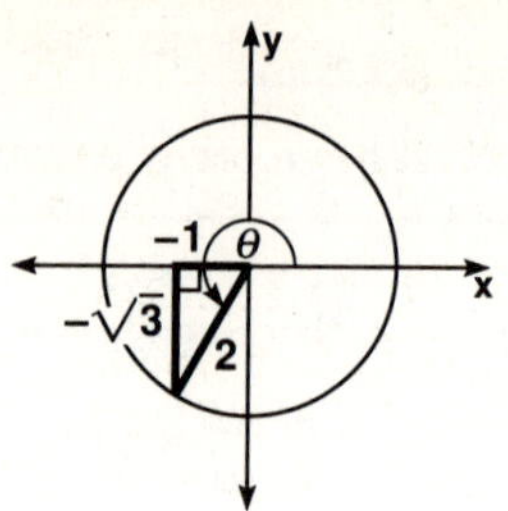

By the Pythagorean Relation: $y = -\sqrt{3}$

Or use the tangent value:

$\tan\theta = \frac{y}{x} = \sqrt{3} = \frac{\sqrt{3}}{1} = \frac{-\sqrt{3}}{-1}$ Since x is known to be −1.

Thus: $y = -\sqrt{3}$

$\csc\theta = \frac{r}{y} = \frac{2}{-\sqrt{3}}$ or $-\frac{2\sqrt{3}}{3}$

EXERCISES

In 1–6, point $A\left(\frac{1}{2}, -\frac{\sqrt{3}}{2}\right)$ is on a unit circle whose center is the origin. If θ is an angle in standard position whose terminal ray passes through point A, find the value of:

1. $\sin\theta$ **3.** $\cos\theta$ **5.** $\tan\theta$

2. $\csc\theta$ **4.** $\sec\theta$ **6.** $\cot\theta$

In 7–12, point $P\left(-\frac{\sqrt{3}}{2}, -\frac{1}{2}\right)$ is on a unit circle whose center is the origin. If θ is an angle in standard position whose terminal ray passes through point P, find the value of:

7. $\tan\theta$ **9.** $\sin\theta$ **11.** $\sec\theta$

8. $\csc\theta$ **10.** $\cot\theta$ **12.** $\cos\theta$

In 13–18, point $Q(-\sqrt{3}, -1)$ is on a circle of radius r whose center is at the origin. If θ is an angle in standard position whose terminal ray passes through point Q, find the value of:

13. $\cos\theta$ **15.** $\csc\theta$ **17.** $\tan\theta$

14. $\sin\theta$ **16.** $\cot\theta$ **18.** $\sec\theta$

19. If the terminal side of angle θ passes through the point (−4, 3), what is the value of $\cos\theta$?
(1) $\frac{3}{5}$ (2) $-\frac{3}{5}$ (3) $\frac{4}{5}$ (4) $-\frac{4}{5}$

20. If $\tan x = -\frac{2}{3}$ and angle x lies in the second quadrant, what is the value of $\cos x$?
(1) $\frac{3\sqrt{5}}{5}$ (2) $-\frac{3\sqrt{5}}{5}$ (3) $\frac{3\sqrt{13}}{13}$ (4) $-\frac{3\sqrt{13}}{13}$

21. If $\sin x = \frac{5}{13}$ and $\angle x$ is in Quadrant II, find $\cos x$.

22. If $\angle\theta$ is in Quadrant III and $\cos\theta = -\frac{4}{5}$, find $\csc\theta$.

23. If $\sec\theta = \frac{17}{15}$ and $\angle\theta$ is in Quadrant IV, find $\tan\theta$.

24. If $\sin\theta = \frac{2}{3}$ and θ is in Quadrant I, what is the value of $(\tan\theta)(\cos\theta)$?
(1) $\frac{2}{3}$ (2) $\frac{\sqrt{5}}{3}$ (3) $\frac{3\sqrt{5}}{5}$ (4) $\frac{2\sqrt{5}}{3}$

25. If $\cos x = -\frac{4}{5}$ and $\tan x > 0$, the value of $\sin x$ is
(1) $\frac{3}{5}$ (2) $\frac{5}{3}$ (3) $-\frac{5}{3}$ (4) $-\frac{3}{5}$

26. If $\sin\theta = -\frac{3}{5}$ and $\cos\theta > 0$, find $\tan\theta$.

27. Find the value of $\tan x$ if $\cos x = \frac{3}{5}$ and $\sin x < 0$.

28. If $\sin\theta = \frac{5}{13}$ and $\tan\theta = -\frac{5}{12}$, find $\sec\theta$.

29. If $\cos\theta = -\frac{3}{5}$ and $\csc\theta = -\frac{5}{4}$, find $\cot\theta$.

30. If $\tan\theta = \frac{8}{15}$ and $\sec\theta = -\frac{17}{15}$, find $\csc\theta$.

31. If $\tan\theta = -\sqrt{3}$ and $\sec\theta = -2$, find $\csc\theta$.

32. If $\cot\theta = -1$ and $\csc\theta = \sqrt{2}$, find $\sec\theta$.

33. If $\tan\theta = 1$ and $\cos\theta = -\frac{1}{\sqrt{2}}$, find $\csc\theta$.

34. If $\sin\theta = \frac{3}{5}$ and $\cos\theta < 0$, find $\cot\theta$.

35. If $\csc\theta = -\frac{13}{12}$ and $\sec\theta > 0$, find $\tan\theta$.

36. If $\sec\theta = \sqrt{2}$ and $\tan\theta > 0$, find $\sin\theta$.

37. If $\cot\theta = \frac{15}{8}$ and $\sin\theta < 0$, find $\sec\theta$.

38. If $\cot\theta = \sqrt{3}$ and $\sec\theta < 0$, find $\csc\theta$.

39. If θ is a positive acute angle and $\sin\theta = a$, which is an expression for $\cos\theta$ in terms of a?
(1) $\sqrt{a}$ (3) $\sqrt{1-a^2}$
(2) $\frac{1}{\sqrt{a}}$ (4) $\frac{1}{\sqrt{1-a^2}}$

40. If x is a positive acute angle and $\cos x = a$, an expression for $\tan x$ in terms of a is
(1) $\frac{1-a}{a}$ (3) $\frac{\sqrt{1-a^2}}{a}$
(2) $\sqrt{1-a^2}$ (4) $\frac{1}{1-a}$

41. If x is a positive acute angle and $\tan x = R$, then $\cos x$ is equal to
(1) $\frac{R}{\sqrt{R^2-1}}$ (3) $\frac{1}{\sqrt{R^2+1}}$
(2) $\sqrt{R^2-1}$ (4) $\frac{1}{\sqrt{R^2-1}}$

42. If $\sin A = k$, then the value of the expression $(\sin A)(\cos A)(\tan A)$ is equivalent to
(1) 1 (2) $\frac{1}{k}$ (3) k (4) k^2

43. If $\cos\theta = \frac{1}{c}$, then the value of the expression $(\sin\theta)(\cos\theta)(\cot\theta)$ is equivalent to
(1) c^2 (2) $\frac{1}{c^2}$ (3) c (4) $\frac{1}{c}$

6.4 RADIAN MEASURE

Angle Measure

In addition to the unit *degree*, angles are measured in a unit called *radian*.

When a central angle of a circle intercepts an arc equal in length to the radius of the circle, the measure of the angle is ONE RADIAN.

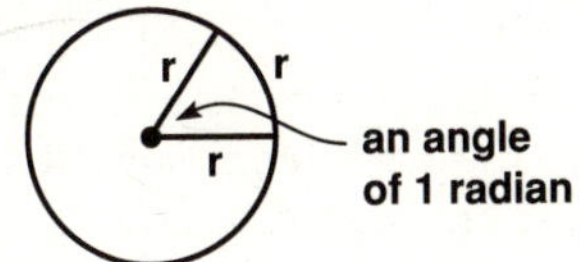

Since the measure of the circumference of a circle is 2π radii, the measure is 2π radians. Since there are 360 degrees in the measure:

$$2\pi \text{ radians} = 360°$$

$$1 \text{ radian} = \left(\frac{180}{\pi}\right)^{\circ} \approx 57°$$

To convert between radian and degree measure, multiply by the appropriate conversion factor.

From radians to degrees, multiply by:

$$\frac{180°}{\pi \text{ radians}}$$

Example: Express in degrees the measure of an angle of $\frac{5\pi}{12}$ radians.

$$\frac{5\pi}{12} \text{ radians} \times \frac{180°}{\pi \text{ radians}} = 75°$$

(with 12 and 180° cancelled to 1 and 15, and π radians cancelled)

From degrees to radians, multiply by:

$$\frac{\pi \text{ radians}}{180°}$$

Example: Express in radians the measure of an angle of 100°.

$$100° \times \frac{\pi \text{ radians}}{180°} = \frac{5\pi}{9} \text{ radians}$$

(with 100° and 180° cancelled to 5 and 9)

In angle measure, it is customary to omit the word "radian."

Example: sin $\frac{\pi}{2}$ means the sine of an angle whose measure is $\frac{\pi}{2}$ radians. When using degrees, the symbol should be included, as in sin 90°.

EXERCISES

In 1–9, express in degrees the angle whose radian measure is given.

1. $\frac{4\pi}{3}$
2. $\frac{3\pi}{4}$
3. $\frac{2\pi}{5}$
4. $\frac{5\pi}{6}$
5. $\frac{5\pi}{9}$
6. $\frac{7\pi}{10}$
7. $\frac{7\pi}{12}$
8. 3π
9. 4π

10. Expressed in degrees, $\frac{8\pi}{3}$ is equivalent to
(1) 240° (2) 300° (3) 420° (4) 480°

In 11–19, express in radians the angle whose degree measure is given.

11. 15°
12. 60°
13. 105°
14. 120°
15. 160°
16. 240°
17. 300°
18. 390°
19. 540°

Arc Measure

In a circle of radius r, the length s of an arc is related to the radian measure of a central angle, θ, and the length of the radius.

The arc length is in the same unit as the radius.

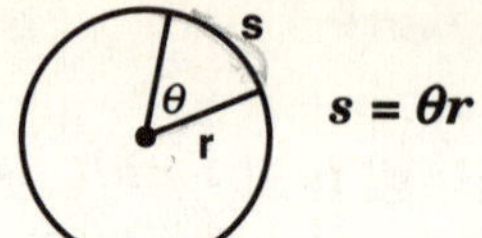

Examples

1. Find the length of the arc that subtends an angle of 2 radians in a circle of radius 5 cm.

   Solution: Since the angle measure is in radians, substitute directly into the formula for arc length.

   $$s = \theta r$$
   $$= 2(5)$$
   $$= 10 \text{ cm}$$

2. To the nearest tenth of a cm, find the length of the arc that subtends an angle of 2 degrees in a circle of radius 5 cm.

   Solution: Convert the angle measure from degrees to radians before substituting into the formula for arc length.

   $$2° \times \frac{\pi \text{ radians}}{180°} = \frac{\pi}{90} \text{ radians}$$

   $$s = \theta r = \frac{\pi}{90}(5) = \frac{\pi}{18} \text{ cm} \approx 0.2 \text{ cm}$$

EXERCISES

1. In a circle of radius 8 inches, find the length of the arc intercepted by a central angle of 1.5 radians.

2. In a circle with radius 3 centimeters, find the length of the arc intercepted by a central angle of 4 radians.

3. In a circle with radius 5 inches, find the length of an arc intercepted by a central angle of 45°.

4. A circle has a radius of 6 centimeters. What is the number of radians in a central angle that has an arc of length 12 centimeters?

   (1) $\frac{1}{2}$ (2) 2 (3) 18 (4) 72

5. In circle O, the length of radius $\overline{OB}$ is 5 centimeters and the length of $\widehat{AB}$ is 5 centimeters. The measure of $\angle AOB$ is

   (1) 1 radian (2) π radians (3) greater than 60° (4) 60°

6. In a circle, a central angle containing 1.5 radians intercepts an arc whose measure is 18 centimeters. The length of the radius is

   (1) 6 cm (2) 12 cm (3) 24 cm (4) 27 cm

7. In circle O, a central angle of 2 radians intercepts an arc of 28 meters. Find the length of the radius.

8. In a circle, a central angle of 30° intercepts an arc of 10 cm. Find the length of the radius.

6.5 DETERMINING VALUES OF THE TRIGONOMETRIC FUNCTIONS

Special Angles: 30°, 45°, 60°

The values of the trigonometric functions of these angles may be obtained from right triangles.

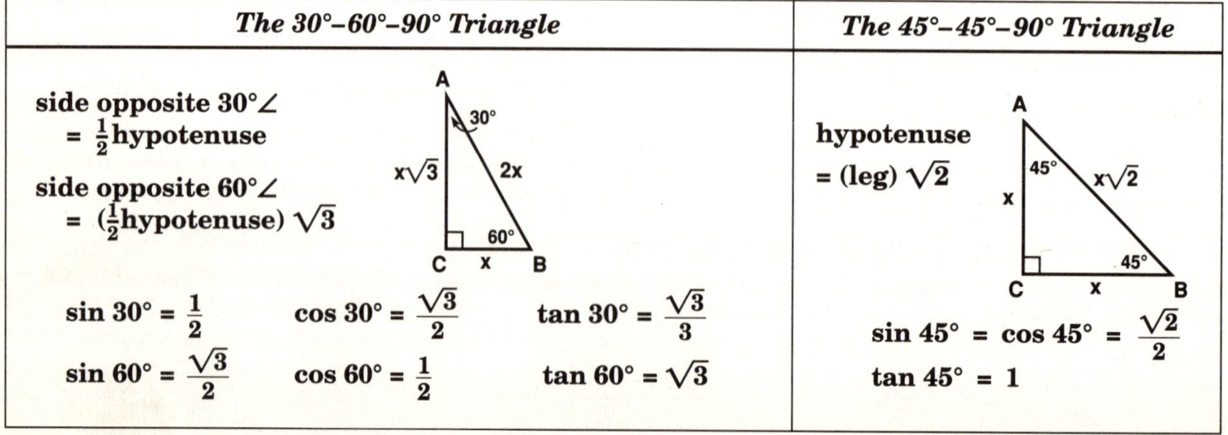

The 30°–60°–90° Triangle	*The 45°–45°–90° Triangle*
side opposite 30°∠ $= \frac{1}{2}$hypotenuse side opposite 60°∠ $= (\frac{1}{2}\text{hypotenuse})\sqrt{3}$ $\sin 30° = \frac{1}{2}$ $\cos 30° = \frac{\sqrt{3}}{2}$ $\tan 30° = \frac{\sqrt{3}}{3}$ $\sin 60° = \frac{\sqrt{3}}{2}$ $\cos 60° = \frac{1}{2}$ $\tan 60° = \sqrt{3}$	hypotenuse $= (\text{leg})\sqrt{2}$ $\sin 45° = \cos 45° = \frac{\sqrt{2}}{2}$ $\tan 45° = 1$

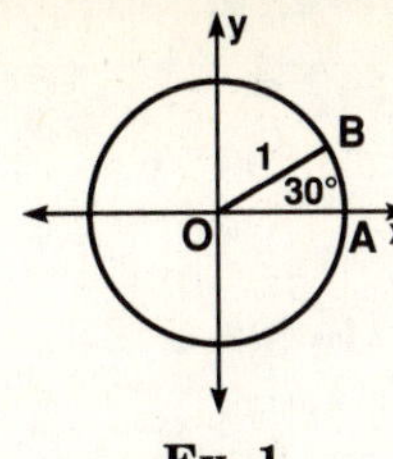

Ex. 1

1. The center of circle O is at the origin, radius $OB = 1$, and $m\angle AOB = 30°$. What are the coordinates of point B?

   (1) $\left(\frac{1}{2}, \frac{\sqrt{3}}{2}\right)$ (3) $\left(\frac{\sqrt{3}}{2}, \frac{1}{2}\right)$

   (2) $\left(\frac{\sqrt{2}}{2}, \frac{\sqrt{2}}{2}\right)$ (4) $(1, 1)$

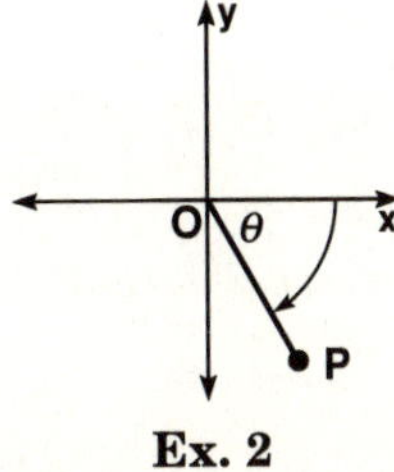

Ex. 2

2. θ is an angle in the fourth quadrant that is generated clockwise. $\overline{OP}$ is drawn and P has coordinates $(1, -\sqrt{3})$. What is the measure of angle θ?

   (1) 30° (2) −30° (3) 60° (4) −60°

3. What is the image of (1, 0) after a counterclockwise rotation of 60°?

   (1) $\left(\frac{1}{2}, \frac{\sqrt{3}}{2}\right)$ (3) $\left(\frac{1}{2}, -\frac{\sqrt{3}}{2}\right)$

   (2) $\left(\frac{\sqrt{3}}{2}, \frac{1}{2}\right)$ (4) $\left(-\frac{\sqrt{3}}{2}, -\frac{1}{2}\right)$

4. What is the image of (1, 0) after a clockwise rotation of 30°?

   (1) $\left(-\frac{1}{2}, \frac{\sqrt{3}}{2}\right)$ (3) $\left(-\frac{\sqrt{3}}{2}, \frac{1}{2}\right)$

   (2) $\left(\frac{1}{2}, -\frac{\sqrt{3}}{2}\right)$ (4) $\left(\frac{\sqrt{3}}{2}, -\frac{1}{2}\right)$

5. Find the numerical value of the expression $\sin 30° + \cos 60°$.

6. The expression $(\cos 60° \cos 30° + \sin 60° \sin 30°)$ is equal to

   (1) 1 (2) $\frac{1}{2}$ (3) $\frac{\sqrt{3}}{2}$ (4) 0

7. If $f(x) = 2 \cos x$, find $f\left(\frac{\pi}{3}\right)$.

8. If $f(x) = 3 \cos \frac{x}{3}$, find $f(\pi)$.

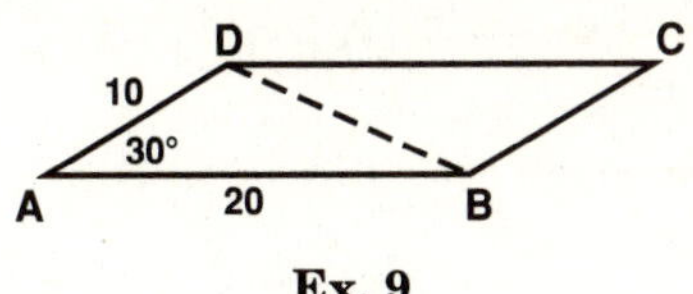

Ex. 9

9. $ABCD$ is a parallelogram with $AB = 20$ cm, $AD = 10$ cm, and $m\angle A = 30°$. Find the area of parallelogram $ABCD$.

10. The lengths of two sides of a triangle are each 10 in., and they include an angle whose measure is 120°. Find the length of the third side of the triangle.

11. The value of $\sin \frac{\pi}{6} + \tan \frac{\pi}{4}$ is

    (1) $\frac{3}{2}$ (3) $\frac{1+\sqrt{2}}{2}$

    (2) $\frac{\sqrt{3}+2}{2}$ (4) $\frac{\sqrt{3}+\sqrt{2}}{2}$

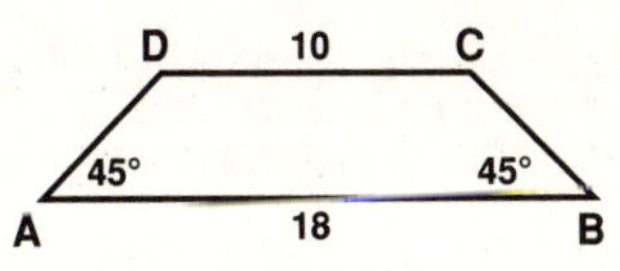

Ex. 12

12. In isosceles trapezoid $ABCD$, base $AB = 18$ cm, base $CD = 10$ cm, and the measure of each base angle A and B is 45°. Find the area of $ABCD$.

13. In an isosceles trapezoid, the measure of each of two base angles is 45°, and the length of an altitude is 6 cm. Find the length of a leg.

14. The midpoints of the sides of a square are joined in consecutive order to form another square. If the length of a side of the outer square is 6 units, find the length of a diagonal of the inner square.

15. In a right triangle, the measure of one of the angles is 30°. If the length of the hypotenuse is 20 ft., find the length of the altitude to the hypotenuse.

Quadrantal Angles: 0°, 90°, 180°, 270°

The values of the trigonometric functions of these angles may be obtained from a unit circle.

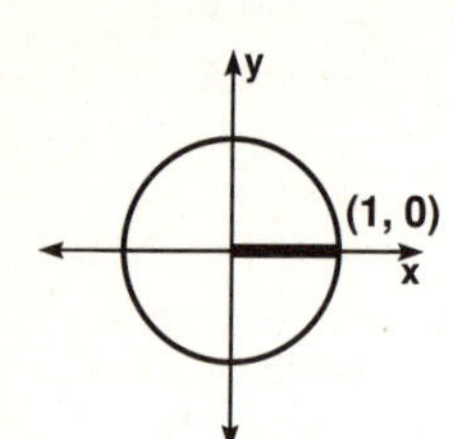

For 0°, use (1, 0).

$x = 1, y = 0, r = 1$

$\sin 0° = \frac{y}{r} = \frac{0}{1} = 0$

$\cos 0° = \frac{x}{r} = \frac{1}{1} = 1$

$\tan 0° = \frac{y}{x} = \frac{0}{1} = 0$

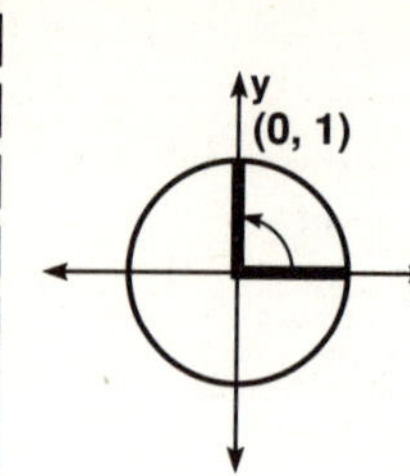

For 90°, use (0, 1).

$x = 0, y = 1, r = 1$

$\sin 90° = \frac{y}{r} = \frac{1}{1} = 1$

$\cos 90° = \frac{x}{r} = \frac{0}{1} = 0$

$\tan 90° = \frac{y}{x} = \frac{1}{0}$ not defined

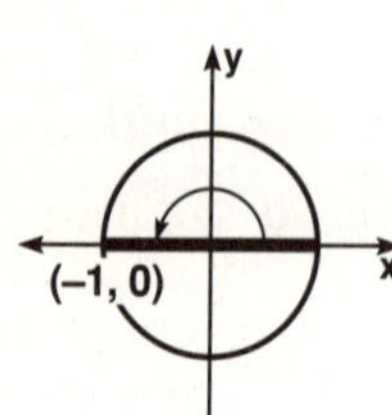

For 180°, use (–1, 0).

$x = -1, y = 0, r = 1$

$\sin 180° = \frac{y}{r} = \frac{0}{1} = 0$

$\cos 180° = \frac{x}{r} = \frac{-1}{1} = -1$

$\tan 180° = \frac{y}{x} = \frac{0}{-1} = 0$

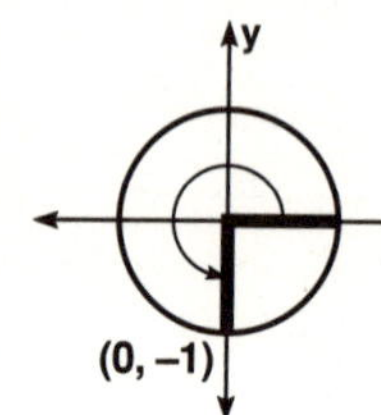

For 270°, use (0, –1).

$x = 0, y = -1, r = 1$

$\sin 270° = \frac{y}{r} = \frac{-1}{1} = -1$

$\cos 270° = \frac{x}{r} = \frac{0}{1} = 0$

$\tan 270° = \frac{y}{x} = \frac{-1}{0}$ not defined

Note: **360° has the same function values as 0°.**

EXERCISES

1. Which is equal in value to sin 180°?
   (1) tan 45° (2) cos 90° (3) cos 0° (4) tan 90°

In 2–5, find the numerical value of the expression.

2. sin 90° + cos 90°
3. cos 90° + sin 180°
4. 2 sin 270° – cos 90°
5. $(\sin 90°)^2$ or $\sin^2 90°$
6. If $f(x) = \cos 2x$, find $f(\frac{\pi}{2})$.
7. If a function f is defined by $f(x) = \sin\left(\frac{x}{2}\right)$, find the numerical value of $f(\pi)$.
8. If $f(x) = 3 \cos x$, find the numerical value of $f(\pi)$.
9. If $f(x) = \sin 2x$, find $f(\frac{\pi}{4})$.
10. If $f(x) = \sin x + \cos 2x$, then $f(\pi)$ equals
    (1) 1 (2) 2 (3) 0 (4) –1
11. If $f(x) = 2 \cos x + \sin 2x$, the numerical value of $f(\frac{\pi}{2})$ is
    (1) –1 (2) 2 (3) 0 (4) –2
12. If $f(x) = \cos x + \tan \frac{x}{3}$, then $f(\pi)$ is
    (1) $\frac{\sqrt{3}+3}{3}$ (2) $\frac{\sqrt{3}-3}{3}$ (3) $\sqrt{3} + 1$ (4) $\sqrt{3} - 1$
13. Find the value of $\sin \frac{\pi}{2} - \cos \frac{3\pi}{2}$.
14. Find the value of $\sin\left(\frac{\pi}{6} + \frac{\pi}{3}\right)$.
15. What is the value of $\sin \frac{\pi}{2} \cos 2\pi$?
    (1) 1 (2) $\frac{1}{2}$ (3) 0 (4) –1
16. For which value of θ is the expression $\frac{1}{1 - \sin\theta}$ undefined?
    (1) 0 (2) $\frac{\pi}{2}$ (3) π (4) $\frac{3\pi}{2}$
17. The value of $\sin^2 \frac{3\pi}{2} + \cos^2 \frac{3\pi}{2}$ is
    (1) 1 (2) –1 (3) 0 (4) undefined
18. The expression $1 - 2\sin^2 30°$ has the same value as
    (1) sin 60° (2) cos 60° (3) cos 90° (4) sin 90°
19. The multiplicative inverse of $\sin^2 90° + \cos^2 90°$ is
    (1) 1 (2) 0 (3) –1 (4) undefined
20. In $\triangle ABC$, angle A is acute and $\sin A = \cos B$. The value of $\sin C$ is
    (1) 1 (2) $\frac{1}{2}$ (3) $\frac{\sqrt{2}}{2}$ (4) $\frac{\sqrt{3}}{2}$

Reference Angles

Since the trigonometric functions are defined in terms of x, y, and r, the functions of an angle of any measure can be related to the functions of a corresponding acute angle, called its REFERENCE ANGLE.

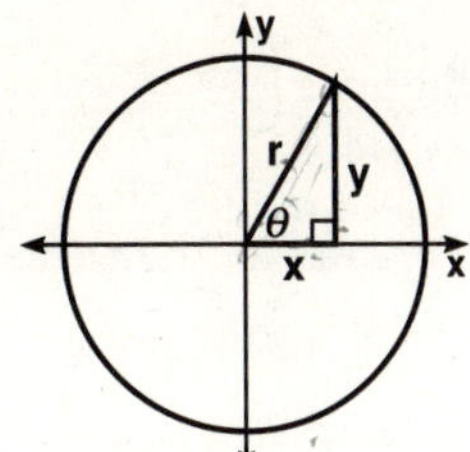

If θ is in Q I, θ is its own reference angle.

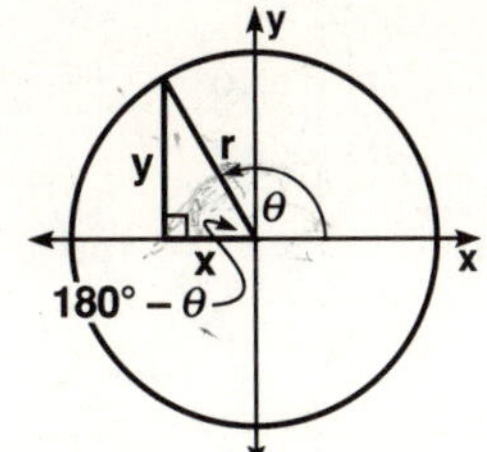

If θ is in Q II, use $180° - \theta$ as the reference angle.

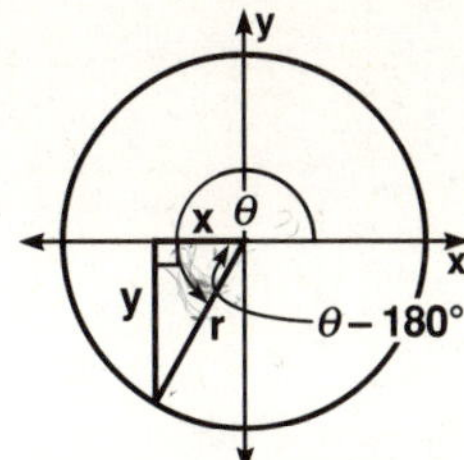

If θ is in Q III, use $\theta - 180°$ as the reference angle.

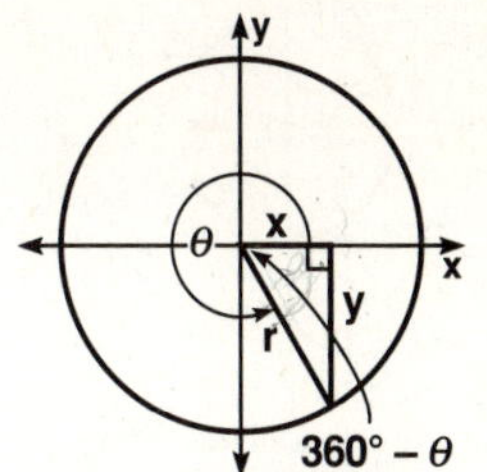

If θ is in Q IV, use $360° - \theta$ as the reference angle.

Once the reference angle has been determined, note the sign associated with the particular function in the given quadrant.

Examples:

sin 120°	sin 240°	sin 300°
In Q II, $\sin\theta > 0$.	In Q III, $\sin\theta < 0$.	In Q IV, $\sin\theta < 0$.
sin 120°	sin 240°	sin 300°
= sin (180 – 120)°	= –sin (240 – 180)°	= –sin (360 – 300)°
= sin 60°	= –sin 60°	= –sin 60°

Summary of Reference Angles in the Quadrants

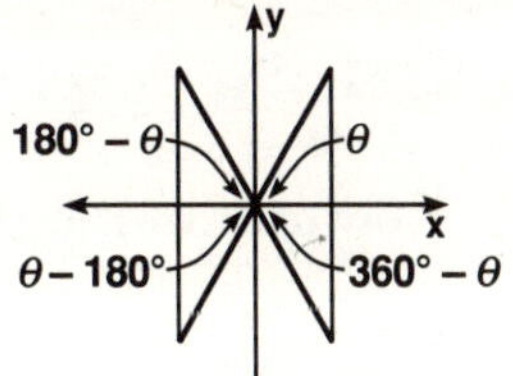

To remember the locations of the reference angles, think of a "bow tie" design, achieved by reflecting the acute angle of Quadrant I.

For Q II: reflect the Q I angle in the y-axis.

For Q III: reflect the Q I angle in the origin.

For Q IV: reflect the Q I angle in the x-axis.

Note that the reference angle is always contained in the right triangle whose horizontal leg is on the x-axis.

Summary of Function Equivalents in the Quadrants

In Quadrant II	In Quadrant III	In Quadrant IV
$\sin\theta = \sin(180° - \theta)$	$\sin\theta = -\sin(\theta - 180°)$	$\sin\theta = -\sin(360° - \theta)$
$\cos\theta = -\cos(180° - \theta)$	$\cos\theta = -\cos(\theta - 180°)$	$\cos\theta = \cos(360° - \theta)$
$\tan\theta = -\tan(180° - \theta)$	$\tan\theta = \tan(\theta - 180°)$	$\tan\theta = -\tan(360° - \theta)$

EXERCISES

In 1–14, rewrite the expression as a function of a positive acute angle.

1. cos 128°

2. sin 230°

3. cot 212°

4. cos 310°

5. tan 115°

6. cot 320°

7. sin 140°

8. $\sin\frac{2\pi}{3}$

9. $\cos\frac{3\pi}{4}$

10. $\tan\frac{7\pi}{6}$

11. $\cot\frac{5\pi}{4}$

12. $\sin\frac{7\pi}{4}$

13. $\cos\frac{4\pi}{5}$

14. $\tan\frac{6\pi}{5}$

In 15–28, find the numerical value of the expression.

15. tan 120°

16. sin 210°

17. tan 315°

18. cos 330°

19. cot 150°

20. sin 300°

21. cot 240°

22. $\sin \frac{3\pi}{4}$

23. $\cot \frac{5\pi}{4}$

24. $\cos \frac{2\pi}{3}$

25. $\sin \frac{7\pi}{4}$

26. $\tan \frac{4\pi}{3}$

27. $\cos \frac{3\pi}{2}$

28. $\sin \frac{5\pi}{3}$

29. Which expression is equivalent to sin 200°?
(1) –sin 20° **(2)** cos 20° **(3)** cos 70° **(4)** –sin 70°

30. The value of cos 305° is
(1) 0.5736 **(2)** 0.8192 **(3)** –0.8192 **(4)** –0.5736

31. If $\angle x$ is an acute angle and $\sin x = \frac{3}{5}$, find the value of $\sin(180° - x)$.

32. If $\angle x$ is an acute angle and $\cos x = t$, express $\cos(180° - x)$ in terms of t.

33. If x is a positive acute angle, then $\tan(180° - x)$ is equal to
(1) $-\tan x$ **(2)** $-\cot x$ **(3)** $\tan x$ **(4)** $\cot x$

34. If $\cos x = \frac{12}{13}$ and x is an acute angle, the value of $\cos(180° - x)$ is
(1) $\frac{5}{13}$ **(2)** $-\frac{5}{13}$ **(3)** $\frac{12}{13}$ **(4)** $-\frac{12}{13}$

35. If x is a positive acute angle, then express $\tan(180° + x)$ as a function of x.

36. The expression $\sin(180° + x)$ is equivalent to
(1) $\sin x$ **(2)** $-\sin x$ **(3)** $\cos x$ **(4)** $-\cos x$

37. The expression $\sin(2\pi - x)$ is equal to
(1) $\sin x$ **(2)** $-\sin x$ **(3)** $\cos x$ **(4)** $-\cos x$

Coterminal Angles

Two angles that have the same terminal side are COTERMINAL ANGLES.
The values of the trigonometric functions of two coterminal angles are the same.

For an angle whose measure is greater than 360°, work with a coterminal angle of measure between 0° and 360°.

Examples: $\sin 420° = \sin(420 - 360)°$
$= \sin 60°$ In Q I, $\sin\theta > 0$.
$= \frac{\sqrt{3}}{2}$

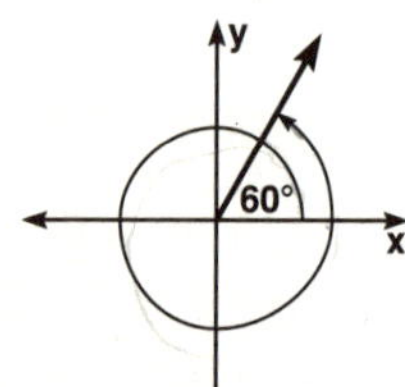

$\cos\frac{8\pi}{3} = \cos\left(\frac{8\pi}{3} - 2\pi\right)$
$= \cos\frac{2\pi}{3}$
$= -\cos\left(\pi - \frac{2\pi}{3}\right)$ In Q II, reference $\angle$ is $\pi - \theta$ and $\cos\theta < 0$.
$= -\cos\frac{\pi}{3}$
$= -\frac{1}{2}$

For an angle whose measure is negative, work with a coterminal angle of positive measure.

Example: $\sin(-60°) = \sin 300°$ coterminal $\angle$
$= -\sin(360 - 300)°$ In Q IV, reference $\angle$ is $360° - \theta$ and $\sin\theta < 0$.
$= -\sin 60°$
$= -\frac{\sqrt{3}}{2}$

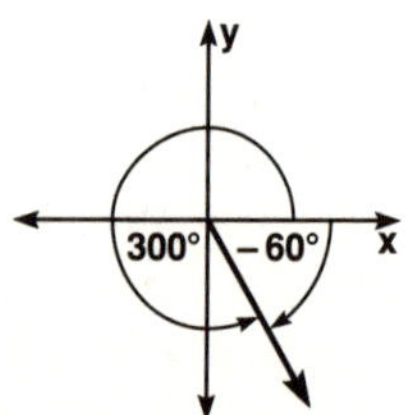

EXERCISES

In 1–24, rewrite the expression using a function of a positive acute angle.

1. sin 430°
2. cos 520°
3. tan 575°
4. cos 680°
5. tan 780°
6. cos $\frac{3\pi}{4}$
7. tan $\frac{4\pi}{5}$
8. cot $\frac{3\pi}{5}$
9. sin $\frac{6\pi}{5}$
10. tan $\frac{11\pi}{9}$
11. sin (–20°)
12. cos (–40°)
13. sin (–70°)
14. tan (–150°)
15. sin (–170°)
16. cos (–200°)
17. sin (–210°)
18. cos (–220°)
19. sin (–275°)
20. cos (–310°)
21. tan (–350°)
22. sin $\left(-\frac{3\pi}{4}\right)$
23. cos $\left(-\frac{5\pi}{6}\right)$
24. tan $\left(-\frac{7\pi}{3}\right)$

25. Which expression is equivalent to sin 490°?
(1) sin 50°
(2) –sin 50°
(3) sin 40°
(4) –sin 40°

26. The expression cos 750° is equivalent to
(1) cos 30°
(2) –cos 30°
(3) cos 60°
(4) –cos 60°

27. The expression tan (–230°) is equivalent to
(1) tan 40°
(2) –tan 40°
(3) tan 50°
(4) –tan 50°

28. Which expression is equivalent to sin (–120°)?
(1) sin 60° (3) cos 30°
(2) –sin 60° (4) –sin 30°

In 29–48, find the numerical value of the expression.

29. sin 480°
30. cos 660°
31. cot 570°
32. sin 750°
33. cos $\frac{5\pi}{2}$
34. tan $\frac{13\pi}{4}$
35. cot $\frac{24\pi}{9}$
36. tan (–135°)
37. sin (–270°)
38. sin (–330°)
39. cos (–90°)
40. sin (–150°)
41. tan (–210°)
42. cos (–330°)
43. sin (–45°)
44. sin $\left(-\frac{3\pi}{4}\right)$
45. cos $\left(-\frac{\pi}{3}\right)$
46. sin $\left(-\frac{3\pi}{2}\right)$
47. tan $\left(-\frac{5\pi}{3}\right)$
48. cos $\left(-\frac{7\pi}{4}\right)$

49. Which expression is not equal to sin 300°?
(1) sin (–60°)
(2) –sin 60°
(3) –cos 30°
(4) cos (–30°)

50. Which expression is not equal to cos 150°?
(1) –cos 30°
(2) –sin 60°
(3) cos (–210°)
(4) –cos 210°

51. Which rotation about the origin is equivalent to $R_{-200°}$?
(1) $R_{200°}$
(2) $R_{-160°}$
(3) $R_{160°}$
(4) $R_{560°}$

Basic Graphs

Since the graph of each trigonometric function is an endless repetition of a basic curve, the functions are called PERIODIC FUNCTIONS.

The PERIOD of the function is the length of the interval needed to produce one basic curve.

The AMPLITUDE of the function is one-half the difference of the maximum and minimum *y*-values.

The Basic Sine Curve

Table of Values for y = sin x

x	0	$\frac{\pi}{6}$	$\frac{\pi}{3}$	$\frac{\pi}{2}$	$\frac{2\pi}{3}$	$\frac{5\pi}{6}$	π	$\frac{7\pi}{6}$	$\frac{4\pi}{3}$	$\frac{3\pi}{2}$	$\frac{5\pi}{3}$	$\frac{11\pi}{6}$	2π
	0°	30°	60°	90°	120°	150°	180°	210°	240°	270°	300°	330°	360°
y	0	0.5	0.87	1	0.87	0.5	0	−0.5	−0.87	−1	−0.87	−0.5	0

This table gives values for one wave of the basic sine curve. It takes 2π radians, or 360°, to draw one full sine wave.

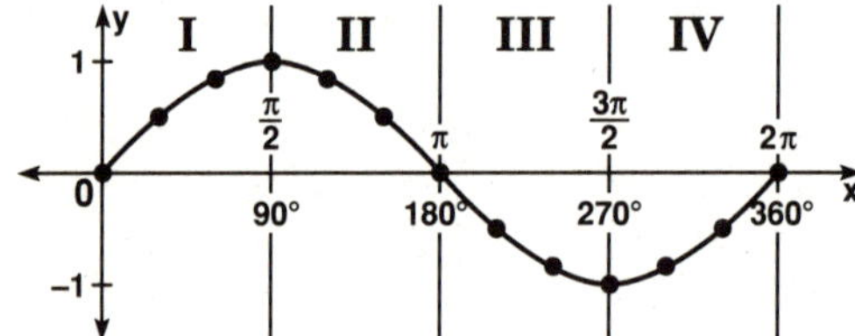

$y = \sin x$
period $= 2\pi$, or $360°$
amplitude $= 1$

The Basic Cosine Curve

Table of Values for y = cos x

x	0	$\frac{\pi}{6}$	$\frac{\pi}{3}$	$\frac{\pi}{2}$	$\frac{2\pi}{3}$	$\frac{5\pi}{6}$	π	$\frac{7\pi}{6}$	$\frac{4\pi}{3}$	$\frac{3\pi}{2}$	$\frac{5\pi}{3}$	$\frac{11\pi}{6}$	2π
	0°	30°	60°	90°	120°	150°	180°	210°	240°	270°	300°	330°	360°
y	1	0.87	0.5	0	−0.5	−0.87	−1	−0.87	−0.5	0	0.5	0.87	1

This table gives values for one wave of the basic cosine curve. It takes 2π radians, or 360°, to draw one full cosine wave.

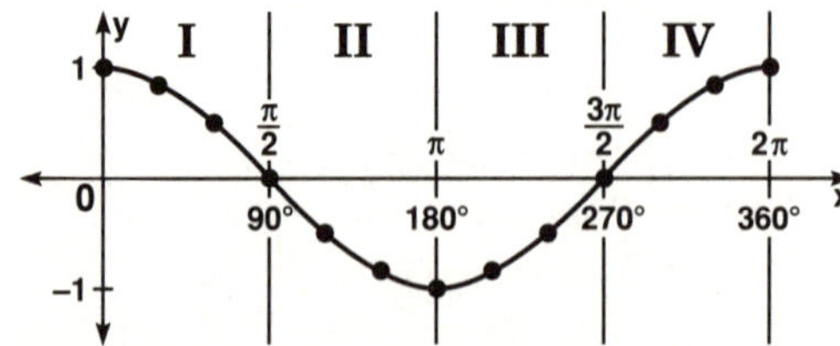

$y = \cos x$
period $= 2\pi$, or $360°$
amplitude $= 1$

The Basic Tangent Curve

Table of Values for y = tan x

x	0	$\frac{\pi}{6}$	$\frac{\pi}{4}$	$\frac{\pi}{3}$	$\frac{\pi}{2}$	$\frac{2\pi}{3}$	$\frac{5\pi}{6}$	$\frac{3\pi}{4}$	π	$\frac{7\pi}{6}$	$\frac{5\pi}{4}$	$\frac{4\pi}{3}$	$\frac{3\pi}{2}$	$\frac{5\pi}{3}$	$\frac{7\pi}{4}$	$\frac{11\pi}{6}$	2π
	0°	30°	45°	60°	90°	120°	150°	135°	180°	210°	225°	240°	270°	300°	315°	330°	360°
y	0	0.58	1	1.73	±∞*	−1.73	−0.58	−1	0	0.58	1	1.73	±∞*	−1.73	−1	−0.58	0

*** These values are undefined.**
∞ means "increases without limit."

The vertical lines at these values are asymptotes to the graph.

This table gives values for two periods of the basic tangent curve. It takes π radians, or 180°, to draw one full tangent curve.

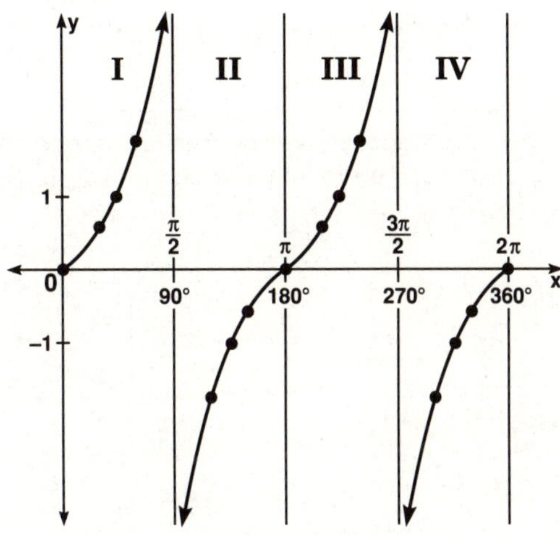

$y = \tan x$
period $= \pi$, or 180°
amplitude is undefined

EXERCISES

1. As angle x increases from 90° to 180°, the value of $\sin x$
(1) increases from −1 to 0
(2) increases from 0 to 1
(3) decreases from 0 to −1
(4) decreases from 1 to 0

2. As angle x increases from 180° to 270°, the value of $\cos x$ will
(1) increase from 0 to 1
(2) increase from −1 to 0
(3) decrease from 0 to −1
(4) decrease from 1 to 0

3. As angle θ increases from 0 to π, the value of $\cos\theta$ will
(1) decrease, only
(2) increase, only
(3) decrease, then increase
(4) increase, then decrease

4. As θ increases from $\frac{\pi}{2}$ to $\frac{3\pi}{2}$, the value of $\cos\theta$
(1) decreases, only
(2) increases, only
(3) decreases and then increases
(4) increases and then decreases

5. As θ increases from $\frac{\pi}{2}$ to π, which statement is true?
(1) $\sin\theta$ decreases from 0 to −1
(2) $\cos\theta$ decreases from 0 to −1
(3) $\cos\theta$ increases from −1 to 0
(4) $\sin\theta$ increases from −1 to 0

6. As θ increases from π to $\frac{3\pi}{2}$, which statement is true?
(1) $\sin\theta$ increases from −1 to 0
(2) $\sin\theta$ decreases from 1 to 0
(3) $\cos\theta$ decreases from 0 to −1
(4) $\cos\theta$ increases from −1 to 0

7. Which is not an element in the domain of $y = \tan x$?

(1) π (2) 2π (3) 0 (4) $\frac{\pi}{2}$

8. Which value is not in the domain of the function defined by $y = 2 \tan x$?

(1) π (2) $\frac{\pi}{2}$ (3) $\frac{\pi}{3}$ (4) $\frac{2\pi}{3}$

9. Which is not an element in the range of the function $y = \cos x$?

(1) 1 (2) 2 (3) $\frac{1}{2}$ (4) $-\frac{1}{2}$

10. Which number is not an element of the range of the function defined by $y = \sin x$?

(1) 1 (2) 2 (3) 0 (4) $\frac{1}{2}$

Amplitude, Period, and Frequency

The amplitude and period of the basic curves are changed by constant factors in the equation.

A constant multiplier of the function affects the amplitude.

A constant multiplier of the angle affects the period.

The number of cycles of the curve within 2π radians is called the FREQUENCY.

$$y = a \sin bx$$
$$\text{amplitude} = |a|$$
$$\text{period} = \frac{2\pi}{|b|}$$
$$\text{frequency} = |b|$$

Examples: In these sine curves, the amplitude is changed from 1, but the period remains at 2π radians, or 360°. Only one cycle of the curve appears in 2π radians.

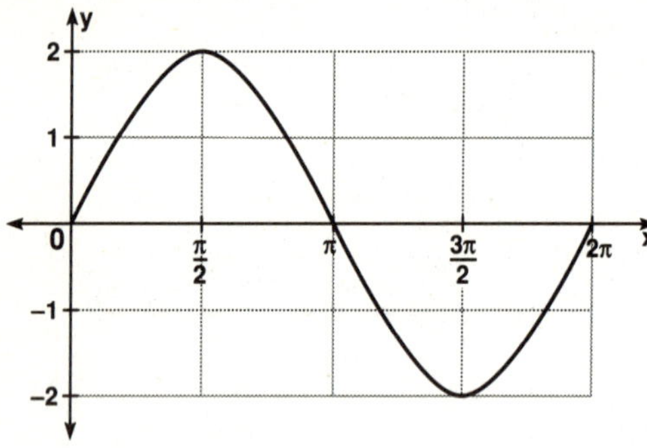

$y = 2 \sin x$
amplitude = 2
period = 2π, or 360°
frequency = 1

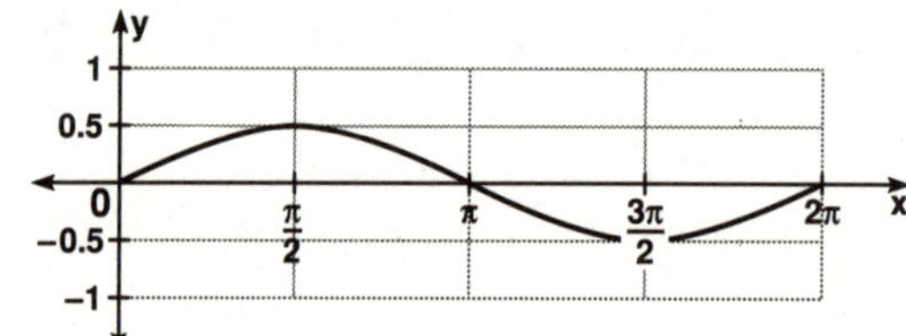

$y = \frac{1}{2} \sin x$
amplitude = $\frac{1}{2}$
period = 2π, or 360°
frequency = 1

Examples: In these sine curves, the amplitude remains at 1, but the period is changed from 2π, or 360°. There no longer is a single cycle of these curves in 2π radians.

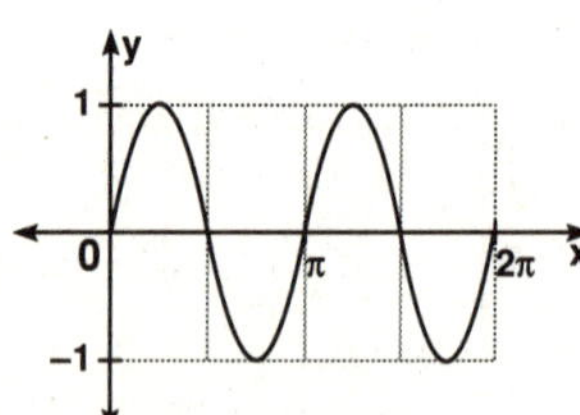

$y = \sin 2x$
amplitude = 1
period = $\frac{2\pi}{2} = \pi$, or 180°
frequency = 2

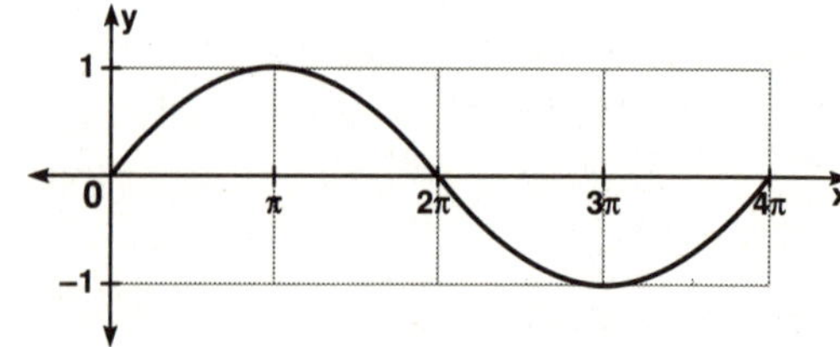

$y = \sin \frac{1}{2}x$
amplitude = 1
period = $\frac{2\pi}{\frac{1}{2}} = 4\pi$, or 720°
frequency = $\frac{1}{2}$

EXERCISES

1. The amplitude of $y = 3 \sin 2x$ is
(1) π (2) 2 (3) 3 (4) 4π

2. What is the amplitude of the function $y = \frac{2}{3} \sin 3x$?
(1) 1 (2) $\frac{2}{3}$ (3) 3 (4) $\frac{2\pi}{3}$

3. The amplitude of the graph of $y = 3 \cos 2x$ is
(1) π (2) 2 (3) 3 (4) 4π

4. What is the amplitude of the graph of the equation $y = 2 \cos 3x$?
(1) $\frac{2\pi}{3}$ (2) 2 (3) 3 (4) 6π

5. What is the range of the function $y = 3 \sin x$?
(1) $y \geq 0$ (3) $y \leq 3$
(2) $-1 \leq y \leq 1$ (4) $-3 \leq y \leq 3$

6. Which is the maximum value of the function $y = 2 \sin 3x$?
(1) 1 (2) 2 (3) 3 (4) 4

7. The maximum value of $f(\theta) = 2 \sin 3\theta$ is
(1) 1 (2) 2 (3) 3 (4) π

8. What is the maximum value of y for the equation $y = 1 + 3 \sin x$?
(1) 1 (2) 2 (3) 3 (4) 4

9. What is the maximum value of y for the equation $y = 3 - \sin x$?
(1) 1 (2) 2 (3) 3 (4) 4

10. What is the minimum value of $f(\theta)$ in the equation $f(\theta) = 3 \sin 4\theta$?
(1) -1 (2) -2 (3) -3 (4) -4

In 11–16, find the amplitude of the graph of the given function.

11. $y = \sin 2x$
12. $y = \frac{1}{2} \sin 2x$
13. $y = 3 \sin \frac{1}{2}x$
14. $y = \cos x$
15. $y = \cos 2x$
16. $y = 6 \cos 3x$

17. What is the period of $y = \sin 2x$?
(1) 4π (2) 2 (3) π (4) 4

18. What is the period of the graph whose equation is $y = 2 \sin 4x$?
(1) $\frac{4\pi}{3}$ (2) $\frac{\pi}{2}$ (3) 3 (4) 4

19. What is the period of $y = 3 \sin \frac{1}{2}x$?
(1) π (2) 2π (3) 3π (4) 4π

20. The period of the curve $y = \frac{1}{2} \cos 2x$ is
(1) $\frac{1}{2}$ (2) 2 (3) π (4) 4π

21. What is the period of the graph of the equation $y = 3 \cos 2x$?
(1) π (2) 2 (3) 3 (4) 2π

22. What is the period of $y = \tan x$?
(1) $\frac{\pi}{2}$ (2) π (3) 2π (4) $\pi + 2$

23. What is the period of the graph of the equation $y = 2 \tan 3x$?
(1) $\frac{2\pi}{3}$ (2) $\frac{\pi}{3}$ (3) π (4) $\frac{\pi}{2}$

24. What is the frequency of the graph of $y = \cos 2x$?

25. How many cycles of the graph of $y = 4 \sin 3x$ appear in 2π radians?

26. The graph of which equation has amplitude 2 and period π?
(1) $y = 2 \cos 2x$ (3) $y = 2 \sin x$
(2) $y = \frac{1}{2} \sin 2x$ (4) $y = 2 \cos \frac{1}{2}x$

27. The graph of which equation has amplitude 1 and period π?
(1) $y = \tan x$ (3) $y = \sin 2x$
(2) $y = \sin \frac{1}{2}x$ (4) $y = \cos x$

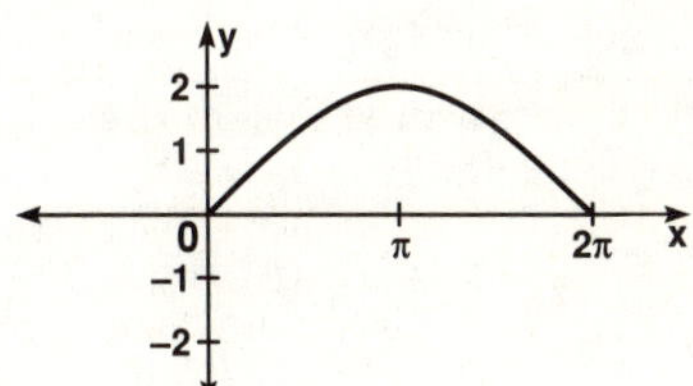

Ex. 28

28. Which is the equation of the graph shown?
(1) $y = 2 \sin \frac{1}{2}x$ (3) $y = 2 \cos \frac{1}{2}x$
(2) $y = \frac{1}{2} \sin 2x$ (4) $y = \frac{1}{2} \cos 2x$

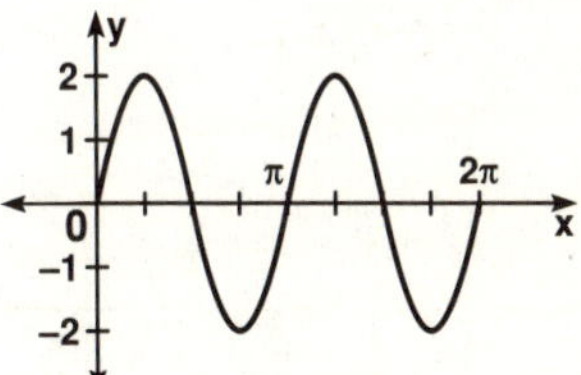

Ex. 29

29. Which is the equation of the function shown?
(1) $y = 2 \sin \frac{1}{2}x$ (3) $y = 2 \sin 2x$
(2) $y = \frac{1}{2} \cos 2x$ (4) $y = 2 \cos 2x$

Sketching a Graph

To sketch a graph of a trigonometric function:

1. **Know the basic trigonometric shapes.**

sine cosine tangent

2. **From the equation, determine the amplitude, period, and frequency.**
3. **Take convenient units on the y-axis to display the amplitude.**
4. **Take convenient units on the x-axis to display the period.**

Example: $y = 3 \sin 2x$ when $0 \le x \le 2\pi$

amplitude = 3

period = $\frac{2\pi}{2} = \pi$

frequency = 2

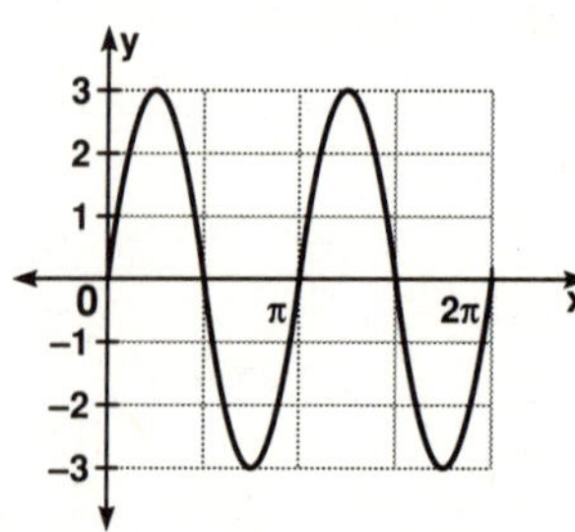

Example

a. On the same set of axes, sketch and label the graphs of $y = 2 \sin 2x$ and $y = \cos x$ for the values of x in the interval $-\pi \le x \le \pi$.

b. How many values of x in the interval $-\pi \le x \le \pi$ satisfy the equation $2 \sin 2x = \cos x$?

c. For which of the given values in the interval $-\pi \le x \le \pi$ does $2 \sin 2x - \cos x = 1$?

(1) $-\pi$ (2) $-\frac{\pi}{2}$ (3) 0 (4) $\frac{\pi}{2}$

Solution:

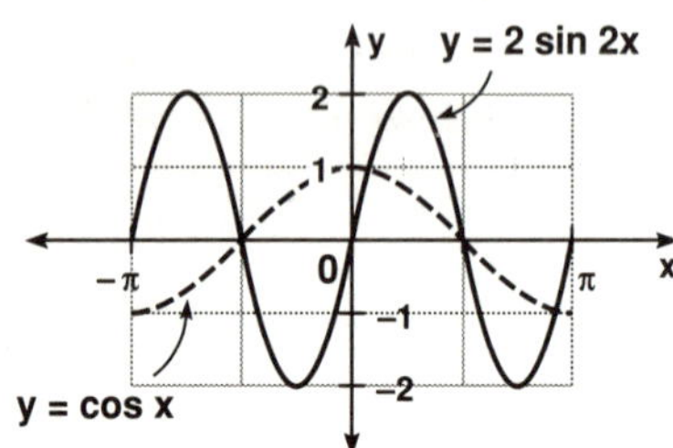

a. $y = 2 \sin 2x$

amplitude = 2, period = $\frac{2\pi}{2}$ or π

Thus, in the given interval between $-\pi$ and π, the frequency will be 2.

Draw one cycle of the sine curve with amplitude 2 between 0 and π.

To draw the second cycle of the curve between $-\pi$ and 0, note how it must be attached to the first cycle to form the repetitive sine pattern.

$y = \cos x$

amplitude = 1, period = 2π

Thus, in the given interval, the frequency will be 1.

Draw a half-cycle of the cosine curve between 0 and π.

To draw the second half-cycle between $-\pi$ and 0, note how it must be attached to form the cosine pattern.

b. The solutions to the equation $2 \sin 2x = \cos x$ occur at the intersection points of the graphs of $y = 2 \sin 2x$ and $y = \cos x$.

Answer: In the interval $-\pi \le x \le \pi$, there are four values of x that satisfy $2 \sin 2x = \cos x$.

c. Look for a point at which the distance between the y-values of the two graphs is 1.

Answer: **(1)**

EXERCISES

In 1–5, sketch the graph of the given function in the given interval.

1. $y = 2 \sin 3x$ $\quad 0 \le x \le 2\pi$

2. $y = 3 \sin 2x$ $\quad -\pi \le x \le \pi$

3. $y = 2 \cos \frac{1}{2}x$ $\quad 0 \le x \le 2\pi$

4. $y = \cos 2x$ $\quad -2\pi \le x \le 2\pi$

5. $y = \tan x$ $\quad -2\pi \le x \le 2\pi$

6. **a.** On the same set of axes, sketch and label the graphs of $y = 2 \cos \frac{1}{2}x$ and $y = -1$ for the values of x in the interval $0 \le x \le 2\pi$.

b. State the number of values of x in the interval $0 \le x \le 2\pi$ that satisfy the equation $2 \cos \frac{1}{2}x = -1$.

7. **a.** On the same set of axes, sketch the graphs of $y = \cos 2x$ and $y = \sin x$ for the values of x in the interval $0 \le x \le 2\pi$.

b. State the number of values of x in the interval $0 \le x \le 2\pi$ that satisfy the equation $\cos 2x = \sin x$.

8. **a.** On the same set of axes, sketch the graphs of $y = 3 \cos x$ and $y = \sin\left(\frac{x}{2}\right)$ for the values of x in the interval $0 \le x \le 2\pi$.

b. State the number of values of x in the interval $0 \le x \le 2\pi$ that satisfy the equation $\sin\left(\frac{x}{2}\right) = 3 \cos x$.

9. **a.** On the same set of axes, sketch and label the graphs of $y = 2 \sin x$ and $y = \cos 2x$ in the interval $0 \le x \le 2\pi$.

b. At $x = \frac{\pi}{2}$, the difference $2 \sin x - \cos 2x$ is

(1) 1 **(2)** 2 **(3)** 3 **(4)** 0

10. **a.** On the same set of axes, sketch and label the graphs of the equations $y = 2 \sin \frac{1}{2}x$ and $y = \cos 2x$ in the interval $0 \le x \le 2\pi$.

b. What is the value of x in the interval $0 \le x \le 2\pi$ for which $2 \sin \frac{1}{2}x - \cos 2x = 1$?

(1) 0 **(2)** $\frac{\pi}{2}$ **(3)** π **(4)** $\frac{3\pi}{2}$

11. **a.** On the same set of axes, sketch and label the graphs of the equations $y = 2 \cos x$ and $y = \sin \frac{1}{2}x$ for the values of x in the interval $0 \le x \le 2\pi$.

b. From the graph drawn in part **a**, determine the value of $(\sin \frac{1}{2}x - 2 \cos x)$ if $x = \pi$.

12. **a.** On the same set of axes, sketch and label the graphs of $y = \tan x$ and $y = 2 \cos x$ for the values of x in the interval $0 \le x \le 2\pi$.

b. State the number of values of x in the interval $0 \le x \le 2\pi$ that satisfy the equation $\tan x = 2 \cos x$.

13. **a.** On the same set of axes, sketch and label the graphs of $y = \cos \frac{1}{2}x$ and $y = \tan x$ for the values of x in the interval $0 \le x \le 2\pi$.

b. How many values of x in the interval $0 \le x \le 2\pi$ satisfy the equation $\cos \frac{1}{2}x = \tan x$?

14. **a.** On the same set of axes, sketch and label the graphs of $y = \cos x$ and $y = \frac{1}{2}\sin x$ in the interval $-\pi \le x \le \pi$.

b. From the graphs made in part **a**, state the number of values of x in the interval $-\pi \le x \le \pi$ that satisfy the equation $\cos x = \frac{1}{2}\sin x$.

15. **a.** On the same set of axes, sketch and label the graphs of $y = \sin \frac{1}{2}x$ and $y = 2 \cos x$ as x varies from $-\pi$ to π radians.

b. From the graphs made in part **a**, how many values of x in the interval $-\pi \le x \le \pi$ satisfy the equation $\sin \frac{1}{2}x = 2 \cos x$?

16. **a.** On the same set of axes, sketch and label the graphs of $y = \frac{1}{2}\cos x$ and $y = \sin 2x$ for the values of x in the interval $-\pi \le x \le \pi$.

b. From the graphs made in part **a**, determine the number of values of x in the interval $-\pi \le x \le \pi$ that satisfy the equation $\frac{1}{2}\cos x = \sin 2x$.

17. **a.** On the same set of axes, sketch and label the graphs of the equations $y = \sin x$ and $y = 2 \cos 2x$ for the values of x in the interval $-\pi \le x \le \pi$.

b. Using the graph drawn in part **a**, find the value of x in the interval $-\pi \le x \le \pi$ for which $\sin x - 2 \cos 2x = 3$.

18. **a.** On the same set of axes, sketch and label the graphs of the equations $y = 2 \sin x$ and $y = \cos 2x$ as x varies from $-\pi$ to π radians.

b. Using the graphs drawn in part **a**, determine the value of x in the interval $-\pi \le x \le \pi$ such that $2 \sin x - \cos 2x = 3$.

19. **a.** On the same set of axes, sketch and label the graphs of the equations $y = 2 \cos x$ and $y = \sin 2x$ as x varies from $-\pi$ to π radians.

b. Use the graphs drawn in part **a** to determine all values of x in the interval $-\pi \le x \le \pi$ that satisfy the equation $2 \cos x = \sin 2x$.

20. **a.** On the same set of axes, sketch and label the graphs of the equations $y = \tan x$ and $y = \cos 2x$ for the values of x in the interval $-\pi \le x \le \pi$.

b. Using the graph drawn in part **a**, determine the number of values of x in the interval $-\pi \le x \le \pi$ such that $\cos 2x = \tan x$.

21. **a.** On the same set of axes, sketch the graphs of $y = 2 \sin x$ and $y = x^2$, for values of x in the interval $-\pi \le x \le \pi$.

b. Using the graph made in part **a**, tell how many values in the interval $-\pi \le x \le \pi$ satisfy the equation $x^2 = 2 \sin x$.

22. The graph of which equation passes through the point (0, 1)?

(1) $y = \sin x$ **(3)** $y = 2^x$

(2) $y = \tan x$ **(4)** $y = \log_2 x$

Transformations of the Trigonometric Graphs

Translations

A periodic function is *symmetric* (is its own image) under the translation $T_{p,0}$ where p is the period of the function, or a multiple of the period.

Examples: $y = \sin x$ and $y = \cos x$ are each symmetric under $T_{2\pi,0}$.
$y = \tan x$ is symmetric under $T_{\pi,0}$.
That is, each of the curves is an endless repetition of its basic pattern.

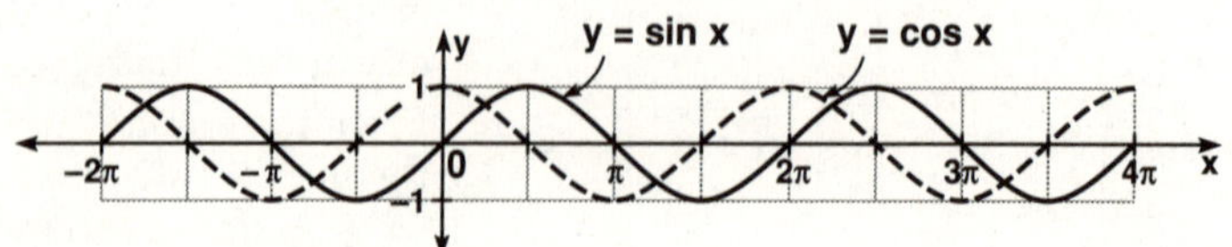

The cosine wave is a translation of the sine wave under $T_{-\frac{\pi}{2},0}$.

Reflections

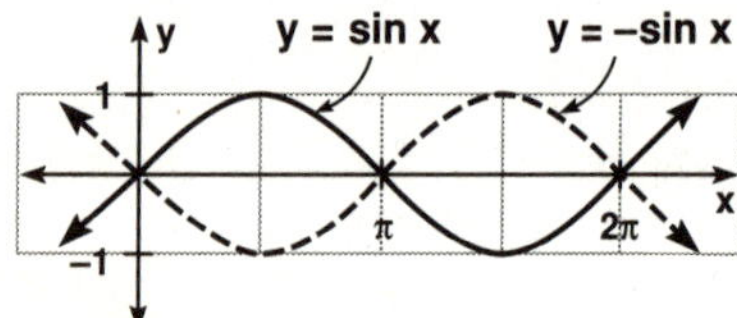

The image of $y = a \sin x$ under a reflection in the x-axis is $y = -a \sin x$.

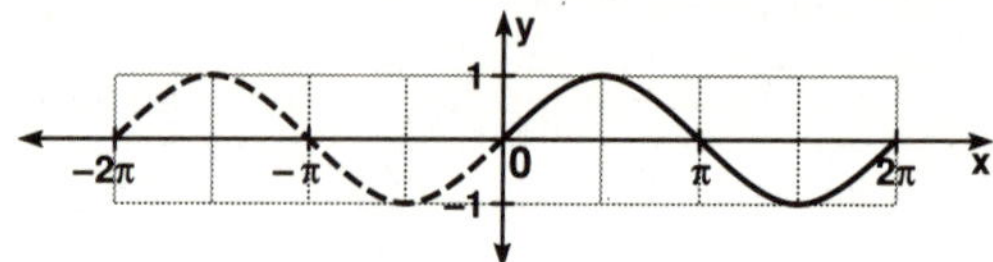

The sine wave is symmetric under a reflection in the origin.

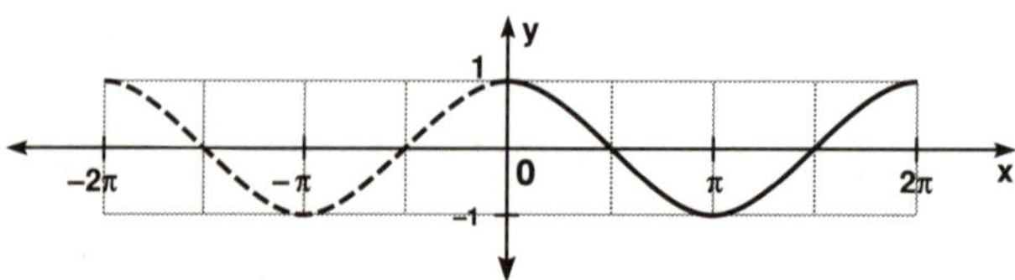

The cosine wave is symmetric under a reflection in the y-axis.

EXERCISES

1. On the same axes, $y = \sin x$ and $y = \cos x$ are graphed. Applying the translation $T_{\frac{\pi}{2},0}$ to $y = \cos x$, the graphs
   (1) coincide
   (2) intersect at one point, only
   (3) intersect at two points, only
   (4) intersect at three points, only

2. The graph of which equation has line symmetry with respect to the y-axis?
   (1) $y = \sin x$ (3) $y = \cos x$
   (2) $y = \tan x$ (4) $y = x$

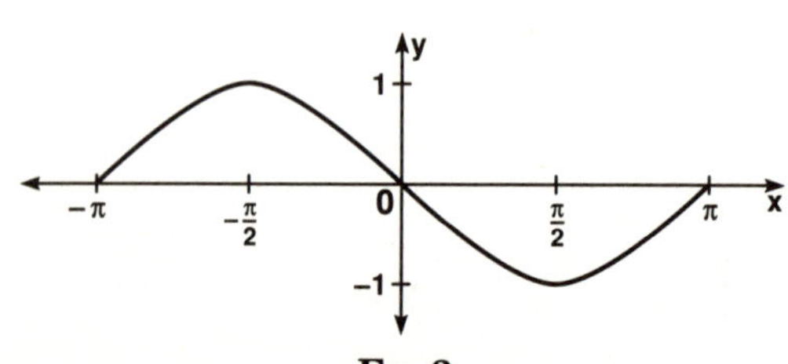

Ex. 3

3. The graph shown is a reflection in the y-axis of
   (1) $y = \sin x$ (3) $y = \cos x$
   (2) $y = \sin 2x$ (4) $y = \cos 2x$

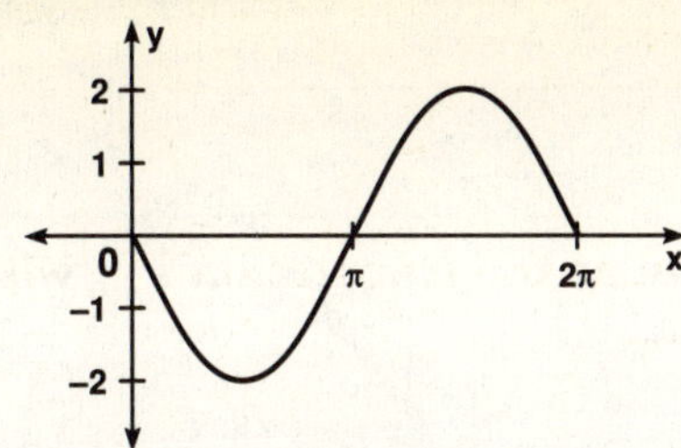

Ex. 4

4. Which is an equation of the graph shown?
   (1) $y = \sin 2x$
   (2) $y = -\sin 2x$
   (3) $y = -2 \sin x$
   (4) $y = 2 \sin x$

5. Which is an equation of the reflection of the graph of $y = \sin x$ in the x-axis?
   (1) $y = \cos x$
   (2) $y = \csc x$
   (3) $y = -\sin x$
   (4) $y = -\sec x$

6. The graph of which equation is symmetric with respect to the origin?
   (1) $y = -3$
   (2) $x = 2$
   (3) $y = \sin x$
   (4) $y = \cos x$

7. Which graph represents the reflection over the x-axis of the curve $y = \sin x$?

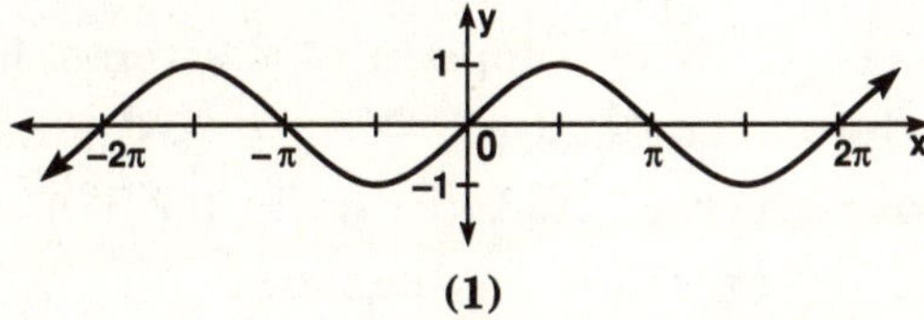

(1)

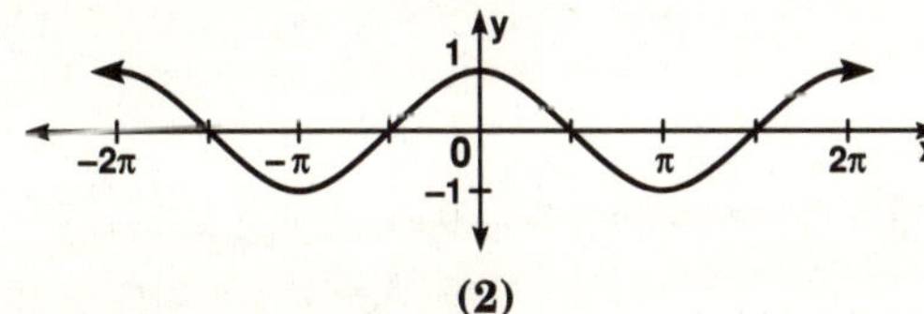

(2)

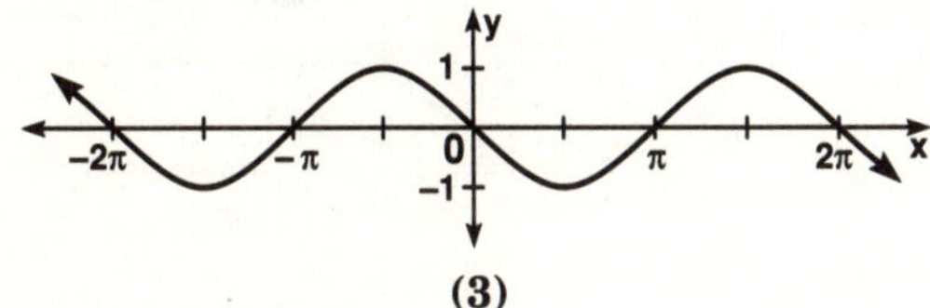

(3)

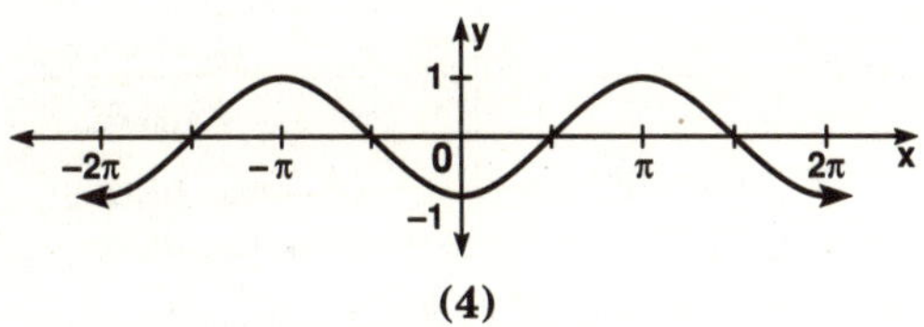

(4)

8. In the interval $0 \le x \le 2\pi$, the graph of $y = \sin x$ is symmetric with respect to the
   (1) origin
   (2) x-axis
   (3) point $(\pi, 0)$
   (4) line $x = \pi$

9. The equation $y = \tan x$ is graphed in the interval $0 \le x \le \frac{\pi}{2}$ and is reflected over the x-axis. On this reflection, point $\left(\frac{\pi}{4}, y\right)$ has which value for y?
   (1) 1
   (2) −1
   (3) 0
   (4) $\frac{\sqrt{3}}{3}$

10. Which graph has line symmetry with respect to the y-axis?
    (1) $y = x$
    (2) $y = x^2$
    (3) $y = \sin x$
    (4) $y = \tan x$

11. **a.** On the same set of axes, sketch and label the graphs of $y = \sin \frac{1}{2}x$ and $y = 2 \cos x$ as x varies from 0 to 2π radians.
    b. Using the same set of axes, sketch the reflection of $y = \sin \frac{1}{2}x$ in the line $y = -1$.

12. **a.** On the same set of axes, sketch and label the graphs of the equations $y = 2 \cos 2x$ and $y = -2 \sin x$ in the interval $0 \le x \le \pi$.
    b. Using the graphs drawn in part **a**, find the value of x in the interval $0 \le x \le \pi$ for which $2 \cos 2x = -2 \sin x$.

13. **a.** On the same set of axes, sketch and label the graphs of the equations $y = 2 \sin 2x$ and $y = -2 \cos x$ in the interval $-\pi \le x \le \pi$.
    b. Use the graphs drawn in part **a** to determine how many values of x in the interval $-\pi \le x \le \pi$ satisfy the equation $2 \sin 2x + 2 \cos x = 0$.

14. **a.** Sketch the graph of the equation $y = 2 \sin x$ in the interval $-\pi \le x \le \pi$.
    b. On the same set of axes, reflect the graph drawn in part **a** in the y-axis and label the graph **b**.
    c. Write an equation of the graph drawn in part **b**.
    d. Using the equation from part **c**, find the value of y when $x = \frac{\pi}{6}$.

Graphs

When the graph of $y = \sin x$ is reflected in the line $y = x$, the resulting inverse relation $x = \sin y$ is not a function.

The inverse relation $x = \sin y$, meaning *y is the angle whose sine is x*, can also be thought of as *y is the arc whose sine is x*, leading to the notation $y =$ *arc sin x*.

Similar inverse relations result when reflecting the graphs of $y = \cos x$ and $y = \tan x$ in the line $y = x$, namely, $y = \text{arc}\cos x$ and $y = \text{arc}\tan x$.

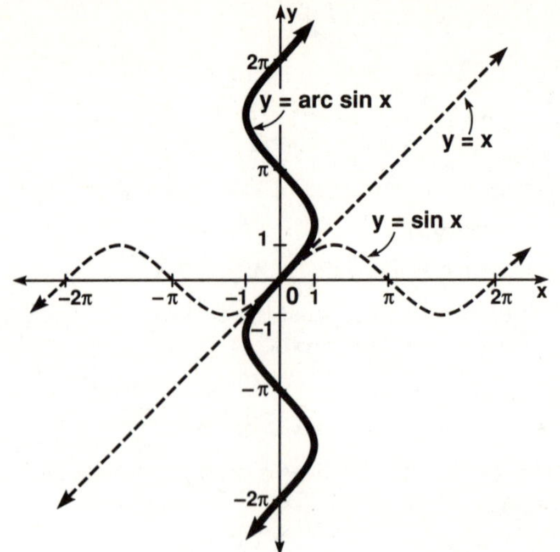

Restricting domains of the original trigonometric functions results in inverse relations that are functions.

If the domain of $y = \sin x$ is restricted to $-\frac{\pi}{2} \le x \le \frac{\pi}{2}$, the inverse relation $y = \text{arc}\sin x$ is a function, $y = \text{Arc}\sin x$.

If the domain of $y = \cos x$ is restricted to $0 \le x \le \pi$, the inverse relation $y = \text{arc}\cos x$ is a function, $y = \text{Arc}\cos x$.

If the domain of $y = \tan x$ is restricted to $-\frac{\pi}{2} < x < \frac{\pi}{2}$, the inverse relation $y = \text{arc}\tan x$ is a function, $y = \text{Arc}\tan x$.

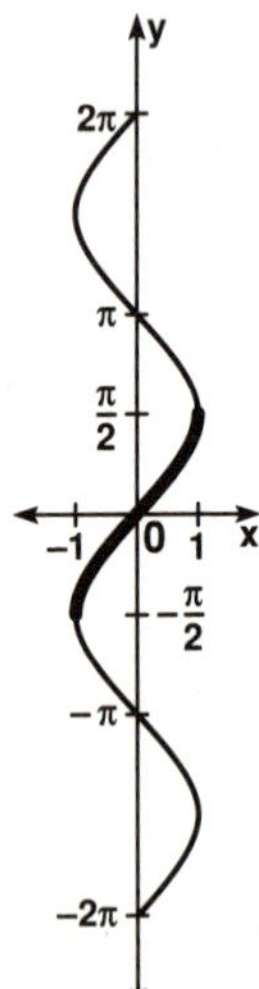

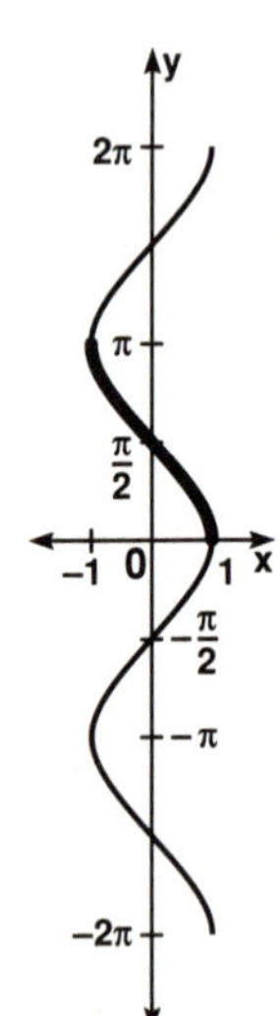

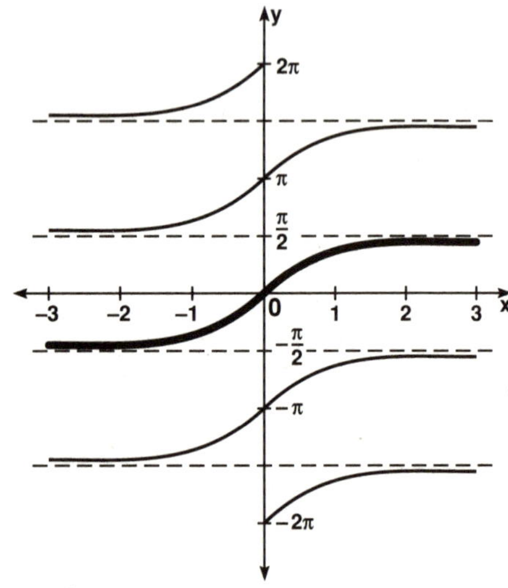

The bold section of each graph represents a part of the inverse relation that is a function.

EXERCISES

1. Which is an equation of the graph shown at the right?
   (1) $y = \text{arc sin } x$
   (2) $y = \text{arc cos } x$
   (3) $y = \sec x$
   (4) $y = \csc x$

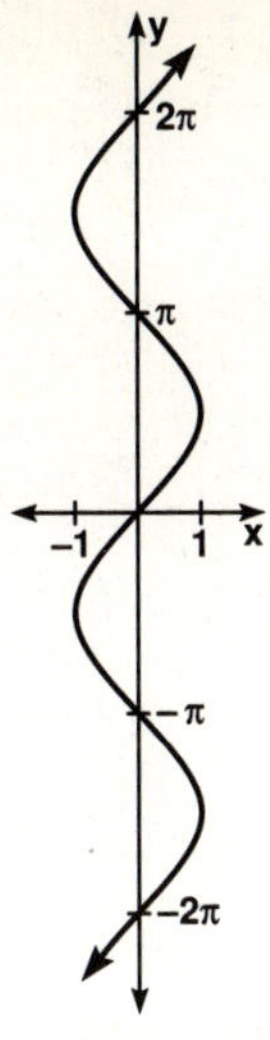

Ex. 1

2. To result in an inverse that is a function, the domain of the trigonometric function $y = \sin x$ is restricted to
   (1) $-2\pi \le x \le 2\pi$
   (2) $-\pi \le x \le \pi$
   (3) $-\frac{\pi}{2} \le x \le \frac{\pi}{2}$
   (4) $0 \le x \le 2\pi$

3. The domain of the inverse function $y = \text{Arc sin } x$ is
   (1) $-1 \le x \le 1$
   (2) {real numbers}
   (3) $-2\pi \le y \le 2\pi$
   (4) $-\frac{\pi}{2} \le y \le \frac{\pi}{2}$

4. The range of both $y = \sin x$ and $y = \cos x$ is
   (1) $-1 \le y \le 1$
   (2) $-1 < y < 1$
   (3) {real numbers}
   (4) {reals ≥ 0}

5. The range of $y = \tan x$ is
   (1) {real numbers}
   (2) $-1 \le y \le 1$
   (3) $-2\pi \le x \le 2\pi$
   (4) $-\frac{\pi}{2} < x < \frac{\pi}{2}$

6. The domain of the inverse function $y = \text{Arc tan } x$ is
   (1) {real numbers}
   (2) $-1 \le x \le 1$
   (3) $-2\pi \le y \le 2\pi$
   (4) $-\frac{\pi}{2} < y < \frac{\pi}{2}$

7. The range of the inverse function $y = \text{Arc sin } x$ is
   (1) $-360° \le y \le 360°$
   (2) $-180° \le y \le 180°$
   (3) $-90° \le y \le 90°$
   (4) $0° \le y \le 360°$

8. What is the range of the inverse function $y = \text{Arc cos } x$?

Finding a Value from Inverse Notation

To find a value written in inverse notation, translate the notation into words.

Examples

1. If $\theta = \text{Arc sin } \frac{1}{2}$, find $m\angle\theta$.

Solution: $\theta = \text{Arc sin } \frac{1}{2}$, means θ is the angle whose sine is $\frac{1}{2}$, where $-90° \le \theta \le 90°$.

Thus, θ must be in Quadrant I or IV.

Since the value of sine is given as positive, θ is in Quadrant I.

The angle in Quadrant I with $\frac{1}{2}$ as its sine is 30°.

Answer: $m\angle\theta = 30°$, or $\frac{\pi}{6}$

2. If $x = \text{Arc cos}\left(-\frac{\sqrt{3}}{2}\right)$, find $m\angle x$.

Solution: $x = \text{Arc cos}\left(-\frac{\sqrt{3}}{2}\right)$ means x is the angle whose cosine is $\left(-\frac{\sqrt{3}}{2}\right)$, where $0° \le x \le 180°$.

Thus, x must be in Quadrant I or II.

Since the value of cosine is given as negative, x is in Quadrant II.

The reference angle is 30° for that value of cosine.

Answer: $m\angle x = 150°$, or $\frac{5\pi}{6}$

3. Find cos [Arc tan (−1)].

Solution: cos [Arc tan (−1)] means the cosine of the angle whose tangent is −1, where the angle is between −90° and 90°.

Thus, the angle must be in Quadrant I or IV.

Since the value of tangent is given as negative, the angle is in Quadrant IV.

In Quadrant IV, cosine is positive.

The reference angle is 45° for a tangent value of 1.

$\cos 45° = \frac{\sqrt{2}}{2}$ *Ans.*

4. Find: $\tan\left(\text{Arc sin } \frac{5}{13}\right)$

Solution: You must find the tangent of the angle whose sine is $\frac{5}{13}$. By definition of Arc sin, the angle is in Quadrant I or IV.

Since the value of sine is given as positive, the angle is in Quadrant I.

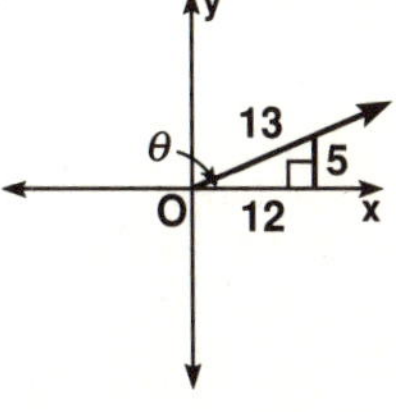

There is no need to know the value of the reference angle.

From the Pythagorean Triple 5, 12, 13,
$x = 12, y = 5, r = 13$

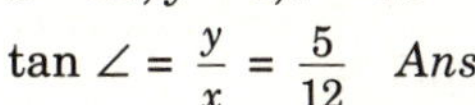

$\tan \angle = \frac{y}{x} = \frac{5}{12}$ *Ans.*

EXERCISES

1. If $\theta = \text{Arc cos } \frac{\sqrt{3}}{2}$, what is the measure of angle θ?

2. If $x = \text{Arc sin}\left(-\frac{1}{2}\right)$, find m$\angle x$.

3. What is the smallest positive value of x that satisfies $x = \text{Arc cos } \frac{1}{2}$?

4. If $\theta = \text{Arc tan }(-1)$, find m$\angle\theta$.

5. If $x = \text{Arc sin }\left(-\frac{1}{\sqrt{2}}\right)$, find m$\angle x$.

6. If $x = \text{arc cos }\left(-\frac{1}{2}\right)$, then x measures
   (1) 30° (2) 60° (3) 120° (4) 150°

7. The value of Arc sin (–1) is
   (1) π (3) $\frac{\pi}{2}$
   (2) $-\frac{\pi}{2}$ (4) $-\frac{\pi}{4}$

8. If $\theta = \text{Arc cos } \frac{\sqrt{2}}{2}$, what is the value of tan θ?
   (1) 1 (3) $\sqrt{3}$
   (2) $\sqrt{2}$ (4) $\frac{\sqrt{3}}{3}$

9. What is the value of sin (Arc tan 1)?
   (1) $-\frac{\sqrt{2}}{2}$ (3) $\frac{\sqrt{3}}{2}$
   (2) $\frac{\sqrt{2}}{2}$ (4) $-\frac{\sqrt{3}}{2}$

10. If $y = \sin\left(\text{Arc cos } \frac{1}{2}\right)$, the value of y is
    (1) $\frac{1}{2}$ (3) 30°
    (2) $\frac{\sqrt{3}}{2}$ (4) 60°

11. The value of $\sin\left(\text{Arc cot } \frac{4}{3}\right)$ is
    (1) $\frac{4}{5}$ (3) $\frac{3\sqrt{7}}{7}$
    (2) $\frac{3}{5}$ (4) $\frac{4}{3}$

12. If $\theta = \text{Arc cos } \frac{\sqrt{3}}{2}$, what is the value of sin θ?

In 13–22, find the indicated value.

13. $\cos\left(\text{Arc sin } \frac{\sqrt{3}}{2}\right)$

14. cos (Arc tan 1)

15. $\tan\left(\text{Arc sin} \frac{3}{5}\right)$

16. $\cos\left(\text{Arc sin } \frac{4}{5}\right)$

17. $\cos\left(\text{Arc sin } \frac{5}{13}\right)$

18. $\tan\left(\text{Arc cos } \frac{5}{13}\right)$

19. $\sin\left(\text{Arc cos } \frac{15}{17}\right)$

20. $\tan\left(\text{Arc sin } \frac{\sqrt{2}}{2}\right)$

21. $\cot\left(\text{Arc tan } \frac{8}{5}\right)$

22. $\csc\left(\text{Arc sin } \frac{11}{12}\right)$

23. The value of $\text{Arc sin } \frac{1}{2} + \text{Arc tan } 1$ is
    (1) 120° (2) 105° (3) 90° (4) 75°

24. The value of 2(Arc sin 1) is
    (1) 0 (2) $\frac{1}{2}$ (3) π (4) $\frac{\pi}{2}$

25. The value of tan (Arc tan 1) is
    (1) 1 (2) 0 (3) $\frac{\pi}{4}$ (4) $\frac{5\pi}{4}$

26. Find the value of $\sin\left(\text{Arc sin } \frac{1}{2}\right)$.

27. The value of sin (Arc sin 1 + Arc cos 1) is
    (1) 1 (2) $\frac{1}{2}$ (3) $\frac{\sqrt{3}}{2}$ (4) 0

28. If 3 sin x = 1, then which is an expression for x in inverse trigonometric form?
    (1) $x = \text{Arc sin } 3$ (3) $x = \text{Arc sin}\left(\frac{1}{3}\right)$
    (2) $x = \text{Arc sin }(-3)$ (4) $x = \text{Arc sin}\left(-\frac{1}{3}\right)$

29. If 5 sin A = –3, express A as an inverse of a trigonometric function.

6.8 SUMMARY EXERCISES

1. Which is a value of x if sin 60° = cos (x + 10°)?
   (1) 10° (2) 20° (3) 50° (4) 60°

2. Find the value of sin 27° 14′ to four decimal places.

3. Find the value of cos 52° 14′ to four decimal places.

4. If tan x = 0.5906, find the measure of positive acute angle x to the nearest 10 minutes.

5. If sin θ = 0.8455, find the value of positive acute angle θ to the nearest minute.

6. If cos θ = 0.9288, find the value of positive acute angle θ to the nearest minute.

7. Find x to the nearest tenth:
   $x = 193\ (\sin 23°\ 20')^2$

8. In right triangle ABC, $\overline{AB}$ is the hypotenuse. If $AC = 5$ and $BC = 12$, express $\frac{\sin B}{\tan B}$ as a fraction in lowest terms.

9. In right triangle ABC, $AB = 5{,}000$ and $m\angle C = 90°$. If the measure of angle A is $20° 40'$, find AC to the nearest unit.

10. A diagonal is drawn in a rectangle whose dimensions are 10 cm by 50 cm. Find the tangent of the angle formed by the diagonal and the longer side.

11. From external point P, tangents $\overline{PA}$ and $\overline{PB}$ are drawn to circle O. If $m\angle APB = 50°$ and $PA = 20$ cm, find the length of the radius, to the nearest tenth.

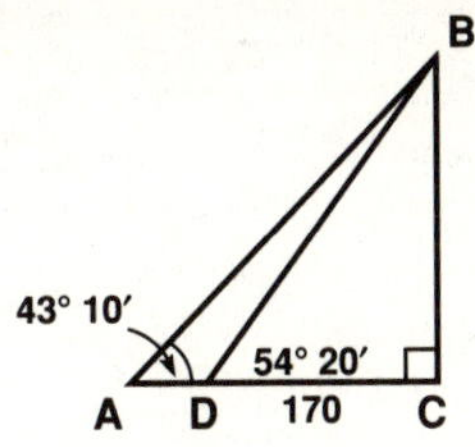

Ex. 12

12. In the diagram, B represents the position of a captive balloon connected by a cable to a ground station at A. Point C is on the ground directly below the balloon, and D is an observation point. Points A, D, and C lie in a straight line on level ground. $m\angle A = 43° 10'$, $m\angle BDC = 54° 20'$, $m\angle C = 90°$, and $DC = 170$ yards. Find, to the nearest yard:

a. the height, BC, of the balloon

b. the length, AB, of the cable

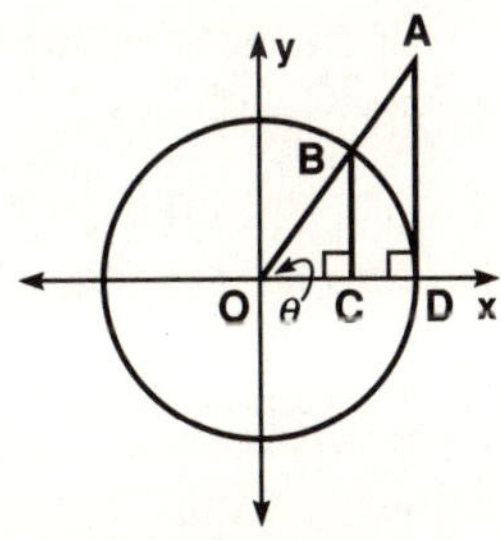

Ex. 13

13. The diagram shows a unit circle with radius $OB = 1$. Angle θ is in Quadrant I, $\overline{BC} \perp \overline{OD}$, and $\overline{AD} \perp \overline{OD}$. From the diagram, select a line segment that represents the given function.

a. $\sin\theta$ **b.** $\cos\theta$ **c.** $\tan\theta$

14. If $\sin\theta = \cos\theta$, in which quadrants may angle θ terminate?

(1) I, II (2) II, III (3) I, III (4) I, IV

15. If $\sin x = -\frac{2}{3}$ and $\cos x > 0$, in which quadrant does angle x terminate?

16. If $\sin\theta < 0$ and $\tan\theta < 0$, the measure of θ may be

(1) $-80°$ (2) $-100°$ (3) $120°$ (4) $220°$

17. If the terminal side of angle θ passes through $(-12, 5)$, what is the value of $\cos\theta$?

(1) $-\frac{5}{12}$ (2) $-\frac{12}{13}$ (3) $\frac{5}{12}$ (4) $\frac{12}{13}$

18. If $\sin x = -\frac{3}{5}$ and angle x lies in Quadrant IV, what is the value of $\tan x$?

(1) $\frac{3}{4}$ (2) $-\frac{3}{4}$ (3) $\frac{4}{3}$ (4) $-\frac{4}{3}$

19. If $\cos x = -\frac{8}{17}$ and $\tan x > 0$, what is the value of $\sin x$?

(1) $-\frac{8}{15}$ (2) $\frac{8}{15}$ (3) $-\frac{15}{17}$ (4) $\frac{15}{8}$

20. One radian is approximately equal to

(1) $57°$ (2) $45°$ (3) π (4) $\frac{\pi}{2}$

21. Express $\frac{2\pi}{9}$ in degree measure.

22. Express $144°$ in radian measure.

23. In a circle with radius 4.5 centimeters, find the length of the arc intercepted by a central angle of 3 radians.

24. In a circle with radius 18 inches, find, to the nearest tenth of an inch, the length of an arc that subtends an angle of $30°$.

25. In a circle, a central angle of 3 radians intercepts an arc of 18 centimeters. What is the radius of the circle?

26. What is the image of $(1, 0)$ after a clockwise rotation of $60°$?

(1) $\left(-\frac{\sqrt{3}}{2}, \frac{1}{2}\right)$ (3) $\left(\frac{\sqrt{3}}{2}, \frac{1}{2}\right)$

(2) $\left(\frac{1}{2}, -\frac{\sqrt{3}}{2}\right)$ (4) $\left(\frac{1}{2}, \frac{\sqrt{3}}{2}\right)$

27. If $f(x) = 3\sin x$, find $f\left(\frac{\pi}{6}\right)$.

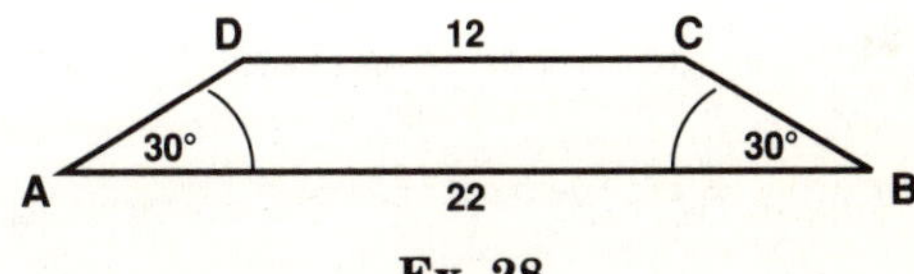

Ex. 28

28. In isosceles trapezoid $ABCD$, base $AB = 22$ cm, base $CD = 12$ cm, and the measure of each base angle A and B is $30°$. Find the area of $ABCD$, to the nearest sq. cm.

29. If $f(x) = 2\sin 2x + 2\cos x$, the numerical value of $f\left(\frac{\pi}{2}\right)$ is

(1) 4 (2) 2 (3) 1 (4) 0

30. The value of $\sin 240°$ is

(1) $\frac{1}{2}$ (2) $-\frac{1}{2}$ (3) $\frac{\sqrt{3}}{2}$ (4) $-\frac{\sqrt{3}}{2}$

31. Find the value of $\tan 150°$.

32. Find the value of $\cos\frac{5\pi}{3}$.

33. Find the value of $\sin 810°$.

34. Express tan (–140°) as a function of a positive acute angle.

35. Which is the value of cos (–240°)?

(1) $-\frac{1}{2}$ **(2)** $\frac{3}{2}$ **(3)** $\frac{1}{2}$ **(4)** $-\frac{3}{2}$

36. Write $(R_{-30^\circ} \circ R_{40^\circ} \circ R_{60^\circ})(A)$ as an equivalent single rotation of A.

37. As angle x increases from 0° to 180°, the value of sin x

(1) decreases, only
(2) increases, only
(3) decreases, then increases
(4) increases, then decreases

38. Which is not an element in the range of the function $y = \cos x$?

(1) 0 **(2)** –1 **(3)** 1 **(4)** 2

39. What is the amplitude of the graph of $y = \frac{3}{2} \cos 2x$?

(1) $\frac{3}{2}$ **(2)** 2 **(3)** π **(4)** 4π

40. Which is the equation for the function sketched?

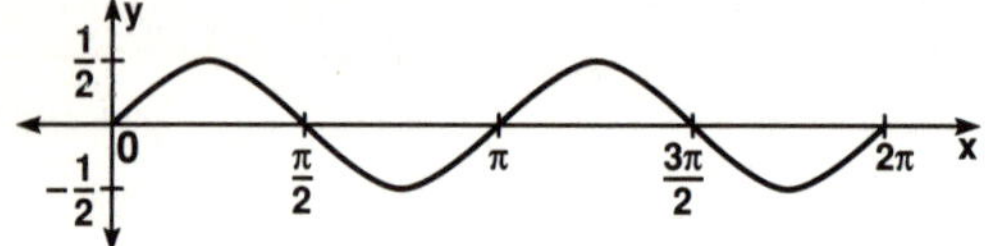

(1) $y = 2 \sin \frac{1}{2}x$ **(3)** $y = \frac{1}{2} \cos 2x$

(2) $y = \frac{1}{2} \sin 2x$ **(4)** $y = \frac{1}{2} \sin \frac{1}{2} x$

41. The maximum value of y for the equation $y = 4 - \cos x$ is

(1) 1 **(2)** –1 **(3)** 3 **(4)** 5

42. a. On the same set of axes, sketch the graphs of $y = \tan x$ and $y = \frac{1}{2} \cos x$, as x varies from 0 to 2π radians.

b. State the number of values of x in the interval $0 \le x \le 2\pi$ that satisfy the equation $\tan x = \frac{1}{2} \cos x$.

43. a. On the same set of axes, sketch and label the graphs of $y = 2 \sin \frac{1}{2}x$ and $y = \cos 2x$ for all values of x in the interval $0 \le x \le 2\pi$.

b. For which value in the interval $0 \le x \le 2\pi$ does $2 \sin \frac{1}{2}x - \cos 2x = 1$?

(1) 0 **(2)** $\frac{\pi}{2}$ **(3)** π **(4)** 2π

44. Which is the graph of the equation $y = -\sin x$?

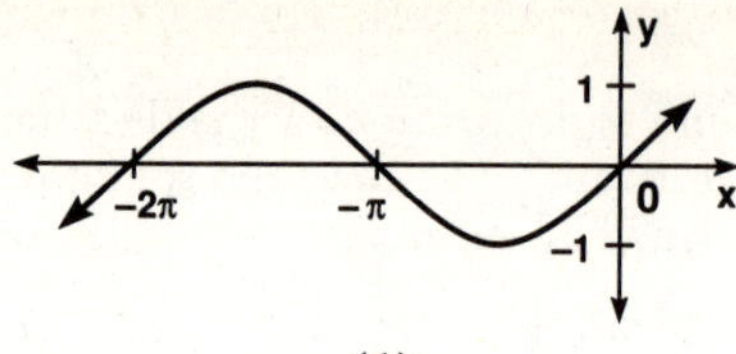

(1)

(2)

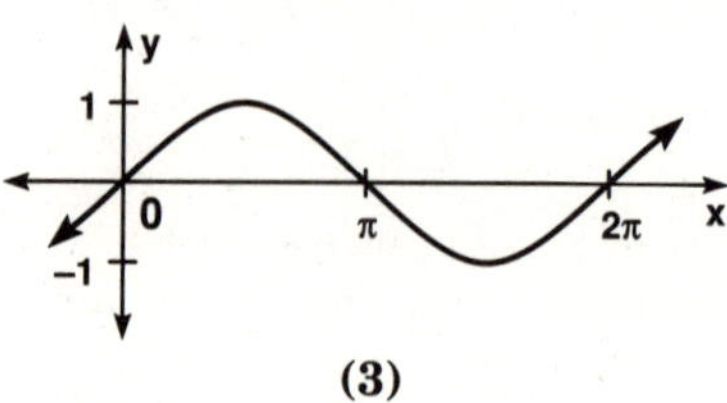

(3)

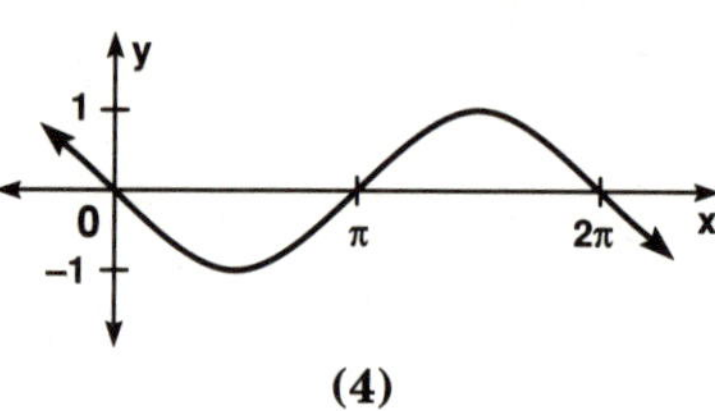

(4)

45. So that its inverse will be a function, the domain of $y = \sin x$ is restricted to

(1) $-\pi \le x \le \pi$ **(3)** $-\frac{\pi}{2} \le x \le \frac{\pi}{2}$

(2) $-\pi < x < \pi$ **(4)** $0 < x < \frac{\pi}{2}$

46. If $\theta = \text{Arc cos}\left(-\frac{1}{2}\right)$, find m$\angle\theta$.

47. Find the value of $\text{Arc sin } \frac{1}{2} + \text{Arc cos } \frac{\sqrt{2}}{2}$.

48. If $\theta = \text{Arc sin } \frac{\sqrt{2}}{2}$, the value of tan θ is

(1) $\frac{\sqrt{2}}{2}$ **(2)** 1 **(3)** –1 **(4)** 0

49. Find $\tan\left(\text{Arc sin } \frac{3}{5}\right)$.

CHAPTER 7

Trigonometry, Part II

7.1 ALGEBRAIC TECHNIQUES APPLIED TO TRIGONOMETRIC EXPRESSIONS

Factoring

To factor in a trigonometric expression, treat the quantity $\sin x$ in the same manner as the variable x is treated in an algebraic expression.

In algebra, x and y are not like terms. In trigonometry, $\sin x$ and $\cos x$ are not like terms.

$\sin^2 x$ means $(\sin x)^2$ or $(\sin x)(\sin x)$. This is not the same as $\sin x^2$ or $\sin (x \cdot x)$.

Common Factor	*Difference of Perfect Squares*	*Factors of a Trinomial*
$x^2 + x$ $= x(x + 1)$	$x^2 - y^2$ $= (x + y)(x - y)$	$x^2 - 3x + 2$ $= (x - 2)(x - 1)$
$\sin^2 x + \sin x$ $= \sin x (\sin x + 1)$	$\sin^2 x - \cos^2 x$ $= (\sin x + \cos x)(\sin x - \cos x)$	$\tan^2 x - 3 \tan x + 2$ $= (\tan x - 2)(\tan x - 1)$

EXERCISES

In 1–6, remove a common factor.

1. $\sin \theta + 2 \sin \theta \cos \theta$
2. $\csc^2 x - 3 \csc x$
3. $\sin^2 x + \sin^2 x \tan^2 x$
4. $\cos y - \cos^2 y$
5. $\tan t + \tan^3 t$
6. $\dfrac{\cos^2 \theta}{\sin^2 \theta} - \cos^2 \theta$

In 7–10, factor the difference of squares.

7. $1 - \sin^2 x$
8. $\cos^2 \theta - \sin^2 \theta$
9. $4 \tan^2 \theta - 1$
10. $1 - \cos^2 x$

In 11–15, factor the trinomial.

11. $\sin^2 A + 2 \sin A + 1$
12. $\tan^2 \theta - 5 \tan \theta - 6$
13. $2 \sin^2 x - 3 \sin x + 1$
14. $2 \cos^2 y + \cos y - 1$
15. $6 \cot^2 \alpha - 7 \cot \alpha - 3$ $\quad$ (α = alpha)

Operations With Fractions

Simplifying a Fraction

Use techniques of factoring, and cancel pairs of common factors from numerator and denominator.

Example

$$\frac{\sin x + \sin^2 x}{\sin x} = \frac{\cancel{\sin x}\,(1 + \sin x)}{\cancel{\sin x}} = 1 + \sin x$$

Combining Fractions by Addition or Subtraction

With Like Denominators

Keeping that denominator, combine numerators.

Example

$$\frac{\sin A}{\cos A} - \frac{1}{\cos A} = \frac{\sin A - 1}{\cos A}$$

With Unlike Denominators

Obtain a least common denominator, L.C.D. Rewrite each fraction using the L.C.D.

Example

$$\frac{\sin x + \cos x}{\sin x} + \frac{\sin x - \cos x}{\cos x}$$ L.C.D. = $(\sin x)(\cos x)$

$$= \frac{\sin x + \cos x}{\sin x} \cdot \frac{\cos x}{\cos x} + \frac{\sin x - \cos x}{\cos x} \cdot \frac{\sin x}{\sin x}$$ Multiply numerator and denominator of each fraction by the missing factor of the L.C.D.

$$= \frac{\sin x \cos x + \cos^2 x}{\sin x \cos x} + \frac{\sin^2 x - \sin x \cos x}{\sin x \cos x}$$ The fractions now have like denominators.

$$= \frac{\cancel{\sin x \cos x} + \cos^2 x + \sin^2 x - \cancel{\sin x \cos x}}{\sin x \cos x}$$ Combine numerators.

$$= \frac{\cos^2 x + \sin^2 x}{\sin x \cos x}$$ Further simplification is possible using an identity, reserved for Section 7.2.

Complex Fractions

To simplify a complex fraction, use either of these techniques.

Multiply each term of the numerator and of the denominator by the L.C.D. of all the denominators.

Example

$$\frac{\frac{\sin x}{\cos x}}{1 - \frac{\sin^2 x}{\cos x}}$$ The L.C.D. of $\cos x$, 1, $\cos x$ is $\cos x$.

$$= \frac{\frac{\sin x}{\cancel{\cos x}} \cdot \cancel{\cos x}}{1 \cdot \cos x - \frac{\sin^2 x}{\cancel{\cos x}} \cdot \cancel{\cos x}}$$

$$= \frac{\sin x}{\cos x - \sin^2 x}$$

Treat the complex fraction as a division.

Example

$$\frac{\frac{\sin x}{\cos x}}{1 - \frac{\sin^2 x}{\cos x}}$$

$$= \left[\frac{\sin x}{\cos x}\right] \div \left[1 - \frac{\sin^2 x}{\cos x}\right]$$ Rewrite as division.

$$= \left[\frac{\sin x}{\cos x}\right] \div \left[\frac{1}{1} \cdot \frac{\cos x}{\cos x} - \frac{\sin^2 x}{\cos x}\right]$$ Combine fractions of divisor.

$$= \left[\frac{\sin x}{\cos x}\right] \div \left[\frac{\cos x - \sin^2 x}{\cos x}\right]$$

$$= \left[\frac{\sin x}{\cancel{\cos x}}\right] \times \left[\frac{\cancel{\cos x}}{\cos x - \sin^2 x}\right]$$ Rewrite division as multiplication by reciprocal.

$$= \frac{\sin x}{\cos x - \sin^2 x}$$

EXERCISES

In 1–5, express the fraction in simplest form.

1. $\dfrac{2\cos^2\theta}{2\sin\theta\cos\theta}$

2. $\dfrac{1 - \sin x}{1 - \sin^2 x}$

3. $\dfrac{\sec\alpha\sin\alpha - \tan\alpha\sec\alpha}{\sec\alpha}$

4. $\dfrac{\cos A - \cos^3 A}{1 + \cos A}$

5. $\dfrac{(1 + \sin\theta)^2}{1 + \sin\theta}$

In 6–14, express the sum or difference as a single fraction in simplest form.

6. $\dfrac{1}{\sin A} - \dfrac{\cos A}{\sin A}$

7. $\dfrac{\sin^2\theta}{\cos^2\theta} + 1$

8. $\dfrac{1}{\cos x} - \cos x$

9. $\dfrac{\sin\theta}{\cos\theta} + \dfrac{\cos\theta}{\sin\theta}$

10. $\dfrac{\sin\alpha}{1 + \cos\alpha} + \dfrac{\cos\alpha}{\sin\alpha}$

11. $\dfrac{1 + \sin y}{\cos y} + \dfrac{\cos y}{1 + \sin y}$

12. $\dfrac{1}{1 + \sin z} - \dfrac{1}{1 - \sin z}$

13. $\dfrac{1 + \sec A}{\sec A - 1} + \dfrac{1 + \cos A}{\cos A - 1}$

14. $\dfrac{\sin\theta + \cos\theta}{\sec\theta + \tan\theta} + \dfrac{\cos\theta - \sin\theta}{\sec\theta - \tan\theta}$

In 15–29, express the complex fraction in simplest form.

15. $\dfrac{\frac{1}{\cos x}}{\frac{1}{\sin x}}$

16. $\dfrac{\frac{1}{\sin y}}{\frac{1}{\cos y}}$

17. $\dfrac{\frac{\cos A}{\sin A}}{\frac{1}{\sin A}}$

18. $\dfrac{\frac{1}{\cos^2 x}}{\frac{\sin^2 x}{\cos^2 x}}$

19. $\dfrac{\sin\theta + \cos\theta}{\frac{1}{\cos\theta} + \frac{1}{\sin\theta}}$

20. $\dfrac{\sin\alpha - \frac{1}{\sin\alpha}}{\frac{1}{\sin\alpha}}$

21. $\dfrac{\frac{1}{\sin x}}{\frac{\cos x}{\sin x} + \frac{\sin x}{\cos x}}$

22. $\dfrac{\sin\theta + \frac{\sin\theta}{\cos\theta}}{1 + \frac{1}{\cos\theta}}$

23. $\dfrac{\sin z + \frac{\cos z}{\sin z}}{\sin z - \frac{\cos z}{\sin z}}$

24. $\dfrac{\frac{1}{\cos\alpha} - \frac{1}{\sin\alpha}}{\frac{1}{\cos\alpha} + \frac{1}{\sin\alpha}}$

25. $\dfrac{\frac{1}{\cos\theta} + \frac{1}{\sin\theta}}{\frac{\sin\theta}{\cos\theta} + \frac{\cos\theta}{\sin\theta}}$

26. $\dfrac{\frac{\cos A}{\sin A} - 1}{\frac{\cos A}{\sin A} + 1}$

27. $\dfrac{1 - \frac{\sin^2 x}{\cos^2 x}}{1 + \frac{\sin^2 x}{\cos^2 x}}$

28. $\dfrac{\frac{1}{\sin\alpha}\left[\sin^2\alpha + \cos^2\alpha \cdot \frac{\sin\alpha}{\cos\alpha}\right]}{\sin\alpha + \cos\alpha}$

29. $\dfrac{\frac{\sin^2 t}{\cos^2 t} \cdot \frac{1}{\sin^2 t} - 1}{\frac{1}{\sin t} \cdot \frac{\sin^2 t}{\cos^2 t} \cdot \sin t}$

In 30–38, express as a single fraction in simplest form.

30. $\dfrac{1}{\cos x} - \dfrac{\sin x}{\cos x} \cdot \sin x$

31. $\dfrac{\sin y}{\cos y} \cdot \sin y + \cos y$

32. $\sin\theta\left[\dfrac{1}{\cos\theta} - \dfrac{1}{\sin\theta}\right]$

33. $\left[1 + \dfrac{1}{\cos A}\right]\left[1 - \cos A\right]$

34. $\dfrac{1}{\frac{1}{\cos^2\theta}} + \dfrac{1}{\frac{1}{\sin^2\theta}}$

35. $\dfrac{\frac{1}{\cos A}}{\cos A} + \dfrac{\frac{\sin A}{\cos A}}{\frac{\cos A}{\sin A}}$

36. $\dfrac{\frac{\cos x}{\sin x}}{\frac{\sin x}{\cos x}} + \dfrac{\frac{\sin x}{\cos x}}{\frac{\cos x}{\sin x}}$

37. $\dfrac{\cos\theta}{1 - \frac{\sin\theta}{\cos\theta}} + \dfrac{\sin\theta}{1 - \frac{\cos\theta}{\sin\theta}}$

38. $\dfrac{1}{\frac{1}{\cos t}}\left[\dfrac{\sin t}{\cos t} + \dfrac{\cos t}{\sin t}\right]$

7.2 TRIGONOMETRIC IDENTITIES

An IDENTITY is an equation that is true for *all* permissible replacements of the variable.
Example: $(x + 1)^2 = x^2 + 2x + 1$ is an identity because it is true for all values of x.

The Basic Trigonometric Identities

RECIPROCAL IDENTITIES	QUOTIENT IDENTITIES	PYTHAGOREAN IDENTITIES
$\csc\theta = \dfrac{1}{\sin\theta}$ where $\sin\theta \neq 0$	$\tan\theta = \dfrac{\sin\theta}{\cos\theta}$ where $\cos\theta \neq 0$	$\sin^2\theta + \cos^2\theta = 1$
$\sec\theta = \dfrac{1}{\cos\theta}$ where $\cos\theta \neq 0$	$\cot\theta = \dfrac{\cos\theta}{\sin\theta}$ where $\sin\theta \neq 0$	$1 + \tan^2\theta = \sec^2\theta$ where $\cos\theta \neq 0$
$\cot\theta = \dfrac{1}{\tan\theta}$ where $\tan\theta \neq 0$		$1 + \cot^2\theta = \csc^2\theta$ where $\sin\theta \neq 0$

EXERCISES

1. Which statement is an example of an identity?
   (1) $(x + y)^2 = x^2 + y^2$
   (2) $(x - y)^2 = x^2 - 2xy + y^2$
   (3) $\dfrac{x^2 - y^2}{x - y} = x - y$
   (4) $\dfrac{(x + y)^2}{x^2 - y^2} = \dfrac{x - y}{x + y}$

2. The identity
   $\sin B\,(\cos B + \sin B) = (\cos B + \sin B)\sin B$
   is an illustration of the
   (1) distributive law of multiplication of real numbers with respect to addition
   (2) identity element with respect to multiplication of real numbers
   (3) commutative law of multiplication of real numbers
   (4) associative law of addition of real numbers

3. The truth of the statement
$\sin A (\cos A + \sin B) = \sin A \cos A + \sin A \sin B$
is guaranteed for all values of A and B by the
(1) commutative law for addition
(2) commutative law for multiplication
(3) distributive law for multiplication over addition
(4) associative law for multiplication

4. Which equation is an identity?
(1) $\sin x + \cos x = 0$
(2) $\sin x + \cos x = 1$
(3) $\sin^2 x = 1 - \cos^2 x$
(4) $\cos x = \dfrac{1}{\sin x}$

5. Which is an example of a trigonometric identity?
(1) $\sin x \cos x = 1$ (3) $\cos x \cot x = 1$
(2) $\cot x \tan x = 1$ (4) $\tan x \sin x = 1$

6. Which is an example of an identity?
(1) $\sec A \csc A = 1$ (3) $\sec^2 A - 1 = \tan^2 A$
(2) $\sin A + \cos A = 1$ (4) $\cos^2 A - \sin^2 A = 1$

7. An example of an identity is
(1) $\sin^2 x - \cos^2 x = 1$ (3) $\tan^2 x = 1 + \sec^2 x$
(2) $\dfrac{1}{\sec^2 x} + \dfrac{1}{\csc^2 x} = 1$ (4) $\sin x + \cos x = 1$

8. An example of an identity is
(1) $(1 + \sec x)(1 - \sec x) = \tan^2 x$
(2) $(\sec x + 1)(\sec x - 1) = \tan^2 x$
(3) $\sec^2 (90° - x) = \tan^2 x$
(4) $1 + \sec^2 x = \tan^2 x$

9. Which is not an identity?
(1) $\sin^2 x + \cos^2 x = 1$ (3) $\dfrac{\tan x}{\sin x} = \sec x$
(2) $\tan x + \cot x = 1$ (4) $\dfrac{1}{\sin x} = \csc x$

10. Find the numerical value of: $\dfrac{\sin^2 \frac{\pi}{2} + \cos^2 \frac{\pi}{2}}{\tan \frac{\pi}{4}}$

11. In $\triangle ABC$, angle C is a right angle. If $\sin A = p$, then $\sin B$ is equal to
(1) 1 (2) p (3) $\sqrt{1 + p^2}$ (4) $\sqrt{1 - p^2}$

Expressing One Function in Terms of Another

One use of the basic identities is to express any function in terms of any other function of the same angle.

Example

Express $\tan\theta$ in terms of $\sin\theta$.

Solution:

$\tan\theta = \dfrac{\sin\theta}{\cos\theta}$ Quotient Identity

$\tan\theta = \dfrac{\sin\theta}{\pm\sqrt{1 - \sin^2\theta}}$ From the Pythagorean Identity, solve for $\cos\theta$ in terms of $\sin\theta$:

$\sin^2\theta + \cos^2\theta = 1$
$\cos^2\theta = 1 - \sin^2\theta$
$\cos\theta = \pm\sqrt{1 - \sin^2\theta}$

Alternate Solution: In a unit circle, identify the sides of a reference triangle in terms of $\sin\theta$.

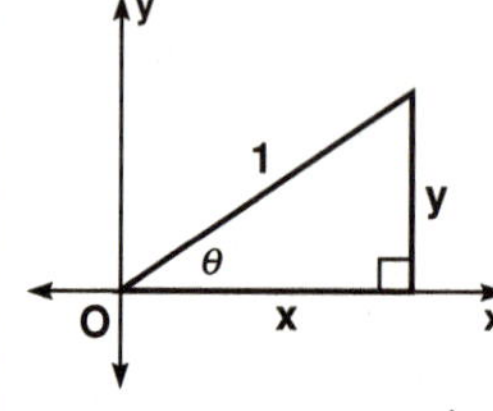

$y = \sin\theta$
$x^2 + y^2 = 1$
$x^2 + \sin^2\theta = 1$
$x^2 = 1 - \sin^2\theta$
$x = \pm\sqrt{1 - \sin^2\theta}$

$\tan\theta = \dfrac{y}{x} = \dfrac{\sin\theta}{\pm\sqrt{1 - \sin^2\theta}}$

EXERCISES

1. Express $\sin\theta$ in terms of $\cos\theta$.
2. Express $\cos\theta$ in terms of $\sin\theta$.
3. Express $\tan\theta$ in terms of $\sec\theta$.
4. Express $\cot\theta$ in terms of $\cos\theta$.
5. Express $\tan\theta$ in terms of $\cos\theta$.
6. Express $\cot\theta$ in terms of $\sin\theta$.
7. Express $\csc\theta$ in terms of $\cos\theta$.
8. Express $\sec\theta$ in terms of $\sin\theta$.
9. Express $\sin\theta$ in terms of $\tan\theta$.
10. Express $\cos\theta$ in terms of $\tan\theta$.

Equivalent Expressions

A second use of the basic identities is to write an expression equivalent to a given expression.

Examples

1. The expression $\frac{\tan\theta}{\sec\theta}$ is equivalent to

(1) $\sin\theta$ (3) $\cos\theta$

(2) $\frac{\sin\theta}{\cos^2\theta}$ (4) $\frac{\cos^2\theta}{\sin\theta}$

Solution: The choices suggest rewriting the given expression in terms of $\sin\theta$ and $\cos\theta$.

$$\frac{\tan\theta}{\sec\theta} = \frac{\frac{\sin\theta}{\cos\theta}}{\frac{1}{\cos\theta}}$$ Quotient Identity; Reciprocal Identity

$$= \frac{\sin\theta}{1}$$ Cancel the denominator $\cos\theta$ in the complex fraction.

Answer: (1)

2. Express as a single function: $\frac{\frac{1}{\cos\theta} - \cos\theta}{\frac{\sin\theta}{\cos\theta}}$

Solution: Simplify the complex fraction.

$$\frac{\frac{1}{\cos\theta} - \cos\theta}{\frac{\sin\theta}{\cos\theta}} = \frac{\frac{1-\cos^2\theta}{\cos\theta}}{\frac{\sin\theta}{\cos\theta}}$$ Combine in the numerator.

$$= \frac{1-\cos^2\theta}{\sin\theta}$$ Cancel the denominator $\cos\theta$.

$$= \frac{\sin^2\theta}{\sin\theta}$$ Pythagorean Identity

$$= \sin\theta$$ Cancel $\sin\theta$.

EXERCISES

In 1–29, for all values of the angle for which the expressions are defined, choose an equivalent expression.

1. $\frac{-1}{\cos A}$ is equivalent to

(1) $\sec A$ (2) $-\sec A$ (3) $\sin A$ (4) $-\sin A$

2. $\frac{\cot\theta}{\csc\theta}$ is equivalent to

(1) $\sec\theta$ (2) $\sin\theta$ (3) $\cos\theta$ (4) $\csc\theta$

3. $\frac{\sec\theta}{\csc\theta}$ is equivalent to

(1) $\sin\theta$ (2) $\cos\theta$ (3) $\tan\theta$ (4) $\cot\theta$

4. $\frac{\sin\theta}{\tan\theta}$ is equivalent to

(1) $-\cos\theta$ (3) $1-\cos\theta$

(2) $\cos\theta$ (4) $1+\cos\theta$

5. $\frac{\sin^2 A}{\tan A}$ is equivalent to

(1) $\frac{\sin A}{\cos A}$ (3) $\frac{1}{\sin A\cos A}$

(2) $\sin A\cos A$ (4) $\frac{\cos A}{\sin A}$

6. $\sin\theta$ is equivalent to

(1) $\frac{\tan\theta}{\sec\theta}$ (2) $\frac{1}{\sec\theta}$ (3) $\sec\theta$ (4) $\frac{\sec\theta}{\tan\theta}$

7. The expression $\frac{\tan x}{\sec^2 x}$ is equivalent to

(1) $\sin x$ (3) $\frac{\sin^3 x}{\cos x}$

(2) $\sin x\cos x$ (4) $\frac{\cos^3 x}{\sin x}$

8. $\sqrt{\frac{2\cos^2\theta}{\sin^2\theta}}$ is equivalent to

(1) $2\tan\theta$ (3) $2\cot\theta$

(2) $\sqrt{2}\tan\theta$ (4) $\sqrt{2}\cot\theta$

9. $(\tan\theta)(\csc\theta)$ is equivalent to

(1) $\sin\theta$ (2) $\cos\theta$ (3) $\csc\theta$ (4) $\sec\theta$

10. $(\cot\theta)(\sec\theta)$ is equivalent to

(1) $\tan\theta$ (2) $\cos\theta$ (3) $\cot\theta$ (4) $\csc\theta$

11. $\tan A \cdot \cos A \cdot \csc A$ is equivalent to

(1) 1 (2) $\frac{1}{2}$ (3) $\sin A$ (4) $\frac{1}{\sin A}$

12. $\csc y + 1$ is equivalent to

(1) $\frac{\cot y}{\csc y - 1}$ (3) $\cot y$

(2) $\frac{\sin y + 1}{\sin y}$ (4) $\frac{1+\cos y}{\cos y}$

13. $\sec x - \tan x$ is equivalent to

(1) 1 (3) $\frac{1-\sin x}{\cos x}$

(2) $\cos x - \cot x$ (4) $\frac{\cos x - \sin^2 x}{\sin x\cos x}$

14. $\sin\theta(\csc\theta - \sin\theta)$ is equivalent to

(1) 1 (3) $\tan\theta - 1$

(2) $\cos\theta$ (4) $\cos^2\theta$

15. $\cos y(\csc y - \sec y)$ is equivalent to

(1) $\cot y - 1$ (3) $1-\tan y$

(2) $\tan y - 1$ (4) $-\cos y$

16. $\cot^2\theta$ is equivalent to

(1) $\dfrac{1}{\sin^2\theta}$ (3) $1-\cos^2\theta$

(2) $\cos^2\theta$ (4) $\dfrac{\cos^2\theta}{1-\cos^2\theta}$

17. $\dfrac{\sin^2 x+\cos^2 x}{\cos x}$ is equivalent to

(1) $\sin x\cos x$ (3) $\csc x$

(2) $\tan x\cos x$ (4) $\sec x$

18. $\cos A+\dfrac{\sin^2 A}{\cos A}$ is equivalent to

(1) 1 (2) $\sec A$ (3) $\csc A$ (4) $\cos A$

19. $4+\cos^2 A$ is equivalent to

(1) $5-\sec^2 A$ (3) $\dfrac{5}{\sec^2 A}$

(2) $5-\sin^2 A$ (4) $5+\sin^2 A$

20. $\dfrac{1}{\sin^2 A}-1$ is equivalent to

(1) $\cot^2 A$ (3) $\sec^2 A-1$

(2) $\cos^2 A$ (4) $\dfrac{\sin^2 A-1}{\sin^2 A}$

21. $\dfrac{\sin\theta}{\cos\theta}+\dfrac{\cos\theta}{\sin\theta}$ is equivalent to

(1) 1 (2) $\sec\theta$ (3) $\dfrac{1}{\csc\theta}$ (4) $\dfrac{1}{\sin\theta\cos\theta}$

22. $\dfrac{\cot^2 x}{1-\sin^2 x}$ is equivalent to

(1) $\cos^2 x$ (3) $\dfrac{1}{\sin^2 x}$

(2) $\tan^2 x$ (4) $1-\sin^2 x$

23. $\dfrac{\cos x-\dfrac{\sin^2 x}{\cos x}}{1+\dfrac{\sin x}{\cos x}}$ is equivalent to

(1) $\cos x+\sin x$ (3) $\dfrac{1}{\cos x+\sin x}$

(2) $\cos x-\sin x$ (4) $\dfrac{1}{\cos x-\sin x}$

24. $\sin\theta\left(\dfrac{1}{\sin\theta}-\sin\theta\right)$ is equivalent to

(1) $-\cos^2\theta$ (3) $1-\cos^2\theta$

(2) $\cos^2\theta$ (4) $1+\cos^2\theta$

25. $\dfrac{2(1+\cos A)}{\sin^2 A+\cos A+\cos^2 A}$ is equivalent to

(1) 1 (2) 2 (3) $\dfrac{2}{\sin A}$ (4) $\dfrac{2}{\cos A}$

26. $\dfrac{\cos^2 B}{\sin B}+\sin B$ is equivalent to

(1) 1 (2) $\dfrac{1}{\csc B}$ (3) $\dfrac{1}{\sin B}$ (4) $\cos^2 B$

27. $\sin^4 B-\cos^4 B$ is equivalent to

(1) $1+\cos^2 B$ (3) $\sin^2 B+\cos^2 B$

(2) $1-\cos^2 B$ (4) $\sin^2 B-\cos^2 B$

28. $\sec^2 x+\csc^2 x$ is equivalent to

(1) $\sin^2 x\cos^2 x$ (3) $1+\tan^2 x$

(2) $\dfrac{1}{\sin^2 x\cos^2 x}$ (4) $1-\tan^2 x$

29. $\dfrac{1-\tan^2\theta}{1+\tan^2\theta+2\tan\theta}$ is equivalent to

(1) $\dfrac{\tan\theta-1}{\tan\theta+1}$ (3) $\dfrac{1}{\tan\theta}+1$

(2) $\dfrac{1-\tan\theta}{1+\tan\theta}$ (4) $1-\dfrac{1}{\tan\theta}$

30. The expression $\tan x$ is not equivalent to

(1) $\sin x\sec x$ (3) $\cot x\sin x$

(2) $\dfrac{\sin x}{\cos x}$ (4) $\dfrac{\cos x\sec x}{\cot x}$

In 31–35, rewrite the expression in terms of $\sin\theta$ and $\cos\theta$. Express the result in simplest form.

31. $\sin\theta\sec\theta\cot\theta$

32. $\dfrac{\cot\theta}{\csc\theta}$

33. $\dfrac{1}{\sec^2\theta}+\dfrac{1}{\csc^2\theta}$

34. $\cot\theta+\tan\theta$

35. $\sec\theta-\tan\theta\sin\theta$

Proving an Identity

To prove that a trigonometric statement is an identity, note:

1. **The object is to show that the two sides of the statement are equivalent.**

   You may work on only one side and show that it is equivalent to the other. Work on the more complicated side.

   You may work on the two sides *independently* until you arrive at equivalent expressions.

   You may not perform operations involving the two sides simultaneously. For example, do not add the same quantity to both sides. As a reminder, use a line between sides.

2. **Use the basic identities to transform one or both sides of the proposed identity.**

   A general starting point is to rewrite expressions in terms of sine and cosine, but be alert to situations when a Pythagorean substitution is appropriate.

3. After replacements have been made, do the algebra suggested by the form of the expression.

If there is a complex fraction, simplify it.

If there are two fractions, combine them.

Look for possibilities of factoring.

Example

For all values of θ for which the expressions are defined, prove that the given statement is an identity.

$$\frac{\tan\theta + \cot\theta}{\cos\theta\,\sin\theta} = \sec^2\theta\,\csc^2\theta$$

Solution: Work on the left side, rewriting the expression in terms of $\sin\theta$ and $\cos\theta$. Then, do the algebra suggested by the form of the expression. Continue until the left side is equivalent to the right side, or transform the right side so that it is equivalent to the reduced expression on the left side.

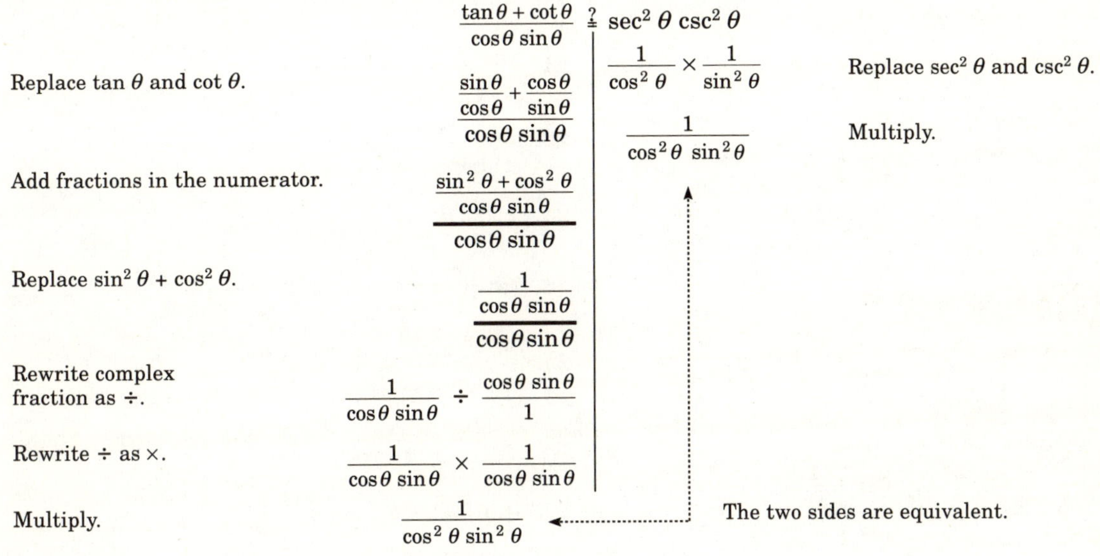

Sometimes, algebraic manipulations are required before replacements can be made.

Examples

1. For all values of θ for which the expressions are defined, prove that the following is an identity:

$$\frac{(\cos\theta + \sin\theta)^2}{1 + 2\sin\theta\cos\theta} = \cos\theta\,\tan\theta\,\csc\theta$$

Solution: On the left, carry out the square. Then, replace $\cos^2\theta + \sin^2\theta$ by 1.

On the right, rewrite in terms of $\sin\theta$ and $\cos\theta$. Then, cancel.

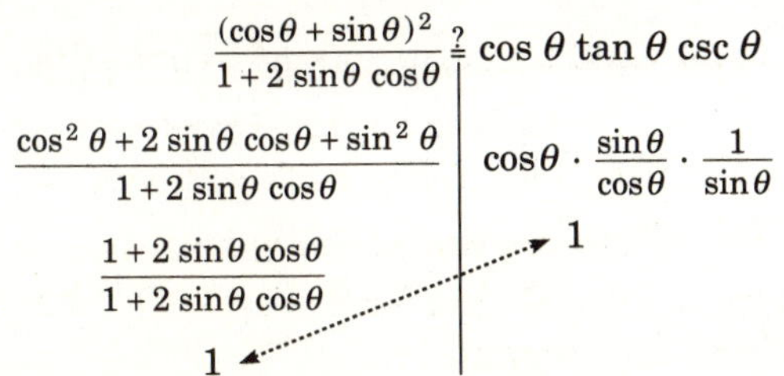

2. For all values of θ for which the expressions are defined, prove that the following is an identity:

$$\frac{1 - \sin\theta}{\cos\theta} = \frac{\cos\theta}{1 + \sin\theta}$$

Solution: Both sides are in simplest form. Multiply the numerator and denominator of one side by a "conjugate."

$$\frac{1 - \sin\theta}{\cos\theta} \stackrel{?}{=} \frac{\cos\theta}{1 + \sin\theta} \cdot \frac{1 - \sin\theta}{1 - \sin\theta}$$

$$\frac{\cos\theta(1 - \sin\theta)}{1 - \sin^2\theta}$$

$$\frac{\cos\theta(1 - \sin\theta)}{\cos^2\theta}$$

$$\frac{1 - \sin\theta}{\cos\theta}$$

EXERCISES

In 1–27, prove that the given statement is an identity for all values of the angle for which the expressions are defined.

1. $\sec\theta - \sin\theta\tan\theta = \cos\theta$
2. $\tan\theta + \cot\theta = \sec\theta\csc\theta$
3. $(\sin A + 1)(\csc A - 1) = \cos A\cot A$
4. $(1 + \csc\theta)(1 - \sin\theta) = \cot\theta\cos\theta$
5. $\dfrac{\tan A + \sin A}{\csc A + \cot A} = \sin A\tan A$
6. $\sin^2 x(1 + \tan^2 x) = \tan^2 x$
7. $\dfrac{1}{\tan x - \cot x} = \dfrac{\sin x\cos x}{2\sin^2 x - 1}$
8. $\dfrac{\cos\theta + \cot\theta}{\cos\theta\cot\theta} = \tan\theta + \sec\theta$
9. $\dfrac{\sin x}{1 + \cos x} + \dfrac{1 + \cos x}{\sin x} = 2\cot x\sec x$
10. $1 + \dfrac{1}{\cos x} = \dfrac{\tan^2 x}{\sec x - 1}$
11. $\dfrac{1 + \tan^2\theta}{1 - \cos^2\theta} = \sec^2\theta\csc^2\theta$
12. $2\cos^2 x - 1 = \dfrac{1 - \tan^2 x}{1 + \tan^2 x}$
13. $\dfrac{\cos x}{\tan x} = \csc x(1 - \sin^2 x)$
14. $\dfrac{\cos\theta\sin\theta + \cos\theta}{\cos^2\theta} = \tan\theta + \sec\theta$
15. $\dfrac{\cos\theta\sin^2\theta}{1 - \cos\theta} = \cos\theta + \cos^2\theta$
16. $\dfrac{\tan\theta - \cot\theta}{\tan\theta + \cot\theta} = 2\sin^2\theta - 1$
17. $\csc x - \sin x = \dfrac{\cot x}{\sec x}$
18. $\dfrac{\tan x\csc^2 x}{1 + \tan^2 x} = \cot x$
19. $\dfrac{\sin x + \tan x}{1 + \sec x} = \sin x$
20. $\dfrac{\sin\theta\tan\theta + \cos\theta}{\cos\theta} = \sec^2\theta$
21. $\dfrac{\sin\theta\cot\theta + \cos^2\theta}{1 + \cos\theta} = \cos\theta$
22. $\dfrac{\cos\theta}{\sin\theta\tan\theta + \cos\theta} = \dfrac{1}{\sec^2\theta}$
23. $2\csc^2\theta = \dfrac{1}{1 + \cos\theta} + \dfrac{1}{1 - \cos\theta}$
24. $\cos\theta(\cos\theta + 1) + \sin^2\theta = \dfrac{\sin\theta + \tan\theta}{\tan\theta}$
25. $\dfrac{\sin x - \cos y}{\sin x + \cos y} = \dfrac{\sec y - \csc x}{\sec y + \csc x}$
26. $\dfrac{1 - \cos\theta}{\sin\theta} = \dfrac{\sin\theta}{1 + \cos\theta}$
27. $(\tan\theta + \sec\theta)^2 = \dfrac{1 + \sin\theta}{1 - \sin\theta}$

7.3 TRIGONOMETRIC EQUATIONS

A TRIGONOMETRIC EQUATION contains a trigonometric function of an angle. Such an equation must first be solved for the function of the angle and then for the measure of the angle.

The same techniques used for solving algebraic equations apply to trigonometric equations. Note the domain of the variable to be sure to include all possible solutions of the angle.

First-Degree Equations

Examples

1. Solve $2\sin\theta - 1 = 0$ for the domains:

a. $0° \le \theta \le 360°$ **b.** all values of θ

Solution: Use the properties of equality to solve first for $\sin\theta$.

$2\sin\theta - 1 = 0$	
$2\sin\theta = 1$	Add 1 to both sides.
$\sin\theta = \frac{1}{2}$	Divide both sides by 2.

From this value of $\sin\theta$, determine the quadrants in which θ lies and the measure of the reference angle.

$\sin\theta > 0$ in Quadrants I and II.

The measure of the reference angle is 30° or $\frac{\pi}{6}$.

In Q I, use 30°.

In Q II, use (180 – 30)° or 150°.

Answers: **a.** For $0° \le \theta \le 360°$, the solutions for θ are 30°, 150°.

b. For all values of θ, the solutions for θ are $30° + n \cdot 360°$, $150° + n \cdot 360°$, where n is an integer.

2. Find θ to the nearest degree, $0° \le \theta \le 360°$:

$$4 \cos \theta = \cos \theta + 2$$

Solution: Use the properties of equality to solve first for $\cos \theta$.

$4 \cos \theta = \cos \theta + 2$
$3 \cos \theta = 2$ Subtract $\cos \theta$.
$\cos \theta = \frac{2}{3}$ or 0.6667

From this value of $\cos \theta$, determine the quadrants in which angle θ lies and the measure of the reference angle.

$\cos \theta > 0$ in Quadrants I and IV.

Use a table or calculator to determine that, to the nearest degree, the measure of the reference angle is 48°.

In Q I, use 48°.
In Q IV, use $(360 - 48)°$ or 312°.

Answers: For $0° \le \theta \le 360°$, the solutions for θ are 48°, 312°.

Additional algebraic techniques may be necessary in the solution of equations in which the trigonometric function is of the first degree.

Examples

1. For $0 \le \theta \le \pi$, solve:

$$\tan \theta \cos \theta - \tan \theta = 0$$

Solution: After removing the common factor, set each factor of the product equal to 0.

$$\tan \theta \cos \theta - \tan \theta = 0$$
$$\tan \theta (\cos \theta - 1) = 0$$

$\tan \theta = 0$	$\cos \theta - 1 = 0$
$\theta = 0, \pi$	$\cos \theta = 1$
	$\theta = 0$

Answer: For $0 \le \theta \le \pi$, the solutions for θ are $0, \pi$.

Note: Remember that setting each factor equal to 0 is possible only when the product is 0.

2. For $0° \le \theta \le 360°$, solve: $|2 \cos \theta - 3| = 5$

Solution: Consider two cases.

If $2 \cos \theta - 3 \ge 0$, replace $\lvert 2 \cos \theta - 3 \rvert$ by $2 \cos \theta - 3$.	If $2 \cos \theta - 3 < 0$, replace $\lvert 2 \cos \theta - 3 \rvert$ by $-(2 \cos \theta - 3)$.
$2 \cos \theta - 3 = 5$	$-(2 \cos \theta - 3) = 5$
$2 \cos \theta = 8$	$-2 \cos \theta + 3 = 5$
$\cos \theta = 4$	$-2 \cos \theta = 2$
Reject (maximum value of cosine is 1)	$\cos \theta = -1$
	$\theta = 180°$

Answer: For $0° \le \theta \le 360°$, the solution for θ is 180°.

EXERCISES

1. The value of θ in the interval $90° < \theta < 270°$ that satisfies the equation $4 \sin \theta + 1 = 3$ is
(1) 120° (2) 150° (3) 210° (4) 240°

2. A root of the equation $2 \sin x + \sqrt{3} = 0$ is
(1) 60° (2) 120° (3) 210° (4) 300°

3. Which value of x satisfies the equation $6 \tan x - 2 = 4$?
(1) $\frac{\pi}{6}$ (2) $\frac{\pi}{2}$ (3) $\frac{\pi}{3}$ (4) $\frac{\pi}{4}$

4. Which is the solution set of the equation $2 \sin x - \sqrt{3} = 0$ when $0 < x < 2\pi$?
(1) $\left\{\frac{\pi}{6}, \frac{5\pi}{6}\right\}$ (3) $\left\{\frac{\pi}{3}, \frac{2\pi}{3}\right\}$
(2) $\left\{\frac{7\pi}{6}, \frac{11\pi}{6}\right\}$ (4) $\left\{\frac{4\pi}{3}, \frac{5\pi}{3}\right\}$

5. Solve the equation $2 \sin x - 1 = 0$ for all values of x between 0 and $\frac{\pi}{2}$.

6. Express the roots of the equation $3 \cos \theta + 1 = 0$ in inverse trigonometric notation.

7. A value of θ that satisfies the equation $\cos \theta (2 \cos \theta - 1) = 0$ is
(1) 0 (2) π (3) $\frac{\pi}{2}$ (4) $\frac{\pi}{6}$

8. What value of x satisfies the equation $\sin x \cos x - 2 \cos x = 0$ for $0° < x < 180°$?

9. Find the value of x greater than 0° and less than 360° that satisfies the equation $2 \tan x + \sin x \tan x = 0$.

10. Find a value of x greater than 0 and less than 2π that satisfies the equation $\sin x \cos x - 2 \sin x = 0$.

In 11–14, find the values of θ in the interval $0° \le \theta < 360°$ that satisfy the given equation.

11. $|\sin \theta - 3| = 2$ **13.** $|2 \tan \theta - 1| = 1$

12. $|2 \cos \theta + 5| = 3$ **14.** $|2 \csc \theta - 3| = 1$

15. In the interval $0° \le x < 360°$, $\sin x = \cos x$ when x is
(1) 45°, only (3) 135° and 315°
(2) 45° and 225° (4) 225°, only

16. If $\cos A - \sin A = 0$, find the measure of the positive acute angle A.

17. Express in degrees the value of x between 180° and 270° that satisfies the equation $\tan x = \cot x$.

18. Which value of A satisfies the equation $\sqrt{\tan A} = 1$?
(1) 30° (2) 45° (3) 60° (4) 90°

19. A solution of the equation $\sqrt{4 \sin x + 7} = 3$ is
(1) $\frac{\pi}{4}$ (2) $\frac{\pi}{3}$ (3) $\frac{\pi}{6}$ (4) $\frac{\pi}{2}$

20. Solve the equation $\sqrt{2 \sin x + 7} = 3$ for the smallest positive value of x.

21. Solve the equation $\sqrt{3 \tan x + 1} = 2$ for the smallest positive value of x.

22. If x is an angle greater than 0° and less than 180°, find the value of x satisfying the equation $\sqrt{3 + \sin x} = 2$.

23. Express the measure of the positive acute angle θ that satisfies the equation $2 \tan \theta \cos \theta - 1 = 0$.

24. Solve for $\sin x$: $\sqrt{1 - \sin x} = \frac{1}{2}$

25. Solve the following set of equations for $\sin A$:
$\sin A + 2 \cos B = -\frac{1}{3}$
$2 \sin A - \cos B = 1$

26. Find the value of y between 0° and 90° that satisfies the following system of equations:
$2 \sec x - 4 \tan y = 0$
$\sec x + \tan y = \sqrt{3}$

Quadratic Equations

As with algebraic quadratics, some trigonometric quadratics may be solved by factoring.

Examples

1. For $0° \le \theta < 360°$, solve: $\cos^2 \theta = \cos \theta$

Solution: Gather terms on one side to remove the common factor. Do not divide both sides by $\cos \theta$.

$$\cos^2 \theta = \cos \theta$$
$$\cos^2 \theta - \cos \theta = 0$$
$$\cos \theta (\cos \theta - 1) = 0$$

$\cos \theta = 0$	$\cos \theta - 1 = 0$
$\theta = 90°, 270°$	$\cos \theta = 1$
	$\theta = 0°$

Answer: For $0° \le \theta < 360°$, the solutions for θ are 0°, 90°, 270°.

2. For $0° \le \theta < 360°$, solve: $2 \cos^2 \theta + 7 \cos \theta - 4 = 0$

Solution: Factor the trinomial. Set each factor equal to 0.

$$2 \cos^2 \theta + 7 \cos \theta - 4 = 0$$
$$(2 \cos \theta - 1)(\cos \theta + 4) = 0$$

$2 \cos \theta - 1 = 0$	$\cos \theta + 4 = 0$
$\cos \theta = \frac{1}{2}$	$\cos \theta = -4$
Q I, IV: $\theta = 60°, 300°$	Reject

Answer: For $0° \le \theta < 360°$, the solutions for θ are 60°, 300°.

---

3. For $0 \le \theta < 2\pi$, solve: $\sin^2 \theta - 1 = 0$

Solution: Factor the difference of squares. Set each factor equal to 0.

$$\sin^2 \theta - 1 = 0$$
$$(\sin \theta + 1)(\sin \theta - 1) = 0$$

$\sin \theta + 1 = 0$	$\sin \theta - 1 = 0$
$\sin \theta = -1$	$\sin \theta = 1$
$\theta = \frac{3\pi}{2}$	$\theta = \frac{\pi}{2}$

Answer: For $0 \le \theta < 2\pi$, the solutions for θ are $\frac{\pi}{2}, \frac{3\pi}{2}$.

Alternate Solution:

$$\sin^2 \theta - 1 = 0$$
$$\sin^2 \theta = 1$$
$$\sin \theta = \pm 1$$
$$\theta = \frac{\pi}{2}, \frac{3\pi}{2}$$

Other trigonometric quadratics require the quadratic formula.
To solve, a trigonometric quadratic must be in terms of a single function.
Be alert to the requirements of the solution set.

Example

a. Solve $2\sec^2 x - 3\tan x - 5 = 0$ for all values of $\tan x$ to the nearest hundredth.

Solution: Use an identity to replace $\sec^2 x$ so that the equation is in terms of $\tan x$.

$$2\sec^2 x - 3\tan x - 5 = 0$$
$$2(1 + \tan^2 x) - 3\tan x - 5 = 0$$
$$2 + 2\tan^2 x - 3\tan x - 5 = 0$$
$$2\tan^2 x - 3\tan x - 3 = 0$$

Treat $\tan x$ as the variable, and use the quadratic formula.

Use: $\dfrac{-b \pm \sqrt{b^2 - 4ac}}{2a}$ with $a = 2$, $b = -3$, $c = -3$

$$\tan x = \frac{-(-3) \pm \sqrt{(-3)^2 - 4(2)(-3)}}{2(2)} = \frac{3 \pm \sqrt{33}}{4} \approx \frac{3 \pm 5.744}{4}$$

$\tan x \approx \dfrac{3 + 5.744}{4}$	$\tan x \approx \dfrac{3 - 5.744}{4}$
$\tan x \approx 2.19$	$\tan x \approx -0.69$

Note: When an answer is to be rounded, intermediate steps should be carried out to one decimal place more than the final answer. Intermediate calculations should be cut off (truncated), not rounded.

b. For $0° \leq x < 360°$, find all values of x, to the nearest degree, that satisfy the given equation.

Solution: Use a table or calculator.

$\tan x \approx 2.19$	$\tan x \approx -0.69$
$x \approx 65°$ in Q I, $245°$ in Q III	$\tan x \approx 145°$ in Q II, $325°$ in Q IV

Answer: For $0° \leq x < 360°$, the solutions for x are $65°$, $145°$, $245°$, $325°$.

EXERCISES

1. What is the value of x in the interval $90° \leq x \leq 180°$ that satisfies the equation $\sin x + \sin^2 x = 0$?
(1) $90°$ (2) $135°$ (3) $180°$ (4) $270°$

2. Which value of x satisfies the equation $\cos^2 x + \cos x = 0$?
(1) π (2) 2π (3) $\frac{\pi}{6}$ (4) $\frac{\pi}{4}$

3. In the equation $2\sin^2 x - \sqrt{3}\sin x = 0$, angle x may equal
(1) $0°$ (2) $30°$ (3) $45°$ (4) $150°$

4. Which value of x does *not* satisfy the equation $\sin^2 x + \sin x = 0$?
(1) $\frac{\pi}{2}$ (2) 2π (3) $\frac{3}{2}\pi$ (4) π

5. Find the positive acute angle θ if $2\sin^2\theta - \sin\theta = 0$.

6. Find the value of x in the interval $0° \leq x \leq 180°$ that satisfies the equation $\cos^2 x - 2\cos x = 0$.

7. Find the positive acute angle that satisfies the equation $\tan^2\theta - \tan\theta = 0$.

8. Which value of x satisfies the equation $2\cos^2 x - 1 = 1$?
(1) $0°$ (2) $30°$ (3) $45°$ (4) $90°$

9. A solution for the equation $2\sin^2 x = 1$ is
(1) π (2) $\frac{\pi}{4}$ (3) $\frac{\pi}{6}$ (4) $\frac{3\pi}{2}$

10. Solve the equation $3\tan^2 x - 1 = 0$ for the smallest positive value of x.

11. Find the number of degrees in the obtuse angle θ that satisfies the equation $4\sin^2\theta = 1$.

12. Find all values of x in the interval $0° \leq x \leq 360°$ that satisfy the equation $\tan^2 x - 1 = 0$.

In 13–16, tell the total number of values of the angle that satisfy the given equation in the specified interval.

13. $2\sin^2 x + \sin x - 1 = 0$ $\quad 0° \leq x \leq 360°$

14. $\tan^2\theta - 3\tan\theta + 2 = 0$ $\quad 0° \leq \theta \leq 360°$

15. $2\sin^2 x + 3\sin x + 1 = 0$ $\quad 0° \leq x \leq 90°$

16. $3\tan^2 A + \tan A - 2 = 0$ $\quad 0 \leq A \leq \pi$

17. If $(\tan x - 2)(\tan x - 1) = 0$, then x may be an angle whose terminal side lies in
(1) the first quadrant, only
(2) the first or third quadrants, only
(3) the second or fourth quadrants, only
(4) any of the four quadrants

18. A value of $\cos x$ that satisfies the equation $6\cos^2 x + \cos x - 2 = 0$ is
(1) $\frac{2}{3}$ (2) $-\frac{1}{2}$ (3) 3 (4) $-\frac{2}{3}$

19. A value of x that satisfies the equation $\sin^2 x - 4\sin x + 3 = 0$ is
(1) $\frac{\pi}{2}$ (2) π (3) $\frac{3\pi}{2}$ (4) 2π

20. Which value of x will satisfy the equation $2\cos^2 x + \cos x - 1 = 0$?
(1) 30° (2) 45° (3) 60° (4) 90°

21. A value of x that satisfies the equation $2\cos^2 x - \cos x - 1 = 0$ is
(1) $\frac{\pi}{3}$ (2) $\frac{4\pi}{3}$ (3) $\frac{3\pi}{4}$ (4) $\frac{\pi}{2}$

22. Solve the equation $\tan^2 x + 3\tan x - 4 = 0$ for the positive value of $\tan x$.

23. Find the measure of the smallest positive angle that satisfies:
$2\cos^2\theta + 5\cos\theta - 3 = 0$

24. Find the measure of the smallest acute angle for which $2\sin^2\theta - 3\sin\theta + 1 = 0$.

25. Find a value of x between 0° and 360° that satisfies:
$\sin^2 x - 3\sin x + 2 = 0$

In 26–30, find all values of θ in the interval $0 \le \theta < 2\pi$ that satisfy the given equation.

26. $2\sin^2\theta - 3\sin\theta + 1 = 0$

27. $\cos^2\theta - \cos\theta - 2 = 0$

28. $\sin^2\theta - \sin\theta - 2 = 0$

29. $2\sin^2\theta = 1 + \sin\theta$

30. $2\cos^3\theta + \cos^2\theta - \cos\theta = 0$

31. Find, to the nearest degree, all values of θ in the interval $0° \le \theta < 360°$ that satisfy the equation $2\tan^2\theta + \tan\theta - 1 = 0$.

In 32–33, find the smallest positive value of x that satisfies the given equation.

32. $\sqrt{\tan^2 x + 1} = 2$

33. $\sqrt{5\tan^2 x + 4} - 3 = 0$

In 34–37, find, to the nearest degree, all values of θ in the interval $0° \le \theta < 360°$ that satisfy the given equation.

34. $8\sin^2\theta + 2\sin\theta - 1 = 0$

35. $6\sin^2\theta = 1 - \sin\theta$

36. $2\cos^2\theta + 3 = 5\cos\theta$

37. $3\tan^2\theta + 5\tan\theta = 2$

38. a. Solve for all values of $\tan\theta$ to the nearest tenth: $2\tan^2\theta = 5\tan\theta - 1$

b. How many different acute angles satisfy the equation in part **a**?

39. a. Solve for all values of $\cos x$ to the nearest tenth: $4\cos^2 x = \cos x + 2$

b. How many values of x between 180° and 360° satisfy the equation $4\cos^2 x = \cos x + 2$?

40. a. Find, to the nearest tenth, the roots of the equation $2x^2 = 5x + 1$.

b. If $x = \csc\theta$, in which quadrant(s) does angle θ lie?

41. a. Solve for all values of $\tan\theta$ to the nearest hundredth: $\tan\theta + \frac{1}{\tan\theta} = 6$

b. Using the answers from part **a**, find, to the nearest degree, all values of θ that satisfy $\tan\theta + \frac{1}{\tan\theta} = 6$ in the interval $0° \le \theta < 360°$.

42. a. Solve for all values of $\cot\theta$ to the nearest hundredth: $\cot^2\theta - 4\cot\theta + 2 = 0$

b. Using the answers in part **a**, find, to the nearest degree, all values of θ that satisfy $\cot^2\theta - 4\cot\theta + 2 = 0$, where $0° < \theta \le 360°$.

43. a. Solve the equation $\tan x + \cot x = 3$ for $\tan x$ to the nearest tenth.

b. How many values of x are there between 0° and 360° that satisfy the equation $\tan x + \cot x = 3$?

In 44–46, find all values of θ in the interval $0° \le \theta < 360°$ that satisfy the given equation.

44. $2\sin\theta + 1 = \csc\theta$

45. $2\cos\theta + 1 = \sec\theta$

46. $\sin^2\theta - \cos^2\theta = 0$

In 47–53, find, to the nearest degree, all values of θ in the interval $0° \le \theta < 360°$ that satisfy the given equation.

47. $\tan\theta - 2\cot\theta = 1$

48. $7\cos\theta + 1 = 6\sec\theta$

49. $\sec^2\theta = 4 - 2\tan\theta$

50. $2\sin\theta - 3\csc\theta = -5$

51. $2\sin\theta - 1 = \csc\theta$

52. $\sin\theta + 1 = 2\cos^2\theta$

53. $3\tan^2\theta + \frac{1}{\cot\theta} = 2$

7.4 TRIGONOMETRIC FORMULAS

Sums and Differences of Angles

Formulas for Sums of Angles	*Formulas for Differences of Angles*
$\sin(x + y) = \sin x \cos y + \cos x \sin y$	$\sin(x - y) = \sin x \cos y - \cos x \sin y$
$\cos(x + y) = \cos x \cos y - \sin x \sin y$	$\cos(x - y) = \cos x \cos y + \sin x \sin y$
$\tan(x + y) = \dfrac{\tan x + \tan y}{1 - \tan x \tan y}$	$\tan(x - y) = \dfrac{\tan x - \tan y}{1 + \tan x \tan y}$

One application of these formulas is to prove other identities.

Examples

1. Use the formula for $\cos(x - y)$ to show:

$$\cos(-\theta) = \cos\theta$$

Solution: In the formula, let: $x = 0$, $y = \theta$

$$\cos(x - y) = \cos x \cos y + \sin x \sin y$$
$$\cos(0 - \theta) = \cos 0 \cos\theta + \sin 0 \sin\theta$$
$$\cos(-\theta) = 1 \cdot \cos\theta + 0 \cdot \sin\theta$$
$$\cos(-\theta) = \cos\theta$$

Note: This relation can also be seen from the graph of $y = \cos x$. That is, since the graph of $y = \cos x$ is symmetric to the line $x = 0$ (the y-axis), then:

$$\cos(-x) = \cos x$$

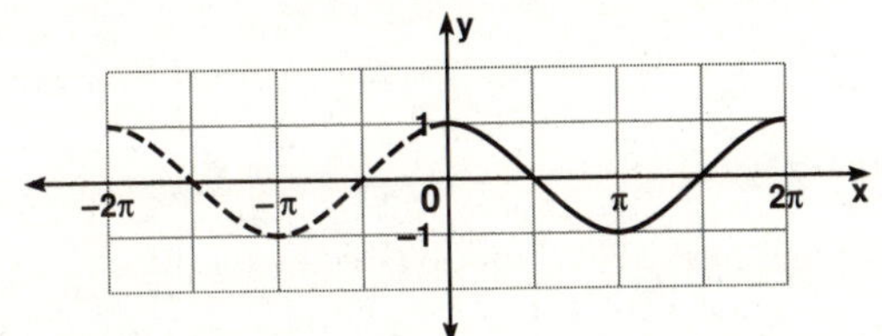

2. Prove that the following is an identity:

$$\tan x + \tan y = \frac{\sin(x + y)}{\cos x \cos y}$$

Solution: Begin on the right side with the formula for $\sin(x + y)$. Since the left side is a sum of tangents, rewrite the right side as the sum of two fractions.

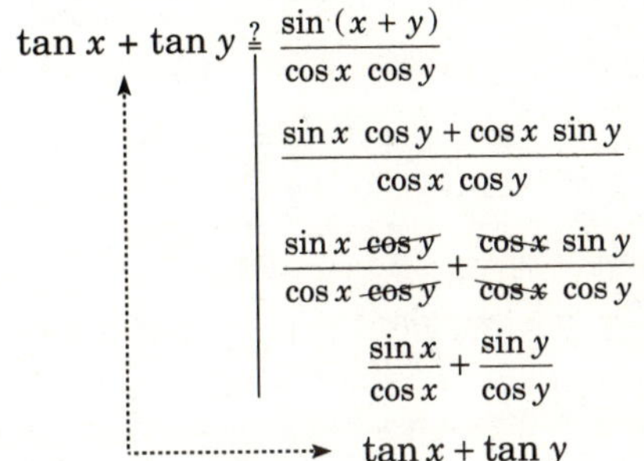

Another application of the formulas is to evaluate trigonometric functions.

Examples

1. Find the exact value of $\tan 15°$. (Recall that a table or calculator gives only an approximate value.)

Solution: Since $15°$ is the difference of two special angles, $45° - 30°$, use the formula for $\tan(x - y)$ with $x = 45°$, $y = 30°$.

$$\tan(x - y) = \frac{\tan x - \tan y}{1 + \tan x \tan y}$$

$$\tan 15° = \tan(45° - 30°) = \frac{\tan 45° - \tan 30°}{1 + \tan 45° \tan 30°}$$

Substitute values for $\tan 45°$ and $\tan 30°$.
$$\tan 15° = \frac{1 - \frac{\sqrt{3}}{3}}{1 + 1 \cdot \frac{\sqrt{3}}{3}}$$

Multiply numerator and denominator of the complex fraction by 3.
$$= \frac{1 - \frac{\sqrt{3}}{3}}{1 + 1 \cdot \frac{\sqrt{3}}{3}} \cdot \frac{3}{3}$$

$$= \frac{3 - \sqrt{3}}{3 + \sqrt{3}}$$

2. *Given:* $\angle w$ in Quadrant I, $\angle t$ in Quadrant II

$$\sin w = \tfrac{2}{3} \qquad \cos t = -\tfrac{4}{5}$$

Find the value of $\sin(w + t)$.

Solution: To apply the formula for $\sin(w + t)$, you must know values for $\cos w$ and $\sin t$. To determine these values:

$\sin^2 w + \cos^2 w = 1$	$\sin^2 t + \cos^2 t = 1$
$\left(\frac{2}{3}\right)^2 + \cos^2 w = 1$	$\sin^2 t + \left(-\frac{4}{5}\right)^2 = 1$
$\frac{4}{9} + \cos^2 w = \frac{9}{9}$	$\sin^2 t + \frac{16}{25} = \frac{25}{25}$
$\cos^2 w = \frac{5}{9}$	$\sin^2 t = \frac{9}{25}$
$\cos w = \frac{\sqrt{5}}{3}$	$\sin t = \frac{3}{5}$
Since w is in Q I, $\cos w > 0$.	Since t is in Q II, $\sin t > 0$.

$$\sin(w + t) = \sin w \cos t + \cos w \sin t$$
$$= \frac{2}{3} \cdot \left(-\frac{4}{5}\right) + \frac{\sqrt{5}}{3} \cdot \frac{3}{5}$$
$$= -\frac{8}{15} + \frac{3\sqrt{5}}{15} = \frac{3\sqrt{5} - 8}{15}$$

EXERCISES

1. Which equation is not a trigonometric identity?

(1) $\sin^2 x + \cos^2 x = 1$

(2) $\tan x = \frac{\sin x}{\cos x}$

(3) $\cos(x + y) = \cos x \cos y + \sin x \sin y$

(4) $\sin(x + y) = \sin x \cos y + \cos x \sin y$

2. $\sin(\theta + 270°)$ is equivalent to

(1) $\cos\theta$ **(2)** $2\cos\theta$ **(3)** $-\cos\theta$ **(4)** $-\sin\theta$

3. $\sin(180° + A)$ is equivalent to

(1) $\cos A$ **(2)** $\sin A$ **(3)** $-\cos A$ **(4)** $-\sin A$

4. $\sin(90° - \theta)$ is equivalent to

(1) $\cos\theta$ **(2)** $\sin\theta$ **(3)** $-\cos\theta$ **(4)** $-\sin\theta$

5. $\cos(\theta + 90°)$ is equivalent to

(1) $\sin\theta$ **(2)** $\cos\theta$ **(3)** $-\sin\theta$ **(4)** $-\cos\theta$

6. $\cos(2\pi - x)$ is equivalent to

(1) $-\cos x$ **(2)** $\cos x$ **(3)** $-\sin x$ **(4)** $\sin x$

7. $\tan(x + 45°)$ is equivalent to

(1) $\frac{\tan x - 1}{1 + \tan x}$ **(3)** $\frac{\tan x}{1 + \tan x}$

(2) $\frac{\tan x + 1}{1 - \tan x}$ **(4)** $\frac{\tan x}{1 - \tan x}$

8. $\tan(180° - y)$ is equivalent to

(1) -1 **(3)** $-\tan y$

(2) $\frac{-\tan y}{1 + \tan y}$ **(4)** $\frac{1 - \tan y}{1 + \tan y}$

9. $\cos(A - B) - \cos(A + B)$ is equivalent to

(1) $-2\sin A \sin B$ **(3)** $2\cos A \cos B$

(2) $-2\cos B$ **(4)** $2\sin A \sin B$

10. $\frac{\sin(x + y)}{\cos x \cos y}$ is equivalent to

(1) $1 + \cot x$ **(3)** $\tan x + \tan y$

(2) $\tan x + 1$ **(4)** $\frac{1}{\cos y} + \frac{1}{\cos x}$

In 11–12, use a sum or difference formula to prove that the given statement is an identity.

11. $\sin(-\theta) = -\sin\theta$ **12.** $\tan(-\theta) = -\tan\theta$

In 13–22, prove that the given statement is an identity for all values of the angles for which the expressions are defined.

13. $\sin(x + 45°) = \frac{\sqrt{2}}{2}(\sin x + \cos x)$

14. $\cos(60° + y) = \frac{1}{2}(\cos y - \sqrt{3}\sin y)$

15. $\tan(45° + x) = \frac{1 + \tan x}{1 - \tan x}$

16. $\tan(45° - B) = \frac{\cos B - \sin B}{\cos B + \sin B}$

17. $\cos(60° + B) + \cos(60° - B) = \frac{1}{\sec B}$

18. $\frac{\sin(A - B)}{\sin A \sin B} = \cot B - \cot A$

19. $\sin(x + y)\sin(x - y) = \sin^2 x - \sin^2 y$

20. $\cot(x + y) = \frac{\cot x \cot y - 1}{\cot x + \cot y}$

21. $\frac{\cos(x - y)}{\cos(x + y)} = \frac{\cot x + \tan y}{\cot x - \tan y}$

22. $\frac{\sin(A + B)\cos C}{\sin(A + C)\cos B} = \frac{1 + \cot A \tan B}{1 + \cot A \tan C}$

23. a. Using the formula for $\cos(x - y)$, find the exact value of $\cos 15°$ in radical form if $m\angle x = 45°$ and $m\angle y = 30°$.

b. Using the formula for $\sin(x - y)$, find the exact value of $\sin 15°$ in radical form if $m\angle x = 45°$ and $m\angle y = 30°$.

c. Find the exact value of $\sin 75°$, using the formula for $\sin(x - y)$ where $m\angle x = 90°$ and $m\angle y = 15°$. Use the values for $\cos 15°$ and $\sin 15°$ found in parts **a** and **b**.

24. Since $\cos 75° = \cos(30° + 45°)$, then $\cos 75°$ equals

(1) $\frac{\sqrt{6} - \sqrt{2}}{4}$ **(3)** $\frac{-\sqrt{2} - \sqrt{6}}{4}$

(2) $\frac{-\sqrt{6} + \sqrt{2}}{4}$ **(4)** $\frac{\sqrt{2} + \sqrt{6}}{4}$

25. $\sin 35° \cos 22° + \cos 35° \sin 22°$ equals

(1) $\sin 13°$ **(2)** $\sin 57°$ **(3)** $\cos 13°$ **(4)** $\cos 57°$

26. $\sin 60° \cos 45° - \sin 45° \cos 60°$ equals

(1) 1 **(2)** 0 **(3)** $\frac{\sqrt{6} - \sqrt{2}}{4}$ **(4)** $\frac{1}{2}$

27. $\cos 70° \cos 40° - \sin 70° \sin 40°$ equals

(1) $\cos 30°$ **(2)** $\cos 70°$ **(3)** $\cos 110°$ **(4)** $\sin 70°$

28. $\sin 13° \cos 17° + \cos 13° \sin 17°$ equals

(1) 1 **(2)** $\frac{1}{2}$ **(3)** $\frac{\sqrt{3}}{2}$ **(4)** 0

29. $\sin 42° \cos 48° + \cos 42° \sin 48°$ equals

(1) 1 **(2)** 0 **(3)** $\sin 6°$ **(4)** $\cos 6°$

30. $\sin 96° \cos 24° + \cos 96° \sin 24°$ equals

(1) $\sin 60°$ **(2)** $-\sin 60°$ **(3)** $\cos 60°$ **(4)** $-\cos 60°$

31. $\sin 210° \cos 30° - \cos 210° \sin 30°$ equals

(1) 1 **(2)** -1 **(3)** 0 **(4)** 180

32. Express in radical form:

$\sin 90° \cos 30° - \cos 90° \sin 30°$

33. If $\sin x = \frac{3}{5}$ and x is a positive acute angle, find $\cos\left(x + \frac{\pi}{2}\right)$.

34. If A and B are positive acute angles and if $\sin A = \frac{3}{5}$ and $\sin B = \frac{4}{5}$, then $\sin(A + B)$ is equal to

(1) 1 (2) 0 (3) $\frac{7}{5}$ (4) $\frac{24}{25}$

35. If x and y are positive acute angles, and $\sin x = \frac{3}{5}$ and $\sin y = \frac{1}{2}$, then $\cos(x + y)$ is equal to

(1) $\frac{4\sqrt{3}+3}{10}$ (3) $\frac{4}{5} + \frac{\sqrt{3}}{2}$

(2) $\frac{4\sqrt{3}-3}{10}$ (4) $\frac{4}{5} - \frac{\sqrt{3}}{2}$

36. If $\tan x = \frac{1}{2}$ and $\tan y = 1$, the value of $\tan(x + y)$ is

(1) $\frac{1}{2}$ (2) $\frac{3}{4}$ (3) 3 (4) $\frac{3}{2}$

37. If x and y are positive acute angles, and $\sin x = \frac{3}{5}$ and $\sin y = \frac{1}{2}$, then $\sin(x + y)$ is equal to

(1) $\frac{3\sqrt{3}-4}{10}$ (3) $\frac{12}{25} + \frac{\sqrt{3}}{4}$

(2) $\frac{3\sqrt{3}+4}{10}$ (4) $\frac{12}{25} - \frac{\sqrt{3}}{4}$

38. If $\sin\alpha = \frac{3}{5}$, $\tan\beta = \frac{5}{12}$, and α and β are in the first quadrant, then the value of $\cos(\alpha + \beta)$ is

(1) $-\frac{16}{65}$ (2) $\frac{33}{65}$ (3) $\frac{56}{65}$ (4) $\frac{63}{65}$

39. If $\sin A = \frac{3}{5}$, $\sin B = \frac{5}{13}$, and angles A and B are acute angles, what is the value of $\cos(A - B)$?

(1) $-\frac{12}{65}$ (2) $\frac{16}{65}$ (3) $\frac{33}{65}$ (4) $\frac{63}{65}$

40. If $\tan x = \frac{1}{2}$ and $\tan y = \frac{1}{3}$, then the value of $\tan(x + y)$ is

(1) 1 (2) $\frac{5}{7}$ (3) $\frac{1}{5}$ (4) $\frac{1}{7}$

In 41–44, express the answer in simplest form.

41. If $\tan x = 1$ and $\tan y = 2$, find the value of $\tan(x + y)$.

42. If x and y are obtuse angles such that $\sin x = \frac{3}{5}$ and $\sin y = \frac{1}{2}$, find the value of $\sin(x + y)$.

43. If x and y are positive acute angles such that $\cos x = \frac{12}{13}$ and $\cos y = \frac{4}{5}$, find the value of $\cos(x + y)$.

44. If A and B are positive acute angles such that $\sin A = \frac{3}{5}$ and $\cos B = \frac{5}{13}$, find the value of $\cos(A + B)$.

Double Angles

Double-Angle Formulas

$$\sin 2x = 2 \sin x \cos x$$

$$\cos 2x = \cos^2 x - \sin^2 x \text{ or } 2\cos^2 x - 1 \text{ or } 1 - 2\sin^2 x$$

$$\tan 2x = \frac{2\tan x}{1 - \tan^2 x}$$

One application of these formulas is in evaluating trigonometric functions.

Example

Given: $\angle x$ is in Quadrant II and $\cos x = -\frac{4}{5}$.

Find the value of $\sin 2x$.

Solution: To apply the formula for $\sin 2x$, you must know the value of $\sin x$. To determine $\sin x$, use a Pythagorean identity.

$\sin^2 x + \cos^2 x = 1$

$\sin^2 x + \left(-\frac{4}{5}\right)^2 = 1$

$\sin^2 x + \frac{16}{25} = \frac{25}{25}$

$\sin^2 x = \frac{9}{25}$

$\sin x = \frac{3}{5}$ Since x is in Q II, $\sin x > 0$.

$\sin 2x = 2 \sin x \cos x = 2\left(\frac{3}{5}\right)\left(-\frac{4}{5}\right) = -\frac{24}{25}$

A second application of these formulas is in solving trigonometric equations.

Example

For $0° \le \theta < 360°$, solve:

$$\cos 2x - 3\cos x - 1 = 0$$

Solution: To solve, you need a single function of a single angle.

$\cos 2x - 3\cos x - 1 = 0$	Replace $\cos 2x$ by $2\cos^2 x - 1$.
$2\cos^2 x - 1 - 3\cos x - 1 = 0$	
$2\cos^2 x - 3\cos x - 2 = 0$	Combine.
$(2\cos x + 1)(\cos x - 2) = 0$	Factor.

$2\cos x + 1 = 0$	$\cos x - 2 = 0$	Set each factor equal to 0.
$2\cos x = -1$	$\cos x = 2$	
$\cos x = -\frac{1}{2}$	Reject	Reference angle is 60°. Since $\cos x < 0$, the solutions are in II and III.
$x = 120°, 240°$		

A third application of these formulas is in proving other identities.

Example

Prove the identity: $\sin 2x = \dfrac{2\tan x}{1 + \tan^2 x}$

Solution: On the left, expand $\sin 2x$. On the right, rewrite in terms of $\sin x$ and $\cos x$.

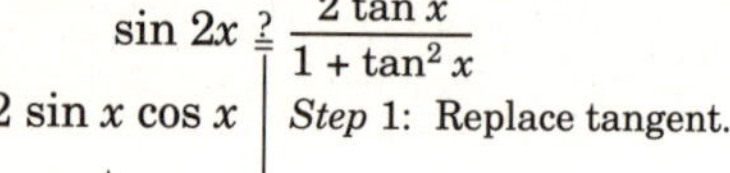

$\sin 2x \overset{?}{=} \dfrac{2\tan x}{1+\tan^2 x}$

$2\sin x\cos x$

Step 1: Replace tangent.

$$\frac{2\,\dfrac{\sin x}{\cos x}}{1 + \dfrac{\sin^2 x}{\cos^2 x}}$$

Step 2: Combine fractions in denominator.

$$\frac{\dfrac{2\sin x}{\cos x}}{\dfrac{\cos^2 x + \sin^2 x}{\cos^2 x}}$$

Step 3: Replace $\sin^2 x + \cos^2 x$.

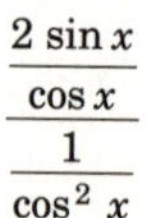

$$\frac{\dfrac{2\sin x}{\cos x}}{\dfrac{1}{\cos^2 x}}$$

Step 4: Rewrite complex fraction as ÷.

$$\frac{2\sin x}{\cos x} \div \frac{1}{\cos^2 x}$$

Step 5: Rewrite ÷ as ×, and cancel $\cos x$.

$$\frac{2\sin x}{\cos x} \cdot \frac{\cos^2 x}{1} = 2\sin x\cos x$$

EXERCISES

1. If A is a positive acute angle and $\cos A = \frac{4}{5}$, what is the value of $\cos 2A$?

(1) 1 **(2)** $\frac{7}{25}$ **(3)** $\frac{9}{25}$ **(4)** $\frac{24}{25}$

2. If $\sin x = \frac{3}{5}$ and angle x is obtuse, then the value of $\sin 2x$ is

(1) $\frac{6}{5}$ **(2)** $-\frac{6}{5}$ **(3)** $\frac{24}{25}$ **(4)** $-\frac{24}{25}$

3. If $\sin x = \frac{3}{5}$ and x is an acute angle, what is the numerical value of $\sin 2x$?

4. If $\sin A = \frac{2}{5}$, find the value of $\cos 2A$.

5. If $\sin x = a$ and $\cos x = b$, express $\sin 2x$ in terms of a and b.

6. If x is a positive acute angle and $\cos x = \frac{5}{13}$, find $\sin 2x$.

7. If $\sin x = \frac{5}{6}$, what is the value of $\cos 2x$?

8. If $\tan A = \frac{1}{3}$, find the value of $\tan 2A$.

9. If $\tan\theta = 1$, then the value of $\tan 2\theta$ is

(1) 1 **(3)** -2

(2) 2 **(4)** undefined

10. $\angle A$ is in Quadrant I and $\sin A = \frac{\sqrt{5}}{3}$. Find, in simplest form, the value of:

a. $\sin 2A$ **b.** $\cos 2A$

11. Which is a solution of the equation $\sin x = \cos 2x$?

(1) 15° **(2)** 60° **(3)** 30° **(4)** 45°

12. Which is a solution of the equation $\sin^2 2x + \sin 2x - 2 = 0$?

(1) 30° **(2)** 45° **(3)** 60° **(4)** 90°

In 13–18, find all values of θ in the interval $0 \le \theta < 2\pi$ that satisfy the given equation.

13. $\cos 2\theta = -\sin\theta$

14. $\cos 2\theta = \cos\theta$

15. $\cos 2\theta + 2 = \sin\theta$

16. $\sin 2\theta - \cos\theta = 0$

17. $\cos 2\theta + \cos\theta + 1 = 0$

18. $2\cos^3\theta + \cos\theta\cos 2\theta = 0$

In 19–22, find all values of θ in the interval $0° \le \theta < 360°$ that satisfy the given equation. As necessary, express values to the nearest degree.

19. $3\cos 2\theta + \sin\theta - 2 = 0$

20. $3\cos 2\theta - \sin\theta - 2 = 0$

21. $3\cos 2\theta + 5\sin\theta - 2 = 0$

22. $5\sin\theta + 2\cos 2\theta - 3 = 0$

In 23–31, for all values of the angle for which the given expression is defined, choose an equivalent expression.

23. $\sin 2\theta\sec\theta$ is equivalent to

(1) $\tan\theta$ **(2)** $\tan 2\theta$ **(3)** $2\cos\theta$ **(4)** $2\sin\theta$

24. $\frac{1}{2}\sec x\sin 2x$ is equivalent to

(1) $\sin x$ **(2)** $-\sin x$ **(3)** $\cos x$ **(4)** $-\cos x$

25. $2\sin^2 A + \cos 2A$ is equivalent to

(1) 1 **(2)** 2 **(3)** $\sin^2 A$ **(4)** $-\sin^2 A$

26. $\dfrac{\sin 2A}{\sin^2 A}$ is equivalent to

(1) 1 **(2)** 2 **(3)** $2\tan A$ **(4)** $2\cot A$

27. $\dfrac{\sin 2A}{2 \sin A}$ is equivalent to

(1) 1 (3) $\dfrac{\sin A}{2}$

(2) $\cos A$ (4) $\dfrac{1 - 2\cos^2 A}{2 \sin A}$

28. $\dfrac{\sin 2A}{\cos A} - \sin A$ is equivalent to

(1) 1 (2) $\cos A$ (3) $\sin A$ (4) $2 \sin A$

29. $\dfrac{2 \cos x}{\sin 2x}$ is equivalent to

(1) $\sin x$ (2) $2 \sin x$ (3) $2 \csc x$ (4) $\csc x$

30. $\sin 2A + \cos A$ is equivalent to

(1) $\cos A(2 \sin A + 1)$ (3) $2(\sin A + \cos A)$

(2) $\cos A(\cos A + 1)$ (4) $\cos A (\sin A + 1)$

31. $(\sin x - \cos x)^2$ is equivalent to

(1) 1 (3) $1 - \sin 2x$

(2) $-\cos 2x$ (4) $1 - \cos 2x$

32. Which statement is true for all real values of θ?

(1) $\cos^2 \theta - \sin^2 \theta = 1$

(2) $\cos \theta + \sin \theta = 1$

(3) $\sin^2 \theta = \dfrac{1 - \cos 2\theta}{2}$

(4) $\cos 2\theta = 2 \cos \theta$

33. Which equation is an identity?

(1) $\sin 4x = 4 \sin x \cos x$

(2) $\cos 4x = \cos^4 x - \sin^4 x$

(3) $\sin^2 4x + \cos^2 4x = 1$

(4) $\sin^4 x + \cos^4 x = 1$

In 34–69, prove that the statement is an identity for all values of the angle for which the expressions are defined.

34. $\sin 2x = \tan x(2 - 2 \sin^2 x)$

35. $2 - \sec^2 x = (\cos 2x)(\sec^2 x)$

36. $\cot x \sin 2x - \cos 2x = \sec^2 x - \tan^2 x$

37. $\sin 2\theta \cot \theta - 2 \sin^2 \theta = 2 \cos 2\theta$

38. $\cot \theta = \dfrac{\sin 2\theta}{2 \sin^2 \theta}$

39. $\cot \theta = \dfrac{\sin 2\theta}{1 - \cos 2\theta}$

40. $\tan 2x \csc x = \dfrac{2 \cos x}{\cos 2x}$

41. $\cos 2\theta = \dfrac{1 - \tan^2 \theta}{1 + \tan^2 \theta}$

42. $\tan \theta = \dfrac{1 - \cos 2\theta}{\sin 2\theta}$

43. $\dfrac{\cos(90° - \theta)}{\sin 2\theta} = \dfrac{\sec \theta}{2}$

44. $\dfrac{\sin 2\theta}{\tan \theta} = \dfrac{2}{1 + \tan^2 \theta}$

45. $\dfrac{2 \tan x - \sin 2x}{2 \sin^2 x} = \tan x$

46. $\dfrac{\cos 2x + 1}{\sec^2 x - \tan^2 x} = 2 \cos^2 x$

47. $\dfrac{1}{2} \sin 2A = \dfrac{\tan A}{1 + \tan^2 A}$

48. $\dfrac{\sin 2\theta}{1 + \cos^2 \theta - \sin^2 \theta} = \tan \theta$

49. $\cos 2x = \dfrac{1 - \tan^2 x}{\sec^2 x}$

50. $\dfrac{\sin 2\theta}{\tan \theta} = \dfrac{2}{1 + \tan^2 \theta}$

51. $\dfrac{\sin \theta + \sin 2\theta}{1 + \cos \theta + \cos 2\theta} = \tan \theta$

52. $\sec x \sin 2x = \dfrac{2 - 2 \cos^2 x}{\sin x}$

53. $\tan \theta + \cot \theta = \dfrac{2}{\sin 2\theta}$

54. $1 + \tan^2 \theta = \dfrac{2 \sin \theta}{\cos \theta \sin 2\theta}$

55. $\dfrac{2 \sin^2 A}{\sin 2A} + \cot A = \sec A \csc A$

56. $\dfrac{\cos 2\theta}{\sin \theta} + \sin \theta = \dfrac{\cot \theta}{\sec \theta}$

57. $\dfrac{1}{2}(\cot A - \tan A) = \dfrac{1}{\tan 2A}$

58. $\dfrac{\sin 2\theta}{\sin \theta} - \dfrac{\cos 2\theta}{\cos \theta} = \dfrac{1}{\cos \theta}$

59. $\dfrac{2 \sin^2 x}{\sin 2x} + \dfrac{1}{\tan x} = \sec x \csc x$

60. $\dfrac{\cos 2x}{\sin x} + \dfrac{\sin 2x}{\cos x} = \csc x$

61. $2 - \tan^2 A = 1 + \dfrac{\cos 2A}{\cos^2 A}$

62. $\dfrac{\cos x}{\sin x} + \dfrac{\sin x}{\cos x} = \dfrac{2}{\sin 2x}$

63. $\dfrac{2 \cos x}{\sin 2x} = \dfrac{1}{\sin x \cos^2 x} - \dfrac{\tan^2 x}{\sin x}$

64. $(\cos 2\theta)(1 + \tan^2 \theta) = 2 - \dfrac{1}{\cos^2 \theta}$

65. $\dfrac{\cos 2\theta}{\cos \theta(\cos \theta - \sin \theta)} = 1 + \tan \theta$

66. $\tan \theta + \dfrac{2 - 4 \sin^2 \theta}{\sin 2\theta} = \cot \theta$

67. $\dfrac{1 + \cos 2A}{\sin 2A} = \cot A$

68. $\csc 2x + \cot 2x = \cot x$

69. $\dfrac{1 + \cos 2\theta}{1 - \cos 2\theta} = \cot^2 \theta$

Half Angles

Half-Angle Formulas

$$\sin\frac{x}{2} = \pm\sqrt{\frac{1-\cos x}{2}} \qquad \cos\frac{x}{2} = \pm\sqrt{\frac{1+\cos x}{2}} \qquad \tan\frac{x}{2} = \pm\sqrt{\frac{1-\cos x}{1+\cos x}}$$

The half-angle formulas are applied in ways similar to the double-angle formulas.

Example

Find the exact value of cos 195°.

Solution: Consider 195° as $\frac{390°}{2}$, and use the formula for $\cos\frac{x}{2}$.

$$\cos\frac{x}{2} = \pm\sqrt{\frac{1+\cos x}{2}}$$

$$\cos 195° = \cos\frac{390°}{2} = -\sqrt{\frac{1+\cos 390°}{2}} = -\sqrt{\frac{1+\cos 30°}{2}} = -\sqrt{\frac{1+\frac{\sqrt{3}}{2}}{2}} = -\sqrt{\frac{2+\sqrt{3}}{4}} = -\frac{1}{2}\sqrt{2+\sqrt{3}}$$

195° is in Q III, where cosine < 0. — Reference ∠ for 390° is 30°. — Replace cos 30°. — Multiply in complex fraction by 2. — Denominator is a perfect square.

EXERCISES

1. The expression $2\sin^2\frac{A}{2}$ is equivalent to
   (1) $1 - \cos A$ (3) $1 + \cos A$
   (2) $\frac{1-\cos A}{2}$ (4) $\frac{1+\cos A}{2}$

2. Which statement is an identity?
   (1) $\cos 2x = 1 - 2\sin^2 x$
   (2) $\sin 2x = 2\sin^2 x$
   (3) $\sin\frac{1}{2}x = \pm\sqrt{1-\cos x}$
   (4) $\cos\frac{1}{2}x = \pm\sqrt{1+\cos x}$

3. Which expression is equivalent to $\sin^2\frac{1}{2}x$?
   (1) $\frac{1-\cos x}{2}$ (3) $\frac{1-\sin x}{2}$
   (2) $\frac{1+\cos x}{2}$ (4) $\frac{1+\sin x}{2}$

4. If $\cos x = -1$, a value of $\sin\frac{1}{2}x$ is
   (1) 1 (2) 2 (3) $\sqrt{3}$ (4) 0

5. If x is a positive acute angle and $\cos x = \frac{1}{2}$, what is the value of $\sin\frac{1}{2}x$?
   (1) 1 (2) 2 (3) $\frac{\sqrt{3}}{2}$ (4) $\frac{1}{2}$

6. If $\cos\theta = \frac{1}{8}$, the positive value of $\cos\frac{1}{2}\theta$ is
   (1) $\frac{\sqrt{7}}{2}$ (2) $\frac{3}{2}$ (3) $\frac{\sqrt{7}}{4}$ (4) $\frac{3}{4}$

7. If θ is a positive acute angle and $\cos\theta = \frac{7}{25}$, then $\sin\frac{1}{2}\theta$ is equal to
   (1) $\frac{4}{5}$ (2) $\frac{-4}{5}$ (3) $\frac{3}{5}$ (4) $\frac{-3}{5}$

8. If $\cos x = 0.8$, what is a value of $\tan\frac{1}{2}x$?
   (1) $\frac{1}{3}$ (2) $\frac{1}{9}$ (3) 3 (4) 9

9. If $\cos A = t$, then $\sin^2\frac{A}{2}$ is equal to
   (1) $\frac{1-t}{2}$ (3) $\frac{1-t}{1+t}$
   (2) $\frac{1+t}{2}$ (4) $\frac{1-t}{4}$

10. If $\cos x = \frac{15}{17}$, what is the positive value of $\sin\frac{1}{2}x$?

11. x is a positive acute angle, $\cos x = \frac{7}{18}$. Find $\cos\frac{1}{2}x$.

12. Find the positive value of $\sin\frac{1}{2}x$ if $\cos x = 0.02$.

13. If $\cos A = \frac{3}{5}$, find the positive value of $\tan\frac{1}{2}A$.

14. If $\cos\theta = -\frac{5}{13}$ and θ is in Quadrant II, find $\sin\frac{1}{2}\theta$.

15. If $\sin\theta = -0.8$ and θ is in Quadrant III, find $\sin\frac{1}{2}\theta$.

16. If $\tan x = \frac{8}{15}$ and x is in Quadrant III, find $\cos\frac{1}{2}x$.

17. If $\sin x = -0.6$ and x is in Quadrant IV, find $\cos\frac{x}{2}$.

18. If $\tan x = \frac{3}{4}$ and x is in Quadrant III, find $\tan\frac{x}{2}$.

19. Find the exact value of $\sin 22\frac{1}{2}°$.

20. Find the exact value of $\sin 112° 30'$.

21. Find the exact value of $\cos 67.5°$.

22. Find the exact value of $\tan(-195°)$.

23. Solve for $\cos\theta$: $\cos\frac{\theta}{2} = \frac{\sqrt{5}}{4}$

In 24–26, find all values of θ in the interval $0 \le \theta < 2\pi$ that satisfy the given equation.

24. $\cos\frac{1}{2}\theta = \sin\theta$

25. $\tan\frac{\theta}{2} = \sin\theta$

26. $\sin\frac{1}{2}\theta - \cos\frac{1}{2}\theta = \frac{\sqrt{2}}{2}$

In 27–33, prove that each statement is an identity for all values of the angles for which the expressions are defined.

27. $1 - \cos x = 2\sin^2\frac{x}{2}$

28. $\tan\frac{1}{2}A = \csc A - \cot A$

29. $\left(\cos\frac{x}{2} - \sin\frac{x}{2}\right)^2 = 1 - \sin x$

30. $\tan\frac{1}{2}\theta = \frac{\sin\theta}{1+\cos\theta}$

31. $\tan\frac{1}{2}A = \frac{1-\cos A}{\sin A}$

32. $\sin x = \frac{2\tan\frac{1}{2}x}{1+\tan^2\frac{1}{2}x}$

33. $1 + \tan\frac{1}{2}\theta\tan\theta = \sec\theta$

7.5 SUMMARY EXERCISES

In 1–4, factor as completely as possible.

1. $4\sin^3\theta - \sin\theta$

2. $9\sin x\tan^2 x - 16\sin x$

3. $3\sin^2 A - \sin A - 2$

4. $2\sin^2\theta + 7\sin\theta - 15$

5. Simplify: $\frac{\sin^3\theta - \sin\theta}{\sin\theta + 1}$

6. Express as a single fraction in simplest form:
$\frac{1}{\cos x + 1} - \frac{1}{\cos x - 1}$

In 7–8, express the complex fraction in simplest form.

7. $\dfrac{\sin A - \cos A}{\frac{1}{\cos A} - \frac{1}{\sin A}}$

8. $\dfrac{\frac{\sin\alpha}{\cos\alpha} - \frac{\cos\alpha}{\sin\alpha}}{\frac{1}{\cos\alpha} - \frac{1}{\sin\alpha}}$

9. Express as a single fraction in simplest form:
$$\frac{\frac{\sin A}{\cos A}}{\frac{\cos A}{\sin A}} + \frac{\frac{\cos A}{\sin A}}{\frac{\sin A}{\cos A}}$$

10. Which is not an identity?
(1) $\sin^2\theta + \cos^2\theta = 1$
(2) $\cos^2\theta = 1 - \sin^2\theta$
(3) $\cos^2\theta = 1 + \sin^2\theta$
(4) $\sin^2\theta = 1 - \cos^2\theta$

11. Which is not an identity?
(1) $\sin\theta \cdot \csc\theta = 1$
(2) $\tan\theta + \cot\theta = 1$
(3) $\tan^2\theta + 1 = \sec^2\theta$
(4) $\csc^2\theta - 1 = \cot^2\theta$

12. Express $\cot\theta$ in terms of $\sec\theta$.

In 13–15, for all values of the angle for which the given expression is defined, choose an equivalent expression.

13. $\frac{1-\sin^2\theta}{\cos\theta}$ is equivalent to
(1) $\sec\theta$ (2) $\tan\theta$ (3) $\cos\theta$ (4) $\sin\theta$

14. $\frac{\tan x\cos x}{\csc x}$ is equivalent to
(1) 1 (2) $\sin^2 x$ (3) $\csc^2 x$ (4) $\tan x$

15. The expression $\sin A + \frac{\cos^2 A}{\sin A}$ is equivalent to
(1) 1 (2) $\cos A$ (3) $\sin A$ (4) $\csc A$

In 16–18, prove that the given statement is an identity for all values of the angle for which the expressions are defined.

16. $\frac{\cot A - \tan A}{\sec A + \csc A} = \cos A - \sin A$

17. $\frac{(\cos\theta + \sin\theta)^2}{1 + 2\sin\theta\cos\theta} = \cos\theta\tan\theta\csc\theta$

18. $(\cot\theta + \csc\theta)^2 = \frac{1+\cos\theta}{1-\cos\theta}$

19. Which value of θ satisfies the equation $\sin\theta = \cos\theta$?
(1) 0 (2) $\frac{\pi}{4}$ (3) $\frac{\pi}{2}$ (4) π

20. Which does not represent a root of the equation $2\sin\theta + 1 = 0$?
(1) $\arcsin\left(\frac{1}{2}\right)$
(2) $\arcsin\left(-\frac{1}{2}\right)$
(3) 210°
(4) $\frac{11\pi}{6}$

21. In the interval $0° \le \theta < 360°$, find all values of θ to the nearest degree: $3\tan\theta = 5 + \tan\theta$

In 22–27, solve the given equation for all values of θ in the interval $0° \le \theta < 360°$.

22. $\sin\theta\cos\theta = \cos\theta$

23. $|3 - 2\sin\theta| = 4$

24. $\sqrt{7 + 2\cos\theta} = 3$

25. $2\cos^2\theta = \cos\theta$

26. $4\cos^2\theta = 1$

27. $2\sin^2\theta - 5\sin\theta = 3$

28. Find, to the nearest degree, all values of θ in the interval $0° \le \theta \le 360°$ that satisfy the equation $3\sin^2\theta + 2\sin\theta - 1 = 0$.

29. **a.** Find, to the nearest tenth, the value(s) of $\tan\theta$ that satisfy the equation:

$$\tan^2\theta - 3\tan\theta + 1 = 0$$

b. Using the answer(s) obtained in part **a**, find the quadrant(s) in which angle θ may lie.

30. $\cos(90° - x)$ is equivalent to

(1) $-\cos x$ **(2)** $\cos x$ **(3)** $-\sin x$ **(4)** $\sin x$

In 31–32, prove that the given statement is an identity for all values of the angles for which the expressions are defined.

31. $\sin\left(x + \frac{\pi}{3}\right) = \frac{1}{2}(\sin x + \sqrt{3}\cos x)$

32. $\cot(x - y) = \dfrac{\cot x \cot y + 1}{\cot y - \cot x}$

33. If $\sin(x - y) = -0.6$ and x and y are both acute angles, in which quadrant will the angle represented by $(x - y)$ lie?

(1) I **(2)** II **(3)** III **(4)** IV

34. Using the formula for $\cos(x + y)$, find the exact value of $\cos 105°$ in radical form if $m\angle x = 60°$ and $m\angle y = 45°$.

35. $\sin 32° \cos 41° - \cos 32° \sin 41°$ equals

(1) $\sin 73°$ **(2)** $-\sin 9°$ **(3)** $\cos 73°$ **(4)** $\cos 9°$

36. If $\tan A = \frac{2}{3}$ and $\tan B = 3$, express $\tan(A - B)$ as a fraction in simplest form.

37. If A and B are both acute angles, $\sin A = \frac{5}{13}$, and $\sin B = \frac{4}{5}$, then $\sin(A - B)$ is

(1) $-\frac{33}{65}$ **(2)** $\frac{63}{65}$ **(3)** $\frac{33}{65}$ **(4)** $\frac{43}{65}$

38. $\cos 2A$ is equivalent to

(1) $2\sin^2 A - 1$ **(3)** $\sin^2 A - \cos^2 A$
(2) $1 - 2\sin^2 A$ **(4)** $1 - 2\cos^2 A$

39. If x is an acute angle and $\cos x = \frac{3}{5}$, then the numerical value of $\cos 2x$ is

(1) $\frac{7}{25}$ **(2)** $\frac{24}{25}$ **(3)** $-\frac{7}{25}$ **(4)** $-\frac{24}{25}$

40. If $\angle\theta$ is in Quadrant II and $\tan\theta = -\frac{4}{3}$, find the value of $\sin 2\theta$.

41. Find all values of θ in the interval $0° \le \theta \le 360°$ that satisfy the equation $\cos 2\theta = \sin\theta$.

42. The expression $(\sin 2x)(\tan x)$ is equivalent to

(1) $2\sin x$ **(3)** $2\sin^2 x$
(2) $2\cos x$ **(4)** $2\cos^2 x$

43. Prove the identity:

$$\sin 2x = \tan x(2 - 2\sin^2 x)$$

44. $\cos^2\frac{1}{2}x$ is equivalent to

(1) $\frac{1 - \cos x}{2}$ **(3)** $\frac{1 - \sin x}{2}$
(2) $\frac{1 + \cos x}{2}$ **(4)** $\frac{1 + \sin x}{2}$

45. If $\cos A = \frac{1}{2}$ and angle A is a positive acute angle, find the value of $\sin\frac{1}{2}A$.

46. If $\cos A = \frac{1}{3}$, then the positive value of $\tan\frac{1}{2}A$ is

(1) $\sqrt{2}$ **(3)** $\frac{\sqrt{3}}{3}$
(2) $\sqrt{3}$ **(4)** $\frac{\sqrt{2}}{2}$

47. If $\cos\theta = -0.6$ and θ is in Quadrant III, find $\sin\frac{1}{2}\theta$.

48. If $\sin x = -\frac{4}{5}$ and x is in Quadrant IV, find $\cos\frac{1}{2}x$.

49. Find the exact value of $\sin 67\frac{1}{2}°$.

50. Find all values of θ in the interval $0° \le \theta < 360°$ that satisfy the equation $\sin\frac{\theta}{2} = \cos\theta$.

51. Prove that the given statement is an identity for all values of the angle for which the expressions are defined:

$$\frac{1 + \sec\theta}{\sec\theta} = 2\cos^2\frac{1}{2}\theta$$

52. $\log\tan\theta$ is equivalent to

(1) $\log\sin\theta \div \log\cos\theta$
(2) $\log\sin\theta \times \log\cos\theta$
(3) $\log\sin\theta + \log\cos\theta$
(4) $\log\sin\theta - \log\cos\theta$

CHAPTER 8

Trigonometry, Part III

8.1 AREA OF A TRIANGLE

The area of a triangle can be expressed as one-half the product of any two sides and the sine of the included angle.

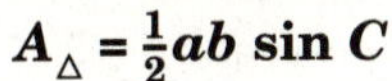

$$A_{\triangle} = \frac{1}{2}ab \sin C$$

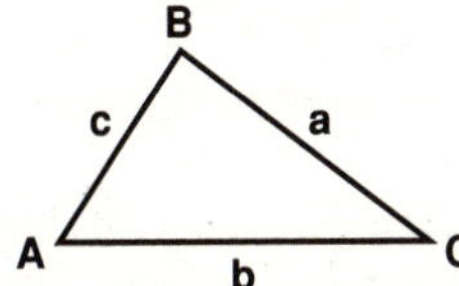

Example

In $\triangle PQR$, $m\angle R = 120°$, $p = 8$ cm, and $q = 10$ cm. Find the area.

Solution:

$$\begin{aligned} A_{\triangle} &= \frac{1}{2}pq \sin R \\ &= \frac{1}{2}(8)(10)(\sin 120°) \\ &= 40 \sin 60° \\ &= 40\left(\frac{\sqrt{3}}{2}\right) = 20\sqrt{3} \text{ cm}^2 \end{aligned}$$

Q
p
120°
P
R
q

EXERCISES

1. In $\triangle ABC$, if $b = 10$, $c = 16$, and $m\angle A = 30°$, the area of the triangle is
   (1) 160 (2) $80\sqrt{3}$ (3) $40\sqrt{3}$ (4) 40

2. If, in $\triangle ABC$, $m\angle A = 45°$, $m\angle B = 45°$, and $a = 3$ cm, find the area of the triangle.

3. The lengths of two sides of a triangle are 8 cm and 7 cm and the included angle measures 60°. In cm^2, what is the area of the triangle?
   (1) 14 (3) 28
   (2) $14\sqrt{3}$ (4) $28\sqrt{3}$

4. In $\triangle ABC$, $a = 6$, $b = 10$, $m\angle C = 120°$. The area is
   (1) $30\sqrt{3}$ (3) $15\sqrt{3}$
   (2) 30 (4) 15

5. What is the area of $\triangle ABC$ if $a = 12$, $b = 10$, and $m\angle C = 150°$?
   (1) 60 (2) 20 (3) 30 (4) 40

6. In $\triangle ABC$, $a = 9$, $c = 8$, and $\sin B = \frac{1}{3}$. The area is
   (1) 6 (2) 12 (3) 24 (4) 36

7. In $\triangle PQR$, $PQ = 5$ cm, $QR = 6$ cm, and $m\angle Q = 30°$. Find the area.

8. In $\triangle ABC$, $a = 6$, $b = 8$, and $\sin C = \frac{1}{4}$. Find the area.

9. In isosceles $\triangle ABC$, vertex angle B measures 30° and each leg has length 10. Find the area.

10. In $\triangle ABC$, $a = 10$ in., $b = 10$ in., and $m\angle A = 75°$. Find the area.

11. In $\triangle ABC$, $m\angle C = 90°$, side $c = 13$ cm, and side $a = 5$ cm. Find the area.

12. Find the area of right $\triangle ABC$, if $m\angle C = 90°$, $m\angle B = 45°$, and $b = \sqrt{3}$ in.

13. In $\triangle ABC$, $m\angle C = 90°$, $a = 6$ ft. and $c = 10$ ft. Find the area.

14. In $\triangle ABC$, $a = 10$, $b = 10$ and $m\angle A = 70°$. Find the area, to the nearest integer.

15. Find, to the nearest tenth, the area of $\triangle ABC$ if $a = 6$ cm, $b = 10$ cm, and $m\angle C = 18°$.

16. The area of $\triangle ABC$ is 100 cm^2. If $c = 20$ cm and $m\angle A = 30°$, then b is equal to
   (1) 20 cm
   (2) 500 cm
   (3) $20\sqrt{3}$ cm
   (4) $10\sqrt{2}$ cm

17. The area of $\triangle ABC$ is 10 sq. in. If $a = 10$ in. and $b = 18$ in., find the value of $\sin C$.

18. The area of acute $\triangle ABC$ is 24 sq. in., with $a = 12$ in. and $b = 8$ in. Find the number of degrees in the measure of angle C.

19. In isosceles $\triangle ABC$, $a = b$. The area is equal to
   (1) $cb \sin A$
   (2) $\frac{1}{2}cb \cos A$
   (3) $b^2 \sin C$
   (4) $\frac{1}{2}b^2 \sin C$

20. The length of each of the equal sides of an isosceles triangle is a and the measure of a base angle is 15°. Express the area of the triangle in terms of a.

21. The area of triangular field ABC is 780 m^2. If the length of $\overline{AC}$ is 52 m and $m\angle A = 68°$, what is the length of $\overline{AB}$ to the nearest meter?

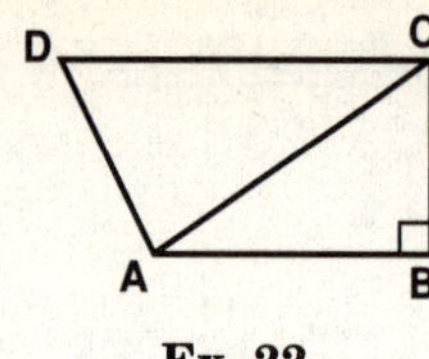

Ex. 22

22. a. In quadrilateral $ABCD$, m$\angle DAB$ = 106°, AB = 18, AD = 12, m$\angle ACB$ = 56°, and m$\angle B$ = 90°. Find AC to the nearest integer.
 b. Using the answer to part **a**, find the area of $\triangle ACD$ to the nearest integer.

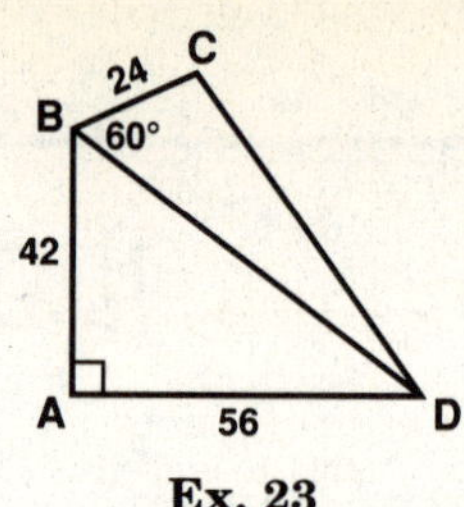

Ex. 23

23. A plot of ground has the shape of the figure shown. AB = 42 rods, AD = 56 rods, BC = 24 rods, m$\angle DAB$ = 90°, and m$\angle CBD$ = 60°. Find, to the nearest hundred square rods, the area of the plot of ground $ABCD$.

8.2 THE LAW OF SINES

In any triangle, the ratio between the sine of an angle and the length of the side opposite that angle is constant.

The Law of Sines can be used to find missing parts of a triangle if the known combination of sides and angles is a.s.a., a.a.s., or s.s.a.

In any $\triangle ABC$:

$$\frac{\sin A}{a} = \frac{\sin B}{b} = \frac{\sin C}{c} \qquad \textit{The Law of Sines}$$

Examples

1. *Given:* In $\triangle ABC$, m$\angle A$ = 72°, m$\angle B$ = 40°, and c = 15 in.

Find: a, to the nearest tenth of an inch

Solution: With a.s.a. as information, apply the Law of Sines.

First, find m$\angle C$.

$$m\angle A + m\angle B + m\angle C = 180°$$
$$72 + 40 + m\angle C = 180$$
$$m\angle C = 68°$$

Since you are looking for a and you know c, use the ratios that involve a and c.

$$\frac{\sin C}{c} = \frac{\sin A}{a}$$
$$\frac{\sin 68°}{15} = \frac{\sin 72°}{a}$$
$$a = \frac{15(\sin 72°)}{\sin 68°}$$
$$a \approx 15.4 \text{ in.} \quad \textit{Ans.}$$

2. In $\triangle ABC$, a = 11 cm, b = 20 cm, and m$\angle B$ = 43°. Find the area of $\triangle ABC$, to the nearest sq. cm.

Solution: To apply the area formula, you must know m$\angle C$. Use the Law of Sines to find m$\angle A$, which will determine m$\angle C$.

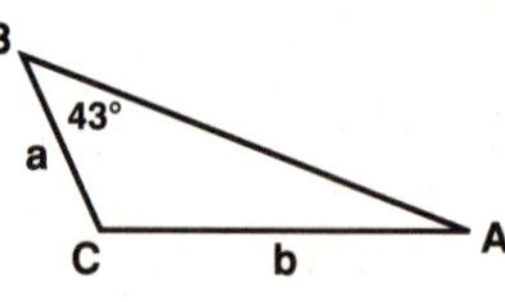

Step 1: Find m$\angle A$.

$$\frac{\sin B}{b} = \frac{\sin A}{a}$$
$$\frac{\sin 43°}{20} = \frac{\sin A}{11}$$
$$\sin A = \frac{11(\sin 43°)}{20}$$
$$\sin A \approx 0.3751$$
$$m\angle A \approx 22° \text{ or } 158°$$

Reject 158° since no triangle could be formed.

Step 2: Use A to find C.

$$m\angle A + m\angle B + m\angle C = 180°$$
$$22 + 43 + m\angle C = 180$$
$$m\angle C \approx 115°$$

Step 3: Use m$\angle C$ in the area formula.

$$A_{\triangle} = \tfrac{1}{2}ab \sin C$$
$$= \tfrac{1}{2}(11)(20) \sin 115°$$
$$= 110 \sin 65°$$
$$\approx 100 \text{ sq. cm} \quad \textit{Ans.}$$

EXERCISES

1. If, in $\triangle ABC$, $\sin A = \frac{1}{4}$ and $\sin B = \frac{1}{2}$, what is the ratio of side a to side b?
(1) $\frac{1}{8}$ (2) 2 (3) $\frac{1}{4}$ (4) $\frac{1}{2}$

2. In $\triangle ABC$, $\sin A$ = 0.8 and a = 4. The value of the ratio $\frac{\sin B}{b}$ is
(1) $\frac{1}{5}$ (2) $\frac{1}{2}$ (3) $\frac{2}{1}$ (4) $\frac{5}{1}$

3. In $\triangle ABC$, $m\angle A = 30°$ and $m\angle B = 60°$. The ratio of a to b is

(1) $\frac{1}{\sqrt{3}}$ (2) $\frac{2}{1}$ (3) $\frac{1}{2}$ (4) $\frac{\sqrt{3}}{1}$

4. In $\triangle RST$, $m\angle R = 45°$ and $m\angle T = 30°$. Find the ratio of t to r.

5. In $\triangle ABC$, $m\angle A = 40°$, $m\angle C = 65°$, and $c = 12$. Which is a correct expression for a?

(1) $\frac{12\sin 40°}{\sin 75°}$ (3) $\frac{12\sin 65°}{\sin 75°}$

(2) $\frac{12\sin 65°}{\sin 40°}$ (4) $\frac{12\sin 40°}{\sin 65°}$

6. In $\triangle RST$, what is the value of r in terms of R, T, and t?

(1) $r = \frac{tR}{T}$ (3) $r = \frac{\sin T}{t \cdot \sin R}$

(2) $r = \frac{t \cdot \sin T}{\sin R}$ (4) $r = \frac{t \cdot \sin R}{\sin T}$

7. Given: $\triangle ABC$, $\angle C$ is an obtuse angle, $m\angle A = 28°$, and $b = 250$. If $\overline{AC}$ is extended, the measure of the exterior angle at C is 44°. Which expression can be used to find the length of a?

(1) $\frac{250\sin 28°}{\sin 136°}$ (3) $\frac{250\sin 16°}{\sin 28°}$

(2) $\frac{250\sin 28°}{\sin 16°}$ (4) $250 \sin 28° - \sin 16°$

8. In $\triangle ABC$, $a = 19$, $c = 10$, and $m\angle A = 111°$. Which statement can be used to find the measure of angle C?

(1) $\sin C = \frac{10}{19}$ (3) $\sin C = \frac{10\sin 21°}{19}$

(2) $\sin C = \frac{19\sin 69°}{10}$ (4) $\sin C = \frac{10\sin 69°}{19}$

9. In $\triangle ABC$, if $m\angle A = 30°$, $a = 6$, and $b = 8$, then $\sin B$ is

(1) $\frac{2}{3}$ (2) $\frac{3}{4}$ (3) $\frac{6}{10}$ (4) $\frac{8}{10}$

10. In $\triangle ABC$, $b = 2$, $c = 3$, and $\sin C = 0.63$. What is the value of $\sin B$?

(1) 0.21 (2) 0.31 (3) 0.42 (4) 0.67

11. In $\triangle ABC$, $a = 10$, $b = 6$, and $\sin B = \frac{2}{5}$. Express $\sin A$ in simplest fractional form.

12. In $\triangle ABC$, $a = \sqrt{2}$, $b = 3$, and $m\angle B = 45°$. Find the value of $\sin A$.

13. In $\triangle ABC$, $a = 5$, $b = 7$, and $\sin A = \frac{3}{7}$. Find the value of $\sin B$.

14. In $\triangle ABC$, $m\angle A = 30°$, $a = 8$, and $b = 12$. Find the value of $\sin B$.

15. In $\triangle ABC$, $b = 4$, $c = 3$, and $\sin B = \frac{1}{2}$. Find the value of $\sin C$.

16. In $\triangle RST$, side $r = 9$, side $s = 8$, and $\sin S = \frac{2}{3}$. Find the value of $\sin R$.

17. In $\triangle RST$, $\sin R = 0.36$, $r = 12$, and $s = 18$. Find the value of $\sin S$.

18. In $\triangle ABC$, $m\angle A = 30°$, $m\angle B = 45°$, and $b = \sqrt{2}$. The value of a is

(1) 1 (2) 2 (3) $2\sqrt{2}$ (4) 4

19. In $\triangle ABC$, $m\angle A = 30°$, $m\angle C = 45°$, and $a = 8\sqrt{2}$. What is the value of c?

(1) 32 (2) 16 (3) $4\sqrt{2}$ (4) 4

20. In right $\triangle ABC$, $m\angle C = 90°$, $a = 4$, and $\sin A = \frac{1}{2}$. What is the length of the hypotenuse?

(1) $4\sqrt{3}$ (2) $\frac{8\sqrt{3}}{3}$ (3) 8 (4) $8\sqrt{2}$

21. In $\triangle ABC$, $\sin A = 0.6$, $\sin B = 0.5$, and $b = 75$ cm. Find the length of side a.

22. In $\triangle ABC$, $\sin A = \frac{1}{3}$, $\sin B = \frac{1}{5}$, and $b = 6$. Find the length of side a.

23. In $\triangle ABC$, $\sin A = 0.8$, $\sin B = 0.3$, and $a = 24$. Find the length of side b.

24. In $\triangle ABC$, $\sin A = \frac{4}{5}$, $\sin B = \frac{3}{4}$, and $a = 16$. Find the length of side b.

25. In $\triangle ABC$, $\sin A = \frac{\sqrt{5}}{3}$, $\sin B = \frac{2}{3}$, and $a = \sqrt{5}$. What is the length of side b?

26. In $\triangle ABC$, $m\angle A = 40°$, $m\angle B = 50°$, and $c = 80$ cm. Find the length of side b to the nearest cm.

27. In $\triangle ABC$, $\sin A = \frac{1}{2}$, $\sin C = \frac{1}{3}$, and $a = 12$. Find the length of side c.

28. In $\triangle RST$, $\sin R = 0.6$, $\sin S = 0.4$, and side $s = 16$. Find the length of side r.

29. In $\triangle RST$, $s = 54$, $\sin S = 0.72$, and $\sin T = 0.28$. Find the value of t.

30. In $\triangle ABC$, $a = 5$, $b = 6$, and $\sin B = \frac{3}{5}$. Find the measure of acute angle A.

31. In $\triangle ABC$, $a = \sqrt{2}$, $b = 1$, and $m\angle A = 90°$. Find the measure of $\angle B$.

32. In $\triangle RST$, $r = 3$, $s = 3\sqrt{2}$, and $m\angle R = 30°$. Find $m\angle S$ if S is an acute angle.

33. In $\triangle ABC$, $m\angle B = 38°$, $m\angle C = 56°\,20'$, and $a = 12$. Find the length of side c to the nearest integer.

34. In $\triangle ABC$, $m\angle A = 27°\,10'$, $m\angle B = 33°\,20'$, and side $\overline{BC} = 12$ cm. Find the length of side $\overline{AB}$ to the nearest cm.

35. In $\triangle ABC$, $m\angle A = 38°$, $a = 11$, $b = 15$, and $\angle B$ is an obtuse angle. Find the measure of $\angle C$ to the nearest degree.

36. In $\triangle ABC$, $a = 15$, $c = 20$, and $m\angle C = 100°$. Find $m\angle A$ to the nearest degree.

37. In $\triangle ABC$, $m\angle A = 28°\,40'$, $a = 16$, $b = 20$, and $\angle B$ is obtuse. Find $m\angle C$ to the nearest ten minutes.

38. In $\triangle ABC$, m$\angle A$ = 16° 30′, m$\angle B$ = 28° 10′, and AB = 34.5 feet. Find AC to the nearest tenth of a foot.

39. In $\triangle ABC$, m$\angle B$ = 35°, m$\angle C$ = 41°, and BC = 23 meters. Find the length of the shortest side of the triangle to the nearest meter.

40. The measures of the angles of a triangle are in the ratio 2:3:4. The length of the shortest side of the triangle is 30 feet. Find the longest side to the nearest foot.

41. The measures of two angles of a triangle are 25° and 58°. The longest side of the triangle is 39 meters. Find the length of the shortest side to the nearest meter.

42. In $\triangle ABC$, m$\angle B$ = 53° 20′, m$\angle C$ = 71° 30′, and BC = 26.1 inches. Find the length of the altitude on $\overline{BC}$ to the nearest tenth of an inch.

43. In $\triangle RST$, m$\angle R$ = 17° 20′, RT = 40, and m$\angle T$ = 34° 50′.
   a. Find RS to the nearest integer.
   b. $\triangle RST$ is enlarged by a dilation to form $\triangle R'S'T'$. If $R'T'$ = 200, what is the length of $\overline{R'S'}$?

44. Two sides of a triangular plot measure 30 meters and 18 meters, respectively, and the angle opposite the 30-meter side measures 58°.
   a. Find, to the nearest degree, the measure of the angle opposite the 18-meter side.
   b. Using the answer to part **a**, find the area of the triangle to the nearest square meter.

45. In $\triangle ABC$, BC = 30 feet, m$\angle A$ = 30° 10′, and m$\angle C$ = 103° 20′.
   a. Find AC to the nearest foot.
   b. Find the area of $\triangle ABC$ to the nearest square foot.

46. In $\triangle ABC$, a = 30, c = 27, and m$\angle A$ = 34°.
   a. Find the measure of $\angle C$ to the nearest degree.
   b. Using the answer obtained in part **a**, find the area of $\triangle ABC$ to the nearest square unit.

47. In $\triangle ABC$, AC = 30 cm, m$\angle B$ = 100°, and m$\angle A$ = 50°. Find the area of $\triangle ABC$ to the nearest square centimeter.

8.3 THE AMBIGUOUS CASE

Usually, when 3 pieces of information (s.s.s., s.a.s., a.s.a., a.a.s., or hy-leg in a right △) are known, all triangles that can be thus constructed are congruent.

In the case of s.s.a., the possibilities for construction depend on the relationships between the given sides and the altitude opposite the given angle.

Let a, b, and m$\angle A$ be known, where $b > h$, the altitude from C.

When $\angle A$ is acute, there are 5 possible situations.

If $a < h$:

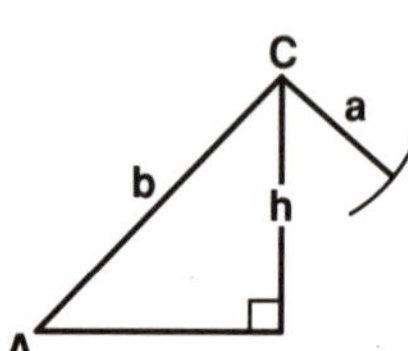

No triangle is possible.

If $a = h$:

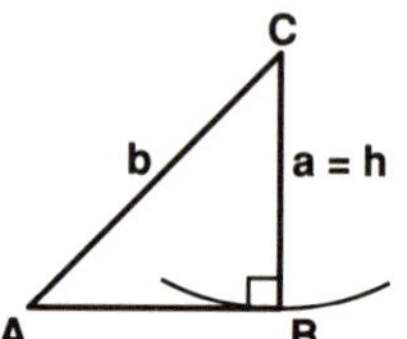

One triangle satisfies, right $\triangle ABC$.

If $a > h$ and $a = b$:

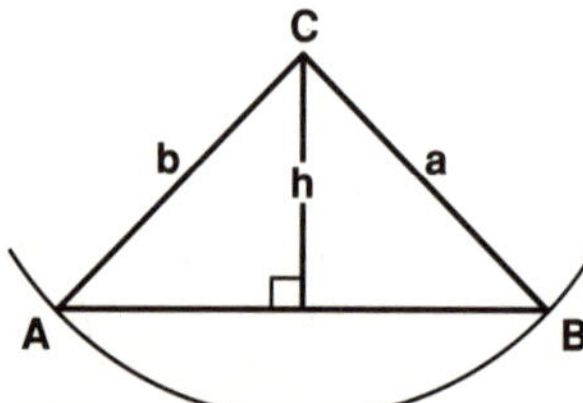

One triangle satisfies, isosceles $\triangle ABC$.

If $a > h$ and $a < b$:

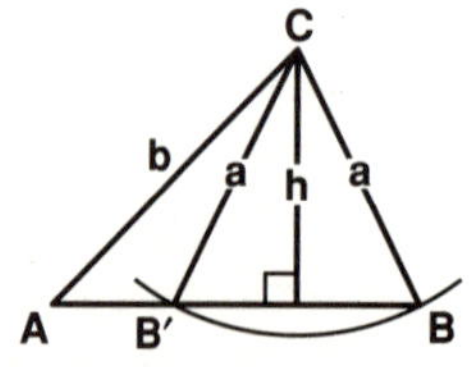

Two triangles satisfy, acute $\triangle ABC$ and obtuse $\triangle AB'C$.

If $a > h$ and $a > b$:

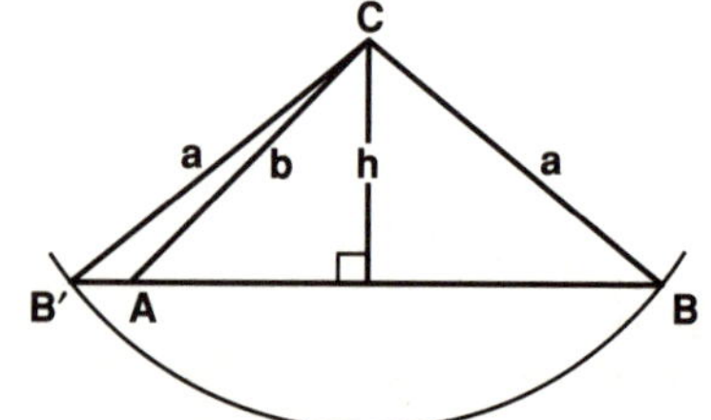

One triangle satisfies, $\triangle ABC$. ($\triangle AB'C$ does not contain acute $\angle A$.)

Examples

1. If m$\angle A = 40°$, side $b = 10$, and side $a = 7$, how many distinct triangles are possible?

Solution: Find the length of h, the altitude from C.

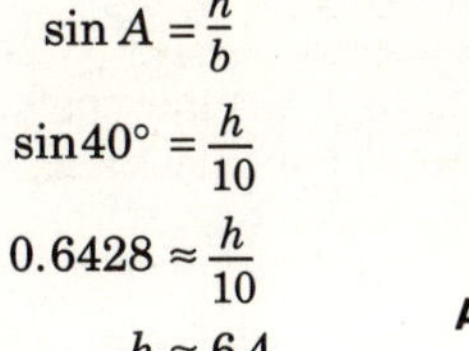

$\sin A = \frac{h}{b}$

$\sin 40° = \frac{h}{10}$

$0.6428 \approx \frac{h}{10}$

$h \approx 6.4$

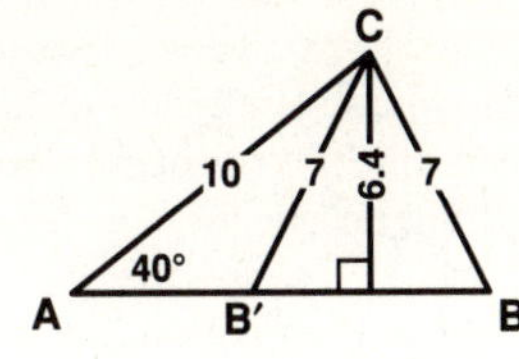

Thus, $a > h$ and $a < b$, or $h < a < b$.

Answer: There are two triangles possible.

2. If m$\angle A = 45°$, $b = 3\sqrt{2}$, and $a = 3$, then $\triangle ABC$

(1) cannot be drawn **(3)** is a right $\triangle$
(2) is an acute $\triangle$ **(4)** is an obtuse $\triangle$

Solution: Find the length of h, the altitude from C.

$h = b \sin A$

$h = 3\sqrt{2} \sin 45°$

$h = 3\sqrt{2} \cdot \frac{\sqrt{2}}{2}$

Thus, $a = h$.

Answer: **(3)**

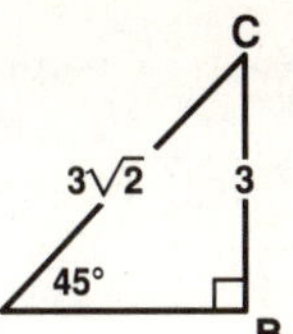

EXERCISES

1. If m$\angle A = 30°$, $a = 11$, and $b = 12$, the number of distinct triangles that can be constructed is

(1) 1 **(2)** 2 **(3)** 3 **(4)** 0

2. If $a = 8$, $b = 8$, and m$\angle A = 30°$, then $\triangle ABC$

(1) must be an acute triangle
(2) must be a right triangle
(3) must be an obtuse triangle
(4) may be either an obtuse or an acute triangle

3. In $\triangle ABC$, if m$\angle A = 30°$, $b = 10$, and $a = 12$, then $\triangle ABC$

(1) must be a right triangle
(2) must be an acute triangle
(3) must be an obtuse triangle
(4) may be either an acute or an obtuse triangle

4. In $\triangle ABC$, m$\angle A = 30°$, $a = \sqrt{5}$, and $b = 4$. Then $\angle B$

(1) may be either obtuse or acute
(2) must be obtuse, only
(3) must be acute, only
(4) may be a right angle

5. How many distinct triangles can be constructed if $a = 5$, $b = 7$, and m$\angle A = 70°$?

(1) 1 **(2)** 2 **(3)** 3 **(4)** 0

6. If m$\angle A = 45°$, $b = 6\sqrt{2}$, and $a = 6$, then $\triangle ABC$

(1) is not unique
(2) is a right triangle
(3) is an obtuse triangle
(4) cannot be constructed

7. Using the data $a = 9$, $b = 10$, and m$\angle A = 60°$, which statement about $\triangle ABC$ is true?

(1) It cannot be constructed.
(2) It must be obtuse.
(3) It must be acute.
(4) It may be either acute or obtuse.

8. In $\triangle ABC$, if m$\angle A = 40°$, $a = 12$, and $b = 10$, $\triangle ABC$ must be

(1) acute **(2)** right **(3)** isosceles **(4)** obtuse

9. In $\triangle ABC$, $a = 12$, $b = 9$, and m$\angle A = 42°$. These data determine for the measure of $\angle B$

(1) two values, one less than 90° and one greater than 90°
(2) two values, both less than 90°
(3) exactly one value, that value being less than 90°
(4) exactly one value, that value being greater than 90°

10. How many triangles, if any, can be constructed using the data m$\angle A = 68°$, $a = 7$, and $b = 9$?

(1) none
(2) two distinct triangles
(3) an obtuse triangle, only
(4) a right triangle, only

11. A student is given the data m$\angle A = 50°$, $a = 10$, and $b = 6$ and asked to construct a triangle if possible. He should find that

(1) no triangle can be constructed with these parts
(2) a triangle can be constructed in which $\angle B$ is acute
(3) a triangle can be constructed in which $\angle B$ is obtuse
(4) two different triangles can be constructed, one having $\angle B$ acute and the other having $\angle B$ obtuse

12. Given acute $\angle B$ such that $\sin B = 0.4$ and $a = 6$. Using this information, two distinct triangles can be constructed when b is equal to

(1) 1 **(2)** 2 **(3)** 6 **(4)** 4

13. If $a = 5$, $b = 6$, and $\sin A = \frac{2}{3}$, which statement about $\triangle ABC$ is true?

(1) It must be an acute triangle.
(2) It must be a right triangle.
(3) It must be an obtuse triangle.
(4) It may be either an acute or an obtuse triangle.

14. In $\triangle ABC$, if $b = 20$ and m$\angle A = 30°$, it is possible to construct two distinct triangles when side a is

(1) 8 **(2)** 10 **(3)** 15 **(4)** 20

15. In $\triangle ABC$, $m\angle A = 30°$, $AB = 10$, and $BC = a$. Two distinct triangles can be constructed if

(1) $5 < a < 10$ (3) $a < 5$
(2) $a > 10$ (4) $a = 5$

16. Two distinct triangles can be constructed if $m\angle A = 34°$, $b = 20$ and a is equal to

(1) 10 (2) 15 (3) 20 (4) 25

17. Two distinct triangles can be constructed if $m\angle A = 40°$, $b = 10$, and a is equal to

(1) 16 (2) 10 (3) 8 (4) 4

18. If $m\angle A = 50°$ and side $c = 10$, for which value of side a can two distinct triangles be formed?

(1) 5 (2) 7 (3) 9 (4) 11

19. In $\triangle ABC$, $m\angle A = 38°$, $a = 18$, and $c = 24$. Then $\angle C$

(1) must be acute
(2) must be obtuse
(3) may be either acute or obtuse
(4) may be a right angle

20. In $\triangle ABC$, $AB = 10$, $BC = 9$, and $m\angle A = 32°$. Then, $\angle C$ can be

(1) an acute angle, only
(2) an obtuse angle, only
(3) a right angle
(4) either an acute or an obtuse angle

In 21–25, use the given data to determine the number of distinct (noncongruent) triangles that can be constructed.

21. $a = \frac{1}{3}$, $b = \frac{2}{3}$, and $m\angle A = 30°$

22. $a = 10$, $c = 11$, and $m\angle C = 60°$

23. $m\angle A = 60°$, $a = 6$, and $b = 8$

24. $a = 7$, $b = 6$, and $m\angle A = 50°$

25. $m\angle B = 52°$, $a = 18$, $b = 16$

8.4 THE LAW OF COSINES

The length of one side of a triangle can be expressed in terms of the lengths of the other two sides and the measure of the included angle.

The Law of Cosines can be used to find missing parts of a triangle if the known combination of sides and angles is s.a.s. or s.s.s.

In any $\triangle ABC$:

$$c^2 = a^2 + b^2 - 2ab \cos C$$

The Law of Cosines

Examples

1. *Given:* In $\triangle ABC$, $m\angle C = 50°$, $a = 10$, and $b = 20$.

Find: c, to the nearest tenth

Solution: With s.a.s. as information, apply the Law of Cosines.

$$\begin{aligned} c^2 &= a^2 + b^2 - 2ab \cos C \\ &= 10^2 + 20^2 - 2(10)(20) \cos 50° \\ &\approx 100 + 400 - 400(0.6428) \\ &\approx 500 - 257.11 \\ c^2 &\approx 242.89 \\ c &\approx 15.6 \end{aligned}$$

Reject the negative value.

2. *Given:* In $\triangle PQR$, $PR = 8$, $QR = 17$, and $PQ = 20$.

Find: $m\angle R$, to the nearest degree

Solution: With s.s.s. as information, apply the Law of Cosines.

$$\begin{aligned} r^2 &= p^2 + q^2 - 2pq \cos R \\ (PQ)^2 &= (QR)^2 + (PR)^2 - 2(QR)(PR) \cos R \\ (20)^2 &= (17)^2 + (8)^2 - 2(17)(8) \cos R \\ 400 &= 289 + 64 - 272 \cos R \\ 47 &= -272 \cos R \\ \frac{47}{-272} &= \cos R \\ -0.1728 &\approx \cos R \\ 100° &\approx m\angle R \end{aligned}$$

Since $\cos R < 0$, $\angle R$ is obtuse.
m reference $\angle = 80°$

EXERCISES

1. In $\triangle ABC$, $a = 2$, $b = \sqrt{3}$, and $m\angle C = 30°$. What is the value of c?

(1) 1 (2) 2 (3) $2\sqrt{3}$ (4) $\frac{\sqrt{3}}{3}$

2. In $\triangle ABC$, $a = 3$, $b = 1$, and $m\angle C = 60°$. What is the length of side c?

(1) $\sqrt{7}$ (2) 2 (3) 3 (4) $\sqrt{5}$

3. In $\triangle ABC$, $a = 2$, $b = 5$, and $\cos C = \frac{1}{2}$. The length of side c is

(1) $\sqrt{19}$ (2) $\sqrt{29}$ (3) $\sqrt{34}$ (4) $\sqrt{39}$

4. In $\triangle ABC$, $a = 6$, $b = 8$, and $\cos C = \frac{3}{8}$. What is the length of side c?

(1) $\sqrt{118}$ (2) $\sqrt{82}$ (3) 10 (4) 8

5. In $\triangle ABC$, $a = 2$, $b = 4$, and m$\angle C = 120°$. What is the length of side c?
(1) $\sqrt{7}$ (2) $2\sqrt{7}$ (3) 28 (4) $4\sqrt{7}$

6. In $\triangle ABC$, if $c = \sqrt{5 - 4\cos 60°}$, what is the length of c?
(1) $\sqrt{\frac{1}{2}}$ (2) $\sqrt{2}$ (3) $\sqrt{3}$ (4) $\sqrt{\frac{1}{3}}$

7. In $\triangle ABC$, $a = 1$, $b = 2$, and $\cos C = \frac{1}{2}$. Find the length of side c in radical form.

8. In $\triangle ABC$, $a = \sqrt{3}$, $b = \sqrt{3}$, and m$\angle C = 120°$. Find the value of c.

9. In $\triangle ABC$, $a = 3$, $b = 5$, and m$\angle C = 120°$. Find the value of c.

10. In $\triangle ABC$, $b = 8$, $c = 5$, and $\cos A = -0.4$. What is the value of a?
(1) 10 (2) 11 (3) $\sqrt{57}$ (4) $\sqrt{105}$

11. In $\triangle ABC$, $b = 5$, $c = 4$, and $\cos A = \frac{1}{8}$. Find the numerical value of a.

12. In $\triangle ABC$, if $a = 4$, $b = 5$, and m$\angle C = 120°$, then
(1) $c^2 > a^2 + b^2$
(2) $c^2 > (a + b)^2$
(3) $c^2 < 2ab$
(4) $c^2 < a^2 + b^2$

13. If the lengths of two sides of a triangle are 7 and 10 and the cosine of the included angle is $-\frac{1}{7}$, what is the length of the third side?

14. In $\triangle ABC$, if $a = 8$, $b = 9$, and $c = 10$, what is the value of $\cos C$?
(1) $\frac{4}{5}$ (2) $\frac{5}{12}$ (3) $\frac{5}{16}$ (4) $\frac{1}{100}$

15. In $\triangle ABC$, $a = 2$, $b = 3$, and $c = 4$. What is the value of $\cos C$?
(1) $-\frac{1}{16}$ (2) $\frac{1}{16}$ (3) $-\frac{1}{4}$ (4) $\frac{1}{4}$

16. In $\triangle ABC$, $a = \sqrt{5}$, $b = \sqrt{5}$, and $c = 2$. What is the value of $\cos C$?
(1) $\frac{3}{5}$ (2) 0 (3) $\frac{-3}{10}$ (4) $\frac{-1}{4}$

17. In $\triangle ABC$, $a = 4$, $b = 3$, and $c = \sqrt{13}$. Find $\cos C$.

18. In $\triangle ABC$, $a = 6$, $b = 6$, and $c = 9$. The value of $\cos B$ is
(1) $\frac{3}{4}$ (2) $-\frac{3}{4}$ (3) $\frac{1}{8}$ (4) $-\frac{1}{8}$

19. In $\triangle ABC$, if $a = 5$, $b = 7$, $c = 6$, find $\cos B$.

20. In $\triangle ABC$, if $a = 7$, $b = 6$, and $c = 5$, what is the value of $\cos A$?
(1) $\frac{1}{49}$ (2) $\frac{1}{10}$ (3) $\frac{1}{5}$ (4) $\frac{5}{8}$

21. In $\triangle ABC$, $a = 5$, $b = 8$, and $c = 9$. Then, $\cos A$ equals
(1) $\frac{1}{12}$ (2) $\frac{5}{6}$ (3) $-\frac{5}{6}$ (4) 25

22. In $\triangle ABC$, if $a = 4$, $b = 3$, and $c = 3$, then the value of $\cos A$ is
(1) $\frac{2}{3}$ (2) $\frac{1}{9}$ (3) $-\frac{1}{9}$ (4) $-\frac{2}{3}$

23. In $\triangle ABC$, $a = 12$, $b = 10$, and $c = 8$. Find the numerical value of $\cos A$.

24. In $\triangle PQR$, $p = 6$, $q = 8$, and $r = 10$. The cosine of the largest angle of the triangle is
(1) 1 (2) -2 (3) 0 (4) $\frac{1}{25}$

25. The sides of a triangle are 2, 3, and 4. Find the numerical value of the cosine of the largest angle.

26. In $\triangle ABC$, $a = 5$, $b = 7$, and $c = 8$. The measure of $\angle B$ is
(1) 30° (2) 60° (3) 120° (4) 150°

27. If $19 = 22 - 21\cos C$, what is the measure of angle C to the nearest degree?
(1) 8 (2) 19 (3) 82 (4) 98

28. In $\triangle ABC$, $a = 15$, $b = 13$, and $c = 8$. Which equation can be used to find m$\angle A$?

(1) $\cos A = \dfrac{8^2 + 13^2 - 15^2}{2(8)(13)}$

(2) $\cos A = \dfrac{8^2 - 13^2 - 15^2}{2(8)(13)}$

(3) $\cos A = \dfrac{13^2 + 15^2 - 8^2}{2(13)(15)}$

(4) $\cos A = \dfrac{15^2 + 8^2 - 13^2}{2(15)(8)}$

29. In $\triangle ABC$, $AB = 25$ feet, $AC = 30$ feet, and m$\angle A = 121°$. Find BC to the nearest foot.

30. In $\triangle ABC$, $AB = 30$ feet, $BC = 24$ feet, and m$\angle B = 40°$. Find to the nearest foot the length of $\overline{AC}$.

31. Two sides of a triangle are 10 and 12, respectively, and the angle included between these two sides measures 130°. Find the length of the third side of the triangle to the nearest integer.

32. In triangular field RST, the length of $\overline{RS}$ is 50 m, m$\angle RST = 142°$, and the length of $\overline{ST}$ is 68 m. Find the length of $\overline{RT}$ to the nearest meter.

33. In $\triangle ABC$, $AB = 51$, $BC = 40$, and $CA = 20$. Find m$\angle C$ to the nearest degree.

34. In $\triangle ABC$, $a = 250$, $b = 150$, and $c = 120$. Find m$\angle A$ to the nearest degree.

35. Three sides of a triangle are 5, 6, and 8. Find to the nearest degree the measure of the largest angle.

36. In $\triangle ABC$, $a = 25$, $b = 31$ and $c = 14$. Find m$\angle B$ to the nearest ten minutes.

37. In $\triangle ABC$, the lengths of sides a, b, and c are in the ratio 4:6:8. Find the ratio of the cosine of $\angle C$ to the cosine of $\angle A$.

38. **a.** In $\triangle ABC$, $AB = 15$ cm, $BC = 10$ cm, and $AC = 6$ cm. Find m$\angle B$ to the nearest degree.
b. Using the answer to part **a**, find the area of $\triangle ABC$ to the nearest square centimeter.

39. The sides of a triangular plot of land are 50, 80, and 100 meters.
   a. Find, to the nearest degree, the measure of the largest angle of the triangle.
   b. Using the answer obtained in part **a**, find the area of the triangle to the nearest square meter.

40. In parallelogram $ABCD$, $AB = 12$ cm, $AD = 20$ cm, and $m\angle A = 50°$.
   a. Find the length of the longer diagonal of the parallelogram to the nearest centimeter.
   b. Find the area of the parallelogram to the nearest square centimeter.

41. a. Two consecutive sides of a parallelogram are 8 cm and 10 cm, respectively. If the length of the longer diagonal of the parallelogram is 14 cm, find the measure of the largest angle of the parallelogram to the nearest degree.
   b. Using your answer to part **a**, find the area of the parallelogram to the nearest square centimeter.

8.5 APPLYING THE LAWS OF SINES AND COSINES

There are many applications of these laws about triangle measure.

Use the Law of Sines when the known information involves a.s.a., a.a.s., or s.s.a.

Use the Law of Cosines when the known information involves s.a.s. or s.s.s.

Familiar Geometric Settings

Examples

1. A surveyor on the ground takes two readings of the angle of elevation of the top of a tower. From 150′ apart, the measures are 50° and 70°. Find the tower's height to the nearest foot.

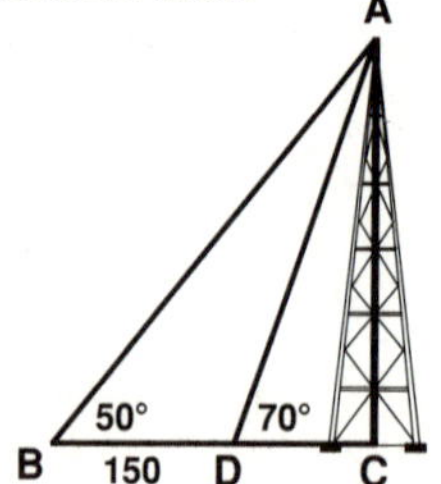

Solution: Use the Law of Sines in $\triangle ABD$ to find AD. Then, work in $\triangle ADC$ to find AC.

In $\triangle ABD$:

$m\angle BDA = 110°$

$m\angle BAD = 20°$

$$\frac{\sin 20°}{150} = \frac{\sin 50°}{AD}$$

$$AD = \frac{150(\sin 50°)}{\sin 20°}$$

$AD \approx 335.9'$

In right $\triangle ADC$:

$$\sin 70° = \frac{AC}{AD}$$

$$\sin 70° \approx \frac{AC}{335.9}$$

$AC \approx 335.9(\sin 70°)$

$AC \approx 316'$ *Ans.*

2. $\overline{PA}$ and $\overline{PB}$ are tangent to circle O at points A and B respectively. If $PA = 10$ cm and $m\angle P = 34°$, find the length of chord $\overline{AB}$ to the nearest centimeter.

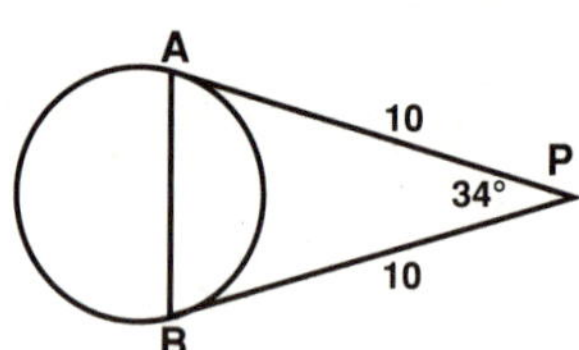

Solution: Tangents to a circle from an external point are congruent, making $PB = 10$ cm.

With s.a.s. known, use the Law of Cosines.

$(AB)^2 = (PA)^2 + (PB)^2 - 2(PA)(PB)\cos P$

$= 10^2 + 10^2 - 2(10)(10)\cos 34°$

$= 100 + 100 - 200(\cos 34°)$

$\approx 200 - 165.8075$

$(AB)^2 \approx 34.1925$

$AB \approx 6$ cm *Ans.*

EXERCISES

1. The diagonals of a parallelogram are respectively 7.0 inches and 10.0 inches long, and they intersect at an angle of 65°. Find the length of one of the longer sides of the parallelogram to the nearest tenth of an inch.

2. A surveyor at point P sights two points X and Y that are on opposite sides of a lake. If P is 200 m from X and 350 m from Y, and $m\angle XPY = 40°$, find the distance from X to Y to the nearest meter.

3. Main Street and Park Avenue intersect at an angle of 74°. Janet lives on Main, 50 meters from the intersection, and Sara lives on Park, 40 meters from the intersection. Find, to the nearest meter, the distance between Janet's house and Sara's.

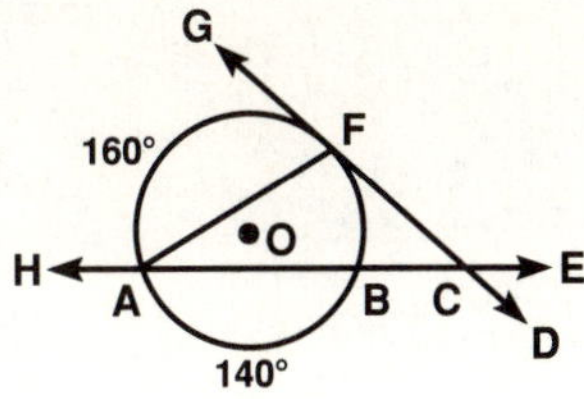

Ex. 4

4. $\overleftrightarrow{DCFG}$ is tangent to circle O at F, $\overleftrightarrow{ECH}$ is a secant intersecting the circle at A and B, $m\widehat{AB} = 140°$, and $m\widehat{AF} = 160°$. If $FC = 10$, find AF to the nearest tenth.

5. A canoe race is to be run over a triangular course marked by buoys A, B, and C. The distance between A and B is 100 yards, that between B and C is 160 yards, and that between C and A is 220 yards. Find, to the nearest degree, $m\angle ABC$.

6. An ice skater starts from point A and skates in a straight line across a frozen lake to point B, which is 630 meters away. Then she skates directly to point C. If $m\angle ABC$ is 47° 30′ and $m\angle CAB$ is 31° 20′, find, to the nearest meter, the distance from C to A.

7. Two straight roads $\overleftrightarrow{RT}$ and $\overleftrightarrow{ST}$ intersect at a town T and form with each other an acute angle of 67°. Towns at R and S are 22 miles and 31 miles respectively from T. Find to the nearest mile the distance between towns R and S.

8. A local airline does not offer a direct connection from city A to city B. Rather, the flight travels 70 miles from city A to city C and then 100 miles from city C to city B. If the angle ACB between the two legs of the flight measures 100°, find to the nearest mile the distance between A and B.

9. Airplane A leaves Chicago, Illinois, on a flight plan to New York City at the same time that airplane B leaves St. Louis, Missouri, on a flight plan to New York City. The directions of the two flight plans make an angle of 55° 40′ with each other. At a given instant, airplane A is 120 miles from New York City while airplane B is 200 miles away. Find to the nearest mile the distance between the planes at this instant.

10. The beam of a searchlight situated at an offshore point W sweeps back and forth between shore points A and B. Point W is located 12 kilometers from A and 25 kilometers from B. The distance between A and B is 29 kilometers. Find the measure of $\angle AWB$ to the nearest ten minutes.

11. Two sides of a parallelogram have lengths of 22 and 29. The measure of one angle of the parallelogram is 12°. Find to the nearest tenth the length of the shorter diagonal.

12. A triangular plot of land is formed by three streets that intersect in pairs at three places. The lengths of the sides of the triangle are 120 meters, 160 meters, and 170 meters. Find, to the nearest degree, the measure of the largest angle formed.

13. A diagonal of a parallelogram is 50 centimeters long and makes angles of 37° 10′ and 49° 20′, respectively, with the sides. Find the length of the shorter side of the parallelogram to the nearest centimeter.

14. A vertical transmitting tower $\overline{AB}$ is located on a slope that is inclined 15° to the horizontal. At a point C, 80 feet down the slope from the foot of the tower, the tower subtends an angle of 40° 10′. Find to the nearest foot the height of the tower.

15. A vertical transmitting tower stands on the side of a hill that is uniformly inclined to the horizontal at an angle of 18°. The tower is partially supported by a cable that reaches from the top of the tower to a point 60 feet up the hill from the base of the tower. If this cable makes an angle of 38° with the tower, find, to the nearest foot, the height of the tower.

16. Engineers are designing a straight tunnel through a hill from point A to point B, which are on opposite sides of the hill. Point C is a point on top of the hill. From A and B, the angles of elevation to C measure 26° 40′ and 38° 10′, respectively. The distance from A to C is 400 meters. If A and B are at the same level and A, B, and C lie in the same vertical plane, find the length of tunnel $\overline{AB}$ to the nearest ten meters.

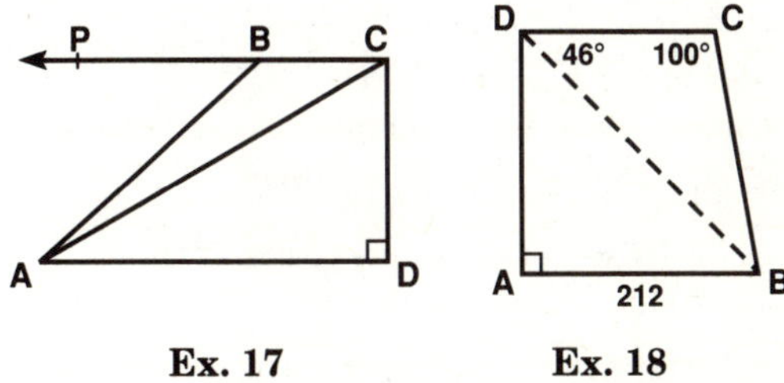

Ex. 17 Ex. 18

17. Trapezoid $ABCD$ has $\overline{BC} \parallel \overline{AD}$ and $\overline{CD} \perp \overline{AD}$. $\overline{CB}$ is extended through B to P and diagonal $\overline{AC}$ is drawn. If $m\angle BCA$ is 29° 40′, $m\angle PBA$ is 41° 20′, and $BC = 1.8$, find CD to the nearest tenth.

18. In trapezoid $ABCD$, $\overline{AB} \parallel \overline{DC}$, $AB = 212$ in., $m\angle A = 90°$, $m\angle C = 100°$, and $m\angle CDB = 46°$. Find DC to the nearest inch.

19. In trapezoid $ABCD$, $\overline{AB}$ and $\overline{DC}$ are parallel bases and $\overline{AD} \perp \overline{AB}$, $m\angle DCB = 128°$, $m\angle DAC = 42°$, and $AD = 26$ ft. Find AB to the nearest foot.

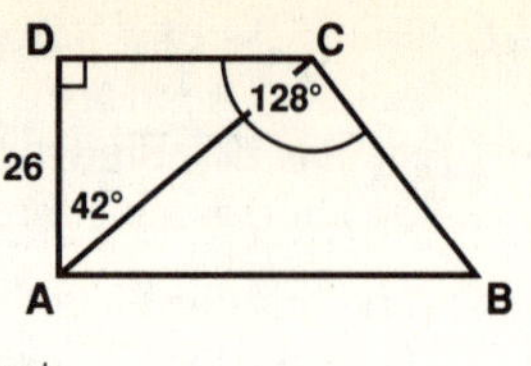

20. In right $\triangle ACD$, B lies on $\overline{AC}$, $\overline{BD}$ is drawn such that $m\angle CDB = 27°$, $m\angle BDA = 30°$, and $BC = 9$. Find AB to the nearest tenth.

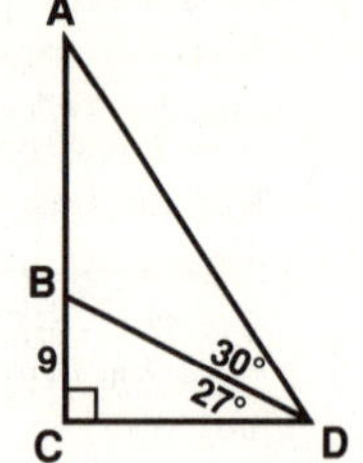

21. From point A on level ground, the angle of elevation of the top of a vertical control tower $\overline{BD}$ measures 43°. At point C, 200 feet closer to the foot of the tower, the angle of elevation measures 56°. Find to the nearest foot the height of the tower.

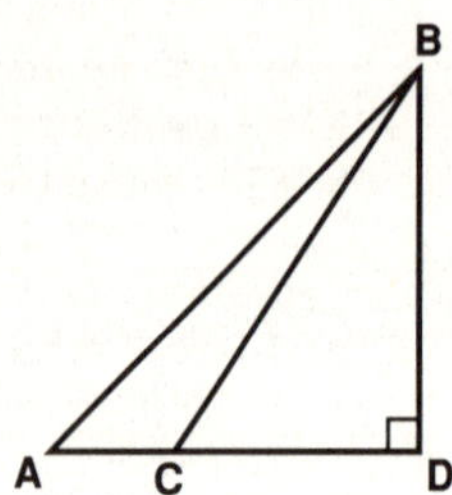

22. A tower $\overline{BA}$ and a flagpole $\overline{CD}$ stand on level ground. From B, the top of the tower, which is 265 feet high, the angle of depression of the top of the flagpole measures 62° 10′. From A, the foot of the tower, the angle of elevation of the top of the flagpole measures 34° 50′. Find the height of the flagpole to the nearest foot.

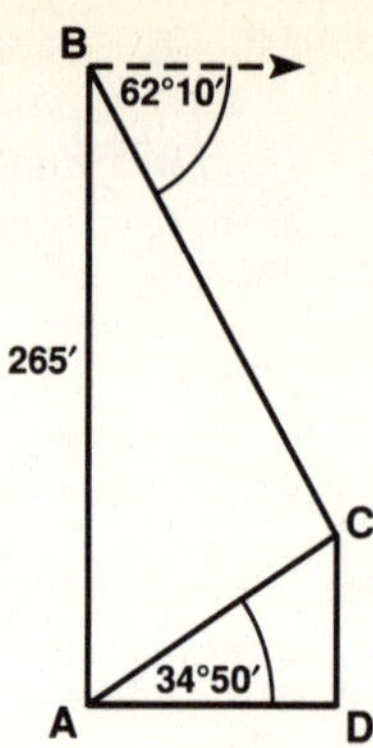

23. From two points 250 yards apart on a horizontal (straight) road running directly toward the launch pad, the angles of elevation of the top of a rocket measure 44° and 28°. Find the height of the rocket to the nearest ten yards.

24. From the top of a tower, the angle of depression of the top of a 70-foot flagpole on level ground is 62° 20′. From the foot of the tower, the angle of elevation of the top of the flagpole is 32° 10′. Find the height of the tower to the nearest tenth of a foot.

A Parallelogram of Forces

When two forces act on an object at a certain angle, the forces are represented by vectors whose magnitudes are the lengths of adjacent sides of a parallelogram.

The magnitude of the RESULTANT FORCE is represented by the length of the diagonal drawn from the object.

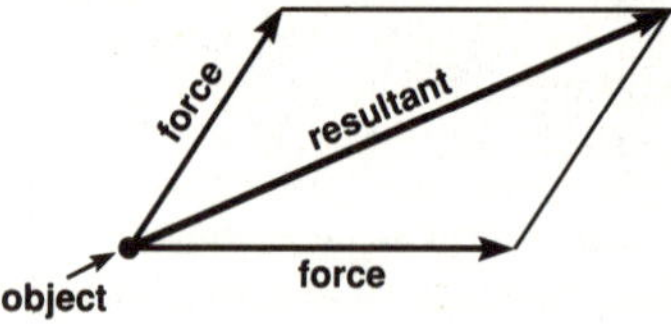

Example

Two forces act on a body at an angle of 72°, resulting in a force whose magnitude is 110 lb. If the magnitude of one of the original forces is 80 lb., find the magnitude of the other, to the nearest pound.

Solution: Draw a parallelogram of forces.
Opposite sides are congruent: $AD = BC = 80$
Consecutive angles are supplementary: $m\angle B = 108°$

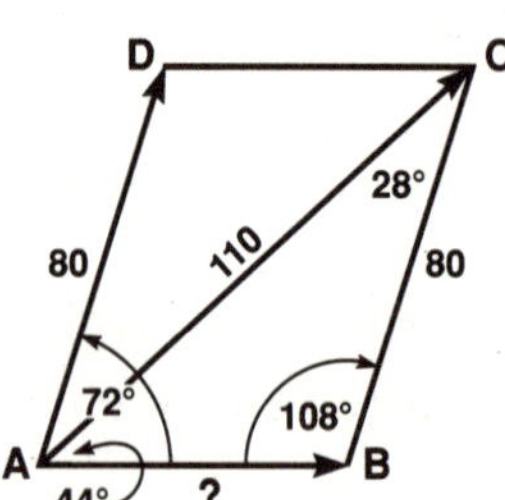

With s.s.a. known in $\triangle ABC$, apply the Law of Sines. To find AB, you must know $m\angle ACB$.

Step 1: Use the Law of Sines to find $m\angle CAB$, which will determine $m\angle ACB$.

$$\frac{\sin 108°}{110} = \frac{\sin \angle CAB}{80} \Rightarrow \frac{\sin 72°}{110} = \frac{\sin \angle CAB}{80}$$

$$\sin \angle CAB = \frac{80(\sin 72°)}{110} \approx 0.6917$$

$$m\angle CAB \approx 44°$$

Step 2: Use $m\angle CAB$ to find $m\angle ACB$.

$$m\angle CAB + m\angle ACB + m\angle B = 180°$$

$$44 + m\angle ACB + 108 \approx 180$$

$$m\angle ACB \approx 28°$$

(continued on next page)

Step 3: Use m$\angle ACB$ in the Law of Sines.

$$\frac{\sin\angle ACB}{AB} = \frac{\sin\angle ABC}{110} \Rightarrow \frac{\sin 28°}{AB} = \frac{\sin 108°}{110}$$

$$AB = \frac{110(\sin 28°)}{\sin 108°}$$

$$AB \approx 54 \text{ lb. } \textit{Ans.}$$

EXERCISES

1. Two forces act on an object. The first force has a magnitude of 76 pounds and makes an angle of 36° with the resultant. The magnitude of the resultant is 118 pounds. Find, to the nearest pound, the magnitude of the second force.

2. Two forces of 11 pounds and 14 pounds, respectively, act on a body. The angle between the two forces measures 28°. Find, to the nearest pound, the magnitude of the resultant force.

3. Two forces act on a point at an angle of 102°. The first is a force of 130 pounds. If the resultant makes an angle of 38° 20′ with the first force, what is the magnitude of the resultant to the nearest pound?

4. Two forces of 17 lb. and 39 lb. act on a body at an angle of 142°. Find, to the nearest pound, the resultant of these two forces.

5. A body is acted upon by two forces, one of 150 pounds and the other of 220 pounds. If the resultant is 280 pounds, find to the nearest ten minutes the measure of the angle between the resultant and the150-pound force.

6. Two forces of 62 pounds and 49 pounds, respectively, act on a body at an angle of 53° 20′ with each other. Find, to the nearest ten minutes, the measure of the angle formed by the resultant and the greater force.

7. A body is acted upon by two forces of 8 and 9 pounds. If the resultant force is 11 pounds, find the measure of the angle between the two forces to the nearest degree.

8. Two forces of 40 pounds and 30 pounds, respectively, act on a body at the same point so that their resultant is a force of 38 pounds. Find, to the nearest degree, the measure of the angle between the two original forces.

9. Two forces of 362 pounds and 529 pounds, respectively, act upon a body at an acute angle with each other. The angle between the resultant force and the 362-pound force is 35° 40′. Find, to the nearest ten minutes, the measure of the angle formed by the two given forces.

10. Two forces of 40 pounds and 55 pounds act on a body, forming an acute angle with each other. The angle between the resultant and the 40-pound force is 22°20′. Find, to the nearest ten minutes, the measure of the angle between the two forces.

11. Two forces act on a body at an angle of 120°. The forces are 28 pounds and 35 pounds.
    a. Find the magnitude of the resultant force, to the nearest tenth of a pound.
    b. Find the measure of the angle formed by the greater of the two forces and the resultant force, to the nearest degree.

12. **a.** Two forces of 8 pounds and 6 pounds, respectively, act on a body so that the magnitude of the resultant is 9 pounds. Find, to the nearest degree, the angle between the two forces.
    b. If the angle between the 8-pound force and the 6-pound force changes, the magnitude of the resultant changes. When the angle between the two forces is 90°, what is the value of the magnitude of the resultant?

Directions in Navigation

At sea or in the air, *bearings* (directions) are specified in either of two ways.

***Compass Directions:* The bearing of a ship or plane from a given point is named by an angle measure between two directions.**

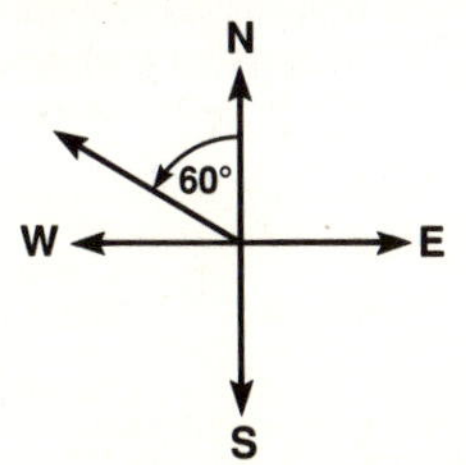

N 60° W means use the North-axis as the initial side of an angle of 60° and draw the terminal side in the direction West.

***Course Angles:* Directions are also given by angle measures between 0° and 360°, beginning at North and moving clockwise.**

***Note:* This system is different from angle measure in which standard position puts the initial side on the x-axis, and a positive measure is in the counterclockwise direction.**

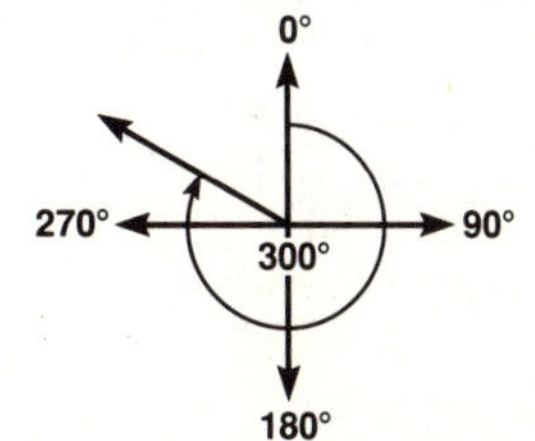

The bearing N 60° W is equivalent to a course angle of 300°.

Example

At 2 P.M. on Monday, a ship sailed from a port on a course 71° (N 71° E) at a speed of 15 mph. At 3 P.M., a second ship left the same port on course 131° (S 49° E) at a speed of 20 mph. Find, to the nearest mile, the distance between the ships at 5 P.M.

Solution: At 5 P.M., ship 1 has traveled for 3 hrs. and is 15(3), or 45 miles, from the starting port.

At 5 P.M., ship 2 has traveled for 2 hrs. and is 20(2), or 40 miles, from the starting port.

$m\angle ACB = (131 - 71)° = 60°$

With s.a.s. known, apply the Law of Cosines.

$c^2 = a^2 + b^2 - 2ab \cos \angle ACB$

$= 40^2 + 45^2 - 2(40)(45) \cos 60°$

$= 1{,}600 + 2{,}025 - 3{,}600(0.5)$

$= 3{,}625 - 1{,}800$

$c^2 = 1{,}825$

$c \approx 43$ miles

EXERCISES

1. Two ships leave a harbor at the same time, one sailing in a direction S 70° E (110°) at a rate of 18 miles per hour and the other in a direction S 85° W (265°) at a rate of 21 miles per hour. Find, to the nearest mile, the distance between them at the end of one hour.

2. At noon on a certain day, a ship sailed from port on a course N 80° E (80°) at a speed of 12 miles per hour. At 1 P.M. a second ship left the same port on a course S 62° E (118°) at a speed of 13.5 miles per hour. Find, to the nearest mile, the distance between the ships at 3 P.M.

3. A ship sails due west from Harbor A for 20 nautical miles to point B. It then sails in the direction 235° 10′ (S 55° 10′ W) for 22 nautical miles to point C. Find, to the nearest nautical mile, the distance from A to C.

4. A ship sails from point A in a direction N 58° 30′ E (58° 30′) for a distance of 28 miles to C. It then changes its course to N 82° 40′ E (82°40′) for a distance of 36 miles to B. Find, to the nearest mile, the distance from A to B.

5. A pilot flies at 333°10′ (N 26° 50′ W) from base B to a landing field C and then flies 319 miles at 42° 40′ (N 42° 40′ E) to an airport A. If the bearing of the airport from the base is 31° 20′ (N 31° 20′ E), find, to the nearest mile, the distance of the airport from the base.

6. A man at point A observes a tower at point B in a direction 20° 20′ (N 20° 20′ E). After traveling 475 feet due north to point C, he observes the same tower in the direction 108° 20′ (S 71° 40′ E). Find, to the nearest foot, the distance from the tower to the first point of observation.

7. Point P is 40 miles directly south of point R. Point S bears N 59° 20′ E (59° 20′) from R and the distance from R to S is 50 miles. Find, to the nearest mile, the distance from P to S.

8. Point B is 20 miles directly west of point A. The bearing of point C from A is 237° 10′ (S 57° 10′ W), and C is 65 miles from A. Find, to the nearest mile, the distance from B to C.

9. Point C is 70 miles directly east of point A. Point B is 60 miles from A and the bearing of B from A is 22° 20′ (N 22° 20′ E). Find, to the nearest mile, the distance from B to C.

10. Two boats, A and B, observe a lighthouse at C. Boat A is 900 yards directly north of boat B. The bearing of the lighthouse from A is 119°20′ (S 60° 40′ E). At the same time, the bearing of the lighthouse from B is 46° 30′ (N46° 30′E). Find, to the nearest yard, the distance from the lighthouse to boat A.

11. Ranger Station B is 27.4 miles due east of Ranger Station A. A fire is located N 21° 40′ E (21° 40′) from Station A and N 33° W (327°) from Station B. Find, to the nearest tenth of a mile, the distance from Station A to the fire.

12. Lighthouse B is 3.7 miles east of lighthouse A. The bearing of ship C from lighthouse A is S 12° 50′ W (192° 50′) and the bearing of C from lighthouse B is S 61° 40′ W (241° 40′). Find, to the nearest tenth of a mile, the distance of the ship from B.

13. Two lighthouses, A and B, are 22 miles apart. Lighthouse A is due north of lighthouse B. The bearing of a ship from lighthouse B is 41° 40′ (N 41° 40′ E), and the bearing of the same ship from lighthouse A is 142° 20′ (S 37° 40′ E). Find, to the nearest mile, the distance from the ship to lighthouse A.

14. A ship at A is 80 miles due west of a ship at B. An S O S is received by both ships showing the bearing of a distressed ship to be N 72° E (72°) from A and N 65° W (295°) from B. Find, to the nearest mile, the distance from the distressed ship to the closer of the other two ships.

15. The bearing of town B from town A is 47° (N 47° E) and the distance between the towns is 120 miles. The bearing of town C from town B is 75° (N 75° E). The bearing of town A from town C is 240° (S 60° W). Find, to the nearest mile, the distance from A to C.

8.6 SUMMARY EXERCISES

1. In $\triangle ABC$, $a = 6$, $b = 8$, and $\sin C = \frac{1}{4}$. Find the area of $\triangle ABC$.

2. Find the area of $\triangle ABC$ if $a = 6$, $b = 12$, and $m\angle C = 150°$.

3. In $\triangle ABC$, $a = 20$ and $m\angle C = 30°$. For which value of b is the area of $\triangle ABC$ equal to 100 square units?

   (1) 10 (2) 20 (3) $\frac{20\sqrt{3}}{3}$ (4) 25

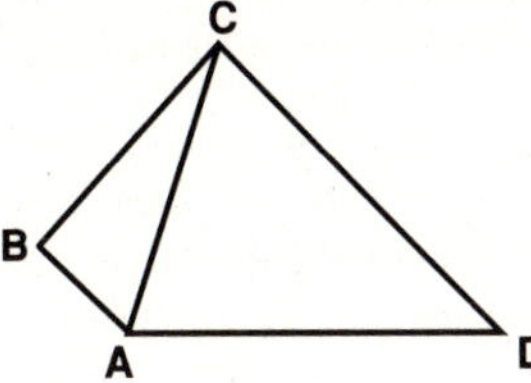

Ex. 4

4. If $\overline{CB} \perp \overline{BA}$, $BA = 10$ cm, $CB = 24$ cm, $AD = 36$ cm, and $m\angle CAD = 72°$, find the area of quadrilateral $ABCD$ to the nearest square centimeter.

5. In $\triangle ABC$, which expression can be used to find the length of side a?

   (1) $\frac{\sin B}{b \sin A}$ (3) $\frac{b \sin A}{\sin B}$

   (2) $\frac{\sin A}{b \sin B}$ (4) $\frac{b \sin B}{\sin A}$

6. If, in $\triangle ABC$, $m\angle A = 60°$ and $m\angle B = 30°$, then $\frac{a}{b}$ equals

   (1) $\frac{1}{2}$ (2) 2 (3) $\sqrt{3}$ (4) $\frac{1}{\sqrt{3}}$

7. In $\triangle ABC$, $m\angle A = 30°$, $b = 14$, and $a = 10$. Find $\sin B$.

8. In $\triangle ABC$, $b = 12$, $c = 8$, and $\sin B = \frac{1}{2}$. Find the value of $\sin C$.

9. In $\triangle RST$, $r = 7$, $\sin R = 0.28$, and $\sin T = 0.44$. Find t.

10. In $\triangle ABC$, $m\angle A = 60°$, $m\angle B = 45°$, and $b = 4$. What is the length of side a?

    (1) $2\sqrt{6}$ (2) $2\sqrt{2}$ (3) $\frac{\sqrt{6}}{2}$ (4) $\frac{16}{3}$

11. In $\triangle ABC$, AB is 22 inches, AC is 15 inches, and $m\angle C$ is 112° 20′. Find, to the nearest ten minutes, $m\angle A$.

12. In $\triangle ABC$, $m\angle A = 16° 30'$, $m\angle B = 28° 10'$, and $AB = 34.5$ m. Find, to the nearest tenth of a meter, the length of $\overline{AC}$.

13. In $\triangle ABC$, $m\angle A = 50°$, $a = 48$, $b = 62$, and $\angle B$ is obtuse. Find $m\angle C$ to the nearest degree.

14. How many distinct triangles can be constructed if $m\angle A = 60°$, $a = 8$, and $b = 10$?

15. If $m\angle A = 30°$, side $a = 8$, and side $b = 10$, what is the total number of noncongruent triangles that can be constructed?

16. In $\triangle ABC$, $a = 5$, $b = 10$, and $\sin A = \frac{1}{2}$. Which is true of $\triangle ABC$?

    (1) It must be a right triangle.
    (2) It must be an acute triangle.
    (3) It must be an obtuse triangle.
    (4) It may be either an acute or an obtuse triangle.

17. In $\triangle ABC$, $m\angle A = 30°$, $a = 6$, and $b = 10$. Then $\angle C$

    (1) must be acute
    (2) must be obtuse
    (3) may be either acute or obtuse
    (4) may be a right angle

18. In $\triangle ABC$, $m\angle A = 30°$, $a = 5$, and $b = 10$. Then $\angle C$

    (1) must be obtuse (3) cannot be 90°
    (2) must be 90° (4) may be 90°

19. Using the data $m\angle A = 38°$, $b = 20$, and $a = 17$, the number of distinct triangles that can be constructed is

    (1) one right triangle (3) one oblique triangle
    (2) two triangles (4) none

20. If the lengths of the sides of a triangle are 3, 4, and 5, respectively, what is the cosine of the largest angle of the triangle?

    (1) 0 (2) $\frac{3}{5}$ (3) $\frac{3}{4}$ (4) $\frac{4}{5}$

21. In $\triangle ABC$, if $a = 6$, $b = 5$, and $c = 8$, then $\cos A$ equals

    (1) $\frac{75}{80}$ (2) $\frac{53}{80}$ (3) $-\frac{3}{80}$ (4) $\frac{53}{60}$

22. In $\triangle ABC$, if $a = 10$, $b = 7$, and $c = 8$, then the value of $\cos C$ is

    (1) $\frac{64}{9}$ (2) $\frac{13}{112}$ (3) $\frac{23}{32}$ (4) $\frac{17}{28}$

23. In $\triangle ABC$, $a = 2$, $b = 4$, and $m\angle C = 60°$. What is the value of c?

    (1) $2\sqrt{7}$ (2) 2 (3) $2\sqrt{3}$ (4) $4\sqrt{7}$

24. In $\triangle ABC$, $a = 3$, $b = 8$, and $m\angle C = 120°$. Find the length of side c to the nearest integer.

25. In $\triangle ABC$, $a = 10$, $b = 12$, and $m\angle C$ is 41° 30′.

    a. Find the length of side c to the nearest integer.

    b. Find the area of $\triangle ABC$ to the nearest tenth.

26. The lengths of the sides of $\triangle ABC$ are 5 m, 7 m, and 8 m.

    a. Find, to the nearest ten minutes, the measure of the smallest angle of the triangle.

    b. Using the result obtained in part **a**, find, to the nearest tenth of a square meter, the area of $\triangle ABC$.

27. Two adjacent sides of a parallelogram measure 10 and 12 centimeters. The angle included between these sides has a measure of 60°.

a. Find, to the nearest centimeter, the length of the shorter diagonal of the parallelogram.

b. What is the area of the parallelogram to the nearest square centimeter?

28. In rhombus *ABCD*, m∠*ABC* = 100° 40′ and the length of each side is 5 in.

a. What is the length of diagonal $\overline{AC}$ to the nearest tenth of an inch?

b. Find the area of *ABCD* to the nearest square inch.

29. Sailboat *S* is 50 meters from a lighthouse located at point *P*. Fishing boat *F* is 65 meters from the same lighthouse. If m∠*SPF* is 102° 30′, find, to the nearest meter, the distance between the two boats.

30. Two sides of a parallelogram measure 17.0 and 20.0 centimeters. The measure of one angle of the parallelogram is 50°. Find, to the nearest tenth of a centimeter, the length of the shorter diagonal.

31. On a level piece of ground, two surveyors establish a baseline running from *A* to *B*, a distance of 120 meters. From *A* and from *B*, a point *C* is sighted and ∠*CAB* and ∠*CBA* are measured to be 51° 30′ and 93° 10′, respectively. Find *AC* to the nearest meter.

32. From a ship, the angle of elevation of point *A* at the top of a cliff measures 22°. After the ship has sailed 2,000 feet directly toward the foot of the cliff, the angle of elevation of *A* measures 48°. Find, to the nearest ten feet, the height of the cliff.

33. Two forces act on a body, making angles of 15° 40′ and 37° 30′ with the resultant. If the larger force is 42 pounds, what is the magnitude of the resultant to the nearest pound?

34. Find, to the nearest degree, the measure of the angle between two forces of 30 lb. and 35 lb. if the magnitude of the resultant is 42 lb.

35. Two forces act on an object. The first force has a magnitude of 80 pounds and makes an angle of 37° with the resultant. The magnitude of the resultant is 120 pounds. Find, to the nearest pound, the magnitude of the second force.

36. A lighthouse *A* is 15 miles from ship *B* and 24 miles from ship *C*. The bearing of *B* from *A* is N 22° 50′ E (22° 50′) and the bearing of *C* from *A* is N 74° 30′ E (74° 30′). Find, to the nearest mile, the distance from *B* to *C*.

CHAPTER 9

Combinatorics and Probability

COMBINATORICS involves computing the number of ways in which r things can be chosen from a total of n things, where $r \le n$. The original n things can be all different or not.

The arrangement, or order, of the chosen r things can matter or not.

If the *arrangement is important*, then *xyz*, *yxz*, and *zxy* are all different choices. Each such choice is called a PERMUTATION.

If the *arrangement is not important*, then *xyz*, *yxz*, and *zxy* are all the same choice. Such a choice is called a COMBINATION.

9.1 PERMUTATIONS

When Things Are All Different

The notation used for the number of possible permutations P of r things chosen from n things is ${}_nP_r$.

If $r = n$,

$${}_nP_n = n(n-1)(n-2)(n-3) \ldots 1 = n!$$

Example: The number of ways to arrange 6 different items is:

$${}_6P_6 = \underset{\text{1st item}}{\underline{6}} \cdot \underset{\text{2nd item}}{\underline{5}} \cdot \underset{\text{3rd item}}{\underline{4}} \cdot \underset{\text{4th item}}{\underline{3}} \cdot \underset{\text{5th item}}{\underline{2}} \cdot \underset{\text{6th item}}{\underline{1}} = 720$$

If $r < n$,

$${}_nP_r = n(n-1)(n-2)(n-3) \ldots (n-r+1)$$

Example: The number of ways to arrange 3 items that are chosen from a set of 6 different items is:

$${}_6P_3 = \underset{\text{1st item}}{\underline{6}} \cdot \underset{\text{2nd item}}{\underline{5}} \cdot \underset{\text{3rd item}}{\underline{4}} = 120$$

The expansion of ${}_nP_r$ has exactly r factors.

When Things Are Not All Different

The number of possible arrangements is reduced when the set of items includes a subset of identical items.

The number of ways to arrange n things in which:

p things are alike is $\dfrac{n!}{p!}$

p things are alike and q things are alike is $\dfrac{n!}{p! \cdot q!}$

This rule extends to any number of subsets.

Example

How many different arrangements are possible using all the letters of MISSISSIPPI?

Solution:

There are 11 letters in the given set of letters.

There are 3 subsets of identical letters:

4 I's, 4 S's, and 2 P's

The number of different 11-letter arrangements is:

$$\frac{11!}{4! \cdot 4! \cdot 2!} = \frac{11 \cdot 10 \cdot \overset{3}{\cancel{9}} \cdot \cancel{8} \cdot 7 \cdot \overset{3}{\cancel{6}} \cdot 5 \cdot \cancel{4 \cdot 3 \cdot 2 \cdot 1}}{\cancel{4} \cdot \cancel{3} \cdot \cancel{2} \cdot 1 \cdot \cancel{4 \cdot 3 \cdot 2 \cdot 1} \cdot \cancel{2} \cdot 1}$$

$= 34{,}650$ *Ans.*

The Counting Principle for Permutations

If one choice can occur in any of m ways and a second choice can occur in any of n ways, then the total number of ways both choices can occur is $m \cdot n$.

Example: From 3 kinds of cheese and 2 kinds of crackers, the total number of cheese-cracker choices is:

$$\underset{\text{cheese}}{\underline{3}} \cdot \underset{\text{crackers}}{\underline{2}} = 6$$

Special Conditions

When there is a special condition, begin by satisfying the condition.

Examples

1. Use the letters in SQUARE and tell how many 6-letter arrangements with no repetitions are possible if the vowels and consonants alternate, beginning with a vowel.

Solution: There are 6 slots to be filled to form 6-letter arrangements.

Beginning with a vowel, every other slot must be filled by a vowel. There are 3 such slots and 3 vowels to arrange in them:

$$\underline{3}\ \_\ \underline{2}\ \_\ \underline{1}\ \_$$

The remaining 3 slots have the 3 consonants to be arranged in them:

$$\underline{3} \cdot \underline{3} \cdot \underline{2} \cdot \underline{2} \cdot \underline{1} \cdot \underline{1} \text{ or}$$

${}_3P_3 \cdot {}_3P_3$ or $3! \cdot 3! = 36$ *Ans.*

2. Allowing no repetition of letters, how many arrangements of MEDIAN can be made using:

a. at most 3 letters **b.** at least 3 letters

Solution:

a. To have *at most* 3 letters, there can be 1, 2, or 3 letters.

Find the number of possible arrangements for each case and take the sum.

${}_6P_1 + {}_6P_2 + {}_6P_3 = 6 + 30 + 120 = 156$ *Ans.*

b. To have *at least* 3 letters, there can be 3, 4, 5, or 6 letters.

Find the number of possible arrangements for each case and take the sum.

${}_6P_3 + {}_6P_4 + {}_6P_5 + {}_6P_6 = 120 + 360 + 720 + 720$

$= 1{,}920$ *Ans.*

EXERCISES

1. $(10 - 7)!$ is equivalent to

(1) $10! - 7!$ **(2)** $10 - 7!$ **(3)** $3!$ **(4)** 3

2. $\frac{(9-3)!}{3!}$ is equivalent to

(1) $2!$ **(2)** $3! - 1$ **(3)** ${}_6P_3$ **(4)** ${}_6P_4$

3. Which of the following is not equivalent to ${}_7P_3$?

(1) $7 \cdot 6 \cdot 5$ **(2)** $\frac{7!}{(7-3)!}$ **(3)** $\frac{7!}{4!}$ **(4)** $7 \cdot 6 \cdot 5 \cdot 4$

In 4–7, no repetition is allowed.

4. How many 3-digit numerals can be formed from the digits 4, 7, and 9?

5. How many 4-digit numerals can be formed from the digits of the numeral 1492?

6. What is the total number of possible 5-letter arrangements of the letters D, I, S, C, O?

7. How many different 2-digit numerals can be made from the digits of 345?

8. How many different arrangements are possible using all the letters of SLEEVELESS?

In 9–12, use the letters of RADIUS and tell how many 6–letter arrangements with no repetitions are possible if the:

9. first letter is R **10.** first letter is a vowel

11. first 3 letters are vowels

12. vowels and consonants alternate, beginning with a vowel

In 13–16, a 3-digit numeral is formed by selecting from the digits 1, 2, 3, 4, 5, and 6 with no repetitions. Tell how many of these 3-digit numerals will have:

13. a number value greater than 300

14. a number value less than 300

15. a number value between 200 and 400

16. digits that are alternately odd and even, beginning with an odd digit

In 17–21, the girls Amy, Ann, and Doris and the boys Al, Abe, Bob, and Roy are in a nursery group. In how many ways can the children be arranged in a line so:

17. a girl is always at the head of the line

18. Roy is always at the head of the line

19. a child whose name begins with the letter A is always at the head of the line

20. the boys and girls alternate, beginning with a boy

21. children whose names begin with the letter A are always at the head and at the rear of the line

In 22–24, use the digits 1, 2, 3, and 4 without repetitions. How many:

22. 3-digit numerals can be formed

23. 2-digit numerals with a number value greater than 40 can be formed

24. 2-digit numerals with a number value greater than 30 can be formed

In 25–28, answers may be left in notation form. The diamond suit of a standard deck of cards is removed from the deck, shuffled, and laid out in a row. How many arrangements are possible so that the:

25. first card is the ace

26. first card is a picture

27. first and last cards are not pictures

28. middle card is a picture and the first and last cards are not pictures

In 29–32, allow no repetition of letters. How many arrangements of the word can be formed using:

a. at most 3 letters **b.** at least 3 letters

29. ARC

30. ANGLE

31. RADIUS

32. BISECTOR

9.2 COMBINATIONS

Simple Combinations

The notation for the number of possible combinations C of r things chosen from n things is:

$$_nC_r = \frac{_nP_r}{r!} = \frac{n(n-1)(n-2)(n-3)\dots(n-r+1)}{r!}$$

Example: The number of ways in which a subcommittee of 4 can be chosen from a committee of 17 is:

$$_{17}C_4 = \frac{17 \cdot \overset{4}{\cancel{16}} \cdot \overset{5}{\cancel{15}} \cdot \overset{7}{\cancel{14}}}{\cancel{4} \cdot \cancel{3} \cdot \cancel{2} \cdot 1} = 2,380 \quad Ans.$$

The selection of r things from a group of n things automatically gives another result as well: the selection of $(n - r)$ things.

$$_nC_r = {_nC_{n-r}}$$

Example: To evaluate $_{20}C_{18}$, avoid working with 18 factors by evaluating the equivalent $_{20}C_2$.

$$_{20}C_{18} = {_{20}C_2} = \frac{\overset{10}{\cancel{20}} \cdot 19}{\cancel{2} \cdot 1} = 190 \quad Ans.$$

Note: $_nC_n = 1 \qquad _nC_0 = 1 \qquad _nC_1 = n$

The Counting Principle for Combinations

If one combination can occur in any of m ways and a second combination can occur in any of n ways, then the total number of ways both combinations can occur is $m \cdot n$.

Examples

1. From 5 teachers and 15 students, in how many ways can a committee be formed containing 2 teachers and 3 students?

Solution: There are 2 different sets to select from: teachers and students. Thus, the choices of teachers and students are independent of each other.

$$\underbrace{_5C_2}_{\text{select teachers}} \cdot \underbrace{_{15}C_3}_{\text{select students}} = 10 \cdot 455 = 4,550 \quad Ans.$$

2. In how many ways can 5 different marbles be placed in 2 boxes so that 3 marbles are in the first box and 2 are in the second?

Solution: Since there is only 1 set to select from, the second selection will depend upon the first.

After a selection has been made for the first box (3 marbles), there is a reduced number of marbles to select from (5 – 3 or 2). Select 2 marbles from the remaining 2 for the second box:

$$\underbrace{_5C_3}_{\text{1st box}} \cdot \underbrace{_2C_2}_{\text{2nd box}} = 10 \cdot 1 = 10 \quad Ans.$$

Special Conditions

When there is a special condition, begin by satisfying the condition.

Examples

1. How many different 4-member committees can be formed from a group of 10 people if Tony, 1 of the 10, must: **a.** always be on the committee **b.** never be on the committee

Solution:

a. Since Tony must always be on the committee:

1. reserve a place for Tony, thereby reducing the number of members to select (4 – 1 or 3), and
2. remove Tony from the selection, thereby reducing the number of people to select from (10 – 1 or 9).

Thus, select 3 members from a group of 9:

$${}_9C_3 = \frac{\overset{3}{\cancel{9}} \cdot \overset{4}{\cancel{8}} \cdot 7}{\cancel{3} \cdot \cancel{2} \cdot 1} = 84 \quad Ans.$$

b. Since Tony is never to be on the committee:

1. exclude Tony, thereby reducing the number of people to select from (10 – 1 or 9), and
2. maintain the number of members to select (4).

Thus, select 4 members from a group of 9:

$${}_9C_4 = \frac{9 \cdot \overset{2}{\cancel{8}} \cdot 7 \cdot \cancel{6}}{\cancel{4} \cdot \cancel{3} \cdot \cancel{2} \cdot 1} = 126 \quad Ans.$$

2. Given a group of 7 people, find the number of ways to select committees of:
a. at least 4 people
b. at most 4 people

Solution:

a. To have *at least* 4 people from the given 7, there can be 4, 5, 6, or 7 people.

Find the number of possible combinations for each case and take the sum:

$$\begin{aligned} &{}_7C_4 + {}_7C_5 + {}_7C_6 + {}_7C_7 \\ &= 35 + 21 + 7 + 1 \\ &= 64 \quad Ans. \end{aligned}$$

b. To have *at most* 4 people from the given 7, there can be 1, 2, 3, or 4 people.

Find the number of possible combinations for each case and take the sum:

$$\begin{aligned} &{}_7C_1 + {}_7C_2 + {}_7C_3 + {}_7C_4 \\ &= 7 + 21 + 35 + 35 = 98 \quad Ans. \end{aligned}$$

Note: In order for a committee to exist, there must be at least one person on it. Therefore, do not consider the case ${}_7C_0$ here.

EXERCISES

In 1–4, evaluate the expression.

1. ${}_{16}C_2$ **2.** ${}_{24}C_1$ **3.** ${}_{24}C_0$ **4.** ${}_{24}C_{21}$

5. Solve for n: ${}_nC_2 = 28$

6. There are 7 different points on a circle. How many straight lines can be drawn through pairs of these 7 points?

7. From a group of 3 teachers and 5 students, how many committees of 3 people can be formed?
(1) 336 (2) 56 (3) 3 (4) 10

8. From an urn containing 6 red marbles, 4 green marbles, and 3 yellow marbles, in how many ways can 3 differently-colored marbles be selected?

9. Three students are chosen to form a committee from the membership of a club of 4 seniors and 6 juniors. How many different committees consisting of 1 senior and 2 juniors can be formed?

10. An urn contains 7 red marbles and 5 yellow marbles. How many selections of 4 marbles will have 2 red and 2 yellow?

11. A congressional committee has 15 Democrats, 12 Republicans, 3 Independents. In how many ways can a 6-member subcommittee be formed that has 1 Independent, 2 Republicans, 3 Democrats?

12. Letters are chosen at random from the English alphabet. Find the number of 6-letter sets possible if the set is to contain 2 vowels and 4 consonants.

In 13–15, cards are drawn at random from a standard deck. Find the number of 5-card hands possible if the hand is to contain:

13. 3 black cards and 2 red cards

14. 4 picture cards and 1 ace

15. 4 picture cards and 1 non-picture card

16. In how many ways can 8 coins be distributed to 3 children so that the first child receives 3 coins, the second child receives 2 coins, and the third child receives 3 coins?

17. In how many ways can 9 prizes be awarded to 4 boys so that the first boy receives 3 prizes and the remaining 3 boys receive 2 prizes each?

In 18–19, find the number of different 6-member committees that can be formed from a group of 12 people if Robin, 1 of the 12, must:

18. always be on the committee

19. never be on the committee

In 20–21, find the number of ways that a committee of 5 can be appointed from the U.S. Senate if the majority leader:

20. is always included **21.** is never included

In 22–23, find the number of ways a 6-member committee can be formed from a group of 8 women and 10 men if there must be the same number of men and women, and if:

22. Jeff, 1 of the men, is always included

23. Nan, 1 of the women, is never included

In 24–27, sets of 2 letters are chosen from the English alphabet. Find the number of 2-letter sets possible if:

24. the set cannot have a vowel

25. the set cannot have a consonant

26. the set must have exactly 1 vowel

27. the set must have a vowel and a consonant

In 28–29, sets of 4 letters are chosen from the English alphabet. Find the number of 4-letter sets possible if there must be the same number of vowels and consonants, and if:

28. A is always included **29.** M is never included

In 30–33, given a group of 6 people. Find the number of ways to select from that group a committee that contains:

30. at least 4 people **32.** at most 4 people

31. 3 or more people **33.** fewer than 4 people

In 34–35, find the number of ways (leaving answers in notation form) to select 5-card hands from a standard deck so that each hand contains:

34. at most 4 red cards **35.** at least 3 black cards

9.3 PROBABILITY

Simple Probability

The PROBABILITY that an event *E* will occur is the *ratio* of the number of ways that the event can occur to the total number of possible outcomes.

$$\text{probability} = \frac{\text{number of successes}}{\text{number of possible outcomes (number in the sample space)}}$$

$$P(E) = \frac{n(E)}{n(S)}$$

Example: The probability that one letter chosen at random from the English alphabet is a vowel is:

$$P(\text{vowel}) = \frac{5}{26} \begin{array}{l}\leftarrow \text{There are 5 vowels.}\\ \leftarrow \text{There are 26 letters in all.}\end{array}$$

Values for Probabilities

The number 1 represents the maximum probability that an event will occur: $P(\textit{certainty}) = 1$

The number 0 represents the minimum probability that an event will occur: $P(\textit{impossibility}) = 0$

Thus, the probability that any event will occur is: $0 \le P(E) \le 1$

If the probability that an event *will* occur is known to be *a*, then the probability that the event will *not* occur is 1 – *a*. $P(\textit{not}) = 1 - P(\textit{will})$

Example

A jar contains 3 red marbles, 4 white marbles, and 5 blue marbles. If one marble is selected at random, what is the probability that the marble selected is: **a.** not black **b.** not red

Solution:

a. There are no black marbles in the jar. Since it is impossible to select a black marble, it is certain that the marble is not black.

Answer: $P(\text{not black}) = 1$

b. $P(\text{red}) = \frac{3}{12}$ ← There are 3 reds. ← There are 12 in all.

$P(\text{not red}) = 1 - P(\text{red})$

$= 1 - \frac{3}{12} = \frac{9}{12}$ or $\frac{3}{4}$ *Ans.*

The Counting Principle for Probability

If two events are *independent*, and if the probability of one event occurring is *m* and the probability of a second event occurring is *n*, then the probability of both events occurring is $m \cdot n$.

This principle can be extended to more than two events.

Example: In three tosses of a fair coin, the probability of getting three heads is:

$$\underbrace{\frac{1}{2}}_{\text{1st toss}} \cdot \underbrace{\frac{1}{2}}_{\text{2nd toss}} \cdot \underbrace{\frac{1}{2}}_{\text{3rd toss}} = \frac{1}{8} \text{ Ans.}$$

Using the Connectives AND, OR

The probability of the event *A and B* is:

$$P(A \wedge B) = \frac{n(A \cap B)}{n(S)}$$

$n(A \cap B)$: The number of elements in the *intersection* of the two sets.

$n(S)$: The number of elements in the sample space.

The probability of the event *A or B* is:

$$P(A \vee B) = \frac{n(A \cup B)}{n(S)}$$

$n(A \cup B)$: The number of elements in the *union* of the two sets.

$n(S)$: The number of elements in the sample space.

Example

In one roll of a fair die, what is the probability of rolling:

a. an even number less than 5 **b.** a number that is even or is less than 5

Solution: Let A represent the set of even numbers on a die: $A = \{2, 4, 6\}$
Let B represent the set of numbers < 5 on a die: $B = \{1, 2, 3, 4\}$

a. The number must be even *and* less than 5. There are two elements in the intersection of the two sets:

$$A \cap B = \{2, 4\} \text{ and } n(A \cap B) = 2$$

$$P(A \wedge B) = \frac{n(A \cap B)}{n(S)} = \frac{2}{6}$$

2: The number of ways the event can occur (the number of elements in the intersection of the sets).

6: The number of possible outcomes (the number of elements in the sample space).

Answer: $\frac{2}{6}$ or $\frac{1}{3}$

Alternate Solution: the Counting Principle

$$\underbrace{\frac{3}{6}}_{\text{probability of 1st event}} \cdot \underbrace{\frac{4}{6}}_{\text{probability of 2nd event}} = \frac{1}{3}$$

b. For "or," use union. There are 5 elements in the union of the sets:

$$A \cup B = \{1, 2, 3, 4, 6\} \text{ and } n(A \cup B) = 5$$

$$P(A \vee B) = \frac{n(A \cup B)}{n(S)} = \frac{5}{6}$$

5: The number of ways the event can occur (the number of elements in the union of the sets).

6: The number of possible outcomes (the number of elements in the sample space).

Answer: $\frac{5}{6}$

Alternate Solution: Add the probabilities of the separate events, and then subtract their overlap, so that outcomes are not counted twice.

$$P(A \vee B) = P(A) + P(B) - P(A \cap B)$$
$$= \frac{3}{6} + \frac{4}{6} - \frac{2}{6} = \frac{5}{6}$$

EXERCISES

In 1–3, find the probability of selecting:

1. an integer divisible by 3 in a random selection from the first 10 positive integers

2. a prime number if one number is chosen at random from $\{2, 3, 4, 5\}$

3. a perfect square if one number is chosen at random from $\{1, 2, 3, 4, 5, 6, 7, 8, 9, 10\}$

In 4–8, the name of a quadrilateral is selected at random from {parallelogram, rhombus, rectangle, square, trapezoid, isosceles trapezoid}. What is the probability of selecting a quadrilateral with:

4. both pairs of opposite sides congruent

5. congruent diagonals

6. perpendicular diagonals

7. both pairs of opposite angles congruent

8. all pairs of consecutive angles congruent

In 9–10, an equation is selected at random from:
$\{y = 0,\ y = x,\ y = x^2,\ x^2 + y^2 = 25\}$
What is the probability that the graph of the equation:

9. is a line 10. passes through the origin

11. A letter is selected at random from the word DEED. What is the probability that the letter selected appears in the word exactly twice?

12. A letter is selected at random from the word SQUARE. What is the probability that the letter selected appears in the word more than once?

13. If the probability that an event will occur is $\frac{x}{y}$, then the probability that the event will not occur is

(1) $-\frac{x}{y}$ (2) $-\frac{y}{x}$ (3) $\frac{1-x}{y}$ (4) $\frac{y-x}{y}$

14. If the probability that an event will not occur is $\frac{1}{x^2}$, then the probability that the event will occur is represented by

(1) -1 (2) 0 (3) x^2 (4) $\frac{x^2-1}{x^2}$

15. If the probability that an event will occur is $\frac{1}{x+1}$, then the probability that the event will not occur is

(1) $x + 1$ (3) $\frac{x}{x+1}$

(2) $-\frac{1}{x+1}$ (4) $-\frac{x}{x+1}$

In 16–21, given the set of functions:

$\{\sin x, \cos x, \tan x\}$

Find the probability that a function chosen at random from this set is:

16. positive in Quadrant I

17. negative in Quadrant I

18. positive in both Quadrants I and III

19. negative in both Quadrants II and IV

20. positive in Quadrant I or II

21. negative in Quadrant II or III

In 22–28, a card is drawn at random from a standard deck of playing cards. What is the probability of drawing:

22. a black king

(1) $\frac{2}{52}$ (2) $\frac{4}{52}$ (3) $\frac{28}{52}$ (4) $\frac{30}{52}$

23. either a black card or a king

(1) $\frac{2}{52}$ (2) $\frac{4}{52}$ (3) $\frac{28}{52}$ (4) $\frac{30}{52}$

24. either an ace or a red king

(1) $\frac{8}{52}$ (2) $\frac{6}{52}$ (3) $\frac{6}{26}$ (4) $\frac{3}{14}$

25. either a king or an ace

(1) $\frac{8}{52}$ (2) $\frac{6}{52}$ (3) $\frac{4}{52}$ (4) $\frac{2}{52}$

26. either a spade or a club

(1) $\frac{8}{52}$ (2) $\frac{2}{52}$ (3) $\frac{13}{52}$ (4) $\frac{26}{52}$

27. either a black card or a red card

(1) $\frac{13}{52}$ (2) $\frac{26}{52}$ (3) 0 (4) 1

28. a black heart

(1) 0 (2) $\frac{1}{3}$ (3) $\frac{1}{2}$ (4) 1

In 29–34, given the set of angle measures:
$\{0°, 30°, 45°, 60°, 90°, 120°, 135°, 150°, 180°\}$
Find the probability that for an angle θ, whose measure is chosen at random from the set:

29. $\sin \theta = 0$

30. $\cos \theta = \frac{1}{2}$

31. $0 \le \tan \theta \le 1$

32. $0 \le \sin \theta \le 1$

33. $-1 \le \cos \theta \le 1$

34. $\sin \theta = \pm\frac{1}{2}$

9.4 PROBABILITY WITH TWO OUTCOMES

The activity of tossing a coin has exactly two distinct possible outcomes, heads or tails. When one of the two possible outcomes is specified as a *success*, say heads, and the probability of heads is traced through a number of tosses of the coin (repetitions of the activity, or TRIALS), this is called a BERNOULLI EXPERIMENT. The outcome of each toss is independent of the previous outcomes.

More generally, this experiment applies to any situation in which the outcome can be designated *success* and *failure*, and $P(\text{success}) + P(\text{failure}) = 1$.

Where *r* Successes Occur First

The probability of getting exactly one 3 followed by four non-3's in five rolls of a fair die is:

$$\frac{1}{6}\cdot\frac{5}{6}\cdot\frac{5}{6}\cdot\frac{5}{6}\cdot\frac{5}{6} \text{ or } \left(\frac{1}{6}\right)^1\left(\frac{5}{6}\right)^4$$

The probability of getting exactly two 3's followed by three non-3's in five rolls of a fair die is:

$$\frac{1}{6}\cdot\frac{1}{6}\cdot\frac{5}{6}\cdot\frac{5}{6}\cdot\frac{5}{6} \text{ or } \left(\frac{1}{6}\right)^2\left(\frac{5}{6}\right)^3$$

The probability of getting exactly *r* 3's followed by $(n - r)$ non-3's in *n* rolls of a fair die is:

$$\left(\frac{1}{6}\right)^r\left(\frac{5}{6}\right)^{n-r}$$

The probability of exactly *r* successes followed by $(n - r)$ failures in *n* trials is:

p^rq^{n-r} where p = probability of success,
q = probability of failure,
and $p + q = 1$

Where Successes Are In Any Order

The probability of getting a certain number of 3's, *in any order*, in five rolls of a fair die is a multiple of getting that number of 3's occurring first.

P(first two 3's)	P(two 3's in any places)
$\left(\frac{1}{6}\right)^2\left(\frac{5}{6}\right)^3$	${}_5C_2\left(\frac{1}{6}\right)^2\left(\frac{5}{6}\right)^3$

Similarly, the probability of getting *r* 3's, *in any order*, in *n* rolls of a fair die is a multiple of getting *r* 3's occurring first:

P(first r 3's)	P(r 3's in any places)
$\left(\frac{1}{6}\right)^r\left(\frac{5}{6}\right)^{n-r}$	${}_nC_r\left(\frac{1}{6}\right)^r\left(\frac{5}{6}\right)^{n-r}$

The probability of exactly *r* successes, in any order, in *n* trials is:

${}_nC_r \cdot p^rq^{n-r}$ where p = probability of success,
q = probability of failure,
and $p + q = 1$

Examples

1. For a certain biased coin, $P(\text{heads}) = \frac{1}{3}$.

   Find the probability of getting 3 heads followed by 2 tails in 5 tosses.

   Solution: Substitute $p = \frac{1}{3}$, $q = 1 - \frac{1}{3}$ or $\frac{2}{3}$, $r = 3$, $n = 5$ into: p^rq^{n-r}

$$P(\text{first 3 heads}) = \left(\frac{1}{3}\right)^3\left(\frac{2}{3}\right)^2 = \frac{1}{27}\cdot\frac{4}{9} = \frac{4}{243}$$

2. For a certain biased coin, $P(\text{heads}) = \frac{1}{3}$.

   Find the probability of getting exactly 3 heads, in any order, in 5 tosses.

   Solution: Substitute $p = \frac{1}{3}$, $q = 1 - \frac{1}{3}$ or $\frac{2}{3}$, $r = 3$, $n = 5$ into: ${}_nC_r \cdot p^rq^{n-r}$

$$P(\text{exactly 3 heads}) = {}_5C_3\cdot\left(\frac{1}{3}\right)^3\left(\frac{2}{3}\right)^2 = \frac{5\cdot4\cdot3}{3\cdot2\cdot1}\cdot\frac{1}{27}\cdot\frac{4}{9} = 10\left(\frac{4}{243}\right) = \frac{40}{243}$$

EXERCISES

1. If a fair coin is tossed 3 times, what is the probability of getting 2 heads in the first 2 tosses?

2. If a fair coin is tossed 3 times, what is the probability of getting exactly 2 heads, in any order?

3. A fair coin is tossed 3 times. What is the probability of obtaining exactly 3 heads?

4. If a fair coin is tossed 4 times, what is the probability of obtaining exactly 3 heads?

5. When a certain biased coin is tossed, the probability of getting a head is $\frac{1}{5}$. If the coin is tossed 3 times, find the probability of getting:

a. 2 heads followed by a tail

b. exactly 2 heads, in any order

6. When a certain biased coin is tossed, the probability of getting a head is $\frac{2}{3}$. If the coin is tossed 3 times, what is the probability of getting no heads?

7. A coin is biased so that the probability of tails is $\frac{1}{3}$. What is the probability of obtaining exactly 2 tails in 5 tosses of the coin?

(1) ${}_5C_2\left(\frac{1}{3}\right)^2\left(\frac{2}{3}\right)^3$ (3) ${}_5C_2\left(\frac{1}{3}\right)^2$

(2) ${}_5C_2\left(\frac{1}{3}\right)^2\left(\frac{1}{3}\right)^3$ (4) $2\left(\frac{1}{3}\right)^2\left(\frac{2}{3}\right)^3$

8. When a certain biased coin is tossed, the probability of getting a tail is $\frac{1}{4}$. If the coin is tossed 2 times, what is the probability of getting 2 heads?

9. A fair die is tossed three times. The probability of obtaining exactly two 5's is

(1) $\frac{1}{72}$ (2) $\frac{5}{72}$ (3) $\frac{25}{72}$ (4) $\frac{67}{72}$

10. In tossing a fair die three times, what is the probability of getting two 6's followed by a number other than 6?

11. What is the probability of obtaining exactly two 6's in seven tosses of a fair die?

(1) $\left(\frac{1}{6}\right)^2\left(\frac{5}{6}\right)^5$ (3) $\left(\frac{2}{6}\right)^7$

(2) $21\left(\frac{1}{6}\right)^2\left(\frac{5}{6}\right)^5$ (4) $\left(\frac{2}{6}\right)^2\left(\frac{4}{6}\right)^5$

12. The four faces of a fair tetrahedron die are numbered 1, 2, 3, and 4. In two tosses of the die, the probability of landing on 4 exactly twice is

(1) $\frac{1}{2}$ (2) $\frac{1}{8}$ (3) $\frac{1}{4}$ (4) $\frac{1}{16}$

13. The probability of guessing the correct answer on a true-false question is $\frac{1}{2}$. If Mary guesses the answers to 5 true-false questions, what is the probability that she will get exactly one wrong answer?

14. The fair spinner shown is spun 3 times. What is the probability of getting a C exactly twice?

B A C D

(1) $\frac{1}{4}$ (3) $\frac{27}{64}$

(2) $\frac{1}{2}$ (4) $\frac{9}{64}$

15. If the probability of a team winning is $\frac{2}{3}$ and the probability of losing is $\frac{1}{3}$, what is the probability that the team will win exactly 1 of 4 games?

16. If the probability of losing a game is $\frac{2}{3}$, what is the probability of losing all 3 games in a 3-game series?

17. If the probability of the Pumas winning is $\frac{2}{5}$, what is the probability that they will win only the first 2 games of the next 5 games they play?

18. The probability that Team A will beat Team B in a sporting event is $\frac{2}{3}$. What is the probability that Team B will win all three games of a three-game series?

19. In a family of 6 children, what is the probability that there will be exactly one male child?

(1) $\frac{6}{64}$ (2) $\frac{7}{64}$ (3) $\frac{32}{64}$ (4) $\frac{58}{64}$

20. From the letters of the word MATH, a letter is drawn at random and replaced. What is the probability of picking exactly 2 A's in 3 tries?

21. If six pennies are tossed, what is the probability that exactly four heads will turn up?

22. When a certain machine makes parts, 10 percent of them are defective. In a sample of 10 parts, what is the probability that 3 will be defective?

(1) ${}_{10}C_3\left(\frac{1}{10}\right)^7\left(\frac{9}{10}\right)^3$

(2) ${}_{10}C_3\left(\frac{9}{10}\right)^7\left(\frac{1}{10}\right)^3$

(3) $\left(\frac{9}{10}\right)^7\left(\frac{1}{10}\right)^3$

(4) $\left(\frac{1}{10}\right)^7\left(\frac{9}{10}\right)^3$

At Least, At Most

Examples

1. Find the probability of getting at least 2 heads in 4 tosses of a fair coin.

Solution: To have *at least* 2 heads, there can be 2, 3, or 4 heads.

Find the probability for each case and take the sum.

$P(\text{at least 2 heads})$
$= P(\text{2 heads}) + P(\text{3 heads}) + P(\text{4 heads})$

$$= {}_4C_2\left(\frac{1}{2}\right)^2\left(\frac{1}{2}\right)^2 + {}_4C_3\left(\frac{1}{2}\right)^3\left(\frac{1}{2}\right)^1 + {}_4C_4\left(\frac{1}{2}\right)^4\left(\frac{1}{2}\right)^0$$

$$= \frac{4\cdot 3}{2\cdot 1}\left(\frac{1}{4}\right)\left(\frac{1}{4}\right) + \frac{4\cdot 3\cdot 2}{3\cdot 2\cdot 1}\left(\frac{1}{8}\right)\left(\frac{1}{2}\right) + 1\left(\frac{1}{16}\right)\left(1\right)$$

$$= \frac{6}{16} + \frac{4}{16} + \frac{1}{16} = \frac{11}{16}$$

2. Find the probability of getting at most 2 heads in 4 tosses of a fair coin.

Solution: To have *at most* 2 heads, there can be 0, 1, or 2 heads.

Find the probability for each case and take the sum.

$P(\text{at most 2 heads})$
$= P(\text{0 heads}) + P(\text{1 head}) + P(\text{2 heads})$

$$= {}_4C_0\left(\frac{1}{2}\right)^0\left(\frac{1}{2}\right)^4 + {}_4C_1\left(\frac{1}{2}\right)^1\left(\frac{1}{2}\right)^3 + {}_4C_2\left(\frac{1}{2}\right)^2\left(\frac{1}{2}\right)^2$$

$$= 1\left(1\right)\left(\frac{1}{16}\right) + 4\left(\frac{1}{2}\right)\left(\frac{1}{8}\right) + \frac{4\cdot 3}{2\cdot 1}\left(\frac{1}{4}\right)\left(\frac{1}{4}\right)$$

$$= \frac{1}{16} + \frac{4}{16} + \frac{6}{16} = \frac{11}{16}$$

EXERCISES

1. Three fair coins are tossed. What is the probability of obtaining at most two heads?

2. Three fair coins are tossed. What is the probability of obtaining at least two tails?

3. In tossing a certain loaded die, the probability of getting a six is $\frac{1}{3}$. If the die is tossed 4 times, what is the probability of getting at least 3 sixes?

4. The probability of rain on any given day is $\frac{2}{3}$. What is the probability of at most one day of rain during the next three days?

5. In each game of a baseball series, a team's probability of winning is $\frac{1}{4}$ and its probability of losing is $\frac{3}{4}$. What is the team's probability of winning at least 2 out of 3 games?

6. Team A and team B play 3 games. If team A's probability of winning a game is $\frac{2}{5}$, what is the probability of team A winning at least two games?

7. The probability of answering correctly by guessing on certain multiple-choice questions is $\frac{1}{3}$. What is the probability of correctly guessing three or more answers out of four?

   (1) $\frac{8}{81}$ (2) $\frac{9}{81}$ (3) $\frac{33}{81}$ (4) $\frac{48}{81}$

8. A coin is loaded so that the probability of obtaining a head is twice as great as that of obtaining a tail.
   - **a.** Find the value of P_{heads} and P_{tails} on a single toss.
   - **b.** Using the probabilities found in part **a**, find the probability of:
     - **(1)** getting exactly 3 heads in 4 tosses
     - **(2)** getting all tails in 5 tosses
     - **(3)** getting at least 2 heads in 3 tosses

9. Team A and Team B are going to play volleyball. The probability that Team A will win a game is $\frac{2}{3}$. In a 3-game series, find the probability that:
   - **a.** Team A will win exactly 2 games
   - **b.** Team A will win at least 2 games
   - **c.** Team B will win exactly 2 games
   - **d.** Team B will win at most 2 games
   - **e.** Team B will not lose all 3 games

10. **a.** The probability of Chris getting a hit is $\frac{1}{3}$. If Chris comes to bat four times, what is the probability that he gets:
     - **(1)** exactly 2 hits
     - **(2)** at least 3 hits
     - **(3)** at most 1 hit

    b. If, in his first two times at bat, Chris does not get a hit, what is the probability that he gets 2 hits in his next two times at bat?

11. In each basketball game played, the Raiders have a probability of winning of $\frac{2}{3}$ and a probability of losing of $\frac{1}{3}$. Find the probability of the Raiders winning:
    - **a.** exactly 4 out of 5 games
    - **b.** at most 4 out of 5 games
    - **c.** exactly 4 out of 5 games if they have already won the first two games

12. A certain part of the country has a 50% chance of rain each day.
    - **a.** What is the probability of not having rain on any given day?
    - **b.** Find the probability of having:
      - **(1)** exactly 5 rainy days in one week
      - **(2)** at most 2 days of rain in one week
      - **(3)** at least 6 days of rain in one week

13. A circle is divided into five equal sections. Assume an unbiased experiment when a spinner is spun.

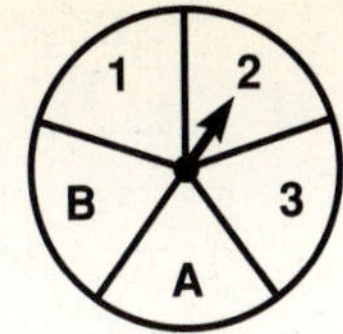

a. If the spinner is spun once, find:
(1) $P(B)$
(2) $P(\text{number})$

b. If the spinner is spun three times, determine the probability it will land on
(1) no B's
(2) at least two numbers
(3) no more than one number

14.

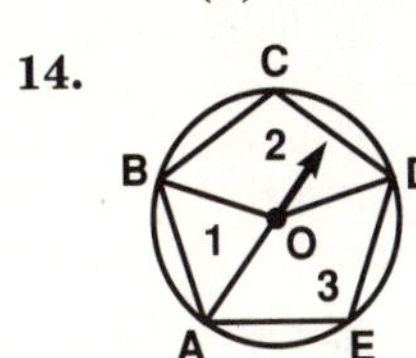

Regular pentagon $ABCDE$ is inscribed in circle O. Radii $\overline{OA}$, $\overline{OB}$, and $\overline{OD}$ divide the pentagon into regions 1, 2, and 3. Assume an unbiased experiment when the spinner is spun.

a. If the spinner is spun once, determine the probability that it will stop:
(1) in region 1 (2) in region 2

b. If the spinner is spun three times, determine the probability it will stop:
(1) in region 1 no more than once
(2) in region 2 at least twice
(3) in region 2 exactly once

15. Circle O is partitioned into four regions as shown, with $\overline{ROS}$ a diameter. Assume an unbiased experiment when a spinner is spun.

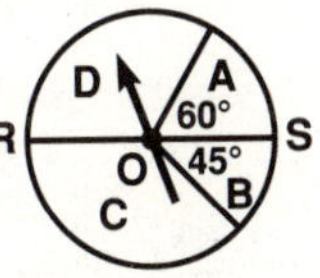

a. If the spinner is spun once, determine the probability that the spinner will stop in:
(1) region A
(2) region C
(3) region D

b. If the spinner is spun three times, what is the probability that:
(1) the spinner will stop in region A exactly twice
(2) the spinner will stop in region D at least twice

16.

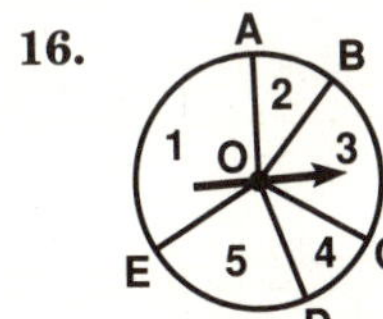

In circle O, $m\widehat{AE} = m\widehat{AC} = m\widehat{EC}$ and $m\widehat{AB} = m\widehat{CD} = 40°$.

a. If the spinner is spun once, determine:
(1) $P(1)$
(2) $P(\text{a number} \geq 2)$

b. If the spinner is spun three times, determine the probability of obtaining:
(1) at most one number ≥ 2
(2) at least one number ≥ 2

17. A circle is divided into four sections as shown, and $m\widehat{AB} : m\widehat{BC} : m\widehat{CD} : m\widehat{DA} = 3 : 4 : 2 : 1$.

a. If the spinner is spun once, find:
(1) $P(\text{red})$
(2) $P(\text{green})$

b. Determine the probability of obtaining:
(1) exactly two green's in three spins
(2) at least three red's in four spins
(3) at most two yellow's in three spins

18.

The wheel is divided into twelve regions of equal area, labeled as shown. On any spin of the wheel, each of the regions is equally likely to stop at the pointer at the bottom.

a. Find:
(1) $P(A)$ (2) $P(B)$

b. Find the probability of:
(1) getting at least three A's in four spins of the wheel
(2) getting no more than one B in three spins of the wheel.

19. The numeric key pad on a calculator is arranged as shown. The probability of pressing any key at random is the same for each key.

7	8	9
4	5	6
1	2	3

a. Find:
(1) $P(6)$
(2) $P(\text{even number})$
(3) $P(\text{odd number})$

b. Find the probability of:
(1) pressing exactly 2 even numbers on three random presses
(2) getting at least 2 even numbers on three random presses

20.

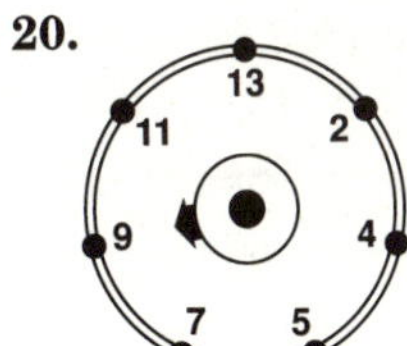

The receivable channels on a TV are indicated on the dial shown. The probability of selecting each channel is the same.

a. Find:
(1) $P(2)$
(2) $P(\text{even channel})$
(3) $P(\text{odd channel})$

b. Find the probability of:
(1) choosing exactly two even channels on three random selections
(2) choosing at least two odd channels on three random selections

1	2	∧
3	4	∨
–	<	>

21. An electronic game contains 9 keys. Four of the keys have numerals and 5 have symbols. Each key is equally likely to be pressed on each move.

a. Find:

(1) $P(4)$

(2) P(numeral key)

(3) P(symbol key)

b. Find the probability of:

(1) pressing exactly 2 numeral keys on 3 random presses

(2) pressing at least 2 symbol keys on 3 random presses

1	2	3	4
5	6	R	Y

22. An electronic game has the form of a calculator as shown. There are eight keys: six of them are numbered 1, 2, 3, 4, 5, 6 and two are colored, one red (R) and one yellow (Y). Each key is equally likely to be pressed.

a. If one key is pressed at random,

(1) what is the probability that a number key will be selected?

(2) what is the probability that a color key will be selected?

b. If three keys are pressed at random,

(1) what is the probability that exactly two number keys will be selected?

(2) what is the probability that at least two number keys will be selected?

9.5 THE BINOMIAL THEOREM

Writing Out an Expansion

Expansion of the binomial $(p + q)^n$

$n = 0$: $(p + q)^0 = 1$

$n = 1$: $(p + q)^1 = p + q$

$n = 2$: $(p + q)^2 = p^2 + 2pq + q^2$

$n = 3$: $(p + q)^3 = p^3 + 3p^2q + 3pq^2 + q^3$

$n = 4$: $(p + q)^4 = p^4 + 4p^3q + 6p^2q^2 + 4pq^3 + q^4$

$n = 5$: $(p + q)^5 = p^5 + 5p^4q + 10p^3q^2 + 10p^2q^3 + 5pq^4 + q^5$

Pascal's Triangle

1

1 1

1 2 1

1 3 3 1

1 4 6 4 1

1 5 10 10 5 1

General Characteristics of the Expansion

1. **There are $(n + 1)$ terms in the expansion of $(p + q)^n$.**
2. **The powers of p descend from n to 0, while the powers of q ascend from 0 to n. In any particular term, the sum of the powers of p and q is n.**
3. **The coefficients can be found from Pascal's Triangle (above right), or by the combination formula ${}_nC_r$, where r = the power of q.**

General Formula

$$(p + q)^n = {}_nC_0 \cdot p^n + {}_nC_1 \cdot p^{n-1}q^1 + {}_nC_2 \cdot p^{n-2}q^2 + {}_nC_3 \cdot p^{n-3}q^3 + \dots + {}_nC_n \cdot q^n$$

Examples

1. Write the expansion of $(2x + y)^6$.

Solution: Write the expansion of $(p + q)^6$. There are 6 + 1, or 7, terms. The powers of p descend from 6 to 0, while the powers of q ascend from 0 to 6. In any particular term, the sum of the powers of p and q is 6. The coefficients are of the form ${}_6C_r$, where r = the power of q.

$$(p + q)^6 = {}_6C_0 \cdot p^6 + {}_6C_1 \cdot p^5q^1 + {}_6C_2 \cdot p^4q^2 + {}_6C_3 \cdot p^3q^3 + {}_6C_4 \cdot p^2q^4 + {}_6C_5 \cdot pq^5 + {}_6C_6 \cdot q^6$$

Let $p = 2x$ and $q = y$. Evaluate the coefficients. Then, simplify.

$$(2x + y)^6 = 1(2x)^6 + 6(2x)^5y + 15(2x)^4y^2 + 20(2x)^3y^3 + 15(2x)^2y^4 + 6(2x)^1y^5 + 1y^6$$

$$= 64x^6 + 192x^5y + 240x^4y^2 + 160x^3y^3 + 60x^2y^4 + 12xy^5 + y^6$$

2. Write the expansion of $(x - 2y)^6$.

Solution: Write the expansion of $(p + q)^6$. Let $p = x$ and $q = -2y$. Evaluate and simplify.

$$(p + q)^6 = {}_6C_0 \cdot p^6 + {}_6C_1 \cdot p^5q^1 + {}_6C_2 \cdot p^4q^2 + {}_6C_3 \cdot p^3q^3 + {}_6C_4 \cdot p^2q^4 + {}_6C_5 \cdot pq^5 + {}_6C_6 \cdot q^6$$

$$(x - 2y)^6 = 1 \cdot x^6 + 6x^5(-2y)^1 + 15x^4(-2y)^2 + 20x^3(-2y)^3 + 15x^2(-2y)^4 + 6x^1(-2y)^5 + 1(-2y)^6$$

$$= x^6 - 12x^5y + 60x^4y^2 - 160x^3y^3 + 240x^2y^4 - 192xy^5 + 64y^6$$

EXERCISES

In 1–8, expand the given binomial to the indicated power.

1. $(x + 2)^4$

2. $(x + 0.1)^3$

3. $(y - 3)^5$

4. $(3a + b)^5$

5. $(2y - 1)^6$

6. $(3x + 2y)^4$

7. $(x - 2y)^5$

8. $(2a - 3b)^4$

Finding a Specific Term

To find the kth term of an expansion, apply the formula: ${}_nC_{k-1} \cdot p^{n-k+1}q^{k-1}$

Examples

1. Write the second term of the expansion $(3a - 1)^4$.

Solution: Use the formula for the kth term of the expansion of $(p + q)^n$.
Let $k = 2$, $n = 4$, $p = 3a$, and $q = -1$.

$${}_nC_{k-1} \cdot p^{n-k+1}q^{k-1} \Rightarrow {}_4C_{2-1} \cdot (3a)^{4-2+1}(-1)^{2-1} = {}_4C_1(3a)^3(-1)^1 = 4(27a^3)(-1) = -108a^3$$

Alternate Solution: You can work out an individual term without memorizing the formula.
In the second term, the power of p, or $3a$, descends from 4 to 3.
Since the sum of the powers must be 4, the corresponding power of q, or -1, is 1.
The coefficient is of the form ${}_4C_r$ where r = the power of q, namely 1. The coefficient is ${}_4C_1$.

$$\text{second term} = {}_4C_1(3a)^3(-1)^1 = 4(27a^3)(-1) = -108a^3$$

2. Write an expression (do not simplify) for the next-to-last term of the expansion of $\left(z^2 + \frac{1}{3}\right)^{30}$.

Solution: Since $n = 30$, there are 31 terms in the expansion. The next-to-last is the 30th term.
In the next-to-last term, the power of p, or z^2, is 1.
Since the sum of the powers must be 30, the corresponding power of q, or $\frac{1}{3}$, is 29.
The coefficient is of the form ${}_{30}C_r$ where r = the power of q.

$$\text{next-to-last term} = \text{30th term} = {}_{30}C_{29}(z^2)^1\left(\frac{1}{3}\right)^{29}$$

EXERCISES

1. What is the numerical coefficient of the second term of the expansion $(x - 2y)^4$?
(1) -8 (2) 8 (3) 24 (4) -32

2. What is the second term in the expansion of $\left(x^2 + \frac{x}{2}\right)^5$?
(1) $\frac{5x^5}{2}$ (2) $\frac{5x^7}{2}$ (3) $\frac{5x^8}{2}$ (4) $\frac{5x^9}{2}$

3. The third term of the expansion of $(\sin x - 1)^3$ is
(1) $3 \sin x$ (2) $-3 \sin x$ (3) $3 \sin^2 x$ (4) $-3 \sin^2 x$

4. What is the third term in the expansion of $(2x + y)^5$?
(1) $20x^3y^2$ (2) $80x^3y^2$ (3) $80x^2y^3$ (4) $-80x^3y^2$

5. The third term of the expansion of $(x - 3)^6$ is
(1) $135x^4$ (2) $-135x^4$ (3) $540x^3$ (4) $-540x^3$

6. Which is the 3rd term in the expansion of $(2x - y)^4$?
(1) $-32x^3y$ (2) $12x^2y^2$ (3) $24x^2y^2$ (4) $-8xy^3$

7. The third term in the expansion of $(a - \sqrt{2})^5$ is
(1) $20a^3$ (2) $20a^2\sqrt{2}$ (3) $-20a^2\sqrt{2}$ (4) $40a^3$

8. The third term of the expansion of $(x - 2y)^6$ is
(1) $60x^4y^2$ (2) $-60x^4y^2$ (3) $160x^3y^3$ (4) $-160x^3y^3$

9. The third term in the expansion of $(a - 2b)^8$ is
(1) ${}_8C_3(a)^6(-2b)^2$ (2) ${}_8C_2(a)^6(-2b)^2$ (3) ${}_8C_3(a)^2(-2b)^6$ (4) ${}_8C_2(a)^2(-2b)^6$

10. Which is the fourth term in the expansion of $(x + 3)^5$?
(1) $270x^2$ (2) $135x^2$ (3) $405x$ (4) $135x$

11. The fourth term in the expansion of $(h + t)^6$ is
(1) ${}_6C_3h^3t^3$ (2) ${}_6C_4h^4t^2$ (3) ${}_6C_4h^2t^4$ (4) ${}_4C_3h^3t^3$

12. The fourth term in the expansion $(a - 3b)^5$ is
(1) $270a^2b^3$ (2) $-270a^2b^3$ (3) $90a^2b^3$ (4) $-90a^2b^3$

13. What is the fifth term of the expansion $(x - 2y)^5$?
(1) $20x^4y$ (2) $40x^4y$ (3) $80xy^4$ (4) $-80xy^4$

14. What is the fifth term in the expansion $(a + bi)^7$?
(1) $35a^3b^4$ (2) $-35a^3b^4$ (3) $21a^2b^5i$ (4) $-21a^2b^5i$

15. Which is the seventh term in the expansion of $(2x - y)^7$?
(1) $7xy^6$ (2) $-7xy^6$ (3) $14xy^6$ (4) $-14xy^6$

16. The last term in the expansion of $(x + 3y)^4$ is
(1) $108xy^3$ (2) $81y^4$ (3) $3y^4$ (4) $243y^5$

17. What is the last term in the expansion of $(x - 2)^5$?
(1) $-32x$ (2) $32x$ (3) -32 (4) 32

18. Which is the last term in the expansion of $(2x - 3y)^5$?
(1) $-3y^5$ (2) $3y^5$ (3) $243y^5$ (4) $-243y^5$

19. The middle term in the expansion $(x + 3y)^4$ is
(1) $54x^2y^2$ (2) $18x^2y^2$ (3) $12x^3y$ (4) $12xy^3$

20. Which is the middle term in the expansion of $(2 \sin x + \cos y)^4$?
(1) $8 \sin^3 x \cos y$ (2) $8 \sin x \cos^3 y$ (3) $12 \sin^2 x \cos^2 y$ (4) $24 \sin^2 x \cos^2 y$

In 21–24, find the middle term of the expansion of the given binomial.

21. $(2x - y)^4$
22. $(3x + 1)^6$
23. $(3x - 2y)^4$
24. $(2a + 4b)^6$

In 25–28, write an expression for the next-to-the-last term of the expansion of the given binomial. (Do not simplify.)

25. $\left(x + \frac{1}{2}\right)^{10}$
26. $(3x - 1)^{19}$
27. $\left(2a + \frac{1}{3}\right)^{40}$
28. $(5y - 0.1z)^{25}$

9.6 SUMMARY EXERCISES

1. How many arrangements of the word NUMBER are possible if the positions of the vowels must remain unchanged?

2. How many numerals with number values between 3,000 and 4,000 can be formed with the digits 3, 4, 6, and 7?

3. If a group consists of 5 boys and 8 girls, how many committees that contain 3 boys and 4 girls can be formed from the group if Joan, 1 of the girls, is always on the committee?

4. If a group consists of 7 men and 5 women, how many 5-person committees containing at least 3 men can be selected from the group?

5. Given the word SYZYGY.
  a. How many different 6-letter arrangements of the word are possible?
  b. In how many 6-letter arrangements of the word will the letter Y be in the first and last positions?
  c. What is the probability that the letter Y is in the first and last positions if 6-letter arrangements are formed from the word?

6. The math department of a certain high school has 5 classes of Course I, 4 classes of Course II, and 3 classes of Course III.
  a. If a teacher's program consists of 5 classes, how many random combinations of 5 classes are possible?
  b. How many 5-class programs will consist of 3 Course I's and 2 Course II's?
  c. If a teacher's program consists of 5 classes, what is the probability that a teacher's program will have 3 Course I's and 2 Course II's?

7. A committee of 4 is to be chosen from a group of 2 men and 4 women.
  a. How many different 4-member committees are possible?
  b. How many of these committees consist of exactly 1 man and 3 women?
  c. What is the probability that the 4-member committee chosen consists of exactly 1 man and 3 women?
  d. What is the probability that a woman will be on the committee?
  e. How many of these committees include at least 2 women?

8. A budget committee consists of 5 Democrats and 4 Republicans.
  a. How many 3-member subcommittees can be formed from the budget committee?
  b. How many of these subcommittees will consist of 1 Democrat and 2 Republicans?
  c. What is the probability that the subcommittee will consist of 1 Democrat and 2 Republicans?
  d. If one of the Democrats on the budget committee is Melodie, what is the probability that she will be a member of one of the subcommittees described in part **b**?
  e. If Ron is one of the Republicans on the budget committee, what is the probability that he will not be a member of one of the subcommittees described in part **b**?
  f. What is the probability that a 5-member subcommittee will have at most 3 Democrats?

9. If the probability that an event will occur is $\frac{y}{x+y}$, then the probability that it will not occur is

(1) $\frac{x+y}{y}$ (2) $\frac{1}{1+y}$ (3) $\frac{x}{x+y}$ (4) $\frac{y}{x+y}$

10. What is the probability that a relation chosen from the following set is a function?
$\{y = x^2,\ x = y^2,\ y = \sin x,\ y = \log x\}$

11. Given the set of angle measures: $\{0°, 90°, 180°, 270°\}$ Find the probability that for an angle θ, whose measure is chosen at random from the set, $\theta = \text{Arc}\cos 0$.

12. If a fair coin is tossed 5 times, what is the probability of getting 3 tails in the first 3 tosses?

13. In a game, the probability of winning is $\frac{1}{4}$ and the probability of losing is $\frac{3}{4}$. If 4 games are played, the probability of winning exactly 3 games is

(1) $\frac{9}{256}$ (2) $\frac{3}{64}$ (3) $\frac{27}{256}$ (4) $\frac{27}{64}$

14. When a certain biased coin is tossed, the probability of getting heads is $\frac{1}{3}$. If the coin is tossed 3 times, what is the probability of getting at least 2 heads?

15. If a fair die is rolled 4 times in a row, what is the probability of getting at most two 5's?

16. The junior class is planning a two-day fair in April. The weather forecast indicates a 60% chance of rain for each of the two days.
  a. Find the probability that it will rain on at least one of the two days.
  b. Find the probability that it will rain on both days.

17. a. In each game of a soccer series, a certain team's probability of winning is $\frac{1}{3}$ and its probability of losing is $\frac{2}{3}$. Find the probability of this team winning
  (1) at least 2 games in a 4-game series
  (2) at most 3 games in a 4-game series
  b. Find a positive value of x for which ${}_xC_2 = 15$.

18. Circle O is partitioned into six regions by diameters $\overline{AOB}$, $\overline{COD}$, $\overline{EOF}$, $\overline{CD} \perp \overline{AB}$, and $m\angle FOB = 45°$.

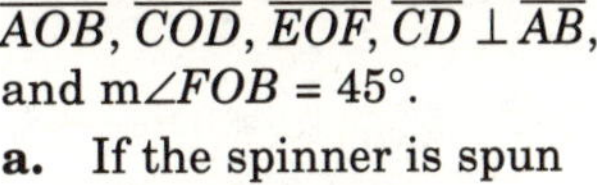

  a. If the spinner is spun once, determine
  (1) $P(3)$ (2) $P(\text{even's})$ (3) $P(7)$
  b. Determine the probability of obtaining
  (1) exactly two even's on three spins
  (2) no more than one 3 on three spins
  (3) exactly one 7 on four spins
  (4) at least three non-even's on five spins

19. Which is the third term in the expansion of $(x - 3)^5$?

(1) $-9x^3$ (2) $9x^3$ (3) $-90x^3$ (4) $90x^3$

20. What is the fourth term in the expansion of $(x - 2y)^5$?

(1) $80x^2y^3$ (2) $60x^2y^3$ (3) $-80x^2y^3$ (4) $-60x^2y^3$

CHAPTER 10

Statistics

10.1 SUMMATION NOTATION

The Greek capital letter *sigma*, Σ, is used to mean "take the sum of what follows." What follows Σ is a general term that represents the nature of each term of the summation. The general term is written with an INDEX, shown by one letter (usually *i*, *j*, *k*, *n*, or *t*). The *limits* for the index are written above Σ (upper limit) and below Σ (lower limit).

The first term of the summation is formed by substituting the lower limit for the index into the general term. Each succeeding term of the summation is formed using successive integral values of the index, until the upper limit is reached.

Example: $\sum_{i=1}^{5} 2^i$ means take the sum of terms of the form 2^i for consecutive integral values of i beginning with $i = 1$ and ending with $i = 5$.

$$\sum_{i=1}^{5} 2^i = 2^1 + 2^2 + 2^3 + 2^4 + 2^5 = 2 + 4 + 8 + 16 + 32 = 62$$

Values for the index may start with a number other than 1.

Example: $\sum_{i=0}^{5} 2^i = 2^0 + 2^1 + 2^2 + 2^3 + 2^4 + 2^5 = 63$

If a constant factor appears inside the summation symbol, the constant may be "factored out."

Example: $\sum_{i=1}^{3} 2x_i = 2\sum_{i=1}^{3} x_i = 2(x_1 + x_2 + x_3)$

EXERCISES

In 1–18, evaluate the summation.

1. $\sum_{k=2}^{5} 4k$
2. $\sum_{k=1}^{3} \frac{6}{k}$
3. $\sum_{k=1}^{3} \frac{k}{k+1}$
4. $\sum_{n=1}^{4} (2n - 1)$
5. $\sum_{k=1}^{4} k^2$
6. $\sum_{k=4}^{6} (k^2 - 8)$
7. $\sum_{k=0}^{3} (k^2 + 1)$
8. $\sum_{k=1}^{3} (3 - k)^2$
9. $\sum_{k=2}^{4} (k^3 + 1)$
10. $\sum_{k=1}^{3} k^k$
11. $\frac{1}{3}\sum_{x=1}^{4} x^2$
12. $\sum_{k=1}^{3} \frac{1}{2}(k^2)$
13. $2\left(\sum_{k=2}^{4} k^2\right)$
14. $3\sum_{k=2}^{4} (k - 2)^2$
15. $\sum_{x=2}^{4} 3(x + 1)$
16. $\sum_{k=1}^{2} \sin\frac{k\pi}{2}$
17. $\sum_{n=0}^{4} \cos\frac{n\pi}{2}$
18. $\sum_{k=1}^{4} \cos\frac{k\pi}{3}$
19. The value of $\sum_{r=2}^{4} {}_6C_r$ is
    (1) 15 (2) 35 (3) 50 (4) 64
20. Find the value of: $\sum_{r=0}^{4} {}_4C_r$

10.2 MEASURES OF CENTRAL TENDENCY

In Statistics, it is useful to represent a set of data by a single number that tends to fall somewhere in the center of the set. Three such MEASURES OF CENTRAL TENDENCY are called the *mean*, the *median*, and the *mode*.

The Mean (Arithmetic Mean)

The MEAN of n numbers $x_1, x_2, ..., x_n$ is the sum of the numbers divided by n.

$$\text{the mean} = \bar{x} = \frac{x_1 + x_2 + \dots + x_n}{n} = \frac{\sum_{i=1}^{n} x_i}{n}$$

(read "x-bar")

Examples

1. For the set of numbers 30, 41, 32, 46, 37, find the mean.

   Solution: The mean of the 5 numbers is their sum divided by 5.

   $$\text{mean} = \frac{30 + 41 + 32 + 46 + 37}{5} = \frac{186}{5} = 37.2$$

2. The arithmetic mean of the numbers 5, 7, $x + 3$, 12 is 10. Find x.

   Solution: The mean is the sum of the 4 values divided by 4.

   $$\text{mean} = \frac{5 + 7 + x + 3 + 12}{4}$$

   $$10 = \frac{27 + x}{4}$$

   $$40 = 27 + x$$

   $$13 - x$$

The Median

The MEDIAN of a set of numbers arranged in numerical order is the "middle" number.

The number of values below the median value is the same as the number above it.

Examples

1. Determine the median value of 4, 3, 1, 4, 4, 6, 3.

   Solution: Arrange the values in ascending order and choose the middle value:

   1, 3, 3, 4, 4, 4, 6
   ↑
   median

   Answer: The median value is 4.

2. Determine the median value of 3, 4, 1, 1, 4, 6.

   Solution: Arrange the values in ascending order. Since there is an even number of values, find the number halfway between the two values surrounding the exact middle.

   1, 1, 3, 4, 4, 6
   ↑
   median

   Answer: The median is 3.5.

The Mode

The MODE of a set of data is the value that appears most frequently.

A set of data may have:

a single mode: For 1, 7, 9, 7, 8, the mode is 7.

more than one mode: For 1, 1, 7, 9, 7, the modes are 1 and 7.

no mode: For 1, 7, 9, 8, 4, there is no mode.

The Most Representative Measure

It is important to recognize the measure that best represents a set of data.

Example: For the data 2, 1, 8, 3, 500, 3, 1, the mean, 74, is not representative of the set because six of the seven values are below 10, and 500 distorts the result.

A better representation of the average value is the median, 3, which is also the mode here.

Working With Grouped Data

A set of data may be presented in a FREQUENCY TABLE that, rather than repeating individual measures, lists each measure once and tells how many times it appears in the data set.

To calculate the mean from a frequency table:

1. **Multiply each measure x_i by its frequency f_i, resulting in the products $x_i \cdot f_i$.**
2. **Find the sum of these products: $\Sigma x_i \cdot f_i$**
3. **Divide by the total frequency Σf_i or N.**

$$\text{mean} = \bar{x} = \frac{\Sigma x_i \cdot f_i}{N}$$

To calculate the median from a frequency table:

1. **Find the total frequency: Σf_i or N**
2. **The median, which is the middle measure, falls in the position that is $\frac{N+1}{2}$ measures from either the bottom or the top measure.**

Example

For the measures shown in this table

Measure x_i	Frequency f_i
70	2
80	3
90	5

find: **a.** the mean
b. the median
c. the mode

Solution:

a. To find the mean, calculate $\Sigma x_i \cdot f_i$ and N.

Measure x_i	Frequency f_i	Product $x_i \cdot f_i$
70	2	140
80	3	240
90	5	450

$\Sigma f_i = N = 10$ $\quad$ $830 = \Sigma x_i \cdot f_i$

$$\text{mean} = \frac{\Sigma x_i \cdot f_i}{N} = \frac{830}{10} = 83$$

b. The median of 10 measures is halfway between the 5th and the 6th measures.

Five measures down from the top of the table, or up from the bottom, locates the median between 80 and 90, at 85.

c. The mode is the measure with the highest frequency. Thus, the mode is 90.

EXERCISES

1. If student heights are 176 cm, 172 cm, 160 cm, and 160 cm, what is the mean height of these students?

2. Express the mean (average) of $x + 1$ and $3x - 3$ as a binomial.

3. A student received test scores of 72, 84, and 86. What score must the student receive on a fourth test so that the mean of these scores will be 85?

4. A set of data consists of four scores: x_1, x_2, x_3, and x_4. If the mean of the four scores is 9, what is the value of x_3 when $x_1 = 5$, $x_2 = 7$, and $x_4 = 11$?
   (1) 9 (2) 13 (3) 3 (4) 12

5. The following data are numbers of minutes a student spent on homework: 25, 35, 30, 50, and 38. What is the median of the data?

6. Find the median measure: 6, 9, 7, 6.5, 8, 7

7. The test scores for five students were 59, 60, 63, 76, and 87. How many points greater than the median is the mean?

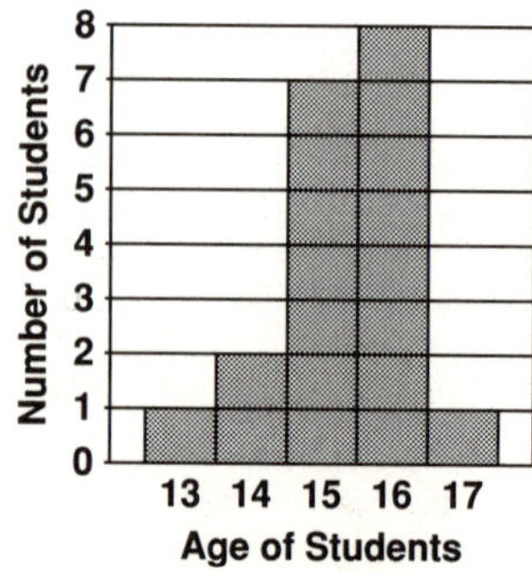

8. The histogram above shows the distribution of student ages in a tenth-grade class. Which age is the mode?

9. Which set of data has more than one mode?

(1) 2, 2, 4, 6, 7, 9 (3) 2, 2, 2, 6, 7, 9
(2) 2, 2, 4, 6, 9, 9 (4) 2, 3, 4, 6, 9, 9

10. For which set of data do the mean, median, and mode all have the same value?

(1) 1, 3, 3, 3, 5 (3) 1, 1, 1, 2, 5
(2) 1, 1, 2, 5, 6 (4) 1, 1, 3, 5, 10

11. If a group of data consists of the numbers 2, 2, 5, 6, and 15, which is true?

(1) median > mean (3) mode < median
(2) mean = mode (4) median = mode

12. If a group of data consists of the numbers 5, 5.5, 7, and 7.5, which is true?

(1) The median and the mean are each 6.5.
(2) The median and the mode are each 6.5.
(3) The median and the mean are each 6.25.
(4) The median and the mode are each 6.25.

Measure x_i	Frequency f_i
8	5
16	1
20	2

13. What is the mean of the data in the table above?

(1) 5.5 (2) 8 (3) 12 (4) 13.3

Measure x_i	Frequency f_i
2	2
5	3
7	4
8	1

14. Find the mean of the measures in the table above.

Measure x_i	Frequency f_i
4	15
5	8
6	13
7	10

15. What is the median of the set of data shown in the table above?

(1) 15 (2) 10.5 (3) 5.5 (4) 4

x_i	f_i
20	2
21	5
23	4
24	4

16. What is the median for the above set of data?

Measure x_i	Frequency f_i
5	3
12	2
13	5
18	4

17. What is the mode of the data shown in the table above?

(1) 12 (2) 12.5 (3) 13 (4) 51.5

Measure x_i	Frequency f_i
8	1
10	3
14	2

18. Use the data in the table above to tell which statement is true.

(1) mean = median (3) mean < mode
(2) mean > median (4) median > mode

Measure x_i	Frequency f_i
60	2
75	4
80	1
90	3

19. Which correctly compares the mean and median of the set of data shown in the table above?

(1) The mean and median are equal.
(2) The mean exceeds the median by 2.
(3) The median exceeds the mean by 2.
(4) The mean exceeds the median by 2.5.

Working With Ungrouped Data

A number that shows the spread, or variation, of values about the mean is called a MEASURE OF DISPERSION.

The simplest measure of dispersion is the RANGE, which is the difference between the highest and lowest data values of the set.

the range = highest value – lowest value

Example: The range of the data 15, 32, 57, 44, is 57 – 15, or 42.

In a set of n data values, the amount by which a value x_i differs from the mean $\bar{x}$ is called the *deviation from the mean:* $x_i - \bar{x}$.

The average of the absolute values of the mean deviations is the MEAN ABSOLUTE DEVIATION:

$$\frac{\sum_{i=1}^{n}|x_i - \bar{x}|}{n}$$

The average of the squares of the mean deviations is the VARIANCE:

$$\frac{\sum_{i=1}^{n}(x_i - \bar{x})^2}{n}$$

The square root of the variance is the STANDARD DEVIATION:

$$\sqrt{\frac{\sum_{i=1}^{n}(x_i - \bar{x})^2}{n}}$$

Example: For the data set 15, 32, 57, 44, the mean $\bar{x}$ is $\frac{15+32+57+44}{4}$, or 37.

$$\text{the mean absolute deviation} = \frac{|15-37|+|32-37|+|57-37|+|44-37|}{4}$$

$$= \frac{22+5+20+7}{4} = \frac{54}{4} = 13.5$$

$$\text{the variance} = \frac{(15-37)^2+(32-37)^2+(57-37)^2+(44-37)^2}{4}$$

$$= \frac{22^2+5^2+20^2+7^2}{4} = \frac{958}{4} = 239.5$$

$$\text{the standard deviation} = \sqrt{239.5} \approx 15.5$$

Example

On an IQ test, the scores of 5 students were 134, 131, 126, 125, and 119. Calculate the standard deviation of these scores to the nearest tenth.

Solution:

Step 1: Find the mean, $\bar{x}$.

$$\bar{x} = \frac{134+131+126+125+119}{5}$$

$$= \frac{635}{5} = 127$$

Step 2: Find the variance, which is the average of the squares of the mean deviations. You may find it convenient to arrange these calculations in tabular form.

x_i	$x_i - \bar{x}$	$(x_i - \bar{x})^2$
134	134 – 127 or 7	7^2 or 49
131	131 – 127 or 4	4^2 or 16
126	126 – 127 or –1	$(-1)^2$ or 1
125	125 – 127 or –2	$(-2)^2$ or 4
119	119 – 127 or –8	$(-8)^2$ or 64

$$\Sigma(x_i - \bar{x})^2 = 134$$

$$\text{variance} = \frac{\Sigma(x_i - \bar{x})^2}{n} = \frac{134}{5} = 26.8$$

Step 3: The standard deviation is the square root of the variance.

$$\text{standard deviation} = \sqrt{\frac{\Sigma(x_i - \bar{x})^2}{n}}$$

$$= \sqrt{26.8}$$

$$\approx 5.2 \quad \textit{Ans.}$$

EXERCISES

1. What is the range for the following data?

52, 32, 61, 82, 63

(1) 50 (2) 58 (3) 11 (4) 61

Score	Frequency
210	1
370	5
640	7
700	4
790	1

2. Given the above table of SAT scores for a class. What is the range of these test scores?

In 3–4, for the given set of data, calculate:
a. the mean absolute deviation
b. the variance
c. the standard deviation, to the nearest tenth

3. 7, 10, 14, 16, 18

4. 92, 86, 98, 88, 96

5. On a certain civil service examination, the grades of five people were 71, 73, 74, 86, and 96.

Compute:

a. the arithmetic mean of their grades

b. the standard deviation, to the nearest tenth

In 6–11, for the given set of data, calculate the standard deviation, to the nearest tenth.

6. The heights in inches of a basketball team are:

81, 73, 75, 80, 71

7. On the PSAT, five students received scores of 50, 52, 53, 59, and 61.

8. During a given week, Pat worked 7 hours on Monday, 10 hours on Tuesday, 7 hours on Wednesday, 8 hours on Thursday, and 10 hours on Friday.

9. 95, 85, 90, 80, 85, 85, 80, 95, 85, 80

10. The ages of ten teachers at George Washington Elementary School are 33, 23, 36, 29, 36, 36, 33, 29, 36, and 29.

11. The shoe sizes of ten players on a basketball team are:

7, 8, $9\frac{1}{2}$, 10, 10, 10, $10\frac{1}{2}$, 11, 11, 13

12. A high school football team scored the following number of points during the ten-game season:

19, 20, 21, 27, 29, 29, 34, 40, 40, 41

a. What is the median?

b. What is the mean?

c. Find the standard deviation of these scores, to the nearest tenth.

13. Given the following ten scores:

61, 65, 65, 65, 67, 69, 71, 74, 75, 78

For these scores, find the:

a. mode
b. median
c. mean
d. standard deviation, to the nearest tenth

Working With Grouped Data

When several data values of a set occur repeatedly, it is convenient to present the data in a frequency table. The frequency table may be given or it may have to be prepared.

To group a set of data in a frequency table and calculate the standard deviation:

1. Order the measures, x_i, and list them in the first column of a table. List the corresponding frequencies, f_i, in the second column.

2. Calculate the mean: $\frac{\Sigma x_i \cdot f_i}{\Sigma f_i}$

3. Calculate the variance.

Find: a. the deviation of each data measure from the mean: $x_i - \bar{x}$

b. the squares of the mean deviations: $(x_i - \bar{x})^2$

c. the products $f_i(x_i - \bar{x})^2$ and their sum

d. the average of the products $f_i(x_i - \bar{x})^2$, that is: $\frac{\Sigma f_i (x_i - \bar{x})^2}{\Sigma f_i}$

4. Calculate the standard deviation: Find the square root of the variance.

Example

1. Given the measures: 7, 1, 7, 3, 10, 7, 0, 1, 3, 6, 4, 0, 7, 7, 3

a. Find the standard deviation, to the nearest tenth.

b. Determine the number of measures that are within one standard deviation of the mean.

Solution:

a. Prepare a table to keep track of all calculations.

x_i	f_i	$x_i \cdot f_i$	$x_i - \bar{x}$	$(x_i - \bar{x})^2$	$f_i(x_i - \bar{x})^2$
0	2	0	$0 - 4.4 = -4.4$	$(-4.4)^2 = 19.36$	$2(19.36) = 38.72$
1	2	2	$1 - 4.4 = -3.4$	$(-3.4)^2 = 11.56$	$2(11.56) = 23.12$
3	3	9	$3 - 4.4 = -1.4$	$(-1.4)^2 = 1.96$	$3(1.96) = 5.88$
4	1	4	$4 - 4.4 = -0.4$	$(-0.4)^2 = 0.16$	$1(0.16) = 0.16$
6	1	6	$6 - 4.4 = 1.6$	$(1.6)^2 = 2.56$	$1(2.56) = 2.56$
7	5	35	$7 - 4.4 = 2.6$	$(2.6)^2 = 6.76$	$5(6.76) = 33.80$
10	1	10	$10 - 4.4 = 5.6$	$(5.6)^2 = 31.36$	$1(31.36) = 31.36$
Totals:	15	66			135.60

mean $= \frac{\Sigma x_i \cdot f_i}{\Sigma f_i} = \frac{66}{15} = 4.4$ variance $= \frac{\Sigma f_i (x_i - \bar{x})^2}{\Sigma f_i} = \frac{135.60}{15} = 9.04$

standard deviation $= \sqrt{\text{variance}} = \sqrt{9.04} \approx 3.0$ *Ans.*

b. For values "within one standard deviation (s.d.) of the mean," look at "mean ± 1 s.d."
For this data, you want to know how many measures are between 4.4 + 3.0, or 7.4, and 4.4 – 3.0, or 1.4.
Four of the measures, namely, 3, 4, 6, and 7, are between 1.4 and 7.4.
The sum of their frequencies is 3 + 1 + 1 + 5, or 10. *Ans.*

EXERCISES

In 1–4, for the given frequency table, find the standard deviation of the set of data, to the nearest tenth.

1.

Score x_i	Frequency f_i
88	6
84	7
76	5
72	2

2.

Measure of Weight x_i	Frequency f_i
91	1
96	1
105	2
111	3
113	2
114	1

3.

Measure of Weight x_i	Frequency f_i
56	1
75	2
82	2
100	3
110	1
120	1

4.

Index i	Measure of Height x_i	Frequency f_i
1	56	1
2	58	2
3	60	2
4	61	2
5	62	3

5. A class of students obtained the following results on a test:

4 students received 90%
5 students received 80%
8 students received 70%
3 students received 60%

For these scores, find the:

a. mean

b. standard deviation, to the nearest tenth

6. Find the standard deviation, to the nearest tenth, for the following data:

4, 9, 8, 10, 11, 10, 13, 13, 12, 12, 15, 12, 16, 16

In 7–10, for the given data set, find the:

a. mean
b. median
c. mode
d. standard deviation, to the nearest tenth

7.

Measure x_i	Frequency f_i
70	3
75	4
80	7
85	6

8.

Height x_i	Frequency f_i
62	2
66	1
68	2
72	3
74	2

9.

Measure x_i	Frequency f_i
50	4
58	4
62	3
64	6
65	2
68	1

10.

Score x_i	Frequency f_i
40	1
50	2
60	4
70	6
80	4
90	2
100	1

11. The table below shows the frequency of the average daily temperatures during the month of June.

Temperature x_i	Frequency f_i
63	5
70	3
78	4
79	3
80	6
84	4
96	5

a. Using this set of data, find

(1) the mode **(2)** the median

b. The mean, $\bar{x}$, for these data is 79. Find the standard deviation, to the nearest tenth.

12. During a 10-week softball season, Jo got the following hits per week:

3, 8, 6, 1, 5, 7, 6, 5, 6, 3

a. Find the standard deviation of the number of hits.

b. The probability of Jo getting a hit is $\frac{1}{4}$. If she comes to bat three times, what is the probability that she will get at least two hits?

13. In Australia, a study of farms with 30 or fewer sheep produced the following data.

Number of Sheep per Farm x_i	Number of Farms f_i
15	6
20	3
22	5
25	4
30	2

a. What is the mean for the number of sheep per farm?

b. Find the standard deviation, to the nearest tenth.

c. What is the total number of farms that lie within one standard deviation of the mean?

14. On a math exam, the scores of ten students were:

66, 81, 95, 97, 86, 58, 76, 73, 88, 80

a. Find the mean.

b. Find the standard deviation, to the nearest tenth.

c. How many scores from the given data differ from the mean by more than one standard deviation?

The statistical graph of the distribution of measures obtained from, for example, a test such as SAT (called a *standardized test*) is known as a NORMAL CURVE.

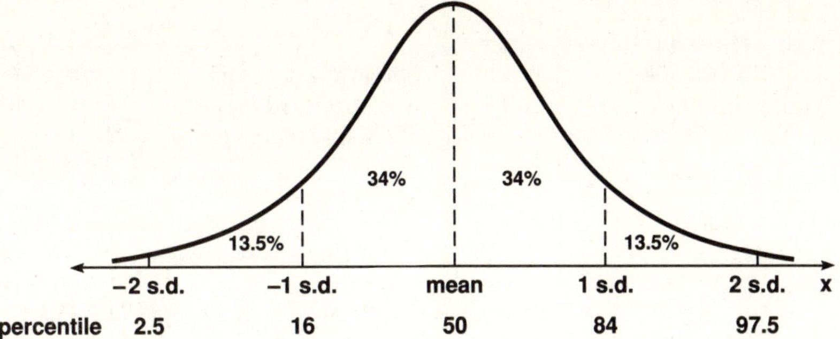

In a normal curve (also called a BELL CURVE because of its shape):

1. **The measures shown on the horizontal axis involve the mean and standard deviation.**
2. **There is symmetry about the line representing the mean value.**
3. **The data fall according to the percentages shown on the graph, so that about 68% of the data fall within one standard deviation of the mean, and 95% within 2 standard deviations. 99.5% of the data fall within 3 standard deviations.**
4. **The corresponding PERCENTILE values (those values that indicate what percent of the total frequency scored *at or below that measure*) are shown at the foot of the graph.**

Note: Symbols used for the standard deviation are s.d., *s*, or σ (lower case Greek sigma). Symbols used for the mean are $\bar{x}$ or μ (lower case Greek mu).

Examples

1. A survey of 16-year-olds in Spruceville showed that they watched an average (mean) of 20.7 hours of TV per week, with a standard deviation of 3.8 hours.

a. Determine how many TV-hours were seen by:
(1) about 68% of the participants
(2) about 95% of the participants

b. What was the minimum number of hours of TV that virtually everyone watched?

Solution: Assume a normal distribution.

a. (1) 68% of the participants fall within one standard deviation of the mean.

20.7 + 3.8 = 24.5
20.7 − 3.8 = 16.9

Answer: 68% watched between 16.9 and 24.5 hours.

(2) 95% of the participants fall within 2 standard deviations of the mean.

20.7 + 2(3.8) = 28.3
20.7 − 2(3.8) = 13.1

Answer: 95% watched between 13.1 and 28.3 hours.

b. "Virtually all" of the participants fall within 3 standard deviations of the mean.

20.7 − 3(3.8) = 9.3 minimum value

Answer: Virtually all watched a minimum of 9.3 hours.

2. On a certain standardized test, the mean score was 50 and the standard deviation 3.

a. About what percent of those taking this test scored between 44 and 47?

b. If Judy's score was 59, approximately how did she do compared to the rest of this group?

Solution: Sketch a normal curve with the given mean and standard deviation.

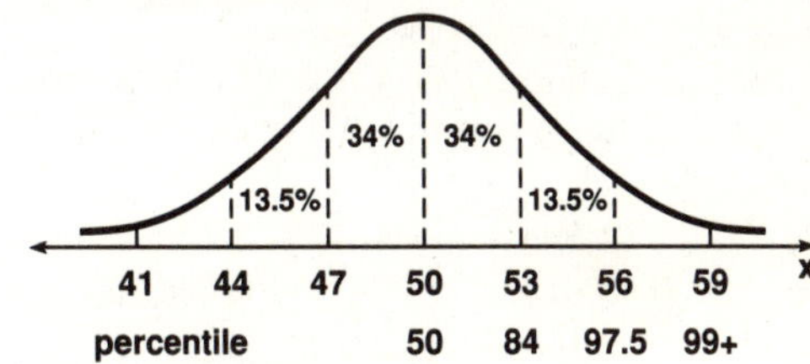

a. 47 = 50 − 3 = the mean − 1 s.d.
44 = 50 − 6 = the mean − 2 s.d.

The interval between −2 s.d. and −1 s.d. contains the scores of about 13.5% of the group. *Ans.*

b. Judy's score of 59 puts her in about the 99th percentile. *Ans.*

EXERCISES

1. The graph of a normal curve has a line of symmetry passing through the point where the deviation from the mean is
(1) 1 (2) 2 (3) −1 (4) 0

2. In a standardized test, approximately what percent of the scores will fall between +1 standard deviation and −1 standard deviation from the mean?
(1) 5% (2) 34% (3) 68% (4) 95%

3. What approximate percentage of the scores of a normal distribution would be expected to fall within two standard deviations from the mean?
(1) 2.5% (2) 34% (3) 68% (4) 95%

4. On a standardized test, the mean is 76 and the standard deviation is 4. Between which two scores will approximately 68% of the scores fall?
(1) 68 and 84 (3) 74 and 78
(2) 72 and 80 (4) 76 and 80

5. The mean of a normally distributed set of data is 52 and the standard deviation is 4. Approximately 95% of all the cases will lie between which measures?
(1) 44 and 52 (3) 48 and 56
(2) 44 and 60 (4) 52 and 64

6. A set of measures that follows a bell curve has a mean of 50 and standard deviation of 5. Approximately what percent of the measures fall between 45 and 55?
(1) 34 (2) 68 (3) 95 (4) 98

7. A set of scores with a normal distribution has a mean of 50 and a standard deviation of 7. Approximately what percent of the scores fall in the range 36 to 64?
(1) 34% (2) 68% (3) 95% (4) 99%

8. A set of test scores is distributed normally with a mean of 80 and a standard deviation of 8. Between what two scores should 68 percent of the scores fall?

9. On a standardized test with a normal distribution, the mean is 20 and the standard deviation is 2.6. In which interval would the greatest number of scores occur?
(1) 12.2 – 14.8 (3) 22.6 – 25.2
(2) 17.4 – 20.0 (4) 27.8 – 30.4

10. For a standardized test, the mean is 30 and the standard deviation is 3.1. Which score could be expected to occur the greatest number of times?
(1) 24.1 (2) 26.7 (3) 33.0 (4) 36.2

11. In a standardized test with a normal distribution of scores, the mean is 63 and the standard deviation is 5. Which score can be expected to occur most often?
(1) 45 (2) 55 (3) 65 (4) 74

12. For a standardized test, the mean is 52.8 and the standard deviation is 5.2. Which score could be expected to occur the least number of times?
(1) 45.3 (2) 64.1 (3) 48.2 (4) 56.3

13. For a standardized test, the mean was 75 and the standard deviation was 5.8. Which score can be expected to occur less than 5% of the time?
(1) 90 (2) 80 (3) 70 (4) 65

14. For a standardized test, if the mean is 20 and the standard deviation is 2.6, which score will occur fewer than 5 times out of 100?
(1) 25.1 (2) 22.6 (3) 18.7 (4) 14.6

15. On a standardized test, the mean is 61 and the standard deviation is 3.2. Which score can be expected to occur less than 3% of the time?
(1) 50 (2) 56 (3) 62 (4) 65

16. On a standardized test with a standard deviation of 2, a score of 26 will occur fewer than 5 times out of 100. Which score could be the mean for this test?
(1) 20 (2) 23 (3) 24 (4) 25

17. On a standardized test, Cathy had a score of 74, which was exactly 1 standard deviation below the mean. If the standard deviation for the test is 6, what is the mean score for the test?
(1) 68 (2) 71 (3) 77 (4) 80

18. In a normal distribution, $\bar{x} + 2\sigma = 80$ and $\bar{x} - 2\sigma = 40$ when $\bar{x}$ represents the mean and σ represents the standard deviation. The standard deviation is
(1) 10 (2) 20 (3) 30 (4) 60

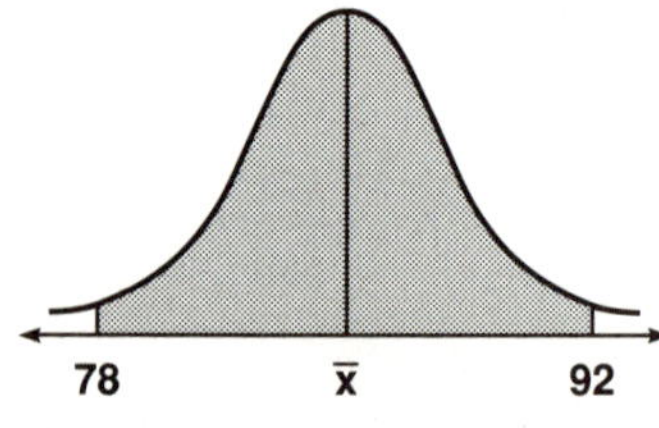

Ex. 19

19. In the diagram, the shaded area represents approximately 95% of the scores on a standardized test. If these scores ranged from 78 to 92, which could be the standard deviation?
(1) 3.5 (2) 7.0 (3) 14.0 (4) 20.0

20. The scores on a test have a normal distribution. The mean of the scores is 40 and the standard deviation is 6. The probability that a score chosen at random lies between 34 and 46 is closest to

(1) 0.34 2) 0.68 (3) 0.95 (4) 0.99

21. On a standardized exam, a student scores 77. The mean for the exam is 70 and the standard deviation is 3. The student's score ranks

(1) below the 75th percentile
(2) between the 75th and the 85th percentiles
(3) between the 85th and the 95th percentiles
(4) above the 95th percentile

22. On a standardized exam, the mean is 29 and the standard deviation is 2. If a student scored 34 on the exam, the student ranks

(1) below the 70th percentile
(2) between the 70th and the 80th percentiles
(3) between the 80th and the 90th percentiles
(4) above the 90th percentile

23. A standardized test has a mean of 55 and a standard deviation of 7.2. A student in the 60th percentile would have a score of

(1) 39 (2) 57 (3) 65 (4) 72

24. a. Find, to the nearest tenth, the standard deviation for the following data.

Measure x_i	Frequency f_i
20	4
21	2
24	5
26	3
30	6

b. The above data do not form a normal distribution. If a measure is selected at random from the above data, what is the probability that it will differ from the mean by less than one standard deviation?

10.5 SUMMARY EXERCISES

In 1–6, evaluate the summation.

1. $\sum_{k=1}^{4} \frac{12}{k}$

2. $\sum_{n=3}^{5} (2n+3)$

3. $\frac{1}{2}\sum_{x=1}^{4} (x-1)^2$

4. $\sum_{k=1}^{3} 2(k+1)$

5. $\sum_{n=1}^{4} \cos \frac{n\pi}{2}$

6. $\sum_{r=1}^{3} {}_5C_r$

7. Which statistical term represents the score that occurs most often in a distribution?

(1) mean (3) mode
(2) median (4) standard deviation

8. What is the mean score for the test results of 60, 60, 70, 75, and 80?

(1) 60 (2) 69 (3) 70 (4) 75

9. If the heights, in centimeters, of 5 students are 176, 172, 160, 158, and 158, find the median height for this group.

10. The high temperatures during 5 days were 82°, 86°, 91°, 79°, and 91°. Find the mode for these temperatures.

11. Express the mean (average) of $3x - 1$, $2x$, and $x + 7$ as a binomial.

12. A student received test scores of 82, 94, and 96. What must she receive as a fourth score so that the mean of these 4 scores will be exactly 90?

13. For which set of numbers will the mean, median, and mode all be equal?

(1) 2, 2, 5 (3) 2, 3, 3, 4
(2) 2, 5, 5 (4) 2, 2, 5, 5

14. The scores on a test were 75, 75, 85, 90, and 100. Which statement about these scores is true?

(1) The mean and the median are the same.
(2) The mode is greater than the median.
(3) The mode is greater than the mean.
(4) The mean is less than the median.

Measure x_i	Frequency f_i
60	2
80	5
100	3

15. What is the mean of the above data?

(1) 78 (2) 80 (3) 80.2 (4) 82

Measure x_i	Frequency f_i
20	4
30	4
50	7

16. What is the median of the above data?

(1) 20 (2) 30 (3) 37 (4) 50

Measure x_i	Frequency f_i
60	5
62	4
63	8
68	6

17. Find the median of the set of data shown in the table above.

18. Given the following scores: 62, 75, 53, 92, 75 What is the range of the scores?
(1) 92 **(2)** 75 **(3)** 62 **(4)** 39

19. Find the range of the following data:
72, 89, 41, 89, 73, 72, 91

20. The set of numbers {4, 7, 12} has
(1) a range of 3 and a median of 7
(2) a range of 8 and a median of 7
(3) a range of 12 and a median of $7\frac{2}{3}$
(4) a range of 8 and a median of $7\frac{2}{3}$

21. On a math test, five students received the following scores: 96, 84, 100, 88, 82. Calculate the standard deviation of these scores, to the nearest tenth.

Measure x_i	Frequency f_i
60	1
75	4
80	3
90	2

22. Find, to the nearest tenth, the standard deviation for the above set of data.

Grade x_i	Frequency f_i
92	2
87	3
82	6
77	9
72	10
67	6
62	4

23. The table above shows the grades for a college statistics class.
a. Find the mean of the data.
b. Find the standard deviation to the nearest tenth.

Measure x_i	Frequency f_i
68	4
76	4
80	3
82	6
83	2
86	1

24. The table above represents the weight, in pounds, of the students in Mrs. Grabenstein's homeroom. Using this set of data, find:
a. the mean
b. the median
c. the mode
d. the standard deviation, to the nearest tenth

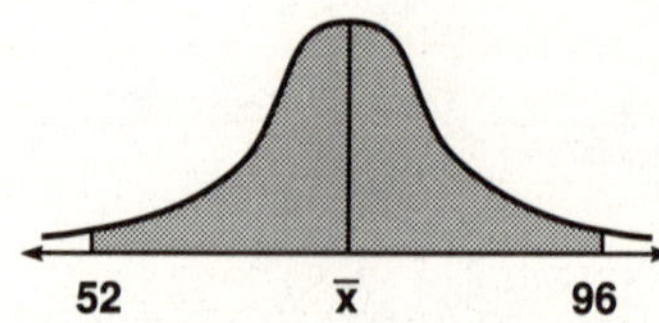

25. In the diagram, the shaded area represents approximately 95% of the scores on a standardized test. If these scores ranged from 52 to 96, which could be the standard deviation?
(1) 11 **(2)** 22 **(3)** 76 **(4)** 44

26. On a standardized test with normal distribution, the mean is 75 and the standard deviation is 3. Within which range should approximately 95% of the scores lie?
(1) 72–78 **(2)** 69–81 **(3)** 66–84 **(4)** 63–87

27. On a standardized test, the mean was 75 and the standard deviation was 4.0. Approximately what percentage of the scores would fall within the range 71 to 79?
(1) 34% **(2)** 68% **(3)** 95% **(4)** 99%

28. The test scores of 50 students resulted in a mean of 82 and a standard deviation of 7.5. If the distribution of scores was normal, which score could be expected to occur less than 5% of the time?
(1) 98 **(2)** 90 **(3)** 74 **(4)** 70

29. On a test, the mean score is 25 and the standard deviation is 2.3. Which score could be expected to occur the least number of times?
(1) 20 **(2)** 28 **(3)** 23 **(4)** 24

30. A student scores 84 on a standardized exam. The mean for the exam is 75 and the standard deviation is 4. Assuming a normal distribution, the student ranks
(1) below the 75th percentile
(2) between the 75th and 85th percentiles
(3) between the 85th and the 95th percentiles
(4) above the 95th percentile

REGENTS EXAMINATIONS

HIGH SCHOOL MATHEMATICS: COURSE III
JUNE 1998

Part I

Answer 30 questions from this part. Each correct answer will receive 2 credits. No partial credit will be allowed. Write your answers in the spaces provided on the separate answer sheet. Where applicable, answers may be left in terms of π or in radical form. [60]

1 If $f(x) = (2x)^2$, find $f(-4)$.

2 Solve for the positive value of x: $x^{\frac{2}{3}} = 9$

3 Solve for x: $\frac{x-3}{5} + \frac{4x}{3} = 4$

4 Solve for x: $\sqrt{2x-8} - 1 = 5$

5 Evaluate: $\sum_{n=1}^{5} n^2$

6 Find the image of $A(-3,2)$ under a dilation with the center at the origin and a scale factor of -2.

7 In $\triangle ABC$, $\sin A:\sin B:\sin C = 4:5:6$. Find the value of c when $a = 10$.

8 Find the value of $\tan\left(\text{Arc sin } \frac{5}{6}\right)$.

9 If a fair coin is flipped three times, what is the probability of obtaining exactly two heads?

10 In the accompanying diagram of circle O, secants $\overline{CBA}$ and $\overline{CED}$ intersect at C. If $AC = 12$, $BC = 3$, and $DC = 9$, find EC.

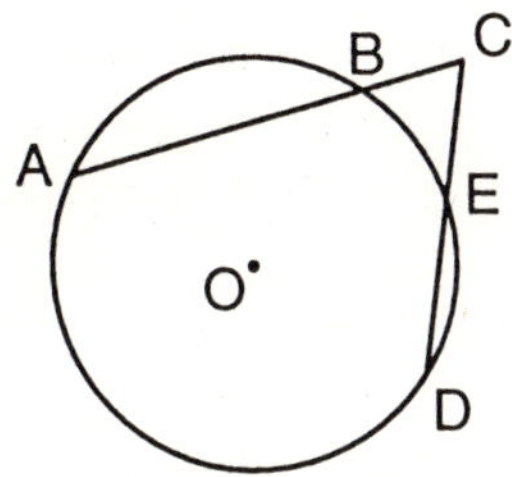

11 In a circle whose radius is 9 centimeters, what is the number of radians in a central angle if the length of the intercepted arc is 18 centimeters?

12 Find, in radical form, the area of $\triangle ABC$ if $a = 6$, $b = 6$, and $m\angle C = 45$.

13 Factor completely: $5x^2y^3 - 180y$

14 If P varies inversely as V and $P = 700$ when $V = 8$, find the value of V when $P = 350$.

Directions (15–35): For *each* question chosen, write on the separate answer sheet the *numeral* preceding the word or expression that best completes the statement or answers the question.

15 In the accompanying diagram of circle O, $m\angle AOB = 80$.

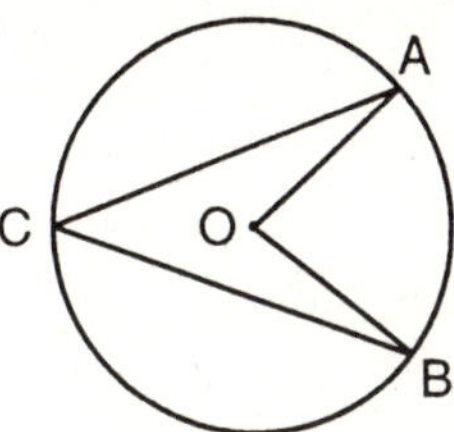

What is $m\angle ACB$?

(1) 80
(2) 160
(3) 20
(4) 40

16 The value of $\cos 16° \cos 164° - \sin 16° \sin 164°$ is

(1) -1
(2) $-\frac{1}{2}$
(3) 0
(4) $\frac{\sqrt{3}}{2}$

17 If the graphs of the equations $xy = 12$ and $y = 2$ are drawn on the same set of axes, what is the total number of common points?

(1) 1 (3) 3
(2) 2 (4) 0

18 The expression $\dfrac{\frac{a}{b}-1}{\frac{a}{b}+1}$ is equivalent to

(1) $\dfrac{a+b}{a-b}$ (3) $\dfrac{1}{a-b}$
(2) $\dfrac{a-b}{a+b}$ (4) $\dfrac{1}{a+b}$

19 The value of $\sin\frac{3\pi}{2} + \cos\frac{2\pi}{3}$ is

(1) $\frac{1}{2}$ (3) $-1\frac{1}{2}$
(2) $1\frac{1}{2}$ (4) $-\frac{1}{2}$

20 The sum of $3\sqrt{-8}$ and $4\sqrt{-50}$ is

(1) $12\sqrt{-58}$
(2) $26i\sqrt{2}$
(3) $7i\sqrt{58}$
(4) $7i\sqrt{2}$

21 What is the solution set of the inequality $|3x + 6| \le 30$?

(1) $-12 \le x \le 8$ (3) $x \le -12$ or $x \ge 8$
(2) $-8 \le x \le 12$ (4) $x \le -8$ or $x \ge 12$

22 The roots of the equation $x^2 + 6x + 11 = 0$ are

(1) real, rational, and unequal
(2) real, rational, and equal
(3) real, irrational, and unequal
(4) imaginary

23 If $\cos x = -\frac{\sqrt{2}}{2}$, in which quadrants could $\angle x$ terminate?

(1) I and IV (3) II and IV
(2) I and III (4) II and III

24 Which expression is equivalent to $\dfrac{\sin 2x}{\cos x}$?

(1) $2 \sin x$ (3) $\cos 2x$
(2) $\tan x$ (4) $2 \cos x$

25 If $\sin (x - 3)° = \cos (2x + 6)°$, then the value of x is

(1) −9 (3) 29
(2) 26 (4) 64

26 Which graph represents the solution set of $x^2 + 5x - 6 > 0$?

(1) 

(2) −6 −5 −4 −3 −2 −1 0 1 2 3 4 5 6

(3) −6 −5 −4 −3 −2 −1 0 1 2 3 4 5 6

(4) −6 −5 −4 −3 −2 −1 0 1 2 3 4 5 6

27 What is the result of $T_{2,-1} \circ r_{y=-1}$ (2,0)?

(1) (2,0)
(2) (2,−1)
(3) (4,−3)
(4) (−4,3)

28 In $\triangle ABC$, $a = 8$, $b = 2$, and $c = 7$. What is the value of $\cos C$?

(1) $-\frac{19}{32}$ (3) $\frac{109}{112}$
(2) $-\frac{11}{28}$ (4) $\frac{19}{32}$

29 What is the domain of $f(x) = \dfrac{1}{\sqrt{(4-x^2)}}$?

(1) $x < 2$
(2) $|x| \le 2$
(3) $-2 < x < 2$
(4) all real numbers

30 In standard position, an angle of $\frac{7\pi}{3}$ radians has the same terminal side as an angle of

(1) 60° (3) 240°
(2) 120° (4) −420°

31 If the mean on a standardized test with a normal distribution is 54.3 and the standard deviation is 4.6, what is the best approximation of the percent of the scores that fall between 54.3 and 63.5?

(1) 34 (3) 68
(2) 47.5 (4) 95

32 In the accompanying diagram of a unit circle, the ordered pair (x,y) represents the point where the terminal side of θ intersects the unit circle.

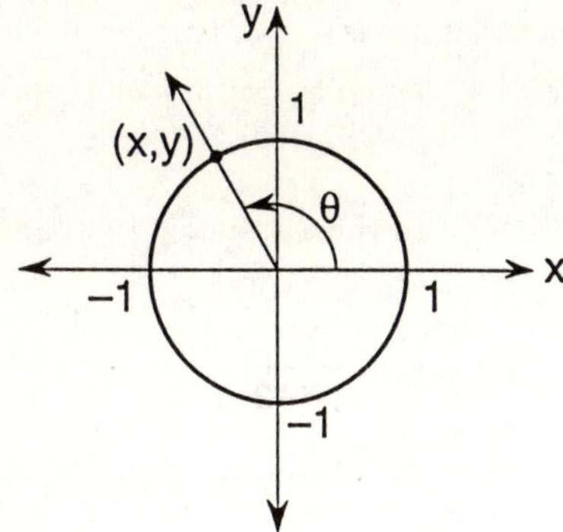

If $\theta = \frac{3\pi}{4}$, what is the value of x?

(1) 1
(2) $-\frac{1}{2}$
(3) $-\frac{\sqrt{2}}{2}$
(4) $\frac{\sqrt{3}}{2}$

33 What is the sum (S) and the product (P) of the roots of the equation $2x^2 - 4x + 1 = 0$?

(1) $S = \frac{1}{2}, P = 2$
(2) $S = 2, P = \frac{1}{2}$
(3) $S = -2, P = \frac{1}{2}$
(4) $S = -4, P = 1$

34 If $a = 5$, $c = 18$, and $m\angle A = 30$, what is the total number of distinct triangles that can be constructed?

(1) 1
(2) 2
(3) 3
(4) 0

35 What is the middle term in the expansion $(x - 3y)^4$?

(1) $54x^2y^2$
(2) $54xy^2$
(3) $9x^2y^2$
(4) $9xy^2$

Part II

Answer four questions from this part. Clearly indicate the necessary steps, including appropriate formula substitutions, diagrams, graphs, charts, etc. Calculations that may be obtained by mental arithmetic or the calculator do not need to be shown. [40]

36 *a* On the same set of axes, sketch and label the graphs of the equations $y = \sin \frac{1}{2}x$ and $y = -2 \cos x$ in the interval $-\pi \leq x \leq \pi$. [8]

b Using the graphs drawn in part *a*, determine the number of solutions to the equation $\sin \frac{1}{2}x = -2 \cos x$ in the interval $-\pi \leq x \leq \pi$. [2]

37 In the accompanying diagram of circle O, diameter $\overline{EOC}$ is extended through C to point P; diameter $\overline{AFOD}$, tangent $\overline{PD}$, and chords $\overline{AC}$, $\overline{CD}$, $\overline{BFE}$ are drawn; $m\angle COD = 60$; and $m\angle AFB = 100$.

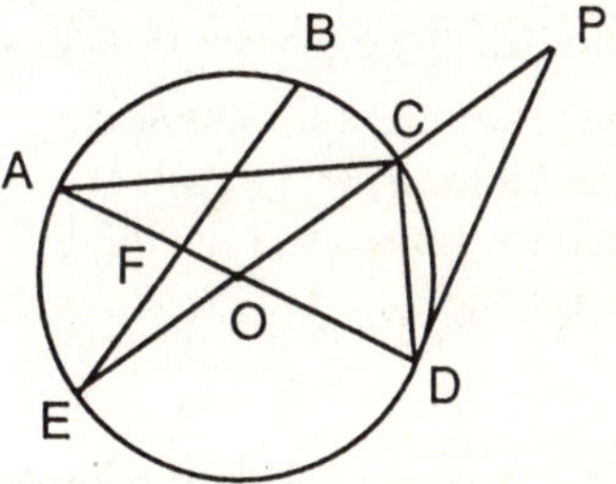

Find:

a $m\overset{\frown}{DE}$ [2]
b $m\angle P$ [2]
c $m\angle ACE$ [2]
d $m\overset{\frown}{AB}$ [2]
e $m\angle ACD$ [2]

38 *a* Given: $\log_b 3 = p$
$\log_b 5 = q$

(1) Express $\log_b \frac{9}{5}$ in terms of p and q. [2]

(2) Express $\log_b \sqrt[3]{15}$ in terms of p and q. [2]

b Solve for x: $\log_4(x^2 + 3x) - \log_4(x + 5) = 1$ [6]

39 *a* Only red cards and black cards are in a box. The probability of drawing a black card is $\frac{3}{5}$. A card is randomly drawn and replaced in the box after each draw. Five such draws are made. Find the probability that

(1) *exactly* two black cards will be drawn [2]
(2) *at least* four black cards will be drawn [4]

b For these measurements, find the standard deviation, to the *nearest hundredth*:

85, 88, 79, 79, 80, 92, 94, 78, 80, 85 [4]

40 Find, to the *nearest ten minutes* or *nearest tenth of a degree*, all values of θ in the interval $0° \leq \theta < 360°$ that satisfy the equation $5 \sin^2 \theta - 7 \cos \theta + 1 = 0$. [10]

41 *a* Solve for x: $\frac{x}{x + 5} + \frac{9}{x - 5} = \frac{50}{x^2 - 25}$ [5]

b Solve for y and express the roots of the equation in simplest $a + bi$ form:

$$5y + \frac{5}{y} = 8 \quad [5]$$

42 *a* Given: $Z_1 = 4 - i$ and $Z_2 = -5 - 2i$.

(1) Using the complex plane, graph and label Z_1 and Z_2. [2]
(2) On the same plane, graph the sum of Z_1 and Z_2. [1]
(3) Express the sum of Z_1 and Z_2 as a complex number. [1]

b Forces of 40 pounds and 70 pounds act on a body at an angle measuring 60°. Find the magnitude of the resultant of these forces to the *nearest hundredth of a pound.* [6]

HIGH SCHOOL MATHEMATICS: COURSE III
AUGUST 1998

Part I

Answer 30 questions from this part. Each correct answer will receive 2 credits. No partial credit will be allowed. Write your answers in the spaces provided on the separate answer sheet. Where applicable, answers may be left in terms of π or in radical form. [60]

1 Express $\frac{7\pi}{5}$ radians in degrees.

2 If $f(x) = x - 2$ and $g(x) = x^2$, find $f(g(3))$.

3 If $\sin A = -1$ and $0° \leq A < 360°$, find $m\angle A$.

4 In $\triangle ABC$, $a = 15$, $c = 10$, and $\sin A = 0.45$. Find $\sin C$.

5 Find the coordinates of P', the image of $P(3,-1)$ under the transformation $(x,y) \rightarrow (-y,-x)$.

6 Find the value of sin 135° in radical form.

7 Evaluate: $\sum_{x=1}^{4}(x^2 - 3)$

8 When the graphs of $2 + 4i$ and $3 - 7i$ are drawn on the same set of axes, in which quadrant will the sum of these expressions lie?

9 Solve for the positive value of x: $\frac{x}{3} - \frac{4}{x} = \frac{4}{3}$

10 If $a = 4$, evaluate $a^{\frac{1}{2}} + a^0 + a^{-2}$.

11 In the accompanying diagram, chords $\overline{AB}$ and $\overline{CD}$ intersect at E. If $m\,\widehat{AC} = 75$ and $m\,\widehat{DB} = 45$, find $m\angle AED$.

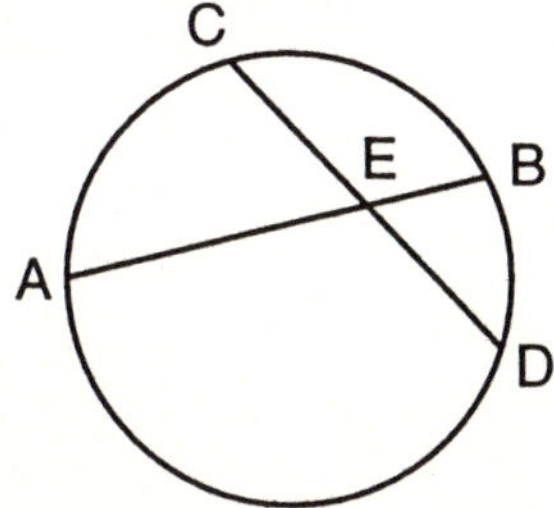

12 What is the image of (6,5) under a counterclockwise rotation of 180°?

13 If $\log_n 8 = 3$, find the value of n.

14 In the accompanying diagram, p and q are lines of symmetry in regular pentagon $ABCDE$. Find $r_p \circ r_q(B)$.

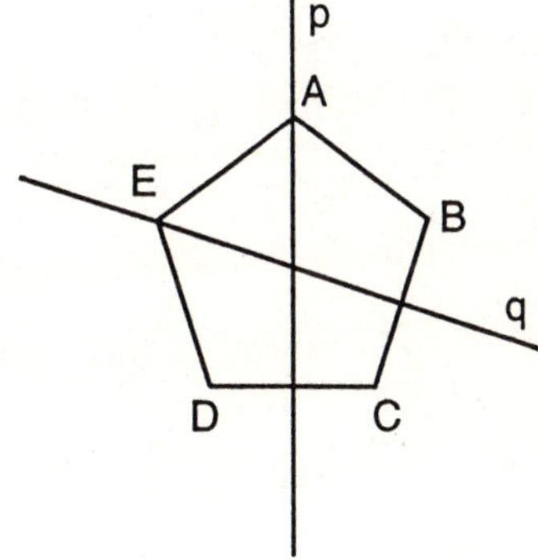

15 If x varies inversely as y and $x = 12$ when $y = 4$, what is the value of y when $x = 16$?

16 For which value of θ is $\frac{\cos\theta}{\sin\theta}$ undefined in the interval $-\pi < \theta < \pi$?

Directions (17–35): For *each* question chosen, write on the separate answer sheet the *numeral* preceding the word or expression that best completes the statement or answers the question.

17 What is the value of y if $y = \sin\left(\text{Arc tan } \frac{5}{12}\right)$?

(1) $\frac{5}{13}$ (3) $\frac{13}{12}$
(2) $\frac{12}{13}$ (4) $\frac{13}{5}$

18 In the accompanying diagram of circle O, $m\angle AOC = 108$.

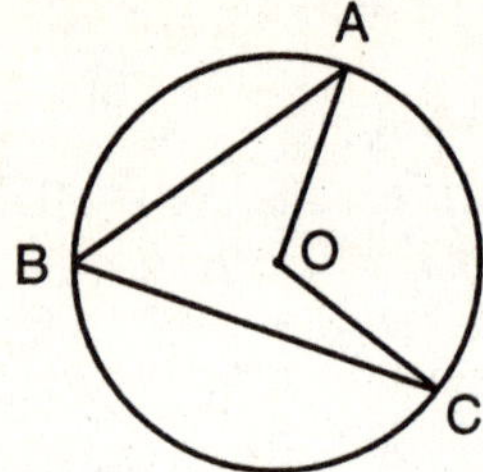

What is $m\angle ABC$?

(1) 27
(2) 54
(3) 108
(4) 216

19 What is the value of x in the equation $3^{x-3} = 1$?

(1) 1
(2) $\frac{1}{3}$
(3) 3
(4) 0

20 Which equation is represented by the graph in the accompanying diagram?

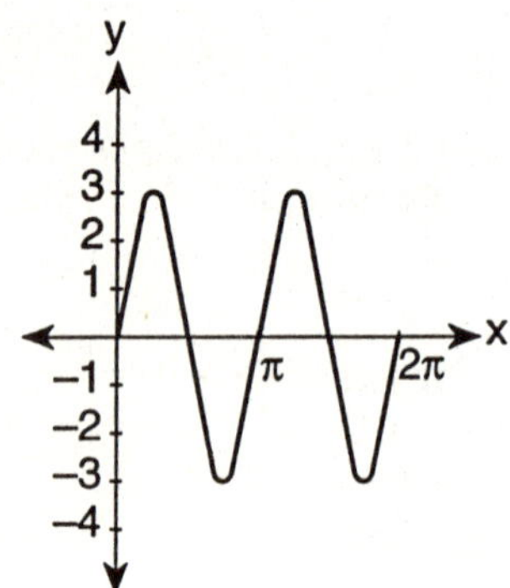

(1) $y = 3 \sin 2x$
(2) $y = 2 \sin 3x$
(3) $y = 3 \sin x$
(4) $y = 2 \sin 4x$

21 The expression $\cos^2 40 - \sin^2 40$ has the same value as

(1) sin 20
(2) sin 80
(3) cos 80
(4) cos 20

22 If a fair die is tossed five times, what is the probability of getting exactly three 6's?

(1) $\frac{125}{7776}$

(2) ${}_5C_3\left(\frac{1}{6}\right)^3\left(\frac{5}{6}\right)^2$

(3) ${}_5C_3\left(\frac{1}{6}\right)^2\left(\frac{5}{6}\right)^3$

(4) $\frac{25}{7776}$

23 What is the solution set for the inequality $x^2 - 2x < 8$?

(1) $-2 < x < 4$
(2) $-4 < x < 2$
(3) $x < -2$ or $x > 4$
(4) $x < -4$ or $x > 2$

24 What is the solution set of the equation $|2x - 5| = 3$?

(1) { }
(2) {−4,4}
(3) {4}
(4) {1,4}

25 The expression $\frac{\sin 2x}{\sin(-x)}$ is equivalent to

(1) $-2 \sin x$
(2) $2 \sin x$
(3) $-2 \cos x$
(4) $2 \cos x$

26 Which equation has both 3 and 6 as roots?

(1) $\sqrt{x-2} = x - 4$

(2) $\sqrt{x-2} = 4 - x$

(3) $\sqrt{x-2} = \frac{3}{x}$

(4) $\sqrt{x-2} = \frac{x}{3}$

27 In $\triangle ABC$, $a = 4$, $b = 3$, and $\cos C = -\frac{1}{2}$. What is the length of c?

(1) 7
(2) $\sqrt{13}$
(3) $\sqrt{37}$
(4) $\sqrt{19}$

28 Which equation has rational roots?

(1) $x^2 + 8x - 8 = 0$
(2) $x^2 + 8x + 9 = 0$
(3) $2x^2 + 4x + 5 = 0$
(4) $3x^2 + 8x + 4 = 0$

29 When drawn on a set of axes, which equation is an ellipse?

(1) $2x^2 + y = 12$
(2) $2x^2 + y^2 = 12$
(3) $2x^2 + 2y^2 = 12$
(4) $2x^2 - y^2 = 12$

30 When simplified, i^{99} is equivalent to

(1) 1
(2) −1
(3) i
(4) $-i$

31 On a standardized test with a normal distribution of scores, the mean score is 82 and the standard deviation is 6. Which interval contains 95% of the scores?

(1) 70–82
(2) 70–94
(3) 76–88
(4) 76–94

32 In the interval $0 \le \theta < 2\pi$, the number of solutions of the equation $\sin \theta = \cos \theta$ is

(1) 1
(2) 2
(3) 3
(4) 4

33 In isosceles triangle ABC, $\overline{AB} \cong \overline{BC}$, $m\angle B = 45$, and $AB = 3\sqrt{2}$. The area of the triangle is

(1) $\frac{9}{2}$
(2) $9\sqrt{2}$
(3) $\frac{9\sqrt{2}}{2}$
(4) $\frac{3\sqrt{2}}{2}$

34 What is the fourth term in the expansion $(a + b)^5$?

(1) $10a^2b^3$
(2) $10a^3b^2$
(3) $5a^2b^3$
(4) $5a^3b^2$

35 Which diagram could represent the graph of an equation with imaginary roots?

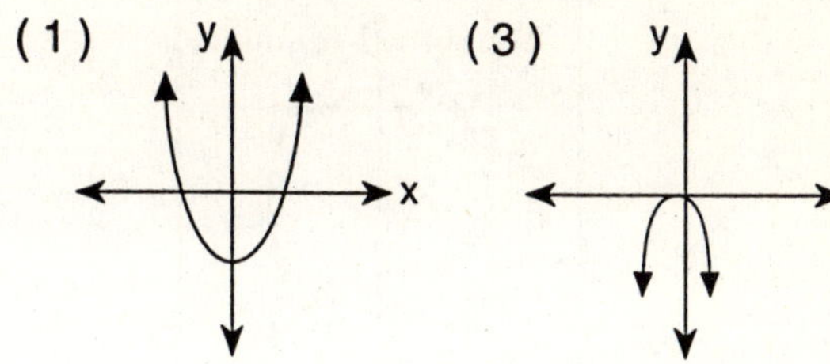

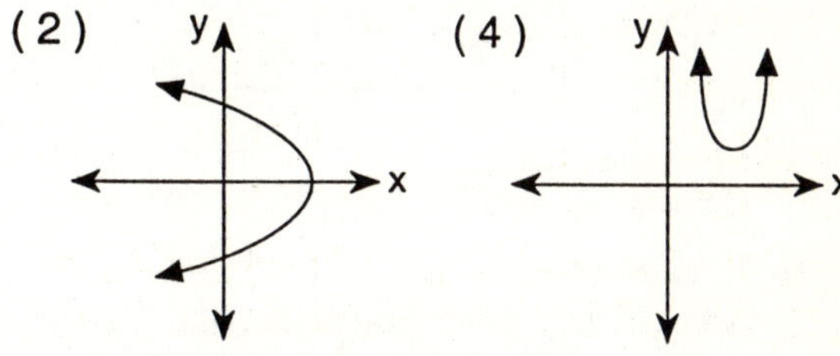

Part II

Answer four questions from this part. Clearly indicate the necessary steps, including appropriate formula substitutions, diagrams, graphs, charts, etc. Calculations that may be obtained by mental arithmetic or the calculator do not need to be shown. [40]

36 *a* On the same set of axes, sketch and label the graphs of the equations $y = 3 \cos \frac{1}{2}x$ and $y = -2 \sin x$ in the interval $0 \le x \le 2\pi$. [8]

b In the interval $0 \le x \le 2\pi$, which value of x satisfies the equation $3 \cos \frac{1}{2}x = -2 \sin x$? [2]

37 Find all values of x in the interval $0° \le x < 360°$ that satisfy the equation $3 \cos 2x + 2 \sin x = -1$. Express your answer to the *nearest ten minutes* or *nearest tenth of a degree.* [10]

38 *a* Simplify: $\dfrac{\frac{x}{x-3} + \frac{4}{x}}{1 - \frac{1}{3-x}}$ [6]

b Solve the equation for x and express the roots in simplest $a + bi$ form:

$4x^2 - 12x + 25 = 0$ [4]

39 *a* (1) On graph paper, sketch and label the graph of the equation $y = 2^x$ in the interval $-2 \le x \le 2$. [2]

(2) On the same set of axes, reflect the graph drawn in part *a* (1) in the y-axis and label it r. [2]

(3) Write an equation of the graph drawn in part *a* (2). [2]

b Solve for x to the *nearest hundredth*:

$2^x = \frac{3}{16}$ [4]

40 In parallelogram $ABCD$, $AB = 14$, $BC = 20$, and $m\angle B = 54$.

a Find, to the *nearest tenth*, the length of diagonal $\overline{BD}$. [6]

b Find $m\angle DBC$ to the *nearest degree.* [4]

41 The table below shows the heights of a group of 20 students.

Height (inches)	Frequency
72	3
71	2
70	1
69	2
68	4
67	2
66	4
65	2

a Find the mean and the standard deviation to the *nearest tenth*. [4]

b If one student's height is chosen at random, what is the probability that the height falls within one standard deviation of the mean? [2]

c If three students' heights are chosen at random, what is the probability that *at most* one of them falls within one standard deviation of the mean? [4]

42 In the accompanying diagram of circle O, $m\widehat{AB}:m\widehat{BC} = 1:2$; diameter $\overline{CA}$ and chord $\overline{AE}$ are drawn; chord $\overline{EC}$ is parallel to chord $\overline{AB}$; chord $\overline{BC}$ is extended through C to D; and tangent $\overline{DE}$ is drawn.

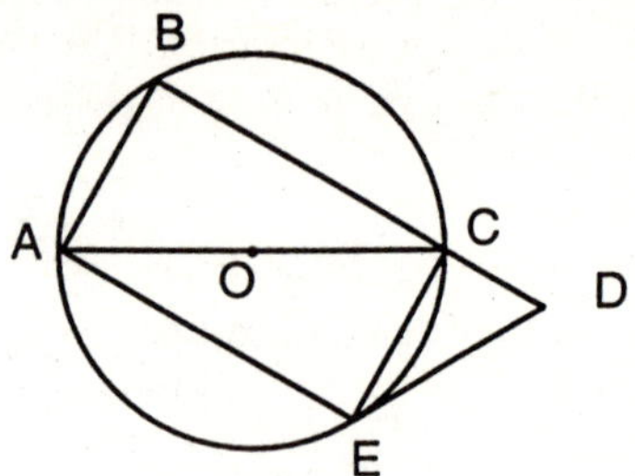

Find:

a $m\widehat{BC}$ [2]

b $m\widehat{CE}$ [2]

c $m\angle AEC$ [2]

d $m\angle CED$ [2]

e $m\angle BDE$ [2]

HIGH SCHOOL MATHEMATICS: COURSE III
JANUARY 1999

Part I

Answer 30 questions from this part. Each correct answer will receive 2 credits. No partial credit will be allowed. Write your answers in the spaces provided on the separate answer sheet. Where applicable, answers may be left in terms of π or in radical form. [60]

1 In the accompanying diagram of circle O, $\overrightarrow{XA}$ and $\overrightarrow{XB}$ are tangents and $m\angle XAB = 75$. Find $m\angle X$.

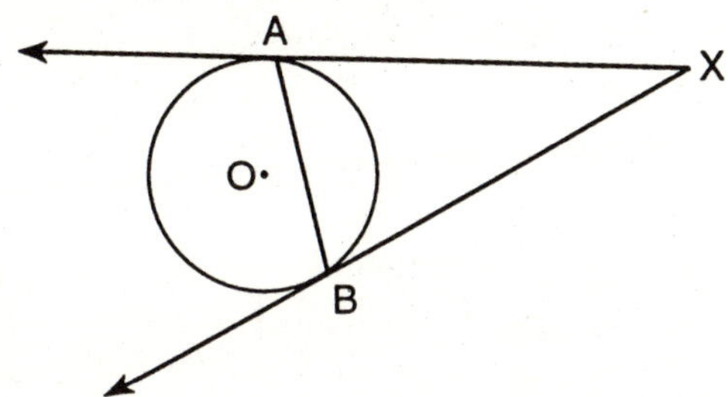

2 Translation T maps point (2,6) to point (4,–1). What is the image of point (–1,3) under translation T?

3 Express the sum of $2\sqrt{-49}$ and $-3\sqrt{-16}$ as a monomial in terms of i.

4 If $f(x) = x^2 - 3x$, find $f(-1.8)$.

5 If $f(x) = \sin 3x + \cos x$, what is $f\left(\frac{\pi}{2}\right)$?

6 Evaluate: $\sum_{k=1}^{3}(k+1)^2$

7 In the accompanying diagram of circle O, diameter $\overline{AB}$ is perpendicular to chord $\overline{CD}$ at E, $CD = 8$, and $EB = 2$. What is the length of the diameter of circle O?

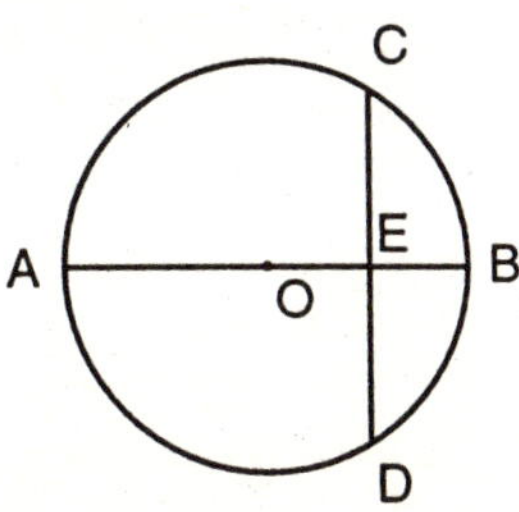

8 Express 75° in radian measure.

9 In the accompanying diagram, tangent $\overline{AB}$ and secant $\overline{ACD}$ are drawn to circle O from point A. If $AC = 4$ and $CD = 12$, find AB.

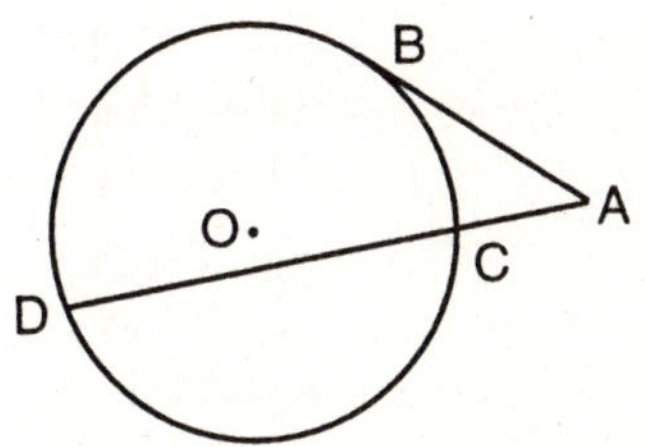

10 Express in simplest form: $\dfrac{\frac{3}{4}+\frac{3}{x}}{\frac{1}{x}+\frac{1}{4}}$

11 In $\triangle ABC$, $m\angle A = 33$, $a = 12$, and $b = 15$. Find $\sin B$ to the *nearest thousandth*.

12 Factor completely: $x^4 - 16$

13 In $\triangle ABC$, $a = 2$, $c = 6$, and $\cos B = \frac{1}{6}$. Find b.

14 The width of a rectangle with constant area varies inversely as its length. If the width is 4 when the length is 12, find the width when the length is 16.

Directions (15–35): For *each* question chosen, write on the separate answer sheet the *numeral* preceding the word or expression that best completes the statement or answers the question.

15 For which value(s) of x is the function $f(x) = \dfrac{x^2-9}{x-7}$ undefined?

(1) 9
(2) 3 and –3
(3) 3, only
(4) 7

16 The solution set of $2^{x+1} = 8$ is

(1) { }
(2) {2}
(3) {3}
(4) {4}

17 The expression cos 70° cos 10° + sin 70° sin 10° is equivalent to

(1) cos 60°
(2) cos 80°
(3) sin 60°
(4) sin 80°

18 If the image of A after a dilation of –2 is $A'(-8,6)$, what are the coordinates of A?

(1) (4,–3)
(2) (–4,3)
(3) (16,–12)
(4) (–16,12)

19 If θ is an angle in Quadrant I and $\tan^2 \theta - 4 = 0$, what is the value of θ to the *nearest degree?*

(1) 1
(2) 2
(3) 63
(4) 75

20 If $\log_4 x = 3$, then x is equal to

(1) 7
(2) 12
(3) 64
(4) 81

21 The value of sin (Arc cos 1) is

(1) 1
(2) $\frac{1}{2}$
(3) $\frac{1}{2}\sqrt{3}$
(4) 0

22 If $\cos A > 0$ and $\csc A < 0$, in which quadrant does the terminal side of $\angle A$ lie?

(1) I
(2) II
(3) III
(4) IV

23 If –1 and 7 are the roots of the quadratic equation $x^2 + kx - 7 = 0$, then k must be

(1) –7
(2) –6
(3) 6
(4) 8

24 The expression $\sec x \sin 2x$ is equivalent to

(1) $\frac{1}{2}$
(2) 2
(3) $2 \cos x$
(4) $2 \sin x$

25 A fair die is tossed five times. What is the probability of obtaining exactly three 4's?

(1) $\frac{250}{7776}$
(2) $\frac{10}{7776}$
(3) $\frac{1250}{7776}$
(4) $\frac{90}{1024}$

26 If $|2x + 3| < 1$, then the solution set contains

(1) only negative real numbers
(2) only positive real numbers
(3) both positive and negative real numbers
(4) no real numbers

27 Which relation is a function?

(1) $y = \cos x$
(2) $x = 4$
(3) $x = y^2$
(4) $x^2 + y^2 = 16$

28 The roots of the equation $x^2 + 4x + 2 = 0$ are

(1) real, rational, and equal
(2) real, rational, and unequal
(3) real, irrational, and unequal
(4) imaginary

29 In the accompanying diagram of a unit circle, $\overline{BA}$ is tangent to circle O at A, $\overline{CD}$ is perpendicular to the x-axis, and $\overline{OC}$ is a radius.

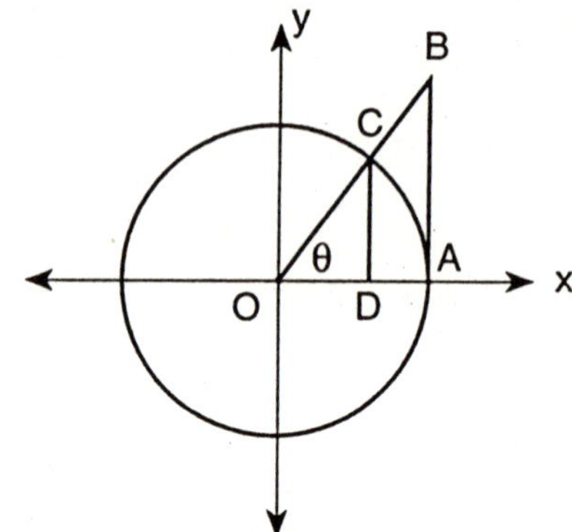

Which distance represents $\sin \theta$?

(1) OD
(2) CD
(3) BA
(4) OB

30 A standardized test with a normal distribution of scores has a mean score of 43 and a standard deviation of 6.3. Which range would contain the score of a student in the 90th percentile?

(1) 30.4–36.7
(2) 36.7–43.0
(3) 43.0–49.3
(4) 49.3–55.6

31 The graph of the equation $xy = 5$ forms

(1) an ellipse
(2) a hyperbola
(3) a line
(4) a parabola

32 The value of $(1 - i)^2$ is

(1) 0
(2) 2
(3) $-2i$
(4) $2 - 2i$

33 The solution set of the equation $\sqrt{2x+15} = x$ is

(1) {5,–3}
(2) {5}
(3) {–3}
(4) { }

34 What are the coordinates of the image of $P(-2,5)$ after a clockwise rotation of 90° about the origin?

(1) (–5,–2)
(2) (–2,–5)
(3) (2,5)
(4) (5,2)

35 What is the best approximation of the standard deviation of the measures –4, –3, 0, 8, and 9?

(1) 1
(2) 2
(3) 5
(4) 10

Part II

Answer four questions from this part. Clearly indicate the necessary steps, including appropriate formula substitutions, diagrams, graphs, charts, etc. Calculations that may be obtained by mental arithmetic or the calculator do not need to be shown. [40]

36 *a* On the same set of axes, sketch and label the graphs of the equations $y = -\sin x$ and $y = 2 \cos x$ in the interval $0 \leq x \leq 2\pi$. [8]

b Using the graphs sketched in part *a*, determine the number of solutions to the equation $2 \cos x = -\sin x$ in the interval $0 \leq x \leq 2\pi$. [2]

37 In the accompanying diagram of circle O, $m\overset{\frown}{AC} = 140$, $m\overset{\frown}{AE} = 130$, $m\overset{\frown}{AB}:m\overset{\frown}{BC} = 6:4$, $\overline{PD}$ is a tangent, secant $\overline{PCE}$ intersects diameter $\overline{AD}$ at F, and secant $\overline{PBA}$ is drawn.

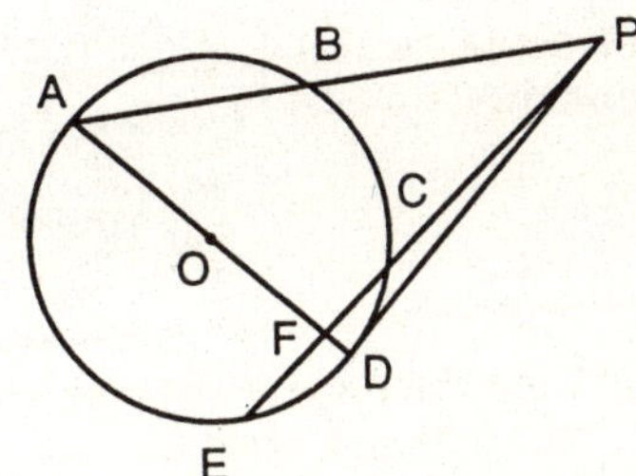

Find:

a $m\overset{\frown}{ED}$ [2]
b $m\overset{\frown}{AB}$ [2]
c $m\angle BAD$ [2]
d $m\angle APE$ [2]
e $m\angle EFD$ [2]

38 *a* Express in simplest form:

$$\frac{2x-8}{x^2+x-12} \div \frac{20-5x}{2x^2-5x-3} \quad [4]$$

b Prove the following identity:

$$\frac{\sin\theta}{1+\cos\theta} + \frac{1+\cos\theta}{\sin\theta} = 2\cot\theta\sec\theta \quad [6]$$

39 *a* On graph paper, sketch the graph of the equation $y = 3^x$ in the interval $-2 \le x \le 2$. [2]

b On the same set of axes, sketch the graph of the equation $y = 6$. [1]

c Based on the graphs sketched in parts *a* and *b*, between which two consecutive integers does the solution of $3^x = 6$ lie? Explain your answer. [1,2]

d Find x to the *nearest hundredth:* $3^x = 6$ [4]

40 In $\triangle ABC$, $AC = 8$, $BC = 17$, and $AB = 20$.

a Find the measure of the largest angle to the *nearest degree.* [6]

b Find the area of $\triangle ABC$ to the *nearest integer.* [4]

41 *a* A mathematics quiz has five multiple-choice questions. There are four possible responses for each question. Jennifer selects her responses at random on every question.

(1) What is the probability she will select the correct response for *at most* one question? [3]

(2) What is the probability she will select the correct response to *at least* three questions? [4]

b Find, in simplest form, the middle term in the expansion of $\left(x^2 + \frac{1}{x}\right)^6$. [3]

42 Find, to the *nearest degree*, all values of θ in the interval $0° \le \theta < 360°$ that satisfy the equation $2\sin^2\theta + 2\cos\theta - 1 = 0$. [10]

HIGH SCHOOL MATHEMATICS: COURSE III
JUNE 1999

Part I

Answer 30 questions from this part. Each correct answer will receive 2 credits. No partial credit will be allowed. Write your answers in the spaces provided on the separate answer sheet. Where applicable, answers may be left in terms of π or in radical form. [60]

1 Solve for x: $\sqrt{3x-8} + 4 = 11$

2 In the accompanying figure of circle O, $m\angle AOC = 52$. Find $m\angle ABC$.

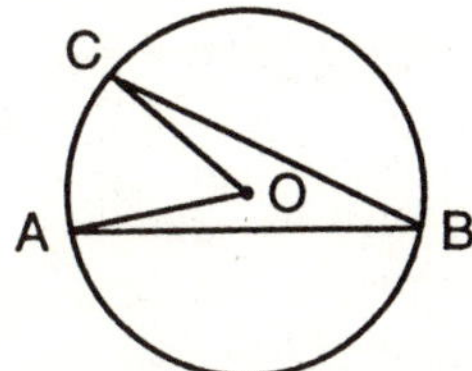

3 Find the value of $\sum_{n=1}^{5} 2n$.

4 If k is a positive integer, what is the greatest value of k that will make $\sqrt{k-4}$ an imaginary number?

5 If $8^{x+1} = 4^{2x}$, what is the value of x?

6 Express 405° in radian measure.

7 In circle O, a central angle of 3 radians intercepts an arc of 27 meters. Find the number of meters in the length of the radius.

8 Solve for all values of x: $|2x + 5| = 4$

9 If $f(x) = \sin \frac{1}{2}x + 2\cos x$, evaluate $f(\pi)$.

10 In $\triangle ABC$, $\cos C = -0.2$, $a = 8$, and $b = 10$. Find the length of side c.

11 Evaluate: $-3x^0 + (8)^{\frac{2}{3}} + \left(\frac{1}{2}\right)^{-2}$

12 If $\cos (2x - 25)° = \sin 55°$, find the value of x.

13 In the accompanying diagram, chords $\overline{DE}$ and $\overline{FG}$ intersect at H. If $DE = 18$, $HE = 8$, and $HF = 5$, find GH.

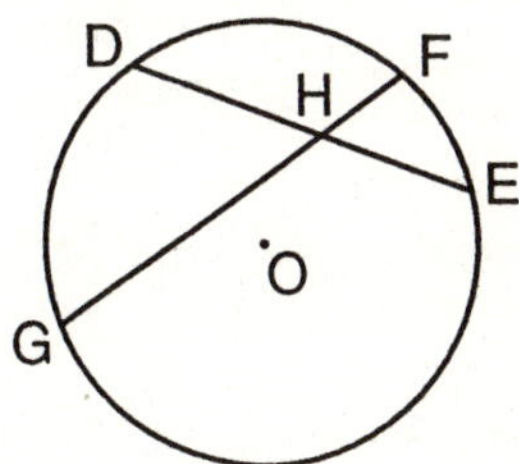

14 If $\sin x = \frac{2}{3}$, find the value of $\cos 2x$ in simplest fractional form.

Directions (15–35): For *each* question chosen, write on the separate answer sheet the *numeral* preceding the word or expression that best completes the statement or answers the question.

15 If $f(x) = 3x^2$ and $g(x) = \sqrt{2x}$, what is the value of $(f \circ g)(8)$?

(1) $8\sqrt{6}$ (3) 48
(2) 16 (4) 144

16 The value of $\cos \left(\text{Arc} \sin \frac{\sqrt{3}}{2}\right)$ is

(1) 1 (3) $\frac{\sqrt{3}}{3}$
(2) $\frac{1}{2}$ (4) $\sqrt{3}$

17 The expression $\log \frac{x^2y^3}{\sqrt{z}}$ is equivalent to

(1) $\frac{(2x)(3y)}{\frac{1}{2}z}$
(2) $2\log x + 3\log y + \frac{1}{2}\log z$
(3) $\log 2x + \log 3y - \log \frac{1}{2}z$
(4) $2\log x + 3\log y - \frac{1}{2}\log z$

18 Which graph represents the inequality $x^2 - 5x - 6 < 0$?

(1) −3 −2 −1 0 1 2 3 4 5 6

(2) −3 −2 −1 0 1 2 3 4 5 6

(3) −3 −2 −1 0 1 2 3 4 5 6

(4) −3 −2 −1 0 1 2 3 4 5 6

19 If $\log_2 (x^2 - 1) = \log_2 8$, then the solution set for x is

(1) {3,−3}
(2) {−3}
(3) {3}
(4) { }

20 In $\triangle ABC$, $\sin A = \frac{1}{2}$, $b = 20$, and $m\angle B = 45$. What is the length of side a?

(1) $\frac{10\sqrt{3}}{3}$
(2) 10
(3) $10\sqrt{2}$
(4) $20\sqrt{2}$

21 Expressed in simplest form, $\csc \theta \bullet \tan \theta \bullet \cos \theta$ is equivalent to

(1) 1
(2) $\sin \theta$
(3) $\cos \theta$
(4) $\tan \theta$

22 For which value of x is the function $f(x) = \frac{1}{1 - \tan x}$ undefined?

(1) 0
(2) π
(3) $\frac{\pi}{3}$
(4) $\frac{\pi}{4}$

23 The expression $\frac{\frac{x}{z} - \frac{z}{x}}{\frac{1}{z} + \frac{1}{x}}$ is equivalent to

(1) $x - z$
(2) $x + z$
(3) xz
(4) $\frac{x - z}{xz}$

24 Which equation is represented in the graph below?

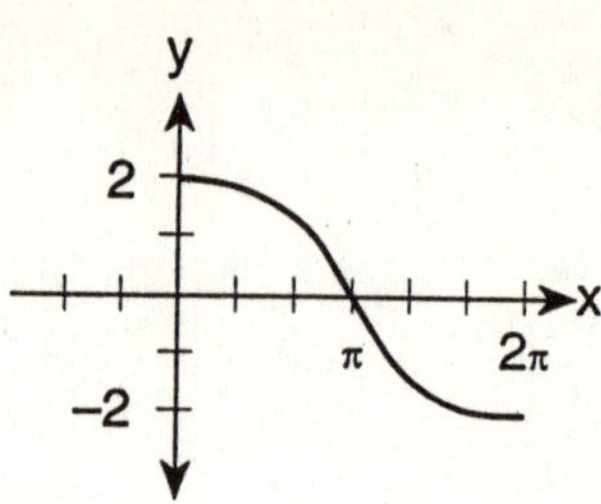

(1) $y = 2 \sin \frac{1}{2}x$
(2) $y = \frac{1}{2} \sin 2x$
(3) $y = 2 \cos \frac{1}{2}x$
(4) $y = \frac{1}{2} \cos 2x$

25 The expression $i^2(2 - i)$ is equivalent to

(1) $-2 - i$
(2) $-2 + i$
(3) $2 - i$
(4) $2 + i$

26 A spinner is divided into five equal sectors labeled 1 to 5. What is the probability of spinning exactly 3 even numbers in 4 spins?

(1) ${}_5C_4\left(\frac{2}{5}\right)^4\left(\frac{3}{5}\right)$
(2) ${}_4C_3\left(\frac{2}{5}\right)^3\left(\frac{3}{5}\right)$
(3) ${}_5C_4\left(\frac{3}{5}\right)^4\left(\frac{2}{5}\right)$
(4) ${}_4C_3\left(\frac{3}{5}\right)^3\left(\frac{2}{5}\right)$

27 The roots of the equation $ax^2 + 4x = -2$ are real and equal if a has a value of

(1) 1
(2) 2
(3) 3
(4) 4

28 If the graph of the complex number $-2 + 5i$ is rotated counterclockwise 90° about the origin, the image will fall in Quadrant

(1) I
(2) II
(3) III
(4) IV

29 If $2\sqrt{-2}$ is subtracted from $3\sqrt{-18}$, the difference is

(1) $7i\sqrt{2}$
(2) $11i\sqrt{2}$
(3) $-7i\sqrt{2}$
(4) $-11i\sqrt{2}$

30 Which value of θ satisfies the equation $2\sin^2\theta - 5\sin\theta - 3 = 0$?

(1) 300° (3) 150°
(2) 210° (4) 30°

31 For which equation does the sum of the roots equal 3 and the product of the roots equal 4.5?

(1) $x^2 + 3x - 9 = 0$ (3) $2x^2 + 6x + 9 = 0$
(2) $x^2 - 3x + 9 = 0$ (4) $2x^2 - 6x + 9 = 0$

32 If θ is an angle in standard position and its terminal side passes through point $\left(-\frac{1}{2}, \frac{\sqrt{3}}{2}\right)$ on the unit circle, then a possible value of θ is

(1) 60° (3) 150°
(2) 120° (4) 330°

33 The expression cot (–200°) is equivalent to

(1) –tan 20° (3) –cot 20°
(2) tan 70° (4) cot 70°

34 A function is defined by the equation $y = 2x + 3$. Which equation defines the inverse of this function?

(1) $y = \frac{1}{2}x + \frac{1}{3}$ (3) $y = -2x - 3$
(2) $x = \frac{1}{2}y - \frac{3}{2}$ (4) $y = \frac{1}{2}x - \frac{3}{2}$

35 The graph of the equation $2x^2 - 5y^2 = 10$ forms

(1) a circle (3) a hyperbola
(2) an ellipse (4) a parabola

Part II

Answer four questions from this part. Clearly indicate the necessary steps, including appropriate formula substitutions, diagrams, graphs, charts, etc. Calculations that may be obtained by mental arithmetic or the calculator do not need to be shown. [40]

36 *a* On the same set of axes, sketch and label the graphs of the equations $y = -3\cos x$ and $y = \frac{1}{2}\sin 2x$ in the interval $-\pi \le x \le \pi$. [8]

b Based on the graphs drawn in part *a*, find all values in the interval $-\pi \le x \le \pi$ that satisfy the equation $-3\cos x = \frac{1}{2}\sin 2x$. [2]

37 *a* Find, to the *nearest ten minutes* or *nearest tenth of a degree*, all values of A in the interval $0° \le A < 360°$ that satisfy the equation $4\sin^2 A + 1 = \sin^2 A + 2$. [6]

b Solve for x and express the roots of the equation $8x^2 - 28x + 29 = 0$ in simplest $a + bi$ form. [4]

38 *a* On graph paper, sketch the triangle formed by points $A(3,-3)$, $B(-1,-5)$, and $C(5,-4)$. [1]

b On the same set of axes, graph and state the coordinates of

(1) $\triangle A'B'C'$, the image of $\triangle ABC$ after the rotation $R_{90°}$ [3]

(2) $\triangle A''B''C''$, the image of $\triangle A'B'C'$ after the translation $T_{-4,-1}$ [2]

(3) $\triangle A'''B'''C'''$, the image of $\triangle A''B''C''$ after the dilation D_3 [2]

c Is the composite transformation $\triangle ABC \rightarrow \triangle A'''B'''C'''$ an isometry? Explain your answer. [1,1]

39 In the accompanying diagram of circle O, diameter $\overline{AE}$ is extended through E to C; tangent $\overline{CB}$, chord $\overline{AB}$, and radius $\overline{OB}$ are drawn; and $m\overset{\frown}{AB}:m\overset{\frown}{BE} = 2:1$.

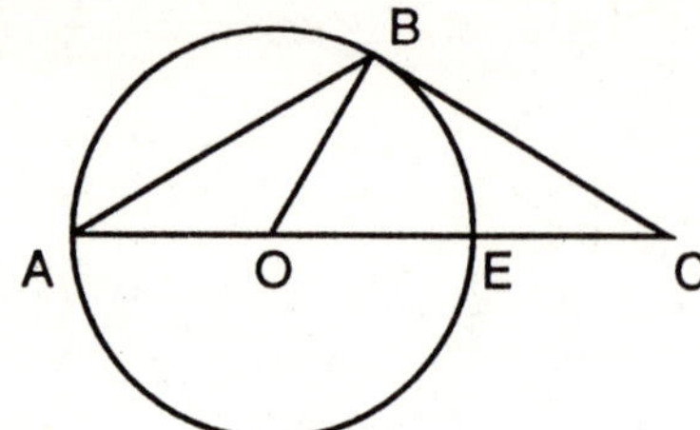

a Find:

(1) $m\overset{\frown}{AB}$ [2]
(2) $m\angle BAC$ [2]
(3) $m\angle C$ [2]
(4) $m\angle ABC$ [2]

b Which term describes $\triangle OBC$? [1]

(1) acute
(2) right
(3) obtuse
(4) equiangular

c Explain how you arrived at your answer for part *b*. [1]

40 *a* In the equation $x^2 - 3x + c = 0$, one value of x is 2.5.

Find:

(1) c [2]
(2) the other value of x [3]

b Expand and express $(i - 3)^4$ in simplest $a + bi$ form, where i is the imaginary unit. [5]

41 *a* The accompanying table represents the PSAT scores of a group of ten students.

Score	*Frequency*
48	1
50	3
53	1
54	2
57	1
62	1
68	1

(1) Find the standard deviation to the *nearest tenth.* [4]
(2) How many scores fall within one standard deviation of the mean? [2]

b The probability of a biased coin coming up tails is $\frac{1}{4}$. When the coin is flipped four times, what is the probability of obtaining *at least* 2 tails? [4]

42 Michael and his friends are plotting a course for a race. They decided to make the course in the shape of a triangle, PQR. Beginning at point P, participants run 1.4 miles to Q, then from Q to R, and finally 2.6 miles from R back to P. Angle QPR measures 38°30'.

a Find, to the *nearest tenth of a mile*, the total number of miles for the entire race. [7]

b Find, to the *nearest tenth of a square mile*, the area of triangle PQR. [3]

HIGH SCHOOL MATHEMATICS: COURSE III
AUGUST 1999

Part I

Answer 30 questions from this part. Each correct answer will receive 2 credits. No partial credit will be allowed. Write your answers in the spaces provided on the separate answer sheet. Where applicable, answers may be left in terms of π or in radical form. [60]

1 If $f(x) = x^0 + x^{\frac{1}{2}} + x^{-1}$, find f(4).

2 If $f(x) = \sin x + \cos x$, evaluate $f(2\pi)$.

3 Express the sum of $2\sqrt{-9}$ and $7\sqrt{-64}$ in simplest form in terms of i.

4 Express 220° in radian measure.

5 Evaluate: $\sum_{x=2}^{5}(x-3)^2$

6 For which *negative* value of x is the fraction $\frac{x+5}{x^2-x-6}$ undefined?

7 If $f(x) = x^2$ and $g(x) = 2x - 1$, find $(f \circ g)(4)$.

8 Point A is rotated 180° in a counterclockwise direction about the origin. If the coordinates of A are (–1,3), what are the coordinates of A', its image?

9 Solve for x: $\log_2 x = 3$

10 In which quadrant does the sum of $-4 + 2i$ and $5 - 6i$ lie?

11 In $\triangle ABC$, $\sin A = \frac{1}{3}$, $m\angle B = 30$, and $a = 12$. What is the length of b?

12 Tangent $\overline{PA}$ and secant $\overline{PBC}$ are drawn to a circle from external point P. If $PA = 9$ and $PC = 27$, find PB.

13 Solve for x: $32^x = 4^{(2x+1)}$

14 What is the number of degrees in the value of θ that satisfies the equation $2 \cos \theta - 1 = 0$ in the interval $180° \leq \theta \leq 360°$?

15 In the accompanying diagram of circle O, chords $\overline{AB}$ and $\overline{CD}$ intersect at E and $\overline{AD}$ is a diameter. If $m\overset{\frown}{CB} = 82$, find $m\angle AED$.

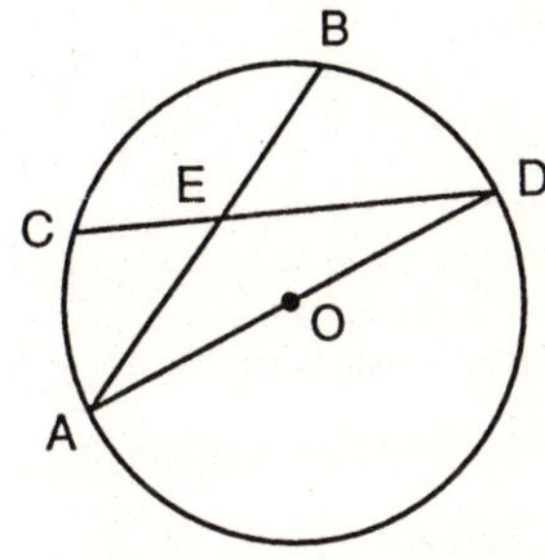

16 Factor completely: $\tan^3 x - 9 \tan x$

Directions (17–35): For *each* question chosen, write on the separate answer sheet the *numeral* preceding the word or expression that best completes the statement or answers the question.

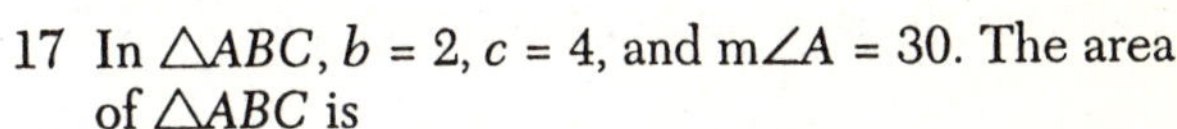

17 In $\triangle ABC$, $b = 2$, $c = 4$, and $m\angle A = 30$. The area of $\triangle ABC$ is

(1) 1
(2) 2
(3) $\sqrt{3}$
(4) 4

18 Which value of c would make the roots of the equation $x^2 + 6x + c = 0$ real, rational, and equal?

(1) 9
(2) –9
(3) 18
(4) –18

19 Expressed as a single fraction, $\frac{5}{x-3} - \frac{1}{x}$ is equivalent to

(1) $\frac{6x-3}{x^2-3x}$
(2) $\frac{4x+3}{x^2-3x}$
(3) $\frac{4x+3}{2x-3}$
(4) $\frac{4}{x^2-3x}$

20 If x varies inversely as y and y is doubled, then x will be

(1) divided by 2 (3) decreased by 2
(2) multiplied by 2 (4) increased by 2

21 If $\tan x = -\sqrt{3}$, in which quadrants could angle x terminate?

(1) I and III (3) II and IV
(2) II and III (4) III and IV

22 If A and B are positive acute angles, $\sin A = \frac{5}{13}$, and $\cos B = \frac{4}{5}$, what is the value of $\sin(A + B)$?

(1) $-\frac{16}{65}$ (3) $\frac{56}{65}$
(2) $\frac{33}{65}$ (4) $\frac{63}{65}$

23 What is the solution set for the equation $2x + |x| = -2$?

(1) $\{1\}$ (3) $\{-1\}$
(2) $\{-2\}$ (4) $\{\ \}$

24 The expression $\frac{\sec\theta}{\csc\theta}$ is equivalent to

(1) $\cot\theta$ (3) $\cos\theta$
(2) $\tan\theta$ (4) $\sin\theta$

25 On a standardized examination, Laura received a score of 85, which was exactly 2 standard deviations above the mean. If the standard deviation for the examination is 4, what is the mean for this examination?

(1) 93 (3) 83
(2) 87 (4) 77

26 What is the solution set for the inequality $x^2 - 2x - 3 \le 0$?

(1) −3 −2 −1 0 1 2 3

(2) −3 −2 −1 0 1 2 3

(3) −3 −2 −1 0 1 2 3

(4) −3 −2 −1 0 1 2 3

27 The domain of $f(x) = x^2 + 2x + 1$ is $-3 \le x \le 3$. The largest value in the range of $f(x)$ is

(1) 20 (3) 3
(2) 16 (4) 4

28 In $\triangle DEF$ if $d = \sqrt{3}$, $e = 4$, and $m\angle F = 30$, the length of f is

(1) 7 (3) $\sqrt{7}$
(2) $\sqrt{17}$ (4) $\sqrt{3}$

29 The maximum value of $3 \sin \frac{1}{3}\theta$ is

(1) 1 (3) 3
(2) $\frac{1}{3}$ (4) 0

30 The graph of the equation $y = 2\cos 2x$, $0 \le x \le 2\pi$, has a line of symmetry at

(1) $x = \pi$ (3) $y = 2$
(2) $x = \frac{\pi}{4}$ (4) the x-axis

31 For the equation $\sqrt{x + 21} = x + 1$, the solution set for x is

(1) $\{\ \}$ (3) $\{-5,4\}$
(2) $\{-5\}$ (4) $\{4\}$

32 If $\sin x = -\frac{\sqrt{2}}{2}$ and $\cos x = \frac{\sqrt{2}}{2}$, the measure of angle x is

(1) 45° (3) 225°
(2) 135° (4) 315°

33 The graph of the equation $y = -(4)^x$ lies in Quadrants

(1) I and II (3) III and IV
(2) II and III (4) I and IV

34 Which quadratic equation has roots of $3 - i$ and $3 + i$?

(1) $x^2 + 6x + 10 = 0$ (3) $x^2 - 6x + 8 = 0$
(2) $x^2 + 6x + 8 = 0$ (4) $x^2 - 6x + 10 = 0$

35 The graph of the equation $y^2 - x^2 = 4$ forms

(1) a circle (3) a hyperbola
(2) an ellipse (4) a parabola

Part II

Answer four questions from this part. Clearly indicate the necessary steps, including appropriate formula substitutions, diagrams, graphs, charts, etc. Calculations that may be obtained by mental arithmetic or the calculator do not need to be shown. [40]

36 *a* On graph paper, sketch and label the graph of the equation $y = 2\cos\theta$ in the interval $0 \leq \theta \leq 2\pi$. [4]

b On the same set of axes, sketch and label the graph of the equation $y = \tan\theta$ in the same interval. [4]

c If $f(\theta) = \tan\theta - 2\cos\theta$, find $f(\pi)$. [2]

37 In the accompanying diagram of circle O, diameter $\overline{AD}$, chord $\overline{AE}$, and secants $\overline{CBA}$ and $\overline{CDE}$ are drawn; $m\angle BAD = 40$; and $m\overset{\frown}{AE} = 5(m\overset{\frown}{ED})$.

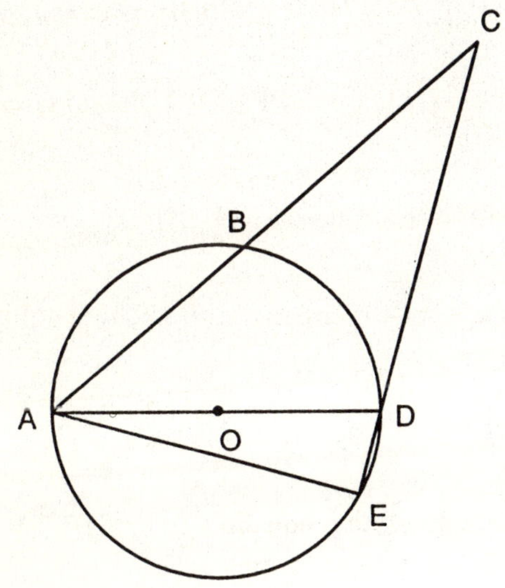

Find:

a $m\overset{\frown}{BD}$ [2]

b $m\overset{\frown}{AE}$ [2]

c $m\angle ACE$ [2]

d $m\angle AED$ [2]

e $m\angle ADC$ [2]

38 *a* On graph paper, draw and label $\triangle PQR$, whose vertices are $P(3,5)$, $Q(9,5)$, and $R(7,7)$. [1]

b On the same set of axes, graph and state the coordinates of

(1) $\triangle P'Q'R'$, the image of $\triangle PQR$ after $R_{90°}$ [3]

(2) $\triangle P''Q''R''$, the image of $\triangle P'Q'R'$ after $r_{x\text{-axis}}$ [2]

(3) $\triangle P'''Q'''R'''$, the image of $\triangle P''Q''R''$ after $r_{y\text{-axis}}$ [2]

c Based on the graphs drawn in parts *a* and *b*, write a single transformation that shows the composition $r_{y\text{-axis}} \circ r_{x\text{-axis}} \circ R_{90°}$. [2]

39 *a* Perform the indicated operations and express in lowest terms:

$$\frac{x^2-9}{2x+4} \bullet \frac{x^2+7x+10}{x^2-3x-18} \div \frac{x^2+2x-15}{2x^2-12x} \quad [6]$$

b Express the roots of the equation $2x^2 + 4x + 5 = 0$ in simplest $a + bi$ form. [4]

40 *a* Prove that the following is an identity for all values of θ for which the expressions are defined:

$$\frac{\sin\theta}{\cot\theta} + \cos\theta = \sec\theta \quad [4]$$

b If θ is in Quadrant II and $\cos\theta = -\frac{3}{4}$, find an exact value for $\sin 2\theta$. [3]

c Solve for x to the *nearest hundredth:*

$$\log_7 75 = x \quad [3]$$

41 To determine the distance across a river, a surveyor marked three points on one riverbank: H, G, and F, as shown below. She also marked one point, K, on the opposite bank such that $\overline{KH} \perp \overline{HGF}$, $m\angle KGH = 41$, and $m\angle KFH = 37$. The distance between G and F is 45 meters. Find KH, the width of the river, to the *nearest tenth of a meter*. [10]

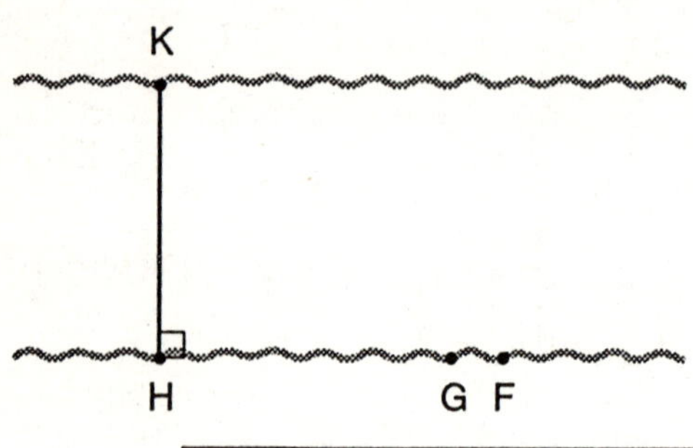

42 *a* A spinner is divided into two regions, green and red. The probability of the pointer landing on the green region is $\frac{2}{3}$. The pointer is spun 5 times.

(1) What is the probability of the pointer landing on the green region *exactly* 2 times? [2]

(2) What is the probability of the pointer landing on the red region *at least* 4 times? [3]

b Find all values of θ in the interval $0° \leq \theta < 360°$ that satisfy the equation $\cos \theta = \cos 2\theta$. [5]

HIGH SCHOOL MATHEMATICS: COURSE III
JANUARY 2000

Part I

Answer 30 questions from this part. Each correct answer will receive 2 credits. No partial credit will be allowed. Write your answers in the spaces provided on the separate answer sheet. Where applicable, answers may be left in terms of π or in radical form. [60]

1 Express $\frac{7\pi}{6}$ radians in degrees.

2 Express the sum of $3 + \sqrt{-49}$ and $2 + \sqrt{-121}$ in simplest $a + bi$ form.

3 Solve for the positive value of x: $|2x - 3| = 11$

4 Solve for x: $3^{2x+1} = 27^x$

5 Which negative real number is *not* in the domain of $\frac{3}{x^2 - 4}$?

6 Evaluate: $\sum_{n=1}^{3} n^2$

7 If $x + 2$ is a factor of $x^2 + bx + 10$, what is the value of b?

8 In $\triangle ABC$, $a = 16$, $c = 14$, and $m\angle B = 30$. What is the area of $\triangle ABC$?

9 In the accompanying diagram, isosceles triangle ABC is inscribed in circle O with diameter $\overline{AOB}$. Find $m\angle CAB$.

10 In $\triangle ABC$, $a = 2$, $\sin A = \frac{2}{3}$, and $\sin B = \frac{5}{6}$. Find the length of side b.

11 If $f(x) = 2\cos^2 x + \sin x - 1$, find the value of $f\left(\frac{\pi}{2}\right)$.

12 Express $\dfrac{\frac{x}{3} - 1}{\frac{x^2}{3} - 3}$ in simplest form.

13 Find the value of $5x^0 + x^{-\frac{1}{2}} - x^{\frac{1}{2}}$ when $x = 16$.

14 Express $\dfrac{\cos 2A + \sin^2 A}{\cos A}$ as a single trigonometric function for all values of A for which the fraction is defined.

15 In circle O, chords $\overline{AB}$ and $\overline{CD}$ intersect at E, $AE = 3$ inches, $BE = 8$ inches, and CE is 2 inches longer than DE. What is the length of $\overline{DE}$, expressed in inches?

16 What is the probability of getting *exactly* two heads in three tosses of a fair coin?

Directions (17–35): For *each* question chosen, write on the separate answer sheet the *numeral* preceding the word or expression that best completes the statement or answers the question.

17 The numerical value of $\sin \frac{3\pi}{2} + \cos \frac{\pi}{4}$ is

(1) $1 + \frac{\sqrt{2}}{2}$
(2) $\frac{\sqrt{2}}{2}$
(3) $-1 + \frac{\sqrt{2}}{2}$
(4) -1

18 If $\tan A = \frac{2}{3}$ and $\tan B = \frac{1}{2}$, what is the value of $\tan (A + B)$?

(1) $\frac{1}{8}$
(2) $\frac{7}{8}$
(3) $\frac{1}{4}$
(4) $\frac{7}{4}$

19 Which trigonometric function is shown in the graph below?

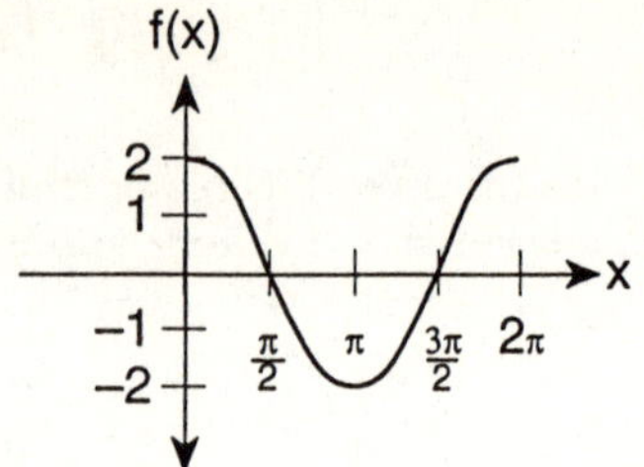

(1) $f(x) = 2 \sin x$
(2) $f(x) = 2 \cos x$
(3) $f(x) = \cos 2x$
(4) $f(x) = \sin 2x$

20 What is the solution set of the equation $\sqrt{x^2 - 3x + 3} = 1$?

(1) {1}
(2) {2}
(3) {1,2}
(4) { }

21 If $\sin \theta = -\frac{3}{5}$ and $\cos \theta > 0$, what is the value of $\tan \theta$?

(1) $\frac{3}{4}$
(2) $-\frac{3}{4}$
(3) $\frac{4}{3}$
(4) $-\frac{4}{3}$

22 The roots of the equation $x^2 - 7x + 15 = 0$ are

(1) imaginary
(2) real, rational, and equal
(3) real, rational, and unequal
(4) real, irrational, and unequal

23 How many distinct triangles can be formed if $a = 20$, $b = 30$, and $m\angle A = 30$?

(1) 1
(2) 2
(3) 3
(4) 0

24 Which expression is *not* an isometry?

(1) $r_{y=x}$
(2) $T_{-2,4}$
(3) D_{-2}
(4) $R_{0,90°}$

25 What is one solution of the equation $(\sin x + \cos x)^2 = 2$?

(1) $\frac{\pi}{4}$
(2) $\frac{\pi}{3}$
(3) $\frac{\pi}{2}$
(4) 0

26 Which equation does *not* represent a function?

(1) $y = 2x$
(2) $y = x^2 + 10$
(3) $y = \frac{10}{x}$
(4) $x^2 + y^2 = 9$

27 In which quadrant does the sum of $2 + 3i$ and $3 - 5i$ lie?

(1) I
(2) II
(3) III
(4) IV

28 If the coordinates of point P are (2,–3), then $(R_{90} \circ R_{180})(P)$ is

(1) (–2,3)
(2) (–2,–3)
(3) (3,–2)
(4) (–3,–2)

29 What is the value of $\sin\left(\text{Arc}\cos \frac{1}{x}\right)$?

(1) $\frac{\sqrt{1-x^2}}{x}$
(2) $\frac{\sqrt{1+x^2}}{x}$
(3) $\frac{\sqrt{x^2-1}}{x}$
(4) $\frac{x}{\sqrt{x^2+1}}$

30 In a normal distribution, what is the greatest percent of the data that falls within 2 standard deviations of the mean?

(1) 95
(2) 81.5
(3) 68
(4) 34

31 In the diagram below, figure b is the reflection of $y = 2^x$ in the line $y = x$.

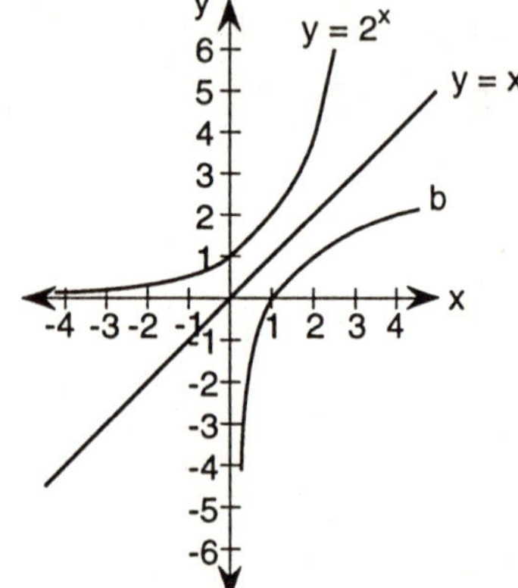

Which is an expression for the equation of figure b?

(1) $y = (-2)^x$
(2) $y = 2^{-x}$
(3) $y = \log_2 x$
(4) $y = \log_x 2$

32 What is the solution set of the inequality $x^2 + 3x - 10 > 8$?

(1) $\{x \mid -6 < x < 3\}$ (3) $\{x \mid -3 < x < 6\}$
(2) $\{x \mid x < -6 \text{ or } x > 3\}$ (4) $\{x \mid x < -3 \text{ or } x > 6\}$

33 What is the third term in the expansion of $(x + 2y)^5$?

(1) $10x^3y^2$ (3) $80x^2y^3$
(2) $40x^3y^2$ (4) $20x^2y^3$

34 If $f(x) = x^2$, what is the value of $f(i^3)$?

(1) 1 (3) i
(2) −1 (4) $-i$

35 If x varies inversely as y and $x = 12$ when $y = 3$, what is the value of x when $y = 9$?

(1) 36 (3) $\frac{1}{4}$
(2) $\frac{1}{3}$ (4) 4

Part II

Answer four questions from this part. Clearly indicate the necessary steps, including appropriate formula substitutions, diagrams, graphs, charts, etc. Calculations that may be obtained by mental arithmetic or the calculator do not need to be shown. [40]

36 In the accompanying diagram of circle O, $\overline{AOED}$ is a diameter, $\overline{PD}$ is a tangent, $\overline{PBA}$ is a secant, chords $\overline{BD}$ and $\overline{BEC}$ are drawn, $m\angle DAB = 43$, and $m\angle DEC = 72$.

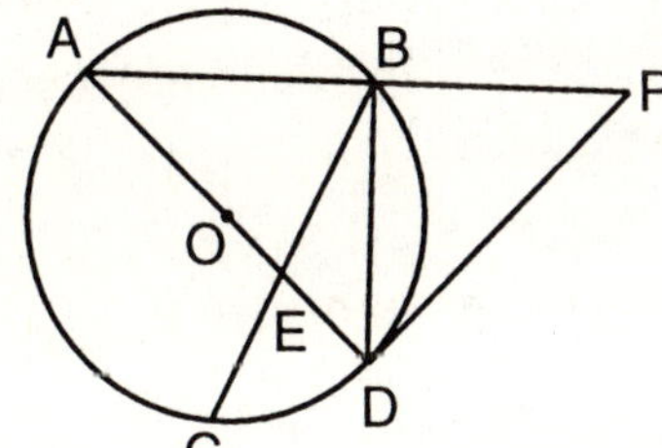

Find:

a $m\angle BDP$ [2]
b $m\widehat{AB}$ [2]
c $m\widehat{AC}$ [2]
d $m\angle P$ [2]
e $m\angle CBD$ [2]

37 *a* In the month of February at a ski resort, the probability of snow on any day is $\frac{3}{4}$.

(1) What is the probability that snow will fall on every day of a 5-day trip to that resort in February? [2]

(2) What is the probability that snow will fall on *at least* 3 days of that 5-day trip in February? [4]

b Using the scores in the table below, find the standard deviation to the *nearest tenth*. [4]

Scores	Frequency
60	2
65	6
70	4
75	8
80	5

38 In parallelogram $ABCD$, $AD = 8$, $AB = 12$, and diagonal $BD = 15$.

a Find $m\angle BAD$ to the *nearest degree*. [6]

b Using the answer obtained in part *a*, find the area of parallelogram $ABCD$ to the *nearest tenth*. [4]

39 *a* Find the period of the graph of $y = 3 \sin 2x$. [2]

b On graph paper, sketch the graph of $y = 3 \sin 2x$ for one period. [4]

c On the same set of axes, sketch the image of the graph drawn in part *b* after it is reflected in the x-axis. Label the graph *c*. [2]

d Write an equation for the graph sketched in part *c*. [2]

40 Find, to the *nearest degree*, all positive values of θ less than 360° that satisfy the equation $2 \tan^2 \theta - 2 \tan \theta = 3$. [10]

41 *a* Given: $\log 2 = x$
$\log 3 = y$

Express in terms of x and y:

(1) $\log \frac{2}{3}$ [2]

(2) $\log 12$ [3]

b Using logarithms, find w to the *nearest hundredth*.

$$5^{2w} + 9 = 40 \quad [5]$$

42 *a* For all values of θ for which the expressions are defined, prove the following is an identity:

$$\frac{\tan \theta - \cot \theta}{\tan \theta + \cot \theta} = 2 \sin^2 \theta - 1 \quad [5]$$

b For all values of x for which the expression is defined, solve for x:

$$\frac{3}{x+3} + \frac{2}{x-4} = \frac{4}{3} \quad [5]$$

HIGH SCHOOL MATHEMATICS: COURSE III
JUNE 2000

Part I

Answer 30 questions from this part. Each correct answer will receive 2 credits. No partial credit will be allowed. Write your answers in the spaces provided on the separate answer sheet. Where applicable, answers may be left in terms of π or in radical form. [60]

1 In $\triangle ABC$, $\sin A = 0.3$, $\sin B = 0.8$, and $b = 12$. Find the length of side a.

2 If $f(x) = \sin 2x + \cos x$, find $f(\frac{\pi}{2})$.

3 An angle inscribed in a circle measures 80 degrees. What is the number of degrees in the intercepted arc?

4 In $\triangle ABC$, $a = 1.3$, $b = 2.4$, and $m\angle C = 30$. Find the area of $\triangle ABC$.

5 Solve for x: $9^{2x} = 27^{x+1}$

6 If $\sin A < 0$ and $\cot A > 0$, in which quadrant does the terminal side of $\angle A$ lie?

7 A translation maps $P(3,-2)$ to $P'(1,1)$. Under the same translation, find the coordinates of Q', the image of $Q(-3,2)$.

8 Factor completely: $9x^3 - x$

9 Solve for all values of x: $|2x + 3| = 7$

10 If $g(x) = 36^x$, evaluate $g\left(-\frac{1}{2}\right)$.

11 Evaluate: $2\sum_{n=1}^{4} n^2$

12 Express in simplest form: $\dfrac{\frac{x-y}{y}}{\frac{1}{y}-\frac{1}{x}}$

13 Express $\sqrt{-2} + \sqrt{-18}$ as a monomial in terms of i.

14 In a circle whose radius is 2 centimeters, a central angle intercepts an arc of 6 centimeters. What is the number of radians in the central angle?

15 Determine the maximum number of triangles possible when $m\angle A = 150$, $a = 14$, and $b = 10$.

16 Solve for x: $x - 1 = \sqrt{2x+13}$

Directions (17–35): For *each* question chosen, write on the separate answer sheet the *numeral* preceding the word or expression that best completes the statement or answers the question.

17 Which transformation is *not* an isometry?

(1) dilation
(2) rotation
(3) reflection
(4) translation

18 The expression $\sin\theta(\cot\theta - \csc\theta)$ is equivalent to

(1) $\cos\theta - \sin^2\theta$
(2) $2\cos\theta$
(3) $-\sin\theta$
(4) $\cos\theta - 1$

19 Which equation is sketched in the accompanying graph?

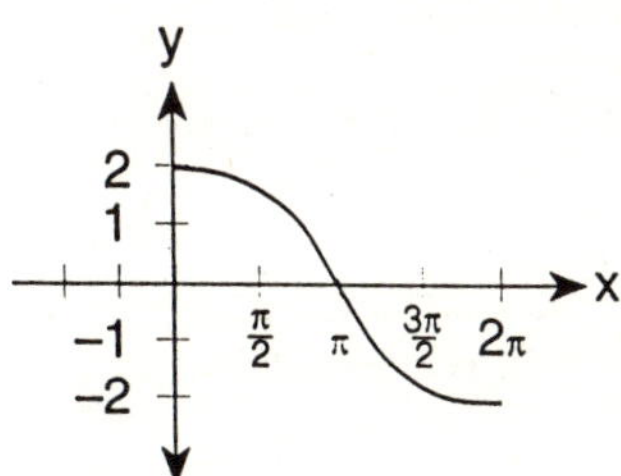

(1) $y = \cos\frac{1}{2}x$
(2) $y = \frac{1}{2}\cos x$
(3) $y = 2\cos\frac{1}{2}x$
(4) $y = 2\cos 2x$

20 As angle x increases from $\frac{\pi}{2}$ to π, the value of $\sin x$ will

(1) increase from −1 to 0
(2) increase from 0 to 1
(3) decrease from 0 to −1
(4) decrease from 1 to 0

21 Which graph represents the solution set for the inequality $x^2 - x - 20 < 0$?

(1) 

(2) 

(3) 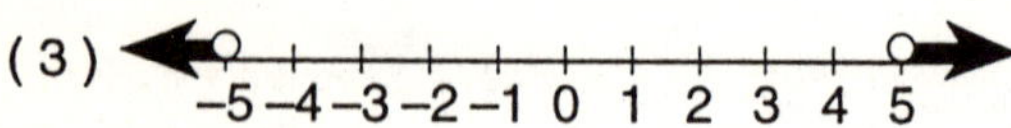

(4) −5 −4 −3 −2 −1 0 1 2 3 4 5

22 If the fraction $\frac{123}{10,000}$ is expressed in the form 1.23×10^n, the value of n is

(1) −1 (3) −3
(2) −2 (4) −4

23 If $f(x) = \sin(\text{Arc} \tan x)$, the value of f(1) is

(1) $\sqrt{2}$ (3) $\frac{\sqrt{3}}{2}$
(2) $\frac{\sqrt{2}}{2}$ (4) $\frac{\sqrt{3}}{3}$

24 A solution of the equation $\cos 2\theta + \sin 2\theta = -1$ is

(1) 240° (3) 45°
(2) 135° (4) −30°

25 In circle O, $\overline{PA}$ and $\overline{PB}$ are tangent to the circle from point P. If the ratio of the measure of major arc AB to the measure of minor arc AB is 5:1, then $m\angle P$ is

(1) 60 (3) 120
(2) 90 (4) 180

26 Which equation is *not* a function?

(1) $3x^2 + 4y^2 = 12$ (3) $y = 2^x$
(2) $y = 2 \cos x$ (4) $y = \log_2 x$

27 When the sum of $4 + 6i$ and $6 - 8i$ is graphed, in which quadrant does it lie?

(1) I (3) III
(2) II (4) IV

28 In the accompanying diagram, point $P(-0.6,-0.8)$ is on unit circle O.

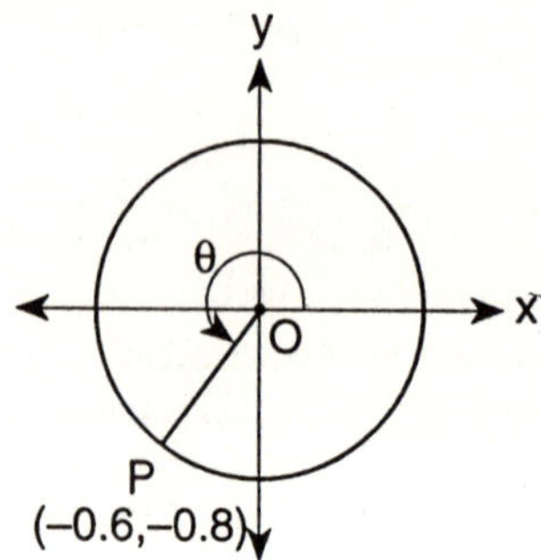

What is the measure of angle θ to the *nearest degree*?

(1) 143 (3) 225
(2) 217 (4) 233

29 The expression log 12 is equivalent to

(1) log 6 + log 6 (3) log 3 − 2 log 2
(2) log 3 + 2 log 2 (4) log 3 • log 4

30 In the equation $x^2 - 7x + 2 = 0$, the sum of the roots exceeds the product of the roots by

(1) 9 (3) −9
(2) 5 (4) −5

31 What is the third term in the expansion of $(a - 3b)^4$?

(1) $6a^2b^2$ (3) $54a^2b^2$
(2) $-6a^2b^2$ (4) $-54a^2b^2$

32 The roots of the equation $2x^2 - 4x + k = 0$ are real and equal if k is equal to

(1) −2 (3) −4
(2) 2 (4) 4

33 The expression cos (270° – A) is equivalent to

(1) cos A (3) sin A
(2) –cos A (4) –sin A

34 The scores on a test approximate a normal distribution with a mean score of 72 and a standard deviation of 9. Approximately what percent of the students taking the test received a score greater than 90?

(1) $2\frac{1}{2}$% (3) 10%
(2) 5% (4) 16%

35 Mr. and Mrs. Douville have six children. What is the probability that there is *exactly one* female child? [Assume that P(male) = P(female).]

(1) $\frac{1}{64}$ (3) $\frac{6}{64}$
(2) $\frac{5}{64}$ (4) $\frac{32}{64}$

Part II

Answer four questions from this part. Clearly indicate the necessary steps, including appropriate formula substitutions, diagrams, graphs, charts, etc. Calculations that may be obtained by mental arithmetic or the calculator do not need to be shown. [40]

36 In the accompanying diagram of circle O, tangent $\overline{BA}$, diameter $\overline{AD}$, secant $\overline{BCE}$, $\overline{AD}$ intersects $\overline{BE}$ at F, chords $\overline{DE}$ and $\overline{DC}$ are drawn, m$\angle AFB$ = 80, and m$\overarc{AC}$ = 100.

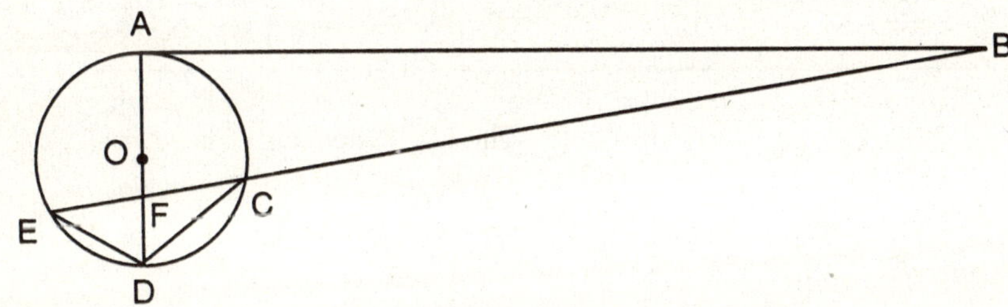

Find:

a m$\angle BED$ [2]
b m$\angle BAF$ [2]
c m$\overarc{ED}$ [2]
d m$\angle B$ [2]
e m$\angle EDC$ [2]

37 *a* On the same set of axes, sketch and label the graphs of the equations $y = \sin \frac{1}{2}x$ and $y = -3 \cos 2x$ in the interval $-\pi \le x \le \pi$. [8]

b Using the graphs drawn in part *a*, find the number of values of x in the interval $-\pi \le x \le \pi$ that satisfy the equation $\sin \frac{1}{2}x = -3 \cos 2x$. [2]

38 *a* Assume that in the United States $\frac{1}{5}$ of all cars are red. Suppose you are driving down the highway and you pass 6 cars.

(1) What is the probability that *at most* one of the cars you pass is red? [3]

(2) What is the probability that *at least* four of the cars you pass are red? [3]

b The scores on a mathematics test are 42, 51, 58, 64, 70, 76, 76, 82, 84, 88, 88, 90, 94, 94, 94, and 97. For this set of data, find the standard deviation to the *nearest tenth*. [4]

39 Find all values of x in the interval $0 \le x < 360°$ that satisfy the equation $4 \cos^2 x - 5 \sin x - 5 = 0$. Express your answer to the *nearest ten minutes* or *nearest tenth of a degree*. [10]

40 *a* On the same set of axes, sketch and label the graphs of the equations $xy = 8$ and $x = 2^y$. [6]

b On the same set of axes used in part *a*, sketch the reflection of $x = 2^y$ in the line $y = x$. Label it *b*. [3]

c Write an equation of the graph drawn in part *b*. [1]

41 *a* Two forces of 50 pounds and 69 pounds act on a body to produce a resultant of 70 pounds. Find, to the *nearest tenth of a degree* or *nearest ten minutes*, the angle formed between the resultant and the smaller force. [6]

b For all values of θ for which the expressions are defined, prove the following is an identity:

$$(\cot \theta + \csc \theta)(1 - \cos \theta) = \sin \theta \quad [4]$$

42 *a* Solve for x and express your answer in simplest $a + bi$ form:

$$x^2 - 10x = -41 \quad [6]$$

b Express in simplest form:

$$\frac{81 - x^2}{6x - 54} \div \frac{x^2 + 9x}{3x} \quad [4]$$

HIGH SCHOOL MATHEMATICS: COURSE III
AUGUST 2000

Part I

Answer 30 questions from this part. Each correct answer will receive 2 credits. No partial credit will be allowed. Write your answers in the spaces provided on the separate answer sheet. Where applicable, answers may be left in terms of π or in radical form. [60]

1 If $f(x) = 3x - 4$ and $g(x) = x^2$, find the value of $f(3) - g(2)$.

2 What is the amplitude of the function $y = 3 \sin 2x$?

3 What is the value of $\sin(\text{Arc tan } \sqrt{3})$?

4 In the accompanying diagram, $\overline{PQ}$ and $\overline{PS}$ are tangents drawn to circle O, and chord $\overline{QS}$ is drawn. If $m\angle P = 40$, what is $m\angle PQS$?

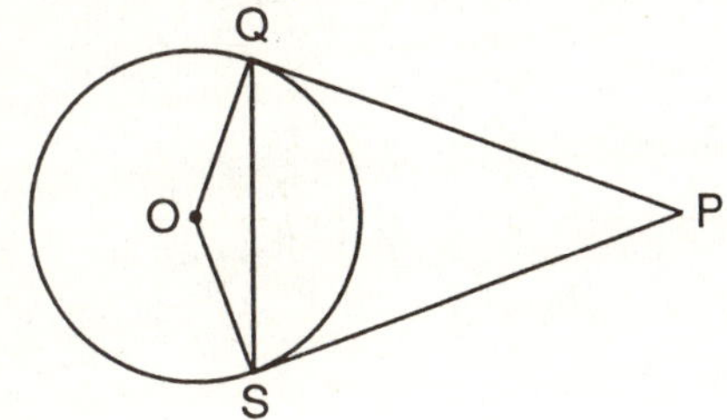

5 An angle that measures $\frac{5\pi}{3}$ radians is drawn in standard position. In which quadrant does the terminal side of the angle lie?

6 Express $4\sqrt{-25} - 2\sqrt{-81}$ as a monomial in terms of i.

7 In $\triangle ABC$, $a = 6$, $b = 10$, and $m\angle C = 30$. Find the area of $\triangle ABC$.

8 Solve for the positive value of x: $x^{\frac{4}{3}} + 2 = 18$

9 What is the solution set of the equation $|2x - 1| = 5$?

10 If point A has coordinates $(-3,4)$, what are the coordinates of A', the image of A under $r_{y\text{-axis}} \circ D_2$?

11 Factor completely: $3x^3 - 192x$

12 Evaluate: $\sum_{k=0}^{3} (2-k)^2$

13 Solve for the *smallest* non-negative value of θ:

$$\sqrt{3 \cos \theta + 1} = 2$$

14 Express $\dfrac{\frac{3}{x^2} + \frac{1}{x}}{1 - \frac{9}{x^2}}$ in simplest form.

15 Circle O has its center at the origin, $OB = 1$, and $\overline{BA} \perp \overline{OA}$. If $m\angle BOA = \theta$, which line segment shown has a length equal to $\cos \theta$?

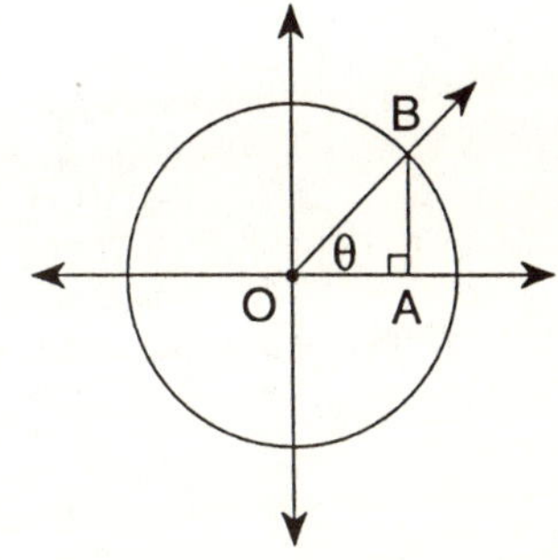

Directions (16–35): For *each* question chosen, write on the separate answer sheet the *numeral* preceding the word or expression that best completes the statement or answers the question.

16 In scientific notation, the number $\frac{9}{1{,}000{,}000}$ is written as

(1) 9.0×10^{-6}
(2) 9.0×10^{-7}
(3) 9.0×10^{6}
(4) 9.0×10^{7}

17 For which value of θ is the fraction $\frac{1}{\cos\theta}$ undefined?

(1) π (3) $\frac{\pi}{4}$
(2) $\frac{\pi}{2}$ (4) 0

18 What is the solution of the inequality $x^2 + 2x - 15 < 0$?

(1) $x < -5$ or $x > 3$ (3) $x < -3$ or $x > 5$
(2) $-5 < x < 3$ (4) $-3 < x < 5$

19 The roots of the equation $x^2 + kx + 3 = 0$ are real if the value of k is

(1) 0 (3) 3
(2) 2 (4) 4

20 The heights of the members of a high school class are normally distributed. If the mean height is 65 inches and a height of 72 inches represents the 84th percentile, what is the standard deviation for this distribution?

(1) 7 (3) 12
(2) 11 (4) 137

21 What is the greatest possible integral value of x for which $\sqrt{x-5}$ is an imaginary number?

(1) 5 (3) 3
(2) 6 (4) 4

22 The expression $\log 4x$ is equivalent to

(1) $\log x^4$ (3) $\log 4 + \log x$
(2) $4 \log x$ (4) $(\log 4)(\log x)$

23 Which value of θ satisfies the equation $2\cos^2\theta - \cos\theta = 0$?

(1) $\frac{\pi}{3}$ (3) $\frac{\pi}{6}$
(2) $\frac{\pi}{4}$ (4) 0

24 If the probability that Mike will successfully complete a foul shot is $\frac{4}{5}$, what is the probability that he will successfully complete exactly three of his next four foul shots?

(1) $\frac{64}{625}$ (3) $\frac{256}{625}$
(2) $\frac{192}{625}$ (4) $\frac{64}{125}$

25 In $\triangle ABC$, $a = 1$, $b = 1$, and $m\angle C = 120$. The value of c is

(1) 1 (3) $\sqrt{2.5}$
(2) $\sqrt{2}$ (4) $\sqrt{3}$

26 In the accompanying diagram, $\overline{PAB}$ and $\overline{PCD}$ are secants drawn to circle O, $PA = 8$, $PB = 20$, and $PD = 16$.

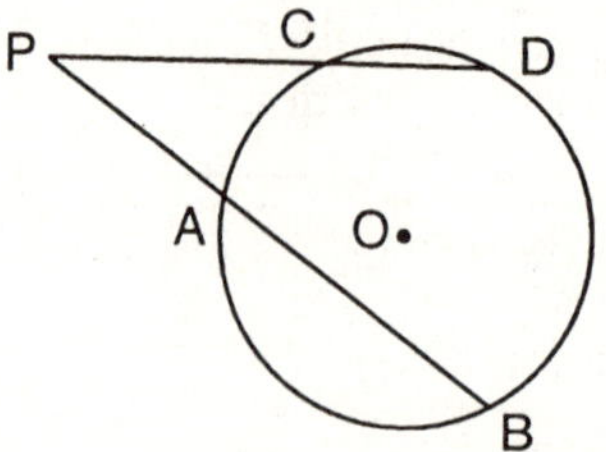

What is PC?

(1) 6.4 (3) 12
(2) 10 (4) 40

27 When the graphs of the equations $xy = -16$ and $y = x$ are drawn on the same set of axes, what is the total number of common points?

(1) 1 (3) 3
(2) 2 (4) 0

28 The inverse of the function $y = 2x - 5$ is

(1) $y = \frac{1}{2}(x + 5)$ (3) $y = 2x + 5$
(2) $y = \frac{1}{2}(x - 5)$ (4) $y = 5 - 2x$

29 As x increases from π to 2π, the value of $\sin x$

(1) increases, only
(2) decreases, only
(3) increases, then decreases
(4) decreases, then increases

30 If $3^x \cdot y = 3^{x+1}$, what is the value of y?

(1) 1 (3) 3
(2) -1 (4) $\frac{1}{3}$

31 If $m\angle A = 32$, $a = 5$, and $b = 3$, it is possible to construct

(1) an obtuse triangle
(2) two distinct triangles
(3) no triangles
(4) a right triangle

32 The expression $\frac{\sin x \cdot \cos x}{\tan x}$ is equivalent to

(1) 1 (3) $\cos x$
(2) $\sin^2 x$ (4) $\cos^2 x$

33 Which field property is *not* satisfied by the set of integers for addition and multiplication?

(1) identity for multiplication
(2) inverses for multiplication
(3) identity for addition
(4) closure for addition

34 What is the fourth term of the expansion $(2x - y)^7$?

(1) $16x^4y^3$ (3) $-560x^4y^3$
(2) $35x^3y^4$ (4) $-560x^3y^4$

35 If $\sec x < 0$ and $\tan x < 0$, then the terminal side of angle x is located in Quadrant

(1) I (3) III
(2) II (4) IV

Part II

Answer four questions from this part. Clearly indicate the necessary steps, including appropriate formula substitutions, diagrams, graphs, charts, etc. Calculations that may be obtained by mental arithmetic or the calculator do not need to be shown. [40]

36 In the accompanying diagram of circle O, diameters $\overline{BD}$ and $\overline{AE}$, secants $\overline{PAB}$ and $\overline{PDC}$, and chords $\overline{BC}$ and $\overline{AD}$ are drawn; m$\widehat{AD}$ = 40; and m$\widehat{DC}$ = 80.

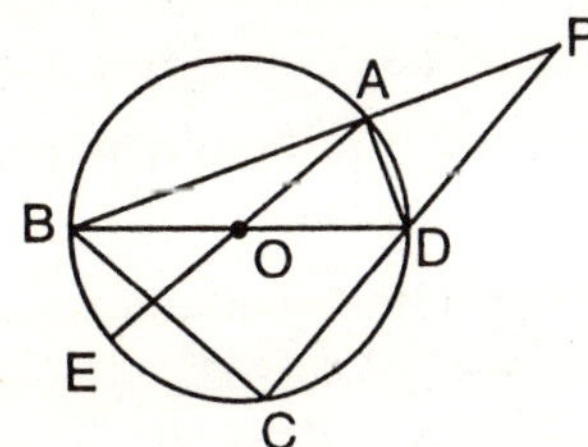

Find:

a m$\widehat{AB}$ [2]
b m$\angle BCD$ [2]
c m$\angle BOE$ [2]
d m$\angle P$ [2]
e m$\angle PAD$ [2]

37 *a* On the same set of axes, sketch and label the graphs of the equations $y = 4 \sin 2x$ and $y = -2 \cos \frac{1}{2}x$ in the inverval $0 \le x \le 2\pi$. [8]

b Based on the graph drawn in part *a*, how many values in the interval $0 \le x \le 2\pi$ satisfy the equation $4 \sin 2x = -2 \cos \frac{1}{2}x$? [2]

38 Given: $f(x) = \log_3 x$

a On graph paper, sketch and label the graph of $f(x) = \log_3 x$. [4]

b On the same set of axes, rotate the graph drawn in part *a* 90° counterclockwise about the origin. Sketch this rotation and label it *b*. [4]

c Write an equation of the function graphed in part *b*. [2]

39 *a* Five marbles are in a jar. Two are red and three are white. Four marbles are selected at random with replacement.

(1) Find the probability that *at most* two red marbles are selected. [4]

(2) Find the probability that *at least* three red marbles are selected. [2]

b Find, to the *nearest tenth*, the standard deviation of this set of data. [4]

x_i	f_i
87	3
89	4
91	3
93	6
95	2

40 *a* In the interval $0° \leq \theta < 360°$, find all values of θ that satisfy the equation $1 + 2 \sin \theta = \csc \theta$. [5]

b Prove the following identity:

$$\frac{\tan \theta}{\cot \theta} + 1 = \sec^2 \theta$$ [5]

41 *a* The roots of a quadratic equation are $r_1 = 3 + 2i$ and $r_2 = 3 - 2i$.

(1) Find the sum of the roots r_1 and r_2. [1]

(2) Find the product of the roots r_1 and r_2. [2]

(3) Write a quadratic equation that has roots r_1 and r_2. [2]

b Solve for x: $\frac{4x}{x+2} - \frac{12}{x} = 1$ [5]

42 *a* Two forces of 130 and 150 pounds yield a resultant force of 170 pounds. Find, to the *nearest ten minutes* or *nearest tenth of a degree*, the angle between the original two forces. [7]

b Given: $z_1 = 1 + 3i$ and $z_2 = 5 + 2i$. Plot z_1, z_2, and $z_1 + z_2$ on graph paper. [3]

HIGH SCHOOL MATHEMATICS: COURSE III
JANUARY 2001

Part I

Answer 30 questions from this part. Each correct answer will receive 2 credits. No partial credit will be allowed. Write your answers in the spaces provided on the separate answer sheet. Where applicable, answers may be left in terms of π or in radical form. [60]

1 If $25 - 3^2 = 2^x$, what is the value of x?

2 If $f(x) = \tan x$, evaluate $f\left(\frac{\pi}{4}\right)$.

3 In the accompanying diagram of circle O, chords $\overline{AB}$ and $\overline{CF}$ intersect at E. If $EB = 16$, $AE = 5$, and $CE = 10$, find EF.

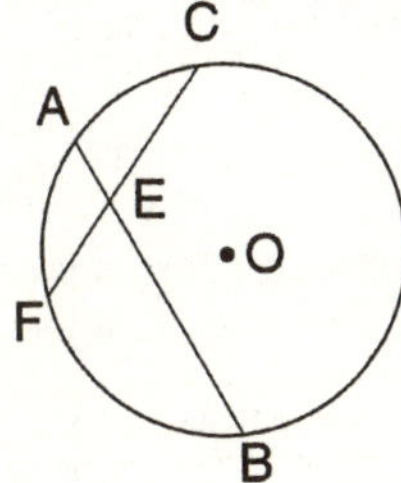

4 If θ is a positive acute angle and $2 \cos \theta + 3 = 4$, find the number of degrees in θ.

5 Solve for x: $5 + \sqrt{3x-2} = 9$

6 If $f(x) = \frac{2}{\sqrt{5-x^2}}$ and $g(x) = x + 1$, evaluate $(f \circ g)(0)$.

7 In which quadrant are both tangent and cosecant negative?

8 Evaluate: $\sum_{k=1}^{4} 2^{k-1}$

9 In $\triangle FUN$, $f = 4$, $m\angle F = 26$, and $m\angle N = 67$. Find the value of n to the *nearest integer*.

10 If the probability of a team winning any game is $\frac{2}{3}$, find the probability that the team would win *exactly* four games in a five-game series.

11 Factor completely: $3t^3 + 5t^2 - 12t$

12 If the coordinates of B are $(1,-5)$, what are the coordinates of B', the image of B after $R_{90} \circ r_{x\text{-axis}} B$?

13 Express the sum of $2\sqrt{-50}$ and $6\sqrt{-162}$ as a monomial in terms of i.

14 Find the value of $\sin\left(\text{Arc} \cos \frac{8}{17}\right)$.

Directions (15–35): For *each* question chosen, write on the separate answer sheet the *numeral* preceding the word or expression that best completes the statement or answers the question.

15 In the accompanying diagram, $\triangle ABC$ is inscribed in circle O and $\overline{AB}$ is a diameter.

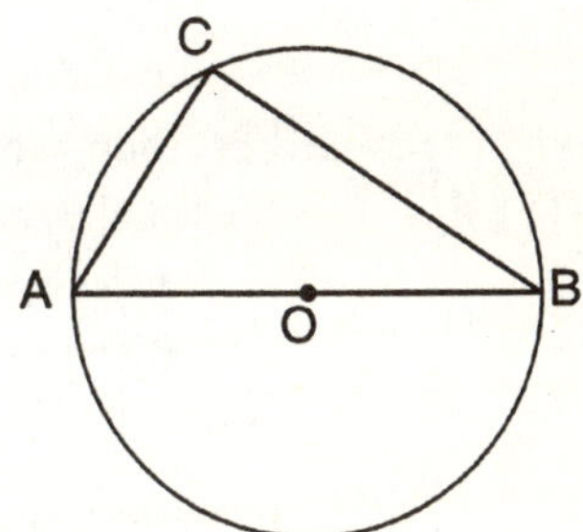

What is the number of degrees in $m\angle C$?

(1) 30
(2) 45
(3) 60
(4) 90

16 The expression $\frac{1}{1-\tan x}$ is undefined when x equals

(1) 0°
(2) 30°
(3) 45°
(4) 60°

17 If $f(x) = x^{-\frac{2}{3}}$, what is f(8)?

(1) $-\frac{16}{3}$ (3) $\frac{1}{4}$
(2) -4 (4) 4

18 Expressed in simplest form, $\frac{5x + 3}{x} - \frac{x - 1}{2x}$ is

(1) $\frac{4x + 4}{3x}$ (3) $\frac{9x + 7}{2x}$
(2) $\frac{2x + 2}{x}$ (4) $\frac{9x - 5}{2x}$

19 Which equation is represented by the graph in the accompanying diagram?

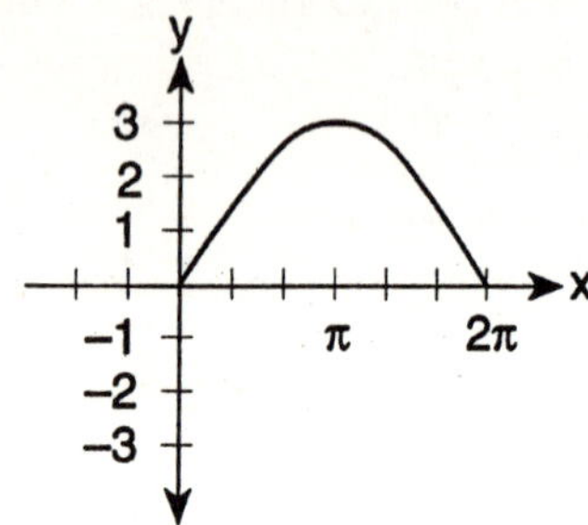

(1) $y = 3 \sin 2x$ (3) $y = 2 \sin 3x$
(2) $y = 3 \sin \frac{1}{2}x$ (4) $y = \frac{1}{2} \sin 3x$

20 Which expression is *not* equivalent to sin 150°?

(1) sin 30° (3) cos 60°
(2) −sin 210° (4) −cos 60°

21 If placed in standard position, an angle of $\frac{11\pi}{6}$ radians has the same terminal side as an angle of

(1) −150° (3) −30°
(2) 150° (4) 240°

22 The expression $(\tan \theta)(\csc \theta)$ is equivalent to

(1) $\cos \theta$ (3) $\csc \theta$
(2) $\sec \theta$ (4) $\csc \theta \cot \theta$

23 Which value of c will make the roots of the equation $x^2 - 8x + c = 0$ real and equal?

(1) −16 (3) 0
(2) −4 (4) 16

24 The expression $\log \frac{\sqrt{xy}}{w}$ is equivalent to

(1) $\frac{2 \log xy}{\log w}$
(2) $\log x + \log y - \log w$
(3) $\frac{1}{2}(\log x + \log y) - \log w$
(4) $\frac{1}{2}(\log xy - \log w)$

25 What is the range of the function $y = 2 \sin 3x$?

(1) all real numbers (3) $-2 \leq y \leq 2$
(2) $-1 \leq y \leq 1$ (4) $-3 \leq y \leq 3$

26 The expression $\dfrac{\frac{2x}{x+1}}{1-\frac{x}{x+1}}$ is equivalent to

(1) $\frac{x}{1 - x}$ (3) $\frac{2x}{x + 1}$
(2) −2 (4) $2x$

27 If the vertex angle of an isosceles triangle measures 30° and each leg measures 4, the area of the triangle is

(1) $8\sqrt{3}$ (3) $4\sqrt{3}$
(2) 8 (4) 4

28 The expression $\frac{5}{4 + 3i}$ is equivalent to

(1) $\frac{4 - 3i}{5}$ (3) $\frac{20 + 15i}{7}$
(2) $\frac{4 + 3i}{5}$ (4) $\frac{20 - 15i}{7}$

29 Which graph represents the solution to the inequality $|3 - 2x| > 7$?

(1) −3 −2 −1 0 1 2 3 4 5 6

(2) −3 −2 −1 0 1 2 3 4 5 6

(3) −3 −2 −1 0 1 2 3 4 5 6

(4) −3 −2 −1 0 1 2 3 4 5 6

30 The graph of the equation $y = 3 \cos x$ is symmetric with respect to the

(1) x-axis
(2) y-axis
(3) origin
(4) line $y = x$

31 The average score for a Latin test is 77 and the standard deviation is 8. Which percent best represents the probability that any one student scored between 61 and 93 on the test?

(1) 95%
(2) 99.5%
(3) 68%
(4) 34%

32 The graph of the equation $\frac{x}{2} = \frac{3}{y}$ is

(1) a circle
(2) an ellipse
(3) a hyperbola
(4) a line

33 What is the third term in the expansion of $(2x - y)^3$?

(1) $6xy^2$
(2) $2xy^2$
(3) $-2xy^2$
(4) $-6xy^2$

34 What is the period of the equation $y = -4 \cos 2x$?

(1) π
(2) 2π
(3) -4π
(4) -2

35 If $a = 5$, $c = 4$, and $m\angle A = 40$, then which type of triangle, if any, can be constructed?

(1) a right triangle, only
(2) an acute triangle, only
(3) an obtuse triangle, only
(4) no triangle

Part II

Answer four questions from this part. Clearly indicate the necessary steps, including appropriate formula substitutions, diagrams, graphs, charts, etc. Calculations that may be obtained by mental arithmetic or the calculator do not need to be shown. [40]

36 In the accompanying diagram of circle O, $\overline{AOEC}$ is a diameter, $\overrightarrow{PC}$ is a tangent, $\overline{PBA}$ is a secant, $\overline{BED}$ is a chord, $AO = 8$, and $m\overset{\frown}{AB}:m\overset{\frown}{BC}:m\overset{\frown}{CD}:m\overset{\frown}{DA} = 3:2:1:4$.

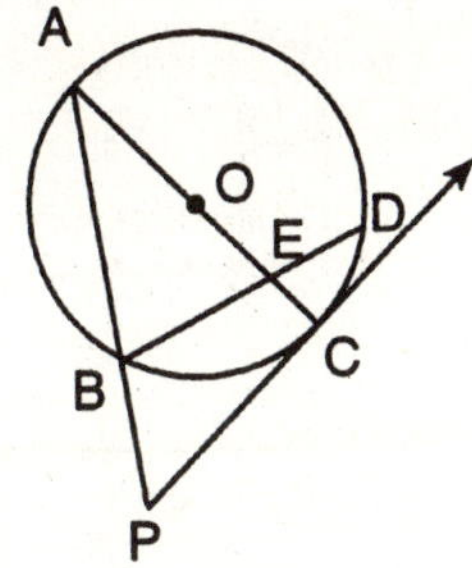

Find:

a $m\overset{\frown}{BC}$ [2]

b $m\angle P$ [2]

c $m\angle BEC$ [2]

d AP to the *nearest tenth* [4]

37 *a* On graph paper, sketch and label the graph of the equation $y = \cos 2x$ in the interval $-\pi \leq x \leq \pi$. [4]

b On the same set of axes, sketch the reflection of $y = \cos 2x$ in the x-axis and label the image *b*. [2]

c Write an equation of the graph drawn in part *b*. [2]

d Using the graphs drawn in parts *a* and *b*, determine one value of x that satisfies both equations. [2]

38 *a* Sketch and label the graph of the equation $y = 3^x$. [4]

b On the same set of axes, sketch the inverse of $y = 3^x$ and label the image *b*. [4]

c Write the equation of the graph sketched in part *b*. [2]

39 In the accompanying diagram of $\triangle ABC$, $AB = 12$ feet, $DC = 17$ feet, $m\angle ABD = 40$, and $m\angle ADB = 110$. Find AC to the *nearest foot*. [10]

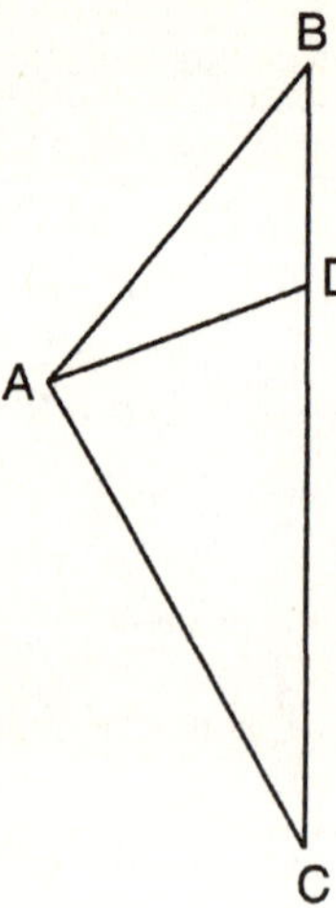

40 Find, to the *nearest ten minutes* or *nearest tenth of a degree*, all values of x in the interval $0° \leq x < 360°$ that satisfy the equation $4 \sin^2 x - 5 \sin x - 6 = 0$. [10]

41 *a* Express in simplest form:

$$\frac{x^2 - 9}{2x - 8} \div \frac{3 - x}{x - 4} \quad [4]$$

b In simplest form, express $\frac{x + y^{-1}}{y + x^{-1}}$ with no negative exponents. [3]

c Solve for x to the *nearest hundredth:* $2^x = 28$ [3]

42 *a* Mel took 12 tests in Sequential Math III and received the following grades:

85, 89, 89, 89, 90, 90, 90, 92, 92, 96, 96, 100

(1) Find, to the *nearest tenth*, the standard deviation. [4]

(2) What percent of the test grades are *more than* one standard deviation above the mean? [2]

b In a baseball game, the probability that Peter gets on base safely is $\frac{3}{7}$. If he comes to bat four times, what is the probability that he will get on base safely *at least* three times? [4]

HIGH SCHOOL MATHEMATICS: COURSE III
AUGUST 2001

Part I

Answer 30 questions from this part. Each correct answer will receive 2 credits. No partial credit will be allowed. Write your answers in the spaces provided on the separate answer sheet. Where applicable, answers may be left in terms of π or in radical form. [60]

1 Solve for the negative value of x: $|3x - 1| = 19$

2 In $\triangle ABC$, $a = 24$, $\sin A = \frac{3}{4}$, and $\sin B = \frac{1}{2}$. Find b.

3 Express 198° in radian measure.

4 Evaluate: $\sum_{k=1}^{3} (3k-1)^2$

5 If $f(x) = 2x - 5$ and $g(x) = \sqrt{x}$, evaluate $(f \circ g)(36)$.

6 If $9^{x+1} = 27^x$, what is the value of x?

7 Express $\frac{1}{2}\sqrt{48} - (2\sqrt{12} - \sqrt{27})$ in simplest radical form.

8 In a circle whose radius is 2, a central angle intercepts an arc whose length is 6. What is the number of radians in the central angle of the arc?

9 If point $P(3,-2)$ is rotated 90° about the origin, what is the image of P?

10 The probability of winning a game is $\frac{3}{5}$ and the probability of losing a game is $\frac{2}{5}$. If the game is played three times, what is the probability of winning *exactly* two games?

Directions (11–35): For *each* question chosen, write on the separate answer sheet the *numeral* preceding the word or expression that best completes the statement or answers the question.

11 The expression $\cos 80° \cos 70° + \sin 80° \sin 70°$ is equivalent to

(1) $\cos 10°$
(2) $\cos 150°$
(3) $\sin 10°$
(4) $\sin 150°$

12 If $\sin A < 0$ and $\tan A > 0$, in which quadrant does the terminal side of $\angle A$ lie?

(1) I
(2) II
(3) III
(4) IV

13 For which value of x is the fraction $\frac{6}{\sin x - 1}$ undefined?

(1) 270°
(2) 90°
(3) 45°
(4) 0°

14 In the accompanying diagram of circle O, diameter $\overline{AB}$ is perpendicular to chord $\overline{CD}$ and intersects $\overline{CD}$ at E, $AE = 9$, and $EB = 4$.

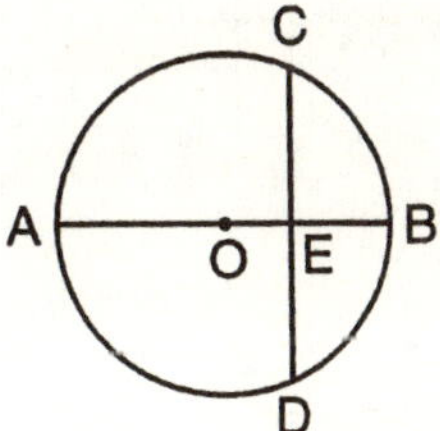

What is ED?

(1) 8
(2) 7
(3) 6
(4) 4

15 The graph of the equation $y = 3 \sin 2x$ is dilated using a factor of 2. The amplitude of the dilated graph is

(1) 1
(2) 6
(3) $\frac{3}{2}$
(4) 4

16 If $f(x) = x^{-\frac{1}{3}}$, then $f(64)$ is equal to

(1) $\frac{1}{4}$
(2) -8
(3) -4
(4) 4

17 The expression $(1 - \cos x)(1 + \cos x)$ is equivalent to

(1) $\sin x$
(2) $-\sin x$
(3) $\sin^2 x$
(4) $-\sin^2 x$

18 If $\tan(x + 20) = \cot x$, a value of x is

(1) 35 (3) 55
(2) 45 (4) 70

19 The expression $\dfrac{\frac{x^2}{y} - y}{\frac{x}{y} + 1}$ is equivalent to

(1) $x^2 - y^2$ (3) $x + y$
(2) $\dfrac{x^2 - y^2}{x + 1}$ (4) $x - y$

20 In $\triangle ABC$, $m\angle C = 30$ and $a = 8$. If the area of the triangle is 12, what is the length of side b?

(1) 6 (3) 3
(2) 8 (4) 4

21 Which equation is represented on the graph shown below?

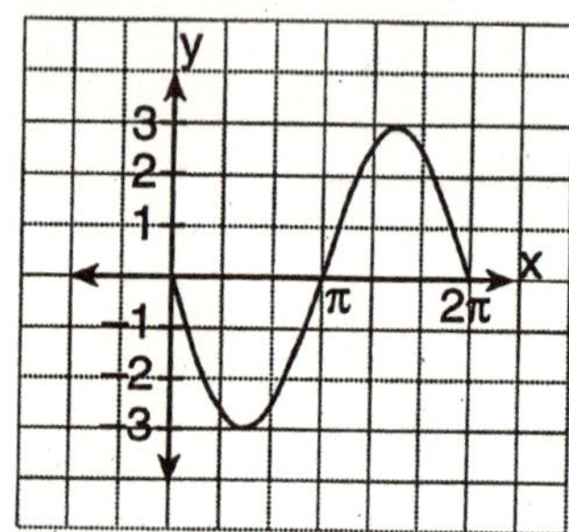

(1) $y = 3 \sin x$ (3) $y = 3 \cos x$
(2) $y = -3 \sin x$ (4) $y = -\sin 3x$

22 The expression $\log \dfrac{\sqrt{x^2y^3}}{z}$ is equivalent to

(1) $\frac{1}{2}(2 \log x + 3 \log y - \log z)$
(2) $\frac{1}{2}(2 \log x + 3 \log y) - \log z$
(3) $2 \log x + 3 \log y - \log z$
(4) $\dfrac{x^2y^3}{z}$

23 What is the value of $\tan\left(\text{Arc cos } -\frac{3}{5}\right)$?

(1) $\frac{5}{3}$ (3) $-\frac{3}{4}$
(2) $\frac{4}{3}$ (4) $-\frac{4}{3}$

24 On a standardized test, the mean is 83 and the standard deviation is 3.5. What is the best approximation of the percentage of scores that fall in the range 76–90?

(1) 34 (3) 95
(2) 68 (4) 99

25 Which graph represents the solution set for $x^2 + x > 12$?

(1) 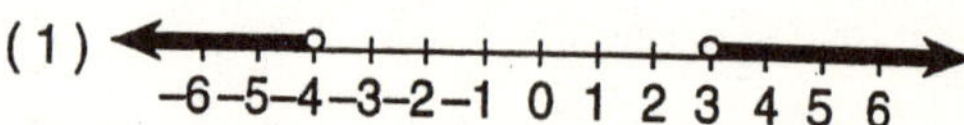

(2) –6–5–4–3–2–1 0 1 2 3 4 5 6

(3) –6–5–4–3–2–1 0 1 2 3 4 5 6

(4) –6–5–4–3–2–1 0 1 2 3 4 5 6

26 The equation $\sqrt{x + 6} + x = 6$ has for its roots

(1) neither 3 nor 10 (3) 3, only
(2) 10, only (4) both 3 and 10

27 In the accompanying diagram of circle O, $m\overset{\frown}{ABC} = 150$.

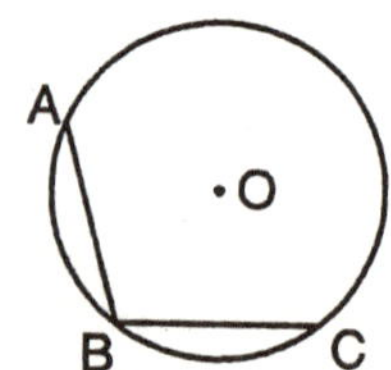

What is $m\angle ABC$?

(1) 210 (3) 95
(2) 105 (4) 75

28 If $f(x) = x^2$, what is the value of $f(2i)$?

(1) –2 (3) –4
(2) 2 (4) 4

29 What is the sum of the roots of the equation $3x^2 - 2x + 5 = 0$?

(1) $-\frac{2}{3}$ (3) $-\frac{5}{3}$

(2) $\frac{2}{3}$ (4) $\frac{5}{3}$

30 In the interval $90° < x < 270°$, what is the solution to $\csc x = -2$?

(1) 120° (3) 210°
(2) 150° (4) 240°

31 Which field property is illustrated by the expression $(\tan \theta)(\cot \theta) = 1$?

(1) closure (3) commutative
(2) identity (4) inverse

32 If the domain of $f(x) = 2x + 1$ is $\{-2 \le x \le 3\}$, which integer is *not* in the range?

(1) −4 (3) 0
(2) −2 (4) 7

33 In $\triangle ABC$, $a = 6$, $b = 7$, and $c = 8$. What is $\cos A$ in simplest fractional form?

(1) $\frac{3}{16}$ (3) $\frac{77}{96}$

(2) $\frac{11}{16}$ (4) $\frac{51}{112}$

34 If $m\angle ABC = 135$, $AC = 9$, and $AB = 10$, what is the maximum number of distinct triangles that can be constructed?

(1) 1 (3) 3
(2) 2 (4) 0

35 If x is a positive acute angle and $\cos x = \frac{1}{9}$, what is the value of $\cos \frac{1}{2}x$?

(1) $\frac{2}{3}$ (3) $\frac{2\sqrt{5}}{3}$

(2) $\frac{1}{3}$ (4) $\frac{\sqrt{5}}{3}$

Part II

Answer four questions from this part. Clearly indicate the necessary steps, including appropriate formula substitutions, diagrams, graphs, charts, etc. Calculations that may be obtained by mental arithmetic or the calculator do not need to be shown. [40]

36 *a* On the same set of axes, sketch and label the graphs of the equations $y = -3 \cos 2x$ and $y = 2 \sin \frac{1}{2}x$ in the interval $-\pi \le x \le \pi$. [8]

b Using the graphs drawn in part *a*, find the number of values of x in the interval $-\pi \le x \le \pi$ that satisfy the equation $-3 \cos 2x = 2 \sin \frac{1}{2}x$. [2]

37 Two forces are applied to an object. The measure of the angle between the 30.2-pound applied force and the 50.1-pound resultant is 25°.

a Find the magnitude of the second applied force to the *nearest tenth of a pound.* [5]

b Using the answer found in part *a*, find the measure of the angle between the second applied force and the resultant to the *nearest degree.* [5]

38 *a* Sketch and label the graph of the equation $\log_3 x = -y$. [5]

b On the same set of axes used in part *a*, sketch the equation $\log_3 x = -y$ reflected in the x-axis and label it *b*. [3]

c Write the equation of the reflection sketched in part *b*. [2]

39 *a* Find all values of x in the interval $0° \le x < 360°$ that satisfy the equation $\cos x \tan x + \cos x = 0$. [5]

b Express in simplest form:

$$\frac{64 - \cos^2 x}{\cos^2 x + 8 \cos x} \div \frac{2 \cos x - 16}{8 \cos x}$$ [5]

40 In the accompanying diagram of circle O, tangent $\overline{PA}$, secant $\overline{PBEC}$, and chords $\overline{AB}$, $\overline{AD}$, and $\overline{CD}$ are drawn; $m\angle C = 30$; $m\widehat{AB} = 100$; and $m\widehat{AC} : m\widehat{CD} = 4:1$.

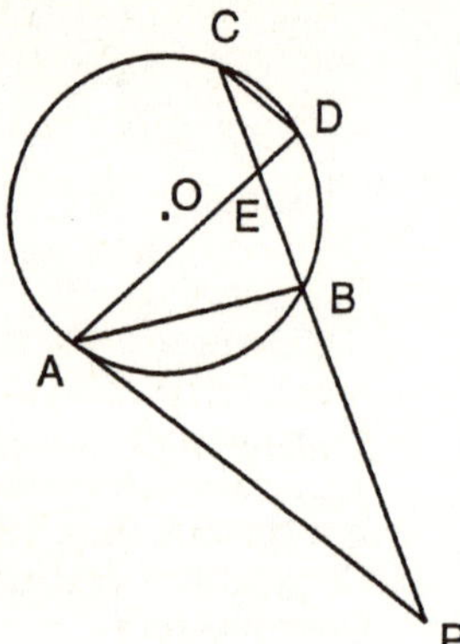

Find:

a $m\widehat{CD}$ [2]
b $m\angle BAP$ [2]
c $m\angle CDA$ [2]
d $m\angle AEB$ [2]
e $m\angle P$ [2]

41 *a* Given $\triangle ABC$ with points $A(4,3)$, $B(4,-2)$, and $C(2,3)$.

(1) On graph paper, sketch $\triangle ABC$. [1]

(2) On the same set of axes, graph and state the coordinates of $\triangle A'B'C'$, the image of $\triangle ABC$ after a reflection in the line $y = x$. [3]

(3) On the same set of axes, graph and state the coordinates of $\triangle A''B''C''$, the image of $\triangle A'B'C'$ after the translation $T_{-4,3}$. [2]

b Where i is the imaginary unit, expand and simplify completely $(3 - i)^4$. [4]

42 *a* The table below shows the age at inauguration of ten presidents of the United States.

President	Age at Inauguration
Harry Truman	60
Dwight D. Eisenhower	62
John F. Kennedy	43
Lyndon B. Johnson	55
Richard M. Nixon	56
Gerald R. Ford	61
Jimmy Carter	52
Ronald Reagan	69
George Bush	64
Bill Clinton	46

Find, to the *nearest tenth,* the standard deviation of the age at inauguration of these ten presidents. [4]

b Solve for x and express your answer in simplest $a + bi$ form:

$$16x = 16 - \frac{13}{x} \quad [6]$$

INDEX